D1665592

Introduction to
DECISION SCIENCE

Introduction to
DECISION SCIENCE

SANG M. LEE
LAURENCE J. MOORE

Virginia Polytechnic Institute and State University

FIRST EDITION

 PETROCELLI / CHARTER   NEW YORK 1975

Library of Congress Cataloging in Publication Data

Lee, Sang M   1939-
    Introduction to decision science.

    Includes bibliographies.
    1. Decision-making--Mathmatical models.
I. Moore, Laurence J., joint author. II. Title.
HD69.D4L435   658.4'03   75-16143
ISBN 0-88405-310-5

To Laura and Nancy

Contents

Preface

Managerial decision problems have increased in both number and complexity over the past thirty years. This change has been due, in large part, to a dramatic change in the nature of management and the environment within which it operates. While organizations have become much larger and more complex, management functions have become more specialized. Natural resources required for operations have become increasingly scarce, forcing managers to evaluate decision problems while considering environmental constraints. Ecology and pollution control have become household words, and governmental and consumer groups have begun to exert greater demands on organizational actions.

As managers have become increasingly held accountable for their decisions, not only to top management and stockholders, but also to government and other outside interest groups, they have looked for more sophisticated approaches to the analysis of overwhelmingly complex problems. There has been an increasing demand not only for techniques of finding the best solution to a problem, but also of presenting a defendable basis for arriving at the course of action selected.

Consequently, we have seen great progress in the field of decision science. Many new problem-solving techniques have been developed as a result of technical breakthroughs. Also, new applications of existing techniques have been developed, and an increasing number of complex problems are being solved with the aid of the computer. The greatest advance in decision science, however, has occurred in the implementation of scientific approaches to real-world problems.

Numerous books have been published in the area of management science, operations research, and decision science. Most of these books

1

can be classified into two broad categories: basic surveys that present concepts of quantitative analysis, and comprehensive theoretical texts that present mathematical foundations of various quantitative tools. Few books have presented comprehensive, introductory, application-oriented, and up-to-date treatment of decision science techniques. This book is intended to fill this void. The authors have attempted to make *Introduction to Decision Science* the following: (1) a comprehensive, yet quite readable presentation of various decision science techniques, (2) an application orientation to real-world problems by emphasizing the model formulation aspect of decision analysis, (3) an up-to-date presentation of goal programming at the introductory level, and (4) a guide to the analysis of complex problems through the inclusion of several computer programs.

The book is directed to those who aspire to become effective decision makers in various organizations, specifically, for students and practitioners of management decision analysis. It presents important decision science techniques and their applications with a minimum of mathematical sophistication. The reader can easily comprehend the entire book with only a good understanding of basic algebra. Wherever there is a need for more complete or sophisticated analysis, an appendix is provided. Also, in order to provide the reader with the opportunity to analyze complex decision problems by using the computer, several computer programs are provided in the Appendix.

This book is intended primarily for undergraduate students of business, administration, social sciences, and engineering. It can also be used as a text or a reference book by graduate students and practicing decision makers. The book provides the necessary background knowledge in decision science so that one could pursue higher level study, using this text as a source of refresher work.

If the book is adopted for an undergraduate introductory course, it is recommended that the following topics be studied in the sequence presented below:

1. Introduction to Decision Science (Chapter 1)
2. Break-even and Optimization Analysis (Chapter 2)
3. Decision Theory (Chapter 3)
4. Linear Programming (Chapters 4 and 5)
5. Goal Programming (Chapter 6)
6. Transportation and Assignment Methods (Chapter 7)
7. Inventory Models (Chapter 8)
8. Waiting Line Analysis—Queueing Theory (Chapter 9)
9. Network Models: PERT-CPM (Chapter 10)

10. Implementation of Decision Science (Chapter 13)
  * Optional Work
    a. Game Theory (Chapter 11)
    b. Simulation Analysis (Chapter 12)
    c. Computer-Based Analysis
      (1) Linear Programming
      (2) Goal Programming

If the book is used at the graduate level, it should be studied in the complete sequence presented. In addition, it is recommended that the course include outside readings (see References) and an independent research project that applies one of the computer programs in the Appendix to analyze a complex managerial decision problem.

The book represents a large portion of the authors' teaching work during the past seven years. In writing the book, we have relied heavily on suggestions and criticisms of our colleagues and students. We have benefited a great deal from our discussions with Edward R. Clayton of Virginia Polytechnic Institute and State University and Ted F. Anthony of the University of Georgia. In writing the goal programming chapter, we relied primarily on works of Sang M. Lee, especially his book, *Goal Programming for Decision Analysis*, Philadelphia: Auerbach Publishers, Inc., 1972. Our graduate assistants provided much needed help in completing this book and the solution manual. We express our thanks to Douglas Hawpe, Boo Ho Rho, and Adley Hemphill. We especially thank David Reemsnyder for the work he did on the linear programming computer program.

Finally, but perhaps most important, we express our love and sincere gratitude to our wives, Laura Lee and Nancy Moore, for their many lost evenings, weekends, and vacations.

S. M. L.
L. J. M.

Blacksburg, Virginia

1 Introduction to Decision Science

This is an introductory text on managerial decision analysis. *Decision science* is concerned with the application of quantitative analysis to managerial decision making. The primary objective of the analysis is to assist the decision maker in finding the best feasible solution to a decision problem by systematically analyzing the ramifications of various decision alternatives. Many decision problems are too complex for the decision maker to analyze all the alternatives and their eventual consequences. The decision scientist analyzes the problem through quantitative techniques and provides pertinent information for the decision maker to use in selecting the best feasible alternative.

DECISION ANALYSIS

Decision analysis has always been the primary task of man. As a matter of fact, the primary distinguishing characteristic of mankind has been the capacity to learn about his environment and transmit such knowledge into action to improve his well-being. Man's desire to make the most effective decision has led to a continuous struggle to comprehend the norms and conditions under which the environment functions. The increase in man's body of knowledge has led to new scientific discoveries, inventions, and innovations. This new knowledge has provided man with the opportunity to manipulate environmental conditions to produce desired consequences. Man has thus acquired much control over nature, providing new horizons of civilization and growth. However, this is also the genesis of the problem of decision making, since different decisions may result in different consequences. Man attempts to select the course of action from a set of alternatives in order to achieve his objectives. Decision analysis is a formalized process for increasing man's understanding and control over environmental conditions. Consequently, every new development in knowledge or science has a potentially practical implication for decision analysis.

Managerial decision analysis is not essentially different from the decision making process of an individual. Here, the decision maker attempts to achieve the objectives of an organization rather than his personal objectives. The general decision process is similar, except that the magnitude of decision consequences may be enormously greater. Since the decision consequences are so important to the firm, the decision maker is justified in using the firm's resources to improve the decision-making process. The primary resources that the decision maker can use are the firm's information systems, facilities, and knowledge of manpower and other resources.

It is only in the past 20 to 30 years that scientific decision analysis has emerged as an important area of management and administration. Today, some leading authorities of management theory have gone so far as to define decision making as synonymous with management. In the process, the basic concept of management has changed drastically from a form of a pure art to that of a combination of art and science.

Increased emphasis on decision analysis is the result of the aggregate effects of advances in management technology, the ever-increasing complexity of environment, and the improved capability of decision scientists. In order to improve the rationality in decision making, greater emphasis has been placed on techniques that would provide more concrete information about the decision environment and the outcomes of alternative courses of action. Hence, the trend of decision making has developed toward the quantitative and computer-oriented approaches. Thus, decision science has been developed as a process that employs scientific method and systematic investigation in order to aid the decision maker in identifying an optimal course of action.

Decision science does not completely replace the intuitive decision-making approach that has been widely practiced in the past and even today. The intuitive approach is based on the experience of the decision maker who has become known for his decision-making abilities. He has a general awareness of the situation and some personal insights about future outcomes. With or without decision science, a decision maker usually exercises some degree of personal judgment. Decision science, therefore, should be intended to enrich and sharpen the judgment of the decision maker in making the final decision.

OPERATIONS RESEARCH, MANAGEMENT SCIENCE, AND DECISION SCIENCE

The beginning of operations research is unknown, as the birth of science is unknown. The roots of operations research are as old as man's curiosity, human organizations, and science. However, the name *operations research* dates back only to the early 1940s. The origin of serious operations research activities was in the United Kingdom early in World War II. For the most effective military tactics and strategies, there was an urgent need for a scientific approach to analyze various logistics problems. The British and later the American military authorities formed groups of scientists to do research on military operations. These teams of researchers were the first operations research teams. It has been said that their studies were instrumental in the victories in the air battle of Britain, the island campaign in the Pacific, the battle of the North Atlantic, and other phases of the war.

After the war, operations research moved into business, government, and other institutions, spurred on by the great success in military operations. This transition was relatively faster in Great Britain than in the United States. However, since 1951 operations research has taken a firm hold in business in the United States and has developed very rapidly indeed.

There are three important factors behind the rapid development of operations research in this country. First, there was an economic boom following World War II. With the industrial boom came continuous mechanization, automation, decentralization of operations, and division of management functions. Such transformations of industrial organizations resulted in complex managerial problems. Many operations researchers, including those management consultants who served in the operations research teams during the war, found these business problems basically the same as the military problems. Thus, application of operations research to managerial decision making became popular. The second factor was that many operations researchers continued their research after the war. Consequently, some important advancements were made in various operations research techniques. For example, Professor George B. Dantzig developed the simplex method of linear programming in 1947 after his continuous research. By 1950, many important operations research techniques were well developed for practical application, such as linear programming, dynamic programming, queueing theory, and inventory models. The third factor affecting the rapid growth of operations research was the staggering analytic power made available by high-speed electronic computers. Complex managerial problems usually require an enormous amount of computation. The computer revolution has made it possible to apply many sophisticated techniques for practical decision analysis.

Synonyms for operations research are numerous; a frequent substitute is management science, and such other terms as systems analysis, systems science, operations analysis, quantitative analysis, managerial analysis, decision analysis, and decision science are also used. We have decided to use the term *decision science* in this book because we are basically concerned with the systematic analysis of the decision environment and the outcomes of decision alternatives. There is no organizational barrier for decision analysis. In other words, we can use decision science for managerial problems in government, military service, business and industry, academic institutions, health-care organizations, and so forth. *Operations research* has a strong connotation of military orientation. *Management science*, on the other hand, seems to suggest that it is appropriate for only private business organizations. We think *decision science* suggests the broad concept that is most appropriate for the application of scientific tools to decision analysis.

Decision science is concerned with the application of scientific tools to provide more concrete information that is relevant to the problem solving on the part of the decision maker. A greater emphasis is placed on the analysis of the nature of the problem, decision environment, objectives of the organization, judgment of the decision maker, and economic as well as noneconomic ramifications of the decision alternatives. Operations research and management science have, on the other hand, put their emphasis on developing abstract models to find the optimum solutions. Decision science attempts to achieve the same. Furthermore, decision science attempts to provide "workable," "implementable," or "satisfactory" solutions to complex problems that do not lend themselves to optimal solutions. Also, decision science recognizes the need for an integration of quantitative analysis with environmental and behavioral aspects of the decision-making process. Therefore, decision science encompasses a broader spectrum of the decision-making process.

THE SYSTEMS APPROACH

As we have already discussed, the essence of decision science is systematic analysis. This systematic analysis employs the "systems approach" and the scientific method. In fact, it is not easy to distinguish the systems approach from the scientific method, as the two are so interwoven. In this section we shall limit our discussion to the systems approach.

Since decision science attempts to be comprehensive, it inevitably involves what is called the systems approach. A system is a whole composed of a set of components with certain relationships between the components and their attributes that serve to perform a function. Thus, an organization is a man-machine system. A television set, on the other hand, is a mechanical system. It is made up of such components as a picture tube, speakers, and transistors, that function to transmit an image and sound. The man-machine organization has some special characteristics because of the psychological and sociological nature of man. The human organization does not allow the exact analysis of the system that is possible in a mechanical system because there exists uncertainty concerning motivation, performance, and cooperation among people. We shall not discuss the philosophical question of whether or not people can be conditioned to function like mechanical components or not. We will simply say that the human organization is a system with interdependent components. Furthermore, the organization itself can be viewed as a component of a larger system in the social environment.

Decision science is concerned with problem solving for the best interest of the organization as a whole, and therefore the problem in question must first be put in proper perspective. Thus, any managerial problem must deserve a broad analysis in terms of its impact on the whole organization and its environment. In other words, decision science should be applied in a systems context.

Decision science applied in a systems context often reveals and uncovers new problems upon the solution of the original problem. This is a very important characteristic of decision science. Therefore, the most beneficial way to apply decision science is through continuous research, rather than the one-shot solution approach. This is why any meaningful systems analysis always includes application of decision science techniques.

The basic objective of decision science is to assist the decision maker of an organization in solving decision problems that involve various components of the organization and its environment. In a theoretical sense, the optimum decision must be one that is the best for the organization as a whole. It is often called the *global optimum*. A decision that is best for one or more parts of the organization is usually called a *suboptimum* decision. Decision science attempts to find the solution that is closest to the global optimum by analyzing interrelationships among the system components that are involved in the problem.

It is an extremely difficult but important task of management to establish criteria for decision analysis. In other words, management must define the objectives and goals of the organization and determine how some of the managerial decisions could contribute to achieving these goals. Suboptimization is often the only feasible solution due to many organizational and/or technical problems.

It is often impossible to analyze the impact of one decision beyond a given component of the organization. For example, an inventory problem is formulated to minimize the total inventory cost. The problem itself may be an extremely complex one. If we attempt to analyze the impact of the solution on production, marketing, finance, personnel, and community reputation of the firm, the problem may become too complex to analyze. In such a case, management may have to simply set the suboptimization (minimization of the total inventory cost) as the objective for decision analysis. Sometimes, suboptimization may be the only solution due to restricted access to higher organizational levels or due to limited resources (personnel, time, or money). However, decision science attempts to analyze the overall effects of a decision as far out as is economically, technically, and chronologically feasible. In this sense, decision science is more concerned with managerial problems rather than repetitive operational problems.

In essence, then, decision science strives to find the optimum solution within the constraints of the decision environment. For example, in a production planning problem, the solution may call for a quick adjustment of manpower and materials according to the demand fluctuations in order to maximize the total profit for the firm. On the other hand, it may be the basic philosophy of top management to maintain a relatively stable employment level. In this case, the solution derived by the decision scientist may be left to top management to make necessary adjustments. Suppose that top management specified 2 percent as the maximum acceptable fluctuation per month in employment level. Then the decision scientist can once again derive the optimum solution within this managerial constraint. Furthermore, he can also identify the economic implications of this management policy. In other words, the final implementation of the decision rests with the decision maker. The decision scientist or the analysis team can only recommend a solution, modify it whenever necessary, and help implement the decision. In the process, the impact of the decision on various components of the organization, on the organization as a whole, and on the environment is pursued continuously. Decision science, therefore, cannot be applied in isolation. It must be put to use in a systems context.

DECISION SCIENCE IN ACTION

In spite of the enormous growth in the application and acceptance of decision science models, there have been very few standard applications. Most organizations do require custom-made type models for decision analysis. It requires, indeed, a great deal of knowledge and experience for the decision scientist to design new custom-made models for a stream of problems. Perhaps it may become possible in the near future that some of the well-known techniques of decision science models can be packaged and be applied to many repetitive-type problems. This practice has been very successful in the industrial engineering and accounting fields. Already, the body of knowledge in decision science is such that it has become all but impossible for any one individual to keep up with all the new developments.

In decision science, problem solving is usually approached by a team rather than by one researcher. There are several reasons for this task-force approach. First, as we have already discussed, as the body of knowledge develops in decision science it becomes impossible for one individual to be a jack-of-all-trades. For example, a researcher may be a nationally known queueing theorist, but he may not know enough linear programming to develop a production planning model. Second, the problem in question may involve several departments in the organization. The researcher may have neither the organizational experience nor the time to comprehend all the interrelationships among the departments. A convenient way to acquire this knowledge and also have the operating personnel participate in the decision analysis is to form a team by selecting a key person from each department. Third, decision science has emerged out of many other sciences. For example, it has borrowed quite heavily from mathematics, industrial engineering, statistics, psychology, economics, and others. Therefore, a decision science team may include an anthropologist, a psychologist, an accountant, a sociologist, a linguist, a mathematician, an engineer, and a decision scientist. Of course, the composition of the team in terms of number of members and their expertise depends upon the problem at hand. By forming a team with competent personnel in various fields, the variety of analytical techniques that can be applied to the problem can be increased.

Managerial problems usually involve economic, biological, psychological, physical, engineering, and environmental aspects. These aspects of the problem can be analyzed best by those who are directly involved in these areas. We shall reiterate that decision science must be used in a systems context. This implies that a team approach is a most effective way to carry out the analysis for the whole organization.

For a successful application of decision science, a considerable amount of artistic creativity is still required. Once the fundamentals of decision science are digested, the real-world application requires creativity to combine such knowledge with the complexities of the problem. Furthermore, the decision scientist must believe in the value of his work. Without this confidence, he cannot effectively communicate his ideas and expertise to the decision maker. The application of decision science requires information such as management philosophy, policies, goals, and relationships among pertinent decision variables. Much of such information can be obtained only from top management. The decision scientist must have the full confidence of the manager, so that his recommendations can be implemented by the decision maker. The final implementation and the analysis of the result are important motivational factors for the decision scientist.

Most decision science applications cut across the formal organization structure. It is imperative, therefore, that top management be part of the important project. For many managerial problems, it is only top management that has broad enough knowledge to judge whether the project is being directed toward the overall organizational objectives rather than the interests of individual departments. In other words, participation of top management assures a system-oriented decision analysis so that suboptimization can be avoided whenever possible. Most executives and administrators have seen the value of decision science. They recognize its potential contribution for the survival and success of the organization in today's technological society. In fact, most dynamic managers have some understanding of the fundamentals of decision science.

THE PROCESS OF DECISION SCIENCE

Every practitioner of decision science may have his own way of doing things. However, there are several major steps that almost everyone agrees are important in decision science. We shall now discuss these phases.

Formulation of the Problem

One of the most important characteristics of the scientific approach to a decision problem is an insistence on determining exactly what one is trying to do. As an old saying goes, a problem well put is half solved. As a matter of fact, identification of the problem is the most difficult part of decision analysis. The decision scientist or a team of decision scientists is usually presented with symptoms rather than a diagnosis. Consequently, he must obtain additional symptoms before he can diagnose (formulate) correctly.

Although decision analysis should begin with the formulation of a problem, this step is a continuous process until a solution is reached. In other words, once an initial formulation of the problem is completed and analysis proceeds, the problem is subjected to continuous modification and refinement. Consequently, it is quite possible that one never can be certain until the end of the analysis process that the problem was correctly formulated, or perhaps not even then.

The decision scientist is often very anxious to get into the "nitty-gritty" part of the decision analysis—model design and solution. This tendency often results in a hurried and superficial effort devoted to problem formulation. This can be very costly to the organization in terms of long-run overall objectives. Therefore, we need a systematic procedure for formulating the problem. Although each problem with its unique characteristics may require different approaches to formulate it, we can list the following generalized phases for the problem-formulation procedure.

The Orientation Period

The orientation period provides an opportunity to the decision maker and the decision scientist(s) to assess the overall picture of the problem. During this period, the decision scientist can obtain a broad understanding of the organizational climate, its objectives, and what is expected of the analysis. It also provides the manager with a similar opportunity. Thus, the orientation period can be used to specify the conditions that are required to carry out the analysis, that is, time requirement, administrative arrangements, resource requirement, and the like.

The Definition of Problem Components

Before the problem can be formulated, its components must be clearly defined. The first component to be defined is the decision maker(s), who is not satisfied with the current state of affairs. The second component to be analyzed is objectives of the decision maker. What are the things that the decision maker is trying to achieve in the analysis? The third component is the decision environment or decision system that embraces the problem in question. Finally, a problem cannot be evaluated unless the decision maker has alternative courses of action. We shall now discuss these components in greater detail.

The decision maker. For any decision analysis, it is necessary to identify the decision maker who has the authority to initiate, modify, and terminate policies that control the system or organization under study. In some instances, the authority of decision making may rest upon more than one individual. In such an event, it is essential to acquire a good understanding about how the decision group reaches certain decisions. Is the decision process based on majority vote or unanimous vote? Who has the authority to approve or veto their decision? These questions must be cleared up at this stage.

The decision objectives. Perhaps the most crucial factor in decision analysis is the identification of decision objectives. The decision maker may have a specific set of objectives that he wants to achieve in the problem. In such a case, analysis of the objectives is relatively simple. However, sometimes the decision maker cannot specify objectives for the problem. In such a case, the decision scientist may attempt to list all possible outcomes of the project and obtain the decision maker's ideas concerning the desirability of obtaining certain outcomes. Based on this analysis, the decision scientist can establish objectives upon the approval of the decision maker.

In analyzing objectives of the decision maker, two distinct types of objectives must be evaluated. First, it is necessary to consider objectives that the decision maker has already obtained and that he wants to retain. For example, he may want to maintain a stable employment level, preserve the good community image of the firm, and the like. The second type of objectives are those the decision maker wants to obtain to a higher degree. For example, he may want to increase the market share, increase profits, decrease personnel turnover, decrease production costs, and so on. In most managerial problems, there are multiple objectives where some are to be obtained and others are to be maintained. In addition to the identification of objectives, it is also essential to obtain the decision maker's priority structure for the objectives. Since it is not always possible to achieve all the objectives to the degree desired by the decision maker, the priority consideration allows concentration of efforts on the higher-priority objectives.

The decision environment. Any organized system involves several key components, such as managers (administrators), employees who carry out policies, equipment and other resources required to carry out policies, outsiders who are affected by the organization, and the social and ecological environment in which the organization functions. It is necessary, therefore, to analyze the effects and repercussions of the decision in the systems perspective. For example, the decision maker's objectives for the problem may be in conflict with the interests of outsiders and the social environment (i.e., profit maximization while neglecting pollution). Through the analysis of the system components and their objectives, the initial set of the decision maker's objectives may be further modified.

Alternative courses of action. A problem cannot exist unless the decision maker has a choice of actions. A number of possible courses of action are usually disclosed in the process of going through the steps of formulating the problem. However, the list of alternatives uncovered in this way may not be exhaustive. It may be necessary, therefore, to develop new alternatives through a thorough systems analysis. It is extremely difficult to determine how exhaustive the alternative search should be, since the process may cost a great deal of money, time, and effort.

Development of the Model

Model developing is the crux of the decision science approach. It is as important as laboratory experiments in physical science. We are getting into the fine details of the problem in this phase. Developing a model allows a comprehensive analysis, as it is a logical expression of the complexities, unique characteristics, and possible uncertainties of the problem. The logical expression requires a mathematical formula to represent the interrelationships among the system elements. Some of these relationships may be expressed by mathematical equations, inequalities, or other constraints that impose restrictions on the decision variables. The model must be capable of representing the most relevant and important characteristics of the problem, such as deterministic or probabilistic (stochastic) nature, static or dynamic elements, input and output requirements, and the measurement of the objective criterion.

The model is a convenient vehicle that helps to analyze the complex reality in a concise and relatively simple manner. A model clarifies the feasible decision alternatives, economic and noneconomic consequences of these alternatives, and the optimum alternative for the problem. The systems approach is only possible when the relationships among the components and their objective criteria are expressed in a comprehensive but manageable mathematical model.

One more consideration requiring close attention in the model-developing phase is the time horizon for the use of the model. The problem at hand may change drastically in time. Therefore, a continuous updating of the model parameters, their relationships, and the objective criteria is necessary. It is imperative to evaluate the objective criteria continuously, as management goals do change in time with the changing decision and organizational environment. A more detailed discussion of the mathematical model will be presented in the next section of this chapter.

It is sometimes necessary to modify a model, even when it is perfectly acceptable, due to the fact that required data are not available or too costly to obtain. Although the initial model development may be simple, its modification may be extremely difficult. Therefore, it is often necessary to go through several cycles of model development and search for data. Each model leads to a search for data that may not always yield the required data. However, the search process often reveals how the model should be modified in order to use the available data.

Solution of the Model

Once a mathematical model is formulated, the next phase is deriving an optimum solution from the model. The optimum solution presents the values for the decision variables that optimize the given decision criterion (objective). As pointed out earlier, a mathematical model is a simple abstract of reality. If the model represents almost every characteristic of the problem, it may be too complex to allow easy formulation, manipulation, and solution. On the other hand, if the model is too simple, it may not represent all the relevant aspects of the problem. Therefore, the model solution phase may point out whether the model is an appropriate one for the problem or not. Consequently, this phase may give rise to a continuous review of the problem-definition/model-development/model-solution cycle until a satisfactory solution is found.

The model does not always yield the optimum solution. Instead, it may give an approximate optimum for the problem when the problem is too complex to allow an analytical solution. Analytic procedures involve the application of various mathematical tools to express the problem in an abstract manner. Its solution usually allows the substitution of values derived from the solution for various model parameters. Sometimes, a model allows only numerical solutions. Numerical procedures are based on three basic steps: (1) Assign certain values to the decision variables in the model; (2) compare the model solutions; and (3) select the set of values for the decision variables that yields the best solution. Numerical procedures may range from a very primitive trial-and-error type analysis to a very systematic iterative analysis. An iterative analysis employs a successive solution that approaches the optimum solution on a step-by-step basis. It is often the case that the problem does not allow either analytic or numerical analysis. In such cases, the only feasible approach may be a computer-based simulation. Simulation will be treated in greater detail in Chapter 12.

Implementation of the Solution

The true value of decision science is realized when the model solution is put to actual use. This phase usually requires a translation of the solution into a set of management policies or operating procedures that is easy to be implemented by the operating personnel. A problem that plagues most decision science practitioners is that the system under investigation keeps changing. Consequently, a control process must be established over the solution so that the model can be updated continuously. Chapter 14 is devoted to the implementation process of decision science.

Decision science has its focal point in the construction and solution of decision models. Therefore, it is characterized by (1) a rational and methodical approach, (2) heavy reliance on quantitative methods, and (3) extensive use of the computer. Although the topics of decision science can be introduced without the use of the computer, it would be impractical or even totally impossible without the use of the computer. Therefore, knowledge of computer science is usually required for a decision scientist to attack real-world problems.

INTRODUCTION TO MODELING

A primary purpose of this book is to acquaint the reader with modeling of business systems. The concept of models for decision analysis is a central issue. A variety of specific models will be presented throughout the text to provide an exposure to the full range of modeling opportunities in the business environment.

Just as an introductory course in statistics does not produce a professional statistician, neither will complete understanding of this text yield a professional model builder. A thorough study of this text, however, will provide the reader with a sound understanding of the methodology of model building and solution, and an exposure to many of the most important models of decision science.

A model is an abstraction of reality. It contains only those elements of reality that are necessary to describe the system of interest. A very abstract form of model, for example, is the *mental image*. A student may formulate a mental model of his professor. He may also have a mental model of his girlfriend. However, the relevant attributes of each model describing the student's mental image of his professor and his girlfriend will likely be quite different. He may, for example, formulate his image of his professor based on whether he is prompt, prepared, fair, competent, and other attributes of importance to the student. On the other hand, his image of his girlfriend may be based on beauty, personality, intelligence, wealth, and the like. It is very important for the model builder to identify the important components of the system to be included in the model as descriptors, and to be able to measure those components on some predefined scale.

A commonly used model of a business problem will now be presented to illustrate another type of model, the graphic model. Figure

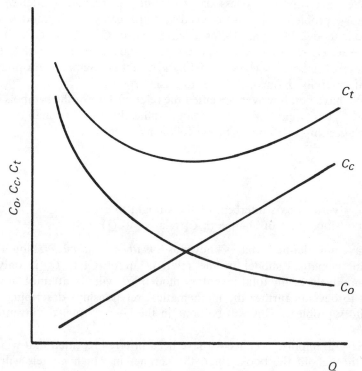

Figure 1.1
Graphic model of the inventory problem

1.1 is a graphic illustration of a model. The first important observation that should be made is that the model has been removed from mere mental image to a form that can be transferred to other persons. One of the more important characteristics of models in business decision analysis is the ability to communicate, in a succinct and exact manner, the system to others in the form of a model.

The graph of Figure 1.1 illustrates the relationship of three variables, C_o, C_c, and C_t, to a fourth variable, Q. The model is a very simplified representation of an inventory situation in which inventory carrying cost C_c, ordering cost C_o, and total inventory cost C_t are related to the quantity to order Q. As the size of orders becomes larger (and thus there are fewer orders), the carrying cost C_c increases, whereas the ordering cost C_o decreases. Total inventory cost C_t first decreases up to a point and then increases. The obvious purpose of such a model is to determine the order size Q that minimizes the sum of the two types of inventory costs.

We have, in the process of presenting the graphic model of an inventory problem, also introduced a third category of model, the symbolic model. The symbols for inventory costs, C_o, C_c, and C_t, and for order size, Q, represent the important components of our model. The language of decision science modeling is symbolic. Symbols are precise and, if carefully defined, difficult to misinterpret.

We have not, however, specified the relationships of the symbols C_o, C_c and C_t to Q in any way other than graphically. Now, we shall express the relationship of C_c to Q in the following form:

$$C_c = a + bQ$$

where

  a = vertical axis intercept of the straight line
  b = slope (rate of change in C_c relative to Q)

We have now defined what is known as a *mathematical model*. Note that this mathematical model of the relationship of C_c to Q is only a subcomponent of the total inventory model. We will not attempt, at this stage, to develop further the mathematical relationships describing our inventory problem. This will be done in the later chapter on inventory models.

Several important concepts have been briefly presented that will be used throughout the book. First, the manner in which models will be presented and discussed has been illustrated, as follows:

1. Graphic models
2. Symbolic models
3. Mathematical models

Wherever possible, models will be first illustrated graphically. Graphical presentation greatly enhances the clarity of communication of decision science models. In fact, an intuitive understanding of the solution process can also be demonstrated in many cases. It is obvious that the optimum value for Q in the inventory modeling case is at the point where the lowest level of total inventory cost, C_r, is achieved.

A second, and critical, set of concepts relating to our inventory model example will be included throughout the text. This is the specific identification of the various elements of the model. These elements are presented below.

Variables of the Model

The Decision Variables—Independent, Controllable Variables
The first and most important type of variable that must be identified in any modeling process is the decision variable or variables. It may also be referred to as a type of input variable. It is the values of these variables for which a solution is desired. They are therefore often referred to as the solution variables. For example, in our inventory model, we wish to reach a decision as to the optimum order size. Thus, the decision variable in this case is Q.

The Exogenous Variables—Independent, Uncontrollable Variables
A second important type of input variable in any model includes those that affect the workings of the model, but cannot be controlled. We have not explicitly identified any such variables in our inventory model. However, an example of an exogenous variable here might be the demand for items in inventory, which affects the solution but cannot be controlled.

The Criterion Variable or Variables—Dependent Variables
The criterion variable may also be referred to as an output variable. The value of the criterion variable is related to the values taken on by the independent, input variables. It is the value of the criterion variable that must be measured in order to determine when an optimum solution has been found. The relationship of the criterion variable to the independent variables is commonly referred to as the objective function. Thus, the

criterion variable may also be termed the objective function variable. In our inventory model example, C_o and C_c are actually both criterion variables; however, they can both be reduced to total inventory cost, C_t. Thus, the real criterion variable of interest here is C_t.

Parameters of the Model

Constants

The parameters of any model are generally constant values included in the functional relationships that describe the model. For example, in our inventory model example the symbols a and b in the functional relationship of C_c to Q are parameters. Likewise, the functional relationship of C_o to Q would also contain associated parameters. Finally, since C_t is simply the sum of ordering cost and inventory holding costs, we have the relationship $C_t = C_o + C_c$, where the parameters of this relationship are 1's: $1 \cdot C_o$ and $1 \cdot C_c$.

Random Variables

In more advanced models, rather than assuming a constant relationship between model components, a more realistic representation may be one in which the parameters themselves vary randomly according to some predefined probability distribution. For example, in our inventory model we might assume that the parameter b was in fact a random variable distributed according to a normal probability distribution. The true constants would then become the mean and variance of the normally distributed random variable. The distinction as to what is a variable and what is a parameter becomes somewhat fuzzy at this stage, and that definitional distinction will not be emphasized in this text.

Relationships of the Model

The essence of any model is the representation of the relationships that the various components have to one another. As was previously pointed out, model relationships may be illustrated graphically; however, in order to make any significant progress toward advanced decision analysis, more explicit statements of the functional relationships must be formulated. These statements of model relationships almost always take the form of mathematical functions. The degree of completeness of the model as to mathematical functional relationships varies considerably, however. Most of the models to be presented in this introductory text will be formulated in a mathematical manner complete enough to derive a solution. This is not always the case, however, and computer programs are an outgrowth of the demonstrated need for tools of analysis for models that cannot always be completely expressed as one grand composite of mathematical functions. A computer program model consists of a combination of logic and smaller subsets of functional relationships.

DECISION SCIENCE TECHNIQUES TO BE STUDIED

This section of the chapter presents the basic structure of the book and gives a brief description of the decision science techniques to be studied. Chapter 1, as has already been seen, is a general introduction to decision science. It presents the philosophic foundation of decision analysis, the role of decision science in today's complex organizations, the process of decision science, and the concept of modeling. Chapter 2 presents elementary break-even analysis, and introduces the concept of classical optimization. A more comprehensive discussion of classical optimization and an introduction to calculus are given in Appendix I. Chapter 3 is devoted to decision theory. In this chapter, the basic probability concept is discussed briefly for decision making under risk. Application of the expected-value criterion is thoroughly examined in two examples. Several important decision-making criteria under uncertainty are also presented. Finally, decision analysis using decision tree concepts is discussed. Chapter 4 presents the basic concepts and the graphical method of linear programming. Various solution approaches and sensitivity analysis are the primary topics of this chapter. Chapter 5 is devoted to the simplex method of linear programming. Illustrations are provided to demonstrate the detailed technique of the simplex method. The computer-based solution of linear programming is the topic of Appendix II. Chapter 6 introduces the concept of goal programming for decision analysis of multiple objectives. Through a simple example, the graphical and simplex solution methods will be presented. The computer-based analysis of goal programming is thoroughly discussed in Appendix III. Chapter 7 presents two special-purpose algorithms—the transportation and assignment methods. Several new developments and techniques are discussed through illustrations. Chapter 8 discusses various inventory models. The basic economic order quantity model is first developed, followed by a multitude of further extensions to this classic model. The classical optimization solution to several inventory models is given in Appendices IV, V, and VI. Chapter 9 introduces the basic concept, assumptions, and various models of waiting-line analysis (queueing theory). The derivations of the basic queueing equations and tables relating to queueing processes are presented in Appendices VII, VIII, IX, and X. Chapter 10 presents the PERT-CPM network models. In addition to project time analysis, PERT-Cost is also presented. Appendix XI presents the table of normal probability values used in PERT analysis. Game theory is the topic of Chapter 11. The underlying assumptions of game theory, the two-person zero-sum game, and mixed strategies will be thoroughly analyzed. Chapter 12 is devoted to a general introduction to simulation. Special emphasis is placed on the generation of random variables as the conceptual basis for most simulation analysis. Appendix XII provides a computer program to generate values of a random variable. Appendix XIII also provides a table of random numbers, which may be used for manual simulation analysis. Chapter 13 is the concluding chapter of the text. It presents a philosophic and qualitative discussion of the role of decision science in managerial decision analysis. The core of the discussion is directed toward the analysis of environmental conditions for an effective implementation of decision science.

REFERENCES

Beer, S., *Management Sciences: The Business Use of Operations Research*, Doubleday, Garden City, N.Y., 1968.

Bierman, H., Bonini, C. P., and Hauseman, W. H., *Quantitative Analysis for Business Decisions*, 4th ed., Irwin, Homewood, Ill., 1973.

Churchman, C. W., Ackoff, R. L., and Arnoff, E. L., *Introduction to Operations Research*, Wiley, New York, 1957.

Lee, S. M., *Goal Programming for Decision Analysis*, Auerbach, Philadelphia, 1972.

Wagner, H. M., *Principles of Management Science*, Prentice-Hall, Englewood Cliffs, N.J., 1970.

QUESTIONS

1. What is decision science?
2. What is the genesis of decision analysis?
3. Are decision science and intuitive decision making mutually exclusive? If yes, why? If not, discuss their relationships.
4. Discuss the origin of operations research.
5. What are the three important factors behind the rapid development of operations research in the early 1950s in the United States?

6. What are some of the synonyms of operations research?
7. What is the systems approach?
8. What is the relationship between decision science and the systems approach?
9. Why is the team approach ideal for decision science studies?
10. Why is it so important to have top management participation in decision analysis projects?
11. Discuss the process of decision science.
12. What are the differences among the mental, graphical, and mathematical models?
13. Discuss various components of a mathematical model.

2 Break-even and Optimization Analysis

INTRODUCTION

This chapter will present some of the key concepts of model construction and solution by extending the introduction to modeling of Chapter 1 to break-even analysis. The elementary break-even model provides a convenient vehicle for introducing these important concepts, which, although included in other decision science models, may become obscured by model detail and complexity. In addition, the technique of break-even analysis, although quite simple conceptually, remains a worthwhile topic for consideration in the study of decision science models.

Since a large portion of decision science is concerned with optimization models, the basic concepts of classical optimization will also be presented, in a summary manner. An extended discussion of classical optimization, including the rules of differentiation, is also provided in Appendix I.

BREAK-EVEN ANALYSIS

Break-even analysis is often referred to as cost-volume-profit analysis. This is because the purpose of the analysis is to study the relationship among cost, volume, and profit in order to determine the point of break-even volume. Break-even is defined as the volume (level of operation in terms of unit quantity, dollar volume, or percentage of capacity) required such that total revenue just equals total costs.

For example, a book publisher is concerned with determining the quantity of book sales required to cover the fixed costs of publishing a new book. If the new book includes costly design and typesetting features, then fixed costs will be high, and the resulting break-even volume will be higher than normal. If the book must compete with several similar books, thus forcing the publisher to price his book competitively at a similar price, then the publisher can undertake the project only if projected sales at the competitive price exceed the computed break-even point.

A manufacturing firm, considering investment in automated equipment for production operations, can make use of break-even analysis to assist in the decision. Although investment in automated equipment may reduce the variable costs of production, the benefits of reduced variable costs may not offset the increase in fixed cost required. Break-even analysis could assist in determining the level of operation required to make such an investment beneficial.

Components of the Break-even Model

The first step of the model construction in any decision science model is to abstract from the system of interest the elements that are essential to the decision analysis. The usual approach is to relate the essential elements or components to various symbols, to facilitate model construction and manipulation.

Identification of System (Model) Components

The major components of the break-even analysis model are total revenue, fixed costs, variable costs, and volume.

Total revenue. Total revenue reflects the sales forecast for the planning period, and consists of the selling price multiplied by the quantity sold.

Fixed costs. Fixed costs are costs not directly related to volume of production or sales. Thus, fixed costs would remain constant in dollar amount regardless of the level of output. Some examples of fixed cost are:

Depreciation on plant and equipment
Executive and office staff salaries
Property insurance and taxes
Property rent
Interest on investment
Lump-sum advertising expenses

Variable costs. Variable costs are often referred to as direct costs and are directly related to the volume of production or sales. Total variable costs would be computed as the variable cost per unit multiplied by the level of operation (quantity). Some examples of variable costs are:

Direct materials
Direct labor
Sales commissions
Packaging
Freight out

Volume (quantity). The volume of the operation is the level of operation, specified as: (1) unit quantity, (2) dollar volume, or (3) percentage of capacity. Both total revenue and total variable costs are related to the level of operation (volume of production or sales).

Specification of the System (Model) Symbols

Whenever possible in decision science, symbolic models are constructed. The two major symbolic components of any model are model variables and model parameters.

Variables of the model. The variables of the model are also subdivided into at least three categories: (1) the decision or solution variable (or variables), (2) the criterion variable, and (3) exogenous or outside variables.

The decision variable is the variable for which a solution is sought. In the case of break-even analysis, it is the break-even volume or quantity that is to be solved for. We will designate Q as our symbol for quantity.

The criterion variable is the variable that is to be measured in order to determine when a solution is reached. In the case of break-even analysis, the objective is to determine at what quantity of output, total revenue just equals total cost. Since profit is equal to total revenue minus total cost, when total revenue equals total cost, profit will equal zero. Therefore, we will designate profit as our criterion variable and denote it by the Greek letter π.

Exogenous variables are sometimes referred to as input variables. Such variables derive their value from outside the system of interest and, generally, cannot be controlled by the decision maker.

The basic break-even model assumes a perfectly competitive market such that price is a value determined by market forces and cannot be manipulated by the decision maker. Additionally, under such conditions, the firm can produce and sell any quantity desired without affecting price. Thus, price, which will be denoted by P, is an exogenous variable to the break-even model.

Parameters of the model. The parameters of the model are the remaining elements of the model that complete the formulation of the relationships among the variables of the model. Parameters are generally constant values, which change only for different cases of the same problem.

If we assume that a model can be represented by a mathematical equation, then the parameters of the model are the coefficients of the equation. The purpose of representing the parameters of the model as symbols is to obtain a solution to the model in a general form. Then for different cases of the same type of problem, the new values of the parameters can be inserted into the general form model solution to obtain a new solution directly.

We will assume, for the time being, that the parameters of the break-even model are fixed cost and variable cost. Fixed cost will be denoted symbolically by FC and variable cost will be denoted by VC.

It should be pointed out here that it often becomes difficult to distinguish between exogenous variables and parameters. The previously given exogenous variable, price, might also be thought of as a model parameter, since it is assumed to be a given constant for the model. Likewise, where a model component may be a parameter or exogenous variable in the model for one decision analysis, it may become the decision variable for another decision analysis. In the case of break-even analysis, both price and fixed cost can take on the roles of decision variables under certain conditions. This condition will be discussed at a later point in the chapter.

Since the break-even model is concerned with the point at which total revenue equals total cost, we will also assign each of these two model components a symbolic representation. Total revenue will be denoted by TR and total cost will be denoted by TC.

Most decision science models are composites of submodels. It is generally simpler to construct each of the submodels separately and then aggregate the submodels into the overall model as a last step. Construction of the break-even model demonstrates this approach by constructing the submodels for total revenue and total cost, and then linking the two together into an overall model.

The model symbols are summarized as follows:

Q = quantity (decision variable)
π = profit (criterion variable)
P = price (exogenous variable)
FC = fixed cost (parameter)
VC = variable cost (parameter)

TR = total revenue (submodel variable)
TC = total cost (submodel variable)

Construction of the Model

The construction of the decision science model consists of identifying the relationships between the system components. Where possible, the functional relationship among the variables and parameters is specified explicitly. This can be done in the case of the break-even analysis model. The model is, in fact, a profit model, where profit equals total revenue minus total cost.

In order to analyze any decision science model and arrive at a decision, the relationship of the criterion variable to the decision variable must be given. In break-even analysis, profit π is the criterion variable, and quantity Q is the decision variable. Thus, the following relationship must be developed:

$\pi = f(Q)$

We know that the following relationship of the criterion variable to the two submodels exists:

$\pi = TR - TC$

We will, therefore, develop each submodel separately, and join the two as our last step.

Total revenue

It was stated previously that total revenue is simply price multiplied by quantity produced or sold. Therefore, our first submodel is given by

$TR = P \cdot Q$

Total cost

Total variable cost was previously given as unit variable cost multiplied by quantity. Fixed cost is a constant dollar value, independent of volume. Thus, the second submodel is

$TC = FC + VC \cdot Q$

The profit model

The profit model is now, therefore, given in terms of the criterion variable, decision variable, exogenous variable, and parameters as

$\pi = P \cdot Q - FC - VC \cdot Q$

or

Profit = (price)(quantity) – fixed cost – (variable cost)(quantity)

Solution of the Model

We must now solve for the value of the decision variable Q in terms of the other model variables and parameters. An objective, in break-even analysis, is to determine the value of Q for which profit π just equals zero (total revenue equals total cost). Therefore, the solution procedure to be employed here is to set the model for profit equal to zero and solve for Q. The solution procedure is illustrated as follows:

$$P{\cdot}Q - FC - VC{\cdot}Q = 0 \qquad \text{Setting profit model equal to 0}$$
$$P{\cdot}Q - VC{\cdot}Q = FC \qquad \text{Transposing } FC$$
$$Q(P - VC) = FC \qquad \text{Collecting } Q \text{ separately}$$
$$Q_{BE} = \frac{FC}{P - VC} \qquad \text{Dividing through by } P - VC$$

We identify Q_{BE} as the break-even point quantity. At the point where the volume of operation equals Q_{BE} profit will equal zero (and total revenue will equal total cost). Note that $P - VC$ is the commonly known term, unit contribution. Thus, break-even is determined by dividing fixed cost by unit contribution.

The model solution illustrates the previously discussed solution in general form; that is, the break-even quantity can, in general, be determined by inserting the values for fixed cost, price, and variable cost for the symbols FC, P, and VC in the Q_{BE} equation and obtaining a solution directly. Not all decision science models can be solved in the general form, but whenever possible it is preferable.

Graphical Model

In most presentations of decision science models, the graphical model will be presented first, in order to give the reader an intuitive understanding of the components and their relationships. However, in this case, the desired emphasis was upon the methodology of model construction and solution rather than the break-even technique itself. In order not to detract from this purpose, presentation of the graphical model was delayed. The preceding model is illustrated graphically in Figure 2.1.

The graph illustrates that the break-even quantity Q_{BE} occurs at the point where profit π just equals zero (and where total revenue equals total cost). If we refer back to the model solution process, we see that break-even occurs where quantity multiplied by unit contribution is equal to fixed cost, or

$$Q(P - VC) = FC$$

Thus, as quantity is increased from zero to Q_{BE}, the total contribution toward fixed cost (quantity times unit contribution) is progressively covering a larger portion of fixed cost, and the loss is being reduced. As quantity is increased beyond Q_{BE}, the expression $Q (P - VC)$ exceeds fixed cost, in the form of increasing profit.

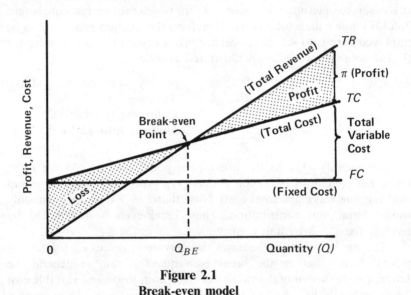

Figure 2.1
Break-even model

Fixed Cost as the Decision Variable

Fixed cost was previously identified as a parameter (uncontrollable constant) of the model. However, for the case in which management is considering investment in fixed assets (i. e., equipment), which will reduce unit variable cost, fixed cost may become a decision variable of sorts. At least, it can no longer be thought of as an uncontrollable constant.

Quantity remains a solution variable (if not a decision variable), since the objective of management for this case will be to determine the volume of operation required to make such an investment worthwhile. Such an analysis is illustrated in Figure 2.2. The subscripts for the various model components correspond to: (1) investment in equipment is not made, and (2) additional investment in equipment is made.

Thus, we see that fixed cost with the additional investment, FC_2, is higher, whereas variable costs increase at a flatter rate, shown by TC_2. The break-even point indicates the volume of operations required to make such an investment outlay beneficial to the firm. The use of increased fixed cost to reduce total costs (beyond a given volume of operation) is often referred to as operating leverage.

Variations in the Solution Results

The solution to the break-even model may be given in several forms. The variations are described as follows:

Break-even Quantity in Units.

The break-even quantity, in units, was previously determined to be

$$Q_{BE} = \frac{FC}{P - VC}$$

Break-even Volume in Dollars.

If one desires the dollar volume (sales) required to break even, it can be computed by multiplying both sides of the initial solution by price P; that is, dollar volume equals $P \cdot Q$, so that dollar-volume break-even, given by $(P \cdot Q)_{BE}$, is

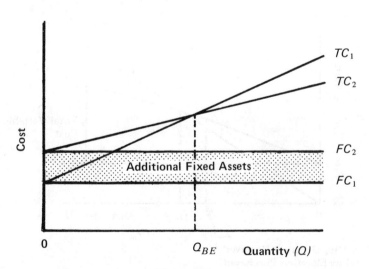

Figure 2.2
Cost break-even for investment in fixed assets

$$(P{\cdot}Q)_{BE} = P{\cdot}\left(\frac{FC}{P - VC}\right)$$

$$= \frac{P{\cdot}FC}{P - VC}$$

$$(P{\cdot}Q)_{BE} = \frac{FC}{1 - (VC/P)} \qquad \text{Break-even in dollars}$$

Break-even as Percentage of Capacity

Break-even as a percentage of total capacity may be determined by dividing both sides of the initial solution by total capacity. If we denote total capacity by Q_{cap}, then break-even as a percentage of total capacity is given by Q_{BE}/Q_{cap} and is computed as

$$\frac{Q_{BE}}{Q_{cap}} = \frac{FC/(P - VC)}{Q_{cap}}$$

$$\frac{Q_{BE}}{Q_{cap}} = \frac{FC}{(P - VC)Q_{cap}} \qquad \text{Break-even as percentage of capacity}$$

Refinements in the Break-even Model

It is reasonable to assume that as the level of operation is increased, the functional relationships may change. An important assumption of

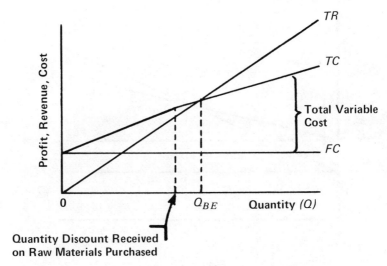

Figure 2.3
Break-even model, with a change in variable cost

simple break-even analysis is that the relationships of revenue and cost to quantity are linear and continuous over the relevant range of analysis. Several variations to the basic model will be presented.

Change in Variable Cost

It is possible that at a certain point in the volume of operation, the variable cost may change. For example, a quantity discount may be allowed on purchased raw materials, if purchased in sufficient volume. This would result in a change in the slope of the total cost function, to a flatter rate of increase relative to Q, as illustrated in Figure 2.3.

Change in Fixed Cost

It is also possible that fixed cost might change at some point as quantity produced or sold is increased. For example, productive capacity might have to be expanded for output levels beyond a certain quantity. This would result in the fixed cost (and total cost) functions moving up step-wise by the amount of increased fixed cost, as shown in Figure 2.4.

A Nonlinear Model

It is not generally valid to assume that quantity sold is unrelated to price. If the commonly assumed functional relationship of quantity sold

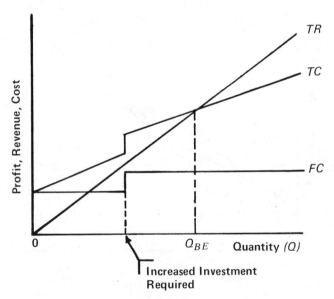

Figure 2.4
Break-even model, with a change in fixed cost

to price is assumed, then we have a downward sloping function (demand curve). This will result in total revenue first increasing, then peaking out, and finally beginning to decline, as quantity sold is increased (through price reductions). The profit model for this situation is developed in Appendix I, Classical Optimization. This analysis also illustrates how price becomes a decision variable, rather than an exogenous variable.

It is also reasonable to expect that average variable cost per unit will fall as economics of scale are realized, and perhaps then increase again as diseconomics of scale are reached. This would result in total costs that rise at a steep level initially, then a reduced rate of increase, followed ultimately by a steeper rate of increase.

A nonlinear model is illustrated in Figure 2.5. In this case, there would be both a lower break-even point and an upper break-even point. However, it is likely that the linear break-even model is more appropriate for the uses for which it is intended. Users of break-even analysis are ordinarily not interested in the high and low extremes, but rather in a

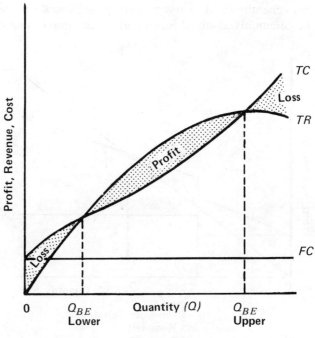

Figure 2.5
Nonlinear break-even model

relevant range within which the linear functions are reasonably good approximations.

OPTIMIZATION ANALYSIS

Some very elementary, but basic, concepts in optimization analysis will be discussed next, as a prelude to the optimization models to be presented in succeeding chapters.

Let us first return to our linear profit model of break-even analysis. It should be apparent that if we wished to maximize profits, the optimum quantity to produce and sell is infinity. By referring to Figure 2.1, one can see that profits continue to increase as the quantity is increased. Thus, the optimum solution value for the decision variable would be: $Q^* = +\infty$, where Q^* denotes the optimum quantity. Of course, reason leads us to the conclusion that after some point, profit would begin to decline (as illustrated in Figure 2.5).

Constrained Optimization

Let us assume that the relationships are approximately linear over the relevant range of analysis. But, in addition to the profit function, let

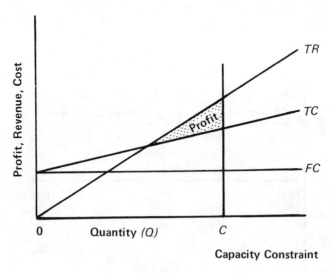

Figure 2.6
Profit model, with capacity constraint

us assume that we also have a capacity constraint, which cannot be altered during the planning period. We will refer to this as C (capacity quantity). The resulting model is illustrated in Figure 2.6.

The mathematical model for this problem is given as follows:

Maximize $\quad \pi = P{\cdot}Q - FC - VC{\cdot}Q$
subject to $\quad Q \leqslant C$

Our model now consists of not only the profit function to be maximized but also the constraint. This example introduces a general form of model often used in decision analysis:

Optimize: $\quad$ objective function
subject to: $\quad$ constraint(s)

The "objective function" is so termed because it includes the objective of the analysis and the criterion variable (i.e., profit).

We note, from observation of Figure 2.6, that the optimum solution value for Q is where it is equal to C. Thus, we have

$Q^* = C$

where

$Q^* =$ optimum value for Q
$C \ =$ capacity of plant

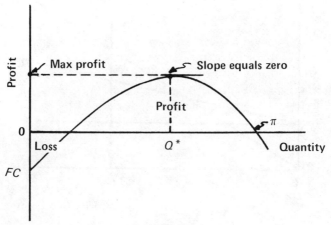

Figure 2.7
Nonlinear profit model, with optimum quantity (Q^*)

Obviously, the model solution is trivial for this example. However, it demonstrates an important point; the solution occurs at a boundary of the range of values that Q can take on, and the solution boundary is formed by the constraint.

The above analysis is the conceptual basis for linear programming, which involves optimizing a linear objective function, including many decision variables, subject to many linear constraints.

Optimization of Nonlinear Models

By referring to Figure 2.5, it is apparent that the maximum profit will be obtained when Q is somewhere about halfway between the lower break-even and the upper break-even points. In order to facilitate the analysis of profit only, the profit function is illustrated in Figure 2.7. Maximum profit is obtained at the highest point on the curve, and the optimum value of Q is associated with this high point.

CLASSICAL OPTIMIZATION

Classical optimization involves the subject of optimizing nonlinear models. Differential calculus is the tool of classical optimization. We will leave this topic for Appendix I. However, the basic concept of classical optimization will be briefly given.

By observing Figure 2.7, we see that the slope of the profit curve changes for various values of Q. It is also apparent that at the highest point on the curve, the *slope* of the curve is zero; that is, a straight line tangent to the profit curve, just touching the highest point, would be exactly parallel to the horizontal axis of the graph (which has zero slope).

If we could obtain a general model of the slope of the curve, for various values of Q, we could then set that slope model equal to zero (slope), and solve for the associated value of Q. Calculus provides this capability.

Through differential calculus, we can obtain from our model of profit as a function of quantity another model of the "rate of change" in profit as a function of quantity. We then simply set this rate-of-change, or slope, model equal to zero and solve for the associated optimum value of Q.

The basic approach of classical optimization is summarized as follows:

1. Formulate the profit model, that is,

$$\pi = f(Q)$$

2. Determine through calculus the slope model,

$$\pi' = f'(Q)$$

where π' and $f'(Q)$ denote the slope, or rate of change in π as a function of Q.

3. Since we know that the maximum profit occurs where the *slope* of the profit function equals zero, we set the slope model equal to zero and solve for the associated value of Q.

4. The solution to step 3 yields Q^*, the optimum value of Q.

The preceding summary of classical optimization is reviewed and extended with an example in the initial discussion of Appendix I, where the basic concepts of classical optimization, along with the rules of calculus, are given. A later example illustrates the case where profit is maximized subject to a linear constraint (the demand function).

REFERENCES

Beveridge, G. S. G., and Schechter, R. S., *Optimization: Theory and Practice*, McGraw-Hill, New York, 1970.

Buffa, E. S., *Operation Management: Problems and Models*, 3d. ed., Wiley, New York, 1972.

Gottfried, B. S., and Weisman, J., *Introduction to Optimization Theory*, Prentice-Hall, Englewood Cliffs, N.J., 1973.

Levin, R. I., and Kirkpatrick, C. A., *Quantitative Approaches to Management*, 2d. ed., McGraw-Hill, New York, 1971.

McAdams, A. K., *Mathematical Analysis for Management Decisions: Introduction to Calculus and Linear Algebra*, Macmillan, New York, 1970.

Wilde, D. J., and Beightler, C. S., *Foundations of Optimization*, Prentice-Hall, Englewood Cliffs, N.J., 1967.

QUESTIONS

1. Define the meaning of the term *break-even* as it is used in this chapter. In what terms may break-even be specified?
2. Describe the major components of the break-even model.

3. Describe the variables of the break-even model, and indicate the general category of variable under which each may be classified.
4. Specify the parameters of the break-even model. Why are symbols used to represent the model parameters?
5. Discuss the relationships of the break-even model. Illustrate graphically. Define all variables, relationships, and axes on the graph. Show regions of profit, loss, and the point of break-even.
6. Discuss how fixed cost may be treated as a decision variable when considering the question of operating leverage. Illustrate graphically.
7. Discuss the conditions under which the relationships of the break-even model might be "kinked" or become "nonlinear."
8. Describe the meaning of "constrained" optimization. Illustrate graphically a simple case.
9. Discuss the derivative obtained by calculus as related to finding a maximum or minimum point on a profit (or cost) curve. What is a "slope model"? What value must the slope model equal at the maximum or minimum point on a curve?
10. Summarize the basic approach of classical optimization. Relate your discussion to a graphical illustration.

PROBLEMS

1. The XZS Corporation has just acquired a new plant at a cost of $875,000. The new plant will be used to produce pipe wrenches. It is estimated that the variable cost per pipe wrench is $2.50. The firm plans to sell the wrenches for $4.25 apiece, to wholesale firms. How many wrenches must the firm produce and sell to break even on their investment?
2. Demonstrate the complete step-by-step development of the model for problem 1. First, define the variables and parameters of the system. Represent all components of the model by symbols, and then define the values of the symbols that represent model parameters. Show the development of the model relationships. Solve the model, in terms of symbols, and discuss why this is desirable where possible.
3. Joe, who owns the "Corner Pizza Parlor," just broke even in his first year of operation. The pizza parlor cost him $10,000, and his average cost per pizza sold was $1.75. What average price did Joe charge if he sold 20,000 pizzas? Joe is not too sophisticated in financial analysis, but he figures that by trading the current pizza oven for a new one he will save 10¢ per pizza. The cost of the trade to Joe is $1000. What will Joe's new break-even quantity be?

4. A hot-dog vendor sold $1800 of products at the football game. His fixed costs included a license to sell, and truck and stand rentals, which totaled $600. The hot dogs, which he sold for 35¢ apiece, cost him an average of 20¢ apiece. Determine break-even sales, in dollars. How much profit did the vendor make?

5. The G.R.H. Manufacturing Company makes ball bearings. Their production capacity is 4 million units per year. They estimate that the annual fixed-cost charges are $800,000. The ball bearings cost 65¢ each to produce, and G.R.H. sells them for 90¢ apiece. At what percent of capacity must the company operate in order to break even?

6. In problem 5, assume that the G.R.H. Company is considering additional investment in more efficient equipment. The incremental investment is $100,000, resulting in a per unit cost reduction of 5¢. At what quantity level must the firm operate to make this additional investment worthwhile? Should the firm make the investment? (Hint: Determine the point of break-even between total cost for the two cases.) Determine the new profit break-even point, in units. Illustrate the entire decision analysis graphically, showing the fixed and variable costs for both cases, and the revenue curve.

7. Assume that the Ezex Corporation must determine whether to purchase or lease cars for its salesmen. The purchase cost is $3000, with associated variable costs of 5¢ per mile. The cost of leasing is a flat 10¢ per mile. Establish a decision rule for the company to follow (lease or buy) based on the estimated miles a man will drive.

8. In problem 7, assume that the lease cost per mile is reduced from 10¢ per mile to 8¢ per mile for any mileage over 50,000 miles per year. Reevaluate the decision rule established for problem 7. Is it still valid? Illustrate the decision model graphically.

9. Suppose the demand curve for a product is downward sloping; that is, there exists an inverse relationship between price charged and quantity demanded. Illustrate the approximate total-revenue curve for this case graphically. Assuming that variable cost is a linear function of quantity sold, show that there would be two break-even points for this situation. Which break-even point would one normally be attempting to determine in standard break-even analysis?

3 Decision Theory

Decision science is primarily concerned with assisting the decision maker in his search for the best course of action. The type of scientific technique to be used in decision analysis is based not only upon the nature of the problem on hand, but also upon the decision environment. Basically, there are four different states of decision environment: certainty, risk, uncertainty, and conflict.

The certainty state exists when all the information required to make a decision is known and available. For example, the analysis of cost, volume, and profit, as presented in Chapter 2, is basically a decision problem under certainty. Here the information concerning the costs and profits is known in relation to the volume of sales. In a linear programming problem, presented in Chapters 4 and 5, we also know exactly how much resources are required to produce a product and its unit profit. The decision science techniques we use for problems under certainty are break-even analysis, deterministic linear and goal programming, transportation and assignment methods, inventory models under certainty, classical optimization technique (use of differential calculus), and the like.

The risk condition refers to the situation where the probabilities of certain outcomes occurring are known. For decision problems under risk, the theory of probability is used extensively. Various stochastic models, such as probabilistic linear programming, chance-constrained programming, stochastic model of goal programming, queueing theory, Markov analysis, simulation models, and probabilistic inventory models have been developed for decision analysis under risk.

The uncertainty state refers to the condition where the probabilities of certain outcomes occurring are not known. There have been several approaches suggested for the decision analysis under uncertainty. However, decision under uncertainty remains the academic virgin land of decision science.

A condition of conflict exists when the interests of two or more decision makers are in a competitive situation. In other words, if decision maker A benefits from a course of action he takes, it is only possible because decision maker B has also taken a certain course of action. Hence, the decision makers are interested not only in what they do individually but also in what both of them do in the decision analysis. Analysis under conflict will be the primary topic of game theory, presented in Chapter 11.

Although the decision environment is never purely certain, decision analysis under certainty provides the fundamental knowledge required for the analysis of risk and uncertainty. In economics, we study price theory under the condition of pure competition, although pure competition never exists in reality. However, the analysis of pure competition provides necessary knowledge for further study of monopolistic competition, oligopoly, and monopolistic situations.

Decision theory is primarily concerned with decision making under the conditions of risk and uncertainty. Decision theory assists the decision maker in analyzing complex problems with numerous alternatives and possible consequences. The basic objective of decision theory is to provide more concrete information concerning the relative likelihood of certain consequences occurring so that he may be able to identify the best course of action.

DECISION MAKING UNDER RISK

For decision making under risk, we must first identify the courses of action that are available and feasible. Next, the possible events that can occur should be examined. Then the conditional payoff for a given course of action under a given possible event should be determined. It is not a simple matter to identify the exact monetary payoffs for the action/event combination. However, accumulated experience or past records often provide relatively accurate estimated payoffs for many decisions. Let us consider a simple decision problem under risk.

A Simple Example

Next Saturday is a football day for Blacksburg High. The game is with the archrival, Radford High. The tickets have been sold out for weeks. A big game with 5000 cheering fans! The Beta Club has been planning to raise some funds by selling a beverage at the game. The club is allowed to sell only one type of beverage, as other student organizations are also trying to sell various beverages. The president of the club is trying to determine whether the members should sell soda or coffee. The payoff is primarily dependent upon the weather condition. If the weather is cold, selling coffee results in a greater payoff. On the other hand, if the weather is relatively warm, soda brings in a greater payoff. The courses of action, possible events, and conditional payoffs are given in Table 3.1.

Table 3.1
Conditional Payoff Table for the Beta Club Problem

	Events	
Action	*Cold weather*	*Warm Weather*
Sell soda	$100	$250
Sell coffee	200	150

The only difficult part of the decision making for the problem is finding out the probabilities of cold or warm weather for the coming Saturday. Wisely, the club president contacted the area weather bureau. The bureau reports that the chance of having cold weather on Saturday is 30 percent. Consequently, the probability of warm weather is 70 percent. The club has decided to accept the weather bureau's report as adequate information for the decision analysis.

The most widely used criterion for decision making under risk is the *expected monetary value* (EMV). The expected monetary value for a given course of action is simply the weighted average payoff, which is the sum of the product of the payoff multiplied by the probability of each event. For example, for the above problem the expected monetary value of selling soda is

$$\text{EMV(soda)} = \$100 \times 0.3 + \$250 \times 0.7 = \$30 + \$175 = \$205$$

The payoff of soda under the cold weather condition is $100. The probability of this conditional payoff (probability of cold weather) is 0.3. The conditional payoff of soda under the warm weather is $250 and its probability to occur is 0.7. The weighted average is simply the sum of the payoffs multiplied by the probabilities, as shown above.

The expected monetary value of selling coffee is

$$\text{EMV(coffee)} = \$200 \times 0.3 + \$150 \times 0.7 = \$165$$

By comparing the expected monetary values associated with each of the two alternatives, the Beta Club decided to sell soda at the game, as the expected payoff for selling soda is $40 more than that for selling coffee.

Now, let us suppose that the area weather bureau could not provide any concrete information concerning the temperature on Saturday. Should the president of the club simply flip a coin to decide what to sell at the game? Suppose he decided to ask the opinions of the club members about the probabilities of cold and warm weather on Saturday. However, before he asks the opinion of each member, he wants to find out the "indifference probabilities." In other words, he wants to determine the probabilities of warm weather and cold weather on Saturday that would cause him to be perfectly indifferent between the two courses of action. In order to be indifferent between selling soda and selling coffee, the expected monetary values must be exactly identical. If we arbitrarily assign P as the probability of cold weather, then the probability of warm weather will be $(1 - P)$, as the sum of two probabilities must be one. The situation described above is summarized in Table 3.2.

Table 3.2
Conditional Payoff Without Probabilities for the Beta Club Problem

	Events	
Action	Cold Weather Probability = P	Warm Weather Probability = $1 - P$
Sell soda	$100	$250
Sell coffee	200	150

Now, we can calculate the expected monetary values as follows:

$$EMV(soda) = \$100P + \$250(1 - P)$$
$$EMV(coffee) = \$200P + \$150(1 - P)$$

Since we are trying to find the indifference probabilities, the two EMVs must be identical. Thus, we can equate the two values:

$$EMV(soda) = EMV(coffee)$$
$$\$100P + \$250(1 - P) = \$200P + \$150(1 - P)$$
$$\$100P + \$250 - \$250P = \$200P + \$150 - \$150P$$
$$\$250 - \$150P = \$150 + \$50P$$
$$-\$200P = -\$100$$
$$P = 0.5$$

The two courses of action will have exactly the same EMVs if the probability of cold weather is 0.5 and the probability of warm weather is also 0.5 $(1 - P = 1 - 0.5)$. We can check this very easily, as follows:

$$EMV(\text{soda}) = \$100 \times 0.5 + \$250 \times 0.5 = \$175$$
$$EMV(\text{coffee}) = \$200 \times 0.5 + \$150 \times 0.5 = \$175$$

Now, the question is whether or not the probability of cold weather is less than or greater than 0.5. If the probability of cold weather is greater than 0.5, the club should sell coffee because its EMV will be greater than that of soda. Accordingly, if the probability of cold weather is less than 0.5, the club should sell soda. The president has asked the opinions of the members, and 90 percent of the members think the probability of cold weather is less than 0.5. Thus, the club decides to sell soda.

We have used the EMV as the decision criterion for the above problem. When we say that the EMV of selling soda is $175, does that mean that we get exactly $175 from the action? No, absolutely not. The eventual payoff of our action is never equal to the EMV, except under conditions of certainty. In fact, the actual payoff will be one of those conditional payoffs listed in the table. For example, if we sell soda and we have warm weather, we will make $250. Then why do we use the EMV as the decision criterion? We use it because we want to maximize the long-run payoff. If the decision problem is a repetitive type, the problem will occur a great number of times. Since the EMV is exactly the same thing as the average payoff of a given course of action when the decision problem is repeated a great number of times, it is a valid criterion for decision making.

When a decision problem under risk is not a repetitive type, the use of the EMV as the decision criterion may be inappropriate. In real-world situations, management frequently avoids a certain course of action which has a very large conditional loss (negative payoff) even when its EMV is greater than that of other courses of action. For example, suppose a firm is contemplating two investment alternatives with the following conditional payoffs under two conditions:

	Conditional Payoffs	
Investment Plan	*Condition 1*	*Condition 2*
A	$-\$1,000,000$	$\$1,060,000$
B	20,000	30,000

Suppose that the two conditions have exactly equal probability of 0.5 to occur. The EMVs for the two plans would be as follows:

$$EMV(\text{plan A}) = -\$1,000,000(0.5) + \$1,060,000(0.5) = \$30,000$$
$$EMV(\text{plan B}) = \quad\ \$20,000(0.5) + \quad\ \$30,000(0.5) = \$25,000$$

Although the EMV of plan A is $5000 greater than that of plan B, the management of the firm is likely to choose plan B over plan A. In other words, management puts a higher priority on the survival of the organization than on the long-run average payoff of certain courses of action. If, however, the conditional payoffs are relatively insignificant in relation to the financial security of the firm, management may well be justified in using the EMV as the decision criterion. For example, if the conditional payoffs of the two plans were as follows, management may use the EMV criterion and choose plan A:

	Conditional Payoffs	
Investment Plan	Condition 1	Condition 2
A	$-$100.00	$106.00
B	2.00	3.00

A Complex Example

The Valley Fish Market sells various sea foods. The demand for most of the foods is relatively easy to predict. However, it is extremely difficult to determine the optimum amount of clams to stock because clams can be stored for only a week and the demand for them fluctuates quite widely. Any clams not sold within a week have to be thrown out at a total loss.

The market purchases clams from a large wholesale dealer in Norfolk at $10 per bushel. The profit per bushel is $5, as the price charged is $15 per bushel. The market has the sales records for the past 100 weeks, as shown in Table 3.3. Demand ranges from 1 to 7 bushels of clams. Based on the number of weeks that the sales equaled a certain number of bushels of clams, we can derive a probability distribution. For example, in 5 weeks out of 100 weeks the demand for clams was 1 bushel. Therefore, the probability of demand for 1 bushel will be $5 \div 100 = 0.05$. Table 3.4 presents the possible demands for clams and their probability distribution based on the past demand. This table represents the possible demand for clams if the past market situation remains constant; in other words, if drastic changes occur in the market situation (i.e., beef shortage, sharp increase in meat prices, etc.), the demand for clams might not be the same as the past records indicate.

The management problem of the Valley Fish Market is to determine the optimum number of bushels of clams to order weekly in order to maximize profit. Clearly, if the market orders more than what will be demanded, profits will be reduced because of the loss on the unsold clams. On the other hand, if the market orders an insufficient amount to

Table 3.3
Valley Fish Market: Past Demand for Clams

Weekly Sales (bushels)	Number of Weeks
1	5
2	10
3	25
4	30
5	20
6	5
7	5
	100

meet the demand, profits will be smaller because of the lost sales due to shortage. The optimum quantity to order will be the one which maximizes the expected profit.

Conditional Profits

Before we can calculate the expected profit, we must construct a table of conditional profits, as shown in Table 3.5. The table presents the possible profits in dollars for a given combination of demand and supply. The conditional profit can be either positive or negative depending upon the combined conditions of specific demand and supply. It should be noted in Table 3.5 that the conditional profits are explicit (out-of-pocket) monetary figures. In other words, conditional

Table 3.4
Demand and Its Probability Distribution

Demand (bushels)	Probability of Demand
1	0.05
2	0.10
3	0.25
4	0.30
5	0.20
6	0.05
7	0.05
	1.00

Table 3.5
Conditional Payoff Table for the Valley Fish Market Problem

				Quantity Stocked				
		1	2	3	4	5	6	7
	1	$5	−5	−15	−25	−35	−45	−55
	2	5	10	0	−10	−20	−30	−40
	3	5	10	15	5	− 5	−15	−25
Demand	4	5	10	15	20	10	0	−10
	5	5	10	15	20	25	15	5
	6	5	10	15	20	25	30	20
	7	5	10	15	20	25	30	35

profits include losses due to overstocking, but they do not include the opportunity (implicit) costs due to understocking.

The conditional profit of stocking a certain amount of clams will be based on two conditions: Demand D is equal to or greater than the quantity Q stocked; and demand D is less than quantity Q stocked.

$D \geq Q$. When the demand is equal to or greater than the quantity stocked, the market can sell all it has in stock. Therefore, the total profit will be $5Q$. It is clear in Table 3.5 that this is how we calculated conditional payoffs along the diagonal and below it. For example, when the market stocks 1 bushel, then demand will be at least 1. Therefore, under any demand condition, all it can sell will be 1 bushel at $5 profit. Hence, the conditional profit will be $5. When the market stocks 2 bushels and if demand is 2 or greater, the total profit will be $5Q = $5 \times 2 = 10.

$D < Q$. When the demand is less than the quantity stocked, the market will have some unsold clams. The total revenue will be $15D$, since it makes a $5 profit per bushel on top of the $10 cost. The total cost will be $10Q$, since the market pays $10 per bushel whether it is sold or not. Then the conditional profit will be total revenue minus total cost, or $15D - $10Q$. This formula is used to calculate the conditional profits above the diagonal. For example, when the market stocks 2 bushels but has only 1 demanded, demand is less than quantity stocked. The conditional profit will be $15D - $10Q = $15 \times 1 - $10 \times 2 = -$5$. If the market stocks 3 bushels but sells only 1, the conditional profit becomes $15 \times 1 - $10 \times 3 = -$15$.

The conditional profit table presents the actual monetary outcomes for specific quantities stocked under various demand conditions. In order to make the stock decision under risk, we must resort to the expected profit criterion.

Expected Profits

In order to calculate the expected profits for stocking various numbers of bushels, we must use the expected monetary value (EMV) concept. First, we have to review the possible demands and their probabilities, as shown in Table 3.4. By combining these probabilities and the conditional profits shown in Table 3.5 we can now calculate the expected profits. For example, for the alternative of stocking 1 bushel, the expected profit can be calculated by multiplying the probabilities of each demand by the conditional profit, as follows:

Demand	Probability of Demand	Conditional Profit	Expected Profit
1	0.05	$5	$ .25
2	0.10	5	.50
3	0.25	5	1.25
4	0.30	5	1.50
5	0.20	5	1.00
6	0.05	5	.25
7	0.05	5	.25
	1.00		$5.00

Since the conditional profit is $5 for all possible demands, we can also calculate the expected profit of stocking 1 bushel by finding $5 × 1.0 = $5. The same approach can be used to calculate the expected profit of stocking 2 bushels:

Demand	Probability of Demand	Conditional Profit	Expected Profit
1	0.05	$ − 5	$ − .25
2	0.10	10	1.00
3	0.25	10	2.50
4	0.30	10	3.00
5	0.20	10	2.00
6	0.05	10	.50
7	0.05	10	.50
	1.00		$9.25

Again, since the conditional profit is $10 for 95 percent of the time and it is − $5 for only 5 percent of the time, we can easily calculate the expected profit by determining $10 × 0.95 + (− $5) × 0.05 = $9.25. Table 3.6 presents the expected profits of various stock decisions. The maximum expected profit is $12.00 when the market stocks 3 bushels of clams. Therefore, the optimum quantity to stock will be 3 bushels. If the

Valley Fish Market has to face the clam inventory problem every week
for a long period of time, stocking 3 bushels per week will provide the
highest average weekly profits under the given demand and its probability distribution, unit cost, and unit profit condition.

Table 3.6
Expected Profit Table for the Valley Fish Market Problem

Demand	Probability	1	2	3	4	5	6	7
				Quantity Stocked				
1	0.05	$5	−5	−15	−25	−35	−45	−55
2	0.10	5	10	0	−10	−20	−30	−40
3	0.25	5	10	15	5	− 5	−15	−25
4	0.30	5	10	15	20	10	0	−10
5	0.20	5	10	15	20	25	30	5
6	0.05	5	10	15	20	25	30	20
7	0.05	5	10	15	20	25	30	35
Expected Profit		$5.00	$9.25	$12.00	$11.00	$5.50	−$3.00	−$12.25

Expected Profit Under Certainty
    If the Valley Fish Market could obtain additional information that
would predict the exact demand for clams for the next week, management could eliminate the condition of risk. In fact, the decision problem
becomes one under the condition of certainty. Demand still fluctuates
from 1 to 7 bushels per week with the given probability distribution.
However, if perfect information is available concerning the demand, the
management of the market can easily determine the optimum quantity to
stock.
    Referring back to Table 3.5, we know that the conditional profit will

Table 3.7
Conditional Payoff Under Certainty for the Valley Fish Market Problem

Demand	1	2	3	4	5	6	7
			Quantity Stocked				
1	$5						
2		$10					
3			$15				
4				$20			
5					$25		
6						$30	
7							$35

be maximum if the quantity stocked is exactly equal to the quantity demanded. In other words, with perfect information concerning demand the only thing management has to do is to order exactly the same quantity as demanded. Then the conditional profits for various demand/stock combinations will be as shown in Table 3.7.

Since the demand and quantity stocked are exactly equal when certainty prevails, there will be no losses due to under- or overstocking. The expected profit (under certainty) can be derived in the same manner, as follows:

Demand	Probability of Demand	Conditional Profit	Expected Profit
1	0.05	$ 5	$ .25
2	0.10	10	1.00
3	0.25	15	3.75
4	0.30	20	6.00
5	0.20	25	5.00
6	0.05	30	1.50
7	0.05	35	1.75
	1.00		$19.25

The expected profit under certainty (with perfect information) is $19.25. This value has some significant meaning; it is the maximum profit possible under the condition of certainty. Without perfect information concerning demand, the best thing management could do was to identify the inventory level that maximized the expected profit. The optimum quantity to stock was found to be 3 bushels with the expected profit of $12.00. How much better off are we with perfect information than we were without it? We can easily determine that the value of perfect information is the difference between the expected profit of the optimum decision without perfect information ($12.00) and that with the perfect information ($19.25). Therefore, the value of perfect information will be $7.25, as this is the amount of profit we can increase with the additional information.

Conditional Loss

The inventory problem of the Valley Fish Market can also be solved by analyzing the expected loss. First, we shall determine the conditional loss associated with the combination of quantity stocked and demanded. The conditional losses are based on two types of losses: actual (accounting) loss and opportunity loss. The actual loss results from overstocking. The opportunity loss is due to understocking.

Loss due to overstocking. In our example, any clams (in bushels) left over after one week must be thrown out at a total loss. If we stock 5 bushels and sell only 4, the 5th bushel must be thrown out at a loss of $10, its initial cost. Consequently, the amount of loss due to overstocking would be $10(Q - D)$.

Loss due to understocking. If we stock less than the quantity demanded, the loss would be the lost profit. For example, if we stocked 4 bushels and there was demand for 5, the 5th bushel demanded could not be satisfied. If we had stocked the 5th bushel we could have made $5 profit from it. Therefore, the opportunity loss due to understocking would be $5(D - Q)$.

From the discussion of the two types of losses above, it should be apparent that there will be no loss whatsoever if we stock exactly the quantity to be demanded. Now we can construct the conditional loss table, as shown in Table 3.8.

Table 3.8
Conditional Loss Table for the Valley Fish Market Problem

Demand	Quantity Stocked						
	1	*2*	*3*	*4*	*5*	*6*	*7*
1	$0	$10	$20	$30	$40	$50	$60
2	5	0	10	20	30	40	50
3	10	5	0	10	20	30	40
4	15	10	5	0	10	20	30
5	20	15	10	5	0	10	20
6	25	20	15	10	5	0	10
7	30	25	20	15	10	5	0

Expected Loss

Once we develop the conditional loss table, the next step is calculating the expected loss for stocking a certain quantity. The possible demands and their probability distribution were shown in Table 3.4.

The expected loss can be found for a given quantity stocked by calculating the weighted average loss, that is, the conditional loss multiplied by its probability. For example, the expected loss of stocking 1 bushel will be:

Demand	Probability of Demand	Conditional Loss	Expected Loss
1	0.05	$ 0	$ 0
2	0.10	5	.50
3	0.25	10	2.50
4	0.30	15	4.50
5	0.20	20	4.00
6	0.05	25	1.25
7	0.05	30	1.50
	1.00		$14.25

Table 3.9 presents the expected loss of various stock decisions. The expected loss is the least amount ($7.25) if we stock 3 bushels. This optimum stock level corresponds with the one we derived in the expected profit section. It does not matter whether we utilize the expected profit or the expected loss criterion; the same optimum stock level can be determined by either. We can now compare the expected profits and expected losses of various stock levels and their changes, as follows:

The optimum quantity is found when expected profit is the maximum, or when the change of expected profit becomes negative. When we look at the expected loss criterion, the optimum quantity is found when expected loss is the minimum, or when change in expected loss becomes positive. Although the signs are opposite, because profit is opposite to loss, the absolute incremental change for both expected values are exactly identical. Of course, this makes very good sense because an increase of $4.25 profit is only possible if a $4.25 decrease of loss occurs (between stock levels of 1 and 2).

Value of Perfect Information

We discussed briefly the value of perfect information in the section on expected profit under certainty. The real value of perfect information is simply the difference between the expected profit ($12.00) of the optimum quantity to stock under risk and the expected profit ($19.25) under certainty, that is $7.25. If we use the expected loss criterion, we find the minimum expected loss to be the same as the value of perfect information.

If the demand for the next week is known in advance, no matter how many bushels it may be, we can reduce the expected loss to zero by simply stocking exactly the same quantity that will be demanded. For example, if perfect information suggests that demand will be 5 bushels, we stock 5 and have no conditional loss. Therefore, the expected loss will be zero when perfect information is available, and the value of perfect information will be exactly equal to the expected loss of the optimum

Table 3.9
Expected Loss Table for the Valley Fish Market Problem

Demand	Probability	Quantity Stocked						
		1	2	3	4	5	6	7
1	.05	$0	10	20	30	40	50	60
2	.10	5	0	10	20	30	40	50
3	.25	10	5	0	10	20	30	40
4	.30	15	10	5	0	10	20	30
5	.20	20	15	10	5	0	10	20
6	.05	25	20	15	10	5	0	10
7	.05	30	25	20	15	10	5	0
Expected Loss		$14.25	$10.00	$7.25	$8.25	$13.75	$22.25	$31.50

↑
Optimum

Quantity Stocked	Expected Profit	Change	Expected Loss	Change
1	$ 5.00		$14.25	
		+4.25		−4.25
2	9.25		10.00	
		+2.75		−2.75
3	12.00		7.25	
		−1.00		+1.00
4	11.00		8.25	
		−5.50		+5.50
5	5.50		13.75	
		−8.50		+8.50
6	−3.00		22.25	
		−9.25		+9.25
7	−12.25		31.50	

stock level under risk. The expected loss of the optimum stock level (3 bushels in Table 3.9) is $7.25. Hence, this is the value of perfect information.

Although it is highly desirable to obtain perfect information about demand, it is extremely difficult to obtain such information in reality. The difficulty arises not only in the analysis of the market situation, but also in the economic feasibility of such an attempt. It requires extensive marketing research through statistical analyses. The costs associated with the sampling, data collection, data analysis, and statistical inference often do not justify the value of perfect information. For example, in the case of the Valley Fish Market, if the total cost of the market analysis exceeds the value of perfect information ($7.25), its economic value is negative. Also, we have to remember that statistical analysis usually does not provide perfect information.

Incremental Analysis

A more convenient shortcut for the inventory problem we have discussed is incremental analysis, first suggested by Professor Robert Schlaifer. In this method we analyze the inventory decision one unit at a time. For example, first we analyze the difference between the expected loss of stocking the first bushel and the expected loss of not stocking the first bushel. Then we proceed with the same analysis for the second bushel, and so on.

Table 3.10 presents the calculation of expected losses for two possible courses of action concerning the first bushel of clams. Regardless of management decisions, there will be only two possible events that can occur; there may be demand for the first bushel, or there may not be demand for it. Referring back to Table 3.4 for the probability distribution for demand, we can easily determine that there always will be demand for the first bushel. Demand ranges from 1 to 7; hence we can

Table 3.10
Incremental Analysis for Stocking the First Bushel

| | | *Courses of Action* | | | |
| | | *Stock 1st Bushel* | | *Don't Stock 1st Bushel* | |
Events	*Probability*	*Cond'l Loss*	*Exp'd Loss*	*Cond'l Loss*	*Exp'd Loss*
Demand for 1st bushel	1.0	$ 0	$0	$5	$5
No demand for 1st bushel	0	10	0	0	0
	1.0		$0		$5

Table 3.11
Incremental Analysis for Stocking the Second Bushel

| | | *Courses of Action* | | | |
| | | *Stock 2nd Bushel* | | *Don't Stock 2nd Bushel* | |
Events	*Probability*	*Cond'l Loss*	*Exp'd Loss*	*Cond'l Loss*	*Exp'd Loss*
Demand for 2nd bushel	0.95	$ 0	$ 0	$5	$4.75
No demand for 2nd bushel	0.05	10	.50	0	0
	1.00		$.50		$4.75

always sell the first bushel if we stock it. The probability of demand is, therefore, 1.0 (and it is zero for no demand for the first bushel). If we stock the first bushel and there is demand for it, the conditional loss will be zero. However, if we stock the bushel but there is no demand for it, the conditional loss will be $10, the cost of the bushel. The expected loss for stocking the first bushel will be $(1.0 \times \$0) + (0 \times \$10) = \$0$. On the other hand, if we do not stock the first bushel but there is demand, the conditional loss will be $5, the lost profit due to understocking. If we do not stock the first bushel and there was no demand, of course, the conditional loss will be zero. The expected loss of not stocking the first bushel, therefore, will be $(1.0 \times \$5) + (0 \times \$0) = \$5$. Since the expected loss of not stocking the first bushel ($5) is greater than that of stocking it ($0), we should stock the first bushel to avoid the loss.

We can analyze the inventory decision whether to stock the second bushel in the same manner, as shown in Table 3.11. It should be apparent when we compare Tables 3.10 and 3.11 that the conditional losses remain the same. For example, if we stock the second bushel and there is demand for it, there will be no loss. But if we stock the second bushel and there is no demand, the loss will be $10 due to overstocking. Now, if we do not stock the second bushel but there is demand for it, the conditional loss will be $5 due to understocking, but if we do not stock the second bushel and there is no demand for it, there will be no loss. The only differences are the probabilities of demand and of no demand for the second bushel. As long as there is demand for two bushels or more, the second bushel will be sold. Therefore, the probability of demand for the second bushel will be 0.95. The only case where there will be no demand for the second bushel is when only one bushel is demanded. Consequently, the probability of no demand for the second bushel will be 0.05. The expected loss of stocking the second bushel ($.50) is still less than that of not stocking the second bushel ($4.75). Therefore, we shall stock the second bushel.

As we progress with the incremental analysis, the expected loss of stocking a certain bushel will gradually increase as the probability of demand for a greater number of bushels decreases. Consequently, the expected loss of not stocking a certain bushel will gradually decrease as the probability of no demand for the bushel increases. Then the optimum stock level will be found at the point where the expected loss of stocking that bushel is still less than the expected loss of not stocking that unit, whereas stocking one more unit will result in greater loss. If the expected loss of stocking a certain bushel is exactly equal to that of not stocking it, we should be indifferent. In other words, we can either stock or not stock the bushel.

We can analyze the problem by formulating a stock decision for the generalized case—stocking the ith bushel—as shown in Table 3.12. The probability that there will be demand for the ith bushel is the same as the probability that demand will be equal to or greater than i bushels. Accordingly, there will be no demand for the ith bushel if demand is less than i bushels. Of course, the sum of the two probabilities is one.

If we stock the ith bushel and there is demand for it, the conditional loss will be zero. But if we stock the ith bushel and there is no demand, the loss, L_o, will be due to overstocking. The expected loss of stocking the ith bushel will be $\$L_o \cdot P(D < i)$. If we do not stock the ith bushel but there is demand for it, the conditional loss, L_U, will be due to understocking. On the other hand, if we do not stock the ith bushel and there is no demand for it, there will be no loss. The expected loss of not stocking the ith bushel is then $\$L_U \cdot P(D \geq i)$.

The condition required for us to stock the ith bushel is that the expected loss of stocking it should be less than or equal to that of not stocking it. In other words, we can express the relationship as: $L_o \cdot P(D < i) \leq L_U \cdot P(D \geq i)$. We can rearrange the relationship further, since the sum of two probabilities is equal to one, or $P(D < i) + P(D \geq i) = 1.0$:

$$L_o \cdot P(D < i) \leq L_U \cdot P(D \geq i)$$

Since $P(D \geq i) = 1 - P(D < i)$,

$$L_o \cdot P(D < i) \leq L_U \cdot [1 - P(D < i)]$$
$$L_o \cdot P(D < i) \leq L_U - L_U \cdot P(D < i)$$

Table 3.12
Incremental Analysis for Stocking the ith Bushel

| | | Courses of Action | | | |
| | | Stock ith Bushel | | Don't Stock ith Bushel | |
Events	Probability	Cond'l Loss	Exp'd Loss	Cond'l Loss	Exp'd Loss
Demand for ith bushel	$P(D \geq i)$	\$0	\$0	$\$L_u$	$\$L_u \cdot P(D \geq i)$
No demand for ith Bushel	$P(D < i)$	L_o	$L_o \cdot P(D < i)$	0	0
	1.0		$\$L_o \cdot P(D < i)$		$\$L_u \cdot P(D \geq i)$

L_o:	Loss due to overstocking
L_u:	Loss due to understocking
$P(D \geq i)$:	Probability that demand will be at least i
$P(D < i)$:	Probability that demand will be less than i

Adding $L_U \cdot P(D < i)$ to both sides,

$$L_O \cdot P(D < i) + L_U \cdot P(D < i) \leq L_U - L_U \cdot P(D < i) + L_U \cdot P(D < i)$$
$$L_O \cdot P(D < i) + L_U \cdot P(D < i) \leq L_U$$

Factoring out $P(D < i)$,

$$P(D < i)(L_O + L_U) \leq L_U$$

Dividing both sides by $(L_O + L_U)$,

$$\frac{P(D < i)(L_O + L_U)}{(L_O + L_U)} \leq \frac{L_U}{(L_O + L_U)}$$

$$P(D < i) \leq \frac{L_U}{L_O + L_U}$$

The above relationship simply says that in order to stock the ith bushel, the probability of demand being less than i bushels should be less than or equal to the ratio of loss due to understocking (L_U) over the sum of losses due to overstocking and understocking ($L_O + L_U$). The probability $P(D < i)$ is a cumulative probability function, as shown in Table 3.13. For example, the probability that demand is less than 1 bushel will be zero because demand is always at least 1 bushel. The probability that demand is less than 2 bushels is the same as the probability that demand is for only 1 bushel, that is, 0.05. The probability that demand is less than 3 bushels is the same as the probability that demand is 1 or 2 bushels. There is 0.05 chance that demand will be 1 bushel and 0.10 chance that demand will be 2 bushels. Therefore, the sum of these two probabilities gives the cumulative probability 0.15 that demand be less than 3 bushels.

Table 3.13
Demand, Probability Distribution of Demand, and Cumulative Probability Distribution $P(D < i)$

Demand (bushels)	Probability	ith Bushel	Cumulative Probability That Demand Is Less Than i, $P(D < i)$
1	0.05	1	0
2	0.10	2	0.05
3	0.25	3	0.15
4	0.30	4	0.40
5	0.20	5	0.70
6	0.05	6	0.90
7	0.05	7	0.95
	1.00		

In our example of Valley Fish Market, loss due to overstocking, L_o, is \$10 and loss due to understocking, L_U, is \$5. Therefore,

$$P(D<i) \leq \frac{L_U}{L_o + L_U}$$

$$P(D<i) \leq \frac{\$5}{\$10 + \$5}$$

$$P(D<i) \leq \frac{\$5}{\$15}$$

$$P(D<i) \leq 0.33$$

In other words, management should keep on stocking as long as the cumulative probability $P(D<i)$ is less than or equal to 0.33. Referring back to Table 3.13, it is evident that the optimum stock level should be 3 bushels. This answer corresponds with those we derived when we utilized the expected profit and expected loss as decision criteria.

Now then, in order to solve the simple inventory problem under risk, the only things we should know to determine the optimum stock level are: loss due to understocking, loss due to overstocking, and the cumulative probability function $P(D<i)$. By using the incremental analysis we can avoid the cumbersome calculative work required by the expected profit or expected loss approach.

Analysis of Salvage Value

In the Valley Fish Market example, we assume that any clams left over at the end of a week were thrown out at a total loss. However in reality, we can often salvage the leftovers. For example, it is quite reasonable to assume that Valley Fish Market can sell the leftover clams to local restaurants for clam chowder at a very low price—say, \$6 per bushel (as opposed to the normal price of \$15). If we accept the salvage value of \$6 per bushel for those left over at the end of the week, our solution may be changed.

Of course, salvage value has no bearing on the solution if demand is equal to or greater than the quantity stocked. In other words, loss due to understocking remains at \$5 per bushel that is short. However, salvage value will change the amount of loss due to overstocking. Any bushel we fail to sell due to overstocking can be salvaged at \$6. Therefore, loss due to overstocking will become only \$4 (\$10 cost − \$6 salvage = \$4) rather than the previous amount of \$10 (cost).

By using the incremental analysis formula, we can determine the optimum stock level. Let us denote L_{ONS} as loss due to overstocking with no salvage value and S as salvage value. Since $L_o = L_{ONS} - S$,

$$P(D < i) \leq \frac{L_U}{(L_{ONS} - S) + L_U}$$

If $L_U = \$5$, $L_{ONS} = \$10$, and $S = \$6$,

$$P(D < i) \leq \frac{5}{(10 - 6) + 5}$$

$$P(D < i) \leq 0.556$$

Referring to the cumulative probability distribution as shown below, we can easily determine the optimum stock level of 4 bushels.

ith bushel	Cumulative Probability $P(D < i)$
1	0
2	0.05
3	0.15
4	0.40
5	0.70
6	0.90
7	0.95

Since loss due to overstocking is not as great as before due to the salvage value of $6 per bushel, the optimum stock level has been increased by one.

Now we can determine what kind of salvage value is required to justify stocking a certain number of bushels. For example, we can determine the range of salvage value required to stock 5 bushels. From the incremental analysis we know that in order to stock 5 bushels, $L_U/(L_O + L_U)$ should be between 0.7 and 0.9 (see Table 3.13). Then by equating the ratio to 0.7, we can determine the minimum salvage value for stocking 5 bushels:

$$0.7 = \frac{L_U}{(L_{ONS} - S) + L_U}$$

$$0.7 = \frac{5}{(10 - S) + 5}$$

$$0.7 = \frac{5}{15 - S}$$

Multiplying both sides by $(15 - S)$,

$$0.7(15 - S) = 5$$
$$10.50 - 0.7S = 5$$
$$0.7S = 5.50$$
$$S = \$7.86$$

Likewise, the maximum salvage value required to justify stocking 5 bushels can be calculated as

$$0.9 = \frac{L_U}{(L_{ONS} - S) + L_U}$$

$$0.9 = \frac{5}{(10 - S) + 5}$$

$$0.9 = \frac{5}{15 - S}$$

$$0.9(15 - S) = 5$$
$$13.50 - 0.9S = 5$$
$$0.9S = 8.50$$
$$S = \$9.44$$

In order to justify stocking 5 bushels, the salvage value must be between \$5.50 and \$9.44. To stock a large number of bushels in relation to the demand distribution, the salvage value must be relatively high. If the salvage value is higher than \$9.44, which is almost as great as the cost of purchasing a bushel, we can stock the quantity of 6 bushels.

Analysis of Goodwill Cost

In the analysis thus far, we have assumed that the loss due to understocking is simply the amount of lost profit. However, in reality, such an assumption is hardly justified. Often, the unsatisfied or unserved customer may cause considerable amount of goodwill cost to the firm by simply not returning to the store or by spreading their bad experiences to other people. For example, suppose that there is a customer who purchases an average of \$50 worth of seafood per month from Valley Fish Market. Let us assume that his demand for clams was not satisfied due to understocking. Hence, he decided not to come back to the market for a whole month. The lost sales is \$50, and possibly the lost profit may be as much as \$10 to the market.

It is extremely difficult to measure the actual goodwill cost. Nevertheless, goodwill cost exists in reality. Goodwill cost affects only the loss due to understocking because it occurs when there is unsatisfied demand. Then the total loss due to understocking, L_U, should include loss due to understocking with no goodwill cost, L_{UNG}, and goodwill cost per bushel that is short, G.

Now, let us suppose the following case: Demand and probability of demand as given in Table 3.13, $L_{UNG} = \$5$, $G = \$2$, $L_{ONS} = \$10$, and $S = \$6$. Then, by employing the incremental analysis formula,

$$P(D<i) \leq \frac{L_U}{L_O + L_U}$$

Since $L_U = L_{UNG} + G$ and $L_O = L_{ONS} - S$,

$$P(D<i) \leq \frac{L_{UNG} + G}{(L_{ONS} - S) + (L_{UNG} + G)}$$

$$P(D<i) \leq \frac{5 + 2}{(10 - 6) + (5 + 2)}$$

$$P(D<i) \leq \frac{7}{4 + 7}$$

$$P(D<i) \leq 0.636$$

Referring to the cumulative probability distribution $P(D<i)$ in Table 3.13, we can easily determine that the optimum stock level is 4 bushels.

By utilizing the approach shown in the salvage value section, we can also determine the range of goodwill cost which will justify stocking a certain number of bushels. For example, let us determine the goodwill cost range required for stocking 5 bushels with the above provided information. In order to stock 5 bushels, the ratio of $(L_{UNG} + G)/[(L_{ONS} - S) + (L_{UNG} + G)]$ should be between 0.7 and 0.9, as shown below.

ith bushel	Cumulative Probability, $P(D<i)$
1	0
2	0.05
3	0.15
4	0.40
5	0.70
6	0.90
7	0.95

First, we can equate the ratio to 0.7 to find the lower limit of goodwill cost:

$$0.7 = \frac{L_{UNG} + G}{(L_{ONS} - S) + (L_{UNG} + G)}$$

Since $L_{UNG} = 5$, $L_{ONS} = 10$, and $S = 6$,

$$0.7 = \frac{5 + G}{(10 - 6) + (5 + G)}$$

$$0.7 = \frac{5 + G}{9 + G}$$

$$0.7(9 + G) = 5 + G$$
$$6.30 + 0.7G = 5 + G$$
$$-0.3G = -1.30$$
$$G = \frac{1.30}{0.3}$$

$$G = 4.33$$

In order to find the upper limit of the range, we can equate the ratio to 0.9, as follows:

$$0.9 = \frac{L_{UNG} + G}{(L_{ONS} - S) + (L_{UNG} + G)}$$

As before, $L_{UNG} = 5$, $L_{ONS} = 10$, and $S = 6$.

$$0.9 = \frac{5 + G}{(10 - 6) + (5 + G)}$$

$$0.9 = \frac{5 + G}{9 + G}$$

$$0.9(9 + G) = 5 + G$$
$$8.10 + 0.9G = 5 + G$$
$$-0.1G = -3.10$$
$$G = 31.00$$

The above calculations indicate that the goodwill cost per bushel that is short should have a range between $4.33 to $31.00 in order for the market to stock 5 bushels. The above analysis clearly points out that in order to stock a relatively large number of bushels, the per unit goodwill cost should be considerably high. Even when the exact amount of goodwill cost is not available, the analysis of goodwill cost provides management with a range of cost that often enables them to make a better inventory decision.

DECISION MAKING UNDER UNCERTAINTY

Situations where the probabilities of certain potential outcomes to occur are not known involve decision making under uncertainty. Even under uncertainty, the conditional payoffs (consequences or outcomes) must be known in advance for a given course of action under a potential state of nature. Therefore, the conditional payoff table under uncertainty should resemble that of a problem under risk.

Suppose a firm is attempting to invest $1 million in a most profitable investment plan. Let us further assume that the firm has to choose only one among the three investment alternatives. The conditional payoff of the investment is primarily based on the future economic condition. The payoff matrix is presented in Table 3.14.

Table 3.14
Payoff Matrix for Investment Plans Under Uncertainty

| Investment Alternative | Economic Conditions | | |
	Fast Growth	Normal Growth	Slow Growth
Stocks	$100,000	$65,000	$ – 40,000
Bonds	80,000	60,000	10,000
Savings	50,000	50,000	50,000

If the firm invests the money in a selected group of stocks, the conditional payoff will be $100,000 if the economic condition is one of a fast rate of growth, $65,000 under a normal growth, and – $40,000 under a slow rate of growth. If $1 million is invested in a selected number of bonds, the conditional payoff will be $80,000 under a fast growth economic condition, $60,000 under a normal growth, and $10,000 under a slow rate of growth. On the other hand, if the money is put in a savings account, the bank guarantees 5 percent interest under any economic condition.

Decision Making with Partial Probabilities

If a certain partial probability is available about the future economic condition, we may be able to exercise our educated judgment into the decision analysis. For example, let us suppose that the Federal Reserve Bank predicts that the probability of normal growth for the next year is 0.4. Then we can at least calculate the indifference probabilities for the three investment alternatives. The payoff of $50,000 for the savings alternative is a certainty. Therefore, we can calculate the probabilities required for the fast growth and the slow growth for us to be indifferent between stocks and savings. If we assign P as the probability of the fast growth condition, then $(0.6 - P)$ will be the probability of the slow growth, so that the sum of all three probabilities will be 1.0 $[0.4 + P + (0.6 - P) = 1.0]$. The expected payoff of stocks will be: $(100,000 \times P) + (65,000 \times 0.4) + (-40,000) \times (0.6 - P)$. In order for us to be indifferent between stocks and savings alternatives, the expected payoff of stocks should be exactly equal to the expected payoff of savings ($50,000). We can equate the two expected values, as follows:

$$100,000P + 65,000 \times 0.4 - 40,000(0.6 - P) = 50,000$$
$$100,000P + 26,000 - 24,000 + 40,000P = 50,000$$
$$140,000P = 48,000$$
$$P = 0.343$$

Therefore, the probability of the fast growth condition should be 0.343 in order for us to be indifferent between stocks and savings. This implies that the probability of the slow growth should be 0.257 $(0.6 - 0.343 = 0.257)$. If the probability of the fast growth condition is greater than 0.343, of course we will prefer stocks over savings.

Now we can proceed to calculate the indifference probabilities between bonds and savings, as follows:

$$80,000P + 60,000(0.4) + 10,000(0.6 - P) = 50,000$$
$$80,000P + 24,000 + 6,000 - 10,000P = 50,000$$
$$70,000P = 20,000$$
$$P = 0.286$$

We should be indifferent between bonds and savings if the probability of the fast growth to occur is 0.286. Consequently, the required probability of the slow growth is 0.314 $(0.6 - 0.286 = 0.314)$. We can also calculate the indifference probabilities between stocks and bonds.

$$100,000P + 65,000(0.4) - 40,000(0.6 - P) = 80,000P + 60,000(0.4)$$
$$+ 10,000(0.6 - P)$$
$$140,000P + 2,000 = 70,000P + 30,000$$
$$70,000P = 28,000$$
$$P = 0.4$$

The required probabilities of the fast growth and the slow growth are 0.4 and 0.2, respectively, in order for us to be indifferent between stocks and bonds.

There is at least one certain payoff we can select among the investment alternatives. It is $50,000 for the savings plan. By analyzing the indifference probabilities we can at least pinpoint the critical probabilities for the investment decision. In order to get the expected return of $50,000 from stocks, the fast growth condition must have 0.343 probability. On the other hand, we can derive the same $50,000 return from bonds if the probability of the fast growth is only 0.286. This implies that if the probability of the fast growth is relatively small, the choice will be between bonds and savings. The indifference probability of the fast growth between stocks and bonds is 0.4. In this case, the expected return of both investment plans is $58,000 (find the exected payoff with 0.4 for the slow growth). Now we can construct the expected return with various probabilities of the fast growth, as shown in Figure 3.1.

The figure presents two critical probabilities. First, if the probability of the fast growth condition is 0.286 or less, the most attractive investment alternative is savings. If the probability is greater than 0.286 but less than 0.4, the best alternative is bonds. If the probability is greater than 0.4, stocks are the best alternative.

In the absence of these critical indifference probabilities, the only thing we can do is ask the management's judgment about the probability of the fast growth condition. Most likely, the answer will be, "It is terribly hard to pinpoint the probability." With the indifference probability information, we can ask a series of questions to the management or a group of experts, such as, "Do you think the probability of the fast growth will be greater than 0.4? If not, will it be greater than 0.286?" When such exact probabilities are put to question, most experts can at least answer "yes" or "no."

The above situation is, however, a very rare case indeed. The

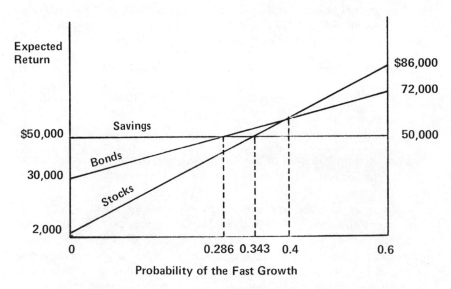

Figure 3.1
Expected return and the probability of the fast growth condition

reasons why we could use the expected monetary value as the decision criterion are: (1) The probability of at least one state of the potential states of nature is known; (2) the investment decision is assumed to be a repetitive type; and (3) the magnitude of payoffs is assumed to be small enough in relation to the current financial situation of the firm. However, if the investment decision we have discussed thus far does not meet all of the three conditions listed above, the problem becomes a pure decision making one under uncertainty. There are several criteria suggested for decision making under uncertainty. We shall examine several better-known criteria.

Decision Making Criteria Under Uncertainty

The Laplace Criterion

The Laplace criterion suggests that, since the probabilities of future states of nature are not known, each potential state of nature should be assigned the same probability. In our example of the investment problem, we should assign the same $\frac{1}{3}$ probability to the fast, normal, and slow growth condition. Hence, the expected monetary value is the only sensible criterion to use in decision making. For our example (see Table 3.14), the expected monetary values for three investment alternatives can be calculated as follows:

$$\text{EMV(stocks)} = \tfrac{1}{3}(100,000) + \tfrac{1}{3}(65,000) + \tfrac{1}{3}(-40,000)$$
$$= \tfrac{1}{3}(100,000 + 65,000 - 40,000) = \tfrac{1}{3}(125,000)$$
$$= 41,666.67$$
$$\text{EMV(bonds)} = \tfrac{1}{3}(80,000 + 60,000 + 10,000) = \tfrac{1}{3}(150,000)$$
$$= 50,000$$
$$\text{EMV(savings)} = 50,000$$

With the Laplace principle, we should be indifferent between bonds and savings, as the expected monetary value for the two alternatives is $50,000. Clearly, stocks is an inferior alternative under this criteria, since its expected monetary value is only $41,666.67.

The Maximin Criterion

The maximin criterion (sometimes referred to as the Wald criterion because Abraham Wald first suggested the approach) is based on a very conservative or pessimistic outlook for the future event. According to this criterion, therefore, all the minimum returns are compared and the alternative which yields the maximum of the minimum returns should be selected. In our example (Table 3.14), the minimum payoffs are as follows:

Alternative	Minimum Payoff
Stocks	− $40,000
Bonds	10,000
Savings	50,000*

Thus, by utilizing the maximin criterion, our choice (indicated by *) will be savings, since it has the maximum-minimum return, $50,000.

The maximin criterion is devised for those who are extremely cautious, conservative, or pessimistic about the future state of nature. In other words, those who are prepared to face the very worst consequences should use the criterion. Quite possibly in a real-world situation, the consequence in question is of such magnitude compared to the financial situation of the firm that management may be forced to be conservative. For example, if a firm cannot survive unless the payoff is at least $20,000, the maximin criterion is a very realistic criterion indeed.

The Maximax Criterion

Since we have the maximin criterion, we ought to have the opposite approach, the maximax criterion. The maximax criterion is based upon a very bold, aggressive, and optimistic outlook for the future event. The concept suggests that the decision maker should select the alternative that has the maximum among the maximum payoffs. In Table 3.14, the maximum payoffs for the three alternative investment plans are as follows:

Alternative	Maximum Payoff
Stocks	$100,000*
Bonds	80,000
Savings	50,000

The best alternative according to the maximax principle is stocks.

The maximax criterion is especially useful for those who tend to be extremely optimistic about the future. This optimism may be the result of several considerations. First, it may stem from the fact that the conditional payoffs are so insignificant in terms of their importance to the firm's financial situation that management can afford to be bold in selecting the course of action. Or, it could be because management has a special information source or a competent group of scientists in the planning area. If the available information indicates a favorable future state of nature, management may attempt to make an agressive move. A third possible reason for using the maximax criterion is in a case of desperation on the part of the decision maker. For example, in our problem if the firm needs at least $85,000 payoff from the investment to stay alive, the decision maker has no choice but to go after the best possible payoff of $100,000 with stocks.

A somewhat similar approach to the maximax criterion is the dominance principle. The dominance principle is useful for the decision maker in reducing the number of alternatives available for decision. However, it does not always yield a unique course of action for the decision maker. An alternative is said to be dominated when another alternative is preferred over it, regardless of the state of nature that may occur. Then the decision maker will gradually eliminate those alternatives that have been dominated by other alternatives. If there is only one alternative remaining after a series of eliminations through the dominance test, the procedure will yield a unique strategy. But if the process yields a number of superior alternatives that cannot be evaluated any further by the dominance test, the decision maker has to use another approach for the final decision.

For example, let us examine the following investment problem under uncertainty:

	Conditional Payoffs Under Economic Conditions		
Investment Plan	*I*	*II*	*III*
A	− $10000	$3000	$6000
B	* − 2000	4000	7000
C	* 3000	4000	5000
D	1000	3000	5000

When investment plans A and B are compared, it is clear that plan B is superior to plan A under every feasible economic condition in terms of conditional payoff. Plan A is, therefore, dominated by plan B. When we compare plans C and D, we find that plan C dominates plan D. By using the dominance principle we have reduced the number of investment plans from the original four to only B and C. We cannot employ the dominance test to compare plans B and C. For a further evaluation of B and C we must use another approach to make the final investment decision. In practice, the decision maker uses the dominance principle quite frequently, either consciously or unconsciously. The dominance principle is a maximizing procedure, as is the maximax criterion.

The Hurwicz Criterion

Professor Leonid Hurwicz has suggested a criterion for decision making under uncertainty. His criterion is somewhat of a compromise between the maximin and maximax criteria. Decision makers in reality are not completely pessimistic as in the maximin criterion and they are not completely optimistic as suggested by the maximax criterion. In fact, decision makers are usually optimistic to a certain degree and also pessimistic to a degree at the same time. Hurwicz devised the coefficient of optimism (σ) to measure the individual decision maker's degree of optimism. The scale used for the coefficient of optimism is 0 to 1. If σ is 0, this implies that the individual is completely pessimistic (zero optimism). On the other hand, if σ is 1, he is completely optimistic (zero pessimism). The coefficient of optimism is σ and the coefficient of pessimism is $1 - \sigma$. Hurwicz suggests that for each alternative the maximum payoff should be multiplied by σ and the minimum payoff should be multiplied by $1 - \sigma$. Accordingly, we can calculate the expected value of each alternative by the above described procedure.

In our example, suppose the decision maker is extremely pessimistic, so that his σ is 0. Then the coefficient of optimism (σ) is 0 and the coefficient of pessimism ($1 - \sigma$) is 1. Then the expected value for the three alternatives will be:

$$EV(\text{stocks}) = \$100,000(0) + (-\$40,000)(1) = -\$40,000$$
$$EV(\text{bonds}) = \$80,000(0) + \$10,000(1) = \$10,000$$
$$EV(\text{savings}) = \$50,000(0) + \$50,000(1) = \$50,000*$$

The extremely pessimistic decision maker will select savings. It can be noted here that when $\sigma = 0$, the Hurwicz criterion is exactly the same as the maximin criterion.

If the decision maker is completely optimistic, $\sigma = 1$ and $1 - \sigma = 0$. Then the expected value for the three alternatives will be:

$$EV(\text{stocks}) = \$100,000(1) + (-\$40,000)(0) = \$100,000$$
$$EV(\text{bonds}) = \$\ 80,000(1) + \$10,000(0) = \$80,000$$
$$EV(\text{savings}) = \$\ 50,000(1) + \$50,000(0) = \$50,000$$

Stocks will be selected in this case. When $\sigma = 1$, the approach is exactly the same as the maximax criterion.

Now, if $\sigma = 0.5$, then the decision maker is only half optimistic and also half pessimistic ($1 - \sigma = 0.5$). The expected value of the three alternatives will be:

$$EV(\text{stocks}) = \$100,000(0.5) + (-\$40,000)(0.5) = \$30,000$$
$$EV(\text{bonds}) = \$\ 80,000(0.5) + \$10,000(0.5) = \$45,000$$
$$EV(\text{savings}) = \$\ 50,000(0.5) + \$50,000(0.5) = \$50,000$$

In the above case, the decision maker should select savings.

It is quite possible in reality that the decision maker cannot specify the exact σ. In this case we can determine several critical σ's and ask the decision maker whether his optimism is greater than these σ's. Based on a series of questions, we can derive the optimum decision. Figure 3.2 presents the Hurwicz criterion problem. On the left-hand side, where $\sigma = 0$, we plot the minimum payoffs for the alternatives. On the right-hand side, where $\sigma = 1$, we plot the maximum payoffs for the alternatives. Now, we connect the minimum and maximum payoffs of each alternative by a straight line. Since there are three straight lines, we can easily determine their intersecting points and solve for the coefficient of optimism σ. For example, at the intersecting point between savings and bonds lines, we shall be indifferent between the two strategies as the expected values will be identical. If we denote the payoff as Y and the coefficient of optimism (σ) as X, then we can derive the functions of three linear lines as follows:

Stocks:	$Y = -40,000 + 140,000X$
Bonds:	$Y = 10,000 + 70,000X$
Savings:	$Y = 50,000$

In order to find σ at the intersecting point between savings and bonds lines, we can equate the two expressions, or

$$10,000 + 70,000X = 50,000$$
$$70,000X = 40,000$$
$$X = 0.571$$

We can do the same for stocks and bonds:

$$-40,000 + 140,000X = 10,000 + 70,000X$$
$$70,000X = 50,000$$
$$X = 0.714$$

In Figure 3.2 we can see clearly that savings will be our choice when σ is less than 0.571. Bonds become the best alternative when σ is between 0.571 and 0.714. The best alternative is stocks when σ is greater than 0.714. We ask the decision maker where his σ is located in relation to 0.571 and 0.714. Based on this information, we can easily find the optimum alternative under the Hurwicz criterion.

One serious problem of the Hurwicz criterion is that it does not work properly for all the cases. For example, let us review a decision problem under uncertainty shown in Table 3.15. If we use the Hurwicz criterion to make the decision, the problem can be depicted as shown in Figure 3.3. Since the minimum payoff of A_1 is 0 and its maximum payoff is \$100, the straight line will be from 0 to \$100 between σ of 0 and 1. The minimum and maximum payoffs of A_2 are exactly the same as that of A_1.

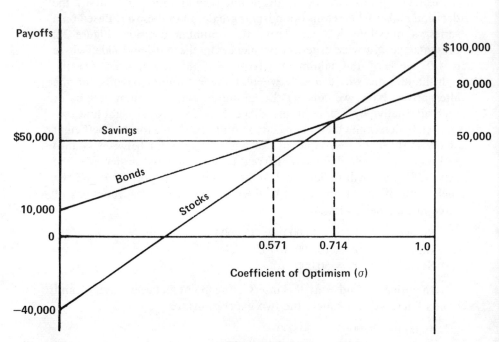

Figure 3.2
The Hurwicz criterion graph

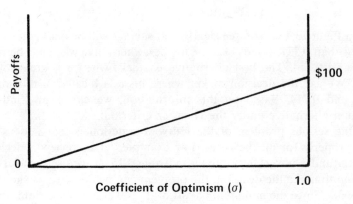

Figure 3.3
Hurwicz criterion problem

Therefore, the straight line for A_2 will simply overlap that for A_1. This implies that we should be indifferent under the Hurwicz criterion, regardless of the value of σ the decision maker may have. Can we ever be indifferent between A_1 and A_2? The payoff for A_1 is always greater than or equal to that for A_2 under any state of nature. Clearly, A_1 is superior to A_2. However, the Hurwicz criterion fails to identify the superiority. Of course, we can easily eliminate A_2 if we use the dominance principle. However, if the payoffs change slightly, as below, the dominance test does not yield a dominant strategy:

	E_1	E_2	E_3	E_4	E_5	E_6
A_1	$100	$100	$0	$0	$100	$100
A_2	0	0	100	100	0	0

The Regret (Minimax) Criterion

Professor L. J. Savage has advanced the concept of regret or opportunity loss as a decision criterion under uncertainty. The basic idea of this criterion is that the decision maker will experience regret when a state of nature occurs and the alternative he has chosen results in a payoff that is less than the maximum. The amount of regret can be computed by finding the difference between the maximum payoff and other payoffs under a given state of nature. Once the regret table is developed, Savage proposes that the decision maker should use the minimax principle—that is, minimize the maximum regret.

Our example is described in the payoff table given as Table 3.14. When we select savings and the fast growth condition occurs, the payoff would be $50,000. However, had we selected stocks, the payoff would have been the maximum payoff of $100,000. Thus, the difference $50,000 is the amount of the decision maker's regret for selecting savings. If the bonds plan was selected, the amount of regret would be $20,000. On the other hand, if the stocks alternative was selected, the regret would be zero, since the payoff is the maximum. Table 3.16 presents the regret table based on the payoff matrix shown in Table 3.14. It should be noted

Table 3.15
A Decision Problem Under Uncertainty

Alternatives	E_1	E_2	E_3	E_4	E_5	E_6
A_1	$100	$100	$100	$100	$100	$0
A_2	100	0	0	0	0	0

Table 3.16
Regret Table for Investment Plans Under Uncertainty

Investment Alternative	Economic Condition		
	Fast Growth	Normal Growth	Slow Growth
Stocks	$ 0	$ 0	$90,000
Bonds	20,000	5,000	40,000
Savings	50,000	15,000	0

that regret is never negative, like the opportunity loss we discussed earlier in this chapter. From Table 3.16 we can easily determine the maximum regret for each investment alternative, as follows:

Alternative	Maximum Regret
Stocks	$90,000
Bonds	40,000*
Savings	50,000

Since the regret criterion advocates the minimization of the maximum regret, bonds will be the alternative we should select.

One problem we face in applying the regret criterion is that the amount of regret is expressed in monetary units (dollars). Since the relative value (marginal utility) of this amount decreases as the total payoff increases, sometimes we may select an inferior alternative when the regret criterion is adopted. For example, let us examine the decision problem described in Table 3.17. The regret table for this problem is developed in Table 3.18. According to the regret criterion, we should be indifferent between alternatives A_1 and A_2, since their maximum regrets are exactly identical. However, are we really indifferent between the two alternatives? We should say not! Under state of nature E_1, the payoff is $150,000 for A_1 and it is $100,000 for A_2. The difference is $50,000. Is this $50,000 worth as much as the difference of $50,000 we see under E_3

Table 3.17
A Decision Problem Under Uncertainty

Alternative	State of Nature		
	E_1	E_2	E_3
A_1	$150,000	$50,000	-$25,000
A_2	100,000	50,000	25,000

Table 3.18
Regret Table for an Investment Problem

Alternative	State of Nature		
	E_1	E_2	E_3
A_1	\$0	\$0	\$50,000
A_2	\$50,000	0	0

between A_1 and A_2? Under E_1, alternative A_2 returns \$100,000. Receiving \$50,000 more on \$100,000 may be nice. Under E_3, A_2 returns \$25,000 and A_1 has $-$\$25,000. The difference is still \$50,000. However, this difference may mean a survival or a bankruptcy. Certainly we will prefer A_2 over A_1.

The above reasoning may be even clearer if we consider the concept of the utility of money. The word *utility* is used in economics as the power to satisfy the wants of humanity. In general, however, the concept of utility refers to a measure of satisfaction from the consumption of a good. Therefore, an individual's utility of a certain good may be quite different from that of others. Suppose a decision maker has an utility function of money as shown in Figure 3.4. The utility of \$50,000 between $-$\$25,000 and \$25,000 (U_1) is substantially greater than the utility of \$50,000 between \$100,000 and \$150,000. Again, it is clear that A_2 is a superior alternative. It is an ideal procedure if we can convert all monetary payoffs to utilities and then apply the regret criterion. However, there is no satisfactory general methodology to develop the utility function of money. Furthermore, people are often not consistent in expressing their perceived value of certain payoffs. Therefore, it is still not practical to use a utility-based regret criterion for decision making under uncertainty.

Subjective Probability

There is one more important concept we should discuss for decision making under uncertainty. It is the concept of subjective probabilities. The traditional concept of probability is based on the mathematical foundation of the law of large numbers. This concept is often called mathematical or objective probability. Subjective probability, on the other hand, is based on the measure of one's degree of belief in the outcomes of his decision. Consequently, it is quite possible that the subjective probability would be quite different from the objective probability, if known. This is easy to understand, for different decision makers may not hold the same expectations concerning future outcomes.

Many experiments conducted in the area of subjective probabilities suggest that decision making under uncertainty is definitely influenced by the decision maker's personal belief concerning the likelihood of future outcomes to occur. These studies reinforce the concept that the individual decision maker is capable of assessing value and probability in the unique decision environment. Consequently, the study of subjective probability and its importance in decision making under uncertainty will provide more knowledge about the actual decision-making process in real-world situations. Another important area of study related to subjective probabilities is the Bayes decision rule. The Bayes decision rule is an orderly and consistent procedure of revising probabilities of the potential states of nature based on additional information, experiments, or personal judgment. The Bayes decision rule is a valuable tool that allows the decision maker to act consistently with his personal judgment concerning the likelihood of the states of nature and conditional payoffs. Nevertheless, there is no unanimous opinion among scholars and practicing managers about its superiority over other decision analysis techniques under uncertainty.

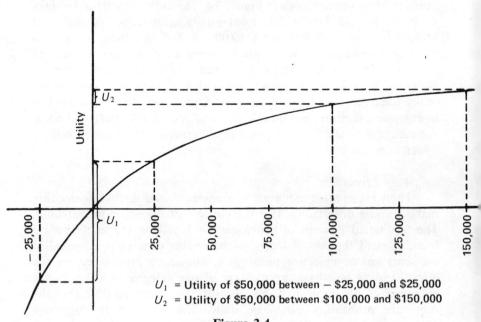

U_1 = Utility of $50,000 between − $25,000 and $25,000
U_2 = Utility of $50,000 between $100,000 and $150,000

Figure 3.4
Utility function for monetary payoffs

DECISION TREES

When the decision problem calls for the selection of a course of action among various alternatives, the above presented techniques and criteria may be appropriate. However, if the decision problem requires a series of decisions rather than a one-shot decision, the use of a decision tree can be a useful tool. A *decision tree* is a schematic presentation of a sequence of decisions and their possible consequences.

Let us review a simple example. The management of a firm is trying to decide whether or not to introduce a new product. The cost of research and development is estimated to be $70,000. The profit from the new product depends primarily on three things: (1) Whether the competitive firm introduces a similar product or not; (2) the type of promotional campaign the firm launches; and (3) the type of promotional campaign the competitor uses. If the competitor does not introduce a similar product, the firm can launch a major promotional campaign and maximize profit. However, if the competitor introduces a similar product, the profit will depend on the promotional efforts of the firm and that of the competitor. Suppose there are three basic types of promotional campaigns based on the costs: major campaign, normal campaign, and minor campaign. The sequence of decisions and their consequences is shown in Figure 3.5 as a decision tree.

At the first decision point, the firm has two alternatives: the firm introduces the product or it does not introduce the product. If the firm does not introduce the product, the conditional profit will be, of course, zero. If the firm introduces the product, the competitor has two alternatives to react: It introduces a similar product or it does not introduce a similar product. The probability of the competitor introducing a product is 0.6, and it is 0.4 for not introducing the product. At the second decision point, the firm has three promotional strategies open: a major campaign, a normal campaign, or a minor campaign. If the competitor does not introduce a similar product, the firm's promotional effort will not bring any response from the competitor. However, if the competitor introduces a similar product, the firm's promotional campaign will be responded by the identical three types of promotional strategies. For example, if the firm employs a major promotional campaign, the competitor's response and their probabilities are: 0.5 for a major campaign, 0.4 for a normal campaign, and 0.1 for a minor campaign. If the firm's major campaign is responded by a major campaign from the competitor, the conditional profit will be $40,000. The major campaign-normal campaign combination results in $60,000

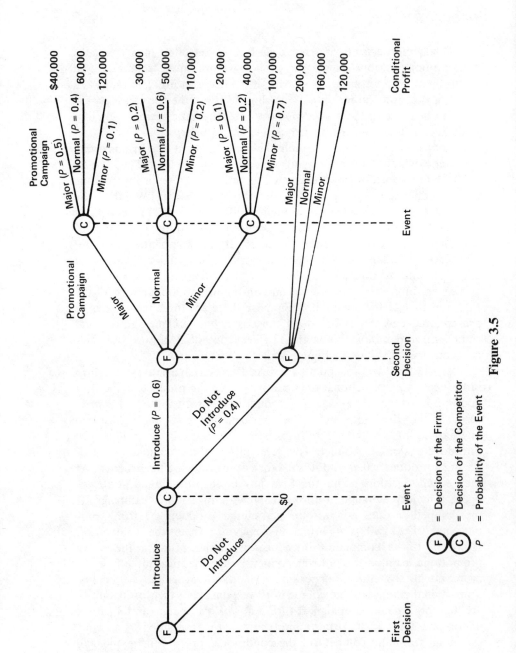

Figure 3.5

78

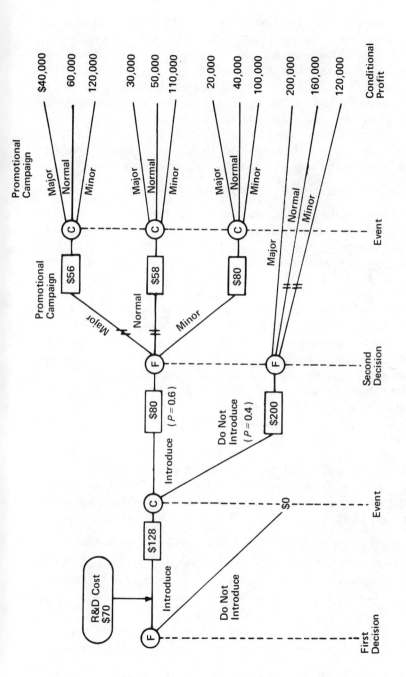

Figure 3.6

and the major-minor combination brings $120,000 conditional profit to the firm. These profit figures do not include the research-development cost of $70,000. Other combinations of campaigns, probabilities, and conditional profits are shown in Figure 3.5.

The best way to analyze this kind of sequential decision problem is to work from the end of the decision tree. We shall calculate the expected profit for each sequence of decisions. For example, the expected profit for the combination of decisions of the firm's to introduce the product, of the competitor to introduce a similar product, and of the firm to use a major promotional campaign will be:

$40,000(0.5) + $60,000(0.4) + $120,000(0.1) = $56,000

Figure 3.6 presents the decision tree with the expected profits for various decision points and events. The expected profits are shown in the rectangular boxes.

When the competitor introduces a similar product, the three promotional strategies result in the following expected profits: major campaign = $56,000; normal campaign = $58,000; minor campaign = $80,000. Since the best promotional strategy is the minor campaign, we can eliminate the other two strategies (as indicated by the sign ||). Then the optimum expected profit is $80,000 when the competitor introduces a similar product and the firm uses a minor promotional strategy.

If the competitor does not introduce a similar product, the highest conditional profit is $200,000 when the firm adopts a major campaign strategy. Therefore, we can eliminate the other two strategies (indicated by || again). Now, the expected profit of the firm's introduction of a new product can be calculated. It is the sum of the expected profit of the event that the competitor introduces a similar product ($80,000) multiplied by its probability (0.6) and the expected profit of the event that the competitor does not introduce a similar product ($200,000) multiplied by its probability (0.4). Thus, it will be:

Expected profit = $80,000(0.6) + $200,000(0.4) = $128,000

The research and development cost for the new product is $70,000. Since the expected net profit of introducing the new product is $58,000, the decision to introduce the product should be made.

REFERENCES

Bierman, H., Bonini, C. P., and Hauseman, W. H., *Quantitative Analysis for Business Decisions*, 4th ed., Irwin, Homewood, Ill., 1973.

Chernoff, H., and Moses, L. E., *Elementary Decision Theory*, Wiley, New York, 1959.

Luce, R. D., and Raiffa, H., *Games and Decisions: Introduction and Critical Survey*, wiley, New York, 1957.

Raiffa, H., *Decision Analysis*, Addison-Wesley, Reading, Mass., 1968.

Schlaifer, R., *Probability and Statistics for Business Decisions*, McGraw-Hill, New York, 1959.

————, *Analysis of Decisions Under Uncertainty*, McGraw-Hill, New York, 1969.

PROBLEMS

1. Your grandfather left a bequest to you in the amount of $100,000. You would like to invest this money in one of two available investment plans: stocks or bonds. The conditional payoffs of each plan under two possible economic conditions are as follows:

	Economic Condition I	*Economic Condition II*
Stocks	$10,000	− $4,000
Bonds	7,000	2,000

   (a) If the probability of economic condition I to occur is 0.8, where should you invest your money?
   (b) What kind of probabilities of economic conditions I and II should there be before you would be indifferent between stocks and bonds?

2. Blue Ridge Winter Sports, Inc. has just opened up a new ski slope. There is a great deal of potential success for the ski business in the area, since it can draw many customers from all over the South. However, the key factor for success is snow. If the winter has an average of 40 inches or more of snow, the season could be a financial success. If the snowfall is between 30 and 40 inches, the firm can operate artificial snow makers and still manage a moderate financial gain. However, if the snowfall is less than 30 inches, as was the case during the past three years in Virginia, the firm will be operating in the red. Recently, a large firm in Vermont has offered $50,000 to Blue Ridge Winter Sports to lease the slope. The president of Blue Ridge is contemplating whether the firm should operate the slope or lease it for the coming winter. The conditional payoffs for operating the ski slope under various snow conditions are as follows:

	Snow 40″ or more	*Snow 30″–40″*	*Snow Less Than 30″*
Operate ski slope	$120,000	$40,000	− $40,000

(a) If the National Weather Bureau forecasts that there is an equal probability of 0.4 for snowfall of more than 40″ and for snowfall of less than 30″, should the firm operate or lease the ski slope?

(b) If the National Weather Bureau can predict only the probability of snowfall of less than 30″ as 0.4, what kind of probability for snowfall of more than 40″ should there be before the firm should operate the ski slope?

3. The Desert Casino has just introduced a new game, dice supreme. The new game involves three dice to be tossed simultaneously by the customer. The casino has put up the following conditions of games and prizes:

A. If the sum of three dice is an odd number, the prize is $10. The ticket to this game is $5.50.

B. If the sum of three dice is at least 15, the prize is $100. The ticket to this game is $12.

C. If the sum of three dice is at most 5, the prize is $120. The ticket to this game is $15.

D. If at least two dice are identical, the prize is $50. The ticket to this game is $20.

In order to break even the firm must sell the tickets at 10 percent above the true break-even level in order to cover operating expenses. Which of the above four are money-making games for the house?

4. The New York Mets are playing the Oakland Athletics in the World Series. According to past records, the Mets have a winning percentage of 60 against any team. The Mets have already played the first two games in Oakland and lost both. Your friend is asking you to make a bet on the Mets. He says if you bet $2 on the Mets to win the Series and if they indeed win, he would pay you $10. If the Mets lose the Series, of course, you lose your $2. Should you take the bet or not?

5. Blacksburg Fish Market sells fresh trout. Trout are bought in Roanoke at $.40 per head and sold for $.75. Any trout left over at the end of the week is sold to a cat-food plant for $.10 per head. According to past experience, demand for trout in a week has been as follows:

Demand	Probability of Demand
15	0.10
16	0.20
17	0.40
18	0.20
19	0.10

(a) If there is no goodwill cost involved for unmet demand, construct a payoff table for various demand and stocking quantities.

(b) Determine the optimum quantity to stock per week.

6. The Bluegrass Market buys T-bone steak from the university's Animal Science Department. The purchasing price is $1.00 per pound and the market sells the steak for $1.50 per pound. Any steak left over at the end of the week is sold to a local cannery for $.40 per pound. According to the sales record during the past 100 weeks, demand has been as follows:

Demand (lb)	Weeks
10	10
11	20
12	20
13	30
14	10
15	10
	100

(a) Construct the payoff table for various quantities of demand and stocking.

(b) If the market can obtain perfect information concerning the following week's demand for T-bone steak, what will be the expected profit?

7. The News Shop buys *Playboy* magazine for $1.00 a copy and sells it for $1.50. Any copies remaining unsold are salvaged for $.20 a copy in the following month. According to the requests for Playboy over the last 100 months, the demand distribution has been as follows:

Number Requested	Relative Frequency
10	0.05
11	0.15
12	0.20
13	0.30
14	0.15
15	0.10
16	0.05

(a) What is the loss due to overstocking?

(b) What is the loss due to understocking?

(c) Construct a conditional loss table and identify the optimum quantity to stock.

(d) What is the value of perfect information about demand for *Playboy* magazine?

8. A newsstand operator buys the Sunday Edition of the Roanoke *Times* for $.15 per copy and sells it for $.25. The distribution of demand for the Sunday paper over the last 100 weeks has been as follows:

Number Demanded	Relative Frequency
Less than 40	0
40	0.02
41	0.04
42	0.07
43	0.10
44	0.12
45	0.13
46	0.14
47	0.12
48	0.10
49	0.08
50	0.05
51	0.02
52	0.01
Over 52	0

(a) Assuming that any paper left over has no value and running short has no effect on any customer's tendency to return, determine the losses due to understocking and overstocking.
(b) On the assumption of part (a), how many copies should be stocked? Use incremental analysis.
(c) If any paper left over can be sold to the fish market for $.05 per copy, how many copies should be stocked?
(d) What is the smallest salvage value of the leftover paper that will justify the operator's actual stocking of 50 copies?

9. Mother's Submarine Shoppe sells various types of cold sandwiches for lunch. According to Selma, the owner, the ordinary check amounts to $1.20 and the profit is about $.50. The shop is planning to sell special $1.50 hot lunches. Selma says that the profit on this special is about $.65. Any remaining hot lunches left over at the end of the day are sold to a local fraternity for $.30. If the shop is short of specials, it loses the extra profit. Any remaining food for cold sandwiches at the end of the day could be saved for several more days. Selma decided to experiment by preparing enough specials

during the past 30 days. The sales of the special lunches on these 30 days were:

Day	Hot Lunch Sale	Day	Hot Lunch Sale
1	25	16	27
2	22	17	24
3	26	18	23
4	25	19	17
5	19	20	20
6	21	21	23
7	20	22	21
8	24	23	22
9	23	24	21
10	22	25	22
11	19	26	20
12	20	27	18
13	24	28	22
14	22	29	26
15	21	30	27

Selma says that if customers cannot get special hot lunches they always buy cold sandwiches.

(a) Assuming that the relative frequencies observed during the past 30 days are good estimates of demand probabilities, determine the optimum number of specials to prepare per day. Use incremental analysis.

(b) If the local fraternity decided not to buy the leftover specials, how many specials should Selma prepare per day?

(c) Under the condition of (b), if the shortage of specials cost $.20 in terms of goodwill cost per customer, how many specials should they prepare?

(d) Again under the condition of (b), what kind of goodwill cost should there be in order to justify stocking 24 hot lunches?

10. A merchant at the farmers market sells avocados. He purchases avocados from a dealer in California at $4 per case (20) and sells them at $8 per case in the first week they are stocked (he sells only in cases). If there are any cases left over after the first week, he reduces the price to $2 per case in the following week. Any avocados that have not been sold by the end of the second week are scrapped at a total loss. The merchant, according to his previous experience, assigns the following probability distributions for the demand for fresh avocados and for week-old avocados:

Fresh Avocados		Week-old Avocados	
Demand	Probability	Demand	Probability
0	0	0	0.15
1	0.3	1	0.25
2	0.4	2	0.30
3	0.3	3	0.20
4+	0	4	0.10

According to the merchant's experience, the demand for the fresh avocados is not related to the demand for the week-old avocados.

(a) Construct a conditional payoff table for various stock levels.
(b) How many cases of avocados should the merchant stock per week?

Hint: The events in the payoff table for this problem are of the type "demand for 1 case of avocados in the first week and demand for 2 cases in the second week.")

11. Colonial Investors, Inc., is considering three alternate investment plans for $1 million retained earnings: motel, theater, or horticultural nursery operation. The single most important factor that determines conditional payoffs of the investment plans is the current energy crisis. The management of the firm feels that if the gasoline shortage becomes severe, the motel operation will result in a financial loss, whereas it will increase the payoff of the theater and nursery operations. The marketing research and financial analysis department cooperated and came up with the following conditional payoff table:

	Gasoline Situation		
	Better	Normal	Worse
Motel	$130,000	$70,000	- $40,000
Theater	40,000	60,000	80,000
Nursery	50,000	60,000	70,000

(a) According to the Energy Control Board, the probabilities are 0.10, 0.60, and 0.30 for the better, normal, and worse gasoline situations, respectively. Where should Colonial Investors invest their $1 million?
(b) If the Federal government says that the only predictable probability is 0.20, for a better gasoline situation, which two investment plans should be selected as possible candidates for the final choice? Why?
(c) What are the indifference probabilities for the normal and worse gasoline situations for the two plans selected in (b)?

12. In problem 11, let us assume that there exists complete uncertainty about the probabilities of the three gasoline situations. However, the conditional payoffs are assumed to remain the same. Identify the optimum investment plan under the Laplace, maximin, maximax, Hurwicz, and regret criteria.

13. Your grandfather left $100,000 in a trust fund for you and you are contemplating four investment plans for the money: land development, stocks, bonds, and savings. According to an investment consultant, conditional payoffs for the four investment plans under three possible economic conditions are as follows:

	Boom	Normal	Recession
Land development	$10,000	$6,000	$ 1,000
Stocks	10,000	6,000	-3,000
Bonds	8,000	6,000	3,000
Savings	6,500	6,500	6,500

(a) Use the dominance principle to eliminate as many inferior investment plans as possible.
(b) Among the remaining investment plans in (a), which will be your choice if your coefficient of optimism under the Hurwicz criterion is 0.65?

14. The Essential Oil Corporation is considering making a bid for the Colorado shale oil development contract to be awarded by the Federal government. Through careful and thorough analysis, management of the firm has decided to set the bidding price of $210 million. The experts estimate that the firm has about a 70 percent chance of winning the contract for $210 million. Once the firm wins the contract, management has three alternatives to process the shale oil: develop a new method to extract oil, use the usual known process, or ship the shale to Japan for processing. The development of the new method to process the shale oil is estimated to cost the firm $30 million. The normal processing method costs $7 million and the shipment to Japan and back will cost about $5 million. The firm's scientists and consultants conclude that if the new process is developed the following possible outcomes and their probabilities are expected:

Event	Probability	Financial Outcome (millions)
Big success	0.7	$450
Normal success	0.2	200
Failure	0.1	20

If the firm employs the usual processing procedure the outcomes are expected as:

Event	Probability	Financial Outcome (millions)
Big success	0.6	$300
Normal success	0.2	200
Failure	0.2	40

The contract in Japan guarantees a return of $230 million for the deal. Construct a decision tree for the problem and determine the optimum decision strategy.

15. The United States is seriously considering a substantial amount of military aid to country A. Country A held a commanding military hardware superiority over the surrounding hostile countries before the recent outbreak. Today, however, the country maintains a relatively small superiority (55 percent on 100 percent rating, where 50–50 is an exact balance). The U.S. government feels that country A must maintain a considerable amount of superiority in military arms in order to maintain a long-term peace in the area. However, any arms aid to country A may result in an immediate Russian aid to hostile countries in the area. The State Department experts estimate that the probability of Russian aid to the hostile countries after the U.S. aid to country A is 0.8. The Central Intelligence Agency has informed the State Department that Russia would most likely wait and see whether the U.S. aid to country A would be a large, medium, or small sum before they make their move to neutralize the U.S. aid. If the U.S. aid to country A is a large sum, the most likely Russian reactions and their consequences are estimated as:

Event	Probability	Country A's Position
Large aid to hostile states	0.7	50%
Medium aid	0.2	60
Small aid	0.1	70

On the other hand, if the United States provides country A a medium amount of arms aid, the expected Russian actions and their consequences are:

Event	Probability	Country A's Position
Large aid to hostile states	0.1	45%
Medium aid	0.6	55
Small aid	0.3	60

If the U.S. arms aid to country A is only a small one, Russian actions are expected to be:

Event	Probability	Country A's Position
Large aid to hostile states	0.1	45%
Medium aid	0.3	50
Small aid	0.6	55

There exists, as mentioned above, 20 percent probability that Russia may not make any equalizing arms aid to the hostile states even when the U.S. provides aid to country A. In such a case, the expected outcomes are as follows:

Event	Country A's Position
Large U.S. aid to country A	90%
Medium aid	75
Small aid	60

If the U.S. government is determined to improve the military superiority of country A in order to maintain the fragile peace in the area, what kind of decisions should it take? Analyze the problem by using decision trees.

4 Linear Programming: Introduction and Graphical Solutions

The origins of mathematical programming techniques go far back in mathematical antiquity to the theories of linear and nonlinear equations. However, George B. Dantzig is generally recognized as the father of linear programming. Dantzig's work was primarily in the search for techniques to solve military logistics problems when he was employed by the U.S. Air Force during World War II. His research was encouraged by other scholars who were working on the same general subject, namely J. von Neumann, L. Hurwicz, and T. C. Koopmans. The original name given to the technique was "programming of interdependent activities in a linear structure," and it was later shortened to "linear programming."

Since 1947 many scholars, such as A. Charnes, W. W. Cooper, A. Henderson, W. Orchard-Hays, have joined Dantzig in developing the technique and exploring the applications of linear programming. Thus, it has become a distinctive management science technique that is probably one of the most widely applied tools in business, government, and other institutions. Linear programming is concerned with optimizing a decision problem by analyzing interrelationships of system components and contributions of these components to the objective function.

BASIC CONCEPTS OF LINEAR PROGRAMMING

A typical decision problem faced by management is the optimum allocation of scarce resources. Resources may represent money, manpower, materials, machine capacity, time, space, or technology. Management's task is to achieve the best possible outcome with the given resources. The desired outcome may be measured in terms of profits, costs, effectiveness, sacrifice, time, space, distance, or welfare of the public. The desired outcome expressed as a linear relationship among the system variables thus becomes the objective function of a linear programming model. The amount of available resources, also expressed as linear functions, represent constraints that define the feasibility area for optimization, Linear programming is used to identify the best combination of limited resources so as to optimize the objective.

Requirements of Linear Programming

The Objective Function

A linear programming problem must have an explicit objective criterion to optimize. The objective function may be one of either maximization or minimization of the criterion, but never both. For example, the objective of the programming may be maximization of profits, effectiveness, or utility, or, it can be minimization of costs, time, or distance.

Limited Resources

If there were unlimited resources, efficient resource allocation would present no managerial problem. In order to apply linear programming, a decision problem must involve activities that require consumption of limited resources. These limited resources may be production capacity, manpower, time, money, space, or technology. The amounts of limited resources are usually expressed as constraints for the linear programming problem.

Decision Variables and Their Relationships

Linear programming is most effective for those problems that involve a large number of decision (or activity) variables. These variables are usually interrelated in terms of utilization of resources and require simultaneous solutions. Let us examine a product-mix problem for a furniture manufacturer, which is a typical linear programming problem, where the firm produces tables, chairs, and desks. Here we have to evaluate various feasible product mixes in relation to their resource requirements and profit contributions. The optimum solution would be the product mix of certain numbers (including zero) of tables, chairs, and desks that maximizes total profit.

Linearity and Additivity

The primary requirement of linear programming is the linearity of the objective function and of the constraints. The word *linear* implies that relationships among the decision variables (products, activities, etc.) must be directly proportional. The proportionality requires that the measure of outcome and resource usage must be proportional to the level of each component activity. For example, if we increase the required resources by 5 percent, it will result in a 5 percent increase in the outcome. Linear programming also requires that the total measure of outcome (the objective criterion) and the total sum of resource usage must be additive. For example, in the case of the furniture manufacturer mentioned above, the total profit will be the sum of the profits earned from tables, chairs, and desks. Also, the total amount of resources utilized for producing the three products must be exactly equal to the sum of resources used for producing tables, chairs, and desks.

Divisibility

Linear programming requires a complete divisibility of the resources utilized and the units of decision variables. In other words, fractional values of the decision variables and resources must be permissible in obtaining an optimal solution. Resources and activities must be considered continuous within a relevant range. In the furniture manufacturer's case, it must be allowed a production program which uses 100 oak boards and 25.67 man-hours to produce 40 tables and 15.25 chairs. In many decision problems it is entirely appropriate to have fractional values in the resource utilization and decision variables. For example, we can use $2\frac{1}{2}$ cups of flour and $1\frac{1}{3}$ cups of sugar to make $\frac{1}{2}$ pound of cake and $2\frac{1}{4}$ pounds of cookies. However, there are occasions in which decision variables have physical significance only if they are in integer values. For example, we cannot assign $1\frac{2}{3}$ persons to a job. Integer programming has been developed for problems that require non-fractional values of resource utilization and decision variables.

Deterministic

In linear programming, all of the model coefficients (i.e., unit profit contribution of each product, the amount of resources required per unit of product, and the amount of available resources) are assumed to be known with certainty. In other words, linear programming implicitly assumes a decision problem in a static time period. In real-world situations, however, model coefficients are never deterministic. A number of techniques have been developed to handle linear programming problems with uncertain coefficients, such as sensitivity analysis, parametric linear programming, and chance-constrained programming. These are, of course, advanced topics of linear programming that are beyond the scope of our discussion.

Linear programming is usually applied to complex decision problems that involve many interacting variables that contribute to the objective criterion function. Indeed, many management problems fall into this category and this is why linear programming has been popular in industry.

Application Areas of Linear Programming

Resource Allocation Problem

Let us assume that there are various input resources that are limited to certain quantities and there are a number of possible outcomes that result from combinations of the resources. The decision problem is to determine a combination of input resources which will result in the optimum outcome. Linear programming is a very effective tool for this type of resource allocation problem, such as product mix, capital budgeting, sales effort allocation, and blending (e.g., concrete mixing, ice cream making, cattle feed production, and sausage blending) problems.

Let us examine an advertising budget allocation problem. A furniture manufacturer has decided to launch a major advertising campaign with a total budget of $10,000 for the next month. The advertising budget is to be spent in four possible media: local newspaper ads, local spot radio ads, local television (daytime) 30-second ads, and local magazine ads. The management of the firm attempts to allocate the advertising budget to the four available media in such a way that the firm can maximize the total "effective" exposures of its products. Suppose that market research studies already available have the following information:

1. The measure of effective exposure per dollar of advertisement in each medium
2. The maximum number of advertisements allowed to a sponsor on a given medium within the period of a month
3. The cost of advertisement per inclusion

In addition, management has certain preference as to the maximum number of ads to be put on a given medium within the period of a month. The programming problem is to determine the advertising dollar to be allocated to each medium in order to maximize the total effective exposure of the firm's products. This problem should be solved within the constraints of the advertising budget, total allowed number of ads on each medium, and management's preference of desirable number of ads on each medium.

Planning and Scheduling Problems

Many decision problems involve some degree of planning and/or scheduling. In order to optimize an objective in the future, a decision must be made concerning present and future actions to be taken. In other words, to accomplish the desired outcome the optimum combination of inputs in a certain time period must be identified. Many problems, such as product scheduling, financial planning, and manpower planning, can be analyzed by linear programming.

Let us examine a simple financial planning decision problem. Suppose the local school has a credit union. The credit union has $50,000 to invest in the following four diversified alternatives: personal loans to the members, government bonds, deposits in a savings and loan association, and preferred stock. As a first step, the credit union attempts to allocate the fund among the four investment alternatives in the most profitable way (they will decide the specific investment choice within the given alternative at a later date). The Federal Credit Union headquarters has provided the following information:

1. Expected annual yield rate for each investment alternative
2. Risk factor (percentage chance of not obtaining the expected annual yield) for each alternative
3. Average length of investment (in years) for each alternative

The credit union wants to invest the $50,000 in these investment alternatives in order to maximize the expected yield. This programming is to be solved subject to the following constraints:

1. The entire sum should be invested.
2. The probability of failing to obtain the expected earnings from the entire investment plan should be less than a given value (say, 0.10).
3. The weighted-average investment period should be less than a given number of years (say, 5).

The above investment decision can be formulated and solved as a linear programming problem.

Diet Problems

The diet problem is so labeled because one of the earliest applications of linear programming was to determine the most economical diet for human beings. Various food-related problems are concerned with the determination of the most economical (least total cost) mix of ingredients while meeting the desired nutrient values.

Let us examine a diet problem in a local hospital. The hospital dietician is planning a special menu for the maternity ward patients. The dietician is considering 50 different types of foods for the menu. The American Medical Association has provided information concerning the minimum nutritional requirements for new mothers and the amount of nutrient in a unit of each food being considered. The local food store has provided discount prices for each type of food. The dietician attempts to formulate a linear programming problem that will specify a menu that meets all nutritional requirements while minimizing the total cost.

Assignment Problems

Assignment problems involve the identification of the most efficient assignment of given subjects (people, machines, tools, etc.) to various destinations so as to minimize the objective criterion. In a machine-loading problem, linear programming is applied to determine the optimum assignment of jobs to various machines so that the total production cost (or production time) can be minimized. Assignment of police patrol cars to various areas of a city in order to minimize the total time required to reach trouble spots is another example. Assignment of snowplows to various spots in an area in order to minimize the total time required to clean up all major roads and assignment of salesmen to various sales districts in such a manner as to minimize the total distance (or time) to travel are also good examples of assignment problems.

Transportation Problems

The transportation problem involves the determination of quantities to be transported from a number of origins to a number of destinations in such a way that the total transportation cost can be minimized. In a transportation problem, it is of course necessary that the capacity of each origin, requirement of each destination, and unit transportation cost from various origins to destinations be predetermined.

The problems discussed above represent only a few of the management decision problems that have been solved by linear programming. It is indeed almost impossible to list all the application areas of linear programming. The type of problems that are most suitable for linear programming solutions are decision problems that involve a clear-cut objective criterion. Strategic and policy decisions that involve multiple, and sometimes conflicting, objectives are not easy to analyze through linear programming. These problems should be solved by goal programming, presented in Chapter 6.

THE GRAPHICAL METHOD OF LINEAR PROGRAMMING

Two basic solution methods of linear programming will be presented in this text: the graphical method and the simplex method. We shall discuss the graphical method in this chapter, since it is the simpler of the two methods and it provides basic knowledge of the linear programming approach.

Since we can effectively depict problems that involve only two dimensions (variables) on the graph, the graphical method will be illustrated through simple problems that involve only two decision variables. It is possible to depict three-dimensional problems graphically, but the procedure becomes quite tedious when there are many functions (constraints). Complex problems, therefore, will be solved by the simplex method in the subsequent chapter. For most complex real-world problems, the graphical method is never used. Instead, the computer-based simplex method is employed for such problems. However, the graphical solution method provides a conceptual framework for understanding the solution process of linear programming.

Linear Equations and Inequalities

In order to facilitate an understanding of the graphical method, it is useful to review some of the properties of linear equations and inequalities. The linear equation is a mathematical expression where two sides of the expression must be equal and all variables must be of the first degree (no exponents). Therefore, all linear equations involving two variables appear geometrically as straight lines in two-dimensional space. Linear equations involving more than two variables will be represented by planes in multidimensional space.

The general form of a linear equation can be expressed by $Y = a + bX$, where a is the Y intercept and b is the slope of the function. Let us examine the following two simple linear equations:

$$Y = 6 - 2X$$
$$Y = -2 + X$$

For the first equation, the Y intercept (or constant) is 6 and the slope (or coefficient) is -2. Similarly, the second equation shows a Y intercept of -2 and a slope of $+1$. The Y intercept indicates the point on the Y axis that the straight line passes through when the value of X is zero. The slope of the linear function is the change in Y associated with one unit change in X, or

$$\text{Slope} = \frac{\text{Change in } Y}{\text{Change in } X}$$

Now, let us plot the above two linear equations on a graph, as shown in Figure 4.1. The first function passes through two points, ($X = 0$, $Y = 6$) and ($X = 3$, $Y = 0$). The second linear function goes through ($X = 0$, $Y = -2$) and ($X = 2$, $Y = 0$). Since the lines intersect, we can find the intersecting point of the two functions by solving two equations simultaneously. For example, since the values of X and Y must be identical at the intersecting point for the two equations, we can write the equation $6 - 2X = -2 + X$, from which we can easily derive $X = 2\frac{2}{3}$. By substituting $X = 2\frac{2}{3}$ in the equation $Y = 6 - 2X$, the value of Y can be calculated, or $Y = \frac{2}{3}$.

Many real-world decision problems cannot be expressed in the

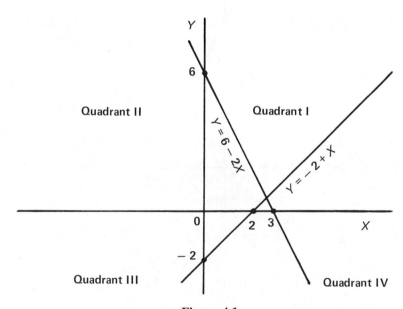

Figure 4.1
Graph of linear equalities

exact form of equations. Therefore, identification and use of linear inequalities become necessary. Inequalities are mathematical expressions that specify certain relationships and conditions. For example, let us consider the following two inequalities:

$$Y \leq 6 - 2X$$
$$Y \geq -2 + X$$

Whereas a straight line is the graphical presentation of a linear equation, a graphical presentation of a linear inequality is a closed half-space. The two inequalities presented above are depicted in Figure 4.2. For the first inequality, any point on the straight line $Y = 6 - 2X$ and to the left of the line, shown as a shaded area, satisfies the inequality condition. Similarly, for the second inequality any point on the straight line $Y = -2 + X$ and in the upper shaded area satisfies the inequality statement.

In linear programming, it is required that all decision variables in the model should be nonnegative; in other words, variables can take on only positive or zero values. This requirement makes good sense, since

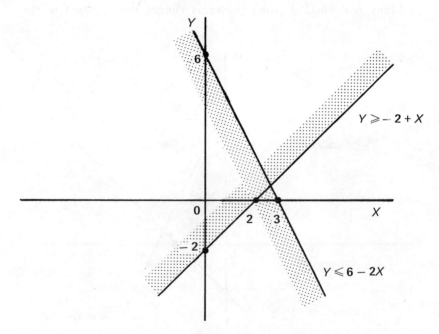

Figure 4.2
Graph of linear inequalities

we cannot think of any negative production of goods when we consider a product mix problem. Because of the nonnegative constraint for variables, the graphical solution requires only the first quadrant of a rectangular coordinate system such as the one shown in Figure 4.1.

The discussion thus far has been limited to examples involving only two variables. However, the concept of equations and inequalities can also be treated for higher dimensional problems. For example, let us examine the following equation, which involves three dimensions:

$$X + Y + Z = 10$$

Since there are three variables, the graphical representation of the equation is a plane in three-dimensional space, as shown in Figure 4.3

Formulating a Linear Programming Model

Example 1

Let us first consider a very simple production problem. An electronics firm produces two types of television sets: color and black-and-white. The production of both types of television sets requires processing in two assembly lines. A color set requires 2 hours in assembly line 1 and 3 hours in assembly line 2. A black-and-white set, on the other hand, requires 4 hours in assembly line 1 and 1 hour in assembly line 2. Assembly line 1 has up to 80 hours of assembly time

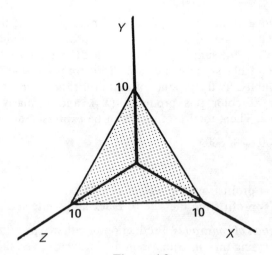

Figure 4.3
Graph of a linear equality with three dimensions (variables)

available for production. Assembly line 2 has a production capacity of 60 hours. The unit profits for color and black-and-white sets are $100 and $80, respectively.

The decision problem requires the determination of the number of color and black-and-white sets to be produced in order to maximize profit. The two decision variables in the problem are the quantity of color sets and quantity of black-and-white sets to be produced. The relationship between the two variables exists because of their competition for resources and differences in processing rates.

The above problem meets all the requirements of linear programming. Now, we shall formulate the problem as a linear programming model. First, all the information necessary for model formulation can be arranged as below. Decision variables are listed in the columns and constraints and the unit profits are shown in the rows. The quantity of color sets to be produced is denoted as X_1 and the quantity of black-and-white sets to be produced is expressed as X_2.

Assembly Line	Hours Required to Produce 1 Unit Color (X_1)	Black-White (X_2)	Resources Available
1	2	4	80
2	3	1	60
Unit Profit	$100	$80	

Formulation of the objective function. The objective of the television manufacturing problem is to maximize total profit. It should be obvious that total profit is the sum of profit from the sale of color sets and profit from the sale of black-and-white sets. Profit from the sale of color sets will be determined by the product of unit profit for color sets ($100) and the quantity of color sets produced (X_1), and similarly for black-and-white sets. Then, total profit, Z, can be expressed as

$$Z = \$100X_1 + \$80X_2$$

Where

$\$100X_1$ = profit from the sale of color sets
$\$80X_2$ = profit from the sale of black-and-white sets

Formulation of constraints. Production of either type of television set requires processing time in both assembly lines. However, the processing time in each assembly line is restricted to certain amount. For example, total production of television sets cannot exceed 80 hours in assembly line 1 and 60 hours in assembly line 2. Total production time required in assembly line 1 will be the sum of total time required to produce color sets and total time required to produce black-and-white sets. Since the required processing time to produce each type of television set is already known, we can formulate the following production constraint for assembly line 1:

$$2X_1 + 4X_2 \leq 80$$

where

$2X_1$ = total time required to produce X_1 color sets in assembly line 1

$4X_2$ = total time required to produce X_2 black-and-white sets in assembly line 1

Similarly, we can formulate the following constraint for the second assembly line:

$$3X_1 + X_2 \leq 60$$

where

$3X_1$ = total time required to produce X_1 color sets in assembly line 2

X_2 = total time required to produce X_2 black-and-white sets in assembly line 2

The directions of inequalities indicate that the left-hand side (total processing time in each assembly line) should be less than or equal to the right-hand side (available production time in each assembly line). There is one more constraint we must remember. That is the nonnegative constraint for the decision variables. This can be expressed as, X_1, $X_2 \geq 0$. Now the complete linear programming model can be presented as

$$
\begin{aligned}
\text{Maximize} \quad & Z = \$100X_1 + \$80X_2 \\
\text{subject to} \quad & 2X_1 + 4X_2 \leq 80 \\
& 3X_1 + X_2 \leq 60 \\
& X_1, \quad X_2 \geq 0
\end{aligned}
$$

Example 2

The credit union in a local school has $500,000 to invest. The credit union does not wish to invest in mutual funds or common stocks, as they view these as risky investments. Instead, they prefer to diversify their investments by allocating the funds among the following alternatives:

personal loans to the members of the credit union, government bonds, deposits in a savings and loan association, and preferred stock. The credit union is trying to determine the amount of money to be invested in the four alternatives in the most profitable way. The actual investment in a specific choice within the given investment alternative will be determined at a later date.

The Federal Credit Union headquarters has provided the current annual yield rate for each of the four alternatives as follows:

	Current Annual Yield
Personal loan to members	7.0%
Government bonds	8.0
Savings and loan	6.5
Preferred stock	7.5

It is believed that the current annual yield rate will persist in the coming year.

The credit union wishes to invest the entire amount of $500,000 so that there will be no idle fund. However, because of the risk elements and the length of investment periods required, management of the union has set the following guidelines:

1. Investment in preferred stock should be at most the amount invested in government bonds or the amount in the savings and loan association.
2. The amount on loan to the members should be at most the total investment in the remaining three alternatives.
3. At least 30 percent of the total investment funds should be allocated to personal loans to the members.

Formulation of the objective function. In this problem, the decision problem is concerned with the amount of money to be invested in each investment alternative. Hence, we have four decision variables, as follows:

X_1 = amount of money to be invested in personal loans to the members
X_2 = amount of investment in government bonds
X_3 = amount of investment in savings and loan
X_4 = amount of investment in preferred stock

The objective of this problem is to maximize the total returns from the four investment alternatives. Since the expected annual yield for each alternative is known, the total returns will be the sum of the amount invested in each alternative times the expected yield rate of the alternative. For example, if $200,000 is invested in personal loans to the members, the return will be $200,000 × 0.07 = $14,000. This return does not include the principal of $200,000. If we want to find the total fund after the investment in personal loans to the members, it will be $200,000 × 1.07 = $214,000. The objective function of this linear programming problem will be

Maximize $\quad Z = 0.07X_1 + 0.08X_2 + 0.065X_3 + 0.075X_4$

Formulation of constraints. First of all, the credit union wishes to invest the entire amount of the available funds into the four alternatives. In other words, the sum of investments in each alternative must be exactly equal to $500,000, or

$$X_1 + X_2 + X_3 + X_4 = 500,000$$

The second constraint comes from the restriction that investment in preferred stock be at most the amount invested either in government bonds or in a savings and loan association. We must formulate two separate constraints for this restriction. First, investment in preferred stock should be less than the amount invested in government bonds, or

$$X_4 \le X_2$$

Next, the amount of investment in preferred stock should be also less than the investment in savings and loan association, or

$$X_4 \le X_3$$

The credit union also wishes to limit the total investment in personal loans to the members to be at most the total amount invested in the remaining three alternatives. Hence we can write

$$X_1 \le X_2 + X_3 + X_4$$

Also, in order to meet the obligation to its members the credit union wishes to invest at least 30 percent of the available funds in personal loans to the members. Since the total amount available for investment is $500,000, 30 percent of this will be $500,000 × 0.30 = 150,000. Now we can write this constraint as:

$$X_1 \ge 150,000$$

We can rearrange the constraints in such a way that all decision variables appear on the left-hand side and all constants on the right-hand side of the equation or inequality. Then, the complete linear programming model will be:

$$
\begin{aligned}
\text{Maximize} \quad & Z = 0.07X_1 + 0.08X_2 + 0.065X_3 + 0.075X_4 \\
\text{subject to} \quad & X_1 + X_2 + X_3 + X_4 = 500{,}000 \\
& X_2 - X_4 \geq 0 \\
& X_3 - X_4 \geq 0 \\
& -X_1 + X_2 + X_3 + X_4 \geq 0 \\
& X_1 \geq 150{,}000 \\
& X_1, \quad X_2, \quad X_3, \quad X_4 \geq 0
\end{aligned}
$$

Example 3

XYZ is a social fraternity at the local university. The coming weekend is the annual Homecoming time. The officers of XYZ are planning a special "Happy Hour" beverage for the alumni and parents coming out to the fraternity house and have decided to provide the "sewer" drink, which contains bourbon and root beer. Based on past experience, XYZ has acquired the following ingredients:

Cheap bourbon	400 ounces
Premium bourbon	360
Cheap root beer	300
Premium root beer	260

XYZ has decided to use the occasion to raise funds for the annual house repair project. They plan to make four different quality drinks:

Type of Drink	Ingredients	Price
Sewer—The Thing	4 oz prem. bourbon; 1 oz prem. root beer	$1.50
Sewer—Supreme	3 oz prem. bourbon; 2 oz cheap root beer	1.20
Sewer—Regular	3 oz cheap bourbon; 2 oz prem. root beer	1.00
Sewer—All the Way	2 oz cheap bourbon; 3 oz cheap root beer	.70

In addition to the above described resource constraints, past experience indicates that demand for the drinks that contain premium bourbon is at most 50. Furthermore, XYZ feels that not more than 80 drinks that contain cheap root beer can be sold.

Formulation of the objective function. The decision problem of XYZ is to determine the number of each type of sewer drink to be produced in order to maximize the total revenue. It is essential to mix the ingredients at least 24 hours in advance to have the real "body" of the sewer flavor. Therefore, mixing the drinks in advance requires a linear programming solution. The total revenue will be a function of price per drink and the number of each drink sold. XYZ officers are confident that they can sell all the drinks they produce as long as they meet the above described six constraints. The objective function, then, will be:

$$\text{Maximize} \quad Z = \$1.50X_1 + \$1.20X_2 + \$1.00X_3 + \$0.70X_4$$

where

X_1 = number of Sewer—The Thing drinks
X_2 = number of Sewer—Supreme drinks
X_3 = number of Sewer—Regular drinks
X_4 = number of Sewer—All the Way drinks

Formulation of constraints. First let us consider the ingredient constraints. There are four ingredients being considered for the drinks:

	Drinks				*Quantity Available*
	X_1	X_2	X_3	X_4	
Cheap bourbon			3	2	400
Premium bourbon	4	3			360
Cheap root beer		2		3	300
Premium root beer	1		2		260

Let us consider cheap bourbon first. The types of drinks that use cheap bourbon are X_3 and X_4. Then, the total amount of cheap bourbon that XYZ will need must be $3X_3 + 2X_4$. This total requirement for cheap bourbon should be less than or equal to the available amount of 400 oz. The constraint can be expressed as

$$3X_3 + 2X_4 \leq 400$$

Following the same reasoning, we can develop the remaining three constraints as

$$4X_1 + 3X_2 \leq 360$$
$$2X_2 + 3X_4 \leq 300$$
$$X_1 + 2X_3 \leq 260$$

There are two additional constraints that are related to sales, since XYZ attempts to use past experience in mixing certain drinks. Drinks that contain premium bourbon should be limited to 50. Drinks that require premium bourbon are X_1 and X_2. Hence, we can write

$$X_1 + X_2 \leq 50$$

Also, drinks that contain cheap root beer should be limited to 80. X_2 and X_4 require cheap root beer. Thus,

$X_2 + X_4 \leq 80$

Now, the complete linear programming model of the XYZ problem can be given as follows:

Maximize $\quad Z = \$1.50X_1 + \$1.20X_2 + \$1.00X_3 + \$.70X_4$

$$
\begin{array}{llllll}
\text{subject to} & & & 3X_3 + & 2X_4 \leq 400 \\
& 4X_1 + & 3X_2 & & \leq 360 \\
& & 2X_2 & + & 3X_4 \leq 300 \\
& X_1 & + & 2X_3 & \leq 260 \\
& X_1 + & X_2 & & \leq 50 \\
& & X_2 & + & X_4 \leq 80 \\
& X_1, & X_2, & X_3, & X_4 \geq 0
\end{array}
$$

Graphic Representation of Constraints

In order to determine the optimum solution to a linear programming problem, we must first identify the area where solutions are feasible. In other words, we must plot the constraints on a graph. For this purpose, we will examine the linear programming problem presented in Example 1. This television production problem has two constraints.

$2X_1 + 4X_2 \leq 80$
$3X_1 + X_2 \leq 60$

We shall treat variable X_1 as the vertical axis and X_2 as the horizontal axis.

The two constraints will be plotted on the graph by treating them as linear equations and then the appropriate inequality conditions will be indicated by shaded areas. For example, the first constraint will be treated as the equation $2X_1 + 4X_2 = 80$. The equation can be solved for X_1, as follows:

$2X_1 + 4X_2 = 80$
$\qquad 2X_1 = 80 - 4X_2 \qquad$ Transposing $4X_2$
$\qquad X_1 = 40 - 2X_2 \qquad$ Dividing both sides by 2

The above equation indicates an X_1 intercept of 40 and a slope of -2. The equation is plotted on the graph as shown in Figure 4.4. Next, the inequality condition of the constraint must be satisfied. If the first constraint is solved for X_1 while maintaining the inequality sign, it becomes $X_1 \leq 40 - 2X_2$. The inequality indicates that X_1 should be to the left of the straight line plotted in Figure 4.4. Thus, the inequality condition can be satisfied by the shaded area shown in Figure 4.5. Any point within the shaded area satisfies the condition and any point outside of it does not meet the requirement. For example, the two points $(X_2=10, X_1=20)$ and $(X_2=5, X_1=10)$ satisfy the inequality condition, but the point $(X_2=20, X_1=10)$ does not meet the requirement. We can verify this statement by substituting the values of X_1 and X_2 in the constraint:

Point $(X_2=10, X_1=20)$:
$$2\times 20 + 4\times 10 \leq 80$$
$$80 = 80$$

Point $(X_2=5, X_1=10)$:
$$2\times 10 + 4\times 5 \leq 80$$
$$40 < 80$$

Point $(X_2=20, X_1=10)$:
$$2\times 10 + 4\times 20 \leq 80$$
$$100 > 80$$

It is apparent that any production combination of color and

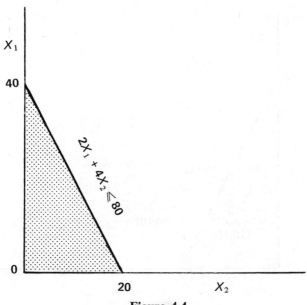

Figure 4.4
Graph of $2X_1 + 4X_2 \leq 80$

black-and-white television sets within the shaded area can be processed in assembly line 1 with the available time. Any production combination outside the shaded area cannot be achieved with the given production capacity.

By following the same procedure, we can solve the second constraint, as follows:

$$3X_1 + X_2 = 60$$
$$3X_1 = 60 - X_2 \qquad \text{Transposing } X_2$$
$$X_1 = 20 - \tfrac{1}{3}X_2 \qquad \text{Dividing both sides by 3}$$

The second equation is also plotted on the graph and the inequality condition $X_1 \leq 20 - \tfrac{1}{3}X_2$ is also indicated by a shaded area, as shown in Figure 4.6.

Since production of either type of television set requires processing time in both assembly lines, the only feasible production area will be the cross-hatched region where the two shaded areas overlap. This area is called the "area of feasible solutions." The area of feasible solutions represents a region that satisfies conditions specified by all the constraints in the model. Any point within the area is a feasible solution and any point external from it is an infeasible solution. Thus, the objective

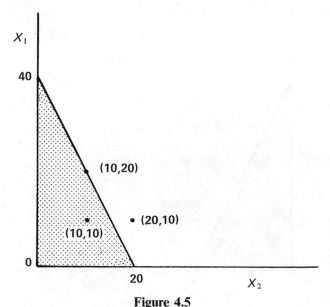

Figure 4.5
Graph of feasible and infeasible solution points of $2X_1 + 4X_2 \leq 80$

function is to be optimized within this restricted area of feasible solutions.

Graphic Solution Method

There are several approaches one can take in solving a linear programming model by the graphic method. Three approaches will be discussed in this text.

The Search Approach

The simplest approach to identify the optimum solution is by searching through certain feasible solutions. At least it is obvious that the origin is not the optimum solution. In other words, if we do not produce any color or black-and-white television sets there would be no profit. Another important point to remember is that the objective function is a linear function. Therefore, total profit increases as we depart from the origin upward. Hence, the point which maximizes total profit will be one of three points, A, B, or C, in Figure 4.7.

Total profits at points A and C are easy to calculate, since the exact values of X_1 and X_2 are already known. At point A ($X_2=0$, $X_1=20$), total

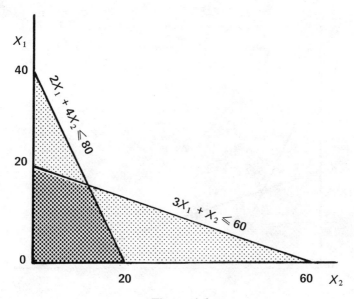

Figure 4.6
Graph of constraints $2X_1 + 4X_2 \le 80$ and $3X_1 + X_2 \le 60$

profit will be $Z = \$100 \times 20 + \$80 \times 0 = \$2000$. At point $C(X_2=20,$ $X_1=0)$, total profit becomes $Z = \$100 \times 0 + \$80 \times 20 = \$1600$. It is thus clear that if we decide to specialize, producing only one type of television set, we should produce 20 color sets.

Now, if total profit at point B is greater than $2000, then it is the optimum point. To calculate the total profit at point B we must first calculate exact values of X_1 and X_2 at the point. This can be done easily by solving the two equations simultaneously, as follows:

$$X_1 = 40 - 2X_2 \tag{1}$$

$$X_1 = 20 - \tfrac{1}{3}X_2 \tag{2}$$

Then,

$$40 - 2X_2 = 20 - \tfrac{1}{3}X_2$$
$$- \tfrac{5}{3} X_2 = -20$$
$$X_2 = 12$$

Substituting this X_2 value in to (1),

$$X_1 = 40 - 2 \times 12$$
$$X_1 = 16$$

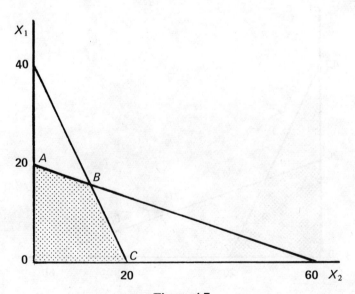

Figure 4.7
Solution area satisfying constraints $2X_1 + 4X_2 \leq 80$ and $3X_1 + X_2 \leq 60$

The total profit at point B can now be derived as $Z = \$100 \times 16 + \$80 \times 12 = \$2560$. The optimum solution to the problem is point B, or production of 16 color sets and 12 black-and-white sets. This solution yields the maximum profit of $2560.

The search approach is probably the simplest and easiest method to determine the optimum solution when the problem has a very small number of constraints. If there are many constraints that bound the area of feasible solutions, there is a large number of points to search. Hence, the search procedure might be extremely cumbersome and time consuming.

The Iso-Profit Function Approach

The second approach of the graphical method of linear programming is concerned with an analysis of the iso-profit function. As the prefix *iso-* implies, the iso-profit function is a straight line on which every point has a same total profit. The iso-profit (or iso-cost in minimization problems) function is derived when the objective function is solved for the variable that is treated as the vertical axis (X_1 in the example). In our example the objective function can be solved for X_1 as follows:

$$Z = \$100X_1 + \$80X_2 \qquad \text{Objective function}$$
$$\$100X_1 = Z - \$80X_2$$
$$X_1 = \frac{Z}{100} - \tfrac{4}{5}X_2 \qquad \text{Iso-profit function}$$

The iso-profit function derived above has an X_1 intercept of $Z/100$ and a slope of $-4/5$. Since the total profit Z is not known, the X_1 intercept cannot be determined. However, the slope of the function is known. The best we can do, therefore, is to plot the iso-profit function according to its slope. As explained earlier, the total profit is zero at the origin and profit increases gradually as we move out as far as possible within the area of feasible solution. In other words, total profit increases as the iso-profit function with $-4/5$ slope moves farther from the origin.

Let us first plot the iso-profit function with an X_1 intercept of 4, as shown in Figure 4.8. Since the slope of the function is $-4/5$, the iso-profit function will go through the two points ($X_2 = 0$, $X_1 = 4$) and ($X_2 = 5$, $X_1 = 0$). By definition, any point on this line has identical total profit. We can check this very simply, as follows:

Point	Z
($X_2 = 0$, $X_1 = 4$)	$400
($X_2 = 5$, $X_1 = 0$)	400
($X_2 = 2\tfrac{1}{2}$ $X_1 = 2$)	400

We can also equate the X_1 intercept of the iso-profit function $(Z/100)$ to the intercept we selected, 4, as follows:

$$4 = \frac{Z}{100}$$

$$Z = \$400$$

Next, we increase the X_1 intercept to 8. This iso-profit function passes through the two points $(X_2=0, X_1=8)$ and $(X_2=10, X_1=0)$. Total profit at any point on this line is \$800. It should be evident that total profit increases gradually as we depart further from the origin with the iso-profit function. Then, the optimum solution must be the *last point* we touch with the iso-profit function within the area of feasible solutions. Figure 4.8 indicates that the optimum solution is found to be the intersecting point of the two constraints when the iso-profit line goes through the two points $(X_2=0, X_1=25\ \frac{3}{5})$ and $(X_2=32, X_1=0)$. At this intersecting point, $(X_2=12, X_1=16)$, the solution satisfies both constraints and the total profit yielded is \$2560.

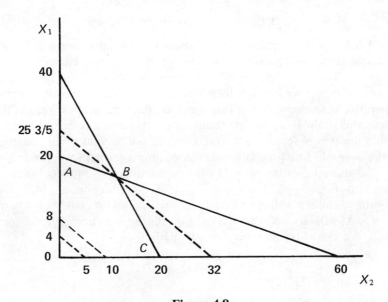

Figure 4.8
Determining the optimum solution using the iso-profit function approach

The Slope Comparison Approach

The iso-profit function approach is effective in most simple linear programming problems where the slope of the iso-profit function is sufficiently different from the slopes of constraints. However, if, for example, the slope of the iso-profit function is $-7/8$ and the slope of a constraint that forms the area of feasible solution is $-8/9$, it is rather difficult to determine the optimum solution when we use our visual judgment. The easiest way to determine the optimum solution in such a case appears to be the slope comparison approach. In this approach, we compare the slope of the iso-profit function with the slopes of constraints that form the area of feasible solutions. In the above television production problem, the slopes of two constraints are $-1/3$ and -2. As long as the slope of the iso-profit function $(-4/5)$ falls between these two slopes, the optimum point is the intersecting point of the two constraints, as shown in Figure 4.9. The slope $-4/5$ is not as steep as -2 but is steeper than $-1/3$, and therefore the iso-profit function will pass through the intersecting point of the two constraints at the tip of the area of feasible solutions.

If the iso-profit function had a slope of -3, which is steeper than either of the two slopes of the constraints, the last point the iso-profit line touches within the feasibility area would be $(X_2 = 20, X_1 = 0)$, as shown in

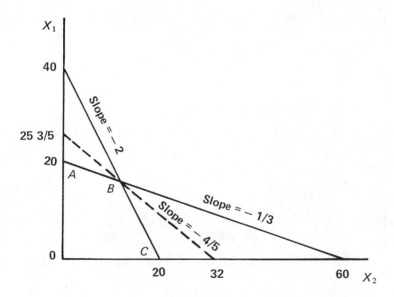

Figure 4.9
Graphical representation of slope comparison approach

Figure 4.10. Therefore, this is the optimum solution. By applying the same reasoning, if the iso-profit function had a slope of $-1/4$, which is flatter than either of the two constraint slopes, the optimum point would be $(X_2=0, X_1=20)$, also shown in Figure 4.10.

If the iso-profit function has a slope identical to one of the slopes of the *critical* constraints, the optimum solution would be a portion of that constraint. For example, if the slope of the iso-profit function were $-1/3$ in our example, any point on the line segment connecting the two points $(X_2=0, X_1=20)$ and $(X_2=12, X_1=16)$ would be the optimum solution. This reasoning is presented in Figure 4.11, where the extra-dark portion of the line connecting $(X_2=0, X_1=20)$ and $(X_2=60, X_1=0)$ indicates the optimum solution. In such a case, obviously, there are multiple optimum solutions.

In the discussion of the slope comparison approach thus far, we have emphasized the fact that we should consider slopes of those constraints that form the border of the area of feasible solution. We can examine this reasoning by analyzing the following problem:

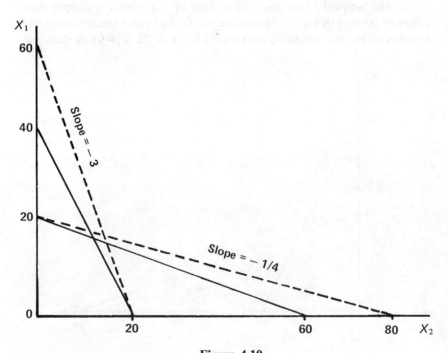

Figure 4.10
Effect of slope changes in the iso-profit function on the optimum solution

$$\text{Maximize} \quad Z = \$100X_1 + \$80X_2$$
$$\text{subject to} \quad 2X_1 + 4X_2 \leq 80$$
$$3X_1 + X_2 \leq 60$$
$$X_1 + X_2 \leq 100$$
$$X_1, \quad X_2 \geq 0$$

The first two constraints and the objective function are identical to the problems we have discussed. The third constraint is added to the problem. The slope of the iso-profit function is $-4/5$ and three slopes of the constraints are $-1/3$, -1, and -2. If we employ the slope comparison approach, the optimum solution should be the intersecting point of the second and third constraints, since $-4/5$ falls between $-1/3$ and -1. The intersecting point of these two constraints is, when the two equations are solved simultaneously, $(X_2 = 120, X_1 = -20)$, as shown in Figure 4.12. This solution clearly violates the nonnegative constraint of the model. It is evident from the figure that the third constraint, $X_1 + X_2 \leq 100$, does not impose any actual restriction on the solution. In fact, the area of feasible solutions is formed by the first two constraints. Consequently, we must compare the slope of the iso-profit function with the slopes of the first two constraints. The optimum

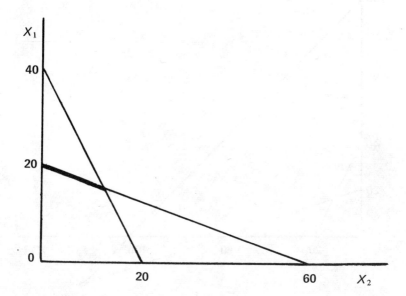

Figure 4.11
Graph of multiple optimum solutions occurring when iso-profit function and a critical constraint have equal slopes

solution for this problem, therefore, is identical to that for the previous problem we discussed.

It should also be noted here that care should be taken in using the slope comparison approach if the problem involves mixed constraints. For example, suppose a problem has the area of feasible solutions shown in Figure 4.13. It is not a simple task to find the optimum solution by just comparing the three slopes. For such problems, it is more appropriate to use the iso-profit (or iso-cost) function approach.

Minimization Problems

Thus far the graphic method of linear programming has been discussed for maximization problems. The same three approaches that

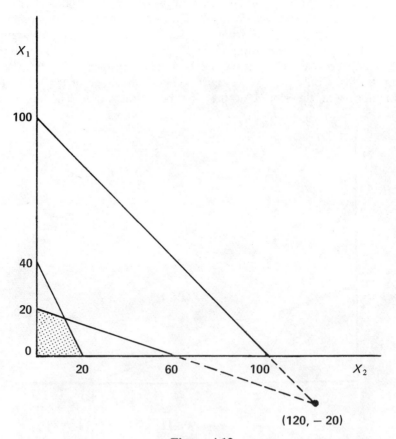

Figure 4.12
Graphical representation of a noncritical constraint

are used for maximization problems can also be applied to minimization problems. Let us consider a very simple diet problem.

A church youth group plans to serve breakfast at a special sunrise service. The group is considering serving only coffee and two types of foods: scrambled eggs and home-fried potatoes. The group received a special request from the congregation of the church that the breakfast meet the minimum Vitamin A and B requirements. Let us assume that information has been obtained concerning the Vitamin A and B contents per egg and per scoop of home-fried potatoes. This information and the minimum Vitamin A and B requirements for breakfast (all fictitious figures) are as follows:

	Vitamin Content (mg)		*Minimum*
Vitamin	*Egg*	*Potato*	*Requirements*
A	2	4	16
B	3	2	12
Unit Cost	4	3	

This diet problem is concerned with the minimization of cost per serving

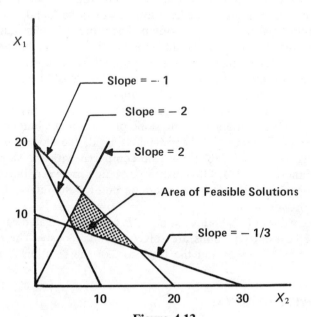

Figure 4.13
Graph of feasible solution of a problem with mixed constraints

while meeting Vitamin A and B requirements. The problem can be easily formulated as a linear programming model

Minimize $Z = 4X_1 + 3X_2$
subject to $2X_1 + 4X_2 \geq 16$
                   $3X_1 + 2X_2 \geq 12$
                   $X_1, \quad X_2 \geq 0$

where

X_1 = number of eggs
X_2 = scoops of potatoes
Z = total costs in cents

The objective function is expressed in terms of cents. The right-hand sides (or constants) of the two constraints specify the minimum requirements. Therefore, the inequalities are shown as "greater than or equal to" rather than "less than or equal to," as we observed in the previous problem. Quite frequently, many constraints of minimization problems indicate "greater than or equal to" type inequalities. The constraints of this problem are plotted on the graph in Figure 4.14.

The problem can be solved by using any of the three approaches we have discussed. The optimum solution can be found at the point where the total cost is minimum. The least total cost can be found, if we ignore the feasibility restrictions, at the origin. Then, the optimum point within the area of feasible solution should be one of those points that are closest to the origin. Therefore, if the search approach is used, the three points to be examined are A, B, and C. If the iso-cost ("cost" because this is a cost minimization problem) function approach is used, the optimum point will be the *first* point we touch within the feasibility area as we move out from the origin with the slope of the iso-cost function, $-3/4$. When the slope comparison approach is used, the slopes of the two constraints, -2 and $-2/3$, should be compared with the slope of the iso-cost function, $-3/4$. Obviously, $-3/4$ falls between the two constraint slopes, and therefore the optimum point is the intersecting point of the two constraints.

Exact values of X_1 and X_2 at point B can be calculated easily when the two constraint equations are solved simultaneously. The optimum point is $(X_2=3, X_1=2)$ and the total cost of the solution is 17 cents.

SENSITIVITY ANALYSIS

Thus far we have discussed the general concept, model formulation, and the graphical analysis of linear programming. One of the important

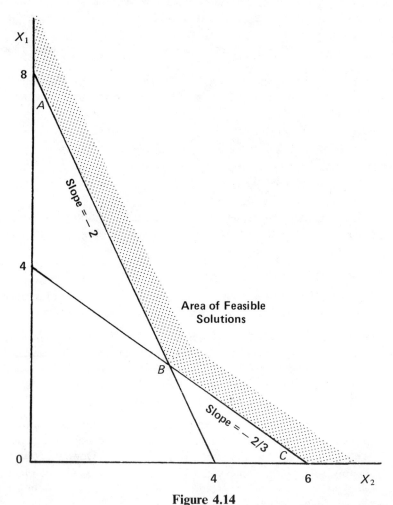

Figure 4.14
Graph of constraints for the diet problem, showing feasible solution area

aspects of linear programming that deserves our attention is sensitivity analysis. Sensitivity analysis is concerned with the sensitivity of the optimum solution to changes in the model parameters. Because there usually exists some degree of uncertainty in real-world situations, certain model parameters are not known with certainty. Therefore, sensitivity analysis, in addition to the derivation of the optimum solution, is of great interest to the decision maker.

If the optimum solution is relatively sensitive to changes in a certain parameter, special efforts should be directed to forecasting the future values of the parameter. By the same token, if the optimal solution has very little sensitivity to change in a certain parameter, it might be a waste of effort and resources to estimate the value of the parameter more accurately.

By way of introducing the sensitivity analysis, let us examine the general model of linear programming for a maximization problem:

$$\text{Maximize} \quad Z = \sum_{j=1}^{n} C_j X_j$$

$$\text{subject to} \quad \sum_{j=1}^{n} a_{ij} X_j \le b_i \quad i = 1,2,...,m$$
$$X_j \ge 0 \quad j = 1,2,...,n$$

In the above model, the values of C_j represent contribution rates (e.g., unit profits in a maximization problem), a_{ij} are technological coefficients (e.g., amount of resources required to produce a unit of a product), b_i are available resources (e.g., total available production capacity in an assembly line), and X_j are decision variables. In sensitivity analysis, we examine the effects of changes in C_j, a_{ij}, and b_i on the optimum solution.

Let us examine the following problem:

$$\text{Maximize} \quad Z = \$100X_1 + \$80X_2$$
$$\text{subject to} \quad X_1 + X_2 \le 100$$
$$2X_1 + X_2 \le 160$$
$$X_1 + 2X_2 \le 160$$
$$X_1, \quad X_2 \ge 0$$

Figure 4.15 depicts the problem on a graph. A brief examination of the figure indicates that the optimal solution of the problem is at point $B(X_2=40, X_1=60)$, with the total profit of $9200. Does the optimal product mix remain the same when there are changes in unit profits, technological coefficients, or resource levels? Let us examine this question by analyzing changes in each parameter.

Change in Contribution Rates C_j

In reality, contribution rates (unit profits for the choice variables) are seldom constant. Sometimes they fluctuate within a certain range and sometimes fluctuations are totally unpredictable. In the above example, suppose the unit profit of X_1 changes from $100 to $120, while the unit profit of X_2 remains at $80. Notice that the only change is in the coefficient of X_1 in the objective function. In other words, the area of feasible solutions remains exactly the same but the slope of the iso-profit

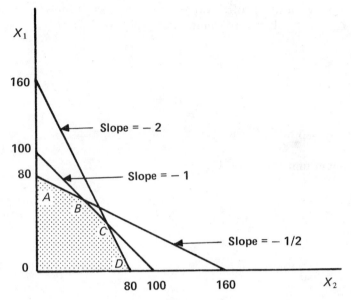

Figure 4.15
Graph of the feasible solution area

function is changed from $-4/5$ to $-2/3$. When we employ the slope comparison method, it is evident that point $B(X_2 = 40, X_1 = 60)$ remains as the optimum solution. Of course, the total profit is increased from \$9200 to \$10,400.

From the discussion of the slope comparison method, it should be clear that point B is the optimal solution as long as the iso-profit function has a slope between -1 and $-1/2$. If the iso-profit function has a slope of $-1/2$, any point on the line segment AB will be an optimal solution. On the other hand, if the slope of iso-profit function is -1, any point on the line segment BC is an optimum solution. Consequently, point C becomes the optimal solution when the slope of the iso-profit line is between -1 and -2.

Now, we can ask a simple question. If the unit profit of X_2 remains at \$80 but the unit profit of X_1 fluctuates, what kind of profit range should we have for X_1 in order for us to select point C as the optimal solution? If we denote C_1 as the unit profit for X_1, and C_2 as the unit profit for X_2, the slope of the iso-profit function becomes $-C_2/C_1$. From our previous discussion, it is clear that the iso-profit function requires a slope between -1 and -2 in order to have point C as the optimal solution. Since the unit profit for X_2 is constant, it is simple to determine the necessary unit profit range for X_1 as follows: Since $-2 \leq -C_2/C_1 \leq -1$, the maximum unit profit for X_1 is

$$\frac{-C_2}{C_1} \leq -1$$

$$\frac{-\$80}{C_1} \leq -1$$

$$C_1 \leq \$80$$

The minimum unit profit for X_1 is

$$\frac{-C_2}{C_1} \geq -2$$

$$\frac{-\$80}{C_1} \geq -2$$

$$C_1 \geq \$40$$

If the unit profit of X_2 remains constant at $80, it is required to have a unit profit range of $40 to $80 for X_1 in order for point $C(X_2=60, X_1=40)$ to be the optimum solution.

Change in Technological Coefficients a_{ij}

Changes in technological coefficients are not only frequent in reality but may also have profound effects on the problem solution. Changes in technological coefficients have no effect on the objective function of the problem, but they affect the constraints and thereby usually bring changes in the area of feasible solutions. In our example, suppose the second constraint is changed from $2X_1 + X_2 \leq 160$ to $2X_1 + \frac{2}{3}X_2 \leq 160$; that is, the coefficient of X_2 is changed from 1 to $\frac{2}{3}$ in the constraint. This change will result in change in the slope of the constraint, as shown in Figure 4.16. It should also be apparent that the area of feasible solution is now $OAECD$.

Change in technological coefficients does not always result in change in the optimal solution. For example, if point C were the previous optimal solution, the change in the coefficient of X_2 in the second constraint discussed above has no effect on the optimal solution. In the original problem, the optimal solution was shown by point $B(X_2 = 40, X_1 = 60)$, with $Z = \$9200$. Now the new optimal solution,

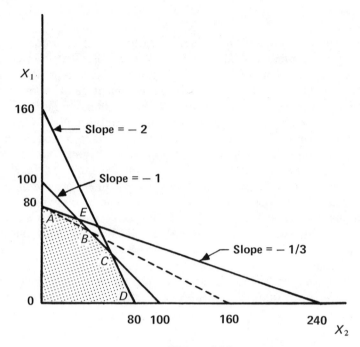

Figure 4.16
Effect of a change in technological coefficients (a_{ij}) on the optimum solution

based on the slope comparison method, will be point $E(X_2 = 30$, $X_1 = 70)$, where $Z = \$9400$.

Change in Resources or Right-hand Side b_i

Changes in the right-hand side of the constraints may have some effect on the optimal solution. Since the right-hand side is the constant value of the constraint, changes in b_i will result in changes in the intercepts of the function. Consequently, it may result in changes in the area of feasible solutions. For example, in our original problem suppose the third constraint is changed from $X_1 + 2X_2 \leq 160$ to $X_1 + 2X_2 \leq 120$. The change in the intercepts and in the area of feasible solutions is shown is Figure 4.17. Note that a change in the right-hand side does not affect the slope of the constraint. The new area of feasible solutions, as shown in Figure 4.17, is $OAFG$. By applying the slope comparison method, it is clear that the optimal solution is point $F(X_2 = 26\frac{2}{3}, X_1 = 66\frac{2}{3})$, where $Z = \$8800$.

SUMMARY

Linear programming is a powerful mathematical technique for determining the optimum solutions of decision problems that involve linear objective functions and linear constraints. Linear programming has been widely applied by industry, government, and nonprofit organizations. The reason for this popularity of linear programming appears to be its relatively simple concept and its applicability to many real-world problems. However, another very important reason is the availability of the simplex technique as a solution algorithm. Today there are numerous simplex-based computer programs available. These programs enable the decision scientist to solve complex linear programming problems with relative ease. The most critical problem in applying linear programming is the model formulation. It requires a good understanding of the basic concept, requirements, and application areas of linear programming.

In this chapter, we have studied these important aspects of linear programming through various examples and the graphical solution method. Linear programming assists the decision maker in selecting the

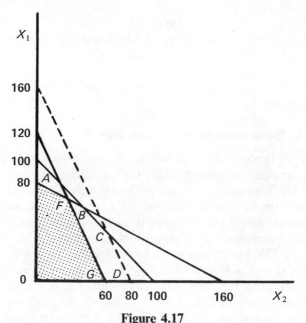

Figure 4.17
Effect of a change in resources on the optimum solution

most effective course of action from various alternatives. Furthermore, the decision maker can gain more clear insight about the nature of the problem by performing sensitivity analysis.

REFERENCES

Bierman, H., Bonini, C. P., and Hauseman, W. H., *Quantitative Analysis for Business Decisions*, 4th ed., Irwin, Homewood, Ill., 1973.

Charnes, A., and Cooper, W. W., *Management Models and Industrial Applications of Linear Programming*, Wiley, New York, 1961.

Hillier, F. S., and Lieberman, G. J., *Introduction to Operations Research*, 2d ed., Holden-Day, San Francisco, 1974.

Kwak, N. K., *Mathematical Programming with Business Applications*, McGraw-Hill, New York, 1973.

Levin, R. I., and Kirkpatrick, C. A., *Quantitative Approaches to Management*, 2d ed., McGraw-Hill, New York, 1971.

Llewellyn, R. W., *Linear Programming*, Holt, New York, 1964.

PROBLEMS

1. Solve the following linear programming problem by using the graphical method:

   Maximize $Z = \$10x_1 + \$8x_2$
   subject to $4x_1 + 6x_2 \leq 48$
   $2x_1 + x_2 \leq 20$

2. Solve the following problem by the graphical method of linear programming:

   Minimize $Z = \$15x_1 + \$25x_2$
   subject to $8x_1 + 6x_2 \geq 72$
   $4x_1 + 6x_2 \geq 48$

3. Due to the shortage of gasoline, more and more people are riding bicycles and the state government sees an opportunity to make some money. They have decided to set up two bicycle production lines at the state penitentiary and have the prisoners manufacture 5-speed and 10-speed bicycles. The maximum number of hours that each assembly line can operate are: assembly line 1, 50 hours per week, and assembly line 2, 40 hours per week. Prisoners working in line 1 produce a 5-speed bicycle in 3 hours and a 10-speed bicycle in 5

hours. Prisoners in line 2 produce a 5-speed bicycle in 2 hours and a 10-speed in 4 hours. The state has determined that a profit of $50 can be realized on each 5-speed bicycle and $80 on each 10-speed bicycle. The state Chamber of Commerce does not wish to drive private bicycle producing firms out of the state. Therefore, they have determined that the state can sell no more than 8 5-speed bicycles and 10 10-speed bicycles each week.

(a) Formulate a linear programming model to determine how many bicycles of each type the prison should produce each week in order to maximize profits.

(b) Solve the above problem using the graphical method.

4. Mr. Jones is the production manager of the Blacksburg Block Company (BBC), which manufactures both bricks and cinder blocks. BBC receives a profit margin of $6.50 and $10.00 per 100 for bricks and cinder blocks, respectively. Mr. Jones is trying to determine the production scheduling for bricks and blocks for the next week. Although he is a profit maximizer, Mr. Jones does have a definite commitment to a customer for 800 bricks. Since there is no inventory of either bricks or blocks, at least 800 bricks must be produced. The production of both bricks and blocks is a two-step process. Both must first be molded and then baked. Molding of 100 bricks requires 2 hours and molding of 100 blocks requires 4 hours. Baking requires 4 hours per 100 bricks or blocks. A maximum of 40 hours per week is available for molding, while the maximum time available for baking is 60 hours per week. Mr. Jones is confident he can sell all the bricks and cinder blocks he produces each week since the primary building season is under way.

(a) Formulate a linear programming model to determine the proper mix of bricks and blocks that will maximize profits.

(b) Solve the above problem using the graphical method.

5. The Peoples Shoe Company is wholly owned by the Peoples Republic of Hahn. Under the government's direction it produces a summer boot and a winter boot for use by the military. Under the current five-year plan and with the existing number of employees, there are 2400 man-hours of production time available each week. Each pair of summer boots requires 3 man-hours of labor and each pair of winter boots requires 4 man-hours of labor. The government can supply the shoe company with a maximum of 1000 square feet of leather each week. Each summer boot requires 1 square foot of leather, while each winter boot requires 2 square feet of leather. Although the govern-

ment could simply take the boots, it has decided that perhaps some incentive can be provided by using the capitalistic notion of profit. Therefore, the company will realize 50¢ profit on each pair of summer boots and 70¢ profit on each pair of winter boots.

(a) Formulate a linear programming model to determine how many pairs of summer and winter boots to produce each week in order to maximize profits.
(b) Solve the above problem using the graphical method.

6. The Neverfail Recorder Company produces two types of tape recorders—a reel-to-reel model and a cassette model—on two assembly lines. The company must process each tape recorder on each assembly line and it has found that the following time is required:

	Reel-to-Reel	*Cassette*
Assembly line 1	6 hours	2 hours
Assembly line 2	4 hours	2 hours

The production manager says that line 1 will be available 40 hours per week while line 2 will be available only 30 hours per week. After these hours of operation each line must be checked for repairs. The company realizes a profit of $30 on each reel-to-reel tape recorder and $12 on each cassette recorder.

(a) Formulate a linear programming model to determine how many recorders of each type should be produced each week in order to maximize profits.
(b) Solve the above problem using the graphical method.

7. The Airwaves Company has been a producer of picture tubes for television sets and certain printed circuits for radios. The company has just expanded into full-scale production and marketing of AM and AM-FM radios. It has built a new plant that can operate 48 hours per week. Production of an AM radio in the new plant will require 2 hours and production of an AM-FM radio will require 3 hours. Each AM radio will contribute $4 to profits while an AM-FM radio will contribute $8 to profits. The marketing department, after extensive research, has determined that a maximum of 15 AM radios and 10 AM-FM radios can be sold each week.

(a) Formulate a linear programming model to determine the optimum production mix of AM and AM-FM radios that will maximize profits.

(b) Solve the above problem using the graphical method.

8. The Hudson Printing Company is facing a tight financial squeeze and is attempting to cut costs wherever possible. At present it has only one printing contract and, luckily, the book is selling well in both the hardcover and paperback editions. It has just received a request to print more copies of this book in either the hardcover or paperback form. Printing costs for hardcover books are $6 per 100 while printing costs for paperbacks are only $5 per 100. Although the company is attempting to economize, it does not wish to lay off any employees. Therefore, it feels obligated to run its two printing presses at least 80 and 60 hours per week, respectively. Press 1 can produce 100 hardcover books in 2 hours or 100 paperback books in 1 hour. Press 2 can produce 100 hardcover books in 1 hour or 100 paperback books in 2 hours.

(a) Formulate a linear programming model to determine how many books of each type should be printed in order to minimize costs.

(b) Solve the above problem using the graphical method.

9. The Arts and Craft Shop is sponsoring a boomerang-throwing contest each week for the next four weeks. Each week's contest will be for only those people who have not participated before. All boomerangs must be purchased from the Arts and Craft Shop. The shop sells two models of boomerang—the regular model and the "Super Bender." Each model requires two processes—carving; and painting and varnishing. There is a maximum of 75 hours available per week for carving and 100 hours available per week for painting and varnishing. Production of a regular boomerang requires 1 hour of carving and 2 hours of painting and varnishing. Production of a "Super Bender" requires 3 hours of carving and 2 hours of painting and varnishing. Profit from the sale of a regular boomerang is $2 while a "Super Bender" provides a $5 profit.

(a) Formulate a linear programming model to determine the number of each type boomerang that should be produced each week in order to maximize profits.

(b) Solve the above problem using the graphical method.

10. The Rawlings Lumber Company cuts raw timber—oak and pine logs—into 2×4 boards. Two steps are required to produce boards from logs. The first step involves removing the bark from the logs. Two hours are required to remove the bark from 1000 feet of oak logs and three hours per 1000 feet of pine logs. After the logs have been

debarked, they must be cut into boards. It takes 2.4 hours to cut 1000 feet of oak logs into boards and 1.2 hours per 1000 feet of pine logs. The bark-removing machines can operate up to 60 hours per week, while the cutting machines are limited to 48 hours per week. The company can buy a maximum of 18,000 feet of raw oak logs and 12,000 feet of raw pine logs each week. The profit per 1000 feet of processed logs is $180 and $120 for oak and pine logs, respectively.

(a) Formulate a linear programming model to determine how many feet of each type of log should be processed each week in order to maximize profits.
(b) Solve the above problem using the graphical method.

11. The Browning Clothing Store is making plans for its annual shirt and pants sale. The owner, Mr. Jarvis, is planning to use two different forms of advertising—radio and newspaper ads—to promote the sale. Based on past experience, Mr. Jarvis feels confident that each newspaper ad will reach 40 shirt customers and 80 pants customers. Each radio ad will reach 30 shirt customers and 20 pants customers, he feels. The cost of each newspaper ad is $100 and the cost of each radio spot is $150. An advertising agency will prepare the advertising and it will require 5 man-hours of preparation for each newspaper ad and 15 man-hours of preparation for each radio spot. Mr. Jarvis' sales manager says that a minimum of 75 man-hours should be spent on preparation of advertising in order to fully utilize the services of the advertising agency. Mr. Jarvis feels that in order to have a successful sale, the advertising must reach at least 360 shirt customers and at least 400 pants customers.

(a) Formulate a linear programming model to determine how much advertising should be done using each media in order to minimize costs and still attain the objectives of Mr. Jarvis.
(b) Solve the above problem using the graphical method.

12. The Kaiser Cattle Ranch prides itself on the high quality of the cattle that it produces. Mr. Kaiser is in the process of preparing a grand champion bull for a cattle show. Mr. Kaiser wants the bull to have a high quality of feed that will contain at least 600 mg of iron and 800 mg of vitamin A per bag. Since no feed sold on the market meets these high standards, Mr. Kaiser has decided to produce his own feed. Mr. Kaiser knows that cattle feed contains ground wheat, soybeans, and fillers. Each pound of ground wheat contains 60 mg of iron and 100 mg of vitamin A. Each pound of soybeans contains 60 mg of iron and 50 mg of vitamin A. Ground wheat will cost Mr.

Kaiser 10¢ per pound, while soybeans will cost 6¢ per pound.

(a) Formulate a linear programming model to determine the optimum mixture of wheat and soybeans that will meet Mr. Kaiser's requirements and still minimize feed costs.

(b) Solve the above problem using the graphical method.

13. Christmas is only a few weeks away and the manager of the Custom Jewelry Company knows that at Christmas his biggest sellers are gold bracelets and gold earrings. There are three full-time goldsmiths who each work 40 hours a week. These men can produce a bracelet with 3 man-hours of labor and a set of earrings with 5 man-hours of labor. The manager has a contract with a supplier for 4000 grams of gold per week until Christmas. Each bracelet will require 200 grams of gold, while a set of earrings will require 80 grams of gold. The profit contribution is $30 for each bracelet and $40 for each set of earrings. The manager knows from past experience that the number of sets of earrings that he will sell will not exceed 20 per week. However, he can sell all the bracelets that his employees can produce.

(a) Formulate a linear programming model to determine how many bracelets and sets of earrings should be produced each week in order to maximize profits.

(b) Solve the above problem using the graphical method.

14. The Cover Girl Company is expanding its operations and attempts to expand its sales territory. The sales manager has a staff of experienced salesladies who are paid $200 per week. He is planning to hire some new sales trainees for $100 per week. Based on past experience, an experienced saleslady can generate $10,000 worth of sales each week. The sales trainee can generate an average of $6000 worth of sales per week. The company has budgeted $800 for the training program of new trainees. The estimated cost of training is $100 per trainee. The sales manager's budget of payroll is $1600 per week. Furthermore, the company has decided that the sales force should be limited to 10 or fewer salesladies. The decision problem of the sales manager is to determine the optimum number of experienced salesladies and new trainees in order to maximize total sales.

(a) Formulate a linear programming model for the problem.

(b) Identify the optimum solution and the total sales by using the graphical method.

(c) If the weekly sales of the experienced salesladies remain relatively constant at $10,000 per week but weekly sales of the trainees fluctuate widely, how much should the trainee sell per week before the company should hire two experienced salesladies and eight trainees?

(d) In the original problem, ignoring (c), if the training cost per trainee is $200 rather than $100, how would the optimum solution be changed?

(e) In the original problem, if the company increases the number of salesladies from 10 to 12, how would the solution be changed?

15. The Champion Sporting Goods Company is the largest producer of baseball and softball equipment in the world. The sales manager is making plans to produce bats and he knows that because of the high quality of the company's bats he can sell all that can be produced. His problem is that he cannot decide how many softball and how many baseball bats should be produced. Each bat must be processed in two different assembly lines. Assembly line 1 can operate up to 70 hours per week while line 2 can operate no more than 60 hours per week. To produce 100 softball bats requires 7 hours on line 1 and 3 hours on line 2, while 100 baseball bats require 5 hours on line 1 and 6 hours on line 2. The sale of 100 softball bats contributes $40 profit while the sale of 100 baseball bats contributes $50 profit.

(a) Formulate a linear programming model to determine how many bats of each type should be produced each week in order to maximize profits.

(b) Solve the above problem using the graphical method.

16. The Global Chemical Company produces only one product, Compound X, which it can produce using either of two processes. Both processes not only produce Compound X, but also a byproduct known as Compound Y. Until recently Compound Y was worthless, but a new, quite profitable market has developed for it. Using process 1, the company can produce 60 grams of Compound X per hour and 15 grams of Compound Y per hour. The second process produces 40 grams of Compound X and 30 grams of Compound Y each hour. Global must produce at least 3600 grams of Compound X per month due to its contract commitments. The company would also like to produce at least 1200 grams of Compound Y per month in order to gain a substantial share of the new market. The cost of using either process to produce Compound X and Compound Y is $30 per hour.

(a) Formulate a linear programming model to determine how many hours per month each process should be operated to produce the desired products and still minimize costs.

(b) Solve the above problem using the graphical method.

17. The Pleasant Valley Truck Farming Association has an agreement with a local grocery store chain to supply them with at least 200 tons of white potatoes this year. In addition, there is an agreement to supply the grocery chain with at least 120 tons of sweet potatoes next year. The association has two fields that it uses to grow potatoes. Field 1 will, on the average, yield 20 tons of white potatoes per acre, whereas field 2 yields an average of 25 tons of white potatoes per acre. Because of differences in soil content, field 1 will be capable of yielding 15 tons of sweet potatoes per acre next year in that ground used the preceding year for growing white potatoes. Field 2 will yield 10 tons of sweet potatoes per acre in that ground used the preceding year to grow white potatoes. Apparently white potatoes add certain ingredients to the soil in which they are grown, which improves the yield of sweet potatoes grown the next season in the same ground. Past experience has shown that whenever sweet potatoes were not alternated with white potatoes, the sweet potato yield per acre was less than 50 percent of what is was otherwise. The association plans to fertilize both fields this year at a cost of $150 per acre for both fields.

(a) Formulate a linear programming model to determine how many acres of each field should be planted with white potatoes this year (and sweet potatoes next year) in order to minimize costs and still produce the contracted amounts of white and sweet potatoes for the next two years.

(b) Solve the above problem using the graphical method.

18. During a recent fire a 20-acre section of Brush Mountain was destroyed. The U.S. Forest Service is planning to reseed this section. It requires 5000 seedlings. Regulations require that at least 50 percent of the seedlings be white pine and the remainder be yellow pine. White pine seedlings cost $4 per 100 and yellow pine seedlings cost $4.05 per 100. The cost of planting the white pine is $10 per 100; the cost of planting the yellow pine is $9.50 per 100. The Forest Service has been allocated $700 to reseed this area, of which only $225 may be used to purchase seedlings.

(a) Formulate a linear programming model to determine how many trees of each type should be planted if the Forest Service wishes to minimize costs.

(b) Solve the above problem using the graphical method.

19. The Appalachian Mining Company operates two gold mines. The mines are located in different parts of the country and they have different production capacities. After crushing, the ore is graded into three classes: premium, good, and regular. There is some demand for each grade of ore. The company has a contract to provide a plant with 12 tons of premium, 8 tons of good, and 24 tons of regular grade ore per week. The first mine costs $200 per day to operate, whereas the second mine costs only $160 per day. The average production per day for the first mine is 6 tons of premium, 2 tons of good, and 4 tons of regular grade ore. The second mine produces daily 2 tons of premium, 2 tons of good, and 12 tons of regular grade ore. The management's problem is to determine how many days a *week* the company should operate each mine in order to fulfill its contract obligations most economically.

(a) Formulate a linear programming model.
(b) Illustrate the model graphically by identifying the following: Axis of graph; Constraints Area of feasible solution; Point of optimum solution; Values of decision variables at the optimum point
(c) Given the optimum solution, determine the cost per week, and for each mine the number of tons of each grade of ore produced each week.
(d) Would there be any change in the optimum solution if the daily operation cost of mine 1 is reduced to $150 while the daily operation cost of mine 2 remains at $160?
(e) In the original problem (ignore d) what would be the effect if the firm has to ship only 6 tons of good grade ore instead of 8 tons?

20. Lee Fortune Cookies, Inc., produces two types of fortune cookies: love and happiness. The major decision problem to be solved is the product mix determination in order to maximize profit. The production of a dozen fortune cookies requires the following processes. The available resources or capacity are presented on the right.

Required per dozen	*Love*	*Happiness*	*Available*
Cookie mix	1.0 lb	0.6 lb	120 lb
Icing mix	0.4 lb	0 lb	32 lb
Labor	0.15 hour	0.10 hour	15 hours
Oven capacity	1 dozen	1 dozen	120 dozen

The expected profit for love cookies is $.40 per dozen and for happiness cookies it is $.30 per dozen.

(a) Formulate a linear programming model for the problem.
(b) Solve the above problem graphically.

(c) Provided that the profit per dozen for love cookies remains at
$.40, what kind of profit range should happiness cookies have in
order to have 80 love cookies and 30 happiness cookies as the
optimum solution?

5 Simplex Method of Linear Programming

The graphical method of linear programming introduced in Chapter 4 is a straightforward technique for solving simple linear programming problems. However, most real-world management problems are too complex to be solved by the graphical method. As a matter of fact, many resource allocation problems faced by management may involve several thousand variables and several hundred constraints. Clearly, these types of problems cannot be solved by the graphical method because of their complexity. Systematic procedures have been developed to solve complex linear programming problems. The best known technique is the simplex method.

The simplex method of linear programming was developed by Professor George B. Dantzig in 1947 and has been further refined since then by many other contributors. This method is a mathematical procedure that employs an iterative process so that the optimum solution is achieved through progressive operations. In other words, in a maximization problem the last solution yields a total profit that is greater than the profit yielded by the previous solution. The simplex procedure is based on matrix algebra. A set of simultaneous equations of constraints is solved through the matrix inverse procedure. Although it may sound like a formidable task, the basic procedure is quite simple. In fact, if students follow the simplex procedure outlined in this chapter, lack of knowledge in matrix manipulation may not be a problem.

Some students may ask, "Why should I learn the complex procedure of the simplex technique when we have the computer to solve linear programming problems?" This question is a very valid one in view of the fact that the manual solution is almost never used in practical applications of linear programming. It is difficult to find a good answer to the question. We pursue knowledge, however, not simply to learn what has been developed by others but to develop our own imagination from the understanding of the existing knowledge as fully as possible. For example, pilots who fly commercial airplanes should know more about the airplane than just how to take-off, fly, and land. To master the skill of flying commercial airliners he should know something about aeronautical engineering, physics, electronics, and even psychology. The same analogy can be applied to astronauts, car drivers, subway operators, computer operators, and so on. In short, knowing more about the fundamentals of the system makes one more proficient in applying the system. This is especially true in emergencies. Suppose the computer provided a very strange solution to a linear programming problem for some reason. This occurs quite frequently. If we did not have the knowledge of the simplex procedure, it would be extremely difficult to evaluate the solution.

As we mentioned in Chapter 1, a good manager should be familiar with the basic mechanism of decision science applications. After all, the objective of decision science courses is to provide more fundamental knowledge about the tools so that it can broaden the perspective and insight of the reader (the future decision maker). Certainly, the simplex method is one of the most powerful techniques that have been developed in the area of decision sciences.

FORMULATION OF THE SIMPLEX MODEL

Let us review the television manufacturer problem first discussed in the previous chapter, so as to facilitate a comparative analysis between the graphical and the simplex solutions. The firm produces color and black-and-white television sets. The production of both types of television sets requires processing in two assembly lines. A color set requires 2 hours in assembly line 1 and 3 hours in assembly line 2. A black-and-white set, on the other hand, requires 4 hours in assembly line 1 and 1 hour in assembly line 2. Assembly line 1 has up to 80 hours of assembly time available for production and assembly line 2 has a production capacity of 60 hours. The unit profits for color and black-and-white sets are $100 and $80, respectively. The management problem is to determine the optimum product mix of color and black-and-white television sets in order to maximize total profit.

The above problem is illustrated in a schematic form in the following table:

	Color	Black-and-White	Production Capacity
Assembly 1	2	4	80 hours
Assembly 2	3	1	60 hours
Unit Profit	$100	$80	

The complete linear programming model for the above problem can be formulated as:

Maximize $Z = \$100X_1 + \$80X_2$
subject to
$$2X_1 + 4X_2 \leq 80$$
$$3X_1 + X_2 \leq 60$$
$$X_1, \quad X_2 \geq 0$$

where

X_1 = number of color television sets
X_2 = number of black-and-white television sets

There are several logical steps to follow in formulating a simplex model of linear programming.

Convert the Constraints to Equations

As explained in the preceding chapter, the optimum solution may not be at the intersection point of the two constraint lines. In other words, the optimal solution does not always use all of the available resources. It is quite possible that at the optimum solution there could be some unused resources. In order to make the model general enough to take care of unused resources, we should introduce an additional variable to represent the slack resources. By introducing the *slack variables* we can convert the inequality constraints to equations. We need as many slack variables as the number of inequality constraints. For the above problem, we need the following two slack variables:

S_1 = slack variable for assembly 1 (unused production capacity)
S_2 = slack variable for assembly 2 (unused production capacity)

The two inequality constraints can be converted to the following equations:

$2X_1 + 4X_2 + S_1 = 80$ Assembly 1
$3X_1 + X_2 + S_2 = 60$ Assembly 2

Since the two constraint inequalities are "less than or equal to," the two equations shown above would hold by assigning appropriate values to the slack variables. For example, if the plant is completely idle, there would be no production of color and black-and-white television sets. Consequently, for assembly line 1 the equation becomes $2(0) + 4(0) + S_1 = 80$, or $S_1 = 80$. For assembly line 2, the equation would be $3(0) + 1(0) + S_2 = 60$, or $S_2 = 60$. It should be evident that the two equations hold by assigning $S_1 = 80$ (unused production capacity in assembly $1 = 80$ hours) and $S_2 = 60$ (unused production capacity in assembly $2 = 60$ hours). Now, let us suppose that the firm is producing 10 color and 5 black-and-white sets. Then the two equations will become

$$2X_1 + 4X_2 + S_1 = 80$$
$$2(10) + 4(5) + S_1 = 80$$
$$S_1 = 40$$

and

$$3X_1 + X_2 + S_2 = 60$$
$$3(10) + 5 + S_2 = 60$$
$$S_2 = 25$$

Express the Objective Function

The original objective function for the problem was $Z = \$100X_1 + \$80X_2$. Since we have introduced two slack variables in the constraints, we must add them in the objective function. If we can assume that no profit or cost is associated with the slack variables (unused production capacity), the objective function becomes

Total profit $= Z = \$100X_2 + \$80X_2 + \$0S_1 + \$0S_2$

If some costs are associated with the slack variables (available but unused resources), the coefficients of the slack variables would be negative values. For this problem, the objective function is as follows:

Maximize $\quad Z = \$100X_1 + \$80X_2 + \$0S_1 + \$0S_2$

Set up the Initial Solution

In the graphical method, the basic approach we took to identify the optimum solution was to start from the origin and move out gradually to the optimum point with the slope of the iso-profit function. In the simplex method, we also initiate the solution procedure from the origin (where we do not produce any product). Since the values of the two decision variables are zero at the origin $(X_1=0, X_2=0)$, the two constraint equations will be

$$2X_1 + 4X_2 + S_1 = 80$$
$$2(0) + 4(0) + S_1 = 80$$
$$S_1 = 80$$

and

$$3X_1 + X_2 + S_2 = 60$$
$$3(0) + 0 + S_2 = 60$$
$$S_2 = 60$$

In the initial solution, the slack variables take on the values shown on the right-hand side (rhs). In other words, the only variables with nonzero values are S_1 ($S_1 = 80$) and S_2 ($S_2 = 60$). The objective function, then, becomes

$$\text{Total profit} = Z = \$100X_1 + \$80X_2 + \$0S_1 + \$0S_2$$
$$= \$100(0) + \$80(0) + \$0(80) + \$0(60) = 0$$

Obviously, the total profit is zero when the plant is completely idle and there is no production.

The Simplex Tableau

The simplex method is based on an iterative process. It is essential, therefore, to employ a simplified tableau for analysis and iteration. Although many different formats of the simplex tableau have been suggested by many authors, the functions of the simplex tableau are basically identical. In this book, we shall adopt the format shown in Figure 5.1.

The First Simplex Tableau

The first simplex tableau contains the initial solution of the linear programming problem. It should be apparent that in the initial solution slack variable S_1 takes the rhs value of 80 and slack variable S_2 takes the rhs value of 60. Consequently, the basic variables (v) in the initial tableau will be S_1 and S_2. Their rhs values are 80 and 60, respectively, as shown in Figure 5.2.

The next procedure involves the identification of all the variables included in the linear programming problem and their C_j values. In our television production problem, there is a total of four variables in the model: X_1 (number of color television sets to be produced), X_2 (number of black-and-white sets to be produced), S_1 (unused production capacity hours in assembly line 1), and S_2 (unused production capacity hours in assembly line 2). First we list these four variables in the appropriate columns, as shown in Figure 5.3. Now, we identify C_j values for each variable in the objective function and list them in the C_j row and C_j column. The objective function of the linear programming model is

$$\text{Total profit} = Z = \$100X_1 + \$80X_2 + \$0S_1 + \$0S_2$$

C_j			C_1	C_2	C_3	C_4
	v	rhs	X_1	X_2	S_1	S_2
	Z_j					
	$C_j - Z_j$					

C_j: Contribution per unit of each variable (e.g. unit profit, unit cost, etc.). C_j applies to the row and the column. In the row, C_j will be represented by C_1, C_2, ..., which indicate the unit profit (or unit cost) we have identified in the objective function. In the column, C_j indicates the unit profit (or unit cost) of the variables in the solution base.

v: Variables in the solution base (product mix in our problem).

rhs: Constant (quantity), or right-hand, side of the variables in the solution base.

X_j, S_i: Decision variables and slack variables. There should be as many columns as the number of variables (including slack variables) on the right-hand side of the double lines.

Z_j: Total contribution of the given solution in the rhs column. In the variable columns, Z_j represents costs associated with the production of one unit for each product (variable).

$C_j - Z_j$: $C_j - Z_j$ is calculated only for the variable columns and not for the rhs column. $C_j - Z_j$ indicates the net increase of profit (or cost) associated with one unit of each product (variable).

Figure 5.1
The simplex tableau

The C_j value of \$100 should be recorded in the X_1 column, \$80 in the X_2 column, \$0 in S_1 column, and \$0 in S_2 column, as shown in Figure 5.4. In the C_j column, C_j values of the variables in the solution base (basic variables) should be recorded. Since S_1 and S_2 are the basic variables in the initial solution, their C_j values (both zero) are recorded, as seen in Figure 5.4

The next step is to list the coefficients of the model variables in the main body of the tableau. The two model constraints of our problem are

$$2X_1 + 4X_2 + S_1 = 80$$
$$3X_1 + X_2 + S_2 = 60$$

We list the coefficients in appropriate columns and rows. For example, in the first constraint equation the coefficient of X_1 is 2; therefore it should be listed in the X_1 column of the first row. All the variable coefficients are listed in Figure 5.5. All the zero coefficients (e.g., the coefficient of S_2 in the first equation) are left blank in the tableau in order to leave the tableau as simple to read as possible.

The next step is to calculate Z_j values. As explained earlier, Z_j in the rhs column represents total contribution with the given solution mix.

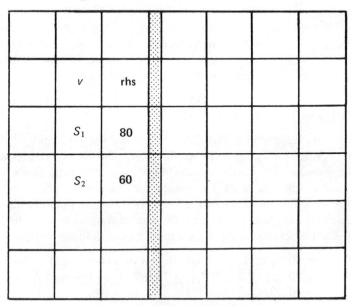

Figure 5.2
Basic variables and rhs values in the simplex tableau

v	rhs	X_1	X_2	S_1	S_2
S_1	80				
S_2	60				

Figure 5.3
Variable columns in the simplex tableau

The procedure we must follow is to find the sum of C_j of each basic variable times the values of rhs of the basic variable. In other words, the Z_j value in the rhs column of the initial solution is

$$Z = \$0 \ (C_j \text{ of } S_1) \times 80 \text{ (rhs of } S_1) + \$0 \ (C_j \text{ of } S_2) \times 60 \text{ (rhs of } S_2)$$
$$Z(\text{rhs}) = 0 \times 80 + 0 \times 60 = \$0$$

Of course, we remember that the initial solution is at the origin, where we do not produce anything. Since we have only the slack variables in the solution base and they do not contribute any profits, total contribution of the initial solution is $0. To calculate Z_j values in various variable columns, we follow the same procedure except that we multiply the C_j of the basic variables with coefficients in each variable column rather than rhs values. For example, the Z_j value in the X_1 column will be

$$Z(X_1) = \$0(C_j \text{ of } S_1) \times 2 \text{ (coefficient in } S_1 \text{ row and } X_1 \text{ column)} +$$
$$\$0 \ (C_j \text{ of } S_2) \times 3 \text{ (coefficient in } S_2 \text{ row and } X_1 \text{ column)}$$
$$= \$0 \times 2 + \$0 \times 3 = \$0$$

By following the same calculation procedure, Z_j of the X_2 column will be $Z(X_2) = \$0 \times 4 + \$0 \times 1 = \$0$. Since the C_j values of S_1 and S_2 are

C_j				100	80	0	0
	v	rhs		X_1	X_2	S_1	S_2
0	S_1	80					
0	S_2	60					

Figure 5.4
Contribution rates (C_j) in the simplex tableau

both zero, the Z_j values will be all zero, as shown in Figure 5.6

The last step required to complete the initial tableau is calculating $C_j - Z_j$. As explained earlier, $C_j - Z_j$ values are calculated only for the variable columns. C_j values are listed on the top of the table right above each variable and Z_j values are listed on the bottom. Therefore, $C_j - Z_j$ will be very simple to calculate indeed. For the X_1 column, C_j is \$100 and Z_j is \$0, as shown in Figures 5.7 and 5.8. $C_j - Z_j$ for the X_1 column, therefore, will be \$100 - \$0 = \$100. With the $C_j - Z_j$ values added to the tableau, we can find the complete tableau of the initial solution in Figure 5.7. The detailed explanation of the simplex tableau will be presented in the following section.

SIMPLEX SOLUTION PROCEDURE

Before the simplex solution procedure is examined, we should review the initial simplex tableau shown in Figure 5.7. In the initial simplex tableau the solution is at the origin. Hence, there is no production. Consequently, the slack variables (unused production capacities) appear in the solution base. The total amount of unused production capacity in assembly line 1, S_1, is 80 and the value of S_2 is 60. Z_j in the rhs column indicates that total profit of the initial solution is zero.

Now let us examine the variable columns. In the X_1 column, we find coefficients of 2 in the S_1 row and 3 in the S_2 row. These coefficients indicate that to produce one unit of X_1 (color television set) it requires 2 units of S_1 and 3 units of S_2. This is nothing new. A color television set requires 2 hours in assembly line 1 and 3 hours in assembly line 2. Similarly, a unit of X_2 (black-and-white set) requires 4 units of S_1 and 1 unit of S_2.

Z_j in the X_1 column is calculated by finding $0 \times 2 + 0 \times 3 = 0$. To produce a color set it requires $(2S_1 + 3S_2)$. Since we have assumed that slack variables, both S_1 and S_2, have no monetary value or cost, the Z_j value in the X_1 column simply represents costs associated with the production of one unit of X_1 (color television set). In this case this cost is zero. Using the same logic, a unit of X_2 (black-and-white set) requires $(4S_1 + 1S_2)$, and the Z_j value in the X_2 column is also zero.

$C_j - Z_j$ represents the net increase of profit (or cost in minimization

C_j				100	80	0	0
	v	rhs		X_1	X_2	S_1	S_2
0	S_1	80		2	4	1	
0	S_2	60		3			1

Figure 5.5
Coefficients (a_{ij}) in the simplex tableau

problems) associated with one unit of each product. A color television set brings in $100 profit ($C_j$). However, at the initial solution where the firm has idle production plant, it costs nothing to produce a color set (Z_j value in X_1 column). Therefore, the net increase of profit per color television set ($C_j - Z_j$) we produce is $100. The same logic can be applied to all other variable columns.

The simplex solution procedure requires the following steps.

Determine the First Product to Introduce

The initial solution of the linear programming problem is simply a starting point. In order to maximize total profit we must introduce some products and depart from the origin. The question is, then, which product we should introduce first. Since our objective is profit maximization, the product we should produce first should be one which will increase total profit at the fastest rate. The net increase of profit per unit of each product is represented by $C_j - Z_j$. The product to be introduced first will be the one with the largest positive value of $C_j - Z_j$. Examining Figure 5.8, the largest positive $C_j - Z_j$ value is $100 in the X_1 column.

C_j				100	80	0	0
	v	rhs		X_1	X_2	S_1	S_2
0	S_1	80		2	4	1	
0	S_2	60		3	1		1
	Z_j	0		0	0	0	0

Figure 5.6
Z_j **values in the simplex tableau**

C_j				100	80	0	0
	v	rhs		X_1	X_2	S_1	S_2
0	S_1	80		2	4	1	
0	S_2	60		3	1		1
	Z	0		0	0	0	0
	$C_j - Z_j$			100	80	0	0

Figure 5.7
$C_j - Z_j$ **values in the simplex tableau**

This indicates that X_1 (color television sets) be produced first in order to increase total profit at the fastest rate. This column, X_1, with the largest $C_j - Z_j$, is usually called the "key column" or "pivot column." The variable in the key column is the incoming variable to the solution base in the second tableau. The key column is marked in Figure 5.8. It should be noted that $C_j - Z_j$ values for the first solution are simply C_j.

Determine the Outgoing Variable

After the key column has been determined, the next step is determining the outgoing variable. We have decided to produce X_1 as the first product in the solution. A unit of X_1 requires 2 hours of S_1 and 3 hours of S_2, as shown in Figure 5.8. The available idle capacities (rhs) in the two assembly lines are 80 and 60, respectively. Then, by dividing the rhs values by the coefficients we can determine the maximum number of X_1 (color television sets) that each assembly line can process. For example, in assembly line 1 there are 80 hours of capacity. It requires 2 hours in assembly line 1 to process one X_1. Therefore, up to 40 units can be processed with the existing production capacity $(80 \div 2 = 40)$. In assembly line 2, we can process only up to 20 units of X_1 $(60 \div 3 = 20)$. Remembering that production of either type of television set requires

C_j				100	80	0	0	
	v	rhs		X_1	X_2	S_1	S_2	
0	S_1	80		2	4	1		$80/2 = 40$
0	S_2	60		③	1		1	$60/3 = 20$ ← Key Row
	Z_j	0		0	0	0	0	
	$C_j - Z_j$			100	80	0	0	

Key ↑
Column

Figure 5.8
Identifying the key column and key row

production time in both assembly lines, we can easily determine that the maximum number of X_1 that can be produced is 20.

In order to determine the quantity of a variable that can be introduced to the solution, the only thing we have to do is identify the *minimum nonnegative* value when the rhs values are divided by the coefficients in the key column. However, the rows with zero coefficients in the key column should be excluded. This procedure assures that rhs values will never be negative, thereby satisfying the nonnegative constraint of the model. The row that contains the minimum non-negative value is called the "key row," as shown in Figure 5.8. The variable in the key row, S_2 in this example, is the outgoing variable. In other words, in the second solution X_1 (color television sets) will replace S_2 (idle production capacity in assembly line 2) in the solution base.

The Second Simplex Tableau

Production of 20 color television sets (X_1) requires a total of 60 hours in assembly line 2 ($3 \times 20 = 60$). Obviously, this will use all of the available production time and exhaust the capacity of assembly line 2.

Consequently, S_2 (slack time in assembly line 2) will become zero. This is the reason why X_1 replaces S_2 in the solution base of the second simplex tableau. Figure 5.9 shows the introduction of X_1 in the solution base and changes in the rhs and C_j columns for the X_1 row. Since X_1 has replaced S_2 in the solution base, the C_j of X_1 ($100) should also replace the C_j of S_2 ($0). The new rhs for the X_1 row is 20, as explained earlier.

Now we shall proceed to find new coefficients in the X_1 row. The procedure we used to find the new rhs value in the X_1 row was dividing the old rhs by the coefficient at the intersection of the key column and the key row. To find the new coefficients in the X_1 row for variable columns, the same procedure should be used, as shown in Figure 5.10.

As explained earlier, the simplex method is based on the matrix inverse procedure. However, knowledge of the matrix algebra is not necessary to see the logic behind the simplex method. For example, the rate of substitution between S_2 (idle production capacity in assembly line 2) and X_1 (number of color television sets to be produced) is 3 to 1. In other words, it requires 3 hours in assembly line 2 to produce 1 color set. That is how we determined the rhs value of 20 in the X_1 row in Figure 5.9. Dividing all coefficients by the pivot element of 3 will provide new rates of substitution between X_1 (the new basic variable) and all other variables in the simplex tableau. Figure 5.10(a) shows the old rela-

C_j				100	80	0	0
	v	rhs		X_1	X_2	S_1	S_2
0	S_1						
100	X_1	20					

Figure 5.9
Finding the new rhs values in the key row

(a)

C_j			100	80	0	0
	v	rhs	X_1	X_2	S_1	S_2
0	S_1					
0	S_2	60	③	1		1

(b)

C_j			100	80	0	0
	v	rhs	X_1	X_2	S_1	S_2
0	S_1					
100	X_1	20	1	1/3		1/3

$60 \div 3 = 20 \qquad 3 \div 3 = 1 \qquad 1 \div 3 = 1/3 \qquad 1 \div 3 = 1/3$

Figure 5.10
Finding the new coefficients in the key row

tionships of the second constraint and Figure 5.10(b) presents the new relationships of the row after X_1 replaces S_2. For example, the coefficient of 1 in the X_1 column and X_1 row indicates that the rate of substitution of X_1 by itself is 1. The coefficient $\frac{1}{3}$ that we find in the S_2 column and the X_1 row indicates that the rate of substitution between X_1 and S_2 is 1 to 3. Of course, this makes good sense because we just substituted S_2 by X_1 with the same substitution rate. The coefficient $\frac{1}{3}$ in the X_2 column is a little harder to explain because we do not have new coefficients in S_1 row. We shall explain this coefficient in the latter part of this section.

The next step in completing the second simplex tableau is to calculate new rhs values and coefficients in the other constraint equation. First, let us calculate the new rhs value of the S_1 row. In the initial solution there were 80 hours of idle production capacity in assembly line 1 (S_1). However, when we process 20 color television sets, the idle production capacity in assembly line 1 must be decreased, as shown in Figure 5.11. Since it requires 2 units of S_1 and 3 units of S_2 to produce a color television set, production of 20 color sets will require 40 units of S_1 and 60 units of S_2. We started the simplex solution with 80 units of S_1 (80 hours of idle production capacity in assembly line 1). Therefore, the leftover S_1 after the production of 20 color sets (X_1) will be $80 - (2 \times 20) = 40$. The calculation of the new rhs for the S_1 row is shown clearly in Figure 5.11.

Now the new relationship of the first constraint should be completed by calculating new coefficients. But first let us review the procedure we used for calculating the new rhs value of S_1, $80 - (2 \times 20) = 40$. The calculational procedure we used was: old value in the row (80) − [coefficient in the key column (2) × new value in the key row in the same column (20)] = new value in the row (40). In order to maintain consistency, we must use the same procedure for calculating the new coefficients, as shown in Figure 5.12. After a period of practice one becomes so proficient in calculating the new coefficients that he may not need any scrap paper to write out the calculations. However, until that time comes we can use the following easy procedure:

Columns	Old Values in the Row		Coefficient in the Key Column	$\times$	New Value in the Key Row		New Values for the Row
rhs	80	−	(2	×	20)	=	40
X_1	2	−	(2	×	1)	=	0
X_2	4	−	(2	×	$\frac{1}{3}$)	=	$3\frac{1}{3}$
S_1	1	−	(2	×	0)	=	1
S_2	0	−	(2	×	$\frac{1}{3}$)	=	$-\frac{2}{3}$

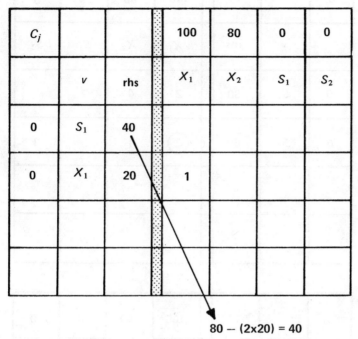

C_j			100	80	0	0
	v	rhs	X_1	X_2	S_1	S_2
0	S_1	40				
0	X_1	20	1			

80 – (2x20) = 40

Figure 5.11
Calculating the new rhs values for other rows

Now that we have established new relationships in the two constraints, we can proceed to complete the second simplex tableau, as shown in Figure 5.13. Z_j in the rhs column ($2000) indicates total profit of the second solution, where we produce 20 color sets and have 40 hours of idle capacity in assembly line 1. Figure 5.14 presents the procedure for calculating Z_j in various columns. For example, in column X_1 we have coefficients 0 in the S_1 row and 1 in the X_1 row. These coefficients indicate that production of 1 unit of X_1 (color television set) requires, at this stage of the simplex solution, 0 unit of S_1 and 1 unit of X_1. In other words, the only way we can produce one additional color set is by sacrificing a color set we have produced. This logic is clear because we have already used up the production capacity of assembly line 2 by producing 20 color television sets (X_1). Then, the cost of producing one additional unit of X_1 will be $100, as shown in Figure 5.14(b).

In the original problem, production of a black-and-white set (X_2) required 4 hours in assembly line 1 and 1 hour in assembly line 2. Then, why do we have coefficients of $3\frac{1}{3}$ in the S_1 row and $\frac{1}{3}$ in the X_1 row? Remembering once again that at the second simplex solution we are producing 20 units of X_1 by using 40 hours of S_1 and 60 hours of S_2,

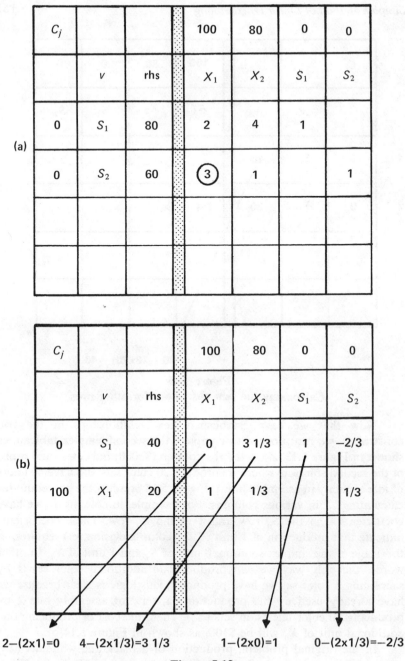

Figure 5.12
Calculating the new coefficients in the S_1 row

C_j			100	80	0	0
	v	rhs	X_1	X_2	S_1	S_2
0	S_1	40		3 1/3	1	−2/3
100	X_1	20	1	1/3		1/3
	Z_j	2000	100	33.33	0	33.33
	$C_j − Z_j$		0	46.67	0	−33.33

Figure 5.13
Calculating Z_j and $C_j − Z_j$ values

there is no production capacity left over in assembly line 2 to produce any X_2. That implies that the only way we can produce X_2 is by sacrificing some units of X_1. We have idle capacity of 40 hours in assembly line 1 (S_1). Therefore, the critical constraint is assembly line 2, where we have no slack time left over. Knowing that a unit of X_2 requires 1 hour and a unit of X_1 requires 3 hours in assembly line 2, we can get 1 hour that is required to produce one unit of X_2 if we sacrifice ⅓ unit of X_1. This rate of substitution is shown in the X_2 column and X_1 row. How about the coefficient 3 ⅓ in the S_1 row? When we sacrifice ⅓ of X_1 we also get back some production time in assembly line 1. Since a whole unit of X_1 requires 2 hours in assembly line 1, if we sacrifice ⅓ unit of X_1 it would free ⅔ of an hour in assembly line 1. A unit of X_2 requires 4 hours in assembly line 1. If we use ⅔ of an hour we get back from sacrificing ⅓ unit of X_1, then the actual use of S_1 required to produce one X_2 will be 3 ⅓ (⅔ + 3 ⅓ = 4). Now, the whole thing makes sense. The total cost of producing a unit of X_2 is 3⅓×0 + ⅓×100 = \$33.33. The same logic applies to the S_1 and S_2 columns, as shown in Figure 5.14(d) and Figure 5.14(e).

Let us review the calculation procedure of $C_j − Z_j$ in Figure 5.13 and then proceed to identify the key column and key row to be used in preparation of the third solution. Calculation of the net increase of profit associated with one unit of each product is shown following:

Variable Columns

	X_1	X_2	S_1	S_2
C_j	$100	$80	$0	$0
Z_j	100	33.33	0	33.33
$C_j - Z_j$	$ 0	$46.67	$0	-$33.33

Obviously, the only product (variable) that can increase total profit is X_2. The unit profit of X_2 is $80 ($C_j$). However, the cost associated with the production of one X_2 (Z_j) is $33.33 because we have to sacrifice $\frac{1}{3}$ of X_1 ($\frac{1}{3} \times $100 = 33.33). Therefore, the net increase of profit from production of one X_2 will be $46.67.

Now, we can trace our solution step on a graph as shown in Figure 5.15. We started the simplex solution at the origin (point O). After determining that the product which increases total profit at the fastest rate is X_1, we jumped to point A. The two constraint lines shown in Figure 5.15 represent the maximum production capacities of the two assembly lines. Point A is exactly on the second constraint line but it is under the first constraint line. Therefore, at point A we use the full capacity of assembly line 2 but only part of the capacity of assembly line 1. This analysis should be clear from the values of $S_1 = 40$ and $S_2 = 0$ at point A.

Optimum Solution of the Problem

Now that we have learned all about the mechanics of the simplex method, we shall proceed to identify the optimum solution of the problem, as shown in Figure 5.16. The key column in the second simplex tableau is X_2 ($C_j - Z_j = 46.67) and the key row is S_1 (the row with the minimum nonnegative value when rhs is divided by the coefficient in key column). By employing the simplex procedure explained earlier we can derive the third solution. The solution indicates that the basic variables are $X_1 = 16$ and $X_2 = 12$ and total profit is $2560. Since no slack variables are in the solution base (v column), we are using the full capacity in both assembly lines. There are no positive values in the $C_j - Z_j$ row. This implies that there is no variable that can be introduced to the solution base and increase total profit. In fact, negative $C_j - Z_j$ values in the S_1 and S_2 columns suggest that if we introduce either one of these variables into the solution, total profit will decrease. Therefore, we have reached the optimum solution. One thing we should remember is that total profit (Z_j value in the rhs column) should be at least equal to or greater than the previous profit (Z_j value in rhs column in the preceding simplex tableau) in maximization problems. If total profit decreases, that certainly suggests that there is some error in the solution process.

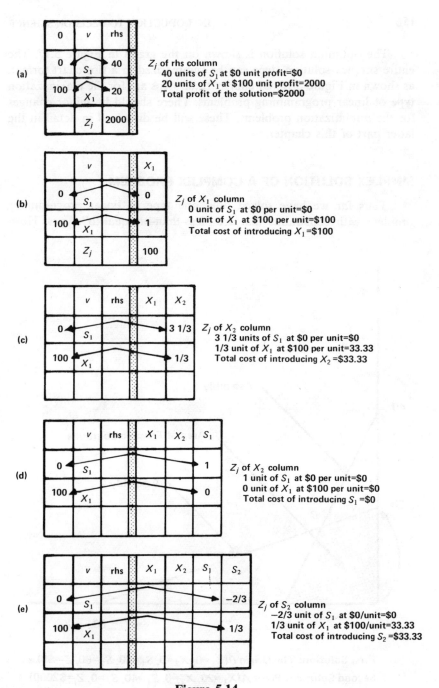

Figure 5.14
Calculating Z_j values

The optimum solution is shown on the graph in Figure 5.17. The entire simplex solution steps can be summarized in a flowchart format, as shown in Figure 5.18. Of course, these steps are for the maximization type of linear programming problems. There should be minor changes for the minimization problems. These will be discussed in detail in the latter part of this chapter.

SIMPLEX SOLUTION OF A COMPLEX PROBLEM

Thus far we have solved only one type of linear programming problem with constraints that are "less-than-or-equal-to" types. How-

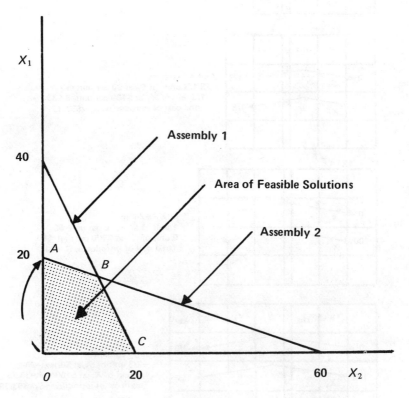

First Solution: The Origin $O(X_1=0, X_2=0, S_1=80, S_2=60, Z_j=\$0)$
Second Solution: Point $A(X_1=20, X_2=0, S_1=40, S_2=0, Z_j=\$2000)$

Figure 5.15
Graphical illustration of the first simplex iteration

(a) THE SECOND SIMPLEX TABLEAU (FIRST ITERATION)

C_j			100	80	0	0	
	v	rhs	X_1	X_2	S_1	S_2	Key Row, ↓
0	S_1	40		③ 1/3	1	– 2/3	40/(3 1/3)=12
100	X_1	20	1	1/3		1/3	20/(1/3)=60
	Z_j	2000	100	33.33	0	33.33	
	C_j-Z_j		0	46.67	0	–33.33	

Key Column

(b) THE THIRD SIMPLEX TABLEAU (SECOND ITERATION)— OPTIMUM SOLUTION

C_j			100	80	0	0
	v	rhs	X_1	X_2	S_1	S_2
80	X_2	12		1	3/10	–1/5
100	X_1	16	1		–1/10	2/5
	Z_j	2560	100	80	14	24
	C_j-Z_j		0	0	–14	–24

New Values (X_2 row)

```
40    ÷  3 1/3 =  12
0     ÷  3 1/3 =  0
3 1/3 ÷  3 1/3 =  1
1     ÷  3 1/3 = 3/10
-2/3  ÷  3 1/3 = – 1/5
```

New Values (X_1 row)

```
20   – (1/3 x  12)  =  16
1    – (1/3 x  0)   =  1
1/3  – (1/3 x  1)   =  0
0    – (1/3 x  3/10) = – 1/10
1/3  – (1/3 x –1/5) =  2/5
```

Figure 5.16

157

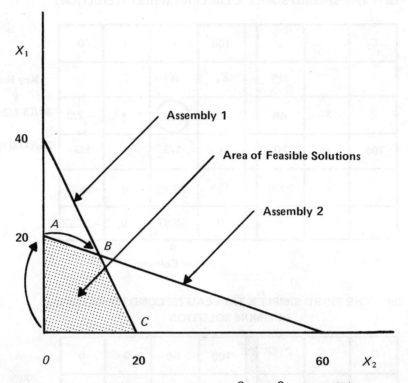

First Solution: The Origin 0 (X_1=0, X_2=0, S_1=80, S_2=60, Z_j=$0)
Second Solution: Point A (X_1=20, X_2=0, S_1=40, S_2=0, Z_j=$2000)
Third Solution (Optimum): Point B (X_1=16, X_2=12, S_1=0, S_2=0, Z_j=$2560)

Figure 5.17
Graphical illustration of the simplex solution

ever, many linear programming problems have different types of constraints. For example, in addition to the "less-than-or-equal-to" types, there are "greater-than-or-equal-to" type constraints. Also, it is quite possible that a constraint may have an "exactly-equal-to" relationship. Let us examine the following relatively simple example with all three types of constraints:

$$
\begin{array}{lrll}
\text{Maximize} & Z = \$20X_1 + \$10X_2 \\
\text{subject to} & X_1 + & X_2 = & 150 \\
& X_1 & \leq & 40 \\
& & X_2 \geq & 20 \\
& X_1, & X_2 \geq & 0
\end{array}
$$

The first constraint of the problem may be a production constraint. It implies that once we decide to produce X_1 and/or X_2 we have to

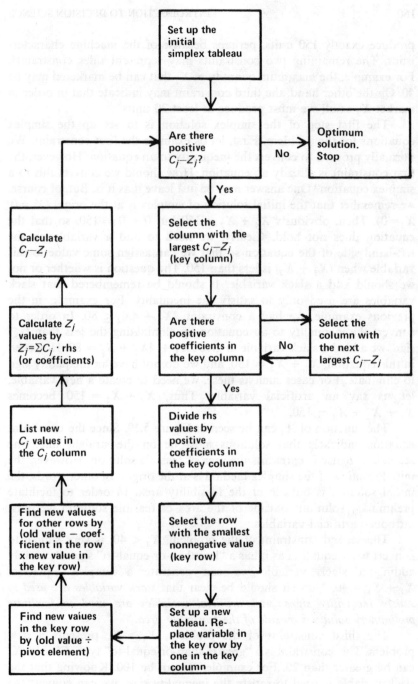

Figure 5.18
Flowchart of the simplex procedure

159

produce exactly 150 units, perhaps because of the machine characteristics. The remaining two constraints may represent sales constraints. For example, the maximum quantity of X_1 that can be marketed may be 40. On the other hand, the third constraint may indicate that in order to market X_2 at all we must produce at least 20 units.

The first step of the simplex solution is to set up the simplex equations for the problem. First, let us examine the first constraint. We normally proceed to convert the inequality to an equation. However, the first constraint is already an equation. How should we convert this to a simplex equation? One answer may be just leave it as it is. But, of course, we remember that the initial solution of simplex is at the origin ($X_1 = 0$, $X_2 = 0$). Then, obviously $X_1 + X_2 = 150$ but $0 + 0 \neq 150$, so that the equation does not hold. Clearly, we need to add a variable on the left-hand side of the equation so that we can assign some value to this variable when ($X_1 + X_2$) is less than 150. The question is whether or not we should add a slack variable. It should be remembered that slack variables are used only to satisfy the inequality. For example, in the previous example, we had a constraint $2X_1 + 4X_2 \leq 80$. In order to convert the inequality to an equation by eliminating the less than ($<$) sign, we added a slack variable to give $2X_1 + 4X_2 + S_1 = 80$. However, in this equation, $X_1 + X_2 = 150$, and we do not have an inequality sign to eliminate. For cases such as these, we need to create a new variable, let us say an artificial variable. Thus, $X_1 + X_2 = 150$ becomes $X_1 + X_2 + A_1 = 150$.

The function of A_1 can be seen in Figure 5.19. Since the constraint equation indicates that solutions must be on the straight line, line segment AB itself represents the area of feasible solution. However, the initial solution of the simplex method is at the origin. In other words, the initial solution is outside of the feasibility area. In order to facilitate preliminary solutions outside of the area of feasible solution we must introduce artificial variables.

The second constraint of the problem, $X_1 \leq 40$, is very simple to convert to an equation as it has a "less-than-or-equal-to" sign. By simply adding a slack variable we can generate a simplex equation, $X_1 + S_1 = 40$. Now, it should be clear that *slack variables are used to satisfy inequality signs* and *artificial variables are used to facilitate preliminary solutions outside of the feasibility area.*

The third constraint of the problem, $X_2 \geq 20$, presents a new problem. This constraint is a "greater-than-or-equal-to" type. Clearly, X_2 can be greater than 20. For example, X_2 can be 100. Knowing that the slack variable is used to satisfy the inequality sign, we can convert the constraint to an equation by subtracting a slack variable, as

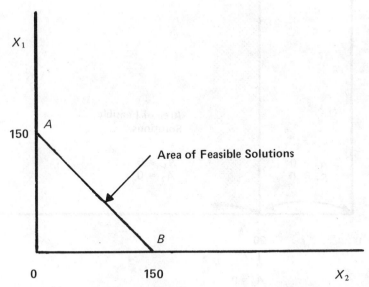

Figure 5.19
Graphical representation of an equation constraint

$X_2 - S_2 = 20$. If X_2 has a value of 100, the equation becomes $100 - S_2 = 20$ and $S_2 = 80$, so that the equation holds. However, there is one more problem. At the initial solution $X_2 = 0$, and therefore $0 - S_2 = 20$ or $S_2 = -20$. But the nonnegative constraint applies to all variables in the model, including the slack variables. Hence, the equation does not hold. Figure 5.20 depicts the problem. At the origin, the solution is evidently outside of the feasibility area. In order to facilitate preliminary solutions outside of the area of feasible solution we should introduce an artificial variable. Then, the equation becomes $X_2 - S_2 + A_2 = 20$. At the origin, the equation will be $0 - 0 + A_2 = 20$, or $A_2 = 20$. If $X_2 = 100$, $100 - S_2 + 0 = 20$, or $S_2 = 80$. The equation holds in either case. It is clear in Figure 5.20 that A_2 and S_2 are complementary to each other. In other words, if A_2 is positive, then S_2 becomes 0, and if S_2 is positive, A_2 becomes zero. Therefore, $S_2 \times A_2 = 0$. As long as X_2 is less than 20, A_2 takes a positive value and S_2 becomes zero. If X_2 is greater than 20, S_2 takes a positive value and A_2 becomes zero. If X_2 happens to be exactly 20, of course both S_2 and A_2 are zero.

If we express linear programming constraints in a general mathematical form, $\Sigma a_{ij} X_j = b_i$ (a_{ij} = technological coefficients, X_j = deci-

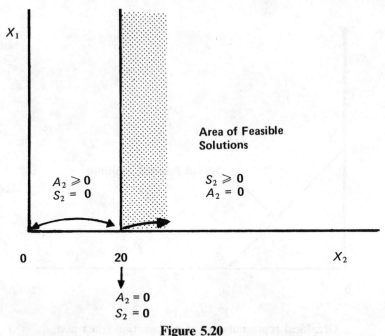

Figure 5.20
Graphical representation of a "greater-than-or-equal-to" type constraint

sion variables, b_i = rhs), then the standard convention of converting these to simplex equations is as follows:

Constraint Type	*Required Adjustment*	*Simplex Equation*
$\Sigma a_{ij} X_j \leq b_i$	Add a slack variable	$\Sigma a_{ij} X_j + S = b_i$
$\Sigma a_{ij} X_j = b_i$	Add an artificial variable	$\Sigma a_{ij} X_j + A = b_i$
$\Sigma a_{ij} X_j \geq b_i$	Subtract a slack variable and add an artificial variable	$\Sigma a_{ij} X_j - S + A = b_i$

Now, we should be able to convert any model constraints to simplex equations. The problem we presented above can be formulated as:

$$\text{Maximize} \quad Z = \$20X_1 + \$10X_2 + \$0S_1 + \$0S_2$$
$$\text{subject to} \quad X_1 + X_2 + A_1 = 150$$
$$X_1 + S_1 = 40$$
$$X_2 - S_2 + A_2 = 20$$

The solution of the above problem by the simplex procedure should be a simple task. However, we have one more problem to resolve before we attempt a simplex solution. The slack variable does not contribute to total profit, and therefore C_j of zero should be assigned to S_i. But, how about C_j for the artificial variable? If we assign zero C_j, it is quite possible that artificial variables may be in the solution base of the optimum solution. How can we interpret the optimum solution? What we do not want and need is having artificial variables in the final solution. We must devise a scheme that ensures an optimum solution without artificial variables in the solution base. One way we can accomplish this is by assigning a very large negative unit profit (C_j) to the artificial variable. This way the artificial variable is so costly that we may never end up with it in the final solution. This method is known as the "Big M" method because we assign a large negative unit profit, $-M$, (negative million dollars, let us say) to the artificial variable. The problem can now be solved as shown in Figure 5.21. It should be simple enough to follow the solution, so that the detailed explanation of the solution will be limited to only the first iteration.

In the initial solution, once again we are at the origin ($X_1 = 0$, $X_2 = 0$). Therefore, the three simplex equations will be:

Constraint 1: $X_1 + X_2 + A_1 = 150$
$$0 + 0 + A_1 = 150$$
$$A_1 = 150$$

Constraint 2: $X_1 + S_1 = 40$
$$0 + S_1 = 40$$
$$S_1 = 40$$

Constraint 3: $X_2 - S_2 + A_2 = 20$
$$0 - 0 + A_2 = 20$$
$$A_2 = 20$$

The basic variables (variables in the solution base) in the initial solution are A_1, S_1, and A_2. It *must* be remembered that whenever there is an artificial variable in a simplex equation, it appears in the solution base in the initial solution. The rhs values for A_1, S_1, and A_2 are 150, 40, and 20, respectively.

In the initial tableau, Z_j values are calculated in the usual manner, as described earlier. For example, in the rhs column, Z_j will be calculated by finding the sum of C_j of the basic variables (A_1, S_1, and A_2) multiplied by the rhs values. Hence, $Z_j(\text{rhs}) = (-M \times 150) + (0 \times 40) + (-M \times 20) = -170M$. Using the same procedure, Z_j of the X_1 column can be determined as $Z_j(X_1) = (-M \times 1) + (0 \times 1) + (-M \times 0) = -M$. The Z_j values of the remaining columns are calculated in the same manner. Now, again, $C_j - Z_j$ can be derived in the usual manner. For example, in the X_1 column C_j is 20 and Z_j is $-M$. Therefore, $C_j - Z_j = 20 - (-M) = 20 + M$. Then, $C_j - Z_j$ for the X_2 column will be $C_j - Z_j = 10 - (-2M) = 10 + 2M$.

(a) INITIAL SOLUTION

C_j			20	10	0	0	$-M$	$-M$	
	v	rhs	X_1	X_2	S_1	S_2	A_1	A_2	
$-M$	A_1	150	1	1			1		150/1 = 150
0	S_1	40	1		1				
$-M$	A_2	20		①		-1		1	20/1 = 20
	Z_j	$-170M$	$-M$	$-2M$	0	M	$-M$	$-M$	Key Row
	C_j-Z_j		20+M	10+2M	0	$-M$	0	0	

Key Column

(b) SECOND SOLUTION

C_j			20	10	0	0	$-M$	
	v	rhs	X_1	X_2	S_1	S_2	A_1	
$-M$	A_1	130	1			1	1	130/1 = 130
0	S_1	40	①		1			40/1 = 40
10	X_2	20		1		-1		Key Row
	Z_j	400– 130M	$-M$	10	0	$-10-M$	$-M$	
	C_j-Z_j		20+M	0	0	10+M	0	

Key Column

(c) THIRD SOLUTION

C_j			20	10	0	0	$-M$	
	v	rhs	X_1	X_2	S_1	S_2	A_1	
$-M$	A_1	90			-1	①	1	← Key Row
20	X_1	40	1		1			
10	X_2	20		1		-1		
	Z_j	1000– 90M	20	10	20+M	$-10-M$	$-M$	
	C_j-Z_j		0	0	$-20-M$	10+M	0	

Key Column

(d) FOURTH SOLUTION (OPTIMUM)

C_j			20	10	0	0
	v	rhs	X_1	X_2	S_1	S_2
0	S_2	90			-1	1
20	X_1	40	1		1	
10	X_2	110		1	-1	
	Z_j	1900	20	10	10	0
	C_j-Z_j		0	0	-10	0

Figure 5.21
Simplex solution of a problem with mixed constraints

164

Once we complete the initial tableau, we select the variable column with the largest positive $C_j - Z_j$. In this example, it is X_2, as shown in Figure 5.21(a). The incoming variable is X_2. In order to identify the outgoing variable, we divide the rhs values by the coefficients in the key column. The smallest nonnegative value is found in the A_2 row. Therefore, A_2 is the outgoing variable. In the second tableau, A_2 will be replaced by X_2 in the solution base. Now, it should be simple enough to follow the simplex procedure shown in the entire Figure 5.21.

There is one more thing that may need some explanation. When an artificial variable is replaced by either a decision or a slack variable in the solution base, that artificial variable column is no longer necessary in the simplex tableau. This is only logical if we remember that the artificial variable is used only to facilitate preliminary solutions outside of the feasible solution area. For example, in the second solution A_2 is replaced by X_2 in the solution base. The quantity of X_2 being produced in the second solution is 20. The third constraint of the problem, $X_2 \geq 20$, suggests that the quantity of X_2 we produce should be at least 20. We began the solution at the origin and therefore we needed to use A_2 in the simplex equation. Now, however, we no longer need A_2 since we are within the feasibility area of the third constraint, $X_2 \geq 20$. The reasoning can be clearly seen in Figure 5.22.

The simplex solution shown in Figure 5.21 indicates that total profit (Z_j in the rhs column) increases gradually after each iteration. The optimum solution is reached when we produce $X_1 = 40$, $X_2 = 110$, and $S_2 = 90$. It is difficult to interpret S_2 value of 90 when the third simplex equation indicated a negative sign for S_2, $X_2 - S_2 + A_1 = 20$. The slack variable we subtracted can be interpreted as a "surplus" variable rather than the standard "idle" slack variable. For example, the third constraint specifies that we must produce the minimum of 20 units of X_2. The optimum solution indicates 110 units of X_2. Therefore, the "surplus" production of X_2 would be 90 units. The simplex solution process of the problem can be seen clearly in Figure 5.23. When value of the artificial variable becomes zero, we no longer need to carry that artificial variable column in the simplex table, as seen in the second and the fourth solutions.

SIMPLEX SOLUTION OF THE MINIMIZATION PROBLEM

Thus far we have solved only maximization problems by the simplex procedure of linear programming. The same solution procedure can be

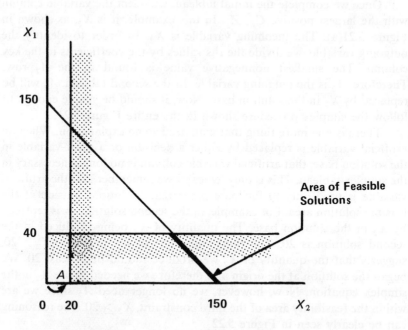

First Solution: The Origin O (X_1=0, X_2=0, S_1=40, S_2=0,
A_1=150, A_2=20, Z=\$0)
Second Solution: Point A (X_1=0, X_2=20, S_1=40, S_2=0,
A_1=130, A_2=0, Z=\$400−130M)

Figure 5.22
Graphical illustration of the first solution (problem with mixed constraints)

applied to minimization problems. Let us review the minimization linear programming problem discussed in Chapter 4. The problem can be illustrated in a schematic form as follows:

| | Foods | | Minimum |
	Egg	Potato	Requirements
Vitamin			
A	2 mg	4 mg	16 mg
B	3 mg	2 mg	12 mg
Unit Cost	4 cents	3 cents	

The above diet problem is concerned with the minimization of total cost per serving of breakfast while meeting the minimum Vitamin A and B requirements. The model we formulated in the preceding chapter was

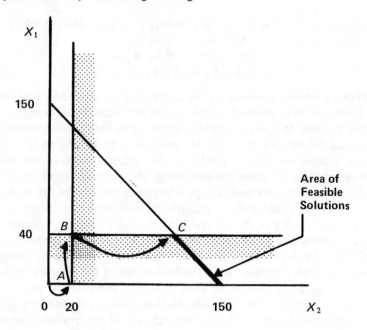

First Solution: The Origin
Second Solution: Point A
Third Solution: Point B ($X_1=40$, $X_2=20$, $S_1=0$, $S_2=0$,
$A_1=90$, $A_2=0$, $Z=\$1000-90M$)
Fourth Solution (Optimum): Point C ($X_1=40$, $X_2=110$,
$S_1=0$, $S_2=90$, $A_1=0$,
$A_2=0$, $Z=\$1900$)

Figure 5.23
Graphical illustration of the simplex solution (problem with mixed constraints)

Minimize $Z = 4X_1 + 3X_2$
subject to $2X_1 + 4X_2 \geq 16$
$3X_1 + 2X_2 \geq 12$
$X_1, \quad X_2 \geq 0$

where

X_1 = number of eggs
X_2 = number of scoops of potato
Z = total cost in cents

The first step of the simplex solution is, of course, to convert the model to a simplex model by introducing appropriate slack and/or artificial variables, as follows:

Minimize $\quad Z = 4X_1 + 3X_2 + 0S_1 + 0S_2 + MA_1 + MA_2$
subject to $\qquad 2X_1 + 4X_2 - S_1 + A_1 = 16$
$\qquad\qquad\quad 3X_1 + 2X_2 - S_2 + A_2 = 12$
$\qquad\qquad\quad X_1, X_2, S_1, S_2, A_1, A_2 \geq 0$

The above problem is solved by using the simplex procedure in Figure 5.24. There are three points that deserve our attention. First, note that we assigned positive M's to the artificial variables in the objective function. The reason we employ the "big M" method is to ensure an optimum solution without artificial variables in the solution base. In the minimization problem of linear programming, the objective is to minimize total cost. Therefore, we must assign a large positive cost to the artificial variable. Secondly, the simplex criterion we use in the minimization is $Z_j - C_j$ rather than $C_j - Z_j$. By reversing the calculations procedure we can still identify the key column by finding a column with the largest $Z_j - C_j$. Thirdly, it should be noted that total cost (Z_j in the rhs column) decreases at each iteration. With the knowledge of the simplex method we have acquired it should be easy to follow the solution procedure shown in Figure 5.24. The optimum solution indicates that the breakfast should consist of 2 eggs and 3 potatoes with a total cost per serving of 17 cents. This answer corresponds to the graphical solution we derived in Chapter 4.

SOME COMPLICATIONS AND THEIR RESOLUTION

Thus far, the discussion of the simplex method has focused on the standard format of linear programming problems. In real-world problems, however, often we have to make various adjustments in order to solve them by linear programming. Some of these complications and their resolution will be discussed in this section.

Nonpositive Right-hand Side

To explain the nonpositive rhs (resources) problem, let us consider the following constraint:

$$-5X_1 + X_2 \leq -25$$

If the above is one of the constraints of the problem, it cannot be solved by the simplex method. In the initial solution of the simplex method it is assumed that the solution is at the origin. Consequently, even when we add a slack variable, the constraint would appear as: $-5X_1 + X_2 + S_1 \leq -25$, $-5(0) + 0 + S_1 = -25$, or $S_1 = -25$. The

(a) FIRST SOLUTION

C_j			4	3	0	0	M	M	Key Row
	v	rhs	X_1	X_2	S_1	S_2	A_1	A_2	
M	A_1	16	2	④	−1		1		↓ 16/4 = 4
M	A_2	12	3	2		−1		1	12/2 = 6
	Z_j	28M	5M	6M	−M	−M	M	M	
	Z_j C_j		5M−4	6M−3	−M	−M	0	0	

Key Column

(b) SECOND SOLUTION

C_j			4	3	0	0	M	
	v	rhs	X_1	X_2	S_1	S_2	A_2	
3	X_2	4	1/2	1	−1/4			4/(1/2) = 8
M	A_2	4	②		1/2	−1	1	4/2 = 2
	Z_j	4M+12	2M+3/2	3	1/2M−3/4	−M	M	↑ Key Row
	Z_j−C_j		2M−5/2	0	1/2M−3/4	−M	0	

Key Column

(c) THIRD SOLUTION (OPTIMUM)

C_j			4	3	0	0
	v	rhs	X_1	X_2	S_1	S_2
3	X_2	3		1	−3/8	1/4
4	X_1	2	1		1/4	−1/2
	Z_j	17	4	3	−1/8	−5/4
	Z_j−C_j		0	0	−1/8	−5/4

Figure 5.24
Simplex solution of a minimization problem

rhs value of S_1 will appear as -25. Clearly this violates the nonnegative constraint, X, S, $A \geq 0$. One way we can resolve this problem is readjusting the constraint by multiplying both sides by -1. The constraint then becomes

$$-5X_1 + X_2 \leq -25$$
$$(-1)(-5X_1 + X_2) \geq (-1)(-25)$$
$$5X_1 - X_2 \geq 25$$

Now we can introduce appropriate slack and/or artificial variables to the constraint to convert it to a simplex equation, as follows:

$$5X_1 - X_2 - S_1 + A_1 = 25$$

Tie for the Key Column

In any linear programming problem it can easily happen during the iteration that two or more columns have exactly identical largest $C_j - Z_j$ (or $Z_j - C_j$) values. When this case occurs, the selection of the key column may be made arbitrarily. However, in order to minimize the number of iterations required to reach the optimum solution, the following basic rules may help the resolution:

1. If there is a tie between two decision variables, choice can be made arbitrarily.
2. If there is a tie between a decision variable and a slack (or surplus) variable, select the decision variable as the entering variable.
3. If there is a tie between two slack (or surplus) variables, selection can be made arbitrarily.

Regardless of the variable column chosen as the key column, the optimum solution will be found eventually, if there is one.

Tie for the Key Row (Degeneracy)

In order to determine the key row, we divide the rhs values by the coefficient in the key column and then determine the minimum positive quotient. If there are two or more rows with identical minimum positive values, this raises the problem of degeneracy. Suppose we have the following programming problem.

Maximize $Z = \$4X_1 + \$6X_2 + \$0S_1 + \$0S_3$
subject to
$$6X_1 + 4X_2 + S_1 = 40$$
$$X_1 \qquad + S_2 = 16$$
$$\tfrac{1}{2}X_1 + X_2 + S_3 = 10$$

Since the X_2 column has the largest $C_j - Z_j$, as shown in Figure 5.25, the key row will be determined between the first and the third rows based on their quotient of rhs/coefficient. Clearly we have a tie in this case, as $40/4 = 10$ and $10/1 = 10$. If we choose the S_3 row as the key row, the solution will be as Figure 5.25. The solution procedure we used is based on the method of resolving degeneracy suggested by A. Charnes and W. W. Cooper (see the reference at the end of this chapter). The method involves the following three steps:

1. Select the rows where ties are found when rhs values are divided by coefficients in the key column.
2. Find the coefficients of the slack variables and divide each coefficient by the coefficients in the key column, starting from S_1 to S_n columns in order to break the tie. If the ratios do not break the tie, find similar ratios for the coefficients of the decision variables.
3. Select the row with the smallest ratio when the S_1 coefficients are divided by the coefficients in the key column. This row becomes the key row.

Now, let us examine our solution in Figure 5.25. From the analysis of $C_j - Z_j$ in the first solution it is apparent that X_2 is the key column. When the rhs values are divided by the coefficients in the key column, identical values are found for the S_1 and S_3 rows and thus a case of degeneracy has occurred. In order to break this tie we divide the coefficients of the slack variables by the coefficients of the key column, as follows:

		Column		
		S_1	S_2	S_3
Row	S_1	1/4	0/4	0/4
	S_3	0/1	0/1	1/1

The tie is broken at the first division. When we divide the coefficient of the S_1 column and S_1 row by the coefficient of the key column in the S_1 row, we derive 1/4. When the same procedure is followed for the S_3 row, the value we get is $0/1 = 0$. Since we select the row with the smallest

C_j			4	6	0	0	0	
	v	rhs	X_1	X_2	S_1	S_2	S_3	
0	S_1	40	6	4	1			40/4 = 10
0	S_2	16	1			1		
0	S_3	10	1/2	①			1	10/1 = 10 Key Row
	Z_j	0	0	0	0	0	0	
	C_j-Z_j		4	6	0	0	0	

Key Column

(b) SECOND SOLUTION

C_j			4	6	0	0	0	
	v	rhs	X_1	X_2	S_1	S_2	S_3	Key Row
0	S_1	0	④		1		-4	0/4 = 0
0	S_2	16	1			1		16/1 = 16
6	X_2	10	1/2	1			1	10/(1/2) = 20
	Z_j	60	3	6	0	0	6	
	C_j-Z_j		1	0	0	0	-6	

Key Column

(c) THIRD SOLUTION (OPTIMUM)

C_j			4	6	0	0	0
	v	rhs	X_1	X_2	S_1	S_2	S_3
4	X_1	0	1		1/4		-1
0	S_2	16			-1/4	1	1
6	X_2	10		1	-1/8		3/2
	Z_j	60	4	6	1/4	0	5
	C_j-Z_j		0	0	-1/4	0	-5

Figure 5.25
Simplex solution of a degenerate problem

ratio, S_3 is selected as the key row. By following the regular simplex procedure, the optimum solution is found in the third solution. It should be noted that total profit is identical in the second and the third solutions.

The procedure we employed to break a tie in determining the key row is a convenient way to resolve the problem of degeneracy. However, fortunately, in most real-world problems only rarely do we face the problem with degeneracy.

Multiple Optimum Solutions

Sometimes a linear programming problem has multiple optimum solutions, as explained in the graphical method section of linear

(a) FIRST SOLUTION

C_j			4	2	0	0	
	v	rhs	X_1	X_2	S_1	S_2	
0	S_1	20	②	1	1		← Key Row
0	S_2	24	2	3		1	
	Z_j	0	0	0	0	0	
	$C_j - Z_j$		4	2	0	0	

Key Column

(b) SECOND SOLUTION (OPTIMUM)

C_j			4	2	0	0
	v	rhs	X_1	X_2	S_1	S_2
4	X_1	10	1	1/2	1/2	
0	S_2	4		2	−1	1
	Z_j	40	4	2	2	0
	$C_j - Z_j$		0	0	−2	0

Figure 5.26
A problem with multiple optimum solutions

programming in Chapter 4. For example, let us examine the following problem:

$$\text{Maximize} \quad Z = \$4X_1 + \$2X_2$$
$$\text{subject to} \quad 2X_1 + X_2 \leq 20$$
$$2X_1 + 3X_2 \leq 24$$
$$X_1, \quad X_2 \geq 0$$

The above problem is solved by the simplex method in Figure 5.26. After only one solution the simplex algorithm stops because total profit cannot be improved any further. How do we find out whether there are multiple optimum solutions to the problem? The way we can check is to examine the $C_j - Z_j$ values of nonbasic variables (variables not in the solution base) in the final solution. Recall that $C_j - Z_j$ values indicate the rates at which total profit increases as the nonbasic variables are entered into the solution. Therefore, bringing S_1 into the solution will certainly decrease total profit as its $C_j - Z_j$ value is -2. However, entering X_2 will neither increase nor decrease total profit. Therefore, if we enter X_2 into the solution base, this solution must also be optimal.

No Feasible Solution

It is quite possible, although very rare, that a certain linear programming problem has no feasible solution at all! If a problem has incompatible constraints, there will be no feasible solution area. In other words, in a simple problem with two decision variables, constraints may not overlap to form a feasibility area. For example, let us examine the following problem:

$$\text{Maximize} \quad Z = \$10X_1 + \$15X_2$$
$$\text{subject to} \quad 2X_1 + 3X_2 \leq 18$$
$$2X_1 + X_2 \geq 20$$
$$X_1, \quad X_2 \geq 0$$

If we use the graphical method, we can ascertain immediately that this problem has no feasible solution, as shown in Figure 5.27. However, if we use the simplex procedure it is not immediately obvious that this is an infeasible problem. For example, let us revise the problem as follows by introducing appropriate slack and artificial variables:

$$\text{Maximize} \quad Z = \$10X_1 + \$15X_2 + 0S_1 + 0S_2 - MA_1$$
$$\text{subject to} \quad 2X_1 + 3X_2 + S_1 = 18$$
$$2X_1 + X_2 - S_2 + A_1 = 20$$

The simplex solution of the problem is presented in Figure 5.28. Since we have introduced slack and artificial variables, there will be an initial

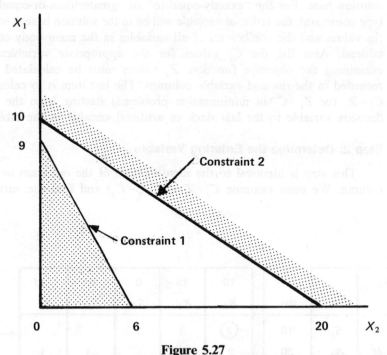

Figure 5.27
Graphical illustration of a problem with no feasible solution

solution at the origin. However, the optimum solution in Figure 5.28(b) still contains the artificial variable in the solution base. What does this mean? This means that the problem has no feasible solutions. In other words, if the optimum solution contains at least one of the artificial variables as a positive basic variable, the problem has no feasible solutions.

STEPS OF THE SIMPLEX METHOD

Now that we have illustrated how to solve a linear programming problem by the simplex method, we can summarize the solution steps to aid in future solutions.

Step 1: Set up the Initial Tableau

We assume that the initial solution is at the origin. Therefore, slack and/or artificial variables should enter the solution base initially. For the "less-than-or-equal-to" type constraint, the slack variable will be in the solution base. For the "exactly-equal-to" or "greater-than-or-equal-to" type constraint, the artificial variable will be in the solution base. List the rhs values and the coefficients of all variables in the main body of the tableau. Also list the C_j values for the appropriate variables by examining the objective function. Z_j values must be calculated and recorded in the rhs and variable columns. The last item is to calculate $C_j - Z_j$ (or $Z_j - C_j$ in minimization problems) starting from the first decision variable to the last slack or artificial variable in the tableau.

Step 2: Determine the Entering Variable

This step is identical to the identification of the optimum or key column. We must examine $C_j - Z_j$ (or $Z_j - C_j$) and find the variable

(a)

C_j				10	15	0	0	$-M$	
	v	rhs		X_1	X_2	S_1	S_2	A_1	
0	S_1	18		②	3	1			←Key Row
$-M$	A_1	20		2	1		-1	1	
	Z_j	$-20M$		$-2M$	$-M$	0	M	$-M$	
	$C_j - Z_j$			$10+2M$	$15+M$	0	$-M$	0	

Key Column

(b)

C_j				10	15	0	0	$-M$
	v	rhs		X_1	X_2	S_1	S_2	A_1
10	X_1	9		1	3/2	1/2		
$-M$	A_1	2			-2	-1	-1	1
	Z_j	$90-2M$		10	$15+2M$	$5+M$	M	$-M$
	$C_j - Z_j$			0	$-2M$	$-5-M$	$-M$	0

Figure 5.28
Simplex analysis of an infeasible problem

column with the largest positive value. The variable in that column will enter the solution base in the next tableau. If there is a tie between the largest positive values in $C_j - Z_j$, use the following guidelines:

1. If the tie is between two decision variables, choice can be made arbitrarily.
2. If the tie is between a decision variable and a slack or an artificial variable, select the decision variable as the entering variable.
3. If there is a tie between two slack (or artificial) variables, selection can be made arbitrarily.

Regardless of the variable chosen as the entering variable, the optimum will be found eventually, if there is one.

Step 3: Determine the Outgoing Variable

This process is identical to finding the key row. Calculate the value of the rhs constants divided by the coefficients in the key column. Select the row that has the minimum nonnegative value. However, exclude rows that have either zero or negative coefficients. (For example, if the rhs value is zero and the coefficient is also zero, this row cannot be qualified as the key row.) The variable in the key row is the outgoing variable.

Step 4: Determine the New Solution

First, find the new rhs value and coefficients in the key row by: new value (key row) = old value/pivot element, where the pivot element is the coefficient at the intersection of the key column and the key row. Second, find the new rhs values and coefficients for all other rows by subtracting from each old value the product of the corresponding new value in the key row multiplied by the coefficient at the intersection of the key column and the given row.

Step 5: Determine Whether the Solution Is Optimal

First, check $C_j - Z_j$ values ($Z_j - C_j$ in minimization problems). If there still exist positive $C_j - Z_j$ values, go to step 2 and continue on the simplex iteration. If there is no positive $C_j - Z_j$ value, check basic variables and their values. If the artificial variable remains a positive basic variable, the problem has no feasible solutions. If there are only decision and slack variables in the solution base, the optimal solution has been found.

DUALITY THEORY OF LINEAR PROGRAMMING

One of the important extensions of linear programming is the development of the concept of duality. The term *duality* implies that every linear programming problem can be analyzed by two different ways. For example, a profit maximization problem can be viewed as a problem of cost minimization. Or a cost minimization can be viewed as a problem of maximizing the efficiency of using resources.

Linear programming problems we have discussed thus far are concerned with only one aspect of the optimization, namely finding the optimum solution with the given relationships among the variables in the model. This approach is called the *primal* solution. Each primal linear programming problem has a corresponding *dual* problem. For example, a maximization problem has a corresponding dual problem of minimization, and a primal minimization problem has a corresponding dual maximization problem. Therefore, the dual of a dual problem is the primal of the given problem. One may ask "why should we worry about another way to solve the same problem?" The answer is that the dual solution provides significant information concerning economic ramifications of the problem. Before we try to interpret the dual solution of a problem, let us discuss the familiar television manufacture problem:

$$\text{Maximize} \quad Z = 100X_1 + 80X_2$$
$$\text{subject to} \quad 2X_1 + 4X_2 \leq 80$$
$$3X_1 + X_2 \leq 60$$
$$X_1, \quad X_2 \geq 0$$

The above is a primal problem where we attempt to maximize total profit within the bounds of two constraints. The dual approach of the problem is to minimize the cost of producing color (X_1) and black-and-white (X_2) television sets with 80 hours of available production capacity in assembly line 1 and 60 hours of capacity in assembly line 2. Then, the decision variables we attempt to determine will be the hourly costs of operating assembly line 1 and assembly line 2. These decision variables can be defined as U_1 and U_2. Then, the objective function will be to minimize total cost of production, or

$$\text{Minimize} \quad Z = 80U_1 + 60U_2$$

Now, let us consider the constraints for the dual. From the primal problem it has been shown that production of one color set (X_1) requires 2 hours in assembly line 1 and 3 hours in assembly line 2. Since U_1 and U_2 represent the costs of operating 1 hour in assembly lines 1 and 2 respectively, the costs required to produce one unit of X_1 will be

$2U_1 + 3U_2$. The requirement necessary to commit $2U_1 + 3U_2$ resources is that they produce at least \$100 profit. If the resources invested in producing a unit of X_1 ($2U_1 + 3U_2$) do not return at least \$100 profit, then management should use resources for some other purposes. Then the first constraint of the dual model can be expressed as: $2U_1 + 3U_2 \geq 100$.

The second constraint can be formulated in the same manner. Production of one black-and-white set (X_2) requires 4 hours in assembly line 1 and 1 hour in assembly line 2. Therefore, the costs required for producing 1 unit of X_2 will be $4U_1 + U_2$. Hence, the constraint becomes $4U_1 + U_2 \geq 80$. Now the complete dual model can be formulated as follows:

$$
\begin{aligned}
\text{Minimize} \quad & Z = 80U_1 + 60U_2 \\
\text{subject to} \quad & 2U_1 + 3U_2 \geq 100 \\
& 4U_1 + U_2 \geq 80 \\
& U_1, \quad U_2 \geq 0
\end{aligned}
$$

In order to solve the above problem by the simplex procedure, the two constraints can be converted to equations as below:

$$
\begin{aligned}
2U_1 + 3U_2 - S_1 + A_1 &= 100 \\
4U_1 + U_2 - S_2 + A_2 &= 80
\end{aligned}
$$

The dual problem is solved in Figure 5.29. The optimum solution of the dual problem indicates that the total cost of maintaining available production capacity hours in the two assembly lines is \$2560. The total cost derived in the dual problem must be always identical with the total profit of the primal (Figure 5.16). The values of the decision variables $U_1 = 14$ and $U_2 = 24$ indicate that an hour of operation time in assembly line 1 is worth \$14 to the firm and an hour is worth \$24 in assembly line 2. This result implies that if the firm is able to increase production capacity at less than \$14 per hour in assembly line 1, it should increase the production time because it will result in an increase of total profit. The same reasoning applies to assembly line 2. If the firm can increase productive time in assembly line 2 at less than \$24 per hour, it should increase the production capacity.

When we compare the simplex solutions of the primal and dual problems, several interesting observations can be made. Referring to Figures 5.16 and 5.29, it can be noted that the values of U_1 (14) and U_2 (24) in the optimization dual solution are exactly identical to the $C_j - Z_j$ values of the two slack variables without the negative sign in the optimum primal solution. The $C_j - Z_j$ values of the slack variables in the final primal solution indicate the reduction of total profit associated with

(a) FIRST SOLUTION

C_j			80	60	0	0	M	M
	v	rhs	U_1	U_2	S_1	S_2	A_1	A_2
M	A_1	100	2	3	-1		1	
M	A_2	80	④	1		-1		1
	Z_j	$180M$	$6M$	$4M$	$-M$	$-M$	M	M
	Z_j-C_j		$6M-80$	$4M-60$	$-M$	$-M$	0	0

← Key Row

↑ Key Column

(b) SECOND SOLUTION

C_j			80	60	0	0	M
	v	rhs	U_1	U_2	S_1	S_2	A_1
M	A_1	60		⑤⁄₂	-1	1/2	1
80	U_1	20	1	1/4		$-1/4$	
	Z_j	$60M+$	80	$5/2M+20$	$-M$	$1/2M-20$	M
	Z_j-C_j	1600	0	$5/2M-40$	$-M$	$1/2M-20$	0

← Key Row

↑ Key Column

(c) THIRD SOLUTION

C_j			80	60	0	0
	v	rhs	U_1	U_2	S_1	S_2
60	U_2	24		1	$-2/5$	1/5
80	U_1	14	1		1/10	$-3/10$
	Z_j	2560	80	60	-16	-12
	Z_j-C_j		0	0	-16	-12

Figure 5.29
Simplex solution of a dual model

one hour of idle capacity in the two assembly lines. Clearly, these figures should be identical to the hourly costs of operating the two assembly lines. It can also be noted that for this problem the values of the decision variables in the final primal solution ($X_1 = 16$ and $X_2 = 12$) are identical to the $Z_j - C_j$ values of the slack variables without the negative sign in the final dual solution. Then, the primal-dual relationships for those problems that are feasible can be summarized as follows:

Primal	*Dual*
Z_j(rhs)	Z_j(rhs)
Value of basic variables	$-(Z_j - C_j)$ in nonbasic columns
$-(C_j - Z_j)$ in nonbasic columns	Value of basic variables

In addition to the economic analysis of the problem, the dual is often formulated for computational purposes. Let us consider a problem with 10 decision variables and 25 constraints. The number of constraints usually determines the number of iterations required to solve the problem. The primal solution, therefore, can take the maximum of 25 iterations. However, if we formulate a dual model for the problem it will involve 25 decision variables and 10 constraints. Thus, the amount of computation time required to solve it, either by hand or by the computer, can be reduced significantly.

Linear programming is a field of study in itself. Indeed, many scholars specialize in this specific tool of management science. An extensive discussion of linear programming requires several books. In this chapter, we have discussed most of the essential parts of linear programming. Those who desire to study more advanced topics of linear programming should consult the references at the end of this chapter. Sensitivity analysis on the basis of the simplex method is an advanced topic of linear programming. We will discuss this topic in Appendix II in conjunction with the computer-based solution of linear programming.

COMPUTER-BASED ANALYSIS OF LINEAR PROGRAMMING

The popularity and wide applications of linear programming are primarily due to the standardized solution procedure on the basis of electronic computers. These standardized solution programs are often referred to as linear programming codes or canned linear programming packages. Almost every major computer manufacturer has developed a linear programming package for its computer system. This certainly indicates that linear programming is a very popular technique. For example, there are linear programming computer codes available from IBM, UNIVAC, RCA, NCR, Control Data, Honeywell, and others.

Appendix II presents a computer-based solution procedure of linear programming. It provides a detailed instruction for input data arrangement, discussion of the solution procedure, and an analysis of the output. The use of the program may provide the student with the first-hand experience in the use of computers for decision analysis.

REFERENCES

Ackoff, R. L., and Sasieni, M. W., *Fundamentals of Operations Research*, Wiley, New York, 1968.

Charnes, A., and Cooper, W. W., *Management Models and Industrial Applications of Linear Programming*, Wiley, New York, 1961.

Churchman, C. W., Ackoff, R. L., and Arnoff, E. L., *Introduction to Operations Research*, Wiley, New York, 1958.

Hillier, F. S., and Lieberman, G. J., *Introduction to Operations Research*, 2d. ed., Holden-Day, San Francisco, 1974.

Kim, C., *Introduction to Linear Programming*, Holt, New York, 1971.

Kwak, N. K., *Mathematical Programming with Business Applications*, McGraw-Hill, New York, 1973.

Levin, R. I., and Lamone, R., *Linear Programming for Management Decisions*, Irwin, Homewood, Ill., 1969.

Llewellyn, R. W., *Linear Programming*, Holt, New York, 1964.

PROBLEMS

1. Solve the following linear programming problem by using the simplex method:

$$\text{Maximize} \quad Z = \$20x_1 + \$15x_2$$
$$\text{subject to} \quad x_1 + x_2 \leq 120$$
$$x_1 \leq 60$$
$$x_2 \geq 40$$

2. Solve the following linear programming problem by using the simplex method:

$$\begin{aligned}
\text{Minimize} \quad & Z = \$2x_1 + \$3x_2 \\
\text{subject to} \quad & 2x_1 + 5x_2 \geq 30 \\
& 4x_1 + 2x_2 \geq 28
\end{aligned}$$

3. Consider the following linear programming problem:

$$\begin{aligned}
\text{Maximize} \quad & Z = \$70x_1 + \$80x_2 \\
\text{subject to} \quad & -2x_1 + x_2 \geq -20 \\
& x_1 + x_2 \leq 14 \\
& x_1 + 2x_2 \leq 20
\end{aligned}$$

(a) Solve the above problem by the simplex method.
(b) Formulate a dual model and also solve it by the simplex method.

4. The Uptown Haberdashery is having its annual sale (Spring Clearance) of unsold winter garments. Due to a very mild winter, Mr. Brown, the store manager, has the following inventory for sale: 5000 men's overcoats, 7500 women's wool sweaters, and 2250 children's wool sweaters. Mr. Brown is in the process of designing an advertising campaign for the sale. The types of advertising he plans to use and how many customers each type will reach are: newspaper —1000 customers per ad; radio—750 customers per ad; and mail —1500 customers per ad. The cost of each type of advertising is: newspaper—$120 per ad; radio—$90 per spot; and mail—$200 per ad. The Hutter Advertising Agency has done an advertising survey and found the percentage of the market—men, women, and children —reached by each type of advertising to be:

	Newspaper	Radio	Mail
Men	45%	20%	50%
Women	40	55	40
Children	15	25	10

Mr. Brown has decided that in order to sell his inventory he must reach at least 6000 men customers, 8500 women customers, and 3500 children customers.

(a) Formulate a linear programming model to determine how much of each type of advertising Mr. Brown should use in order to minimize advertising expense and still sell his inventory.
(b) Solve the problem through one iteration (two simplex tableaus including the initial tableau) using the simplex method.
(c) Solve the problem by using the computer.

5. The Gateway Air Conditioning Company manufactures two air conditioners—the Arctic and the Sub-Zero—at two different factory

locations. Factory 2 is a new plant that has not been completely finished due to material shortages. However, it can produce for a maximum of 25 hours per week. Factory 1 is the older plant but it has full production capabilities and can produce for a maximum of 40 hours per week. The production time in hours for each unit at each factory has been determined by the production manager to be:

	Factory 1	Factory 2
Arctic	3.5	3.0
Sub-Zero	2.0	2.5

The accounting department has determined that the standard costs for each unit at each factory are:

	Factory 1	Factory 2
Arctic	$250	$260
Sub-Zero	$200	$180

In order to provide the necessary profit margin and be competitive, the selling price of the Arctic has been set at $350 while the Sub-Zero is priced at $275. Gateway has been experiencing cost overruns lately and the production manager has set a weekly budget ceiling on production costs. The weekly budget for the Arctic is $2000 while the budget for the Sub-Zero is $2200.

(a) Formulate a linear programming model to determine how many of each unit should be produced at each factory in order to maximize profits.

(b) Solve the above problem using the simplex method.

6. Mr. Manning, Manager of Sales, has two salesmen working for him. The ability of each salesman to secure new accounts had historically been as follows: salesman 1—4 new accounts per 10 visits to prospects; and salesman 2—3 new accounts per 10 visits to prospects. As of May 1, Salesman 1 has 20 established customers that he must call on each month if he is to retain their monthly orders. Salesman 2 has 15 established accounts that he must try to maintain. The average time in hours each salesman spends with each type of customer per visit is:

	New Account	Established Account
Salesman 1	10	5
Salesman 2	8	6

Each new order yields the company an average profit of $150, whereas orders from established accounts are usually smaller and yield an average profit of $50 an order. Salesman 1 has a larger area to cover and as a result has only 120 hours of time (net of traveling time) to spend with his customers each month. Salesman 2 has 135 hours available to spend with his customers, since his traveling time is less.

(a) Formulate a linear programming model to determine how many new and old customers each salesman should call on in May in order to maximize profits.

(b) Solve the above problem using the simplex method.

7. The Fairway Corporation produces and distributes a line of golf equipment and accessories. One of its most profitable items is a one-man golf cart, which it produces on three assembly lines. The output of carts on each line and the time available on each line are:

	Output	Time Available
Assembly line 1	15 units/hr	25 hours per week
Assembly line 2	10 units/hr	40 hours per week
Assembly line 3	12 units/hr	30 hours per week

The primary raw materials used in producing the golf carts are steel and copper wire. The amount of raw material needed to produce a golf cart on each assembly line is:

	Steel (lb)	Copper Wire (ft)
Assembly line 1	50	15
Assembly line 2	35	25
Assembly line 3	40	20

At the present time the company has a contract for 40,000 pounds of steel and 20,000 feet of copper wire each week. After all expenses, the company receives a profit margin of $20 on each golf cart.

(a) Formulate a linear programming model to determine how many hours each assembly line should be run in order to maximize profits.

(b) Solve the above problem through two iterations using the simplex method.

8. The McCoy brothers live in the hills of West Virginia and produce three potent alcoholic mixes. The annual square dance is scheduled in one month and the McCoys always sell large quantities of their three mixes. The quantity of each ingredient for each mix and the name of each mix are:

	Potatoes	Peaches	Raisins
Old Buzzard	60	30	10
Mule Kick	50	25	25
Lady's Friend	30	40	30

Ralph McCoy has estimated that the brothers will be able to sell 500 Mason jars of Old Buzzard, 750 jars of Mule Kick, and 1000 jars of Lady's Friend. Based on his estimate, Jud McCoy has bought 65,000 pounds of potatoes, 30,000 pounds of peaches, and 25,000 pounds of raisins. "Old Man" McCoy has determined that the profit on each mix will be: $1.50/jar for Old Buzzard, $1.25/jar for Mule Kick, and $0.75/jar for Lady's Friend.

(a) Formulate a linear programming model to determine how many jars of each mix to produce in order for the McCoys to maximize profits.

(b) Solve the above problem using the simplex method.

9. Mr. Jarvis, the marketing manager of the Ready Typewriter Co., is trying to decide how to allocate his salesmen to the company's three primary markets. Market 1 is an urban area and the salesmen can sell, on the average, 40 typewriters a week. Salesmen in the other two markets can sell, on the average, 36 and 25 typewriters per week, respectively. For the coming week, three of the salesmen will be on vacation, leaving only 12 men available for duty. Also, because of the lack of company cars, a maximum of 5 salesmen can be allocated to market area 1. The selling expenses per week for salesmen in each area are: $80/week for area 1, $70/week for area 2, and $50/week for area 3. The budget for the next week is $750. The profit margin per typewriter is $15.

(a) Formulate a linear programming model to determine how many salesmen should be assigned to each area in order to maximize profits.

(b) Solve the above problem through two iterations using the simplex method.

10. The annual Handmade Furniture Show and Sale occurs next month and the Giles Vocational School is planning to make furniture for the sale. There are three woodworking classes—beginning, intermediate, and advanced—at the school and they have decided to make three styles of chairs—rocker, straight back, and captain. Each chair must receive work in each class and the time in hours required for each chair in each class is:

	Beginning	Intermediate	Advanced
Rocker	2	4	3
Straight Back	3	3	2
Captain	2	1	4

During the next month there will be 120 hours available in the beginning class, 160 in the intermediate class, and 100 hours in the advanced class to produce the chairs. The teacher of the woodworking classes feels that a maximum of 40 chairs can be sold at the show. The teacher has determined that the profit from each type of chair will be: rocker, $40; straight back, $35; and captain, $30.

(a) Formulate a linear programming model to determine how many chairs of each type should be made in order to maximize profits at the show and sale.

(b) Solve the above problem using the simplex method.

11. The new cars for the upcoming year are about to be introduced and Mr. Weimer, the sales manager of Roadside Motors, has a very large stock of last year's cars. Almost all of the current stock are large, luxury cars that are not selling because of the gas shortage. In order to move these cars Mr. Weimer is planning a large advertising campaign and sale. He plans to use the following types of advertising: (1) radio spots, which cost $40 per spot and reach an estimated 200 potential customers per ad; (2) newspaper ads, which cost $50 per ad and reach an estimated 300 potential customers per ad; and (3) mail ads, which cost $45 per ad and reach an estimated 325 potential customers per ad. Mr. Weimer has estimated that he must reach at least 5000 potential customers in order to reduce his inventory. At the present time the company has a contract for 10 radio spots, 5 newspaper ads, and 5 mail ads each month.

(a) Formulate a linear programming model to determine how many ads of each type Mr. Weimer should purchase in order to minimize costs.

(b) Solve the above problem using the simplex method.

12. The Downing Plastics Company has just received a government contract to produce three different plastic valves that will be used in the Apollo spacecraft. These valves must be highly heat- and pressure-resistant and the company has developed a three-stage production process that will provide the valves with the necessary properties, involving work in three different chambers. Chamber 1 provides the necessary pressure resistance and can process valves for

1200 minutes each week. Chamber 2 provides heat resistance and can process valves for 900 minutes a week. Chamber 3 tests the valves and can work for 1300 minutes a week. The three valve types and the time in minutes required in each chamber are:

	Chamber 1	Chamber 2	Chamber 3
Exhaust	5	7	4
Intake	3	2	10
Bypass	2	4	5

The government will buy all the valves that can be produced and the company will receive the following profit margin on each valve: exhaust, $1.50; intake $1.35; and bypass $1.00.

(a) Formulate a linear programming model to determine how many valves of each type the company should produce each week in order to maximize profits.
(b) Formulate a dual model for the problem.
(c) Solve the above problem through one iteration using the simplex method.

13. A new book has just been written and sent to the publisher. The Underground Printing Company has obtained the contract for printing and binding the books. They have decided to produce the book with three types of binding: paperback for the drugstore patrons; hard cover for the bookstore patrons; and ring-bound for the student patrons who want to appear studious. The minimum quantity of each type to be bound are: paperbacks, 5500 copies; hard cover, 3700 copies; and ring-bound, 2500 copies. The company has two binding machines to process the books. The company has the maximum operating hours of 150 for machine 1 and 200 hours for machine 2. Binding machine 1 costs $12 per hour to operate and can produce either 50 paperbacks per hour, 40 hard covers per hour, or 30 ring-bound books per hour. Binding machine 2 costs $15 per hour to operate and can produce either 65 paperbacks per hour, 35 hard covers per hour, or 25 ring-bound books per hour.

(a) Formulate a linear programming model to determine how many hours each type of book should be processed on each machine if Mr. Read, the operating manager, wishes to minimize production costs.
(b) Solve the above problems through two iteration using the simplex method.

14. The Willis Office Furniture Company is a small business operating in the state of Rhode Island. It has two warehouses in the state from which it fills customers' orders. Due to a recent business slump, the company is attempting to institute a cost reduction campaign. A customer has just ordered 10 desks and 8 tables and Mr. North, the distribution manager, wishes to minimize shipping costs. The shipping costs of tables and desks from each warehouse are:

	Warehouse 1	*Warehouse 2*
Desk	$15	$12
Table	$ 7	$ 9

The company delivers all orders using their own trucks. Trucks coming from warehouse 2 can haul no more than 7 tables and desks but trucks coming from warehouse 1 can haul up to 14 tables and desks. Mr. North has also instituted another policy that he hopes will reduce shipping costs. He has decided that the inventories at the two warehouses should be approximately equal. Therefore, he says that the difference in the number of tables and desks shipped from either warehouse cannot exceed 2.

(a) Formulate a linear programming model to determine how many tables and desks should be shipped from each warehouse in order to minimize shipping costs.
(b) Solve the problem through one iteration (two simplex tableaus including the initial tableau) using the simplex method.
(c) Solve the problem by using the computer.

15. The kite-flying contest is a very important part of the forthcoming county fair. Students at the New River Vocational School have decided to make and sell kites for the occasion. There are three types of kites students have designed: Dragon, Whistle, and Orbiter. The accounting group has reported the following profit margins for the kites: Dragon, 25¢; Whistle, 40¢; and Orbiter, 35¢. The students have contacted a local supply house and found that they can get no more than 12,000 stick-feet of wood and 40,000 square feet of paper. The students have decided to use the following amounts of paper and wood to produce each kite:

	Wood (ft)	*Paper (sq ft)*
Dragon	5.0	12
Whistle	6.5	14
Orbiter	9.0	17

From past fair attendance and participation in the kite contest, the students have estimated that they can sell 1200 Dragon kites and 800 Whistle kites. Their estimate for the Orbiter is that an almost unlimited number can be sold.

(a) Formulate a linear programming model to determine the optimum quantity of each type of kite to produce in order to maximize profit.

(b) Solve the above problem by using the simplex method.

16. Wearever Shoes is an exclusive distributor of Stefano shoes, Italian-style ladies' shoes. The store sells only three styles, which yield the following per unit profits: Ms, $5; Stefano I, $7; and Stefano II, $8. According to past records, the maximum weekly demand for each style is expected to be as follows: Ms, 20 pairs; Stefano I, 15 pairs; and Stefano II, 18 pairs. Stefano, Inc., has informed Wearever that the maximum supply per week would be limited to 32 pairs, regardless of their styles.

(a) Formulate a linear programming model to determine the optimum quantity of each style shoe that Wearever should order per week in order to maximize total profit.

(b) Solve the above problem by using the simplex method.

17. The Dotsun Corporation manufactures and distributes four grades of golf balls: Dot 80, Dot 85, Dot 90, and Dot 100. The profits per dozen balls for each ball are as follows: $3 for Dot 80, $3.50 for Dot 85, $4.25 for Dot 90, and $4.50 for Dot 100. The production process for these golf balls involves four assembly processes, which can operate only a certain amount of time per week, as follows: assembly process 1—40 hours, assembly process 2—55 hours, assembly process 3—45 hours, and assembly process 4—60 hours. The time in minutes required to process a dozen of each grade of ball on each assembly line is as follows:

	Assembly 1	Assembly 2	Assembly 3	Assembly 4
Dot 80	1.5	1.0	2.0	4.0
Dot 85	1.6	1.0	2.5	5.0
Dot 90	1.7	1.0	2.5	6.0
Dot 100	1.9	1.0	3.0	6.5

The sales department has forecast that during the summer months a maximum of 250 dozen/week of Dot 80's, 300 dozen/week of Dot 85's, 180 dozen/week of Dot 90's, and 200 dozen/week of Dot 100's can be sold.

(a) The Dotsun Corporation wants to determine the quantity of each type of ball it should manufacture each week in order to maximize profits. Formulate a linear programming model for the problem.

(b) Solve the problem through one iteration (two simplex tableaus including the initial tableau) by the simplex method.

(c) Solve the problem by using the computer.

18. The Venus Candy Company makes three different candy bars. The ingredients in grams for each candy bar are as follows:

	Chocolate	Nuts	Caramel
Candy Bar 1	12	4	15
Candy Bar 2	6	10	8
Candy Bar 3	10	2	15

Venus' suppliers have limited the company to the following ingredients per week: chocolate, 25,000 grams; nuts, 15,000 grams; and caramel, 30,000 grams. The marketing department estimates that the maximum demand for Candy Bar 1 will be 900 per week and 700 per week for Candy Bar 2. Candy Bar 3 is a relatively new product and demand for this bar appears to be very large at the present time. Per unit profit contributions for each candy bar are as follows: Candy Bar 1, 2¢, Candy Bar 2, 2.5¢, and Candy Bar 3, 1.5¢. Mr. Sweet wants to know how many candy bars of each type he should produce next week in order to maximize profits. Solve the problem by the simplex method.

19. Formulate a dual model for the following linear programming problem:

$$\text{Minimize} \quad Z = \$5X_1 + \$8X_2$$
$$\text{subject to} \quad 2X_1 + X_2 \geq 18$$
$$2X_1 + 2X_2 \geq 26$$
$$X_1 + 2X_2 \leq 32$$

20. The Radford Bulb Company produces three kinds of light bulb: a 60-watt soft-lite bulb, a 60-watt regular bulb, and a 100-watt bulb. The bulbs each take one hour per case in production line 1. In production line 2, a case of the soft-lites takes 2 hours and a case of each of the others takes 1 hour. Production line 1 has 25 hours per week available and line 2 has 40 hours per week available. The company has determined that the two 60-watt bulbs are considered substitute products by most people and that their combined demand will not be more than 25 cases per week. The demand for 100-watt

bulbs will never be greater than 60 cases per week. If the soft-lite bulbs earn a profit of $7 per case and the other two bulbs earn a profit of $5 per case, how many cases per week should the company produce of each type in order to maximize profits?

21. Consider the following linear programming problem:

$$\text{Minimize} \quad Z = \$15X_1 + \$25X_2$$
$$\text{subject to} \quad 3X_1 + 4X_2 \geq 12$$
$$2X_1 + X_2 \geq 6$$
$$3X_1 + 2X_2 \leq 9$$

(a) Solve the above problem by the simplex method.
(b) Is the optimum solution valid? Why or why not?

22. The Inland Oil Company is faced with a problem. It has only enough oil to keep its refineries operating for one more year. The company has determined that it has three possible alternatives for increasing its oil supply. The company has decided that it can spend no more than $5 million and that this investment must provide them at least 2.5 million barrels of oil a year for at least the next 150 years. Alternative 1 is to invest in more oil wells in this country. The company has determined that the total cost of a new well is $200,000 with an expected yield of 500,000 barrels a year for 10 years. Alternative 2 is to invest in oil wells in other countries (South America). A well there costs $800,000 initially and will yield 1 million barrels a year for 25 years. Alternative 3 is to invest in research for the recovery of shale oil. It is estimated that this research will cost $2 million but will yield 1.5 million barrels a year for 75 years. Unlike the other alternatives only one research project is possible.

(a) Formulate a linear programming model to determine the optimum choice of alternatives that will maximize the company's oil supply.
(b) Solve the above problem using the simplex method.

23. The Selective Service System has received orders from the Executive Branch to develop an emergency draft plan in case the Middle East and/or South East Asia situations should worsen. The Selective Service System has passed the task on to the local boards and Local Board 1 is trying to determine how many men would have to be sent draft notices in case of an emergency. The board knows that it will have to actually enlist at least 200 men. Of these men, no less than 50 and no more than 150 should be 19 years old. Of the remainder there should be no more than 50 20-year-olds and no less than 30 and no

more than 50 21-year-olds. From the past experience the board knows that 90 percent of the 19-year-olds called, 80 percent of the 20-year-olds, and 60 percent of the 21-year-olds called passed their physicals. At the present time there is an almost unlimited number of men who could be called for physicals. The board, however, would want to call only enough men to fulfill its quota.

(a) Formulate a linear programming model to determine the number of draft notices that would be sent to each age group in an emergency in order to minimize the total number sent.

(b) Solve the above problem through one iteration (two simplex tableaus including the initial tableau) using the simplex method.

24. Metropolitan Airport Services, Inc., is considering the purchase of new cars for the transportation service between the Municipal Airport and hotels in the downtown area. There are three vehicles under consideration: station wagons, minibuses, and large buses. The purchase price would be $4500 for each station wagon, $9000 for the minibus, and $20,000 for the large bus. The Board of Directors has authorized a maximum amount of $500,000 for these purchases. Because of the heavy air travel in the area, the new vehicles would be utilized at maximum capacity regardless of the type of vehicles purchased. The expected net annual profit would be $1500 for the station wagon, $3500 for the minibus, and $5000 for the large bus. The company has hired 30 new drivers for the new vehicles. They are qualified drivers for all three types of vehicles. The maintenance department has the capacity to handle an additional 80 station wagons. A minibus is equivalent to $1\frac{2}{3}$ station wagons and each large bus is equivalent to 2 station wagons in terms of their use of the maintenance department. Formulate a linear programming model that will determine the optimum number of each type of vehicle to purchase in order to maximize profit.

25. Your grandfather has just left you $1 million. You plan to invest this amount of money in four alternative investment plans: stocks, bonds, savings, and real estate. Investments in stocks and bonds are available at the beginning of each of the next six years. Each dollar invested in stocks at the beginning of each year returns an average of $1.20 (a profit of $.20) two years later, in time for immediate reinvestment. Each dollar invested in bonds at the beginning of one year returns $1.40 three years later for reinvestment. In addition, money-making investments in savings (in a credit union) and in real estate will be available only at one time in the future. Each dollar invested in the credit union at the beginning of the second year hence

returns $1.80 four years later. Each dollar invested in real estate at the beginning of the fifth year hence returns $1.50 two years later. You would also like to invest in various areas in order to minimize the risk. The total amount invested in stocks should not exceed 30 percent of total investment in other investment alternatives. Further, you wish to invest at least 25 percent of the total investment in the credit-union savings plan. In addition, you are planning to get married at the end of the third year. Therefore, you would like to make sure that the amount of cash you have (to show off to your bride but not to spend) would be at least $150,000. If you are attempting to maximize the amount of money (cash) you have at the end of the sixth year, how would you formulate a linear programming model?

26. The International Chef, Inc., markets three blends of oriental tea: premium, fine, and regular. The firm uses three types of tea leaves in the production process, from Korea, Japan, and Taiwan. The following table lists the composition of the three blends:

	Tea Leaves		
	Korean	Japanese	Taiwanese
Premium	40%	20%	40%
Fine	30	30	40
Regular	20	40	40

The firm's net profit per pound for each blend is: premium, 50 cents; fine, 30 cents; and regular, 20 cents. The firm's regular weekly supplies of the Korean and Japanese tea leaves are 20,000 and 22,000 pounds, respectively. However, due to the strained relationship between the United States and Taiwan, if the firm decides to use Taiwanese leaves, it must purchase *at least* 16,000 pounds. The marketing research department reports that there is almost unlimited market for the premium and fine blends. However, the maximum expected sale for the regular blend is 2000 pounds. Formulate a linear programming model that will determine the optimum product mix to maximize total profit.

27. The Barn House is planning a special drink for the Executive Forum dinner party. They have decided to make Deluxe Martinis (special 5-oz drinks). The bartender reports that due to local liquor control the maximum quantities of gin he can obtain are: premium gin, 400 oz; cheap gin, 500 oz. The maximum quantities of vermouth that can be purchased for the occasion are: premium vermouth, 800 oz; cheap vermouth, 400 oz. The bartender mixes four different quality martinis. He mixes cheap gin and cheap vermouth to make Barn

Delight which sells for $.80. Barn Special requires cheap gin and premium vermouth and it sells for $1.00. The bartender mixes premium gin and cheap vermouth to make Barn Jumbo which sells for $1.20. Barn Supreme requires premium gin and premium vermouth. The price for Supreme is $1.50. The mixing quantities for the four types of drinks are as follows:

Drink	Price	Gin	Vermouth
Barn Delight	$ .80	2 oz.	3 oz.
Barn Special	$1.00	3 oz.	2 oz.
Barn Jumbo	$1.20	3 oz.	2 oz.
Barn Supreme	$1.50	4 oz.	1 oz.

From past experience, the bartender knows that the maximum number of drinks he can sell are: 125 drinks that contain cheap gin; 150 drinks that contain cheap vermouth. Formulate a linear programming model to determine the optimum quantities of gin, vermouth, and drinks to maximize total revenue.

28. Old Dominion Chemicals, Inc., produces two products: Formula A and Formula B. Production of both products requires the same two processes. A unit of Formula A requires 3 hours in process one and 4 hours in process two. A unit of Formula B requires 5 hours in process one and 2 hours in process two. The maximum available production time in the two processes is: process one, 60 hours; process two, 70 hours. The production of Formula B results in a byproduct, Formula B1. Some of Formula B1 can be marketed at a profit. However, production of Formula B1 in excess of 10 units is prohibited due to the danger involved. The production process of Formula B yields 4 units of Formula B1 for each unit of Formula B. The unit profits of Formula A and Formula B are $5 and $10, respectively. The byproduct, Formula B1, yields a $3 unit profit. If Formula B1 cannot be sold, it should be destroyed, at a unit cost of $2. The marketing department reports that the demand for Formula A and Formula B is unlimited. However, only 10 units of Formula B1 can be sold. Formulate a linear programming model that will determine the maximum number of units of Formula A, Formula B, and Formula B1 to be produced in order to maximize total profit.

6 Goal Programming

Organizational objectives vary according to the character, type, philosophy of management, and particular environmental conditions of the organization. There is no single universal goal for all organizations. Profit maximization, which is regarded as the sole objective of the business firm in classical economic theory, is one of the most widely accepted objectives of management. In today's dynamic business environment, profit maximization is not always the only objective of management. In fact business firms quite frequently place higher priorities on noneconomic goals than on profit maximization. Or, firms often seek profit maximization while pursuing other noneconomic objectives. We have seen, for example, firms place a great emphasis on social responsibilities, social contributions, public relations, industrial and labor relations, and so on. Whether such objects are sought because of outside pressure or voluntary management decisions, noneconomic objectives exist and they are gaining a greater significance. The recent public awareness of the need for ecological management and the gaining momentum of consumerism may have forced many firms to reevaluate their organizational objectives.

It appears that in reality the decision maker is one who attempts to achieve a set of multiple objectives to the fullest possible extent in an environment of conflicting interests, incomplete information, limited resources, and limited ability to analyze the complex environment.

The problem of multiple conflicting objectives is real in business, the public sector, and nonprofit organizations. Suppose the government is studying the feasibility of constructing a new airport near Washington, D.C. Here, there are many conflicting objectives and interests. The study must consider the capacity of the airport, accessibility of the location, traffic-flow planning, architectural style for the national prestige, noise level for the nearby residents, conservation of natural life in the area, and so forth. Many of today's decision problems that require scientific analysis do not lend themselves to a clear-cut solution by certain criterion variables (i.e., profits, costs, effectiveness, etc.) For example, many social problems involve multiple incompatible objectives in the jungle of conflicting interests. The question is not that of selecting the "social good" over "social evil," but it is often a choice between social evil vs. social evil or social good vs. social good.

Let us consider the example of the strip-mining controversy. In this day of environmental concern, any sensible person, not necessarily a naturalist or conservationist, can easily enumerate many of the problems involved in strip mining. However, we should not forget the increasing energy demands in the United States. It is estimated that the national energy demand will double by early 1980's. With the rapidly diminishing natural gas reserves and the remoteness of the possibility of sufficient nuclear energy production for total energy demand, increased coal production is an important national concern. We simply cannot afford the luxury of deciding whether we should or should not mine coal. Rather, the decision problem is that of determining the most efficient way to mine coal, that is, by conventional underground mining, strip mining, or some combination of both methods. Both methods of mining contribute to social problems. Strip mining, although it is in most cases the more economical method of producing coal, involves many ecological problems. On the other hand, conventional underground mining creates health problems for workers, such as black-lung disease, the constant danger, working in a cramped space, and so on. Should we say, then, that strip mining ought to be banned altogether to preserve the environment? That implies that we would rather allow greater danger to miners working underground to satisfy the greater demand for coal. At least one thing is certain. Unless a new technological breakthrough is realized, the national demand for coal has to be met in some way. In satisfying this demand, there are multiple conflicting objectives and interests.

The point of this discussion is that problems involving multiple objectives cannot easily be solved by traditional techniques using only one predominant objective criterion. Many contemporary decision problems faced by industry, government, and other institutions will increasingly require identification of more elusive and abstract objective functions. The objective function no longer will be restricted to a cardinal criterion (i.e., profits, costs, etc.); rather it will involve general criteria related to the common good. Certainly, cost will remain an important decision variable because it determines the resource requirements. However, its function will be shifted from that of the objective function to that of a decision constraint.

The question still remains as to whether or not we can use the conventional numerical objective function approach (i.e., linear programming) for today's complex decision problems. It is apparent that solution methods based on numerical criteria are not capable of producing acceptable solutions to problems that involve highly abstract objective criteria such as welfare to the taxpayer, public health, consumer protection and satisfaction, community image of the firm, and the like. It should be pointed out that numerical solution techniques are still being used for contemporary decision problems by estimating the numerical measures of abstract objective criteria in terms of a convenient numerical value, that is, utilities, profits, costs, and so on. However, the process often results in a considerable degree of fabrication and distortion of information in order to express abstract criteria in numerical values. Hence, the model solution is of very little value to the decision maker. The only alternate method to the numerical approach for problems involving multiple conflicting objective criteria is the ordinal solution approach. Goal programming, based on the ordinal solution approach, appears to be the most appropriate, flexible, and powerful technique for complex decision problems involving multiple conflicting objectives.

THE GOAL PROGRAMMING APPROACH

As discussed above, most real-world decision problems involve multiple conflicting objectives. If we decide to use linear programming to solve decision problems with multiple objectives, we may introduce other objectives (other than the objective function) as model constraints. The linear programming model, however, requires that the optimum solution must satisfy all constraints. Furthermore, we are assuming that all constraints have equal importance in solving the problems. However, in reality such assumptions are absurd. First of all, it is quite possible that all constraints of the problem cannot be satisfied. Such a problem is called "infeasible." Should we abandon a very important management problem because it cannot be solved by linear programming? Next, all constraints do not have equal importance. For example, let us suppose that the model contains the machine capacity, manpower, and union-contract constraints. The machine capacity and union contract constraints may be more important and rigid than the manpower constraint. In other words, it is easier to add more employees than to add new heavy machinery or renegotiate with the union. Goal programming has been developed to solve decision problems that involve multiple conflicting objectives.

The concept of goal programming was first introduced by A. Charnes and W. W. Cooper as a tool to resolve infeasible linear programming problems. This technique has been further refined by Y. Ijiri, V. Jaaskelainen, S. M. Lee, and others. Goal programming, which is a special extension of linear programming, is capable of solving decision problems with a single goal or multiple goals. Often goals set by management are achievable only at the expense of other goals. Furthermore, these goals may be incommensurable, in other words, unable to be measured on the same unit basis. Thus, there is a need to establish a hierarchy of importance among these conflicting goals so that low-order goals are considered only after the higher-order goals are satisfied or have reached the point beyond which no further improvements are desirable. If management can provide an ordinal ranking of goals in terms of their contributions or importance to the organization and all relationships of the model are linear, the problem can be solved by goal programming.

In goal programming, instead of trying to maximize or minimize the objective criterion directly, as in linear programming, the deviations among goals and what can be achieved within the given set of constraints are to be minimized. In the simplex algorithm of linear programming, such deviations are called "slack" variables. These deviational variables take on a new significance in goal programming. The deviational variable is represented in two dimensions, positive and negative deviations from each subgoal or goal. Then, the objective function becomes the minimization of these deviations, based on the relative importance or priority assigned to them.

The solution of any linear programming problem is limited by quantification. Unless management can accurately quantify the relationship of the variables in cardinal numbers, the solution is only as good as the inputs, if that good. The distinguishing characteristic of goal programming is that it allows an ordinal solution. Stated differently, management may be unable to obtain information on the cost or value of a goal or a subgoal, but often upper or lower limits may be stated for each subgoal. Usually the manager can determine the priority of the desired attainment of each goal or subgoal and rank the priorities in ordinal sequence. Economically speaking, the manager faces the problem of allocation of scarce resources. Obviously, it is not always possible to achieve every goal to the extent desired by management. Thus, with or without goal programming the manager attaches a certain priority to the achievement of a particular goal.

Professor Herbert A. Simon, an authority on decision theory, sates that today's manager is not-trying to "optimize"; instead he tries to "satisfice." An optimizer usually seeks the best possible outcome for a given objective, such as profit maximization in linear programming. A satisficer, on the other hand, attempts to achieve a "satisfactory" level of multiple objectives. Goal programming is, if we accept Professor Simon's theory, an appropriate technique for modern decision analysis.

THE GOAL PROGRAMMING MODEL

Goal programming is a linear mathematical model in which the optimum attainment of multiple goals is sought within the given decision environment. The decision environment determines the basic components of the model, namely, the decision variables, constraints, and the objective function.

Let us now consider the goal programming model through a simple illustration. First, goal programming involving a simple goal with multiple subgoals will be discussed, followed by an analysis of multiple goals.

Single Goal with Multiple Subgoals

Example 1

A furniture manufacturer produces two kinds of products, desks and tables. The unit profit of a desk is $80 and of a table is $40. The goal of the plant manager is to earn a total profit of exactly $640 in the next week.

We can interpret the profit goal in terms of subgoals, which are sales volumes of desks and tables. Then, a goal programming model can be formulated as follows:

$$\text{Minimize} \quad Z = d_1^- + d_1^+$$
$$\text{subject to} \quad \$80X_1 + \$40X_2 + d_1^- - d_1^+ = \$640$$
$$X_1, X_2, d_1^-, d_1^+ \geq 0$$

where,

$$X_1 = \text{number of desks sold}$$
$$X_2 = \text{number of tables sold}$$

$d_1^- =$ underachievement of the profit goal of \$640
$d_1^+ =$ overachievement of the profit goal of \$640

If the profit goal is not completely achieved, then obviously the slack in the profit goal will be expressed by d_1^-, which represents the under-achievement of the goal (or negative deviation from the goal). On the other hand, if the solution shows a profit in excess of \$640, then d_1^+ will show some value. If the profit goal of \$640 is exactly achieved, both d_1^- and d_1^+ will be zero. It should be noted that d_1^- and d_1^+ are complementary to each other. If d_1^- takes a nonzero value, d_1^+ will be zero, and vice versa. Since at least one of the deviational variables will always be zero, $d_1^- \times d_1^+ = 0$. In the above example, there are an infinite number of combinations of X_1 and X_2 that will achieve the goal. The solution will be any linear combination of X_1 and X_2 between the two points ($X_1 = 8$, $X_2 = 0$) and ($X_1 = 0$, $X_2 = 16$). This straight line is exactly the iso-profit function when total profit is \$640.

In the above example we did not have any model constraints. Now let us suppose that in addition to the profit goal constraint considered in Example 1, the following two constraints are imposed. The marketing department reports that the maximum number of desks that can be sold in a week is six. The maximum number of tables that can be sold is eight.

Now the new goal programming model can be presented in the following way:

$$\text{Minimize} \quad Z = d_1^- + d_1^+$$
$$\text{subject to} \quad \$80X_1 + \$40X_2 + d_1^- - d_1^+ = \$640$$
$$X_1 \le 6$$
$$X_2 \le 8$$
$$X_1, X_2, d_1^-, d_1^+ \ge 0$$

The solution to the above problem can be easily calculated on the back of an evelope. The solution is $X_1 = 6$ and $X_2 = 4$. With this solution the deviational variables d_1^- and d_1^+ will both be zero. The plant manager's profit goal can be achieved under the new constraints imposed on the subgoals.

Analysis of Multiple Goals

The model illustrated above can be extended to handle cases of multiple goals. Let us assume that these goals are conflicting and incommensurable.

Example 2

Let us consider the furniture manufacturer case illustrated in Example 1. Now the manager desires to achieve a weekly profit as close to \$640 as possible. He also desires to achieve sales volume for desks and tables close to six and to four respectively. The manager's decision problem can be formulated as a goal programming model as follows:

$$\text{Minimize} \quad Z = d_1^- + d_2^- + d_3^- + d_1^+$$
$$\text{subject to} \quad \$80X_1 + \$40X_2 + d_1^- - d_1^+ = 640$$
$$X_1 + d_2^- = 6$$
$$X_2 + d_3^- = 4$$

where d_2^- and d_3^- represent underachievements of sales volume for desks and tables, respectively. It should be noted that d_2^+ and d_3^+ are not included in the second and third constraints, since the sales goals are given as the maximum possible sales volume. The solution to this problem can be found by a simple examination of the problem: If $X_1 = 6$, and $X_2 = 4$, all goals will be completely attained. Therefore, $d_1^- = d_2^- = d_3^- = d_1^+ = 0$.

Ranking and Weighting of Multiple Goals

In Example 2 we had a case in which all goals are achieved simultaneously within the given constraints. However, in a real decision environment this is rarely the case. Quite often, most goals are competitive in terms of need for scarce resources. In the presence of incompatible multiple goals the manager needs to exercise his judgment about the importance of the individual goals. In other words, the most important goal must be achieved to the extent desired before the next goal is considered.

Goals of the decision maker may simply be meeting a certain set of constraints. For example, the manager may set a goal concerning a stable employment level in the plant, which is simply a part of the production constraint. Or the goal may be an entirely separate function from the constraints of the system. If that is the case, the goal constraint must be generated in the model. The decision maker must analyze the system and investigate whether all of his goals are expressed in the goal programming model. When all constraints and goals are completely identified in the model, the decision maker must analyze each goal in terms of whether over- or underachievement of the goal is satisfactory or not. Based on this analysis he can assign deviational variables to the regular and/or goal constraints. If overachievement is acceptable, positive deviation from the goal can be eliminated from the objective function. On the other hand, if underachievement of a certain goal is acceptable, negative deviation should not be included in the objective function. If the exact achievement of the goal is desired, both negative and positive deviations must be represented in the objective function.

In order to achieve the ordinal solution—that is, to achieve the goals according to their importance—negative and/or positive deviations about the goal must be ranked according to the "preemptive" priority factors. In this way the low-order goals are considered only after high-order goals are achieved as desired. If there are goals in several ranks of importance, the preemptive priority factor P_j ($j = 1, 2, \ldots, k$) should be assigned to the negative and/or positive deviational variables. The preemptive priority factors have the relationship of $P_1 >>> P_2 >>> P_3 \cdots P_j >>> P_{j+1}$, where $>>>$ means "very much greater than." The priority relationship implies that multiplication by n, however large it may be, cannot make the lower-level goal as important as the higher goal. It is, of course, possible to refine goals even further by means of decomposing (subdividing) the deviational variables. To do this, additional constraints and additional priority factors may be required.

One more step to be considered in the goal programming model formulation is the weighting of deviational variables at the same priority level. For example, if the sales goal involves two different products, there will be two deviational variables with the same priority factor. The criterion to be used in determining the differential weights of deviational variables is the minimization of the opportunity cost or regret. This implies that the coefficient of regret, which is always positive, should be assigned to the individual deviational variable with the identical P_j factor. The coefficient of regret simply represents the relative amount of unsatisfactory deviation from the goal. Therefore, deviational variables on the same priority level must be commensurable, although deviations that are on different priority levels need not be commensurable.

Example 3

Consider the following modified case of the illustration given in the previous examples. Production of either a desk or a table requires one hour of production capacity in the plant. The plant has a normal maximum production capacity of 10 hours a week. Because of the limited sales capacity, the maximum number of desks and tables that can be sold are six and eight per week, respectively. The unit profit for a desk is $80 and for a table $40.

The plant manager has set the following goals, arranged in order of importance.

1. He wants to avoid any underutilization of production capacity (providing job security to the plant employees).

2. He wants to sell as many desks and tables as possible. Since the unit profit from the sale of a desk is twice the amount of profit from a table, he has twice as much desire to achieve the sales goal for desks as for tables.
3. He wants to minimize overtime operation of the plant as much as possible.

In the above example, the plant manager is to make a decision that will achieve his goals as closely as possible with the minimum sacrifice. Since overtime operation is allowed in this example, production of desks and tables may take more than the normal production capacity of 10 hours. Therefore, the operational capacity can be expressed as

$$X_1 + X_2 + d_1^- - d_1^+ = 10$$

where

X_1 = number of desks to be produced
X_2 = number of tables to be produced
d_1^- = idle (underutilization of) production capacity
d_1^+ = overtime operation

Accordingly, the sales capacity constraints can be written as

$$X_1 + d_2^- = 6$$
$$X_2 + d_3^- = 8$$

where

d_2^- = underachievement of sales goal for desks
d_3^- = underachievement of sales goal for tables

It should be noted that d_2^+ and d_3^+ are not in the equation, since the sales goals given are the maximum possible sales volume.

In addition to the variables and constraints stated above, the following preemptive priority factors are to be defined:

P_1: The highest priority, assigned by management to the underutilization of production capacity (i.e., d_1^-).
P_2: The second priority factor, assigned to the underutilization of sales capacity (i.e., d_2^- and d_3^-). However, management puts twice the importance on d_2^- as that on d_3^- in accordance with respective profit figures for desks and tables.
P_3: The lowest priority factor, assigned to overtime in the production capacity (i.e., d_1^+).

Now the complete model can be formulated. The objective is the minimization of deviation from goals. The deviant variable associated with the highest preemptive priority must be minimized to the fullest possible extent. When no further improvement is desirable or possible in the highest goal, then the deviations associated with the next highest priority factor will be minimized. The model can be expressed as:

$$\text{Minimize} \quad Z = P_1 d_1^- + 2P_2 d_2^- + P_2 d_3^- + P_3 d_1^+$$
$$\text{subject to} \quad X_1 + X_2 + d_1^- - d_1^+ = 10$$
$$X_1 + d_2^- = 6$$
$$X_2 + d_3^- = 8$$
$$X_1, X_2, d_1^-, d_2^-, d_3^-, d_1^+ \geq 0$$

From the simple investigation of the model we can derive the following optimal solution: $X_1 = 6$, $X_2 = 8$, $d_1^- = d_2^- = d_3^- = 0$, $d_1^+ = 4$. The first two goals are completely attained, but the third goal is only partially achieved, since the overtime operation could not be minimized to zero. This result is due to the direct conflict between the second (sales) goal and the third (minimization of overtime) goal. This kind of result reflects the everyday problem experienced in business when there are several conflicting goals.

THE GRAPHICAL METHOD OF GOAL PROGRAMMING

In this section, building on what we have learned thus far in this chapter, a graphical solution introduced by S. M. Lee will be discussed. Let us recall that the objective of goal programming is not the maximization or minimization of a single objective criterion. Instead, the objective is to attain a certain set of goals, which are rated by priority factors, as closely as possible. The solution procedure we will follow is the minimization of deviation from the goals and what we can achieve within the given decision environment. Deviation from the goal with the highest priority factor will be minimized to the fullest possible extent, and the deviation for the second goal will be minimized after considering the first goal, and so on.

The goal programming problem is, therefore, always a minimization problem. To explain the graphical method of goal programming, let us consider the following example.

A textile company produces two types of linen materials, a strong upholstery material and a regular dress material. The upholstery material is produced according to direct orders from furniture manufacturers. The dress material, on the other hand, is distributed to retail fabric stores. The average production rate for the upholstery material and for the dress material are identical: 1000 yards per hour. By running two shifts, the operational capacity of the plant is 80 hours per week.

The marketing department reports that the estimated *maximum* sales for the following week are 70,000 yards of the upholstery material and 45,000 yards of the dress material. According to the accounting department, the approximate profit from a yard of upholstery material is $2.50, and from a yard of dress material $1.50.

If we assume that the president of the firm simply trys to maximize profit within the bounds of the production capacity and the estimated sales for the week, a linear programming problem can be formulated as follows:

$$\text{Maximize} \quad Z = \$2500X + \$1500X_2$$
$$\text{subject to} \quad X_1 + X_2 \leq 80$$
$$X_1 \leq 70$$
$$X_2 \leq 45$$
$$X_1, \quad X_2 \geq 0$$

where

X_1 = amount of upholstery material produced (in 1000 yards)
X_2 = amount of dress material produced (in 1000 yards)

The problem is presented on the graph in Figure 6.1 and the area of feasible solutions is indicated by the shaded area. The constraints form the boundaries of the feasible solution area, and their slopes are -1, 0, and ∞. The slope of the iso-profit line is $-3/5$. Since this slope lies between 0 and -1, the optimum point will be the intersection point between the production capacity constraint $(X_1 + X_2 \leq 80)$ and the sales constraint for the upholstery material $(X_1 \leq 70)$. The optimum solution is identified as $X_1 = 70$ and $X_2 = 10$ and the total profit is $190,000.

If the president of the firm has only the one objective of profit maximization, goal programming is not required. However, the rest of the case reads as follows:

The president of the company believes that a good management-employee relationship is an important factor for business success. Hence, he decides that a stable employment level is a primary goal for the firm. Therefore, whenever there is demand exceeding normal production capacity, he simply expands production capacity by providing overtime. However, he also feels that overtime operation of the plant of more than 10 hours per week should be avoided because of the accelerating costs. The president has the following four goals, listed in order of importance:

P_1: Avoid any underutilization of production capacity (i.e., maintain stable employment at normal capacity)

P_2: Limit overtime operation of the plant to 10 hours

P_3: Achieve the sales goals of 70,000 yards of upholstery material and 45,000 yards of dress material

P_4: Minimize the overtime operation of the plant as much as possible

Since the above problem involves multiple incompatible goals, linear programming is not an effective approach to the case. A goal programming model should be developed for the solution. The case presents three basic constraints: production, sales, and overtime operation of the plant.

Production Capacity

The production capacity at present is limited to 80 hours by running two shifts. However, since overtime operation of the plant is allowed to a certain extent, the constraint can be expressed as

$$X_1 + X_2 \gtrless 80$$

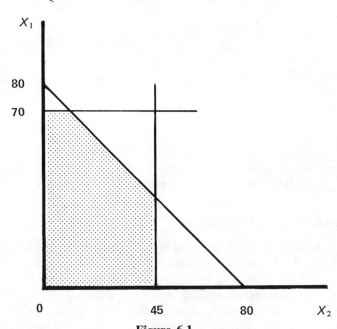

Figure 6.1
Feasible solution area using linear programming

By introducing deviational variables to the constraint, it can be expressed as

$$X_1 + X_2 + d_1^- - d_1^+ = 80$$

where

X_1 = number of hours used for producing the upholstery material
X_2 = number of hours used for producing the regular dress material
d_1^- = underutilization of production capacity, below 80 hours
d_1^+ = overutilization of normal production capacity, above 80 hours

It should be noted that d_1^- takes on a nonzero value only when d_1^+ is zero, and vice versa.

Sales Constraints

The maximum sales for upholstery and dress materials are set at 70,000 and 45,000 yards, respectively. Hence, it is assumed that overachievement of sales beyond the maximum limits are impossible. Then, the sales constraints will be (with X_1 and X_2 expressed in thousands):

$$X_1 \le 70$$
$$X_2 \le 45$$

which can be converted to equations, using deviational variables:

$$X_1 + d_2^- = 70$$
$$X_2 + d_3^- = 45$$

where

d_2^- = underachievement of sales goal of upholstery material
d_3^- = underachievement of sales goal of dress material

Overtime Operation Constraint

From the case itself, only production and sales constraints can be formulated. However, the analysis of goals indicates that overtime operation of the plant is to be limited to 10 hours or less. To solve the problem by goal programming, we need a deviation variable that represents the overtime operation of the plant beyond 10 hours. By minimizing this deviational variable to zero we can achieve the goal. Since there is no such deviational variable in the three constraints presented above, we must create a new constraint.

The overtime operation of the plant, d_1^+, should be limited to 10 hours or less. However, it may not be possible to limit the overtime operation to 10 hours or less in order to meet higher order goals. Therefore, d_1^+ can be smaller than, equal to, or even greater than 10 hours. By introducing some new deviational variables, a constraint regarding overtime can be expressed as

$$d_1^+ + d_4^- - d_4^+ = 10$$

where

$d_4^- =$ negative deviation of overtime operation from 10 hours
$d_4^+ =$ overtime operation beyond 10 hours

The above overtime operation constraint can be expressed in terms of only the decision variable if desired. This can be accomplished by solving the above equation for d_1^+ and substituting it into the production capacity constraint, as follows:

$$d_1^+ = 10 - d_4^- + d_4^+ \qquad \text{Overtime constraint}$$
$$X_1 + X_2 + d_1^- - d_1^+ = 80 \qquad \text{Production constraint}$$
$$X_1 + X_2 + d_1^- - (10 - d_4^- + d_4^+) = 80$$
$$X_1 + X_2 + d_1^- + d_4^- - d_4^+ = 90$$

In the above equation, the value of d_1^- is obviously zero, since the (right-hand-side) value exceeds 80. Consequently, the overtime constraint can also be expressed as

$$X_1 + X_2 + d_4^- - d_4^+ = 90$$

Now the complete model can be formulated. The objective is the minimization of deviations from goals with certain assigned priorities. The deviant variable with the highest priority must be minimized to the fullest possible extent. When no further improvement is possible for the highest goal, the other deviational variables are to be minimized according to their assigned priority factors. One thing to be noted here is the priority factor P_3 that is assigned to the underachievement of sales goals for two types of materials. Sales goals for both materials are considered equally important. However, the profit contribution rate of each material differs somewhat. A yard of upholstery material contributes $2.50 profit, and a yard of dress material only $1.50 profit. Therefore, differential weights must be assigned to sales goals of these materials, even though they are on the same priority level. The profit contribution ratio between the upholstery and dress materials is 5 to 3. Hence, these are assigned as differential weights. The differential weights imply that management is relatively more concerned with the achievement of the sales goal for the upholstery material than that for the dress material. Now, the model can be formulated:

Minimize $Z = P_1d_1^- + P_2d_4^+ + 5P_3d_2^- + 3P_3d_3^- + P_4d_1^+$
subject to $X_1 + X_2 + d_1^- - d_1^+ = 80$
                            $X_1 + d_2^- = 70$
                            $X_2 + d_3^- = 45$
          $X_1 + X_2 + d_4^- - d_4^+ = 90$
     $X_1, X_2, d_1^-, d_2^-, d_3^-, d_4^-, d_1^+, d_4^+ \geq 0$

The decision variables are expressed in terms of thousands of yards in the model.

In order to solve this goal programming problem by the graphical method, the constraints must first be plotted on a graph, as shown in Figure 6.2. Since production capacity may be less than or equal to or even greater than 80 hours, the feasible solution area can be on either side of the straight line, as noted by the arrow signs. The same approach is used to plot the sales goal constraints and the overtime production constraint. If we are to achieve our goals within the sales constraints, the area of feasible solutions should be *ABDO*.

We have plotted all constraints on the graph. The next step is the analysis of the objective function. The first goal is to avoid the underutilization of production capacity or the minimization of d_1^- to

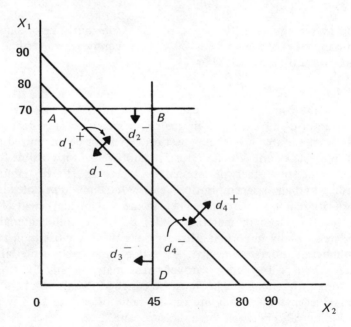

Figure 6.2
Graph of constraints of a goal programming model

zero. In order to achieve this goal, the production capacity constraints of $X_1 + X_2 + d_1^- - d_1^+ = 80$ must be analyzed. The arrow pointing toward the origin from the above function must be minimized to zero. The area of feasible solution is now the upper part from the straight line, as shown in Figure 6.3.

The second goal is to limit the overtime operation of the plant to 10 hours. To achieve this goal the area of feasible solution must be limited to the shaded area shown in Figure 6.4. Now, the first two most important goals will be attained as long as production takes place within the shaded area.

The third goal presented by the president is to achieve maximum sales. Since the profit ratio between the upholstery material (X_1) and dress material (X_2) is 5 to 3, we should try to sell as much upholstery material as possible before trying to sell dress material. The maximum quantity of upholstery material we can sell is, of course, 70,000 yards. This sales goal can be met on the line EF within the shaded area. Next, we should try to achieve the maximum sales for the dress material, 45,000 yards. However, in order to achieve this goal we have to reach point B. This point is outside the shaded area, and therefore our first two

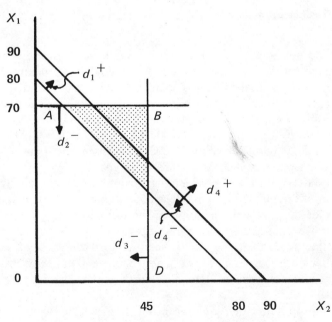

Figure 6.3
Feasible solution area with d_1^- minimized to zero (P_1)

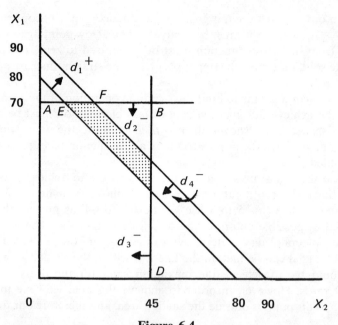

Figure 6.4
Feasible solution area with d_1^+ minimized to 10 hours (P_2)

goals could not be attained at that point. We have no desire to achieve the third goal at the expense of the first two goals. The maximum sales goal for dress material obviously cannot be achieved within the given decision environment. The maximum possible sales goal for dress material must be found on the straight line segment EF.

At point E, X_1 is of course 70,000 and X_2 will be 10,000. At point F, X_1 remains 70,000 but X_2 will be 20,000. It is evident that point F will be the optimum point to meet the firm's three goals.

The last goal of the president is to minimize the total overtime operation of the plant. This goal does not actually change our optimum point, since the overtime operation of the plant has been limited to 10 hours. If we eliminate the overtime operation of 10 hours, this will achieve the fourth goal, but only by sacrificing 10,000 yards of the dress material. In other words, we are going back to point E from F. Of course, we do not wish to attain the fourth goal at the expense of the third goal.

At the optimum point F, the production will be 70,000 yards of upholstery material and 20,000 yards of dress material, and the profit will be $205,000. At this point, our first two goals are attained completely, but the last two goals could not be achieved completely, since there exists the underachievement of the sales goal for the dress material by 25,000 yards and the overtime operation of 10 hours. However, the solution achieves all the goals as closely as possible according to the stated priorities and within the given decision environment.

One may think that linear programming could solve the problem if we treated the first two goals as constraints and maximized the profit within the constraints. In other words, formulate the linear programming problem as:

$$\text{Maximize} \quad Z = 2500X_1 + 1500X_2$$

$$\text{subject to} \quad \begin{aligned} X_1 & & \leq 70 \\ & X_2 & \leq 45 \\ X_1 + & X_2 & \leq 90 \\ X_1, & X_2 & \leq 0 \end{aligned}$$

The solution to the problem is to produce 70,000 yards of upholstery material and 20,000 yards of dress material for a profit of $205,000. As expected, the optimum solution is identical in this case. Does this mean that linear programming would yield the identical answer if we converted some of the management goals to constraints? The answer is "absolutely not." First of all, it may be quite possible that none of the goals set by the decision maker involve financial goals, that is, profit maximization or cost minimization. Second, the constraints set by certain goals will not form a convex set or a single area of feasible solution, so that there might be no solution to the linear programming model.

To illustrate the above statement, let us change the case we have discussed very slightly. Suppose the best customer of the textile company ordered 100,000 yards of upholstery material. For various reasons the president does not wish to fail to meet this order; therefore, the highest priority is assigned to this goal. P_1 is then assigned to d_2^-, the underachievement of this sales goal. The second goal of the president is to avoid any underutilization of production capacity; therefore, P_2 is assigned to d_1^-. The third goal is to minimize the overtime operation of the plant as much as possible. The fourth goal is assigned to the achievement of the sales goal for dress material, so P_4 is assigned to d_3^-.

If we attempt to utilize linear programming to maximize profit, the model would be developed as:

$$\text{Maximize} \quad Z = 2500X_1 + 1500X_2$$

$$\text{subject to} \quad \begin{aligned} X_1 & & \geq 100 \\ & X_2 & \leq 45 \\ X_1 + & X_2 & \leq 90 \\ X_1, & X_2 & \geq 0 \end{aligned}$$

The graphical presentation of the model is shown in Figure 6.5. Obviously, there is no area of feasible solution and consequently the above problem is unsolvable by linear programming.

If we utilize goal programming, the above problem can easily be solved. The goal programming model is formulated as follows:

$$\text{Minimize} \quad Z = P_1 d_2^- + P_2 d_1^- + P_3 d_1^+ + P_4 d_3^-$$

$$\text{subject to} \quad
\begin{aligned}
X_1 + X_2 + d_1^- \qquad\quad - d_1^+ \qquad\quad &= 80 \\
X_1 \qquad\quad + d_2^- \qquad\quad - d_2^+ &= 100 \\
X_2 \qquad\quad + d_3^- \qquad\qquad &= 45 \\
X_1, X_2, d_1^-, d_2^-, d_3^-, d_1^+, d_2^+ &\geq 0
\end{aligned}$$

The graphical presentation of the model is shown in Figure 6.6.

Now, the first goal is to meet the sales goal of 100,000 yards of upholstery material ordered by the best customer. Therefore, the area of feasible solution will be on and above the straight line of $X_1 = 100$. The

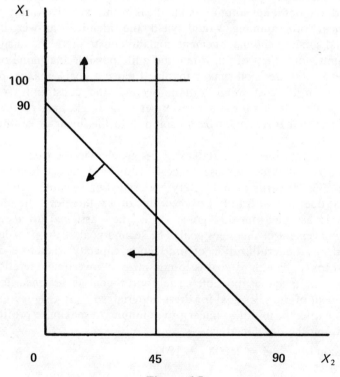

Figure 6.5
Graphical representation of the linear programming model

second goal is to minimize the underutilization of production capacity, which is set at 80 hours. By satisfying the first goal the second goal is automatically attained. The third goal is to minimize the overtime operation of the plant as much as possible. It is clear that in order to satisfy the first goal we have to run the plant 100 hours, an overtime operation of 20 hours. Hence, the third goal cannot be completely attained, but may be partially attained by moving X_2 to zero. Our last goal is to meet the sales goal for the dress material (i.e., $X_2 = 45$). The only way to meet this goal, however, is by providing more overtime hours for the plant. This implies that trying to attain the fourth goal sacrifices the third goal. Therefore this goal has to be ignored.

The goal programming solution of the problem is $X_1 = 100$ and $X_2 = 0$. At this point A, our first two important goals are satisfied; however, the third goal is not completely attained, and the last goal is not achieved at all. From this example, it should be clear that goal programming attempts to solve the problem by identifying the optimum

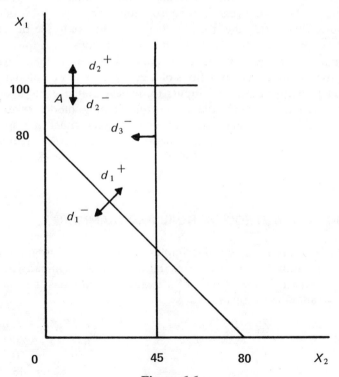

Figure 6.6
Graphical representation of the goal programming model

point according to specified environmental conditions and stated priority structures. However, linear programming could not be used even to attempt to solve the problem when there is no single area of feasible solution.

Some questions may be raised as to why the decision maker sets goals that are beyond the normal operating constraints. However, in reality management often sets such goals even when they are unattainable within the limits of normally available resources, for a variety of reasons. For example, such goals may be established to analyze additional resource requirements and improve the current position of the organization. Or they may be established in order to ensure that long-run goals are not obliterated by short-run objectives. It is also possible that such goals are established to provide incentive to the employees or to judge organizational performance. The point is that management does quite frequently establish goals that may not be attainable within the normal organizational capacity.

Thus far, we have discussed the graphical analysis of goal programming. The goal programming solution is not usually a one-shot procedure. Quite often the decision maker would like to see the change in the output according to various combinations of inputs. Goal programming is a very suitable technique for such sensitivity analysis. In fact, there are three basic functions of a goal programming model. First, the model identifies required inputs to achieve stated goals under the given conditions. Second, the goal programming model reveals the degree of goal attainment with the given inputs under the specified conditions. Third, but not least important, the model facilitates a simulation analysis of various combinations of inputs, constraints, and priority structures of goals.

THE SIMPLEX METHOD OF GOAL PROGRAMMING

The best way to explain the simplex method of goal programming is through an example. Thus, let us examine the textile company problem presented earlier. The president of a textile company has the following goal programming problem:

$$
\begin{aligned}
\text{Minimize} \quad & Z = P_1 d_1^- + P_2 d_4^+ + 5P_3 d_2^- + 3P_3 d_3^- + P_4 d_1^+ \\
\text{subject to} \quad & X_1 + X_2 + d_1^- \qquad\qquad\quad - d_1^+ \qquad = 80 \\
& X_1 \qquad\qquad + d_2^- \qquad\qquad\qquad\quad = 70 \\
& \qquad X_2 \qquad\quad + d_3^- \qquad\qquad\qquad = 45 \\
& X_1 + X_2 \qquad\qquad\quad + d_4^- \quad - d_4^+ = 90 \\
& X_1, X_2, d_1^-, d_2^-, d_3^-, d_4^-, d_1^+, d_4^+ \geq 0
\end{aligned}
$$

The reason we formulated the last constraint (minimization of overtime operation of the plant in excess of 10 hours) by using a decision variable was that we must have all constraints expressed in terms of decision variables in order to solve the problem by the graphical solution method. However, since we now utilize the simplex procedure, we can also solve the problem if the constraint is formulated as below:

$$d_1^+ + d_{11}^- - d_{11}^+ = 10$$

where

d_1^+ = overtime operation of the plant
d_{11}^- = difference between the actual overtime operation of the plant and 10 hours of overtime
d_{11}^+ = overtime operation of the plant in excess of 10 hours.

If we use the above constraint, of course, the second goal in the objective function should read $P_2 d_{11}^+$. Either model is perfectly acceptable for the simplex solution of the problem.

Before the first simplex tableau is presented for the above problem, there are several things we must consider.

First, in goal programming, the purpose of the objective function is to minimize the total unattained goals. This is achieved by minimizing the deviational variables through the use of certain preemptive priority factors or differential weights. There is no profit maximization or cost minimization per se in the objective function. Therefore, the preemptive factors and differential weights take the place of the C_j as used in linear programming.

Second, the objective function is expressed by assigning priority factors to certain variables. These preemptive priority factors are multidimensional, as they are ordinal rather than cardinal values; in other words, priority factors at different levels are not commensurable. This implies that the simplex criterion (Z_j or $Z_j - C_j$) cannot be expressed by a single row, as is done in the case of linear programming. Rather, the simplex criterion becomes a matrix of $m \times n$ size, where m represents the number of preemptive priority levels and n is the number of variables including both decision and deviational variables.

Third, since the simplex criterion is expressed as a matrix rather than a row, we must design a new procedure in identifying the key column. The relationship between the preemptive priority factors is $P_j >>> P_{j+1}$, which means P_j always takes priority over P_{j+1}. It is, therefore, clear that the selection procedure of the key column must consider the level of priorities.

Figure 6.7 presents the initial tableau of this goal programming problem. The basic assumption in formulating the initial tableau of goal programming is identical to that of linear programming. We assume that the initial solution is at the origin, where values of all the decision variables are zero. In the first constraint, therefore, the total operation hours of the plant are of course zero, since $X_1 = X_2 = 0$. Naturally, there cannot be any overtime operation of the plant $(d_1^+ = 0)$. Therefore, underutilization of the normal plant capacity (d_1^-) will be 80 hours. Hence, the variable d_1^- is entered in the solution base and the right-hand side (rhs) becomes 80. By the same token, d_2^- and d_3^- are also in the solution base. In the last constraint $(d_1^+ + d_{11}^- - d_{11}^+ = 10)$, since the plant is not in operation, d_1^+ has to be zero. Then, overtime operation of the plant in excess of 10 hours (d_{11}^+) must also be zero. Consequently, d_{11}^- takes the rhs value of 10, as shown in Figure 6.7. It is always the rule that in the initial tableau of goal programming, negative deviational variables (d_i^-) will appear in the solution base.

C_j						P_1	$5P_3$	$3P_3$		P_4	P_2
	v	rhs		X_1	X_2	d_1^-	d_2^-	d_3^-	d_{11}^-	d_1^+	d_{11}^+
P_1	d_1^-	80		1	1	1				−1	
$5P_3$	d_2^-	70		①			1				
$3P_3$	d_3^-	45		1				1			
	d_{11}^-	10							1	1	−1
$Z_j - C_j$	P_4	0								−1	
	P_3	485		5	3						
	P_2	0									−1
	P_1	80		1	1					−1	

Figure 6.7
Initial goal programming tableau

Now let us examine C_j. In goal programming C_j is represented by the preemptive priority factors and the differential weights as shown in the goal programming objective function. Most goal programming problems involve a large number of variables. For that reason, in order to make the table easier to read, empty spaces are left in the table where zero should appear.

The simplex criterion $(Z_j - C_j)$ is a 4×8 matrix because we have four priority levels and eight variables (2 decision, 6 deviational) in the model. The goal programming procedure first achieves the most important goal to the fullest possible extent and then considers the next-order goal, and so forth. It should be readily apparent that the selection of the key column should be based on the per unit contribution rate of each variable in achieving the most important goal. When the first goal is completely attained, then the key column selection criterion will be based on the achievement rate for the second goal, and so on. That is why we listed the preemptive priority factors from the lowest to the highest, so that the key column can be easily identified at the bottom of the table. To make the simplex table relatively simple, we have omitted the matrix of Z_j altogether. It requires a little more calculation this way but the simplified tableau is well worth that inconvenience.

The goal programming problem is a minimization problem. In the minimization problem of linear programming, the values in the rhs column of the simplex criterion represent the total cost of the solution. In goal programming those Z_j values ($P_4 = 0$, $P_3 = 485$, $P_2 = 0$, and $P_1 = 80$) in the rhs column represent the unattained portion of each goal. For example, in the initial tableau where the textile plant is not even in operation, the second and fourth goals are already completely attained. How could this be possible? Examining the objective function, we can find that the second goal is to minimize the overtime operation of the plant in excess of 10 hours and the fourth goal is to minimize the total overtime operation of the plant. It should be evident by now to the reader that since we are not even operating the plant at this point (at the origin), naturally there is no overtime operation. Consequently, we have already attained the second and fourth goals. The underachievement of the first goal is 80 because the underutilization of the normal plant operation capacity is 80 hours. For the third goal, the underachievement of the goal is 485. We remember that differential weights of 5 and 3 are assigned to the underachievement of sales goals for the upholstery and dress materials. Since these two goals are commensurable and are at the same preemptive priority level, this procedure is absolutely appropriate. However, it is not as easy to interpret the underachievement of 485 for the third goal as other unattained goals where no differential weights are assigned.

Now, let us examine the calculation of $Z_j - C_j$ in Figure 6.7. We have already noted that the C_j values represent the priority factors assigned to deviational variables and the Z_j values are the sum of the C_j times the rhs (or coefficients). Thus, the Z_j value in the X_1 column will be $(P_1 \times 1 + 5P_3 \times 1)$, or $P_1 + 5P_3$. The C_j value in the X_1 column is zero as shown by the blank in the C_j row. Therefore, $Z_j - C_j$ for the X_1 column is $P_1 + 5P_3$. Since P_1 and P_3 are not commensurable, we must list them separately in the P_1 and P_3 rows in the simplex criterion $(Z_j - C_j)$. Consequently, the $Z_j - C_j$ value will be 1 at the P_1 row and 5 at the P_3 row in the X_1 column. By employing the same procedure, $Z_j - C_j$ for the X_2 column can be derived. It will be $(P_1 \times 1 + 3P_3 \times 1) - 0$, or $P_1 + 3P_3$. For the following three columns, d_1^-, d_2^-, and d_3^-, $Z_j - C_j$ will be zero, since the Z_j values are identical to the respective C_j values.

For the d_{11}^- column $Z_j - C_j$ is zero because Z_j and C_j are both zero. For the d_1^+ column, we can easily calculate the Z_j value of $-P_1$ from the table. Since the C_j value of the column is P_4, $Z_j - C_j$ will be $-P_1 - P_4$. Therefore, -1 is listed at the P_1 row and also at the P_4 row in the column. The last column, d_{11}^+, indicates zero Z_j. However, its C_j value is P_2. Thus, $Z_j - C_j$ for the column becomes $-P_2$. Accordingly, we list -1 at the P_2 row for the d_{11}^+ column.

As mentioned earlier, we have combined the calculational procedure for identifying Z_j and $Z_j - C_j$ values in the modified simplex tableau. The procedure requires more calculations in our heads, but it certainly makes the tableau simpler to handle. It is especially true if the problem under consideration is a very complex one. For example, if a problem containing 5 preemptive priorities and 25 variables is being analyzed, we can save the 5×25 matrix by calculating $Z_j - C_j$ in one shot.

Now, let us move on to selection of the key column and key row. The criterion used to determine the key column is the rate of contribution of each variable in achieving the most important goal (P_1). In other words, the column with the largest positive value at the P_1 level in $Z_j - C_j$ will be selected as the key column. In Figure 6.7, there are two identical positive values in the X_1 and X_2 columns. In order to break this tie, we check the next-lower priority levels. Since there is a greater value in the X_1 column at the P_3 level as compared to the X_2 column, we select X_1 as the key column. The key row is the row that has the minimum nonnegative value when we divide the rhs constants by the coefficients in the key column. The coefficient of 1 is circled in Figure 6.7 to indicate that it is at the intersection of the key column and the key row. By entering X_1 into the solution base, the underutilization of the regular plant capacity and the underachievement of sales goal for the upholstery material will be affected. This is clear from an observation of coefficients existing in the d_1^- and d_2^- rows.

By utilizing the regular simplex procedure of linear programming, the first tableau is revised to obtain the second tableau, as shown in Figure 6.8. The plant is in operation for 70 hours in order to produce 70,000 yards of upholstery material. Therefore, the underutilization of regular plant capacity is now 10 hours, as shown by the rhs value in the d_1^- row. We have also completely achieved the sales goal for upholstery material, and therefore d_2^- has been removed from the solution base. The calculation of new coefficients in goal programming is usually easier than in linear programming because in goal programming there are many coefficients with unit (1) value. In the d_3^- and d_{11}^- rows in Figure 6.8, the coefficients will remain exactly as they were in Figure 6.7. This is because the intersectional elements, that is, the elements at the intersection of the key column and each row in question, are zero.

C_j					P_1	$5P_3$	$3P_3$		P_4	P_2
	v	rhs	X_1	X_2	d_1^-	d_2^-	d_3^-	d_{11}^-	d_1^+	d_{11}^+
P_1	d_1^-	10		①	1	−1			−1	
	X_1	70	1			1				
$3P_3$	d_3^-	45		1			1			
	d_{11}^-	10						1	1	−1
Z_j-C_j — P_4		0							−1	
P_3		135		3		−5				
P_2		0								−1
P_1		10		1		−1			−1	

Figure 6.8
Second goal programming tableau

Calculating the new values for the key row (X_1) is achieved by dividing old row values by the pivot element of 1. The only row where some additional calculation is required is the d_1^- row, but this is also relatively easy, since there are no complex fractions involved.

Let us examine Figure 6.8 more closely. The Z_j values in the rhs column ($P_4=0$, $P_3=135$, $2=0$, $P_1=10$) indicate that the unattained portion of the first goal has decreased considerably, 70 to be exact. This is a good sign because the goal programming model is a minimization problem and the value of Z_j should decrease at each step toward the optimum point. As our immediate concern is the achievement of the most important goal, we should simply examine whether Z_j has decreased at the P_1 level at the end of each step. When Z_j at the P_1 level is completely minimized to zero, our attention should then be focused on the Z_j value at the P_2 level, and so on. In Figure 6.8, Z_j at the P_3 level has also decreased by the amount of 350, as the production of 70,000 yards of the upholstery material automatically enables the achievement of the sales goal for the upholstery material.

The key column is identified as X_2 in Figure 6.8. The key row of d_1^- is determined by the usual procedure. The best way to achieve the most important goal completely is by producing 10,000 yards of dress material. The production of 70,000 yards of upholstery and 10,000 yards of dress material will require 80 hours of plant operation.

Figure 6.9 presents the third-stage solution. The solution indicates that production of 70,000 yards of upholstery and 10,000 yards of dress materials is sufficient to achieve the first, second, and fourth goals. However, the third goal is not completely attained, since the sales goal of dress material is still 35,000 yards short of complete attainment; d_3^- of 35 shown in the solution base indicates this. As there is no further goal attainment required at the P_1 and P_2 levels, all coefficients in the $Z_j - C_j$ are either zero or negative, as shown in the table.

The selection of the key column should be determined at the P_3 level. The d_1^+ column is obviously the key column as the only positive value at the P_3 level of $Z_j - C_j$ is in this column. The key row is d_{11}^-. The procedure is both rational and sensible. It employs overtime operation of the plant to attain the third goal to a greater extent. Since we assigned the fourth priority factor to the minimization of overtime operation of the plant, in essence we are attaining the third goal at the expense of the fourth goal.

Figure 6.10 presents the optimum solution to the problem. It is optimum in the sense that this solution enables the decision maker to attain his goals as closely as possible within the given decision constraints and priority structure. Note the decrease of the Z_j value at

C_j			P_1	$5P_3$	$3P_3$			P_4		P_2
	v	rhs	X_1	X_2	d_1^-	d_2^-	d_3^-	d_{11}^-	d_1^+	d_{11}^+
	X_2	10		1	1	−1			−1	
	X_1	70	1			1				
$3P_3$	d_3^-	35			−1	1	1		1	
	d_{11}^-	10						1	①	−1
	P_4	0							−1	
$Z_j - C_j$	P_3	100			−3	−2			3	
	P_2	0								−1
	P_1	0			−1					

Figure 6.9
Third goal programming tableau

the P_3 level from 100 to 75. In order to decrease the underachievement of the third goal we sacrificed the complete attainment of the fourth goal by 10 units, as shown at the P_4 level. The optimum solution is $X_1 = 70, X_2 = 20, d_1^+ = 10, d_3^- = 25$. In other words, the company should produce 70,000 yards of upholstery material and 20,000 yards of dress material with 10 hours of overtime operation of the plant, resulting in 25,000 yards of underachievement in the sales goal of the dress material. With this solution the president of the firm is able to attain his two most important goals completely, and the next two goals as completely as possible under the given constraints.

In Figure 6.10, since the third goal is not completely attained, there is a positive value in $Z_j - C_j$ at the P_3 level. We find it (3) in the d_{11}^+ column. Obviously, we can attain the third goal to a greater extent if we introduce d_{11}^+ in the solution. We find, however, a negative value (-1)

C_j			P_1	$5P_3$	$3P_3$				P_4	P_2
	v	rhs	X_1	X_2	d_1^-	d_2^-	d_3^-	d_{11}^-	d_1^+	d_{11}^+
	X_2	20		1	1	−1		1		−1
	X_1	70	1			1				
$3P_3$	d_3^-	25			−1	1	1	−1		1
P_4	d_1^+	10						1	1	−1
$Z_j - C_j$	P_4	10						1		−1
	P_3	75	−3	−2				−3		3
	P_2	0								−1
	P_1	0	−1							

Figure 6.10
Optimum solution of the goal programming model

at a higher priority level, that is, at the P_2 level. This implies that if we introduce d_{11}^+, we would improve achievement of the third goal at the expense of achieving the second goal. Thus, we cannot introduce d_{11}^+ into the solution. The same logic applies to the d_{11}^- column, where we find a positive value at the P_4 level. The rule is that if there is a positive element at a lower priority level in $Z_j - C_j$, the variable in that column cannot be introduced into the solution as long as there is a negative element at a higher priority level.

There is one more bit of analysis that we can derive from Figure 6.10. From an analysis of the $Z_j - C_j$ values we can point out where conflict exists among the goals. Conflict exists between the second and third goals in column d_{11}^+, and between the third and fourth goals in column d_{11}^-. Now the decision maker can precisely determine how he must rearrange the priority structure if the underachieved goals at the lower levels are to be completely attained. This process provides the decision maker an opportunity to evaluate the soundness of his priority structure for the goals. Furthermore, from an analysis of the coefficients in the main body of the table the decision maker can identify the exact trade-offs between goals. For example, in Figure 6.10 we can see that if we introduce 25 units of d_{11}^+ into the solution, the third goal will be completely attained. However, this procedure will "undo" the second goal by the same quantity. The marginal substitution rate in this case is one to one. The same type of conflict exists between the third and fourth goals, as the coefficients of the d_3^- and d_1^+ rows in the d_{11}^- column indicate. An analysis of the final solution table provides a great deal of information and insight about the decision environment and the decision maker's priority structure of goals.

STEPS OF THE SIMPLEX METHOD OF GOAL PROGRAMMING

Now that we have illustrated how to solve a goal programming problem by the modified simplex method, we can summarize the solution steps to aid in future solutions:

Set up the Initial Tableau from the Goal Programming Model

We assume that the initial solution is at the origin. Therefore, all the negative deviational variables in the model constraints should enter the solution base initially. List the rhs values and the coefficients of all variables in the main body of the table. Also list the preemptive priority factors and differential weights to the appropriate variables by examining the objective function. In the simplex criterion $(Z_j - C_j)$, list priority levels in the v column from the lowest at the top to the highest at the bottom. The Z_j values must be calculated and recorded in the rhs column. The last step is to calculate $Z_j - C_j$ values for each column starting from the first decision variable to the last positive deviational variable.

Determine the New Entering Variable

This step is identical to the identification of the key column. First, we find the highest priority level that has not been completely attained by examining the $Z_j - C_j$ values in the rhs column. When the priority level is determined, we proceed to identify the variable column that has the largest positive $Z_j - C_j$ value. The variable in that column will enter the solution base in the next iteration. If there is a tie between the largest positive values in $Z_j - C_j$ at the highest priority level, check the next lower priority levels and select the column that has a greater value at the lower priority level. If the tie cannot be broken, choose one on an arbitrary basis. The other column will be chosen in subsequent iterations.

Determine the Outgoing Variable from the Solution Base

This process is identical to finding the key row. Calculate the value of the rhs constant divided by the coefficients in the key column. Select the row that has the minimum nonnegative value. The variable in that row will be replaced by the variable in the key column in the next iteration. If there exists a tie when constants are divided by coefficients, find the row that has the variable with the higher priority factor. This procedure enables the attainment of higher-order goals first, and thereby reduces the number of iterations.

Determine the New Basic Feasible Solution

First, find the new rhs and coefficients of the key row by dividing old values by the pivot element, that is, the element at the intersection of the key row and the key column. Second, find the new values for all other rows by using the calculation procedure [old value − (intersectional element of that row × new value in the key row in the same column)]. Now, complete the table by finding Z_j and $Z_j - C_j$ values for the priority rows.

Determine Whether the Solution is Optimal

First, analyze the goal attainment level of each goal by checking the Z_j value in the rhs column for each priority row. If the Z_j values are all zero, this is the optimal solution. Second, if there exists a positive value of Z_j, examine the $Z_j - C_j$ coefficients for that row. If there are positive $Z_j - C_j$ values in the row, determine whether there are negative $Z_j - C_j$ values at a higher priority level in the same column. If there are negative values, the solution is optimum. Third, if there exists a positive $Z_j - C_j$ value at a certain priority level and there is no negative $Z_j - C_j$ value at a higher priority level in the same column, this is not the optimum solution. Therefore, return to Step 2 and continue. Figure 6.11 illustrates the simplex solution procedure for goal programming problems.

APPLICATION AREAS OF GOAL PROGRAMMING

An important property of goal programming is its capability to handle managerial problems that involve multiple incompatible goals according to the assigned importance of the goals. If management is

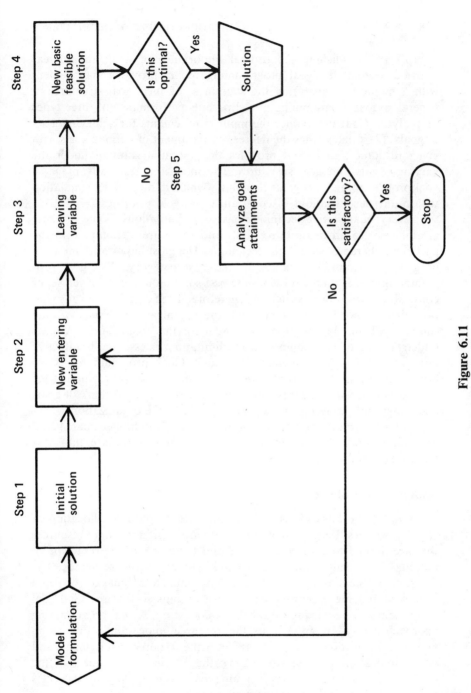

Figure 6.11
Flowchart of the simplex procedure of goal programming

capable of establishing the ordinal importance of goals in a linear decision system, the goal programming model provides management with a method of analyzing the soundness of their goal structure. In general, a goal programming model permits performance of three types of analysis: (1) It determines the input requirements for achieving a set of goals; (2) it determines the degree of attainment of defined goals with given resources; and (3) it provides the optimum solution under the varying inputs and goal structures. The most important advantage of goal programming is its great flexibility, which allows model simulation with numerous variations of constraints and goal priorities.

Every quantitative technique has some limitations. Some of these are inherent to all quantitative tools and some are attributable to the particular characteristics of the technique. The most important limitation of goal programming belongs to the first category. The goal programming model simply provides the best solution under the given set of constraints and priority structure. Therefore, if the decision maker's goal priorities are not in accordance with the organizational objectives, the solution will not be the global optimum for the organization. A clear understanding of its assumptions and limitations is essential to effective application of any mathematical model. Goal programming is no exception to this prerequisite. The application of goal programming for managerial decision analysis forces the decision maker to think of goals and constraints in terms of their importance to the organization.

Goal programming can be applied to almost unlimited managerial and administrative decision areas. The following three are the most readily applicable areas of goal programming.

Allocation Problems

One of the basic decision problems is the optimum allocation of scarce resources. Let us assume that there are n different input resources that are limited to certain quantities and there are m different type of outputs that result from various combinations of the resources. The decision problem is to determine the optimum combination of input resources to achieve certain goals set for outputs so that the total goal attainment can be maximized for the organization. A goal programming approach has been applied to the resource allocation problems in nonprofit institutions. The study analyzes the resource requirements and actual allocation in order to achieve the administrative goals of the organization. Also, goal programming has been applied to the sales effort allocation problem in the marketing area.

Planning and Scheduling Problems

Many decision problems involve some degree of planning and/or scheduling. In order to achieve certain goals in the future, decisions must be made concerning present and future actions to be taken. To accomplish desired outputs, the optimum combination of inputs in a certain time period must be identified. These inputs may include manpower, materials, time, production capacity, technology, and the like. Many problems such as production scheduling, location determination, financial planning, personnel planning, and marketing strategy planning, can be analyzed by goal programming.

Policy Analysis

For government agencies and nonprofit organizations, the basic decision problem involves the assignment of priorities to various goals and development of programs to achieve these goals. Such a decision process constitutes the policy analysis of the organization. Through the application of goal programming the organization is able to ascertain the soundness of its policies, input requirements for the achievement of set goals, and the degree of goal attainment with the given resources. This review and evaluation process is an integral part of policy analysis. Therefore, goal programming is particularly well suited for decision analysis in public and nonprofit organizations.

Here we have discussed but three apparent application areas of goal programming. No single list could possibly exhaust all the potential application fields of goal programming. Goal programming can be utilized in those areas where linear programming has been extensively applied. The real value of goal programming is realized for complex linear decision problems that involve multiple incompatible goals in multiple dimensions.

COMPUTER-BASED ANALYSIS OF GOAL PROGRAMMING

For any decision science technique to be a truly valuable tool for decision analysis, it must accommodate itself to a computer-based solution. The complexity of real-world problems usually compels the use of computers. Many simple hypothetical problems being discussed and taught in classrooms exist only in textbooks. This by no means suggests that simple examples are of no value. Actually, they provide the foundation for understanding complex concepts of various decision science techniques. Nevertheless, in order to apply a technique to practical problems, which is indeed the very purpose of decision science training, computer-based analysis is usually required.

In order for goal programming to be a useful decision science technique for decision analysis, a computer-based solution is an essential requirement. Appendix III presents a computer-based solution procedure of goal programming.

CONCLUSION

Virtually all models developed for managerial decision analysis have neglected or often ignored the unique organizational environment, bureaucratic decision process, and multiple conflicting nature of organizational objectives. However, in reality these are important factors that greatly influence the decision process. In this chapter the goal programming approach is presented as a tool for the optimization of multiple objectives while permitting an explicit consideration of the existing decision environment.

Developing and solving the goal programming model points out where some goals cannot be achieved under the desired policy and, hence, where trade off must occur due to limited resources. Furthermore, the model allows the decision maker to review critically the priority structure in view of the solution derived by the model.

The goal programming approach is not the ultimate solution for all managerial decision problems. It requires that the decision maker be capable of defining, quantifying, and ordering objectives. The goal programming model simply provides the best solution under the given constraints and priority structure of goals. Therefore, some research questions concerning the identification, definition, and ranking of goals still remain.

REFERENCES

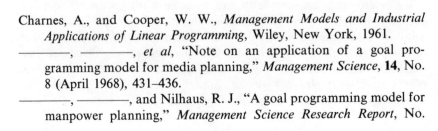

Charnes, A., and Cooper, W. W., *Management Models and Industrial Applications of Linear Programming*, Wiley, New York, 1961.

————, ————, *et al*, "Note on an application of a goal programming model for media planning," *Management Science*, **14**, No. 8 (April 1968), 431–436.

————, ————, and Nilhaus, R. J., "A goal programming model for manpower planning," *Management Science Research Report*, No.

115 (Also see No. 188), Carnegie-Mellon University (August 1968).

Courtney, J., Klastorian, T., and Ruefli, T., "A goal programming approach to urban-suburban location preferences," *Management Science*, **18**, No. 6 (Feb. 1972), 258–268.

Ijiri, Y., *Management Goals and Accounting for Control*, Rand-McNally, Chicago, 1965.

Lee, Sang M., *Goal Programming for Decision Analysis*, Auerbach, Philadelphia, 1972.

————, "Goal programming for decision analysis of multiple objectives," *Sloan Management Review*, **14**, No. 2 (1973), 11–24.

————, "Decision analysis through goal programming," *Decision Sciences* **2**, No. 2 (April 1971), 172–180.

————, and Bird, M., "A goal programming model for sales effort allocation," *Business Perspectives*, **6**, No. 4 (Summer 1970), 17–21. Also published in William C. House (ed.), *Operations Research: An Introduction to Modern Applications*, Auerbach, Princeton, N.J., 1972; and Bruce Gunn (ed.), *Marketing Systems: A Dynamic Synthesis Approach*, Holden-Day, San Francisco, forthcoming.

————, and Clayton, E. R., "A goal programming model for Academic resource allocation," *Management Science*, **18**, No. 8 (April 1972), 395-408.

————, and Jaaskelainen, V., "Goal programming: management's math model," *Industrial Engineering*, (January 1971), 30-35.

————, Lerro A., and McGinnis, B., "Optimization of tax switching for commercial banks," *Journal of Money, Credit and Banking* **3**, No. 2 (May 1971), 293-303.

————, and Nicely, R., "Goal programming for marketing decisions: a case study," *Journal of Marketing*, **38**, No. 1 (January 1974), 24-32.

————, and Sevebeck, W., "An aggregative model for municipal economic planning," *Policy Sciences* **2**, No. 2 (June 1971), 99-115.

PROBLEMS

1. The manufacturing plant of an electronics firm produces two types of television sets, color and black-and-white. According to past experience, production of either a color or a black-and-white set requires an average of 1 hour in the plant. The plant has a normal production capacity of 40 hours a week. The marketing department reports that, because of limited sales opportunity, the *maximum* number of color and black-and-white sets that can be sold are 24 and 30, respectively, for the week. The gross margin from the sale of a color set is $80,

whereas it is $40 from a black-and-white set. The president of the company has set the following goals, arranged in the order of their importance to the organization:

I.   Avoid any underutilization of normal production capacity (no layoffs of production workers).
II. Sell as many television sets as possible. Since the gross margin from the sale of a color television set is twice the amount from a black-and-white set, he has twice as much desire to achieve sales for color sets as for black-and-white sets.
III. Minimize the overtime operation of the plant as much as possible.

(a) Formulate a goal programming model for the above problem.
(b) Solve the problem by using the graphical method of goal programming.

2. The manager of the only record shop in a college town has a decision problem that involves multiple goals. The record shop employs five full-time and four part-time salesmen. The normal working hours per month for a full-time salesman are 160, and for a part-time salesman, 80 hours per month. According to performance records of the salesmen, the average sales have been five records per hour for full-time salesmen and two records per hour for part-time salesmen. The average hourly wage rates are $3 for full-time salesmen and $2 for part-time salesmen. Average profit from the sale of a record is $1.50. In view of past sales records and increased enrollment at the college, the manager feels that the sales goal for the next month should be 5500 records. Since the shop is open six days a week, overtime is often required of salesmen (not necessarily overtime but extra hours for the part-time salesmen). The manager believes that a good employer-employee relationship is an essential factor of business success. Therefore, he feels that a stable employment level with occasional overtime requirement is a better practice than an unstable employment level with no overtime. However, he feels that overtime of more than 100 hours among the full-time salesmen should be avoided because of the declining sales effectiveness caused by fatigue. The manager has set the following goals:

I.   Achieve a sales goal of 5500 records for the next month.
II. Limit the overtime of full-time salesmen to 100 hours.
III. Provide job security to salesmen. The manager feels that full utilization of employees' regular working hours (no layoffs)

is an important factor for a good employer-employee relationship. However, he is twice as concerned with the full utilization of full-time salesmen as with the full utilization of part-time salesmen.

IV. Minimize the sum of overtime for both full-time and part-time salesmen. The manager desires to assign differential weights to the minimization of overtime according to the net marginal profit ratio between the full-time and part-time salesmen.

Formulate a goal programming model for the above problem and Solve it by the graphical method of goal programming.

3. American Computer Hardwares, Inc., produces three different types of computers: Epic, Galaxie, and Utopia. The production of all computers is conducted in a complex and modern assembly line. The production of an Epic requires 5 hours in the assembly line, a Galaxie requires 8 hours, and a Utopia requires 12 hours. The normal operation hours of the assembly line are 170 per month. The marketing and accounting departments have estimated that profits per unit for the three types of computers are $100,000 for the Epic, $144,000 for the Galaxie, and $252,000 for the Utopia. The marketing department further reports that the demand is such that the firm can expect to sell all the computers it produces in the month. The president of the firm has established the following goals, listed according to their importance:

I. Avoid underutilization of capacity in terms of regular hours of operation of the assembly line.

II. Meet the demand of the northeastern sales district for five Epics, five Galaxies, and eight Utopias (differential weights should be assigned according to the net profit ratios among the three types of computers).

III. Limit overtime operation of the assembly line to 20 hours.

IV. Meet the sales goal for each type of computer: Epic, 10; Galaxie, 12; and Utopia, 10 (again assign weights according to the relative profit function for each computer).

V. Minimize the total overtime operation of the assembly line.

(a) Formulate a goal programming model for the above problem.
(b) Solve the problem through two iterations (three tableaus) by the simplex method of goal programming.

4. A production manager faces the problem of job allocation between his two teams. The processing rate of the first team is 5 units per hour and the processing rate of the second team is 6 units per hour. The normal working hours for both teams are 8 hours per day. The production manager has the following goals for the next day, arranged in order of importance:

    I.   The manager wants to avoid any underachievement of the production level, which is set at 120 units of product.

    II. Any overtime operation of team 2 beyond 3 hours should be avoided.

    III. The sum of overtime should be minimized (assign differential weights according to the relative cost of overtime hours—assume that the operating cost of the two teams is identical).

    IV. Any underutilization of regular working hours should be avoided (again assign weights according to the relative productivity of the two teams).

(a) Formulate a goal programming model for the above problem.
(b) Solve the problem by the graphical method.
(c) Solve the problem by the simplex method.

5. Modern Fashions, Inc., produces two types of ladies' bathing suits: regular and bikini. The production of all bathing suits is done in a modern sewing center. A regular bathing suit requires an average of 5 minutes and a bikini requires an average 8 minutes in the sewing center. The normal operation hours of the center are, by running two shifts, 80 hours per week. The unit profits for the bathing suits are: regular, $2.00, bikini, $2.50. The president of the company wishes to achieve the following goals, listed in order of importance:

    I.   Achieve the profit goal of $2000 for the week.

    II. Limit the overtime operation of the sewing center to 8 hours.

    III. Meet the sales goal for each type of bathing suit: regular, 500; bikini, 400.

    IV. Avoid any underutilization of regular operation hours of the sewing center.

(a) Formulate a goal programming model from the above problem.
(b) What will be the change in the objective function if the president decides to achieve the sales goal *exactly* as stated?
(c) Solve the original problem (ignore b) by the graphical method.

(d) Solve the original problem through one iteration using the simplex method.

6. Lee Electronics produces two types of radios: AM and FM. According to past experience, production of either type of radio requires an average of 1 hour in the plant. The plant has a normal production capacity of 40 hours a week. The marketing department reports that because of the limited sales force, the *maximum* number of AM and FM radios that can be sold are 24 and 28, respectively, for the week. The unit profits are: AM, $15; FM, $10. The president of the company has set the following multiple goals, listed in theorder of their importance:

   I.   Avoid any underutilization of normal production capacity.
   II. Achieve the sales goals of 24 AM and 28 FM radios (assign differential weights according to the unit profits).
   III. Minimize the overtime operation of the plant as much as possible.

   (a) In the above problem, if the president of the firm had only a single goal of profit maximization *within the normal production capacity and sales constraints*, how would you set up a goal programming model?
   (b) Formulate a goal programming model for the above problem and solve it by the simplex method.

7. Glory Furniture, Inc., produces three products: tables, chairs, and desks. The production process takes place in two machine centers. For the production of the next week, the company has secured 240 man-hours in machine center 1 and 180 man-hours in machine center 2. To produce a table it requires 10 minutes in machine center 1 and 15 minutes in machine center 2; a chair requires 5 minutes in machine center 1 and 8 minutes in machine center 2; and a desk takes 20 minutes in machine center 1 and 12 minutes in machine center 2. The marketing department reports that the estimated sales for the coming week are: tables, 350; chairs, 700; and desks, 500. The president of the company has listed the following goals in order of priority:

   I. Avoid underutilization of production capacities in the two machine centers (no differential weights).
   II. Limit overtime operation of machine center 1 to 10 hours and overtime of machine center 2 to 15 hours (no differential weights).

    III. Achieve the estimated sales (no differential weights).
    IV. Minimize overtime operation of the two machine centers (no differential weights).

    Formulate a goal programming model for the above problem.

8. American Electronics, Inc., produces the most sophisticated color television sets. The company has two production lines. The production rate of line 1 is 2 sets per hour, whereas it is $1\frac{1}{2}$ sets per hour in line 2. The regular production capacity is 40 hours a week for both lines. The expected profit from an average color television set is $100. The top management of the firm has the following goals for the week (in ordinal ranking):

    I.   Meet the production goal of 180 sets for the week.
    II. Limit the overtime of line 1 to 10 hours.
    III. Avoid the underutilization of regular working hours for both lines (assign differential weights according to the production rate of each line).
    IV. Limit the sum of overtime operation for both lines. (Assign weights according to the relative cost of overtime hour. Let us assume that the cost of operation is identical for the two production lines).

    (a) Formulate the above problem as a goal programming model.
    (b) If the top management desires to put the profit goal of $19,000 for the week as the top priority goal above the stated four goals, how would the model be changed?
    (c) If top management has only the one goal of profit maximization subject to the regular production capacity for both lines, how would the goal programming model be formulated?

9. Colonial Furnitures, Inc., produces three products; desks, tables, and chairs. All furniture is produced in the central plant. To produce a desk requires 3 hours in the plant, a table takes 2 hours, and a chair requires only 1 hour. The regular plant capacity is 40 hours a week. According to the marketing department, the maximum number of desks, tables, and chairs that can be sold are 10, 10, and 12, respectively. The president of the firm has established the following goals according to their importance:

    I. Avoid any underutilization of production capacity.
    II. Meet the order of the Gatewood store for seven desks and five chairs.

III. Avoid overtime operation of the plant beyond 10 hours.

IV. Achieve the sales goals of 10 desks, 10 tables, and 12 chairs.

V. Minimize the overtime operation as much as possible.

(a) Formulate a goal programming model for the problem.

(b) Solve the problem through two iterations (three tableaus) by the simplex method.

10. Midwestern Foods, Inc., specializes in the sale of wheat. The firm has definite information concerning the cost at which it can buy and the price at which it can sell the wheat in the next four months. The sale of wheat is restricted by the storage capacity of the firm. The normal capacity of the firm's storage facility is 3000 bushels (overloading of 2000 is allowed in emergencies). The estimated cost c_i and the price P_i during the next four months are given as follows:

Months	1	2	3	4
Cost (c_i)	\$4	\$4	\$4	\$7
Price (P_i)	6	7	5	6

The quantity of the purchase is assumed to be entirely based upon the revenue generated from sales. It is also assumed that sales are made at the beginning of the month, followed by purchases. At the beginning of the first month there are 2000 bushels of wheat in the warehouse. The president of the firm has the following multiple goals, listed in ordinal importance with respect to what he desires to achieve in the next four months:

I. In the first month, only the normal capacity of the warehouse should be used.

II. The firm should have at least \$20,000 at the beginning of the fourth month for purchases.

III. The firm should reserve at least \$2000 for emergency purposes in each month.

IV. The firm should maximize total profit during the entire four-month period.

Formulate a goal programming model for the above problem.

11. Your grandfather has just left you \$1 million. You plan to invest this money in four alternative plans: stocks, bonds, savings and loan, and real estate. Investments in stocks and bonds are available at the beginning of each of the next six years. Each dollar invested in stocks at the beginning of each year returns an average of \$1.20 (a profit of \$.20) two years later, in time for immediate reinvestment. Each dollar

invested in bonds at the beginning of one year returns $1.50 three years later for possible reinvestment. Each dollar invested in the savings and loan association returns $2.00 ($1.00 profit) five years later. You can invest in savings and loan only at the beginning of the second year. The investment opportunity in real estate is available only at the beginning of the fifth year. It returns $1.75 ($.75 profit) two years later. Any money not in use can be put on the regular passbook savings at an interest rate of 5 percent. You have established the following goals, in order of importance:

I.   Minimize the risk by diversifying the investment. No more than 35 percent of the total investment should be put into one investment plan.

II. Since real estate is such an attractive plan, try to invest at least $250,000 in this plan.

III. Make sure that at least $50,000 is available for float account (it can be in the passbook savings) at all times.

IV. You are planning to get married at the end of the third year. You wish to have at least $200,000 to show off to your bride (not to spend but for immediate reinvestment).

V.   Maximize the amount of money (cash) you have at the end of the sixth year.

Formulate a goal programming model that will determine the amount of money to be invested in various investment plans at different time periods.

12. The Blacksburg Men's Store, which is a branch of a larger store in a nearby city, specializes in sales of quality men's clothing. Presently the store is operating with the full-time manager, who works on salary, and eight part-time salesemen, who earn an hourly wage of $1.40 plus a 20 percent discount on any clothes they purchase in the store. Among the part-time salesmen, four are experienced in selling men's clothing and the others are new to the job.

Each month the store receives a sales quota. The manager breaks it down into his quota and the quota for his part-time salesmen as a group. For the next month the store has received a quota of $25,000. The manager has allotted $13,000 for himself and $12,000 for the part-time team. From records of past experience, the manager sells an average of $54.40 worth of clothing per hour. The group of four experienced part-time salesmen sell an average of $32.25 per hour and the group of inexperienced salesmen sell an average of $26.25 per hour.

The manager's regular working schedule per month has been 188 hours, and for each part-time salesman it has been 50 hours. The manager realizes, however, that he has to put in many extra hours to meet the monthly quotas. He would like to limit his overtime hours to 44, so that his part-time salesmen get enough hours to meet their quota and to earn the money they desire.

As an incentive to the manager and other employees, the main store offers them bonus and commission plans. The manager receives 3 percent bonus on the total sales volume that the store achieves above its sales quota for each month. The manager's objective is to earn an average $50 per month from this bonus plan. The part-time salesmen receive a 5 percent commission on all sales that they make over their quota. The bonus is then split equally among the salesmen. The manager feels that if part-time salesmen put forth some effort, they should be able to earn about $10 each in commission per month.

The manager's goals are listed below in ordinal ranking of importance:

I. The store must meet its sales quota for the month of $25,000.

II. The manager desires to meet his sales quota of the month of $13,000.

III. The manager would like to limit his overtime to 44 hours for the month.

IV. The part-time salesmen must meet their group sales quota for the month of $12,000.

V. The manager wants the part-time salesmen to work at least 400 hours for the month.

VI. The manager would like to earn $50 in bonus. He would also like to see his part-time salesmen earn a commission of $10 each.

VII. If possible, the manager would like to work no more than 188 hours for the month.

VIII. He wants to minimize the total extra hours that part-time salesmen work in the month.

Formulate a goal programming model for the above problem.

13. A state-supported university faces the problem of admission planning for the coming academic year. The primary problem results from multiple conflicting goals of the institution concerning the desired student body. The university administration has had a long-standing policy that requires that at least 80 percent of the entering new

students meet the state residence requirement (i.e., be in-state students). Another important criterion for granting admission is the applicant's college board examination scores and his rank in his high school graduating class. Past college work and records are evaluated to determine the eligibility of transferring and readmitted students. The university estimates that the number of eligible applicants for the coming year are:

	In-State	*Out-of-State*
Freshmen men	2400	1500
Freshmen women	1000	500
Transfer men	400	300
Transfer women	225	75
Readmitted men	250	50
Readmitted women	50	20

The university has an enormous investment in its physical facilities. The institution also supports a large number of faculty, administrative, and staff members to operate the total university system. The volume of these two activities is largely determined by the number of students attending the university. A wide fluctuation in either direction from the projected enrollment needed to support these facilities and personnel will result in either overcrowding of the facilities and overworking the personnel, or underutilization of the facilities and laying off of personnel. With these considerations in mind, the university has projected that between 3000 and 4500 new students must be admitted if the correct level of operation is to be maintained. The university has made an effort to develop long-range projections concerning the classes of students to be admitted during each academic year. These projections apply primarily to the admission of males against females and the admission of freshmen against transfers. These ratios determine the long-term growth patterns of the university. During the academic year under consideration, the university has decided that it must not admit more than 1000 new women students. The university receives many more applications for admission from women than it can possibly accept.

In addition to the male-female ratio, the university must also consider the ratio between freshmen and transfers in the entering group of new students. While the university receives a large number of applications from students desiring to transfer from other institutions, the number of transfers must be limited. For the coming year, the university believes that it can admit no more than 600 transfer students. The university maintains a large number of on-campus residence halls for undergraduate students. These facilities are self-supporting, with the residents paying the cost of retiring the bonded debt plus the normal operating expenses. With no outside funds coming into the system to cover operating deficits, the system must not lose money. Thus it is most important to achieve the desired level of occupancy. In order to achieve the optimum level for the coming year, the university must admit 3500 new students (1100 females and 2400 males). The actual numbers of students can exceed these estimates by 3 percent or be 1.5 percent lower without causing serious overcrowding or revenue loss. The various classes of students tend to choose to live in the residence halls in different proportions. Generally, the university requires all freshmen and sophomore men to reside on campus and all women under the age of 21 to live on campus. With this in mind, the following percentages of students choose to live in the university residence halls.

	Men	Women
Freshmen	100%	100%
Transfers	60	90
Readmitted	30	60

The director of admissions lists the following goals for admission planning in the rank of importance:

I.   At least 80 percent of the total number of new students must meet the state residence requirement.
II. Avoid lowering the university admission standards.
III. Avoid residence hall occupancy less than 98.5 percent of capacity.
IV. Avoid underutilization of the physical facilities.
V.   Avoid overadmission of women.
VI. Avoid overutilization of physical facilities.
VII. Avoid occupancy of the residence halls beyond 103 percent of capacity.
VIII. Avoid overutilization of admission of transfer students.

(a) Solve the above goal programming problem using the computer program. Determine the number of students in each of the following classifications, for both in state and out-of-state students, and discuss the goal attainment: freshmen men, freshmen women, transfer men, transfer women, readmitted men, and readmitted women.

(b) The director of admissions has decided to introduce an additional goal, as follows: The male-female Ratio should be male students—70 percent, and female students—30 percent, and the status of these students should be freshmen students, 80 percent; transfer students, 15; and readmitted students, 5.

This goal should be attained while meeting the 80-percent state residence requirement. If the director places this new goal as the third priority goal, how would it change the solution? Solve this problem using the computer.

7 Transportation and Assignment Methods

The graphical and simplex methods we discussed in the preceding three chapters are for the general linear and goal programming problems. Some special types of linear programming problems may be analyzed more efficiently by using special techniques. Such special linear programming problems to be discussed in this chapter are the *transportation* and *assignment* models.

THE TRANSPORTATION METHOD

The transportation model is concerned with the transportation of a good (or service) from a number of sources to a number of destinations with the minimum total cost. For example, a department store chain may have 20 warehouses (sources) and 100 stores (destinations) in various geographical locations. For a given point in time, each warehouse has a specific capacity of supply and each store has a specific demand for given merchandise. With the unit transportation cost from each warehouse to each store, we may be able to determine the quantity of the merchandise to be transported from warehouses to stores in such a manner as to achieve the minimum total transportation cost.

The transportation model has a wide spectrum of real-world applications. However, mathematical analysis of the transportation problem was not undertaken until 1941, when F. L. Hitchcock published his now-famous study, "Distribution of a Product from Several Sources to Numerous Localities." Since then, the transportation problem has been further studied by such scholars as T. C. Koopmans, George B.

Dantzig, A. Charnes and W. W. Cooper, and many others. In fact, many variations of the transportation method have been developed. In this chapter we shall discuss the most widely used techniques for transportation problems.

THE BALANCED TRANSPORTATION PROBLEM

To illustrate the transportation method, we will examine a problem where the total supply at the sources and the total demand at the destinations are exactly equal (balanced).

The Blacksburg Concrete Company has a contract to supply concrete for three construction projects, in the towns of Pulaski, Christiansburg, and Radford. The amounts of concrete required per day at the three construction sites are as follows:

Site	Location	Daily Demand (truckloads)
1	Pulaski	150
2	Christiansburg	70
3	Radford	60
Total		280

The Blacksburg Concrete Company has three concrete mixing plants, in the towns of Blacksburg, Roanoke, and Hillsville. The maximum production capacities per day of these three plants are:

Plant	Location	Daily Production (truckloads)
A	Blacksburg	120
B	Roanoke	80
C	Hillsville	80
Total		280

Each of the above three plants can supply the required concrete to each of the three construction projects. This transportation problem is a balanced one, since the total supply of the three plants is exactly equal to the total demand of the three construction projects. Certainly, it is rare in reality to observe a balanced transportation problem. However, an analysis of the balanced problem is a good starting point to study the transportation method. Once we learn to analyze the balanced problem, it will be an easy task to attack the unbalanced problem by making minor adjustments.

The cost accounting department of Blacksburg Concrete has

estimated the transportation cost per truckload of concrete from the plants to the construction sites as shown in Figure 7.1. Given the production capacity of the plants, the amount of concrete demanded by the construction projects, and the unit transportation costs, the company seeks to determine the optimum transportation scheme that will minimize the total transportation cost. We have all the information we need to analyze the transportation problem of the Blacksburg Concrete Company.

The transportation method involves the following steps:

1. Define the problem and set up the transportation tableau.
2. Develop an initial solution.
3. Evaluate the solution for improvement.
4. Develop a better solution, if possible.
5. Repeat steps 3 and 4 until the optimum solution is reached.

Now, we shall follow the above steps to solve the Blacksburg Concrete Company case.

Define the Problem and Set up the Transportation Tableau

First, let us set up the complete transportation tableau for the problem, as shown in Figure 7.2. We list the concrete plants (sources) as rows and the construction sites (destinations) as columns. Since we have three plants and three construction sites, the tableau has $3 \times 3 = 9$ cells. In each cell, the unit transportation cost is recorded in the small box at the upper left corner. In the bottom row, the total demand of each construction site is recorded. In the last column, the total supply (production capacity) of each plant is listed. Therefore, in the cell at the lower right corner we can find the total supply and total demand (280) of the problem.

The management problem of Blacksburg Concrete is to determine

Figure 7.1
Estimated Transportation Costs

From	Cost per Truckload		
	To Site 1	To Site 2	To Site 3
Plant A	$8	$5	$6
Plant B	15	10	12
Plant C	3	9	10

To From	1	2	3	Supply
A	8 X_{11}	5 X_{12}	6 X_{13}	120
B	15 X_{21}	10 X_{22}	12 X_{23}	80
C	3 X_{31}	9 X_{32}	10 X_{33}	80
Demand	150	70	60	280

Figure 7.2
Complete transportation tableau

the quantity of concrete to be transported from each plant to each construction site in the most economic manner. If we denote the quantity to be transported from each plant to each construction site as X_{ij} (from the ith plant to the jth construction site), as shown in Figure 7.2, the quantity to be transported can be interpreted as follows:

X_{11} = quantity to be transported from plant A to construction site 1
X_{12} = quantity to be transported from plant A to construction site 2
. . .
X_{33} = quantity to be transported from plant C to construction site 3

Then, the objective function of the problem (minimization of total transportation cost) can be described as:

Minimize $Z = 8X_{11} + 5X_{12} + 6X_{13} + 15X_{21} + 10X_{22} + 12X_{23}$
$+ 3X_{31} + 9X_{32} + 10X_{33}$

The above objective function is to be minimized subject to the supply and demand constraints. Since this problem is a balanced case, where total supply is exactly equal to total demand, we will have "exactly-equal-to" type constraints. Plant A has a total production capacity (supply) of 120 truckloads of concrete. The total amount of concrete we can transport from plant A to construction sites 1, 2, and 3 will be $X_{11} + X_{12} + X_{13}$. Therefore, the supply constraint of plant A becomes

$X_{11} + X_{12} + X_{13} = 120$

By employing the same approach, we can easily determine the supply constraints of plant B and plant C, as follows:

$$X_{21} + X_{22} + X_{23} = 80$$
$$X_{31} + X_{32} + X_{33} = 80$$

The total amount of concrete that construction site 1 receives will be the sum of X_{11}, X_{21}, and X_{31}. Hence, the demand constraint for construction site 1 becomes

$$X_{11} + X_{21} + X_{31} = 150$$

For construction sites 2 and 3, the demand constraints will be

$$X_{12} + X_{22} + X_{32} = 70$$

and

$$X_{13} + X_{23} + X_{33} = 60$$

Now, we can formulate the complete linear programming model for the transportation problem of the Blacksburg Concrete Company:

Minimize $\quad Z = 8X_{11} + 5X_{12} + 6X_{13} + 15X_{21} + 10X_{22} + 12X_{23}$
$$+ 3X_{31} + 9X_{32} + 10X_{33}$$

subject to
$$X_{11} + X_{12} + X_{13} = 120$$
$$X_{21} + X_{22} + X_{23} = 80$$
$$X_{31} + X_{32} + X_{33} = 80$$
$$X_{11} + X_{21} + X_{31} = 150$$
$$X_{12} + X_{22} + X_{32} = 70$$
$$X_{13} + X_{23} + X_{33} = 60$$
$$X_{ij} \geq 0 \quad i, j = 1, 2, 3$$

In the above linear programming problem, we have nine decision variables and six constraints. If we decide to solve the above problem by the simplex procedure, it may take a considerable amount of time. Therefore, we will instead use the transportation method.

Develop an Initial Solution

In the transportation method, as in the linear and goal programming methods, we must develop the initial solution as the starting point for the iterative algorithm. There are several methods available to develop an initial solution. It is obvious, however, that the better the initial solution (in terms of total transportation cost), the fewer the number of iterations required to reach the optimum solution. In this book, we shall examine three different methods to develop the initial solution: the northwest-corner method, the minimum-cell-cost method, and the Vogel's approximation method.

The Northwest-Corner Method

The simplest way to set up the initial solution is the northwest-corner method first suggested by George Dantzig. This is a systematic, but not so scientific, method. However, this method is extremely useful if a computer program is readily available for the transportation problem. The northwest-corner method can be summarized as follows:

1. Start at the northwest corner (upper left corner) of the tableau and allocate as many units as possible into each cell as we move toward the southwest corner of the tableau.
2. Check whether supply and demand are met.

For the Blacksburg Concrete problem, the initial solution by the northwest-corner method is shown in Figure 7.3. The initial solution via the northwest-corner method is achieved by following these steps:

Step 1 (cell A1). Transport as much as possible from plant A to site 1. Cell A1 is the northwest-corner cell in the tableau. The supply capacity of plant A is 120 and demand of site 1 is 150. Therefore, the maximum quantity we can transport to A1 will be 120. By transporting 120 to A1 we have exhausted the supply capacity of A. However, the demand of site 1 has not been completely met as yet, since we are short 30 truckloads.

Step 2 (cell B1). The unsatisfied demand of 30 truckloads of site 1 should be supplied by plant B as we follow the northwest-corner

From \ To	1	2	3	Supply
A	8 A1 (120)	5 A2	6 A3	120
B	15 B1 (30)	10 B2 (50)	12 B3	80
C	3 C1	9 C2 (20)	10 C3 (60)	80
Demand	150	70	60	280

Figure 7.3
Initial solution using the northwest-corner method

procedure. The total quantity being transported to site 1 from plants A (120) and B (30) satisfies the total demand.

Step 3 (cell B2). Since we have satisfied the demand of construction site 1, we move on to the next column, construction site 2. The total demand of site 2 is 70 truckloads. After transporting 30 truckloads to site 1, plant B can ship only the remaining supply capacity of 50 truckloads to site 2.

Step 4 (cell C2). Construction site 2 still requires 20 additional truckloads to meet the total demand of 70. Since plants A and B have already exhausted their supply capacities, this amount has to be shipped from plant C.

Step 5 (cell C3). Because this problem is a balanced case where total demand is exactly equal to total supply, the demand of construction site 3 (60 truckloads) must be exactly equal to the remaining supply capacity of plant C (60 truckloads).

Now, we can check each column and row to see whether or not demand and supply requirements are completely satisfied. The initial solution shown in Figure 7.3 clearly indicates that we have indeed met all the demand and supply requirements. In this problem we have nine cells altogether and we have transported to (filled in) five cells. Consequently, there are four empty cells where we did not transport any quantity.

Let us now calculate the total transportation cost of the initial solution derived by the northwest-corner method, mutiplying the quantity transported by the unit cost as follows:

Cell	Quantity Transported	Unit Transportation Cost	Total Cost
A1	120	8	$960
B1	30	15	450
B2	50	10	500
C2	20	9	180
C3	60	10	600
		Total Transportation Cost =	$2690

The total transportation cost of this initial solution is $2690. One distinctive feature of the northwest-corner solution is that the occupied cells generally form a stair-step effect from the upper left corner of the tableau.

The Minimum Cell-Cost Method

As we have observed, the northwest-corner method is a simple procedure, but it is not a scientific way to set up an initial solution. Consequently, it may require a large number of iterations to find the optimal solution when we start the solution with the northwest-corner method. One way to reduce the number of iterations is to use good common sense in formulating the initial solution. For example, since the objective of the problem is to minimize total cost, we should try to transport as much as possible to those cells with the minimum unit costs. This approach is called the minimum cell-cost method and can be summarized as follows:

1. Select the cell with the minimum cell-cost and allocate as much to this cell as possible.
2. Select the cell with the next minimum cell-cost and allocate as much as possible.
3. Repeat the procedure until the entire rim requirements (demand and supply requirements) are satisfied. In case of a tie, it is recommended to select the cell that can accommodate the greater quantity.

Now, let us go back to the Blacksburg Concrete case. The cell with the minimum unit transportation cost is $3 in C1. The maximum quantity we can allocate to this cell is 80, as the maximum supply capacity of plant C is 80 although site 1 requires 150. First, we allocate 80 to C1, as shown in Figure 7.4. The requirement of site 1 is now reduced to 70. The cell with the next minimum cell-cost is A2 with $5.

To From	1	2	3	Supply
A	8	5 70	6	~~120~~ 50
B	15	10	12	80
C	3 80	9	10	~~80~~
Demand	~~150~~ 70	~~70~~	60	280

Figure 7.4
Allocations to cells C1 and A2 using the minimum cell-cost method

The maximum we can allocate to A2 is 70, since the requirement of site 2 is only 70, although plant A has a supply capacity of 120, as shown in Figure 7.4. The next cell we allocate to is A3, as shown in Figure 7.5. By allocating 50 to A3 we will exhaust the capacity of plant A. It is clear in Figure 7.5 that the only plant that still has some supply capacity is B. Plant B has 80 available. On the other hand, sites 1 and 3 require 70 and 10, respectively. This implies that we have no further choice but to allocate 70 to B1 and 10 to B3, as shown in Figure 7.6. As we crossed out all the rim requirements, we can be assured that we have satisfied the total demand and supply. The total transportation cost of the initial solution by the minimum cell-cost method shown in Figure 7.6 is $2060, calculated as follows:

Cell	Quantity Transported	Unit Transportation Cost	Total Cost
A2	70	5	$ 350
A3	50	6	300
B1	70	15	1050
B3	10	12	120
C1	80	3	240
		Total Transportation Cost =	$2060

As we compare the total transportation costs derived by the northwest-corner and the minimum cell-cost methods, it should be apparent that

To From	1	2	3	Supply
A	8	5 70	6 50	~~120~~ 50
B	15	10	12	80
C	3 80	9	10	~~80~~
Demand	~~150~~ 70	~~70~~	~~60~~ 10	280

Figure 7.5
Allocations to cells C1, A2, and A3 and the resulting supply and demand

To \ From	1	2	3	Supply
A	8	5 70	6 50	~~120~~ ~~50~~
B	15 70	10	12 10	~~80~~
C	3 80	9	10	~~80~~
Demand	~~150~~ ~~70~~	~~70~~	~~60~~ ~~10~~	280

Figure 7.6
Initial solution using the minimum cell-cost method

the use of common sense has reduced the total cost by $630. This implies that the optimal solution can be reached faster by using the initial solution we just derived by the minimum cell-cost method.

The Vogel's Approximation Method

The Vogel's approximation method (sometimes referred to as the penalty or regret method) involves making allocations in such a manner as to minimize the penalty (regret) cost for not selecting certain cells for transportation. In other words, this method is based on the use of the difference between the smallest and next smallest unit transportation costs in each row and each column. This difference figure indicates the penalty (or regret) cost we have to pay per unit if we fail to allocate to the cell with the minimum transportation cost. The Vogel's approximation method can be summarized as follows:

1. Set up the transportation tableau with all the cells empty.
2. Calculate the penalty cost for each row and each column.
3. Select the row or column with the largest penalty cost (tie can be broken by selecting the cell that can accommodate the greatest quantity).
4. Allocate as much as possible to the minimum cost-cell in the chosen row or column.
5. Adjust the demand and supply requirements after the allocation.

6. Eliminate rows and columns that have fully met either demand or supply.
7. Recalculate the penalty cost for each row and each column.
8. Stop if no rows or columns remain to be evaluated; otherwise go to step 3.

Now, let us use the penalty method to set up the initial solution of the Blacksburg Concrete problem. In Figure 7.7, we have calculated the penalty costs for the rows and columns. For example, in the first row (plant A), the minimum cell cost is $5 in A2 and the next smallest cost is $6 in A3. Therefore, the penalty cost will be $6 - $5 = $1. This penalty cost of $1 is the amount we have to pay per unit if we fail to allocate to A2 and subsequently choose A3. The same procedure is used for calculating penalty costs for all the rows and columns.

The largest penalty cost in Figure 7.7 is $6 in the third row (plant C). This penalty indicates that if we fail to allocate to the cell with the minimum cost (C1), we have to pay a $6 penalty per unit to allocate to the next best cell (C2). In order to avoid paying this penalty, we should allocate to C1 as much as possible. The maximum quantity we can allocate to C1 is 80 units, since the capacity of C is only 80. After allocating 80 to C1, as shown in Figure 7.8, we cross out row C, since we

To From	1	2	3	Supply	Row Penalty
A	8	5	6	120	1
B	15	10	12	80	2
C	3	9	10	80	6*
Demand	150	70	60	280	
Column Penalty	5	4	4		

Figure 7.7
Transportation tableau with associated penalty costs

have exhausted the capacity of plant C. Next, we adjust the demand of site 1 from 150 to 70 (150 − 80 = 70). The penalty cost of the columns must be recalculated, since we have eliminated the third row.

In Figure 7.8, it should be clear that column 1 has the largest penalty cost. In order to avoid paying this penalty, we should allocate as much as possible to A1. The maximum quantity we can allocate to completely satisfy the demand of site 1 is 70.

After transporting 70 to A1, we can eliminate column 1. We repeat the procedure of adjusting the supply and/or demand figure and recalculating the penalty costs, as shown in Figure 7.9. The maximum penalty cost now appears in column 3. Therefore, we should allocate to A3 as much as possible. The maximum quantity we can allocate to A3 is 50. Figure 7.10 presents the adjustments after this allocation. Now, there are only two empty cells left in the entire tableau. Therefore, we do not have any further choice left but to allocate 70 to B2 and 10 to B3. Checking the entire tableau, we have completely satisfied the demand and supply requirements. The total transportation cost of this initial solution derived by the penalty method is $1920, calculated as follows:

Cell	Quantity Transported	Unit Transportation Cost	Total Cost
A1	70	$ 8	$560
A3	50	6	300
B2	70	10	700
B3	10	12	120
C1	80	3	240
		Total Transportation Cost =	$1920

The penalty method takes the relative cost (opportunity cost) into account in analyzing the solution. This method is more logical than the minimum cell-cost method, which is based on good common sense. This is readily apparent from the total transportation cost of $1920 derived by the penalty method. In general, Vogel's method greatly reduces the subsequent number of iterations required to reach the optimal solution. As a matter of fact, it often yields the optimal solution itself for simple transportation problems. As we shall see later, this solution shown in Figure 7.10 is in fact the optimum solution to the Blacksburg Concrete problem.

The Evaluation for Solution Improvement

Once we obtain the initial solution to the given transportation problem, the next step is to evaluate whether or not the solution can be further improved in terms of reduced total cost. The evaluation process

To \ From	1	2	3	Supply	Row Penalty
A	8	5	6	120	1
B	15	10	12	80	2
~~C~~	3 ~~80~~	9	10	~~80~~	
Demand	~~150~~ 70	70	60	280	
Column Penalty	7*	5	6		

Figure 7.8
Transportation tableau after one allocation using the penalty cost method

To \ From	1	2	3	Supply	Row Penalty
A	8 70	5	6	~~120~~ 50	1
B	15	10	12	80	2
~~C~~	3 ~~80~~	9	10	~~80~~	
Demand	~~150~~ 70	70	60	280	
Column Penalty		5	6*		

Figure 7.9
Transportation tableau after two allocations using the penalty cost method

255

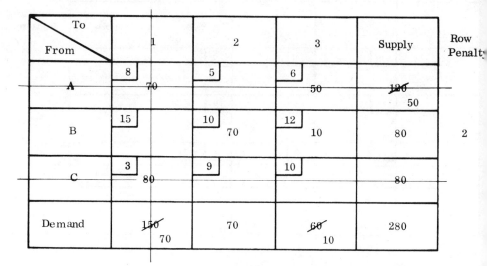

Figure 7.10
Initial solution using the penalty cost method

involves an analysis of the empty cells (cells where no allocations are made) to determine whether it is desirable to make a transfer to one of these empty cells. In order to evaluate all the empty cells in the tableau we must meet one requirement. The number of occupied cells (cells where allocations are already made) must be exactly equal to the sum of the number of rows and columns minus one, or number of occupied cells = number of rows + number of columns −1. If a solution does not meet the above requirement, the solution is called a degenerate case. The problem of the degeneracy will be discussed later in this chapter. We will now discuss two alternative methods to evaluate the solution for improvement: the stepping-stone method and the modified-distribution (MODI) method.

The Stepping-Stone Method

When we walk into a Japanese garden, we often see a beautiful pond. There are water lilies, goldfish, frogs, and dragon flies. Then, no doubt, we will notice a set of stepping stones going across the pond. We can go across the pond if we step carefully on these stepping stones. The stepping-stone method, which was first suggested by A. Charnes and W. W. Cooper, is based on this picturesque image of a Japanese garden. We evaluate all the empty cells by carefully stepping on the occupied cells. We should always remember that if we ever step on an empty cell, we will be in the water screaming "help!"

Let us evaluate the initial solution we derived by the northwest-corner method, as shown in Figure 7.11. We select A2 as the first empty cell to evaluate whether we can improve the solution by transferring some units from A1 to A2. We must always remember that we can transport some concrete only from plants to construction sites but never from a site to itself; in other words, a transfer must be initiated within the given row.

Suppose that we transfer 1 truckload of concrete from A1 to A2 (that is, we ship only 119 from plant A to site 1 and ship 1 from plant A to site 2). In order to allow this transfer of 1 unit from A1 to A2 while satisfying the supply and demand requirements, we have to also transfer 1 unit from column 2 to column 1, as can be seen clearly from the following calculation:

	Site 1	*Site 2*	*Supply*
A	119	1	120
B	30	50	80
C	0	20	
Demand	149	71	

The question is from which cell in column 2 to which cell in column 1 should the transfer of 1 unit be made. Remembering that we can step only on the stepping stones (occupied cells), the transfer has to be made from B2 to B1. Since C1 is an empty cell, the transfer cannot be made

From \ To	1	2	3	Supply
A	[8] (120) −	[5] +	[6]	120
B	[15] (30) +	[10] (50) −	[12]	80
C	[3]	[9] (20)	[10] (60)	80
Demand	150	70	60	280

Figure 7.11
Closed path of cell A2 using the stepping-stone method

from C2 to C1. When we make this transfer, we can still satisfy the demand and supply requirements, as follows:

	Site 1	Site 2	Supply
A	119	1	120
B	31	49	80
C	0	20	
Demand	150	70	

Now, referring back to Figure 7.11, we indicate the flow of the transfer by arrow lines. The change of quantity transported to each cell is indicated by + (increase) or − (decrease) sign. The path we follow (the arrow lines) in order to evaluate the empty cell is called the "closed path." The closed path involves vertical and horizontal movements but never diagonal shortcuts. Thus, the closed path for A2 will be: $A2 = -A1 + A2 - B2 + B1$.

The reason we trace the closed path is to determine whether the transfer of 1 unit will decrease or increase the total transportation cost. From the closed path we identified above, we can determine the net effect in terms of the change in transportation cost. By shipping 1 unit from plant A to site 2, we have to incur $5 cost. But by shipping 1 unit less (only 119 units) from plant A to site 1 we can save $8. Likewise, by transferring 1 unit from B2 to B1 we increase $15 cost at B1 and decrease $10 cost at B2. By following the closed path and analyzing the unit transportation cost in each cell, we can derive the cost improvement index for cell A2 as follows:

$$A2 = -A1 + A2 - B2 + B1$$
$$= -8 + 5 - 10 + 15 = +2$$

The amount +2 indicates that if we make a transfer of 1 unit from A1 to A2 it will increase the total transportation cost by $2. Certainly, we are not willing to make that kind of a transfer. Therefore, we should evaluate all the empty cells first and select a cell with the largest negative cost improvement index. If there is no negative cost improvement index, the existing solution is the optimum solution.

We now continue on to evaluate other empty cells. Let us select C1 because it is an easy cell to evaluate as it is surrounded by three occupied cells. The closed path of C1 is shown in Figure 7.12. The cost improvement index of C1 can be found by tracing the closed path, as follows:

$$C1 = -C2 + C1 - B1 + B2$$
$$= -9 + 3 - 15 + 10 = -11$$

To From	1	2	3	Supply
A	8 ⓒ120	5	6	120
B	15 ③30	10 ⑤50	12	80
C	3	9 ②20	10 ⓒ60	80
Demand	150	70	60	280

Figure 7.12
Closed path of cell C1 using the stepping-stone method

The cost improvement index indicates that if we transfer some units from C2 to C1 we can reduce the total transportation cost by \$11 per unit.

We can evaluate B3 in a similar manner as it is also surrounded by three occupied cells, as shown in Figure 7.13:

$$B3 = - B2 + B3 - C3 + C2$$
$$= - 10 + 12 - 10 + 9 = +1$$

The analysis of A3, which we have put off long enough, is a rather difficult task as its closed path is relatively hard to trace. Observing row A, it is clear that the only occupied cell from which we can transfer 1 unit to A3 is A1. Now, we have to increase 1 unit in column (site) 1. The only occupied cell other than A1 that can accept an additional unit is B1. Analyzing row B, the only occupied cell that can transfer 1 unit to B1 is B2. If we transfer a unit from B2 to B1, we need 1 additional unit in column 2. The only cell where we can accept a transfer of 1 unit other than B2 in column 2 is C2. Investigating row C, this unit must come from C3. Now, we can depict the closed path for A3 in Figure 7.14. The closed path and cost improvement index for A3 are

$$A3 = - A1 + A3 - C3 + C2 - B2 + B1$$
$$= - 8 + 6 - 10 + 9 - 10 + 15 = +2$$

It should be apparent from the above discussion that we can jump over empty cells to step on the occupied cells when we trace the closed path.

To From	1	2	3	Supply
A	8 (120)	5	6	120
B	15 (30)	10 (50) −	12 → +	80
C	3	9 (20) + ←	10 (60) − −	80
Demand	150	70	60	280

Figure 7.13
Closed path of cell B3 using the stepping-stone method

To From	1	2	3	Supply
A	8 (120) −	5	6 → +	120
B	15 (30) + ←	10 (50) − −	12	80
C	3	9 (20) + ←	10 (60) − −	80
Demand	150	70	60	280

Figure 7.14
Closed path of cell A3 using the stepping-stone method

Now, we have evaluated all the empty cells. We can list their cost improvement indices in the tableau, as shown in Figure 7.15. Clearly, the best empty cell to which we can make some transfer is C1. This cell indicates that the total transportation cost could be reduced by $11 per truckload of concrete that we transfer from C2. The next question we have to answer is, How much can we transfer to C1? The closed path for C1 has positive stones (cells with + sign) at B2 and C1 and negative stones (cells with − sign) at B1 and C2, as shown in Figure 7.16(a). The maximum quantity we can transfer to C1 is exactly the minimum quantity we find in the negative stones of the closed path. B1 has 30 and C2 has 20. Therefore, the minimum quantity we find is 20, and 20 is the maximum quantity we can transfer to C1. It should be obvious that if we transfer more than 20 units to C1, we have to assign some negative value to C2 in order to meet the demand and supply requirements. Since we cannot transport negative quantity, the maximum quantity to be transferred to C1 has to be 20, as shown in Figure 7.16(b). The new solution is shown in Figure 7.17. We now have completed one iteration.

The total transportation cost of the improved solution is $2470, as shown in Figure 7.17, a reduction of $220 from $2690 of the initial solution. Since the cost improvement index of C1 was −$11 and the quantity we transferred to C1 was 20, total cost improvement has to be $220 ($11×20 = $220). Now, we shall start the second iteration by evaluating all the empty cells. Before evaluating all the empty cells, we

To From	1	2	3	Supply
A	8 ⑫⓪	5 +2	6 +2	120
B	15 ㉚	10 ㊿	12 +1	80
C	3 −11	9 ⑳	10 ⑥⓪	80
Demand	150	70	60	280

Figure 7.15
Initial solution showing cost improvement indices of empty cells

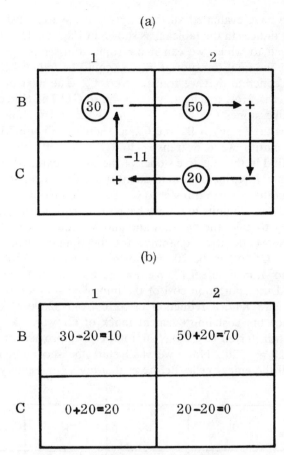

Figure 7.16
Determining maximum quantity transferable to C1

can easily determine the cost improvement index (CII) of C2, the cell
that we just emptied in the first iteration. We emptied C2 because C1 had
a cost improvement index of − $11. Therefore, if we evaluate C2 by using
exactly the same closed path, its cost improvement index will be + $11.
We can easily determine the cost improvement indices of all the
remaining empty cells, as shown in Figure 7.18. The cell with the best
cost improvement index is B3 with − $10. We can reduce the total
transportation cost by $10 per truckload if we transfer from B1 to B3.
The maximum quantity we can transfer is 10 because this is the
minimum quantity in the negative stones of the closed path. Thus, the
total transportation cost will be reduced by $100 ($10 × 10 = 100) and

To From	1	2	3	Supply
A	8 ⑫⓪	5	6	120
B	15 ⑩	10 ⑦⓪	12	80
C	3 ⑳	9	10 ⑥⓪	80
Demand	150	70	60	280

Total transportation cost of the solution:

$$
\begin{array}{rcl}
120 \times 8 & = & \$960 \\
10 \times 15 & = & 150 \\
70 \times 10 & = & 700 \\
20 \times 3 & = & 60 \\
60 \times 10 & = & 600 \\
\hline
& & \$2470
\end{array}
$$

Figure 7.17
New solution after one iteration

hence the total cost becomes $2370. The result of the second iteration is shown in Figure 7.19.

We shall now begin the third iteration. Without calculating we already know that the CII of B1 is +$10, since we just emptied this cell. We can evaluate the remaining empty cells in the manner shown in Figure 7.20. Clearly, A3 has the best cost improvement index with −$9. Now, analyzing the minimum quantity in the negative stones, we can easily determine that the maximum quantity that can be transferred to A3 is 50 (50 units in C3). The solution we derive after the third iteration is shown in Figure 7.21. The total transportation cost will be reduced by $450 ($9 × 50 = $450). Hence, the new total transportation cost is $1920.

We repeat the procedure of evaluating the empty cells. Of course, we need not evaluate C3 because we already know that this cell has a +$9 cost improvement index. The remaining three empty cells are analyzed in Figure 7.22. It is readily evident that no empty cell has a negative cost improvement index. In other words, there is no way we can improve the solution shown in Figure 7.21. Therefore, we have reached the optimum solution. It should be noted here that in a balanced

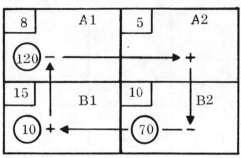

Closed Path: A3 = − A1 + A3 − C3 + C1
CII: A3 = − 8 + 6 − 10 + 3 = − 9

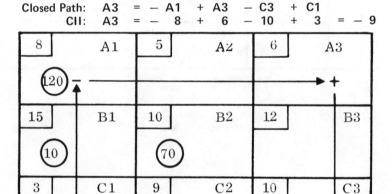

Closed Path: B3 = − B1 + B3 − C3 + C1
CII: B3 = − 15 + 12 − 10 + 3 = − 10

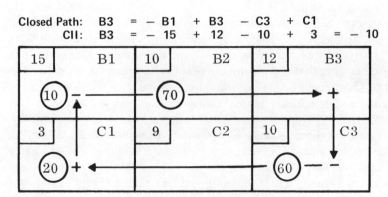

Figure 7.18
Determining cost improvement index (CII) for each empty cell

To	1	2	3	Supply
From				
A	8 (120)	5	6	120
B	15	10 (70)	12 (10)	80
C	3 (30)	9	10 (50)	80
Demand	150	70	60	280

Total transportation cost of the solution:

120 x 8	=	$960
70 x 10	=	700
10 x 12	=	120
30 x 3	=	90
50 x 10	=	500
		$2370

Figure 7.19
New solution after two iterations

transportation problem when all supplies and demands are integer values, the solution will also be in integer values. The transportation schedule and the total transportation cost of the optimum solution are as follows:

Plant	Transported to	Quantity	Unit Cost	Total Cost
A	1	70	$ 8	$560
A	3	50	6	300
B	2	70	10	700
B	3	10	12	120
C	1	80	3	240

Total Transportation Cost = $1920

The stepping-stone method we have applied can be summarized as follows:

1. Be sure that the number of occupied cells is exactly equal to $M + N - 1$, where M = number of rows and N = number of columns.
2. Evaluate each empty cell by following its closed path and

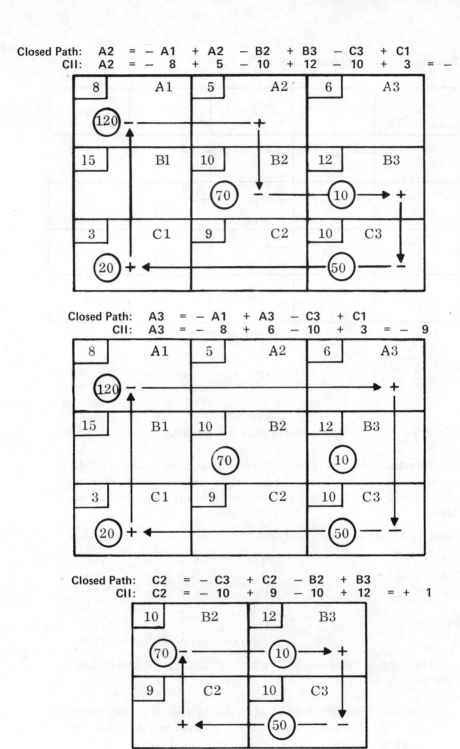

Closed Path: A2 = − A1 + A2 − B2 + B3 − C3 + C1
CII: A2 = − 8 + 5 − 10 + 12 − 10 + 3 = − 8

8 A1	5 A2	6 A3
120		
15 B1	10 B2	12 B3
	70	10
3 C1	9 C2	10 C3
20		50

Closed Path: A3 = − A1 + A3 − C3 + C1
CII: A3 = − 8 + 6 − 10 + 3 = − 9

8 A1	5 A2	6 A3
120		
15 B1	10 B2	12 B3
	70	10
3 C1	9 C2	10 C3
20		50

Closed Path: C2 = − C3 + C2 − B2 + B3
CII: C2 = − 10 + 9 − 10 + 12 = + 1

10 B2	12 B3
70	10
9 C2	10 C3
	50

Figure 7.20
Determining the CII of the remaining empty cells

To From	1	2	3	Supply
A	8 (70)	5	6 (50)	120
B	15	10 (70)	12 (10)	80
C	3 (80)	9	10	80
Demand	150	70	60	280

Figure 7.21
New solution after three iterations

determining its cost improvement index. If all indices have zero or positive, the solution is optimum. If there exist negative indices (or index), find the cell with the largest negative index. This is the cell where a transfer should be made.

3. Determine the quantity to be transferred to the selected empty cell. Trace the closed path for the cell and identify the minimum positive quantity in the minus stones. Transfer this quantity and find the new solution after the iteration. Go to step 1.

The Modified-Distribution (MODI) Method

The MODI method is a more efficient procedure of evaluating the empty cells. Instead of evaluating the empty cells one at a time by tracing the closed path, as in the stepping-stone method, in the MODI method it is possible to evaluate all of the empty cells simultaneously. Consequently, in the MODI method we do not have to trace all the closed paths of the empty cells. Instead, we trace the closed path of only one empty cell, which indicates the best cost improvement index. Certainly, we can eliminate the major portion of the cumbersome task of tracing the closed path!

In order to demonstrate the MODI method, let us go back to the initial solution we obtained by the northwest-corner method for the Blacksburg Concrete problem. To illustrate the MODI method, however, we have to alter the transportation tableau slightly by assigning an additional row and column. The modified transportation tableau of the

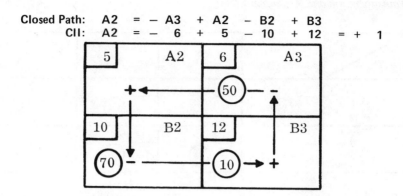

Closed Path: A2 = − A3 + A2 − B2 + B3
CII: A2 = − 6 + 5 − 10 + 12 = + 1

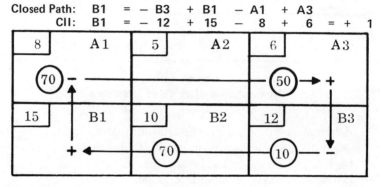

Closed Path: B1 = − B3 + B1 − A1 + A3
CII: B1 = − 12 + 15 − 8 + 6 = + 1

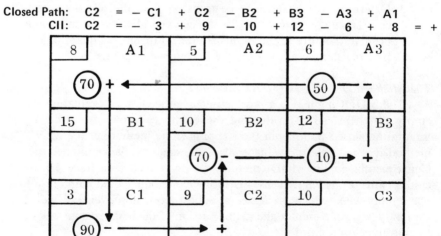

Closed Path: C2 = − C1 + C2 − B2 + B3 − A3 + A1
CII: C2 = − 3 + 9 − 10 + 12 − 6 + 8 = + 10

Figure 7.22
Determining the CII of the remaining empty cells

268

initial solution is shown in Figure 7.23. Note that we added column r_i to indicate row values and row v_j to indicate column values. Now, let us define several variables before we proceed any further:

r_i = value for the ith row (plant)
v_j = value for the jth column (construction site)
C_{ij} = unit transportation cost in the ith row and jth column cell.

For the *occupied* cells (cells where some quantity of concrete has been transported, e.g., A1, B1, B2, C2, and C3), the following relationship exists:

$$C_{ij} = r_i + v_j$$

That is, the unit cost at cell ij = value for row i + value for column j. For example, the unit transportation cost for the five occupied cells can be described as:

$$C_{11} = r_1 + v_1 = 8 \qquad \text{Cell A1}$$
$$C_{21} = r_2 + v_1 = 15 \qquad \text{Cell B1}$$
$$C_{22} = r_2 + v_2 = 10 \qquad \text{Cell B2}$$
$$C_{32} = r_3 + v_2 = 9 \qquad \text{Cell C2}$$
$$C_{33} = r_3 + v_3 = 10 \qquad \text{Cell C3}$$

In the above equations, we have six unknown variables (row and column values) and five equations. In order to obtain a solution to determine the row and column values, one of the variables must be selected and given an arbitrary value. We can select any variable and assign any convenient value. We shall select r_1 and assign a zero value to it. With $r_1 = 0$, it is a very simple task to identify the values of the remaining variables, as follows:

$$r_1 + v_1 = 8 \qquad 0 + v_1 = 8 \qquad v_1 = 8$$
$$r_2 + v_1 = 15 \qquad r_2 + 8 = 15 \qquad r_2 = 7$$
$$r_2 + v_2 = 10 \qquad 7 + v_2 = 10 \qquad v_2 = 3$$
$$r_3 + v_2 = 9 \qquad r_3 + 3 = 9 \qquad r_3 = 6$$
$$r_3 + v_3 = 10 \qquad 6 + v_3 = 10 \qquad v_3 = 4$$

All the row and column values are now determined. It should be pointed out that these values are not always positive. In fact, it is quite possible to have several negative values. We now proceed to evaluate all the empty cells by using the following cost improvement index formula:

$$\text{Cost improvement index} = C_{ij} - r_i - v_j$$

As in the stepping-stone method, if a cell has a negative index, it

v_j		v_1	v_2	v_3	
r_i	To / From	1	2	3	Supply
r_1	A	8 (120)	5	6	120
r_2	B	15 (30)	10 (50)	12	80
r_3	C	3	9 (20)	10 (60)	80
	Demand	150	70	60	280

Figure 7.23
Initial solution modified for the MODI method

indicates that an improved solution is possible. When all indices have zero or positive values, the optimal solution is reached.

Figure 7.24 presents the initial solution of the problem with the calculated row and column values. The empty cells are evaluated as follows:

Empty Cell	$C_{ij} - r_i - v_i$	Cost Improvement Index
A2	$5 - 0 - 3 = 2$	$+2$
A3	$6 - 0 - 4 = 2$	$+2$
B3	$12 - 7 - 4 = 1$	$+1$
C1	$3 - 6 - 8 = -11$	-11

The cost improvement indices derived above correspond with those we calculated in the stepping-stone method. The only empty cell with a negative cost improvement index is C1. The quantity we can transfer to C1 can be determined by analyzing the quantities transported to the negative stones in the closed path. This procedure is exactly identical with the stepping-stone method. From the previous analysis, we know that the closed path for C1 is $-$ C2 + C1 $-$ B1 + B2, as shown in Figure 7.24, and the maximum quantity we can transfer is 20 (in C2).

After we implement this transfer, we derive the second solution and recalculate the row and column values, as shown in Figure 7.25. The procedure of calculating the new row and column values is as follows:

Occupied Cell	$C_{ij} = r_i + v_j$	Value Derived
A1	$C_{11} = r_1 + v_1, 8 = 0 + v_1$	$v_1 = 8$
B1	$C_{21} = r_2 + v_1, 15 = r_2 + 8$	$r_2 = 7$
B2	$C_{22} = r_2 + v_2, 10 = 7 + v_2$	$v_2 = 3$
C1	$C_{31} = r_3 + v_1, 3 = r_3 + 8$	$r_3 = -5$
C3	$C_{33} = r_3 + v_3, 10 = -5 + v_3$	$v_3 = 15$

Now we can proceed to calculate the cost improvement indices for all the empty cells. With the practice we have had, we can easily determine these indices mentally and list them in the tableau, as shown in Figure 7.25. The cell with the best cost improvement index is B3 with $-\$10$. By tracing its closed path, as shown in the figure, we can easily determine that the quantity we can transfer to B3 is 10.

We repeat the process and derive the third solution, shown in Figure 7.26. The new row and column values are determined as follows:

Occupied Cell	$C_{ij} = r_i + v_j$	Value Derived
A1	$C_{11} = r_1 + v_1, 8 = 0 + v_1$	$v_1 = 8$
C1	$C_{31} = r_3 + v_1, 3 = r_3 + 8$	$r_3 = -5$
C3	$C_{33} = r_3 + v_3, 10 = -5 + v_3$	$v_3 = 15$
B3	$C_{23} = r_2 + v_3, 12 = r_2 + 15$	$r_2 = -3$
B2	$C_{22} = r_2 + v_2, 10 = -3 + v_2$	$v_2 = 13$

v_j		$v_1=8$		$v_2=3$		$v_3=4$		
r_i	To From	1		2		3		Supply
$r_1=0$	A	8 (120)		5	+2	6	+2	120
$r_2=7$	B	15 (30)		10 (50)		12	+1	80
$r_3=6$	C	3	-11	9 (20)		10 (60)		80
	Demand	150		70		60		280

Figure 7.24
Initial solution using the MODI method

v_j	$v_1=8$	$v_2=3$	$v_3=15$	
r_i / To / From	1	2	3	Supply
$r_1=0$ A	8 ⑫⓪	5 +2	6 −9	120
$r_2=7$ B	15 ⑩ −	10 ⑦⓪	12 −10 +	80
$r_3=-5$ C	3 ㉒ +	9 +11	10 ⑥⓪ −	80
Demand	150	70	60	280

Figure 7.25
Second solution with recalculated row and column values

v_j	$v_1=8$	$v_2=13$	$v_3=15$	
r_i / To / From	1	2	3	Supply
$r_1=0$ A	8 ⑫⓪ −	5 −8	6 −9 +	120
$r_2=-3$ B	15 +10	10 ⑦⓪	12 ⑩	80
$r_3=-5$ C	3 ㉚ +	9 +1	10 ㊿ −	80
Demand	150	70	60	280

Figure 7.26
Third solution with recalculated row and column values

Figure 7.26 also presents the cost improvement indices for the empty cells. A3 indicates the best cost improvement index with $-\$9$. A brief examination of the closed path suggests that the quantity we can transfer to A3 is 50 (50 units in C3).

The fourth solution is presented in Figure 7.27. Now we should be able to calculate the row and column values mentally by examining the transportation tableau. The cost improvement indices calculated for all the empty cells indicate that there is no negative value. Therefore, we have reached the optimal solution. This solution is exactly identical with the one we derived through the stepping-stone method.

The MODI method we have applied to the Blacksburg Concrete problem can be summarized as follows:

1. Compute the row (r_i) and column (v_j) values by using the relationship $C_{ij} = r_i + v_j$ for the occupied cells in a given solution. Assign a zero value for a row or column variable that appears most frequently in the cost relationship formulas.
2. Compute the cost improvement indices for all the empty cells by using the formula $CII = C_{ij} - r_i - v_j$.
3. Trace the closed path for the empty cell that has the largest negative cost improvement index. If there is no empty cell with a negative improvement index, the optimum solution has been found.

v_j		$v_1=8$	$v_2=4$	$v_3=6$	
r_i	To ⟍ From	1	2	3	Supply
$r_1=0$	A	8 ⟨70⟩	5 +1	6 ⟨50⟩	120
$r_2=6$	B	15 +1	10 ⟨70⟩	12 ⟨10⟩	80
$r_3=-5$	C	3 ⟨80⟩	9 +10	10 +9	80
	Demand	150	70	60	280

Figure 7.27
Optimum solution using the MODI method

4. Transfer the minimum quantity in the negative stones of the closed path to the empty cell selected.

5. Develop a new solution after the iteration and go back to step 1.

THE UNBALANCED TRANSPORTATION PROBLEM

Thus far we have discussed a transportation problem that has balanced rim requirements—that is, supply and demand have exactly the same totals. However, in most real-world transportation problems such a balanced case is a rare exception. As a matter of fact, most problems are unbalanced problems where supply may exceed demand or demand may exceed supply. Since the transportation method requires balanced row and column requirements, we must make a slight modification. First, we shall discuss the case where demand exceeds supply, followed by the case where supply exceeds demand.

Demand Exceeds Supply

Let us consider the original problem of the Blacksburg Concrete Company. Suppose a new apartment complex has been added to the project in construction site 3 and its requirement has been increased from 60 to 90 truckloads of concrete. The total demand is now 310 truckloads, while total supply remains at 280. The scheme we can use to balance the rim requirements for this type of problem is to create an imaginary plant that can take up the excess demand. We introduce a dummy plant D to supply the increased demand of 30 truckloads at site 3.

By creating a new row for plant D we can now balance supply and demand. Since D is only an imaginary plant, the unit transportation costs to the three sites are zero. The initial solution of the problem via the northwest-corner method is shown in Figure 7.28. Now we can proceed to solve the problem by using either the stepping-stone or MODI methods. If the optimum solution calls for plant D (dummy) to transport some quantity to a certain construction site (or sites), this implies that the site (or sites) will receive less than the quantity they demand. For example, if the optimum solution shows plant D supplying 30 truckloads to site 3, in reality construction site 3 can receive only 60 truckloads rather than the 90 it demanded.

Supply Exceeds Demand

Now we can analyze the opposite case, where supply exceeds demand. Suppose, again in the original Blacksburg Concrete problem,

From \ To	1	2	3	Supply
A	8 (20)	5	6	120
B	15 (30)	10 (50)	12	80
C	3	9 (20)	10 (60)	80
D Dummy	0	0	0 (30)	30
Demand	150	70	90	310

Total transportation cost:

120 x 8	=	$960
30 x 15	=	450
50 x 10	=	500
20 x 9	=	180
60 x 10	=	600
30 x 0	=	0
		$2690

Figure 7.28
Initial solution when demand exceeds supply

that the project in construction site 1 now requires only 100 truckloads instead of the original 150. The total demand now amounts to only 230, whereas the total supply remains 280. Clearly, this is a case where supply exceeds demand.

In order to balance the row and column requirements for the problem, we must create a dummy construction site that can absorb the excess supply of 50 truckloads. Let us label this dummy construction site as site 4. We have added a new column to the tableau, as shown in Figure 7.29. The unit transportation costs from various plants to site 4 should be zero. The figure presents the initial solution by using the northwest-corner method. As usual, we can proceed to improve the solution by using either the stepping-stone or MODI methods.

If site 4 receives some quantity from a plant (or plants) in the final solution, this implies that the plant (or plants) is not supplying up to its capacity. For example, if site 4 receives 50 truckloads from plant C, as shown in Figure 7.29, plant C in reality is supplying only 30 truckloads, 50 truckloads below its supply capacity of 80 truckloads.

To From	1	2	3	Dummy 4	Supply
A	8 (100)	5 (20)	6	0	120
B	15	10 (50)	12 (30)	0	80
C	3	9	10 (30)	0 (50)	80
Demand	100	70	60	50	280

Total transportation cost:
$$
\begin{array}{rcl}
100 \times 8 &=& \$800 \\
20 \times 5 &=& 100 \\
50 \times 10 &=& 500 \\
30 \times 12 &=& 360 \\
30 \times 10 &=& 300 \\
50 \times 0 &=& 0 \\
\hline
&& \$2060
\end{array}
$$

Figure 7.29
Initial solution when supply exceeds demand

SOME COMPLICATIONS AND THEIR RESOLUTION

In any transportation problem, we may face several complications. In this section, we shall discuss these problems and the ways to resolve them.

Degeneracy

In order to evaluate all the empty cells for an improved solution, the number of occupied cells must be equal to $M + N - 1$ (M = number of rows, N = number of columns). If a transportation problem does not meet this requirement, it is called a degenerate case. Unless there is an error in the transportation solution, the degeneracy is caused only by the insufficient number of occupied cells. Degeneracy can occur either at the initial solution or during subsequent iterations. In applying the stepping-stone method, the degeneracy will prohibit the analysis of all the empty cells due to insufficient stepping stones to complete the closed path. If we use the MODI method, in a degenerate case it becomes impossible to compute all the row and column values.

Degeneracy in the Initial Solution

Suppose we have a transportation problem as described in Figure 7.30. If we use the northwest-corner method to set up the initial solution, allocations will be as given in the figure. Since the demand of site 1 and supply of plant A are exactly equal, the assignment of 100 to A1 will meet both requirements simultaneously. Consequently, the chain of occupied cells (the stair-step effect) of the northwest-corner method is broken. The number of occupied cells is only four, while we need five $(3 + 3 - 1 = 5)$ occupied cells to evaluate all the empty cells. Clearly, we have a degenerate solution.

To remedy this problem, the quantity ϵ (epsilon) should be assigned to an empty cell that will connect the broken chain of the occupied cells. In our problem there are two candidates: A2 and B1. By assigning ϵ to either one of these two empty cells, we will be able to evaluate all the empty cells. The quantity ϵ is so small by definition that it does not add anything to the rim requirements. But it is sufficiently large to transform the cell to an occupied cell. After assigning ϵ to A2, as shown in Figure 7.31, we can proceed with the solution process in the usual manner.

Degeneracy in Subsequent Iterations

Suppose the Blacksburg Concrete problem has been modified slightly due to the change in demand. The initial solution shown in Figure 7.32(a) based on the northwest-corner method is not degenerate. From a brief analysis of the cost improvement indices, it is apparent that

To From	1	2	3	Supply
A	8 (100)	5	6	100
B	15	10 (100)	12 (20)	120
C	3	9	10 (80)	80
Demand	100	100	100	300

Figure 7.30
Example of a degenerate initial solution

To From	1	2	3	Supply
A	8 (100)	5 (ε)	6	100
B	15	10 (100)	12 (20)	120
C	3	9	10 (100)	80
Demand	100	100	100	300

Figure 7.31
Use of ε to remove degeneracy in initial solution

C1 is the empty cell to be selected for the solution improvement. The closed path for C1 is also shown in the figure.

The maximum quantity we can transfer to C1 is 30. However, when this transfer is made, both B1 and C2 become empty, since these two negative cells have identical quantities of 30, as shown in Figure 7.32(b). The result of the iteration is a degenerate solution, as shown in Figure 7.33. In a usual case of transfer, an empty cell becomes occupied while the negative cell with the minimum quantity in the closed path becomes an empty cell. However if there are two or more negative cells with the identical minimum quantity, a degeneracy will occur. Consequently, sometimes the number of occupied cells may be $M + N - 3$, or two occupied cells are short for the solution evaluation. In such a case ϵ should be assigned to two of the negative cells that have become empty, so that there are $M + N - 1$ occupied cells. In our example shown in Figure 7.33, where we are one cell short, we can assign ϵ to either B1 or C2 and proceed with the usual solution procedure.

Multiple Optimum Solutions

The optimum solution is found to a given transportation problem when all the cost improvement indices are zero or positive. However, if some cost improvement indices are zero, this implies that alternative solutions can be found with reallocation without increasing the total

(a) Initial Solution

To From	1	2	3	Supply
A	8 (120)	5 +2	6 +2	120
B	15 (30)	10 (50)	12 +1	80
C	3 −11	9 (30)	10 (50)	80
Demand	150	80	50	280

(b) Effect of Transfer from C2 to C1

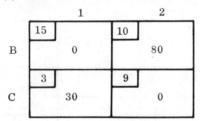

	1	2
B	15 0	10 80
C	3 30	9 0

Figure 7.32

transportation cost. For example, suppose that the optimum solution to a given problem is as shown in Figure 7.34 (the unit cost of B1 has been changed from $15 to $14). The cost improvement indices for the empty cells are all positive, except for cell B1, which has a zero cost improvement index. Therefore, if we make a transfer to B1, it should result in an alternative solution while the total transportation cost remains unchanged.

From a brief analysis of the closed path for cell B1, shown in Figure 7.34, we can easily determine that the maximum quantity we can transfer to B1 is 10. After this change, the new solution is derived as in Figure 7.35. The total transportation cost remains $1920. If management has a preference for a given solution due to road conditions, union contracts, or other nonmonetary factors, an analysis of alternative solutions may be valuable.

To \ From	1	2	3	Supply
A	8 (120)	5	6	120
B	15	10 (80)	12	80
C	3 (30)	9 (ε)	10 (50)	80
Demand	150	80	50	280

Figure 7.33
Use of ε to remove degeneracy after first iteration

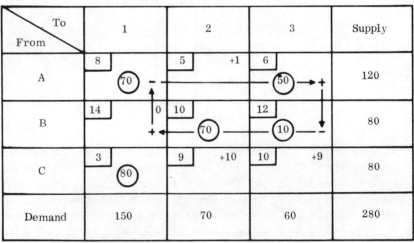

To \ From	1	2	3	Supply
A	8 (70) –	5 +1	6 (50) → +	120
B	14 0	10 (70)	12 (10) –	80
C	3 (80)	9 +10	10 +9	80
Demand	150	70	60	280

Total transportation cost:

70 x 8	=	$560
50 x 6	=	300
70 x 10	=	700
10 x 12	=	120
80 x 3	=	240
		$1920

Figure 7.34
First optimum solution

280

To From	1	2	3	Supply
A	8 ⑥⓪	5	6 ⑥⓪	120
B	14 ⑩	10 ⑦⓪	12	80
C	3 ⑧⓪	9	10	80
Demand	150	70	60	280

Total transportation cost:

60 x	8	=	$480
60 x	6	=	360
10 x	14	=	140
70 x	10	=	700
80 x	3	=	240
			$1920

Figure 7.35
Second optimum solution

Prohibited Transportation Routes

In many real-world situations, it is not possible or practicable to transport from certain sources to certain destinations. There are many possible reasons for prohibited transportation routes, such as union strikes, road construction, seasonal hazards of the road (snow, flood, mud, etc.), weight limits on bridges or roads, limited heights of bridges over the road, or traffic regulations of local governments. A transportation problem with prohibited routes can be handled in the usual manner by assigning large unit transportation costs (assign M as in linear programming) to those prohibited cells. Of course, the same result can be obtained if we block out those cells altogether. In such cases, the blocked-out cells are skipped in the evaluation of the empty cells.

Transportation Problems with Multiple Objectives

In many instances, management may have multiple conflicting objectives to achieve in a given transportation problem. In such a case, we must depart from the usual transportation method, since it handles only one objective criterion, the transportation cost. It is possible to apply the goal programming approach to such transportation problems. However, this topic belongs to the advanced management science course. The reader who is interested in exploring this area should read the paper by Lee and Moore in the references at the end of the chapter.

The Transshipment Problem

An important extension of the transportation method is the transshipment approach. In the transshipment problem, each source (plant) or destination (construction site) is allowed to become an intermediate point of shipments from other sources to other destinations. In real-world situations we frequently confront such transshipment problems. A special procedure is available that can solve the transshipment problem by the regular transportation method with some minor adjustment. The interested reader should refer to the work of Alex Orden in the references.

THE ASSIGNMENT METHOD

Another special-purpose algorithm of linear programming is the assignment method. The assignment method is an efficient technique based on a theorem first proved by a Hungarian mathematician, D. König, and is, therefore, sometimes referred to as the *Hungarian method of assignment*. The assignment method is very closely related to the transportation method; in fact, the assignment method is just a special case of the transportation problem where there are exactly equal number of sources and destinations and each supply and demand must equal one. Consequently, the quantity we transport (assign) must be either zero or one. Because of such a simple structure, the assignment problem can be solved more efficiently by its own unique method than by the transportation method. The early developers of the assignment method were P. S. Dwyer, M. M. Flood, and H. W. Kuhn. However, several variations have been developed for the assignment method.

THE ASSIGNMENT PROBLEM

To present the assignment method, let us consider a simple case. There are four qualified employees to be assigned to four different machines. Because of different individual training and experience, the cost of successful completion of the given task on each machine is different for the employees. Let us assume that only one employee can be assigned to each machine. Further, it is assumed that each task is completed independently by one individual. The above assignment problem, along with the unit costs to complete each task on each machine by the employees, is given in Figure 7.36. It should be noted that there are the same number of rows and columns. Also, the amount of supply and demand for each row and each column is exactly one. These are unique characteristics of the assignment problem.

In Figure 7.36, we can easily see that it costs $10 for employee 1 to complete the task by using machine A, $15 using machine B, and so on. The unit costs to complete each task by each employee may be determined by the amount of time required and the amount of other resources (i.e., materials) used to complete the task. The objective of the above assignment problem is to find the optimum assignment schedule of the employees to each machine so as to minimize the total cost to complete the tasks. The problem can be solved by the regular trans-portation method studied earlier. For example, by using the northwest-corner method we can derive the initial transportation solution shown in Figure 7.37. Since we have identical supply and demand requirements, a

Machine / Men	A	B	C	D	Supply
1	$10	$15	$16	$18	1
2	14	13	16	10	1
3	11	9	8	18	1
4	13	13	11	9	1
Demand	1	1	1	1	4

Figure 7.36
Assignment problem tableau

degenerate solution results. By assigning ϵ to 1B, 2C, and 3D we can avoid the degeneracy and proceed to determine whether an improved solution is possible.

The Opportunity-Cost Table

The first step of the assignment method is to develop a table of opportunity costs. The concept of opportunity cost is important in any decision analysis. The amount of opportunity cost represents the implicit cost associated with the failure of taking the best course of action. For example, in our problem shown in Figure 7.36, if employee 1 is assigned to machine B it will cost the firm $15. The best possible assignment, while disregarding other employees for time being, is clearly to machine A. The failure to assign employee 1 to machine A, assigning him instead to B, will cost the firm $5 (15 − 10 = 5). Since we are trying to minimize the total cost, our strategy should be to minimize the opportunity cost. It should be noted that opportunity costs also exist for each column. For

Machine Men	A	B	C	D	Supply
1	10 ①	15 ⓔ	16	18	1
2	14	13 ①	16 ⓔ	10	1
3	11	9	8 ①	18 ⓔ	1
4	13	13	11	9 ①	1
Demand	1	1	1	1	4

Figure 7.37
Initial solution of assignment problem with degeneracy avoided

example, any employee can be assigned to machine C. If we assign employee 4 to machine C, we have to absorb the opportunity cost of $3 (11 − 8 = 3) because we failed to assign employee 3 to the machine.

It should be clear now that the opportunity cost should be calculated for both rows and columns. First, let us find the initial opportunity cost table by analyzing each row. If we assign an employee to a machine with the minimum unit cost, obviously we choose the best alternative. Consequently, the opportunity cost will be zero. The procedure we should follow in determining the row opportunity costs is to subtract the minimum cost in each row from each of the other costs in that row. For example, we can calculate the opportunity costs for the first row as follows:

	Cost	*Minimum Row Cost*	*Opportunity Cost*
1A	$10	$10	$0
1B	15	10	5
1C	16	10	6
1D	18	10	8

Figure 7.38(a) presents the initial row opportunity-cost table. Now, we can proceed to calculate the column opportunity costs from the initial opportunity-cost table shown in Figure 7.38(a). For example, the final opportunity costs for column A can be calculated as follows:

	Cost	*Minimum Column Cost*	*Final Opportunity Cost*
1A	$0	$0	$0
2A	4	0	4
3A	3	0	3
4A	4	0	4

The second column costs will be:

	Cost	*Minimum Column Cost*	*Final Opportunity Cost*
1B	$5	$1	$4
2B	3	1	2
3B	1	1	0
4B	4	1	3

The complete opportunity-cost table is shown in Figure 7.38(b).

(a) Initial Row-Wise Opportunity Costs

Machine / Men	A	B	C	D
1	0	5	6	8
2	4	3	6	0
3	3	1	0	10
4	4	4	2	0

(b) Opportunity Costs after Column Consideration

Machine / Men	A	B	C	D
1	0	4	6	8
2	4	2	6	0
3	3	0	0	10
4	4	3	2	0

Figure 7.38

Analysis of the Assignment Possibilities

The second step of the assignment method is to determine whether the optimum assignment can be made based on the complete opportunity-cost table. The optimum assignment is possible if the final opportunity-cost table has four "independent" zeros in the table. The "independent" zero indicates that assigning an employee to a cell with zero opportunity cost will not exclude other assignments to cells with zero costs. A convenient way of analyzing the optimum assignment possibility is to draw a minimum number of straight lines, either horizontally or vertically, to cross out all zero values in the opportunity-cost table. If the number of straight lines required to cross out all zeros is exactly equal to the number of rows (employees) or columns (machines), an optimum assignment is possible.

Figure 7.39(a) and Figure 7.39(b) present two different ways to cross out all zeros in the table. It is evident that we need only three straight lines to cross out all zeros. Consequently, an optimum assignment is not possible.

The Revised Opportunity-Cost Table

Since we need only three straight lines to cover all zeros, we need to assign one of the employees to a cell where the opportunity cost is not zero. In order to identify this cell, we must revise the opportunity-cost table. The procedure we should follow is; first select the smallest opportunity cost in the table that is not crossed out by a straight line, and then subtract this cost from all other opportunity costs that are not crossed out by straight lines. This procedure will provide an opportunity-cost table within the opportunity-cost table. The final step required is to add the same minimum opportunity cost to those opportunity costs that are at the intersection of two straight lines. All other opportunity costs crossed out by one straight line will remain unchanged in the revised opportunity-cost table. If we use Figure 7.39(a), the revised opportunity-cost table will be as shown in Figure 7.40.

Figure 7.40(a) and Figure 7.40(b) present two different ways to cross out all zeros for the revised opportunity-cost table. Obviously, we need four straight lines to cover all zeros on the table. Consequently, it is possible to obtain an optimum assignment for the problem. In the revised opportunity-cost table shown in Figure 7.40, there are two zeros in each row and each column except the first row and first column. The zero opportunity-cost appears in 1A. Therefore, in order to minimize the total opportunity cost we must assign employee 1 to machine A. Now three rows (2, 3, and 4) and three columns (B, C, and D) remain. There

Machine Men	A	B	C	D
1	0	4	6	8
2	4	2	6	0
3	3	0	0	10
4	4	3	2	0

(b)

Machine Men	A	B	C	D
1	0	4	6	8
2	4	2	6	0
3	3	0	0	10
4	4	3	2	0

Figure 7.39
Use of straight lines to determine if optimum solution exists

(a)

Machine / Men	A	B	C	D
1	0	4	6	10
2	2	0	4	0
3	3	0	0	12
4	2	1	0	0

(b)

Machine / Men	A	B	C	D
1	0	4	6	10
2	2	0	4	0
3	3	0	0	12
4	2	1	0	0

Figure 7.40
Use of straight lines in revised opportunity cost table

are two optional assignments we can make. First, we can assign employee 2 to machine B. Then, the remaining assignments in the one-to-one pairing will be 3 to C and 4 to D. The second way to make the assignment is to assign employee 2 to machine D. Then, again, we do not have any other choice but to assign 3 to B and 4 to C. The two possible optimum assignments and their total costs are as follows:

Assignment 1

Men	Machine	Cost
1	A	$10
2	B	13
3	C	8
4	D	9

Total Assignment Cost = $40

Assignment 2

Men	Machine	Cost
1	A	$10
2	D	10
3	B	9
4	C	11

Total Assignment Cost = $40

There are two optimum solutions for this problem, since the total cost of assignment is exactly identical for the two solutions.

The solution procedure of the assignment method can be summarized as follows:

1. Develop the opportunity-cost table. First, subtract the smallest cost in each row from each cost in that row to determine the initial row opportunity-cost table. Next, subtract the smallest cost in each column from each cost of that column in the initial opportunity-cost table to develop the complete opportunity-cost table.

2. Draw a minimum number of horizontal or vertical straight lines to cross out all zeros in the complete opportunity-cost table. If the number of straight lines required equals the number of rows or columns, an optimum assignment can be found.

3. If the required number of straight lines is less than the number of rows or columns, develop a revised opportunity-cost table. First,

the smallest opportunity cost not crossed out by straight lines must be identified. Second, this minimum cost is subtracted from all other costs that are not crossed out by straight lines. Finally, the same minimum cost is added to all costs that are at the intersection of two straight lines. Go back to step 2 and repeat until an optimum assignment is possible.

SOME COMPLICATIONS AND THEIR RESOLUTION

As in the transportation problem, we face many complications in the assignment problem. We shall discuss them briefly.

A Case with Impossible Assignments

There are many instances where certain employees cannot be assigned to certain tasks. The reasons for such impossible assignments may be due to physical requirements of the task, special technical skills required of the task, or personal preference of the employee. As in the transportation problem with prohibited routes, we can assign large costs (M) to the impossible assignments and solve the problem by the usual assignment method, or we can block-out those impossible assignments from the solution.

A Case with Uneven Requirements

One very important requirement of the assignment method is that the number of rows must be exactly equal to the number of columns. In the real-world situation, however, such an assignment problem is only a very rare case indeed. Quite frequently, the number of employees may be greater than the number of jobs to which they can be assigned, or there may be more jobs that must be performed than the number of employees to do the work. In such cases, we can introduce either dummy employees or dummy jobs and thus balance the requirements. The procedure is exactly the same as the one we utilized for the unbalanced transportation problems. The unit assignment costs for the dummy rows or columns will all be zero.

A Case with Multiple Objectives

It is quite possible that management may wish to achieve a set of multiple objectives in a given assignment problem. It may be possible to apply goal programming for such assignment problems. However, the assignment problem requires zero-one programming (assignment of an employee to machines must be either zero when no assignment is made or one when the assignment is made). At present, integer goal programming is at the early development stage by S. M. Lee.

A Case with Multiple Optimum Solutions

It is quite possible that, as we have observed previously, there are two or more ways to cross out all zero elements in the final opportunity cost table for a given problem. This implies that there are more than the required number of independent zero elements. In such a case, there will be multiple optimum solutions with the same total cost of assignment. Management has the opportunity to exercise its judgment or preference and select one particular optimum solution for the problem.

REFERENCES

Ackoff, R. L., and Sasieni, M. W., *Fundamentals of Operations Research*, Wiley, New York, 1968.

Charnes, A., and Cooper, W. W., *Management Models and Industrial Applications of Linear Programming*, Wiley, New York, 1961.

Churchman, C. W., Ackoff, R. L., and Arnoff, E. L., *Introduction to Operations Research*, Wiley, New York, 1958.

Hillier, F. S., and Lieberman, G. J., *Introduction to Operations Research*, 2d ed., Holden-Day, San Francisco, 1974.

Hitchcock, F. L., "The distribution of a product from several sources to numerous localities," *Journal of Mathematics and Physics* **20** (1941), 224–230.

Hoffmann, T. R., *Production: Management and Manufacturing Systems*, Wadsworth, Belmont, Cal., 1967.

Koopmans, T. C. (ed.), *Activity Analysis of Production and Allocation*, Cowles Commission Monograph No. 13., Wiley, New York, 1951.

Kwak, N. K., *Mathematical Programming with Business Applications*, McGraw-Hill, New York, 1973.

Lee, S. M., and Moore, L. J., "Optimizing transportation problems with multiple objectives," *AIIE Transactions*, **5**, No. 4 (December 1973), 333–338.

Levin, R. I., and Lamone, R., *Linear Programming for Management Decisions*. Irwin, Homewood, Ill., 1969.

Llewellyn, R. W., *Linear Programming*, Holt, New York, 1964.

Orchard-Hays, W., *Advanced Linear Programming Computing Techniques*, McGraw-Hill, New York, 1968.

Orden, A., "The transshipment problem," *Management Science* **2**, (1956), 276–285.

Reinfeld, V., and Vogel, R., *Mathematical Programming*, Prentice-Hall, Englewood Cliffs, N. J. 1958.

PROBLEMS

1. The Sinclair Publishing House is the largest producer of textbooks for high school use in the United States. It produces books at three publishing plants and then stores them there until a school district orders them. Mr. Lewis, the distribution manager, says that he has the following inventories at each plant of a book called *Introductory Geometry*: plant A, 17,000 books; plant B, 25,000; and plant C, 27,000. Three school districts have placed orders for this book and they require the following quantities: district 1, 20,500 books; district 2, 24,500; and district 3, 24,000. The company has done business with these three districts before and Mr. Lewis says that the shipping costs per 100 books from each plant to each district are:

	District 1	District 2	District 3
Plant A	$5	$6	$3
Plant B	4	2	5
Plant C	7	4	6

(a) Find the initial solutions of the above problem (exact allocation and total transportation cost) by the northwest-corner, minimum cell-cost, and Vogel's approximation methods.

(b) Formulate a linear programming model for the problem.

(c) Starting with the initial solution derived by the northwest-corner method, find the optimum solution through the stepping-stone method.

2. The Wilcox Stone Company has a contract to supply the gravel for all road repairs in the county. The company maintains three stock piles in the county and each contains the following amount of gravel: stock pile 1, 100 tons; stock pile 2, 60; and stock pile 3, 80. Due to recent flooding there are numerous roads that need repair. The company has received instructions to deliver the following amounts to the designated locations: Harrisonburg, 40 tons; Johnstown, 90; and Marion, 110. The company has had this contract for many years and they know that the transportation cost per ton from each stockpile to each location is as follows:

	Harrisonburg	Johnstown	Marion
Stock pile 1	$4	$6	$2
Stock pile 2	8	7	10
Stock pile 3	6	1	4

(a) Formulate a linear programming model for the above problem.
(b) Formulate a goal programming model for the transportation problem.
(c) Develop initial solutions by the minimum cell-cost and Vogel's approximation methods.
(d) Starting with the initial solution derived by the northwest-corner method, find the cell with the best cost improvement index and the quantity that can be transferred to the cell.
(e) Find the optimum solution by using the stepping-stone method.
(f) Is there an alternate optimum solution? If so, identify it.

3. The Owens Tree Farm is the primary supplier of Christmas trees for a tri-city region. Christmas trees are grown at three different farm locations and shipped to the three cities when they place their orders. Shipping costs per tree from each farm to each city have been estimated to be:

	Roanoke	Radford	Dublin
Farm 1	25¢	9¢	18¢
Farm 2	13	15	12
Farm 3	20	17	22

This year's supply of trees is very good and each farm has the following number of trees: farm 1, 1500; farm 2, 800; and farm 3, 1000. Mr. Owens has received orders from tree distributors in the tri-city area and they have requested the following number of trees: Roanoke, 700; Radford, 1200; and Dublin, 1600.

(a) Formulate the initial solution by the minimum cell-cost method.
(b) Find the optimum solution by the MODI method.

4. The Electric Motor Company specializes in producing compact, electric cars. It is a relatively new, small company and has only three plants. These three plants have the following production capacity: plant 1, 800 cars per week; plant 2, 500 cars per week; and plant 3, 600 cars per week. Small electric cars are becoming increasingly popular for travel in and around big cities. As a result, three of Electric's dealers in the following cities have placed large orders for

the next week: Los Angeles, 1050 cars; Houston, 500 cars; and Atlanta, 650 cars. The orders are rush orders and the shipping costs will be higher. The distribution manager says that the following costs per car are associated with shipping from each plant to each city:

	Los Angeles	Houston	Atlanta
Plant 1	$40	$10	$20
Plant 2	15	20	10
Plant 3	20	25	30

(a) Formulate a linear programming model for the above problem.
(b) Set up the initial solutions by the northwest-corner, minimum cell-cost, and Vogel's approximation methods.
(c) Starting with the initial solution derived by the northwest-corner method, solve it through two iterations by the MODI method.

5. REBAL is an organization of students and staff at various local high schools who are interested in rebalancing the environment. REBAL groups in three high schools have conducted a very extensive paper recycling drive during the holidays. They have collected the following amounts of waste paper: Blacksburg High, 175 tons; Pulaski High, 150 tons; and Radford High, 125 tons. There are three firms in the area that buy and process solid waste. However, they are relatively small firms and they can process a very limited quantity per month. The three firms report that they can buy only up to the following quantity of waste paper: Colonial Recycling, 200 tons; Systems Environment, 100 tons; and Valley Ecology, 100 tons. The companies have their own trucks for transportation. Their shipping costs per ton of waste paper from the three high school locations are as follows:

	Colonial	Systems	Valley
Blacksburg	$20	$19	$17
Pulaski	23	21	20
Radford	18	24	22

(a) Formulate a linear programming model for the above transportation problem.
(b) Set up the initial solution by the Vogel's approximation method.
(c) Is the initial solution derived in (b) degenerate? If so, what are some of the cells where ϵ should be assigned?
(d) Find the optimum solution by using the MODI method.

6. The Mason Brick Company manufactures bricks for home builders. There is currently a housing boom and the company's three plants are producing the following number of bricks each month: plant 1, 36,000; plant 2, 25,000; and plant 3, 30,000. There are four major builders in the area which Mason supplies. These builders have the following orders for the next month: Arrow, 26,000 bricks; Long, 40,000 bricks; Sims, 25,000 bricks; and Terrace, 30,000 bricks. Mr. Mason has estimated the shipping cost per 1000 bricks from each plant to each construction site to be as follows:

	Arrow	Long	Sims	Terrace
Plant 1	$12	$10	$9	$15
Plant 2	10	8	2	10
Plant 3	9	5	13	8

(a) Set up the initial solution by the northwest-corner method.
(b) Is the initial solution degenerate? If so, identify those cells where ϵ should be assigned to avoid degeneracy.
(c) Now, solve the problem through one iteration by the MODI method.
(d) Is the solution after one iteration degenerate? If so, where should ϵ be assigned to avoid degeneracy?

7. The Grover Brewing Company brews an extremely popular brand of beer. However, in order to preserve quality, it produces this beer in only three plants where spring water is available. From these plants it ships to only three wholesalers. The current inventory of beer at the three plants is: Colorado plant, 18,000 cases; Minnesota plant, 12,500 cases; and Washington plant, 9500 cases. The three wholesalers have just placed orders for the following quantities of beer: wholesaler 1, 15,000 cases; wholesaler 2, 8500 cases; and wholesaler 3, 16,500 cases. Since these are the only customers, the company knows the shipping costs per 100 cases from each plant to each wholesaler:

	Wholesaler 1	Wholesaler 2	Wholesaler 3
Colorado	$8	$6	$4
Minnesota	4	7	3
Washington	5	8	6

The Colorado plant reports that due to a recent snowstorm in the area, it is impossible to ship beer to wholesaler 3.

(a) Formulate a linear programming model for the above problem.

(b) Set up the initial solution by the minimum cell-cost method.

(c) Find the optimum solution by the MODI method.

8. The Midwest Grain Company owns three grain elevators in which it stores grain. Presently, the company has the following inventories at each location: elevator 1, 125 tons; elevator 2, 60 tons; and elevator 3, 75 tons. The company supplies four grain dealers, who have placed the following orders: dealer A, 45 tons; dealer B, 60 tons; dealer C, 90 tons; and dealer D, 85 tons. The shipping costs (per ton) from each of the elevators are as follows:

	Dealer A	Dealer B	Dealer C	Dealer D
Elevator 1	$20	$18	$12	$19
Elevator 2	25	16	17	21
Elevator 3	18	23	19	18

Due to a recent flood in the area, it has become impossible to ship any grain from elevator 3 to dealer A. The president of the firm lists the following goals in order of importance:

I. Avoid any shipment from elevator 3 to dealer A.

II. In order to meet the contract delivery time, it is extremely important to meet the demand of dealer C completely.

III. Minimize the total transportation cost.

Formulate a goal programming model for the above problem.

9. The Charmelle Dress Company has been producing summer dresses for the past several months in anticipation of receiving orders from its customers. Charmelle stores its dresses in three warehouses and at the present time they have the following inventories: warehouse 1, 2600 dresses; warehouse 2, 3500 dresses; and warehouse 3, 1850 dresses. Orders have begun to come in and three large customers have placed the following orders to be shipped to the following cities: Chicago, 2400 dresses; New York, 1750 dresses; and Tampa, 3350 dresses. The distribution manager says that he has computed the following shipping costs per 100 dresses from each warehouse to each city:

	Chicago	New York	Tampa
Warehouse 1	$15	$10	$13
Warehouse 2	15	14	12
Warehouse 3	11	12	15

(a) Starting with the initial solution derived by the minimum cell-cost method, solve the problem through the MODI method.

(b) Are there any alternate optimum solutions? If so, identify them.

10. The Wilmar Tool Company has a sales force of 25 men who work out of three regional offices. The company produces four basic lines of hand tools. Mr. James, the sales manager, feels that 6 salesmen are needed to distribute product line 1, 10 salesmen to distribute product line 2, 4 salesmen for product line 3, and 5 salesmen for product line 4. The cost per day of assigning salesmen from each of the offices to selling each of the product lines are as follows:

	Product Lines			
	1	2	3	4
Regional office A	$20	$21	$16	$18
Regional office B	17	28	14	16
Regional office C	29	23	19	20

At the present time, 10 salesmen are allocated to office A, 8 salesmen to office B, and 7 salesmen to office C. How many salesmen should be assigned from each office to selling each product line in order to minimize costs?

(a) Starting with the initial solution derived by the minimum cell-cost method, find the optimum solution by the MODI method.

(b) Identify alternate optimum solutions.

11. The management of the Blacksburg Discount Store plans to advertise summer sales to be held in its four stores through local radio stations in August. The cost of advertising per minute varies because of differences in the size of the audience reached. The management has information on the available time for advertising at each of four radio stations, required advertising time by the stores, and costs as shown in the following table:

Radio Stations	Discount Stores				Available Time
	1	2	3	4	
WAAA	$50	$70	$65	$50	30
WBBB	45	60	75	60	40
WCCC	60	50	55	70	50
WDDD	65	50	60	75	50
Required Time	30	30	40	50	

Determine the amount of advertising time of each radio station to be used while minimizing total cost by the MODI method.

12. Consider a transportation problem having the following costs and requirements table:

		Destination					
		A	*B*	*C*	*D*	*E*	*Supply*
	1	$21	$12	$28	$17	$9	50
	2	15	13	20	50	12	60
Source	3	18	17	22	10	8	40
	4	X	2	10	5	1	70
	5	33	29	35	27	23	30
	Demand	40	30	50	60	50	

(X in 4A indicates that transportation is prohibited in that cell.)

(a) Set up the initial solutions of transportation by using the minimum cell-cost and Vogel's approximation methods.
(b) With the initial solution derived by the Vogel's approximation method, solve it through one iteration by the MODI method.
(c) If the president of the firm has the following multiple goals, as arranged in the ordinal ranking of importance, how would you set up a goal programming model?

  I. Sources 3 and 5 should be in full-capacity operation (unionized plants).
  II. Any under-capacity operation that may be required should be equally (in terms of percentage) shared among sources 1, 2, and 4.
  III. Minimize the total transportation cost.

13. Mr. Morris is trying to decide where to locate the four new machines that he ordered for his shop. Some locations are more desirable than others for particular machines because of their proximity to work centers that would have heavy work flow to and from these machines. Mr. Morris has come up with the following estimated costs per unit time of materials handled for each location and machine:

	Location A	Location B	Location C
Machine 1	$11	$5	$13
Machine 2	8	10	11
Machine 3	9	12	7

Which machines should be placed at which locations in order to minimize material handling costs?

14. The Matthews Insurance Company has been given four additional districts in which to attempt to sell life insurance. Mr. Matthews has four agents with varying degrees of training and experience that he can assign to handle this new business. Of course, he wants to assign only one agent to each district. Mr. Matthews has estimated what the costs per 10 customers contacted would be if each agent were assigned to each district:

	District 1	District 2	District 3	District 4
Agent 1	$18	$30	$16	$19
Agent 2	25	24	22	17
Agent 3	30	26	19	20
Agent 4	28	21	29	19

Which agent should be assigned to each district in order to minimize total costs?

15. The Williams Glass Company produces glass bottles and jars for commercial use. Mr. Williams has recently enlarged his plant and he has purchased four new glass molding machines. He has had his personnel department interviewing people to find the most qualified people to run these machines. The personnel department has found that there is a shortage of machine operators for glass molding machines and so they have hired four men with varying experience. From a review of their work experience the production manager has estimated that the production cost per case for each combination of man and machine will be:

	Machine 1	Machine 2	Machine 3	Machine 4
Worker 1	$10	$12	$9	$11
Worker 2	5	10	7	8
Worker 3	12	14	13	11
Worker 4	8	15	11	9

Which worker should be assigned to each machine in order to minimize total production cost?

16. The Overland Bus Company is trying to improve its service to large cities. It is particularly interested in assigning one additional bus to each of four cities. It has four buses of varying age and service that it has removed from cross-country service due to the gas shortage. The company transportation division has estimated that the operating cost of each bus in each city will be:

	Roanoke	Washington	Richmond	Norfolk
Bus 1	$150	$110	$130	$125
Bus 2	140	135	150	110
Bus 3	125	120	115	135
Bus 4	130	115	120	145

(a) Which bus should be assigned to each city in order to minimize total operating cost?

(b) Are there alternate optimum solutions? If so, identify them.

17. The Ralston Candy Company produces four kinds of candy bars. The company has four machines that it uses to produce these candy bars. Mr. Ralston has noticed that production costs per type of candy bar vary from month to month. This has an effect on the profit contribution of each type and Mr. Ralston is wondering if there is a best machine to use for producing each candy bar. The accounting department has been studying past records and has estimated the following costs per case of producing each type of candy bar with each machine:

	Venus	Joy	Choice-Nut	Tasty
Machine 1	$7	$3	$4	$8
Machine 2	5	4	6	5
Machine 3	6	7	9	6
Machine 4	8	6	7	4

Which machine should be used to produce each candy bar in order to minimize total production cost?

18. Piedmont Electronics, Inc., supplies television components to various television manufacturers. The past records indicate that a certain number of components assembled by the workers were returned because of their defects. The average number of defects produced by each worker per month on various component production jobs is given in the following matrix:

Men \ Job	1	2	3	4	5	6
A	30	24	16	26	30	22
B	22	28	14	30	20	13
C	18	16	25	14	12	22
D	14	22	18	23	21	30
E	25	18	14	16	16	28
F	32	24	10	14	28	20

Determine the optimum assignment of the workers to various jobs to minimize the total number of defects.

19. The public works department of Roanoke has seven snowplows. The director wants to assign these plows to seven districts of the city in order to clean up the new snow in the shortest possible time. The amount of time (in minutes) required to clean up all the major streets in each district by different types of snowplows is as follows:

| | | | | Districts | | | |
	1	*2*	*3*	*4*	*5*	*6*	*7*
A	35	22	60	41	27	52	44
B	51	39	42	33	65	47	58
C	25	32	53	41	50	36	43
Snowplows D	32	28	40	46	34	55	49
E	43	36	45	63	57	49	42
F	27	18	31	46	35	42	34
G	48	50	72	59	43	64	58

Solve the above assignment problem.

20. The New York Police Department has seven investigating teams. The chief wants to assign these teams to eight cases under investigation while minimizing the total time required to conclude the cases. The average amount of time (in days) required to complete the different types of cases for each team has been calculated according to past performance, as follows:

| | | | | Cases | | | | |
	A	*B*	*C*	*D*	*E*	*F*	*G*	*H*
1	35	28	55	49	30	25	48	35
2	28	45	20	32	55	37	42	18
3	45	28	55	49	32	44	60	56
Investigation 4	62	37	42	48	55	60	39	45
Team 5	38	32	44	50	70	42	28	47
6	20	35	37	27	32	48	22	29
7	33	40	37	66	53	44	60	X

Each team has a different composition of personnel, expertise, equipment, and so on, and this is part of the problem. For example, Lieutenant Kojak's team (team 7) is very effective in murder cases but they tend to be almost useless for narcotics cases (case H). In fact, the chief has decided not to assign Kojak to case H under any circumstances. Solve the above problem by using the assignment method.

8 Inventory Models

INTRODUCTION

Inventory analysis was one of the first areas of application of decision science models. For example, an economic lot-size equation was first developed by F. W. Harris in 1915. Models of inventory systems were further developed by F. E. Raymond in the early 1930s. Since World War II the literature of decision science has included virtually every possible condition under which inventories might be analyzed.

It is not surprising that inventory analysis has held such a prominent place in decision science when one considers the fact that inventory often represents as much as 25 to 40 percent of the total invested capital of industrial organizations. In addition to being a major component of the total current assets in many businesses, inventory represents an important decision variable at all stages of product manufacturing, distribution, and sales.

When one considers the fact that inventories in some of the world's major corporations are in the billions of dollars, it becomes apparent that improvements in inventory management, by even a few percentage points, can represent very large dollar savings.

The study of inventory models is important not only because inventory often represents such a large portion of total assets but also because inventory analysis offers a wide range of exposure to decision science modeling concepts in general, which may be transferred to other areas of application as well.

INVENTORY FUNCTIONS

Inventory is, broadly defined, any stock of economic resources that are idle at a given point in time. This may include raw materials awaiting use in manufacturing operations, semifinished goods temporarily stored during the manufacturing process, finished goods awaiting distribution, and finished goods awaiting sale in wholesale or retail outlets. Inventories may also include such nonphysical assets as cash, inventories of accounts receivable, or inventories of human resources.

Although inventory is generally considered to be a nonearning asset, the optimum managerial decision is not simply to reduce inventory to the lowest possible level. Inventories are necessary to achieve workable systems of production, distribution, and marketing of physical goods. For example, raw materials must be accumulated in inventory for further processing into finished goods. Also, raw materials inventories are often accumulated as a hedge against price inflation or union strikes in industries supplying these materials. During the process of production, inventory serves the function of decoupling successive stages of manufacturing. This allows the various production departments to operate more independently, without direct reliance on the schedule of output of prior departments in the productive process. The distribution of finished goods almost always requires certain quantities of inventory in transit and accumulations at intermediate delivery points.

It may be more economical to carry a certain amount of inventory in order to produce or purchase in large lots so as to achieve reduced production set-up costs or quantity discounts on items purchased. Inventories may be accumulated in order to smooth out the level of production operations, so that employees do not have to be temporarily laid-off and later rehired and retrained.

The most obvious function of inventory is seen at the retail store level, where inventory is carried to absorb random fluctuations in demand. The objective of inventory at the retail level is to meet demand as it occurs and avoid stock-outs. Additionally, inventory on display serves as a promotional device.

Thus, although inventories are generally considered to be nonearning assets, it is also apparent that inventories serve many functions that are vital to the overall production-distribution-marketing system. The important point is that since inventories are found throughout the system and constitute a major segment of total investment, it is crucial that good inventory management be practiced. The purpose of this chapter is to present the basic concepts of optimum inventory management.

BASIC INVENTORY DECISIONS

The basic inventory decisions are what quantity to order, and when to order. Thus, when attempting to model inventory systems, these are the important decision variables. Throughout the chapter, it will be shown that in many cases it is possible to consider each of these decisions separately. However, in some cases the two decisions are interdependent, and the optimum values for the two decision variables must be obtained simultaneously. The key to which approach must be taken is the assumptions that are implicit in the model.

EVALUATION CRITERIA—INVENTORY COSTS

The most common criteria considered in inventory analysis are inventory-related costs, which may be categorized as (1) ordering costs, (2) carrying costs, and (3) shortage costs.

Ordering Costs

Ordering costs are those costs associated with replenishing the stock of inventory on hand. These are costs that vary with the number of orders made, and are expressed in terms of dollar cost per order. The following are sample costs incurred each time an order is made:

Requisitioning
Purchase order
Transportation
Receiving
Inspection
Placing in storage
Accounting and auditing
Payment to supplier

Carrying Costs

Carrying costs are those costs associated with holding a certain stock of inventory on hand. Carrying costs are often referred to as holding costs. These costs vary with the level of inventory held, and sometimes vary with the time the item is held (such as in the case of perishable goods). There are several components of carrying cost, and the relative impact of each depends upon the inventory goods considered. The following are commonly considered components of carrying cost:

Foregone profit on investment tied up in inventory

Direct storage costs (rent, heat, lights, refrigeration, record keeping, security, etc.)

Product obsolescence or deterioration

Depreciation, taxes, and insurance

Carrying costs may be specified in several ways. The most general form is the dollar cost of carrying one unit in inventory per unit time. The time horizon commonly considered is one year; that is, carrying cost is the cost of carrying one unit in inventory for one year. Another approach commonly used for practical reasons is to specify carrying cost per year as a percentage of average inventory value; for example, carrying cost may equal 15 to 20 percent of average inventory value.

Shortage Costs

Shortage costs are often referred to as stock-out costs. Inventory shortages occur when demand exceeds the supply of inventory on hand. Shortages may either be accidental or be a planned policy on the part of the company.

If inventory shortages result in the permanent loss of sales for items demanded but not filled, then the shortage cost includes lost profits due to unsatisfied demand. Additionally, shortages may result in an ill-will cost, due to permanently lost customers and the associated long-run lost profits of future sales.

On the other hand, the firm may simply back-order demands not filled when shortages occur. This is common practice in most mail-order houses. Thus, the relevant cost of shortage then becomes the clerical and paperwork costs associated with back orders. However, back-ordered shortages may also result in some lost customers, and thus some ill-will costs are usually included in this case also.

CLASSIC INVENTORY MODEL

The discussion of inventory models is organized into a series of steps. Each step will present a different model of inventory. Actually, step one (classic inventory model) will present the basic inventory model, and succeeding models will simply reflect one or more changes in the basic assumptions of the initial model. Also, the set of models will represent a logical development of inventory models, from the simplest case to the more complex cases.

Managerial Objectives

In the construction and solution of inventory models, it will be assumed that the objective of the decision maker is to minimize total inventory costs. It must be recognized that this objective might result in suboptimization in terms of the overall objectives of the organization. Thus, in application, inventory analysis must be conducted using the so-called "systems" concept. The study of inventory models is, nevertheless, a valuable component of any introduction to systems modeling and decision science.

Assumptions of the Classic Inventory Model

The classic model is the simplest of inventory models and is often referred to as the EOQ model (economic order quantity). Although it is generally too oversimplified to reflect most real-world situations, it is a good basis from which to launch a study of inventory models.

The assumptions of the classic EOQ model are as follows:

1. Inventory usage rate (demand) is constant over time.
2. Inventory demand is known with certainty.
3. Inventory replenishment is instantaneous (entire order is received simultaneously).
4. Inventory is replenished when inventory is exactly zero (no excess stock is carried and no shortages are allowed).
5. Reorder lead-time is zero (order is received at the same instant it is placed).

The last assumption is unnecessary, since we could assume a constant, known reorder lead-time without affecting our model results; however, in order to simplify the initial presentation we will include this assumption.

Inventory Level Model

The assumptions of the classic inventory model are illustrated graphically in Figure 8.1, referred to as the *inventory level* model. This distinction in model title is made since inventory models will be illustrated graphically in two ways: (1) graphical model of inventory level, and (2) graphical model of inventory costs.

Note, in Figure 8.1, the downward sloping line shows the level of inventory being reduced at a constant rate over time (constant and known demand). Also, since demand is constant and known exactly, and since receipt of goods ordered is instantaneous, the reorder point is when the inventory level falls to exactly zero.

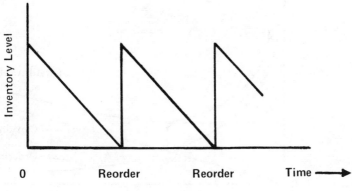

Figure 8.1
Classic inventory level model

Formulation of the Classic Inventory Model

The objective of inventory analysis will be to determine the optimum order quantity such that total inventory costs are minimized. Since it has been assumed that shortages never occur, shortage costs are not considered. The two classes of costs included in the inventory model are: (1) ordering costs, and (2) carrying costs. The objective is to minimize the sum of these two costs.

The Decision Model

We will start by first illustrating the model graphically, in Figure 8.2. We refer to this graphical model of inventory costs as the *decision* model, since the optimum order quantity (optimum decision) can be determined visually from this graphical model. It is important to remember that the inventory model can be illustrated graphically two ways: the inventory *level* model, showing the inventory level over time; and the inventory *decision* model, showing the relationships of inventory costs to the decision variable, order quantity.

Note, in Figure 8.2, that as the quantity ordered (per order) increases, fewer orders will be necessary and, therefore, ordering costs will decrease. However, as order sizes increase there will be more time between orders, and inventory carried will increase, resulting in increased carrying costs. Total inventory costs first decease, as the order size increases, but begin to rise again after a point. The objective of inventory analysis is to solve for the value of order quantity that corresponds to minimum total inventory costs.

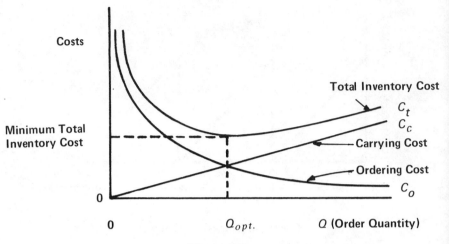

Figure 8.2
Classic inventory decision model

Model Symbols

The first step in constructing the inventory model is to define the variables and parameters (generally constants) of the model. Actually, some of the parameters of the model are initially given as variables. The approach of inventory analysis is to define model parameters as variables, when possible, and solve for the general case. Thus, one can then simply substitute into the general case model solution the values of the parameters and obtain an optimum solution for a specific problem, without having to rework the entire model. The model symbols are defined as follows:

C_t = total annual inventory cost
C_o = total annual ordering costs
C_c = total annual carrying costs
Q = quantity ordered, per order
D = demand (usage) for goods in inventory, expressed on an annual basis.
C_1 = ordering cost, per order
C_2 = carrying cost, per unit of inventory held, for one year

It is important to identify, in any model, the decision variable—that variable for which a solution value is desired. In this case, the decision variable is Q, the quantity ordered. The criterion variable, the value of which must be measured in order to determine the extent to which the objective is achieved, is C_t, total inventory costs. Thus, C_t is a dependent variable, and it is a function of Q, the quantity ordered. This is written in the general mathematical form $C_t = f(Q)$.

However, total inventory costs are affected by more than just order quantity. The other factors affecting the inventory costs are the parameters of the model. In this case, the parameters are C_1 (ordering cost per order), C_2 (carrying cost per unit held for a year), and D (the annual demand for goods in inventory.) Thus, total inventory costs are a function of the decision variable and the model parameters, of $C_t = f(Q, C_1, C_2, D)$.

The whole purpose of decision science is to recognize explicitly the decision variable, the criterion variable, and the parameters, and then to construct a model that expresses their relationship. A general statement of the model at this point, including the objective of the analysis, which is to minimize total inventory costs, is:

Minimize $\quad C_t = C_o + C_c \quad$ Criterion or objective function

where C_o and C_c are actually both variables that are simply sub-components of the overall criterion variable, C_t. However, by expressing our model in this form, and then expressing each of these sub-components of C_t in terms of the parameters and decision variable, the solution to the inventory problem is most easily obtained.

Prior to construction of the model, the concept of average inventory will be examined. Note that since the usage (demand) of goods in inventory is constant, the average inventory held will be $\frac{1}{2}Q$, where Q (quantity ordered) is the maximum level of inventory held at the time of each order receipt. The average inventory level is illustrated graphically in Figure 8.3

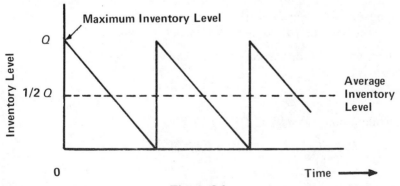

Figure 8.3
Average inventory level

Construction of the Symbolic Model

The inventory model is constructed by analyzing each of the cost categories, as follows:

Ordering cost. Total ordering cost per year, C_o, will simply be the cost per order, C_1, times the number of orders. Since total usage or demand is known to be D, then the number of orders per year will be D/Q. Thus, the total ordering cost is

$$C_o = C_1 \cdot \frac{D}{Q}$$

Carrying cost. Total carrying cost, C_c, is the carrying cost per unit held per year, C_2, times the average number of units held. Thus, the total carrying cost is

$$C_c = C_2 \cdot \frac{Q}{2}$$

The model may now be formulated in terms of the decision variable and the relevant parameters, as follows:

$$C_t = C_o + C_c = C_1 \cdot \frac{D}{Q} + C_2 \cdot \frac{Q}{2}$$

Solution of the Classic Inventory Model

The model may now be solved for the optimum value of the decision variable Q. The approach that may be taken, for this model, is to simply equate total carrying cost to total ordering cost, and solve for Q. This approach will not work for all types of inventory models, but in general holds true for equations of the form $y = ax^{-1} + bx$. A more general solution approach, that of classical optimization (using calculus), is illustrated in Appendix IV.

The solution to the inventory model is as follows:

Equating total ordering cost to total carrying cost,

$$C_1 \cdot \frac{D}{Q} = C_2 \cdot \frac{Q}{2}$$

Dividing both sides by $C_1 Q$,

$$\frac{D}{Q^2} = \frac{C_2}{2C_1}$$

Inverting,

$$\frac{Q^2}{D} = \frac{2C_1}{C_2}$$

Multiplying through by D,

$$Q^2 = \frac{2C_1 D}{C_2}$$

$$Q_{opt} = \sqrt{\frac{2C_1 D}{C_2}}$$

Note that in the final solution, the decision variable Q is given in terms of the model parameters, C_1, C_2, and D. The value 2 may also be thought of as a constant parameter of the model. The solution value of Q is the optimum value of Q, which corresponds to the minimum total inventory cost. This is the lowest point on the C_t curve of Figure 8.2, and it is at the point where C_o equals C_c.

In order to solve for any specific inventory problem satisfying the assumptions of the model, one need simply insert the values of C_1, C_2, and D into the general solution model, $Q = \sqrt{2C_1 D / C_2}$. For example, assume that one had determined that the assumptions of the classic inventory model fit some real-world inventory situation. Further, assume that the values of the model parameters had been determined to be

$C_1 = \$ 50$ Cost per order
$C_2 = \$100$ Cost per unit held in inventory on
             an annual basis
$D = 4900$ Demand for goods in inventory on
             an annual basis

Then, the solution for the optimum order quantity is

$$Q = \sqrt{\frac{2C_1 D}{C_2}}$$

$$= \sqrt{\frac{(2)(50)(4900)}{100}}$$

$$= \sqrt{4900}$$
$$Q_{opt} = 70 \text{ units}$$

The order quantity should be 70 units in order to minimize total inventory costs.

Some Further Solution Results

Several additional types of information may be desired regarding the inventory model. For example, what is the value of the minimum total inventory costs? Other values that are often of interest are (1) how often to order per year, and (2) how long a time between orders.

The nature of the inventory model is such that when the value of Q has been solved for, the other values just mentioned are directly available also. Let us define these values symbolically as

N = number of orders per year
T_b = time between orders
T = total time (in this case one year)

Total inventory cost is already defined as C_t.

In the development of the model it was shown that the number of orders per year was annual demand divided by order size, or $N = D/Q$. Thus, the solution value for N will be

$$N_{opt} = \frac{D}{Q_{opt}} = \frac{4900}{70} = 70 \text{ orders}$$

Also, the solution value for time between orders is simply the total time horizon divided by the number of orders, or $T_b = T/N$. Thus, we have

$$(T_b)_{opt} = \frac{T}{N_{opt}} = \frac{365}{70} = 5.214 \cong 5 \text{ days}$$

The value used for T may be 1 (for one year), or it could be in months, weeks, or days, depending upon the form of solution desired.

Finally, the minimum total inventory cost for the optimum value of Q may be derived by referring to the original model, that is,

$$C_t = C_1 \cdot \frac{D}{Q} + C_2 \frac{Q}{2}$$

It is interesting to note that this may be solved for in a general form, analogous to the general form of the solution for Q, as follows:

$$(C_t)_{opt} = C_1 \frac{D}{Q_{opt}} + C_2 \frac{Q_{opt}}{2}$$

Substituting for Q the optimum solution in terms of model parameters,

$$(C_t)_{opt} = \frac{C_1 D}{\sqrt{2C_1 D/C_2}} + \frac{C_2 \sqrt{2C_1 D/C_2}}{2}$$

Combining fractions over a common denominator,

$$(C_t)_{opt} = \frac{2C_1 D + C_2(2C_1 D/C_2)}{2\sqrt{2C_1 D/C_2}}$$

$$= \frac{4C_1 D}{2\sqrt{2C_1 D/C_2}}$$

$$= \frac{2C_1 D}{\sqrt{2C_1 D/C_2}}$$

Combining all terms under the radical,

$$(C_t)_{opt} = \frac{\sqrt{(2C_1D)^2}\sqrt{C_2}}{\sqrt{2C_1D}}$$

$$= \sqrt{\frac{(2C_1D)^2C_2}{2C_1D}}$$

$$= \sqrt{(2C_1D)C_2}$$

$$(C_t)_{opt} = \sqrt{2C_1C_2D}$$

Thus, one may simply substitute the parameter values for the model into this equation to obtain the minimum total inventory cost. For the example solution, this would yield:

$$(C_t)_{opt} = \sqrt{(2)(50)(100)(4900)}$$

$$= \sqrt{49,000,000}$$

$$= \$7000$$

Reorder Point

The second step in our discussion of inventory models actually does not involve a new model at all. However, one assumption of the previous model is modified and a new assumption is added. The assumption that goods ordered are received at the same instant as ordered is now discarded (assumption 5). The other assumptions of the initial model remain the same, and it is now assumed that the time to receive an order is known and constant.

By discarding the last assumption of the initial model, the concept of reorder lead-time is introduced. Thus, an additional consideration for model analysis is added, but the basic cost model previously presented is unchanged.

Inventory Level Model

The inventory level model is again illustrated graphically, in Figure 8.4. However, in this case it is assumed that there is some time lag from the time at which goods are ordered to the time at which the order is received. This is generally called lead time. Figure 8.4 illustrates the lead time for each of the orders of the figure. Note that in this case, goods are now ordered before the level of inventory falls to zero. The inventory level at which an order is placed is termed the *reorder point*.

With the assumptions of this model—constant and known demand and constant and known lead time—it is a simple matter to compute the reorder point (inventory level at which to reorder goods). The reorder point is simply the product of the demand during lead time (in units per day) times the lead time (in days). Let us define the reorder point as I_r, and the lead time (in days) as T_L. The demand per day (assuming a 365-day-a-year operation) will be $D/365$. Thus, the reorder point is simply

$$I_r = T_L \frac{D}{365}$$

Suppose the demand per day is 15 units and the lead time is 5 days; then the reorder point would be 75 units, or $I_r = 75$ and one would reorder when the inventory level falls to 75 units. It is important to point out that the solution value for Q (the optimum order quantity) is not affected by the assumption that there is some lead time involved in receipt of goods. Therefore, the classic model may include the requirement that one solve for Q by the method illustrated initially, and also solve for I_r, the reorder point.

Example
    Assume that the lead time for the previous example was three days. If the system operated 365 days per year, then the average demand per day would be $4900/365 \cong 13.4$ units. Thus, the proper reorder point would be:

$$I_r = (3)(13.4) = 40.2 \text{ units}$$

In other words, one should reorder when the inventory level reaches 40 units.

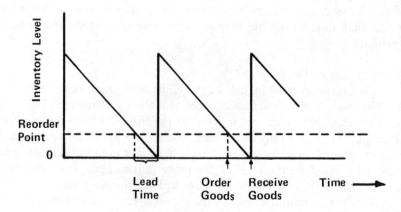

Figure 8.4
Inventory level model, with reorder lead time

Parameter Variations in the Classic Model

The purpose of this step of the inventory discussion is to point out that different approaches may be taken with regard to describing inventory models. Two modifications to the previous model approach will be illustrated.

Carrying Cost as a Percentage

Carrying cost may be expressed as a percentage of average dollar value of inventory held rather than some specified dollar carrying cost per unit held. If the percentage approach is used, the unit price (or value) of inventory in stock must also be specified, in order to determine the average value of inventory held. The development of the model for the percentage carrying cost approach will now be illustrated.

Carrying cost. The variables for the carrying-cost portion of the model are now as follows:

C_2 = carrying cost as a percentage of average dollar value of
      inventory on an annual basis

P = price (or value) per unit of inventory held in inventory

Therefore, we can see that the equation for total annual carrying cost may now be expressed as

$$C_c = C_2 P \frac{Q}{2}$$

that is, the annual carrying cost equals the percentage carrying cost times the average inventory value.

The inventory model and solution. The entire inventory model will now be

$$C_t = C_o + C_c$$

$$C_t = C_1 \frac{D}{Q} + C_2 P \frac{Q}{2}$$

The same solution procedure will be used here as was followed for the initial model, that is, equate the two types of inventory cost, and solve for Q. Thus, we obtain

$$C_1 \frac{D}{Q} = C_2 P \frac{Q}{2}$$

or,

$$Q_{opt} = \sqrt{\frac{2C_1 D}{C_2 P}}$$

The resulting model approach has introduced a new parameter, price of goods in stock, and it has changed the definition of C_2 to a percentage value versus the dollar value definition of the initial model.

Suppose, for example, that the values of the model parameters were found to be the following:

C_1 = \$50   Cost per order
C_2 = 20%   Carrying cost as a percent of average inventory
                              on annual basis
D = 4900   Annual demand for goods in inventory
P = \$500   Cost or value per unit of goods in inventory

Then the solution value for Q would be

$$Q = \sqrt{\frac{2C_1D}{C_2P}}$$

$$= \sqrt{\frac{(2)(50)(4900)}{(0.20)(500)}}$$

$$= \sqrt{4900}$$

$$Q_{opt} = 70$$

Time as a Variable

Another fairly common practice in inventory models is to specify the time horizon over which the inventory analysis is to apply as a variable. The symbol commonly used to denote the time horizon is T. One will often find in this case that the demand for goods in inventory is specified as demand during time T. Also, the holding or carrying cost in this case is often specified as cost of holding one unit in inventory "per unit time" (such as days). Thus, for this case, it is necessary to include the variable T in the construction of the inventory model.

The model. The inventory model will now be specified, where the total time horizon is simply identified as T, and the following definitions apply:

D = demand during time T
C_2 = carrying cost per unit of inventory per unit time (e.g., per day)

Thus, the model is as follows:

$$C_o = C_1\frac{D}{Q} \qquad \text{Ordering cost}$$

$$C_c = C_2\frac{Q}{2}T \qquad \text{Carrying cost}$$

$$C_t = C_1\frac{D}{Q} + C_2\frac{Q}{2}T \qquad \text{Overall inventory model}$$

The solution to the preceding model is determined in a manner similar to the initial model, yielding the following:

$$C_1 \frac{D}{Q} = C_2 \frac{Q}{2} T$$

$$Q_{opt} = \sqrt{\frac{2C_1 D}{C_2 T}}$$

where Q_{opt} is the optimum inventory order quantity for the system evaluated over the time horizon T (e.g., over T days).

Suppose that we take the previous example but modify it such that the time horizon is six months (or 182.5 days). For this example the demand over that period would be 2450 units. The cost of carrying inventory, per day, would be 27.4¢ per unit per day. Recall that ordering cost equals $50. Thus, the model solution would yield

$$Q = \sqrt{\frac{2C_1 D}{C_2 T}}$$

$$= \sqrt{\frac{(2)(50)(2450)}{(0.274)(182.5)}}$$

$$= \sqrt{4900}$$

$$Q_{opt} = 70 \text{ units}$$

As expected, we obtained the same solution as previously obtained.

NONINSTANTANEOUS RECEIPT MODEL

The following step in the development of inventory models will consider the case in which goods are received in a constant stream over time, rather than at one point in time. All other assumptions of the initial model remain unchanged (i.e., only assumption 3 is changed).

Model Symbols

The parameters unique to this model are defined as follows:

r_1 = rate at which goods are received over time, assumed to start at the time the reorder is made, and assumed to be a constant rate

r_2 = usage rate of goods—demand per unit time (e.g., per day), assumed to be a constant rate

All other model symbols are unchanged from the original model.

Average Inventory

Special consideration will be given to the average inventory, for this model. First, recall from the initial classic model that average inventory was half the maximum inventory level, which in that case was Q, the reorder quantity. In this model, the maximum inventory level must be adjusted for the fact that the goods are received over time. This is achieved as follows:

$$\frac{Q}{r_1} = \text{number of days required to receive one entire order (order receipt period)}$$

$$\frac{Q}{r_1} \cdot r_2 = \text{number of units in inventory demanded (usage rate) during order receipt period}$$

$$Q - \left(\frac{Q}{r_1} \cdot r_2\right) = \text{maximum level of inventory for any given order}$$

$$\frac{1}{2}\left[Q - \left(\frac{Q}{r_1} \cdot r_2\right)\right] = \text{average inventory level}$$

The above expression for average inventory can be modified to

$$\frac{Q}{2}\left(1 - \frac{r_2}{r_1}\right)$$

Inventory Level Model

The inventory level model for this case is illustrated graphically in Figure 8.5. Note that it is assumed that the rate at which an order is received is greater than the usage rate (i.e., $r_1 > r_2$). Thus, immediately after an order is placed, the inventory level rises at a constant rate, $r_1 - r_2$, up to the point $Q - (Q/r_1 \cdot r_2)$, and then falls at the constant demand rate r_2.

The Decision Model

The decision model may now be developed as follows:

$$C_o = C_1\frac{D}{Q} \qquad\qquad \text{Ordering cost}$$

$$C_c = C_2\frac{Q}{2}\left(1 - \frac{r_2}{r_1}\right) \qquad\qquad \text{Carrying cost}$$

$$C_t = C_1\frac{D}{Q} + C_2\frac{Q}{2}\left(1 - \frac{r_2}{r_1}\right) \qquad\qquad \text{Overall inventory model}$$

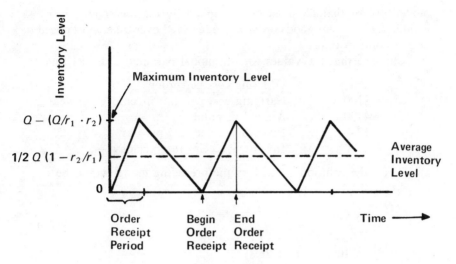

Figure 8.5
Inventory level model, with noninstantaneous receipt of goods

Model Solution
  The solution is obtained in a fashion similar to the initial model, as follows:

$$C_1\frac{D}{Q} = \frac{C_2 Q}{2}\left(1 - \frac{r_2}{r_1}\right)$$

Dividing through by $C_1 Q$,

$$\frac{D}{Q^2} = \frac{C_2(1 - r_2/r_1)}{2C_1}$$

Inverting,

$$\frac{Q^2}{D} = \frac{2C_1}{C_2(1 - r_2/r_1)}$$

Multiplying through by D,

$$Q^2 = \frac{2C_1 D}{C_2(1 - r_2/r_1)}$$

$$Q_{opt} = \sqrt{\frac{2C_1 D}{C_2(1 - r_2/r_1)}}$$

  Thus, the solution is the same as was obtained for the classic EOQ model, except that C_2 must be multiplied by the factor $(1 - r_2/r_1)$ to include the fact that goods ordered are received over time, as opposed to at one point in time.

Suppose that the values for the model parameters are as follows:

C_1 = \$50   Ordering cost per order
C_2 = \$100   Carrying cost per unit inventory per year
D = 4900 units   Annual demand
r_2 = 13.4   Inventory usage rate per day
r_1 = 26.8   Inventory receipt rate per day

Thus, the solution yielded by the preceding model would be

$$Q = \sqrt{\frac{2C_1D}{C_2(1 - r_2/r_1)}}$$

$$= \sqrt{\frac{(2)(50)(4900)}{100(1 - 13.4/26.8)}}$$

$$= \sqrt{\frac{490,000}{50}}$$

$$Q_{opt} = \sqrt{9800} \cong 99 \text{ units}$$

Note that since the goods ordered are received over time, there will be no carrying cost associated with those goods received and used immediately during that time. In the case of the example, exactly half of the goods received are used during the order receipt period. Thus, the total carrying costs will be reduced for this model. Therefore, it becomes economical to order in larger quantities for this case than for the initial model.

PRODUCTION LOT-SIZE MODEL

This step of inventory analysis will reconsider the immediately preceding model by simply considering it within the framework of a different application. Suppose the firm under consideration manufactures its own goods for inventory rather than ordering from outside the firm. Thus, if we consider the order quantity as a production lot size, we can cast this problem within the framework of the preceding model.

Model Symbols

Let us respecify the model variables and parameters for this type of application as follows:

C_t = total annual production and inventory costs
C_o = total annual production set-up costs
C_c = total annual inventory carrying costs
Q = production lot size
D = demand for goods produced for inventory on an annual basis
C_1 = production run set-up costs per production run
C_2 = inventory carrying cost per unit per year
r_1 = production rate
r_2 = demand rate

The model formulation and solution for this application would be identical to the previously given noninstantaneous receipt model.

Production Lot-Size Example

Consider the following example. Suppose a firm has an annual demand for goods produced of 6500 units. The set-up cost for each production run is assumed to be $200. Inventory carrying cost per unit per year is $3.20. The production rate is 50 units per day, while the demand rate is 26 units per day. (Assume approximately 250 operating days per year.)

The optimum production lot size, therefore, should be determined as follows:

$$Q = \sqrt{\frac{2C_1 D}{C_2(1 - r_2/r_1)}}$$

$$= \sqrt{\frac{(2)(200)(6500)}{(3.20)(1 - 26/50)}}$$

$$= \sqrt{\frac{2,600,000}{1.536}}$$

$$= \sqrt{1692708}$$

$Q_{opt} \cong 1301$ units per production run

Thus, the optimum production lot size is approximately 1300 units. The optimum number of production runs may be determined as follows:

$$N = \frac{D}{Q_{opt}}$$

$N_{opt} = 6500/1300 = 5$ production runs per year

The length (in days) between the start of each production run will be

$$T_L = \frac{T}{N_{opt}} \qquad \text{where } T = 250$$

$\cong 50$ working days between run starts

Thus, the optimum solution to this production-inventory problem is to produce 1300 units per production run, with 5 production runs per year, starting every 50 working days. Note that since the production rate is 50 units per day, it will take $1300/50 = 26$ days to complete a run. Thus, 24 working days will remain before the start of the next production run for this product. During this time other goods can be produced. Also, the maximum inventory level reached will be $Q(1 - r_2/r_1)$, or $1300(1 - 26/50) = 1300(.48) = 624$ units.

By using the same approach used in the initial model to develop the general model for total cost, it can be seen that the minimum total production-inventory cost will be given by

$$(C_t)_{opt} = \sqrt{2C_1C_2D\left(1 - \frac{r_2}{r_1}\right)}$$

$$= \sqrt{(2)(200)(3.20)(6500)\left(1 - \frac{26}{50}\right)}$$

$$(C_t)_{opt} \cong \$1998.00$$

QUANTITY DISCOUNT MODEL

The following phase in the development of inventory models includes the case where there is a price discount for goods purchased to replenish inventory, if purchased in sufficient quantity. For example, the normal price for goods might be \$50, whereas, if purchased in order sizes of at least 100 units, the quantity discount price might be \$48. This model is formulated in the same manner as the modified classic model in which carrying cost (C_2) was specified as a percentage of average dollar value of inventory held. Thus, the price is also included in the carrying cost equation in order to yield the dollar value of inventory. If there are price breaks allowed for large quantity orders, the inventory model must consider not only ordering cost and carrying cost, but also cost of goods purchased.

The Symbolic Model

The model for the quantity discount case would, therefore, be:

C_t = total ordering cost + total carrying cost + total cost of goods

$$C_t = C_1\frac{D}{Q} + C_2P\frac{Q}{2} + PD$$

where

C_t = total inventory cost plus cost of goods
C_1 = ordering cost per order
C_2 = carrying cost, as percentage of average value of inventory
   held (on annual basis)
P = price of goods purchased
D = demand for goods per year
Q = quantity ordered per order

Note that there are no new variables introduced in this model. However, the definition of C_t now includes the total value of goods purchased per year, and that value has been added (as the term PD) to the model.

Model Solution

The model is solved in the following manner:

Case I. Quantity discount is received:

1. Determine the optimum order quantity. The optimum order quantity will be the same as the general solution to the classic EOQ model (where inventory cost is specified as a percentage of average inventory value):

$$Q_{opt} = \sqrt{\frac{2C_1 D}{C_2 P}}$$

Since the last term of the total cost function does not include Q, that term has no affect on the solution for Q, and thus the solution here is the same as was obtained for the classic EOQ model. This is proved to be true in Appendix V.
2. Calculate the value of Q_{opt} by substituting into the solution formula the values of C_1, C_2, D, and P. Since this phase of the solution procedure is for the case in which the quantity discount *is* taken, P would be the discount price (the *lower* price).
3. Determine whether the value of Q_{opt} is less than the quantity required to receive the discount price. If the value of Q_{opt} is less than the required quantity, then specify the quantity order size as the minimum order size required to receive the price discount. If the value of Q_{opt} is greater than the required quantity to obtain the price discount, then this order size may be retained as it satisfies the specified requirements.
4. Compute the value of C_t by substituting the values of C_1, C_2, D, P, and Q into the cost model. Recall that the value of P is the discount price and Q must be equal to or greater than the minimum required quantity to receive the discount.

Case II. Quantity discount is not received:

1. Determine the optimum order quantity. This is simply a re-statement of step 1 under Case I. Thus, again we have

$$Q_{opt} = \sqrt{\frac{2C_1 D}{C_2 P}}$$

2. Calculate the value of Q_{opt} by substituting into the solution formula the values of C_1, C_2, D, and P. In this case, the value of P is for the case in which the quantity discount is *not* received (the *higher* price).
3. Compute the value of C_t by substituting the values of C_1, C_2, D, P, and Q into the cost model. Recall that the value of P is the nondiscount price and Q is the solution value (there are no restrictions on the value of Q, if discount is not received).

Final step. Compare the values of C_t for Case I, in which the quantity discount is received, and for Case II, in which the quantity discount is not received. Select the minimum of the two C_t values and order the associated quantity.

The Graphic Model

The previously discussed modeling situation is illustrated graphically in Figure 8.6. The curve of C_t for the nondiscount case will be higher than for the discount case, since a higher product price is included if no discount is assumed. The minimum order quantity required to receive the price discount is indicated by the vertical line.

Note that the actual curve that is relevant for analysis is the darkened portion of the two curves. That is, if Q is less than the discount quantity, then the higher price is charged and the upper cost curve is relevant. If Q is equal to or greater than the discount quantity, then the lower price is charged and the lower cost curve is relevant.

The objective is to determine whether the lowest point on the upper curve is less than the lowest *allowable* point on the lower curve. In the graphical illustration, the quantity discount would be taken, since point *b* is lower than point *a*.

Example

Assume that one is faced with determining the optimum ordering policy for the following situation:

$C_1 = \$20$ Order cost per order

$C_2 = 20\%$ Carrying cost as a percentage of average inventory per year

$D = 300$ units   Total annual demand for goods

$P_1 = \$50$ Price per unit, with *no* quantity discount received

$P_2 = \$48$ Price per unit, with a quantity discount received

In order to receive the quantity discount price, *order sizes must equal or exceed 50 units.*

The solution is computed as follows:

Case I: Quantity discount received:

1. Determine Q_{opt}:

$$Q_{opt} = \sqrt{\frac{2C_1 D}{C_2 P_2}}$$

2. Calculate the value of Q_{opt}, using the discount price (P_2):

$$Q_{opt} = \sqrt{\frac{(2)(20)(300)}{(0.20)(48)}}$$

$$= \sqrt{\frac{12{,}000}{9.6}}$$

$$= \sqrt{1250}$$

$$Q_{opt} \cong 35$$

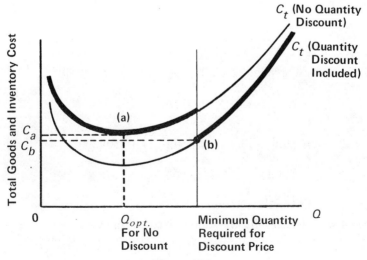

Figure 8.6
Inventory decision model, with quantity discount

3. If the value of Q_{opt} is less than the minimum quantity to receive the discount price, we must set Q equal to the required order quantity to receive the discount; thus, we set Q equal to 50.
4. Compute the value of C_t, for $Q = 50$ and $P_2 = 48$:

$$C_t = C_1\frac{D}{Q} + C_2P_2\frac{Q}{2} + P_2D$$

$$= (20)\left(\frac{300}{50}\right) + (0.20)(48)\left(\frac{50}{2}\right) + (48)(300)$$

$$= 120 + 240 + 14{,}400$$

$$C_t = 14{,}760$$

Case II: Quantity discount not received:

1. Determine Q_{opt}:

$$Q_{opt} = \sqrt{\frac{2C_1D}{C_2P_1}}$$

2. Calculate the value of Q_{opt} using the nondiscount price (P_1):

$$Q_{opt} = \sqrt{\frac{(2)(20)(300)}{(0.20)(50)}}$$

$$= \sqrt{\frac{12{,}000}{10}}$$

$$= \sqrt{1200}$$

$$Q_{opt} \cong 35$$

3. Compute the value of C_t, for $Q = 35$ and $P_1 = 50$:

$$C_t = C_1\frac{D}{Q} + C_2P_1\frac{Q}{2} + P_1D$$

$$= (20)\left(\frac{300}{35}\right) + (0.20)(50)\left(\frac{35}{2}\right) + (50)(300)$$

$$= 171.43 + 175 + 15{,}000$$

$$C_t \cong 15{,}346$$

Final step. The results are summarized as follows:

	Order Size = 50 *Receive Discount*	Order Size = 35 *No Discount Received*
Ordering cost	120	171
Carrying cost	240	175
Cost of goods	14,400	15,000
Total Cost	14,760	15,346

When the discount is received, the order size is larger and thus fewer orders are made and the ordering costs are less. Also, since the price is lower for the quantity discount case, the cost of goods is less. Carrying costs are more, since with fewer orders the average level of inventory is higher (although this is somewhat offset by the lower price, which tends to reduce the average value of inventory held). The total inventory and goods cost is less when the discount is taken; therefore, the order quantity decided upon is 50.

INVENTORY MODEL WITH SHORTAGES

It was assumed in all models previously presented that an order was received precisely at the instant when the level of inventory reached zero. Thus, shortages were not allowed to occur, and shortage cost was ignored in the inventory analysis.

We will now relax this assumption, and allow inventory shortages to occur. However, it will be assumed that all demands not met when there is an inventory shortage will be *back-ordered*. Thus, all demands will eventually be met.

The assumptions of the original classic inventory model will be retained here, except for assumption 4, which precludes shortages. We continue to assume constant and known demand, instantaneous replenishment (entire order is received simultaneously), and zero reorder lead time (receipt of goods at the instant an order is placed).

The Graphic Inventory Level Model

The inventory level model with shortages is illustrated in Figure 8.7. Since back orders (shortages) are filled when an order is received, the maximum inventory level does not reach the level of Q (the order quantity). Rather back orders (B) are filled immediately upon receipt of an order, and the inventory level returns to a level of S (which is equal to

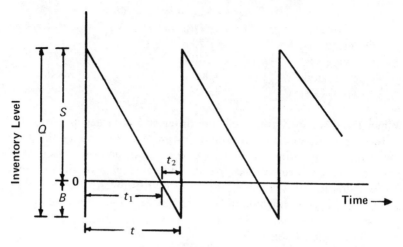

Figure 8.7
Inventory level model, with shortages

$Q - B$). Since the maximum inventory level is lowered, the inventory carrying cost will likewise be reduced. An extreme case would be where all demands are back-ordered, resulting in no inventory and carrying costs of zero. However, the reduction of carrying costs must be balanced against the shortage costs associated with back orders.

The Inventory Decision Model

We also continue with the same description for previously defined model variables, with some additions, as follows:

C_t = total annual inventory cost
C_o = total annual ordering cost
C_c = total annual carrying cost
C_s = total annual shortage cost
Q = quantity ordered per order
B = back-order quantity (shortages) per order
S = maximum inventory level ($Q - B$)
D = demand, on annual basis
C_1 = ordering cost per order
C_2 = carrying cost per unit of inventory per year
C_3 = shortage cost per unit of shortage per year
t_1 = time during which inventory is on hand
t_2 = time during which there is a shortage
t = time between receipt of orders ($t_1 + t_2$)

The Model

The overall cost function for the inventory model with shortages is

$$C_t = C_o + C_c + C_s$$

When specified completely in terms of all model parameters and variables, the model is

$$C_t = \text{ordering cost} + \text{carrying cost} + \text{shortage cost}$$

$$C_t = \frac{C_1 D}{Q} + \frac{C_2 S^2}{2Q} + \frac{C_3 (Q - S)^2}{2Q}$$

Derivations of the model terms are given in Appendix VI.

Model Solution

For the inventory model with shortages there are now two decision variables: order quantity (Q), and maximum inventory level (S). The value of B may be obtained by simply computing $Q - S$. The optimum solutions for the model are as follows:

$$Q_{opt} = \sqrt{\frac{2C_1 D}{C_2}} \cdot \sqrt{\frac{C_2 + C_3}{C_3}}$$

$$S_{opt} = \sqrt{\frac{2C_1 D}{C_2}} \cdot \sqrt{\frac{C_3}{C_2 + C_3}}$$

$$B_{opt} = Q_{opt} - S_{opt}$$

Also, the optimum solutions for t and C_t are

$$t_{opt} = \sqrt{\frac{2C_1}{C_2 D}} \cdot \sqrt{\frac{C_2 + C_3}{C_3}}$$

$$(C_t)_{opt} = \sqrt{2C_1 C_2 D} \cdot \sqrt{\frac{C_3}{C_2 + C_3}}$$

The method for obtaining the solutions to the inventory shortage model involves partial differentiation of the total cost function with respect to each of the two decision variables, setting each partial derivative equal to zero, and simultaneous solution of the resulting equations. This is beyond the scope of this chapter, but may be found in *Introduction to Operations Research*, by Churchman, Ackoff, and Arnoff.

Example

Let us return to the example problem used for the original classic EOQ model, but we will now assume that shortages are allowed (to be back-ordered), with a unit shortage cost of \$200. The model parameter values are given as:

$C_1 = \$50$ Order cost per order
$C_2 = \$100$ Carrying cost per unit per year
$C_3 = \$200$ Shortage cost per unit per year
$D = 4900$ Annual demand

Thus, the optimum solution for the problem is:

$$Q = \sqrt{\frac{2C_1D}{C_2}} \cdot \sqrt{\frac{C_2 + C_3}{C_3}} = \sqrt{\frac{(2)(50)(4900)}{100}} \cdot \sqrt{\frac{100 + 200}{200}}$$

$$= 70\sqrt{\frac{300}{200}} = 70\sqrt{1.5} = 70(1.22)$$

$Q_{opt} \cong 85$ units

Note that the solution for Q in the shortage model is simply the classic EOQ solution multiplied by $\sqrt{(C_2 + C_3)/C_3}$. Further solution results are as follows:

$$S = \sqrt{\frac{2C_1D}{C_2}} \cdot \sqrt{\frac{C_3}{C_2 + C_3}} = 70\sqrt{\frac{200}{300}}$$

$$= 70(0.82) = 57.4$$
$S_{opt} \cong 57$ units

$$B_{opt} = Q_{opt} - S_{opt}$$
$$= 85 - 57$$

$B_{opt} = 28$ units

Thus, the optimum decision is to allow shortages of 28 units to accumulate before ordering 85 units, raising the inventory level to 57 units. The optimum time, in years, between orders is

$$t = \sqrt{\frac{2C_1}{C_2D}} \cdot \sqrt{\frac{C_2 + C_3}{C_3}} = \sqrt{\frac{(2)(50)}{(100)(4900)}} \cdot (1.22)$$

$$= \sqrt{1/4900} \cdot (1.22) = (0.014)(1.22)$$
$t_{opt} = 0.017$ year

By multiplying 0.017 by 365, we find that the optimum time between order receipts is approximately six days. The optimum total inventory cost associated with the preceding solution values is

$$C_t = \sqrt{2C_1C_2D} \cdot \sqrt{\frac{C_3}{C_2 + C_3}}$$

$$= \sqrt{(2)(50)(100)(4900)} \cdot \sqrt{\frac{200}{100 + 200}}$$

$$= 7000(0.8165)$$

$$C_{t_{opt}} = \$5715.50$$

Note the following comparison between the results of the original classic EOQ model, in which shortages were not allowed, and the same model where shortages are allowed:

	Classic EOQ Model No Shortages	Shortage Model
Q (order quantity)	70 units	85 units
S (max. inventory level)	same is Q (70)	57 units
B (shortage—back orders)	0	28 units
C_t (total inventory cost)	$7000	$5715.50
t (time between orders)	5 days	6 days

Thus, it is apparent that under certain circumstances it is economical to allow shortages. It should be pointed out that if shortage cost (C_3) were assigned the value of infinity in the shortage model, the solution results would be identical to the original classic EOQ model.

INVENTORY MODELS WITH SAFETY STOCKS

All inventory models presented up to this point have assumed that demand was constant and known with certainty (assumptions 1 and 2 of the classic model). For these cases, when there is a lead time associated with receipt of goods ordered, the reorder point is easily calculated as the demand per day times the number of days lead time.

Uncertain Demand

We now consider the case where demand is not necessarily constant or known with certainty. We will, however, continue to assume that the lead time is constant and known with certainty. With regard to computing the order quantity, we can still obtain an approximation to the optimum solution by *assuming* that demand is constant, and that no stock-outs will occur. Thus, the optimum order quantity is approximated by using the classic EOQ formula.

However, since demand is actually a random variable, the computation of the reorder point is not so simple. One approach is to take the *expected* (average) demand during lead time and reorder when we reach that inventory level. This is analogous to assuming that demand during lead time is also known and constant. This approach would invariably lead to stock-outs (shortages) a certain portion of the time.

Safety Stocks

Business firms often hold *safety stocks* (buffers) of inventory in order to avoid inventory shortages, where the demand during order lead time is not known with certainty. The decision question, then, becomes one of, what is the optimum safety stock to hold in order to avoid inventory stock-outs.

Demand During Lead Time

It will be assumed that although the demand during lead time is not known with certainty, it can be described as a probability distribution. For example, the firm may have kept records of the relative frequency of various levels of demand during lead time in the past. An example of a probability distribution of demand during lead time is as follows:

Demand During Lead Time	Probability (Relative Frequency)
80	0.10
90	0.20
100	0.40
110	0.20
120	0.10

Model Analysis

Whereas all previous inventory models presented were *deterministic* (assumed certainty), we have now developed a component of our model that involves probabilities, and the model will be termed *probabilistic*. As previously stated, we will approximate the optimum order quantity by using the deterministic EOQ model solution.

The reorder point, which may include allowance for a safety stock to guard against stock-outs, will be determined separately as a probabilistic model. The cost trade-off that must be considered is the carrying cost for inventory safety stocks versus inventory stock-out (shortage) costs.

Inventory Level Model

A graphic illustration of the inventory level model is given in Figure 8.8. In the first and third cycles of the model, inventory shortages would have occurred if no safety stock were carried. In the second cycle of the model, a surplus of inventory would have occurred, even without a safety stock. An implicit assumption of the model is that these surpluses and deficits would balance out over a year, so that on the average the excess inventory held would be the indicated shaded area (safety stock level).

Decision Costs

Since, on the average, the inventory safety stocks would be unused, the unit carrying cost for safety stock would be multiplied times the entire safety stock level. If we denote annual safety stock costs as C_{ss}, and the safety stock inventory level as I_s, then the annual safety stock carrying costs would be

$$C_{ss} = C_2 I_s$$

where C_2 = carrying cost per unit held per year.

The safety stock costs must be balanced against the stock-out costs, which are a function of the probabilistic demand and the safety stock held.

Returning to the probability distribution of demand during lead time, we see that if a reorder point of 120 units is used, we would never expect a stock-out. Thus, stock-out costs would be zero for this case. However, if 110 units is used as the reorder point, we would expect to have a demand of 120 units 10 percent of the time, resulting in stock-outs 10 percent of the time. If 100 units is specified as the reorder point, we

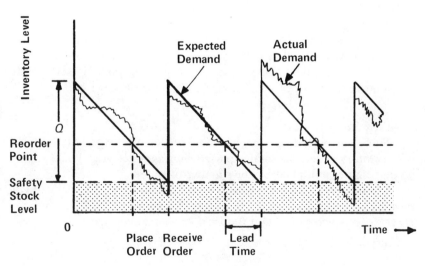

Figure 8.8
Inventory level model, with safety stock

would expect stock-outs of 10 units 20 percent of the time, and stock-outs of 20 units 10 percent of the time.

Expected Shortages

Since the expected (average) demand during lead time is 100 units (weight average of demand levels times associated probabilities), if a reorder point of over 100 units is selected, the excess is considered the safety stock. The expected number of shortages for reorder points of 100, 110, and 120 (and associated safety stocks of 0, 10, and 20) are summarized as follows:

Reorder Point	Safety Stock	Actual Lead-time Demand	X Resulting Shortage	P_i Probability of Demand (Shortage)	XP_i	$E[X]$ Expected Shortage (ΣXP_i)
100	0	100	0	0.4	0	
		110	10	0.2	2	4
		120	20	0.1	2	
110	10	110	0	0.2	0	
		120	10	0.1	1	1
120	20	120	0	0.1	0	0

Thus, we see that the expected number of shortages incurred when we allow no safety stock is 4. If a safety stock of 10 units is provided, the expected shortage is 1. Of course, if the reorder point is set at 120, providing a safety stock of 20 units, there is no shortage incurred.

Expected Shortage Costs

Since the preceding computations yielded the expected shortages per inventory order, the total expected shortages per year would simply be that figure multiplied by the number of orders.

We saw previously that when Q_{opt} is determined by the classic EOQ formula, we also can determine N, the optimum number of orders, as D/Q_{opt}. Thus, we can obtain the total expected shortage costs:

$$C_S = C_3 \cdot N \cdot E[X]$$

where

C_S = total annual shortage cost
C_3 = cost per unit shortage
N = number of orders per year
$E[X]$ = expected number of shortages per order

Example

Let us assume that inventory carrying cost has been determined to be $10 per unit per year ($C_2 = 10$). We further assume that shortage costs have been estimated at $3 per unit shortage ($C_3 = 3$). Finally, the classic EOQ solution model has yielded a solution value for N of 12 (orders per year). Assuming that the previously given probability distribution of demand is appropriate, the cost analysis is as follows:

Safety stock carrying cost. Safety stock inventory carrying cost is computed by simply multiplying the safety stock level times the unit carrying cost ($10). This is summarized as follows:

I_S Safety Stock	C_2 Inventory Level Carrying Cost	$C_{SS} = I_S C_2$ Total Annual Safety Stock Carrying Cost
0	10	0
10	10	100
20	10	200

Expected shortage cost. Expected shortage costs are computed as the combined product of the cost per unit shortage, the number of orders per year, and the expected shortage per order period. This is summarized as follows:

Safety Stock Level	C_3 Cost Per Unit Shortage	N Number of Orders Per Year	$E[X]$ Expected No. Short Per Order Period	$C_S = C_3 N E[X]$ Expected Annual Shortage Cost
0	3	12	4	144
10	3	12	1	36
20	3	12	0	0

Decision analysis. The decision analysis consists of comparing the various safety stock levels and their associated total carrying and shortage costs. A summary of the decision analysis is given as follows:

Safety Stock Level I_S	Safety Stock Inventory Carrying Cost C_{SS}	Expected Shortage Cost C_S	Total Expected Costs $C_{SS} + C_S$
0	0	144	144
10	100	36	136
20	200	0	200

Thus, total expected safety stock inventory carrying and shortage costs are minimized when a safety stock of 10 units is carried (reorder point of 110 units). It should be pointed out that the optimum solution is now based on an *expected* cost value, and this would require that the same policy be carried out over a lengthy period of time in order to balance out variations in actual costs.

In reality, the optimum order quantity (and number of orders per year), and the inventory reorder point (and safety stock level), are interdependent. Thus, more sophisticated models would determine the *simultaneous* solution of these decision variables. However, this becomes very difficult in practice, and generally simulation must be resorted to for this type of decision analysis. Also, a further complication that could easily be assumed is that the inventory lead time is also not known with certainty (a random variable). Simulation is the only practical approach to such models.

REFERENCES

Buchan, J., and Koenigsberg, E., *Scientific Inventory Management*, Prentice-Hall, Englewood Cliffs, N.J., 1963.

Buffa, E. S., and Taubert, W. H., *Production-Inventory Systems: Planning and Control*, rev. ed., Irwin, Homewood, Ill., 1972.

Churchman, C. W., Ackoff, R. L., and Arnoff, E. L., *Introduction to Operations Research*, Wiley, New York, 1957.

Hadley, G., and Whitin, T. M., *Analysis of Inventory Systems*, Prentice-Hall, Englewood Cliffs, N.J., 1963.

Magee, J. F., and Boodman, D. M., *Production Planning and Inventory Control*, 2d. ed., McGraw-Hill, New York, 1967.

Starr, M. K., and Miller, D. W., *Inventory Control: Theory and Practice*, Prentice-Hall, Englewood Cliffs, N.J., 1962.

QUESTIONS

1. Define inventory. Discuss areas in which inventories may build up. Describe nonphysical assets that may be thought of as inventory.
2. Describe several functions served by inventory.
3. Discuss two basic inventory decisions.
4. Discuss the three most common inventory costs considered in inventory analysis.
5. Specify the assumptions of the classic (EOQ) inventory model.
6. Would you classify the classic inventory model as probabilistic or deterministic? Why? Would you classify the classic inventory model as an optimization or descriptive model? Why?
7. Describe the classic inventory level model. Illustrate graphically. Give a full definition of the variables, relationships, and axes of the graph.
8. Describe the classic inventory decision model. Illustrate graphically. Give a full definition of the variables, relationships, and axes of the graph. Discuss the objective of the decision analysis, and the trade-offs involved.
9. Discuss how the noninstantaneous receipt inventory model can be adapted to production lot-size analysis. Illustrate the inventory level model for this case.
10. Discuss the inventory decision model for quantity discounts. What is the general procedure for analysis of this model? Illustrate graphically for several different possible solution results.

PROBLEMS

1. The Ajax Corporation is faced with the attractive situation in which it can obtain immediate delivery of an item it stocks for retail sale. The firm has therefore not bothered to order the item in any systematic way. Ajax has recently hired a management consultant to study their inventory control. The consultant has determined that the various costs associated with making an order amount to approximately $30 per order. In addition, he has determined that the costs of carrying one unit of the item in inventory, for one year, would amount to approximately $20 (primarily direct storage cost and foregone profit on investment in inventory). The forecast demand for the item is 19,200 units per year, and is reasonably constant over time. When an order is placed for the item, the entire order is

immediately delivered to the Ajax Corporation from the supplier. Ajax operates six days a week, plus a few Sundays, or approximately 320 days per year. Determine the following:

(a) Optimum order quantity per order
(b) Total annual inventory ordering and carrying costs associated with the optimum order size policy
(c) Optimum number of orders per year to place
(d) Number of operating days between orders, for the optimum ordering policy

Illustrate the inventory *level* model for this problem. Show on the graph the answers to (a) and (d).

2. In problem 1, assume that the consultant hired by the Ajax Corporation wishes to illustrate to the firm's management the nature of the decision analysis employed for the solution to the inventory ordering policy. Illustrate graphically the inventory *decision* model by including along the horizontal axis several order quantities below and above the optimum quantity, and plot the associated ordering and carrying costs. Show graphically that the optimum order quantity is the value computed in problem 1.

3. In problem 1, assume that rather than receiving immediate delivery of an order, Ajax must wait two days for the order to arrive. At what inventory level (reorder point) should the firm reorder? Illustrate on the inventory *level* model the point in time and the inventory level point at which a reorder would be made. Since the firm has to wait two days for the order, should it recalculate the optimum order quantity? Suppose the lead time required to receive an order was 12 days; how many orders would Ajax have outstanding at any given point in time? Shouldn't Ajax simply lump these orders together and receive them all at once? Why, or why not? Complete a table showing the annual ordering costs, annual carrying costs, and total inventory related costs, for the following two cases: (a) order every 12 days; and (b) order at the interval determined in the solution to problem 1.

4. The purchasing manager for a large steel firm must determine the ordering policy for coal to operate 12 converters. Each converter requires exactly 5 tons of coal per day to operate, and the firm operates 360 days per year. The purchasing manager has determined that the ordering cost is $80 per order, and the cost of holding coal is 20 percent of the average level held. The purchasing manager has negotiated a contract to obtain the coal for $12 per ton for the coming year.

(a) Determine the optimum quantity of coal to receive in each order.
(b) Determine the total inventory-related costs associated with the optimum ordering policy (do not include the cost of the coal).
(c) If 5 days' lead time are required to receive an order of coal, how much coal should be on hand when an order is placed?

5. A lumber mill in Georgia processes 10,000 logs annually, operating 250 days per year. Immediately upon order, the logging company supplier begins delivery to the lumber mill, at the rate of 60 logs per day. The lumber mill has determined that the ordering cost per order is $62.50, and the cost of carrying logs in inventory, awaiting processing, is $15 per log, on an annual basis. Determine the following:

(a) The optimum number of log order quantity
(b) The total inventory cost associated with the optimum order quantity
(c) The number of lumber mill operating days between orders
(d) The number of lumber mill operating days required to receive an order

Illustrate the inventory *level* model graphically. Show the answers to (c) and (d) and the maximum inventory level.

6. The General Aluminum Corporation has predicted the demand for aluminum rivets for the coming year to be 20,000 cases. The average demand rate, based on past data, is reasonably constant. General Aluminum produces at the rate of 160 cases of rivets per day, operating 250 working days annually. The production set-up cost for each production run to produce rivets is $144. The annual carrying cost of rivets produced for inventory is $32 per case. Determine the following:

(a) Optimum quantity to produce for each production run
(b) Length (in working days) of each production run
(c) Time (in days) between production run start-ups
(d) Total production set-up and inventory carrying costs

How many days per year are used for production of rivets?

7. A large grocery chain is faced with the following decision: The cost of ordering a particular item is $40 per order. The carrying cost is 25 percent of the average inventory level, on an annual basis. Yearly demand for the item is 20,000 cases, at a constant rate. The grocery firm currently pays $40 per case for the item. However, they have been offered a $1 per case discount if they would order in minimum

lots of 1000 cases. Should the firm take the discount? Show a comparative analysis of all costs involved for the two alternatives.

8. In problem 1, the Ajax Corporation is considering reducing their inventory level further by simply allowing some shortages to occur. They would back-order demand not met, and fill the demand when the stock was replenished. It is estimated that the cost of shortages is $30 per unit, on an annual basis. All other relevant data is given in problem 1. Determine the following:

(a) The new optimum order quantity
(b) The total inventory ordering, carrying, and shortage costs associated with the optimum order quantity
(c) The back-order quantity, per order

Perform a comparative analysis of the solution to problem 1 and the current solution, showing all the various costs involved.

9. The production foreman for a large mill has encountered a problem of stock-outs. On the other hand, he is under pressure from top management to keep the level of inventory down. He faces the difficult problem of fluctuating demand for the product in inventory. The foreman knows that he must keep some safety stock on hand to guard against higher than average demands, but he cannot determine the optimum level to hold. Assume that you have been employed as a consultant to analyze the problem. It will be assumed that the firm has contracted for 20 orders, of 300 units per order. The inventory carrying cost is $5 per unit, per year, and the estimated shortage cost is $4 per unit shortage. Past records show that the relative frequency of various demand levels, during the lead time to receive an order, are as follows:

Demand During Lead Time (units)	Relative Frequency
240	0.05
260	0.10
280	0.20
300	0.30
320	0.20
340	0.10
360	0.05

Determine the following for the production foreman:

(a) The optimum reorder level
(b) The optimum safety stock to hold
(c) The total safety stock inventory carrying and shortage cost, associated with the optimum reorder policy
(d) The inventory carrying cost for the safety stock alone

Illustrate the *decision* model for this problem graphically.

10. Assume that the classic EOQ model was used to determine the order sizes in problem 9. What was the assumed ordering cost, per order?

9 Waiting-Line Analysis – Queueing Theory

INTRODUCTION

Waiting lines are one of the most common occurrences of everyday life. The reader can, no doubt, recall having waited in line for service during college registration, check-out at a grocery store, deposit or withdrawal at a bank, service at a hamburger stand, payment at a toll-bridge, service at a gasoline station, and numerous other situations. Waiting lines, often referred to as *queues*, may consist of people, automobiles, equipment, or other units awaiting service.

Waiting lines may exist in the form of an observable line of individuals or objects waiting for service, or they may occur in a more abstract sense, such as when machines break down in a factory and must wait their turn to be repaired. Oftentimes, customers may enter a shoe store or ice cream parlor and take a number, indicating their turn for service, and then browse around the store to inspect the goods for sale. This, nevertheless, represents a waiting-line type process. Table 9.1 includes several examples of commonly known situations in which waiting lines occur.

The study of waiting lines, known as *queueing theory*, is far from new. Queueing theory can be traced back to the classic work of A. K. Erlang, a Danish mathematician, who studied the fluctuating demands on telephone facilities and associated service delays. Erlang's work was first published in 1913 under the title *Solution of Some Problems in the Theory of Probabilities of Significance in Automatic Telephone Exchanges*. Thus, waiting-line analysis represents one of the oldest of the various topical areas considered in the decision sciences.

344

Table 9.1
Commonly Known Waiting-Line Situations

Situation	Arrivals	Servers	Service Process
School registration	Students	Registration desk	Course slips assigned and signed
Grocery store	Customers	Checkout counter	Bill computation and payment
Bank	Customers	Teller	Deposit, withdrawal, check cashed, etc.
Traffic intersection	Automobiles	Traffic light	Controlled passage through intersection
Doctor's office	Patients	Doctor and staff	Treatment
Machine maintenance	Machine breakdown	Repairmen	Repair machine
Shipping terminal	Trucks	Docks	Unloading and loading
Assembly line	Product components	Assembly workers	Assemble product
Mail order store	Mail orders	Mail order clerks	Process and mail products ordered
Telephone exchange	Calls	Electronic switching equipment	Complete connection
Air terminal	Airplanes	Runways	Airplanes landing and taking off
Tool crib	Workmen	Tool attendants	Check out or check in tools

Basic Components of a Waiting-Line Process

The methodology of decision science attempts to describe the structure of a system being studied by isolating (or abstracting) from the system its basic components. The basic components of a waiting-line process are: arrivals, servers, and waiting lines (queues). The basic components of a waiting line process are illustrated graphically in Figure 9.1.

Arrivals

Every waiting-line problem involves the arrival of items (customers, equipment, telephone calls, etc.) for service. This element of the queuing process is oftentimes referred to as the *input process*. The input process includes: the *source* of arrivals, commonly referred to as the *calling population*; and the *manner* in which arrivals occur, which is generally a *random* process. As we will see, at a later point in the chapter, a precise description of the input process is required in order to analyze the overall queueing problem.

Servers

Equally important in the description of a queueing process are the servers, otherwise referred to as the *service mechanism*. The service mechanism may involve one or more servers, or one or more service facilities. For example, a shoe store may have several sales personnel, or a toll road may have several toll gates. The service mechanism may simply consist of a single server in a single facility, such as the ticket sales person selling seats for the following week's play. In addition to a precise description of the service mechanism in terms of the number and configuration of servers, there must be a description of the *manner* in which services are completed, which is often a *random* process.

Queues

The focal point of waiting-line analysis is, of course, the waiting line itself. The extent to which queues will exist depends primarily upon the nature of the arrival and service processes. However, another important determinant of the nature of the waiting line is the *queue discipline*. The queue discipline is the decision rule that prescribes the order in which items in the queue will be served (i.e., first-come, first-served; last-come, first-served; or possibly some priority rule). Of course, if waiting lines do not exist, this also has important implications for the queueing analysis, since it implies idle servers or excess service capacity.

Figure 9.1
Basic components of a waiting-line process

Basic Structures of Waiting-Line Processes

Waiting-line processes are generally categorized into four basic structures, according to the nature of the service facilities: (1) single-channel, single-phase; (2) multiple-channel, single-phase; (3) single-channel, multiple-phase; and (4) multiple-channel, multiple-phase. Each of the four categories of queueing processes is illustrated graphically in Figure 9.2.

The number of channels in a queueing process is simply the number of parallel servers available for servicing arrivals. The number of phases, on the other hand, indicates the number of sequential service steps each individual arrival must go through. An example of a single-channel, single-phase queueing process would be a drive-in bank teller with only one teller facility. On the other hand, many banks have several drive-in teller windows, which is an example of a multiple-channel, single-phase operation.

When patients go to a doctor or dentist for treatment, they often wait in a reception room prior to entering the treatment facilities. Then, upon being seated (or otherwise situated) in the treatment room, the patient often receives an initial check-up or treatment from a nurse or technician, followed by treatment from a doctor or dentist. This sort of situation constitutes a single-channel, multiple-phase queueing process (if there is only one doctor and one assistant). If there are several doctors and assistants, then it is a multiple-channel, multiple-phase process.

The reader will undoubtedly immediately visualize a familiar waiting situation that fits none of the previous categories of waiting-line process. This is reasonable and expected. The four presented categories of queueing processes are simply the four *basic* categories. All sorts of deviations can be visualized. For example, rather than a single queue preceding the multiple-channel, single-phase case, there might often be separate queues preceding each server. This occurs, for example, in grocery stores, banks, and department stores. Also, in the multiple-phase cases, queues may or may not build up prior to each of the secondary server locations, such as in a manufacturing job-shop operation. In the multiple-channel, multiple-phase case, items might switch back and forth from one channel to the other, between each of the various service phases. It becomes readily apparent that queueing models can become quite complex indeed. However, much of the fundamentals of basic queueing theory are relevant to the analysis of all queueing problems, regardless of complexity. We will concentrate on those fundamentals in this chapter.

(a)   SINGLE-CHANNEL, SINGLE-PHASE

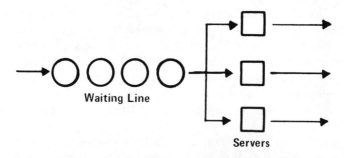

(b)   MULTIPLE-CHANNEL, SINGLE-PHASE

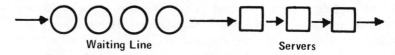

(c)   SINGLE-CHANNEL, MULTIPLE-PHASE

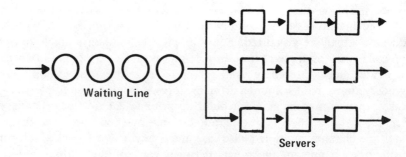

(d)   MULTIPLE-CHANNEL, MULTIPLE-PHASE

Figure 9.2
Four basic structures of waiting-line processes

Queueing Example

The following example of a waiting-line situation is presented to highlight the basic process involved. The First National Bank of Blacksburg has one drive-in teller window, at which customers may make deposits, cash checks, and conduct other miscellaneous bank business. The bank opens for service at 9:00 A.M. Customers arrive in their automobiles for service randomly over time. The time required to service each customer is also a random variable. Of course, customers are served in the order in which they arrive (first-come, first-served basis). The process is illustrated in Table 9.2, for the first hour of operation at the bank drive-in window.

The example of Table 9.2 illustrates that service begins upon each customer's arrival only if no earlier customer is currently being serviced. Otherwise, a waiting line forms and later customers must wait for service. The example should suggest some immediate questions for consideration. For example, is a customer waiting time of 11 minutes acceptable? Such an extensive waiting time at a bank drive-in window could result in highly dissatisfied customers, and possibly the loss of their business. Is a queue length of up to four customers acceptable? The drive preceding the service window may not, in fact, accommodate that many automobiles. Customers may *balk* upon seeing a long waiting line and simply refuse to enter the service queue. This, also, may result in temporary or

Table 9.2
Record of First Hour of Operation at Bank Drive-in Service Window

Time of Customer Arrival	Time Service Begins	Service Time Required	Time Service Ends	Customer Waiting Time	Server Idle Time	Number of Customers Waiting
9:05 A.M.	9:05 A.M.	4 minutes	9:09 A.M.	0 minutes	5 minutes	2
9:06	9:09	3	9:12	3	0	1
9:08	9:12	5	9:17	4	0	0
9:20	9:20	4	9:24	0	3	2
9:22	9:24	2	9:26	2	0	1
9:23	9:26	1	9:27	3	0	0
9:30	9:30	8	9:38	0	3	3
9:32	9:38	3	9:41	6	0	3
9:33	9:41	5	9:45	8	0	3
9:37	9:45	2	9:47	8	0	4
9:40	9:47	1	9:48	7	0	2
9:41	9:48	7	9:55	7	0	1
9:44	9:55	4	9:59	11	0	0
9:59	9:59	2	10:01	0	0	0

permanently lost business. Does the small amount of server idle time imply an overworked drive-in teller, or is the teller simply too slow due to inexperience; or, is it possible that excess service capacity exists?

Questions such as the above require a formal framework for analysis. The following section presents a general decision framework for waiting-line problems.

DECISION FRAMEWORK FOR WAITING-LINE PROBLEMS

As contrasted with linear programming or inventory theory, there is no unified body of knowledge regarding the optimization of waiting-line problems. Thus, most references on queueing theory simply emphasize the development of the queueing system's *operating characteristics*. Operating characteristics simply describe the *performance* of the system in the form of such measures as expected waiting time, percent idle time, and so forth. However, the measures of the system's performance are actually only inputs into a broader conceptual framework, within which most waiting-line problems can be analyzed.

A Decision Model for Queueing Analysis

Most decision analyses of waiting-line problems eventually reduce to the question of, what level of service should be provided (i.e., what service capacity or how many servers)? If the decision variable is to be level of service, then the decision model must formally identify its relationship to other relevant parameters and variables. As is the case with many decision science models, the criterion by which the model solution is evaluated is total expected cost.

The general relationship of the decision variable, level of service, to the evaluation criterion, total expected cost, is shown graphically in Figure 9.3. It can be seen that total expected cost is the sum of two separate costs, (1) service costs and (2) waiting costs.

Service Costs

It should be apparent that as the level of service is increased, the related service cost will increase. For example, if two dock workers are provided to unload trucks at a warehouse depot, instead of one, costs are increased by the amount of the wage for the second worker. The exact shape of the function relating service level to service costs must be determined for each individual case being analyzed.

Another way in which service costs are often included in the

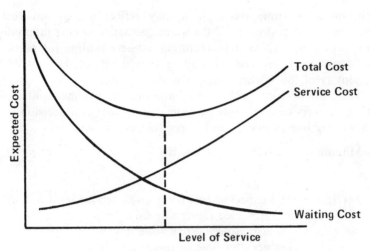

Figure 9.3
Decision model for waiting-line analysis

analysis of waiting-line problems is to include only server idle time costs. As the level of service is increased, the server idle time is also expected to increase. Either approach to including service-related costs should normally yield the same decision results. The decision maker might desire to include some value other than simply server wage to measure the unit cost of increased service level. By considering server idle time, the opportunity cost of not allocating the server to alternative productive activities can be used, rather than server wages. Cases can be made for considering service related costs in either of the two ways discussed.

Waiting Costs

There is generally an inverse relationship between service level and expected customer waiting time. It is, however, much more difficult to arrive at some explicit statement of waiting costs per unit waiting time. This is the reason that this question is often ignored in the literature of queueing theory, and the system's operating characteristics are simply presented, with the ultimate decision analysis left up to the individual manager. However, since the decision must ultimately rest upon relating waiting time to service level, even if no waiting cost is specified, it is implicitly included in the analysis.

Waiting cost may be simply an estimate of the cost of lost business, where customers become impatient and leave the place of service due to excessive waiting times. This type of cost may include the cost of lost profit, on a one-time basis, or it may reflect a long-run cost of permanently lost customers. If the waiting situation occurs internally to an organization, such as manufacturing workers waiting for parts at a parts department, the cost of waiting should reflect the cost of lost productivity of the worker during the waiting time.

Thus, the decision problem becomes one of customer waiting-time costs versus service-level costs. A general statement of a decision model for a waiting-line problem can be specified as follows:

Minimize $\quad E(C|S) = IC_1 + WC_2$

where

$E(C|S) =$ total expected cost for a given service level S
$I =$ total expected server idle time for a
specified period (e.g., one day)
$C_1 =$ cost per unit time of server idle time
$W =$ total expected waiting time for all arrivals for a specified
period (e.g., one day)
$C_2 =$ cost per unit time of customer waiting time

Although the level of service, S, is not explicitly identified in the above functional relationship as a variable, it should be recognized that service level is the decision variable, and the model would be evaluated for each level of service under consideration.

Example

Let us consider the following example of a hypothetical situation in which the above analysis could be used. The Blacksburg National Bank has two drive-in teller windows and wishes to determine the optimum staffing level for a particular day. It is important to note that since arrival rates of customers fluctuate by hour during a day, and by day of the week, this analysis might have to be performed for each hour of operation during the week's operation.

Assume that the waiting-line analysis yields the following information:

	One Teller	*Two Tellers*
Total server idle time (I)	30 minutes	340 minutes
Total customer waiting time (W)	130 minutes	25 minutes
Estimated Cost Per Unit of Server Idle Time (C_1) $ .10		
Estimated Cost Per Unit of Customer Waiting Time (C_2) $3.00		

The resulting computations yield the following:

$$E(C|S=1) = (30)(0.10) + (130)(3.00)$$
$$= 3.00 + 390.00$$
$$= \$393.00$$
$$E(C|S=2) = (340)(0.10) + (25)(3.00)$$
$$= 34.00 + 75.00$$
$$= \$109.00$$

It is apparent from the above analysis that the cost of customer waiting time far outweighs the cost of server idle time. Therefore, even though the addition of a second teller results in much total idle time for the two tellers, the bank should provide two tellers for the day under consideration.

It will again be pointed out that no general optimization theory exists regarding the decision analysis of queueing problems. The purpose of the above formulated model is simply to place the queueing problem within the bounds of a decision making framework. The generally accepted components of decision analysis for queueing problems have been identified. However, the actual analysis of queueing problems may require any one of a large variety of forms, depending upon the actual situation under study. For this reason, queueing theory has been developed to provide a rather wide variety of descriptive measures of the queueing system's performance, previously referred to as operating characteristics. The manner and conditions under which these values are obtained, for input into the decision framework, is the traditional subject of queueing theory.

DEVELOPING THE INPUTS FOR THE DECISION ANALYSIS

The previous discussion of a decision framework for queueing analysis presumes that several important inputs would be provided. These inputs were explicitly identified in the decision model as C_1, C_2, I, and W.

The Cost Inputs

It is assumed in queueing analysis, as well as in all other decision science models, that certain parameters will be provided by the decision maker. For the case of the decision model of waiting-line analysis, it is assumed that management can provide reasonably accurate estimates of the values of C_1 (cost per unit time of server idle time) and C_2 (cost per unit time of customer waiting time). The actual process by which such managerial estimates might be derived constitutes a field of study in itself and will not be pursued further here.

Server Idle Time and Customer Waiting Time Estimates

It is the role of queueing theory to provide such operating characteristics as expected server idle time and expected customer waiting time. The following discussion of queueing theory will present the development of these inputs into the decision analysis model. Queueing theory provides models (formulas) by which to compute the expected waiting time and the expected server idle time, under specified assumptions regarding the nature of the queueing process.

As was previously pointed out, due to the wide range of potential approaches to decision analysis for queueing problems, queueing theory provides many measures of the waiting-line system's performance. The decision analyst must select from among the measures provided those that are relevant to the defined problem in order to arrive at a solution. In addition to the two measures of performance included in the decision model, management might also specify that the expected (average) number in the waiting line should not exceed four. Or, they might specify that the maximum number waiting plus the customer in service (*the number in the system*) should never at any time exceed eight, with a 90 percent degree of certainty. Thus, management would have added certain *constraints* to the decision analysis model. Answers concerning whether these constraints were met or violated could be obtained from queueing theory, in the form of operating characteristics.

The operating characteristics commonly obtained in the analysis of waiting lines are summarized as follows:

1. Probability of any specified number in the system
2. Mean (expected) waiting time
3. Mean (expected) queue length
4. Mean time in the system
5. Mean number of units in the system
6. Probability the service facility will be idle

QUEUEING THEORY—ASSUMPTIONS

All theory is based upon qualifying assumptions. Queueing theory, likewise, has been developed by making a number of assumptions about the several basic components of a waiting-line process. For each change in an assumption, a different theoretical model has evolved. As has been implied in the previous discussions, an almost infinite variety of waiting-line situations may exist. We will consider but a few of the basic theoretical models here; however, the overall conceptual basis for queueing analysis in general should become clear.

Queueing theory models yield measures of performance of the waiting-line process, which provide the basis for decision making. In preparation for the study of queueing theory models, certain fundamental components of the queueing process about which assumptions are made must be considered.

Distribution of Arrivals and Service Times

Queueing models belong to the class of decision science models known as *probabilistic* (or *stochastic*) models. This is because certain elements of the process are included in the model as random variables (as opposed to constant-valued parameters). These random variables are most often described by some associated probability distribution.

Both the arrivals and service times in a queueing process are generally represented as random variables. For example, the number of customers arriving per unit time (e.g., per 5-minute period) at a drive-in bank teller may vary randomly, but according to some definable probability distribution.

Arrival Distribution

The number of arrivals per unit time at a service location may vary randomly according to any one of many probability distributions. However, the most commonly *assumed* distribution fitting customer arrivals is the Poisson distribution. This assumption about the distribution of arrivals is not without empirical basis. Many statistical studies have resulted in the conclusion that arrivals are Poisson-distributed for many queueing processes.

The general model (formula) for the Poisson probability distribution is

$$P(r) = \frac{e^{-\lambda}(\lambda)^r}{r!}$$

where

r = number of arrivals
$P(r)$ = probability of r arrivals
λ = mean arrival rate
e = 2.71828. (the base of natural logarithms)
$r!$ = $r(r-1)(r-2)\cdots3\cdot2\cdot1$ (r factorial)

The commonly used symbol for the mean arrival rate in queueing models is λ (Greek letter lambda). The Poisson distribution corresponds to the assumption of random arrivals, since each arrival is assumed to be independent of other arrivals and also independent of the state of the system. One interesting characteristic of a Poisson distribution, which makes it easier to work with than some other distributions, is that the mean is equal to the variance. Thus, by specifying the mean of a Poisson distribution, the entire distribution is specified.

The Poisson distribution is a *discrete* probability distribution, since it relates to the *number* of arrivals per unit time. Figure 9.4 portrays the Poisson distribution graphically for several different values of the mean, λ. It can be seen that as the mean becomes larger, the distribution becomes flatter and more bell-shaped. For example, if the mean arrival rate λ at a drive-in bank teller per 5-minute period is 2, the probabilities associated with different numbers of arrivals would be:*

r Number of Arrivals	*P(r)* Probability
0	0.1358
1	0.2707
2	0.2707
3	0.1805
4	0.0902
5	0.0361
6	0.0120
7	0.0034
8	0.0009

An interesting feature of the Poisson process is that if the number of arrivals per unit time is Poisson distributed, with a mean rate of λ, then the *time between* arrivals (*interarrival time*) is distributed as a *negative exponential* probability distribution, with mean of $1/\lambda$. Thus, if the mean arrival *rate*, per 5-minute period, is 2, then the mean time between arrivals is 2.5 minutes (5 minutes/2 = 2.5 minutes). (Note that the one in the numerator relates to the time-period reference, i.e., one 5-minute time period.) This relationship is summarized as follows:

---

* A table of Poisson probability values for various values of r and λ is given in Appendix VII.

Arrival Rate	*Time Between Arrivals*
Poisson	Negative exponential
Mean = λ	Mean = $1/\lambda$
λ = 2 arrivals per 5-minute period	$1/\lambda = (1/2)(5 \text{ minutes}) = 2.5 \text{ minutes.}$

Service Time Distribution

Service times in a queueing process may also fit any one of a large number of different probability distributions. The most commonly assumed distribution for service times is the negative exponential distribution. Thus, from the preceding discussion of the relationship between the Poisson and negative exponential distributions, it is apparent that if service times follow a negative exponential distribution, then the service rate follows a Poisson distribution.

The description of arrivals in terms of arrival *rate* (Poisson), and services in terms of service *times* (negative exponential) is simply a matter of convention that has developed in the literature of queueing theory.

Empirical research has shown that the assumption of negative exponential-distributed service times is not valid nearly as often as is the assumption of Poisson-distributed arrivals. Therefore, for actual applications of queueing analysis, this assumption would have to be carefully checked before attempting to use such a model. Other possible distributions of service times will be presented at a later point in the chapter.

The general model (formula) for the negative exponential probability density function is

$$f(t) = \mu e^{-\mu t}$$

where

t = service time
$f(t)$ = probability density associated with t
μ = mean service *rate*
$1/\mu$ = mean service *time*
e = 2.71828, ... (base of natural logarithms)

The commonly used symbol for the mean service *rate* in queueing models is μ (Greek letter mu), and therefore the mean service *time* is $1/\mu$. As in the case of the Poisson arrival rate, the negative exponential service time corresponds to the assumption that service times are completely

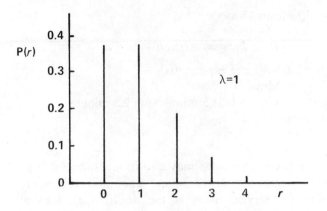

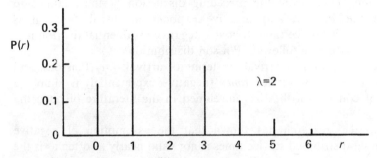

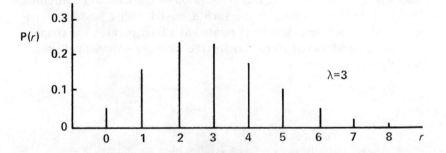

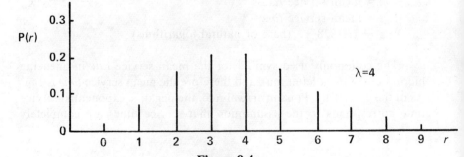

Figure 9.4
Poisson distribution

random. The probability of completing a service for a customer in any subsequent time period after service is begun is independent of how much time has already elapsed on the service for that customer.

The negative exponential distribution is a *continuous* probability distribution, since it relates to *time* of service. Figure 9.5 illustrates graphically the negative exponential distribution. It can be seen that short service times have the highest probability of occurrence, and as service time increases the probability function "tails off" (exponentially) toward zero probability. The area under the curve for the negative exponential distribution is easily determined from its cumulative distribution function, which is determined through integration as follows:

$$F(T) = \int_0^T \mu e^{-\mu t}\, dt = -e^{-\mu t}\big]_0^T = -e^{-\mu T} + e^0 = 1 - e^{-\mu T}$$

This may be further described as:

$$F(T) = f(t \leq T) = 1 - e^{-\mu T}$$

where $F(T)$ is the area under the curve to the left of T. We also have

$$1 - F(T) = f(t \geq T) = e^{-\mu T}$$

where $1 - F(T)$ is the area under the curve to the right of T.

For example, if the mean service time $(1/\mu)$ at a drive-in bank teller is 2 minutes, the probability that service would take T or more minutes, for various values of T, would be:*

T Service Times of at Least	$1 - F(T)$ Probability
0 minutes	1.000
1	0.607
2	0.368
3	0.223
4	0.135
5	0.082
6	0.050
7	0.030
8	0.018
9	0.011
10	0.007
11	0.004
12	0.003
13	0.002
14	0.001

* A table of values of e^x and e^{-x} is given in Appendix VIII.

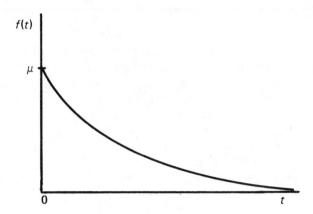

Figure 9.5
Negative exponential probability density distribution

Queue Discipline

As was discussed previously, the queue discipline is a decision rule that determines the order in which waiting customers will be selected for service. Queueing theory models generally assume that customers are serviced on a first-come, first-served basis. If this assumption is not appropriate for the queueing system under study, a different model must be developed.

A feature of customer behavior that can affect the service order is when a customer becomes impatient and decides to leave the system before being served. This is known in the literature of queueing theory as *reneging*.

Infinite Versus Finite Calling Population

The calling population in queueing theory is the source of arrivals to be serviced. If one is considering a waiting-line problem such as a bank drive-in teller operation, it would be reasonable to assume that the calling population is, for all practical purposes, infinite. However, if the source of arrivals for service is 10 machines in a machine shop, which must be serviced when they break down, this is obviously a finite calling population.

The key consideration in this case is whether the probability of customer arrivals is affected by the removal of one customer from the population (by entry into the service system). This question is analogous to the standard probability problem of drawing balls from an urn *without replacement*. If there are five balls in an urn, the probability of drawing a ball of a certain characteristic on the second draw is certainly different than it was on the first draw. However, if there are 500,000 balls in the urn initially, the probabilities would be virtually unaffected by the first draw.

Basic queueing theory models generally include the assumption, initially, of an infinite calling population (source). However, the finite source case is sufficiently abundant in real life that models including each assumption are often developed. Both situations will be presented in this chapter.

Infinite Versus Finite Queue Length

Although queueing theory models always begin with the assumption that waiting lines could theoretically build up to an unlimited length, this is often not the case in reality. There may be limited space prior to the service facility in which queues can build up. For example, the drive preceding a bank drive-in teller can accommodate only a limited number of vehicles, and there may be a city ordinance against queueing up on the adjacent street. On the other hand, customers may simply refuse to enter a long line, even if space is available. This is often referred to as *balking*, in the literature of queueing theory. Although the assumption of infinite queues is more attractive from a mathematical solution stand-point, queues of a finite length are often a more realistic assumption. Finite-length queues are sometimes referred to as *truncated* queues.

Steady State Versus Transient Queueing Systems

A very important assumption of queueing theory is concerned with whether the system reaches an *equilibrium*, or steady-state, condition. Almost all basic models of queueing theory assume a steady-state condition. However, some waiting-line systems can never be expected to operate long enough to achieve a steady state. Some advanced queueing theory models have been developed in which the solution depends directly on the elapsed time since the system begain operation (transient queueing systems analysis). The emphasis, however, in this chapter will be on steady-state models.

Arrival Rate Versus Service Rate

It would seem logical that the rate at which services are completed must exceed the arrival rate of customers, since if this is not the case, the queues would simply continue to grow, and thus there would be no steady-state solution. It is generally assumed that the service rate does exceed the arrival rate.

An interesting relationship between arrival rates, service rates, and expected queue lengths can be illustrated. If the arrival rate must be less than the service rate, then the ratio of arrival rate to service rate will be less than 1. As that ratio approaches 1, the expected queue length will approach infinity (in the steady-state solution, with certain assumptions). This relationship is illustrated graphically in Figure 9.6.

In Figure 9.6, λ represents mean arrival rate and μ represents mean service rate. It can be seen that as the ratio of λ to μ exceeds 0.7 the expected queue length increases very rapidly. The relationship of queue length to arrival rate and service rate, illustrated in Figure 9.6, does assume infinite possible queue lengths (or at least very large). However, if finite (or truncated) queues were assumed, the figure would not be accurate. Thus, if customers balk (do not enter the queue) or if they renege (become impatient and leave), it would, in fact, be possible for the arrival rate to exceed the service rate, and still obtain a steady-state solution.

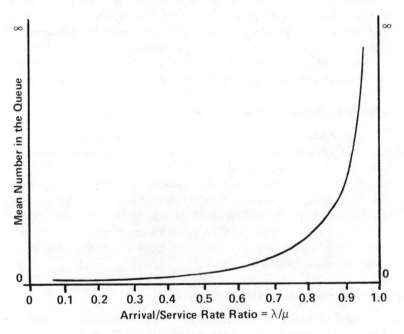

Figure 9.6
Relationship of queue length to arrival/service rate ratio

QUEUEING THEORY—MODELS

Several queueing theory models will now be presented, with the related assumptions identified. Each of the different models will actually be presented in the form of several submodels (equations) that yield the aforementioned operating characteristics for the queueing process. The derivation of the basic components included in the first model is given in Appendix IX. The student planning to pursue queueing theory in any depth should study the derivation of the initial model.

Single-Channel, Single-Phase Models

The most commonly considered case of the single-channel, single-phase queueing process will first be presented, followed by several variations. The negative exponential density function will henceforth be referred to simply as the exponential distribution.

In all of the following cases, the following assumptions will be made, unless otherwise stated within the specific model discussion:

1. Infinite calling population (unlimited arrival source)
2. Infinite queue (unlimited or nontruncated queue)
3. First-come, first-served queue discipline
4. Steady-state solution (equilibrium over time)
5. Service rate exceeds arrival rate ($\mu > \lambda$)

The first model to be presented is almost always the first model presented in any queueing theory discussion.

Poisson Arrivals, Exponential Service Times

This model includes all the most commonly assumed conditions (given above). It is the *classic* model of queueing theory. Before presenting the model equations, the following definitions of model variables will be given:

Operating Characteristics

λ = mean arrival rate   ($1/\lambda$ = mean time between arrivals)

μ = mean service rate   ($1/\mu$ = mean service time)

n = number of customers (units) in the system (includes those waiting and in service)

L = mean number in the system

L_g = mean number in the queue (queue length)

W = mean time in the system
W_g = mean waiting time (in the queue)
ρ = service facility utilization factor
I = percent server idle time

With the above assumptions and variable definitions, the model is given by the following:

1. The probability of no units in the system

$$P_0 = 1 - \frac{\lambda}{\mu}$$

2. The probability of n units in the system

$$P_n = \left(\frac{\lambda}{\mu}\right)^n \left(1 - \frac{\lambda}{\mu}\right)$$

3. The probability of k or more units in the system

$$P_{n \geq k} = \left(\frac{\lambda}{\mu}\right)^k$$

4. Mean (expected) number of units in the system

$$L = \frac{\lambda}{\mu - \lambda}$$

5. Mean number of units in the queue

$$L_q = \frac{\lambda^2}{\mu(\mu - \lambda)}$$

6. Mean time in the system

$$W = \frac{1}{\mu - \lambda}$$

7. Mean waiting time

$$W_q = \frac{\lambda}{\mu(\mu - \lambda)}$$

8. Service facility utilization factor

$$\rho = \frac{\lambda}{\mu}$$

9. Percent server idle time

$$I = 1 - \frac{\lambda}{\mu}$$

It is also of interest to note the following relationships among the various operating characteristics:

$$P_n = P_0 \left(\frac{\lambda}{\mu}\right)^n$$

$$L_q = L - \frac{\lambda}{\mu} = \lambda \cdot W_q$$

$$L = L_q + \frac{\lambda}{\mu} = \lambda \cdot W$$

$$W_q = W - \frac{1}{\mu} = \frac{L_q}{\mu}$$

$$W = W_q + \frac{1}{\mu} = \frac{L}{\lambda}$$

$$I = 1 - \rho = P_0$$

Thus, when any one of the relationships L_q, L, W_q, or W has been obtained, the other three relationships can be determined directly from the first (assuming λ and μ are known). It should also be noted that the percent idle time, I, and the probability of zero customers in the system, P_0, are one and the same.

The preceding basic queueing equations will be illustrated for the following problem. Assume that the system of interest is a drive-in bank teller, with one drive-in window. Further assume that customers arrive in their cars at the average rate of 20 per hour (or one every 3 minutes on the average) according to a Poisson distribution. Assume also that the bank teller takes an average of 2 minutes per customer to complete a service, and that the service time is exponentially distributed. Customers, who arrive from an infinite population, are served on a first-come, first-served basis, and there is no limit to possible queue length. With the above description of the system, we can obtain the queueing system's operating characteristics, for the steady-state condition.

The parameters of the arrival rate and service time distributions are as follows:

Mean Rate	*Mean Time*
Arrivals: Poisson: $\lambda = 20$ per hour	Exponential: $\dfrac{1}{\lambda} = \dfrac{1 \text{ hr}}{20} = 3$ min
Services: Poisson: $\mu = 30$ per hour	Exponential: $\dfrac{1}{\mu} = \dfrac{1 \text{ hr}}{30} = 2$ min

Note that in the following computations, since it is the parameters λ and μ that are used, the time values yielded will be in terms of hours. The values for L, L_q, W, and W_q are as follows:

$$L = \frac{\lambda}{\mu - \lambda} = \frac{20}{30 - 20} = \frac{20}{10} = 2 \text{ persons}$$

There will be an average of two persons (cars) in the system (waiting or being served).

$$L_q = \frac{\lambda^2}{\mu(\mu - \lambda)} = \frac{(20)^2}{30(30 - 20)} = \frac{400}{30(10)} = \frac{400}{300} = 1.33 \text{ persons}$$

There will be an average of 1.33 cars waiting in line.

$$W = \frac{1}{\mu - \lambda} = \frac{1}{30 - 20} = \frac{1}{10} \text{ hour } (= 6 \text{ minutes})$$

The average time in the system, per customer, will be 6 minutes.

$$W_q = \frac{\lambda}{\mu(\mu - \lambda)} = \frac{20}{30(20 - 20)} = \frac{20}{30(10)} = \frac{20}{300}$$

$$= \frac{1}{15} \text{ hour } (= 4 \text{ minutes})$$

The average waiting time per customer will be 4 minutes.

Thus, on the average, each customer will spend 6 minutes in the process of waiting and being serviced, of which 4 minutes will be spent waiting in line. Note that the difference is 2 minutes, spent in service, which is equal to the original value specified for $1/\mu$, the mean service time. There will be an average of 2 cars in the system, and an average of 1.33 cars waiting for service. It might seem, intuitively, that if there are 2 customers in the system, and one in service, the number waiting should be only one. However, recall that arrivals and service times are *random* over time, so that part of the time the drive-in teller is idle, and part of the time more than one customer is waiting. The values obtained are simply the averages, over an *assumed* lengthy period of time.

Some additional operating characteristics are given as follows:

$$P_0 = 1 - \frac{\lambda}{\mu} = 1 - \frac{20}{30} = 1 - \frac{2}{3} = \frac{1}{3} = 0.33$$

The probability of no customers in the system is 0.33. Since the percent idle time of the server (I) is equal to P_0, the bank drive-in teller is idle 33 percent of the time. Of course, the teller would be busy 67 percent of the time, which is the server utilization factor: $\rho = \lambda/\mu = 0.67$. Probability distributions of the exact number in the system, and of some number or greater in the system, are given as follows:

Probability of n *Customers in System*		*Probability of* k *or more Customers in System*	
n $P_n = \left(\dfrac{20}{30}\right)^n\left(1-\dfrac{20}{30}\right)$		k $P_{n\geq k} = \left(\dfrac{20}{30}\right)^k$	
0	0.333	0	1.000
1	0.222	1	0.667
2	0.148	2	0.444
3	0.099	3	0.296
4	0.066	4	0.198
5	0.044	5	0.132
6	0.029	6	0.088
7	0.019	7	0.058
8	0.013	8	0.039
9	0.009	9	0.026
10	0.006	10	0.017

It is of considerable interest to note that 13.2 percent of the time there will be five or more customers in the system ($P_{n\geq 5} = 0.132$). Thus, if the drive preceding the drive-in teller window had a capacity limit of three cars (a capacity of four cars in the system), then the operating system would have sufficient capacity only 87 percent of the time. Thirteen percent of the time, customers would have to line up on the adjacent street. If we assume that customers are lost as a result of insufficient system capacity, a modified queueing model must be used, assuming a finite possible queue length.

Suppose that the bank's management has discovered that by doubling the teller's salary from $3.00 per hour to $6.00 per hour, the teller's service time is reduced from an average of 2 minutes per customer to 1.5 minutes per customer (40 per hour). Management also estimates that the cost of customer waiting time is $5.00 per minute, in terms of customer dissatisfaction. Should they give the teller the raise?

The system operating characteristics required to analyze the problem are W_q and I, which are summarized below:

	Case 1	Case 2
	$1/\mu = 2$ *minutes per customer*	$1/\mu = 1.5$ *minutes per customer*
Mean waiting time: $Wq = \dfrac{\lambda}{\mu(\mu - \lambda)}$	4 minutes	1.5 minutes

Percent idle time: $I = 1 - \dfrac{\lambda}{\mu}$ 33%   50%

Since the mean arrival rate (λ) is 20 per hour, if the drive-in teller operation is open 8 hours per day, the expected number of customers is 160. Thus, the total expected waiting times are: 640 minutes for case 1, and 240 minutes for case 2. The teller will be idle 2.64 hours and 4 hours, respectively, for case 1 and case 2. The relative costs are summarized below:

	Case 1 $1/\mu = 2$ *minutes*	*Case 2* $1/\mu = 1.5$ *minutes*
Customer waiting time cost	$640 \times 5 = \$3200$	$240 \times 5 = \$1200$
Server idle time cost	$2.64 \times 3 = \$7.92$	$4 \times 6 = \$24.00$

Thus, the bank would expect to gain $2000.00 in customer goodwill at a cost of $16.08, by doubling the teller's wage, and thereby reducing customer waiting time. The teller is destined for a raise!

It should be noted that server idle time is the appropriate variable to consider regarding the service level cost only if it can be assumed that the value of lost productivity during idle time was equal to the teller's wage level in each case. If this is not the case, then the correct manner in which to analyze the problem is to simply compare the total cost of each service level. In this case it would be 8 hours at $3.00 per hour ($24.00) versus 8 hours at $6.00 per hour ($48.00). The cost of increased service level is therefore $24.00. Although the value of lost productivity during idle time is the theoretically correct manner in which to analyze a queueing problem, it is about as difficult to estimate as the cost of customer waiting time. Thus, the second manner of simply comparing the total costs of service is probably a best approximation. In any event, the resulting decision would be the same. As an exercise, show that it would still be economically appropriate to double the teller's salary even if it resulted in an increase in the service rate by only ½ of one percent (from 2 minutes to 1.99 minutes).

Poisson Arrivals, Arbitrary Service Times

In many cases, the service time cannot be assumed to fit an exponential distribution. However, if it can be assumed the service times are independent, with some common probability distribution (*any* distribution, as long as it is the same for all services), whose mean $(1/\mu)$ and standard deviation (σ) are known, then the following model equations will yield the system's performance:

$$\rho = \frac{\lambda}{\mu}$$

$$P_0 = 1 - \frac{\lambda}{\mu}$$

$$L_q = \frac{\lambda^2 \sigma^2 + (\lambda/\mu)^2}{2(1 - \lambda/\mu)}$$

$$L = L_q + \frac{\lambda}{\mu}$$

$$W_q = \frac{L_q}{\lambda}$$

$$W = W_q + \frac{1}{\mu}$$

For the previous example of the drive-in bank teller operation, service times might be some arbitrary, nonexponential distribution with mean $1/\mu = 2$ minutes $= 1/30$ hour and standard deviation $\sigma = 4$ minutes $= 1/15$ hour. The following operating characteristics would therefore be obtained:

$$\rho = \frac{20}{30} = 0.67$$

$$P_0 = 1 - \frac{20}{30} = 0.33$$

$$
\begin{aligned}
L_q &= \frac{(20)^2(1/15)^2 + (20/30)^2}{2(1 - 20/30)} \\[2mm]
&= \frac{(400)(1/225) + (400/900)}{2/3} \\[2mm]
&= \frac{(3200 + 800)/1800}{2/3} \\[2mm]
&= \frac{4000}{1800}\left(\frac{3}{2}\right) = \frac{2000}{600} \\[2mm]
&= 3.33 \text{ customers waiting}
\end{aligned}
$$

$$L = 3.33 + \left(\frac{20}{30}\right) = 4.0 \text{ customers in the system}$$

$$W_q = \frac{3.33}{20} = 0.1665 \text{ hour} \cong 10 \text{ minutes waiting}$$

$$W = 0.1665 + \left(\frac{1}{30}\right) = 0.1665 + 0.0333$$

$$= 0.1998 \text{ hours} \cong 12 \text{ minutes in the system}$$

It is interesting to compare the results just obtained to those obtained for the exponential service time case. The comparative results are summarized as follows:

	L_q	L	W_q	W
Exponential service times	1.33	2	4	6
Arbitrary service times	3.33	4	10	12

Recall from the discussion of the exponential distribution that the standard deviation is equal to the mean. For the case of arbitrary service times, we have doubled the standard deviation from 2 minutes to 4 minutes.

Thus, the number in the system and the time in the system have both doubled. The number waiting and the waiting time have both increased by two and a half times. This indicates that, in addition to average service speed, the variance of the services also has an important effect on the performance of the queueing system. As an exercise, show that the arbitrary service time model yields the same results as the exponential service time model when the standard deviation of service time is equal to the mean service time.

Poisson Arrivals, Constant Service Times

Although constant service times may not represent a large number of real situations, it may be the case for services performed by machines. For this case, simply set $\sigma = 0$ and use the preceding model (arbitrary service times). As an exercise, show that L_q for constant service time is equal to $\frac{1}{2}L_q$ for exponential service time.

Poisson Arrivals, Erlang Service Times

The Erlang distribution is a very important distribution in queueing theory because it can be made to fit most empirically determined service times. The Erlang distribution (density function) is

$$f(t) = \frac{(\mu k)^k}{(k - 1)!} t^{k-1} e^{-k\mu t}$$

where μ and k are both parameters of the distribution: μ is the mean, and k is the parameter that determines the dispersion of the distribution.

The Erlang distribution is shown, for several values of k, in Figure 9.7. Note that both the exponential distribution and constant times are special cases of the Erlang distribution.

An intuitive interpretation for k can be given as follows. Suppose a single server performs several functions for a customer during one service operation. If the several (k) respective functions performed have identical exponential distributions with mean $1/k\mu$, then the aggregate service distribution is an Erlang distribution with parameters μ and k. The mean of the Erlang will be $1/\mu$ and the variance σ^2 will be $1/k\mu^2$. However, even if this is not the physical process, the Erlang distribution may fit the service time distribution. It is also of interest to note that k is assumed to be an integer value in the Erlang distribution, and is therefore simply a special case of the *gamma* distribution, where k can be any real value.

In order to solve for the operating characteristics for the Erlang (or gamma) service time model, simply set $\sigma^2 = 1/k\mu^2$, and use the model for arbitrary service times. As an exercise, assume that the bank drive-in teller performed two functions ($k = 2$) for each customer, and solve the example problem given for the Poisson arrivals, exponential service model.

Poisson Arrivals, Exponential Service Times, Finite Queue

For the bank drive-in teller example, suppose that the maximum number of cars the system could contain was four, and that cars could

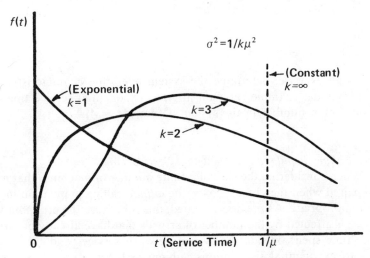

Figure 9.7
Erlang distribution for several values of k

not line up on the adjacent street. This might be due to a city ordinance or customers might simply refuse to enter the queue.

In either event, the model must be modified to consider the truncated (finite) queue system. It should be noted that for this case the service rate does *not* have to exceed the arrival rate ($\mu \not> \lambda$) in order to obtain steady-state conditions. The resultant operating characteristics, where M is the maximum number in the system, would be as follows:

$$P_0 = \frac{1 - \lambda/\mu}{1 - (\lambda/\mu)^{M+1}}$$

$$P_n = (P_0)\left(\frac{\lambda}{\mu}\right)^n \qquad \text{for } n \leq M$$

$$L = \frac{\lambda/\mu}{1 - \lambda/\mu} - \frac{(M+1)(\lambda/\mu)^{M+1}}{1 - (\lambda/\mu)^{M+1}}$$

Since P_n is the probability of n units in the system, if we define M as the maximum number allowed in the system, then P_M (the value of P_n for $n = M$) is the probability that customers are lost from the system. The remaining equations are:

$$L_q = L - \frac{\lambda(1 - P_M)}{\mu}$$

$$W = \frac{L}{\lambda(1 - P_M)}$$

$$W_q = W - \frac{1}{\mu}$$

As an exercise, determine the system operating characteristics for the first model example (Poisson arrivals, exponential service times) if the maximum number in the system is four ($M = 4$).

Finite Calling Population, Exponential Service Times

When considering the case of a finite number of machines that must be repaired when they break down, the *infinite* calling population model is not appropriate. As previously stated, this is because the probability of arrivals is affected by the number of arrivals that have already occurred. If the time spent outside the system between services and the service times are exponential distributions with means $1/\lambda$ and $1/\mu$, respectively, then the operating characteristics are given as follows:

$$P_0 = \frac{1}{\sum_{n=0}^{N} \frac{N!}{(N-n)!} \left(\frac{\lambda}{\mu}\right)^n}$$

where N = population size

$$P_n = \frac{N!}{(N-n)!} \left(\frac{\lambda}{\mu}\right)^n P_0$$

where $n = 1, 2, \ldots, N$

$$L_q = N - \frac{\lambda + \mu}{\lambda} (1 - P_0)$$

$$L = L_q + (1 - P_0)$$

$$W_q = \frac{L_q}{(N - L)\lambda}$$

$$W = W_q + \frac{1}{\mu}$$

The computations associated with the finite calling population model are somewhat unattractive. Fortunately, tables have been developed that yield system operating characteristics for various combinations of input parameters. Thus, by referring to these tables one can analyze the finite queueing process with relative ease.[*]

A number of additional single-server queueing models have been developed. Some examples include systems in which the server works faster as the queue becomes longer, or the arrival rate is reduced as the queue lengthens. Models have also been developed for queue disciplines other than first-come, first-served, such as service in random order, or priority-discipline models. These, and other advanced single-server models, are, however, beyond the scope of this book and will not be considered here.

Multiple-Channel, Single-Phase Models

Since a large number of real-world queueing systems include multiple servers, an introductory presentation of multiple-channel models will be given. Multiple-channel models, however, can become quite complex, and therefore only a limited case will be considered.

Prior to presentation of the multiple-channel model, it should be carefully distinguished from other similar queueing systems. The multiple-channel, single-phase model to be presented assumes that a single waiting line forms prior to the service facility. The service facility contains several servers, who serve customers from the single queue, as

[*] See, Peck, L. G., and Hazelwood, R. N., *Finite Queueing Tables*, Wiley, New York, 1958.

the servers become available. Service is on a first-come, first-served basis. This case was illustrated in Figure 9.2. Such a situation might exist, for example, if there were several attendants operating separate tool check-out counters, in which workmen waited for service in a single line.

This would not be the case for systems such as grocery store check-out counters, where seperate queues form behind each counter. This type of system would actually represent several single-channel, single-phase facilities operating simultaneously. Since customers do not often move from one line to the other (jockey) in the grocery store example, this system could be studied by applying single-server models to each facility. However, when customers commonly jockey from one queue to another, such as from one teller line to another in a bank, neither the multiple-channel model (for all tellers) nor the single-channel model (for each teller independently) is appropriate for analysis of the system. For more complex queueing processes such as this, only simulation can be used.

Poisson Arrivals, Exponential Service Times

The multiple-channel, single-phase model to be presented here assumes Poisson arrivals and exponential service times. Arrivals are assumed to come from an infinite population, and an unlimited (infinite) queue may build up. Service is on a first-come, first-served basis. The mean effective service rate for the overall system is $s{\cdot}\mu$ (where s equals the number of servers) and $s{\cdot}\mu$ exceeds the customer arrival rate (λ). It is further assumed that the service time distribution for each server is the same, regardless of which one of the s servers performs the service for a customer.

The steady-state results for the above described model are given as follows:

$$P_0 = \frac{1}{\left[\sum_{n=0}^{s-1} \frac{(\lambda/\mu)^n}{n!}\right] + \left[\frac{(\lambda/\mu)^s}{s!(1 - \lambda/s\mu)}\right]}$$

$$P_n = \frac{(\lambda/\mu)^n}{n!} P_0 \qquad \text{if } n \leq s$$

$$P_n = \frac{(\lambda/\mu)^n}{s!s^{n-s}} P_0 \qquad \text{if } n \geq s$$

$$\rho = \frac{\lambda}{s\mu}$$

$$L_q = \frac{P_0(\lambda/\mu)^s\rho}{s!(1 - \rho)^2}$$

$$L = L_q + \frac{\lambda}{\mu}$$

$$W_q = \frac{L_q}{\lambda}$$

$$W = W_q + \frac{\lambda}{\mu}$$

Consider the example where trucks arrive at a shipping terminal to be unloaded and loaded. Assume that the terminal dock capacity is three trucks. As trucks enter the terminal the drivers receive numbers, and when one of the three dock spaces becomes available, the truck with the lowest number enters the space. Put in terms of our queueing models, the system can be described as a three-channel, single-phase facility.

Further assume that truck arrivals are Poisson distributed, and unloading and loading (service) times are exponentially distributed. The terminal grounds are sufficiently large that there is no significant limit to the number of trucks that can be waiting at any one time.

If the average truck arrival rate is 5 per hour, and the average service rate per dock space is 2 per hour (30 minutes per truck), the system's steady-state operating characteristics would be as follows:

$$\lambda = 5$$
$$\mu = 2$$
$$s = 3$$
$$s\mu = 6$$

$$\rho = \frac{\lambda}{s\mu} = \frac{5}{(3)(2)} = \frac{5}{6} = 0.8333$$

For computing P_0, we will first compute the first term in the demoninator of the formula, as follows:

$$
\sum_{n=0}^{s-1} \frac{(\lambda/\mu)^n}{n!} = \frac{(\lambda/\mu)^0}{0!} + \frac{(\lambda/\mu)^1}{1!} + \frac{(\lambda/\mu)^2}{2!}
$$

$$
= \frac{(5/2)^0}{0!} + \frac{(5/2)^1}{1!} + \frac{(5/2)^2}{2!}
$$

$$
= \frac{1}{1} + \frac{2.5}{1} + \frac{6.25}{2}
$$

$$
= 1 + 2.5 + 3.125
$$

$$
= 6.625
$$

The second term in the denominator of the P_0 formula is

$$\frac{(\lambda/\mu)^s}{s!(1 - \lambda/s\mu)} = \frac{(5/2)^3}{3!(1 - 5/6)} = \frac{125/8}{6(1/6)} = 15.625$$

Therefore:

$$P_0 = \frac{1}{6.625 + 15.625} = \frac{1}{22.25}$$

$$= 0.0449$$

Since considerable computational effort is involved in calculating the value of P_0, a table of values for P_0 has been provided in Appendix X, for various combinations of $\lambda/\mu s$ (utilization factor) and s (number of channels).

The system's other operating characteristics are as follows:

$$L_q = \frac{P_0(\lambda/\mu)^s\rho}{s!(1 - \rho)^2}$$

$$= \frac{(0.0449)(5/2)^3(5/6)}{3!(1 - 5/6)^2} = \frac{(0.0449)(125/8)(5/6)}{(6)(1/36)}$$

$$= (0.0449)\left(\frac{625}{48}\right)\left(\frac{6}{1}\right) = (0.0449)\left(\frac{625}{8}\right)$$

$$\cong 3.5 \text{ trucks waiting}$$

$$L = L_q + \frac{\lambda}{\mu} = 3.5 + \frac{5}{2}$$

$$= 6.0 \text{ trucks in the system}$$

$$W_q = \frac{L_q}{\lambda} = \frac{3.5}{5} = 0.7 \text{ hour (42 minutes) waiting time}$$

$$W = W_q + \frac{1}{\mu} = \left(0.7 + \frac{1}{2}\right) \text{hours (72 minutes) time in the system}$$

Thus, on the average, there will be 6 trucks in the system, with an average of 3.5 trucks waiting for service. The difference of 2.5 is the average number of trucks in service in the three service locations, reflecting the fact that a portion of the time one or more servers will be idle. In fact, almost 5 percent of the time, the entire system will be idle ($P_0 = 0.0449$). The mean time in the system will be 72 minutes, of which 42 minutes will be spent waiting for a dock space. The difference of 30 minutes is exactly the expected service time, $1/\mu$, originally specified.

It is also of considerable interest to know how many trucks can be

expected to be in the system at any one time. Some probabilities of various numbers of trucks in the system are given as follows:
In general,

$$P_n = \frac{(\lambda/\mu)^n}{n!} P_0 \qquad \text{if } n \leq s$$

$$P_n = \frac{(\lambda/\mu)^n}{s! s^{n-s}} P_0 \qquad \text{if } n \geq s$$

For particular values of n, we find

$$P(n=1) = \frac{(5/2)^1}{1!} (0.0449) = 0.11225$$

$$P(n=2) = \frac{(5/2)^2}{2!} (0.0449) = 0.14031$$

$$P(n=3) = \frac{(5/2)^3}{3!} (0.0449) = 0.11693$$

$$P(n=4) = \frac{(5/2)^4}{3! 3^{4-3}} (0.0449) = 0.09744$$

$$P(n=5) = \frac{(5/2)^5}{3! 3^{5-3}} (0.0449) = 0.08120$$

The preceding values are included in a summary of the number in the system, along with associated individual probabilities and cumulative probabilities, in Table 9.3

Table 9.3 shows that the probability distribution of the number in the system is rather flat and widely dispersed. Thus, even though the expected (mean) number in the system is 6, management may wish to know the chances of having 10 or more trucks in the system (or what is the probability that there will be 7 or more trucks waiting to unload and load?). The former is given as $P(n \geq 10) = 1 - P(n \leq 9)$, where $P(n \leq 9)$ is obtained from Table 9.3 as 0.801. Therefore, there is about a 20 percent chance that there will be 10 or more trucks in the system (or 20 percent of the time there will be at least 10 trucks in the system.)

The example problem involves some interesting questions regarding how one might go about changing the service level. Several possibilities exist. Management could consider increasing the number of service positions at the dock (increase the number of channels). They could also consider trying to increase the service rate with the existing capacity. This might be done by hiring more labor to unload and load trucks, or it might be achieved by installing faster and more efficient equipment. It

Table 9.3

n Number in the System	P_n Probability	N N or less in the System	$P_{n \leqslant N}$ Cumulative Probability
0	0.045	0	0.045
1	0.112	1	0.157
2	0.140	2	0.297
3	0.117	3	0.414
4	0.097	4	0.511
5	0.081	5	0.592
6	0.068	6	0.660
7	0.056	7	0.716
8	0.047	8	0.763
9	0.038	9	0.801
10	0.033	10	0.834
11	0.027	11	0.861
12	0.023	12	0.884
13	0.019	13	0.903
14	0.016	14	0.919
15	0.013	15	0.932

should be noted that even though several persons might be employed at each individual truck position, this could still be thought of as one of the several channels, and μ could be varied by adding or subtracting manpower.

Several other multiple-channel, single-phase models have been developed, such as for the cases of truncated queues and finite calling populations. These, however, are beyond the scope of this chapter.

Multiple-Phase Models

Very little will be said about multiple-phase queueing models, since they become extremely complex very quickly. However, one case should be discussed. If the multiple-phase system satisfies all the assumptions of Poisson arrivals, exponential service times, infinite calling population, infinite queue, and service rate exceeds arrival rate; then the multiple-phase system can be analyzed rather easily.

The fundamental point here is: if a service facility has a Poisson input with parameter λ, and exponential service time distribution with parameter μ, (where $\mu > \lambda$), then the steady-state *output* of this service facility is also a Poisson process with parameter λ. Thus, the facility following the first facility, in a multiple-phase system, will have a Poisson input with parameter λ. This condition will hold for the single-channel model, and for the multiple-channel model just discussed (if $s\mu > \lambda$).

Thus, the individual phases may be evaluated independently of one another, and then the aggregate operating characteristics can be obtained by summing the corresponding values obtained at the respective facilities. The operating characteristics referred to are: total expected waiting time, total expected time in the system, total expected number in queues, and total expected number in the overall system.

Figure 9.8 illustrates three examples of multiple-phase models that can be analyzed by the above procedure, if the previously stated assumptions are met. The first case (a) is simply a single-channel, multiple-phase model. The two phases would be evaluated independently and then the individual phase characteristics would be summed. The second case (b) is simply two stages of a multiple-channel, single-phase process. Thus, each stage would be evaluated independently according to the multiple-channel, single-phase equations, and the resulting operating characteristics would be summed. The third case (c) represents an initial multiple-channel, single-phase stage, with each of the three servers followed by a single-channel, single-phase stage. This system would be evaluated by solving the multiple-channel, single-phase equations for the first stage, and then solving one of the following stage phases as a single-channel, single phase process, with $\lambda_i = \frac{1}{3}\lambda$ (where λ_i = mean arrival rate at the second stage, channel i server). Recall that the multiple-channel, single-phase model assumed that the service rate was identical for each server, yielding the assumption that $\lambda_i = \frac{1}{3}$. Since the results would be the same for each of the three second-stage servers, only one of these need be evaluated.

SIMULATION OF QUEUEING SYSTEMS

Several analytical models of queueing systems have been presented, along with the resulting equations for obtaining measures of the system's performance. However, the reader can quickly appreciate that the number of conceivable waiting-line models is almost infinite.

The purpose of this chapter was to give the reader a feel for the analysis of waiting-line systems, and how to go about obtaining at least rough approximations to the operating characteristics. As a matter of practice, most analyses of waiting lines would include a combination of the aforementioned techniques with the technique of simulation. With

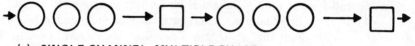

(a) SINGLE-CHANNEL, MULTIPLE-PHASE

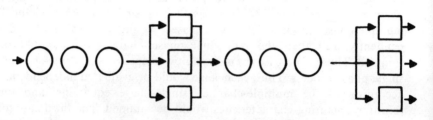

(b) MULTIPLE-CHANNEL, MULTIPLE-PHASE (CASE I)

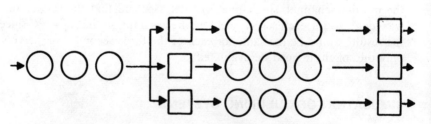

(c) MULTIPLE-CHANNEL, MULTIPLE-PHASE (CASE II)

Figure 9.8
Multiple-phase models

380

the analytical results for insight and guidance, the analyst would generally proceed to develop a computer simulation model that includes all the various facets of the real system. The topic of simulation is presented in a separate chapter.

REFERENCES

Buffa, E. S., *Operations Management: Problems and Models*, 3d. ed., Wiley, New York, 1972.

Feller, W., *An Introduction to Probability Theory and Its Applications, Vol. I*, 3d. ed., Wiley, New York, 1968.

Hillier, F., and Lieberman, G. J., *Introduction to Operations Research*, 2d ed., Holden-Day, San Francisco, 1974.

Morse, P. M., *Queues, Inventories, and Maintenance*, Wiley, New York, 1958.

Saaty, T. L., *Elements of Queueing Theory*, McGraw-Hill, New York, 1961.

Taha, H. A., *Operations Research: An Introduction*, Macmillan, New York, 1971.

QUESTIONS

1. Specify the basic components of a waiting-line process.
2. Describe and illustrate graphically the four basic structures of waiting-line processes.
3. Discuss at least three entirely different systems that may be considered as queueing processes.
4. What is meant by "queue discipline"?
5. Illustrate and describe a general model for decision analysis of queueing processes.
6. Specify at least five operating characteristics commonly obtained in the analysis of waiting lines.
7. Queueing models belong to the general class of models known as "deterministic" models. Is this true or false? If false, into what general class of models do queueing models fall?
8. What is the most commonly assumed distribution for arrivals in a queueing process? Illustrate graphically and describe.
9. What is the most commonly assumed distribution for services in a queueing process? Illustrate graphically and describe.
10. State the assumptions of the first model developed in this chapter.

PROBLEMS

1. Consider a waiting-line process with the following characteristics:

    Infinite calling population
    Infinite possible queue
    First-come, first-served queue discipline
    Steady state condition exists
    Service rate exceeds arrival rate
    Single-channel, single-phase system
    Poisson arrival rate, exponential service times

    Assume that the arrivals occur at a mean rate of three per hour ($\lambda = 3$), and the mean service rate is five per hour ($\mu = 5$).

    (a) What is the probability that during the first hour there will be exactly one arrival? two arrivals? three arrivals? four arrivals? What is the probability there will be four or more arrivals during the first hour?
    (b) What is the probability that the first arrival will require a service time of at least 6 minutes (0.1 hour)? 12 minutes (0.2 hour)? 30 minutes (0.5 hour)?
    (c) What percent of the time will the server be idle?
    (d) What is the expected (mean) waiting time per arrival, in hours and in minutes?
    (e) What is the mean number of arrivals waiting?
    (f) What is the average time in the system (waiting and in service), in hours and in minutes?
    (g) What is the average number of arrivals in the system?
    (h) What value is the utilization factor?

2. In problem 1, construct a probability distribution for k or more units in the system, for values of k ranging from 0 to 6. Suppose it is highly undesirable to have a waiting line of three or more arrivals. What is the probability of this happening?

3. In problem 1, suppose the mean rate for arrivals increased to (a) 4 per hour, (b) 4.5 per hour, (c) 5 per hour. Plot the values of L_q versus values of λ/μ, for the arrival rates of: 3, 4, 4.5, and 5 per hour. What happens as the arrival rate approaches the service rate?

4. Assume that all the conditions of problem 1 are met, except that the service distribution is unknown. The mean service time is known to be 12 minutes, with a standard deviation of 6 minutes (in other words, the mean service rate, μ, equals five per hour, and the

standard deviation of service times in hours, σ, is equal to 0.1). Determine the values for the following operating characteristics:

(a) Utilization factor   (d) L
(b) P_0 (e) W_q
(c) L_q (f) W

Compare these results with the results obtained in problem 1.

5. In problem 1, assume that it is possible to control the service rate (e.g., vary the manpower in the service facility). Assume that the various service rates may be obtained according to the following schedule of associated costs:

Service Rate (μ)	Service Cost Per Hour
4 customers/hour	$3.00
4.5	6.00
5	9.00
5.5	12.00
6	15.00

Further assume that the cost per hour for customers waiting is estimated to be $10.00 per hour. Analyze the system over a period of 8 hours. (Note: It will be assumed here that the system is in steady state at the beginning of the 8-hour period of analysis.)

(a) Determine the optimum service level (service rate) to employ, and the associated expected total cost.
(b) Illustrate the decision analysis graphically, showing service cost, customer waiting cost, and total cost, for the various service rates considered.

6. Assume that a firm has 10 machines that periodically break down and require service. The average time between breakdowns is three days, distributed according to an exponential distribution. The average time to repair a machine is two days, distributed according to an exponential distribution. One repairman repairs the machines in the order in which they break down.

(a) Determine the probability the repairman is idle.
(b) Determine the mean number of machines waiting to be repaired.
(c) Determine the mean time machines wait to be repaired.
(d) Determine the probability that three machines are not operating (being repaired or waiting to be repaired).

7. Customers arrive at a service facility at the mean rate of 8 per hour.

The arrival rate is Poisson distributed. Service times are exponentially distributed, with a mean of 5 minutes. The calling population is infinitely large; however, the maximum possible queue length is three customers. Determine the following:

(a) The probability of zero in the system
(b) The mean number of customers in the system
(c) The mean number of customers waiting
(d) The mean time a customer spends in the system
(e) The mean time a customer spends waiting
(f) The percent of arriving customers lost due to the queue length limitation

8. Assume the same conditions given in problem 1, with the following exceptions: mean arrival rate = 8 per hour; mean service rate per server = 5 per hour; and number of servers = 2 (two-channel, single-phase system). Determine the following operating statistics:

(a) Probability the system is empty
(b) Probability of exactly four in the system
(c) Utilization factor
(d) Mean length of the waiting line
(e) Mean time an arrival spends waiting

9. Assume that an arriving customer must first be serviced in the facility described in problem 1, and proceed directly to a second facility for a second phase of service. The second facility also meets all the assumptions of problem 1, but with a Poisson distributed service rate with a mean of 4 per hour. Thus, the overall system may be described as a single-channel, two-phase process. Determine P_0, L, L_q, W, and W_q for this system.

10. Trucks arrive at a firm's unloading facility according to a Poisson distribution, at the mean rate of 20 trucks per day. Only one truck at a time can be unloaded; however, unlimited space is available for trucks to wait for service. Assume an infinite population of trucks. The firm wishes to determine the optimum number of workers to employ for unloading the trucks (at the single unloading facility). It is known that workers can unload a truck at the mean rate of 5 trucks per man-day, with no diminishing efficiency up to a maximum of eight workers. The unloading rate varies according to a Poisson distribution. Workers are paid $25 per day, while the estimated cost of waiting trucks is $50 per day, per truck. The firm's management

has observed the average number of arriving trucks (20) and the average rate at which workers can unload the trucks (5 per man-day), and they have concluded that they should employ 4 workers (20/5 = 4). Determine whether the firm has arrived at a good decision. What number of workers would you recommend to management? Illustrate your decision analysis as a graphical decision model, to present to the management of the firm. Discuss how you would explain the error in management's decision.

10 Network Models: PERT-CPM

INTRODUCTION

PERT and CPM are two of the best-known network modeling techniques of decision science. PERT (Program Evaluation and Review Technique) and CPM (Critical Path Method) were each developed to aid in the planning, scheduling, and control of large, complex projects. PERT was developed in 1958 to aid in the planning and scheduling of the U.S. Navy's Polaris missile project, involving over 3000 different contracting organizations. Involved in the development of PERT were the Navy's Office of Special Projects, Booz-Allen and Hamilton Company, and the Missile Systems Division of Lockheed Aircraft Corporation. The outstanding success of the Polaris project is largely responsible for the popular acceptance of PERT as a planning and control device by government and business.

CPM was developed independently, and simultaneously, by the DuPont Company in conjunction with the Univac Division of Remington Rand Corporation. Although the purpose of the CPM project was to provide a technique for the control of maintenance of DuPont chemical plants, the two networking techniques are almost identical in concept and methodology. The primary difference between the two techniques, as originally conceived, was the manner in which activity time estimates were derived. In PERT it was assumed that three time estimates would be obtained for each activity, while CPM required only a single estimate for each activity time. All further discussion will relate equally to both techniques, with exceptions to be noted.

PURPOSE OF PERT-CPM NETWORKS

The purpose of PERT-CPM networks is to aid in the planning and control of one-time projects. The network modeling approach requires that the modeler explicitly define the project activities and their interrelationships. This process requires the consideration of: (1) what operations are to be done; (2) how they will be performed; (3) the resources required, such as manpower and equipment; and (4) the time required for each activity or operation.

As is the case with any model, the process of model construction itself assists in clarifying critical relationships and identifying missing elements or unclear aspects. Once constructed, the PERT-CPM network is an aid in the control of the actual project implementation. The PERT-CPM technique provides for the computation of a "critical path," which consists of the sequence of project activities that determines the minimum required project time. Once the critical path is determined, management can consider the possibility of reallocating project resources to reduce project time. In addition, the activities of the critical path must be the most closely controlled activities of the project.

CONSTRUCTION OF THE NETWORK MODEL

As contrasted with other decision science models, the conceptual basis for construction of PERT-CPM network models is quite simple. Of course, this does not imply that obtaining the necessary data or visualizing the relationships of the activities to be performed is simple. However, in the case of the PERT-CPM model, a graphical portrayal of the project activity relationships completes the construction of the model. Thus, no symbolic (mathematical equations) model is required for PERT-CPM models.

Major Components of PERT-CPM Networks

PERT-CPM networks consist of two major components: activities and events. Activities of the network portray the actual operations or activities of the real-world project. As such, activities consume time and resources. Events of the network represent milestones in the project, and occur at a point in time. An event may represent the beginning of an activity, the end of an activity, or both the beginning of one or more activities and the end of one or more other activities.

Events are commonly represented graphically as circles, while activities are represented as arrows. Figure 10.1 illustrates two activities and three events. Activities are identified by their start and end event. Event 1 represents the start of activity 1–2, and event 2 represents the end of activity 1–2. Event 2 also represents the start of activity 2–3, and event 3 represents the end of activity 2–3.

Figure 10.1
Network with two activities and three events

For example, activity 1–2 might represent the construction of concrete forms, while event 2–3 represents the pouring of the concrete, in a building project. Event 1 would represent starting construction of the concrete forms. Event 2 would represent completion of construction of the concrete forms, and begin pouring of the concrete. Event 3 would represent completion of pouring of the concrete.

Precedence Relationships in PERT-CPM Networks

The arrows of the PERT-CPM network show the precedence relationships of activities and events throughout the network. The numbers of the events are simply for purposes of identification and do not indicate the logical flow of the project activities.

Consider, for example, the network described in Table 10.1 and shown graphically in Figure 10.2. Represented is a simple PERT-CPM network in which the point of the preceding paragraph is illustrated. Event 1 represents the start of the project (and the start of activity 1–2). Event 2 represents the completion of activity 1–2, and the start of activities 2–3 and 2–5. Upon completion of activity 1–2, activities 2–3 and 2–5 may begin and be conducted simultaneously. Event 3 represents

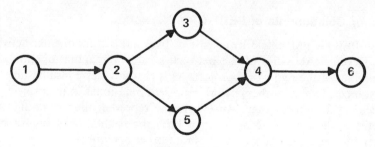

Figure 10.2
Simple PERT-CPM network

Table 10.1
Simple PERT-CPM Network

Activity	Start Event	End Event
1-2	1	2
2-3	2	3
2-5	2	5
3-4	3	4
5-4	5	4
4-6	4	6

the completion of activity 2–3, and the start of activity 3–4. Event 5 represents the completion of activity 2–5, and the start of activity 5–4.

Event 4 represents the completion of activities 3–4 and 5–4, as well as the start of activity 4–6. However, activity 4–6 cannot begin until completion of both activities 3–4 and 5–4. In general, no activity emanating from an event can start until all activities terminating at that event have been completed. Thus, activity 4–6 may begin only when the later finishing activity terminating at event 4 is completed.

Event 6 represents completion of activity 4–6, and completion of the project. Note that the event numbers do *not* indicate the order in which project activities are completed. However, note further that the *network* does show the sequence of the project activities. It is the relationship of the events with the connected arrows that determines the flow of project completion.

Let us further consider the above simple PERT-CPM network, where time values have been associated with each network activity. The assumed time required to complete each project activity is given in Table 10.2, and also shown alongside each activity arrow in Figure 10.3.

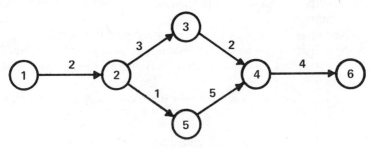

Figure 10.3
PERT-CPM network, with activity times

Table 10.2
Simple PERT-CPM Network, with Activity Times

Activity	Start Event	End Event	Time
1-2	1	2	2
2-3	2	3	3
2-5	2	5	1
3-4	3	4	2
5-4	5	4	5
4-6	4	6	4

We will assume that our time values are in days. Thus, at the end of 2 days (time 2), activities 2–3 and 2–5 may each begin. As soon as activity 2–3 is completed (at the end of 5 days), activity 3–4 can begin. Likewise, when activity 2–5 is completed, at time 3, activity 5–4 begins.

Activity 4–6 cannot begin until the later of the two activities terminating at event 4 has been completed. In the example case, activity 3–4 will be completed at the end of 7 days, while activity 5–4 will be completed at the end of 8 days. Therefore, activity 4–6 starts at time 8, and the project is completed after 12 days.

A Dummy Activity

It may be necessary, in some networks, to include a dummy activity in order to assure the proper precedence relationships. A dummy activity does not consume time or resources, but it does have to be "completed" before any activity can be started from the event at which the dummy terminates.

Let us reconsider the project networks of Figures 10.2 and 10.3, with the following description of required precedence relationships:

1. Activity 1–2 must be completed before activities 2–3 and 2–5 can be started.
2. Activities 2–3 and 2–5 can be started simultaneously.
3. Activity 3–4 can be started only upon completion of activity 2–3.
4. Activity 5–4 can be started only upon completion of *both* activities 2–3 *and* 2–5.
5. Activity 4–6 can be started only upon completion of activities 3–4 and 5–4.

The networks of Figures 10.2 and 10.3 do not correctly portray the fourth requirement that activity 2–3, in addition to activity 2–5, must be completed before starting activity 5–4.

In order to include the requirement that activity 2–3 must be completed prior to starting activity 5–4, we must insert a dummy activity, from event 3 to event 5. This is illustrated in Figure 10.4.

If we assume the same activity times as were previously given for the network of Figure 10.3, the total project time has now changed. Whereas, previously, activity 5–4 could be started after 3 days (completion of activity 2–5), activity 5–4 cannot be started in Figure 10.4 until after 5 days (completion of activity 2–3, and simultaneous completion of the dummy activity from event 3 to event 5). Since activity 5–4 cannot be started until after 5 days, the overall project time will now be 14 days. In general, no activity could be started from event 5 until all activities leading to event 3 had been completed.

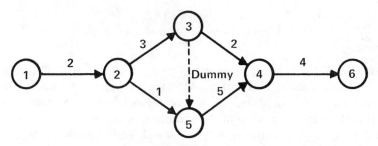

Figure 10.4
PERT-CPM network, with dummy activity

A More Complex Example

Table 10.3 gives a list of several activities, with starting and ending events, from which a PERT-CPM network can be constructed. Con-

Table 10.3
A More Complex Network Example

Activity	Start Event	End Event
1-2	1	2
1-3	1	3
2-4	2	4
2-5	2	5
3-5	3	5
3-6	3	6
4-5	4	5
4-6	4	6
5-6	5	6

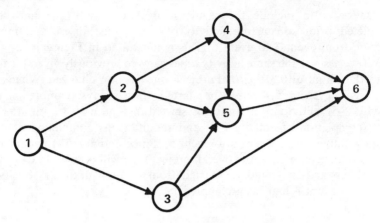

Figure 10.5
A more complex network example

struction of the network diagram, as given in Figure 10.5, illustrates a potential bottleneck at event 5. Activity 5–6 cannot be started until activities 4–5, 2–5, and 3–5 are all completed. One of the purposes of constructing the network prior to execution of the project is to provide the opportunity to consider ways in which to revise the sequence of activities in order to eliminate bottlenecks.

ESTIMATING ACTIVITY TIMES

The CPM network method assumes that a single value estimate of the time required for each activity would be obtained. The PERT technique, on the other hand, includes an explicit recognition of the uncertainty associated with activity time estimates by providing for three time estimates to be made for each activity, as follows:

a = most optimistic (shortest) time
m = most likely (modal) time
b = most pessimistic (longest) time

Beta Distribution

The PERT method then assumes that the distribution associated with the activity time is best approximated by a beta distribution. This distribution was selected due to its flexibility, which allows it to take on a skewed shape. Also, the parameters of such a distribution can be easily approximated by a conversion of the three time estimates provided. Figure 10.6 illustrates the beta distribution for the case in which the distribution is skewed to the right.

Parameters for the Beta Distribution

The parameters that describe the beta distribution are the mean and standard deviation. These parameters can be approximated from the three PERT time estimates according to the following formulas:

Mean: $t_e = \dfrac{a + 4m + b}{6}$

Standard deviation: $\sigma_e = \dfrac{b - a}{6}$

Suppose that the three time estimates for a PERT activity are $a = 3$, $m = 6$, and $b = 15$. Using the formulas given above, the mean and standard deviation would be

$$t_e = \frac{3 + 4(6) + 15}{6} = \frac{42}{6} = 7$$

$$\sigma_e = \frac{15 - 3}{6} = \frac{12}{6} = 2$$

The preceding example represents a case in which the most likely time, m, is much closer to the most optimistic time, a, than it is to the most pessimistic time, b. Therefore, the activity time distribution is skewed to the right, as in Figure 10.6.

Table 10.4 gives the means and standard deviations associated with several PERT activities in which time estimates were provided. As an exercise, the reader should construct the PERT network for Table 10.4.

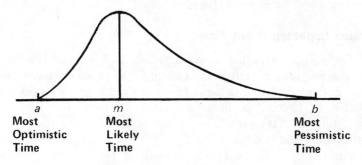

a	m	b
Most Optimistic Time	Most Likely Time	Most Pessimistic Time

Figure 10.6
Beta distribution of a PERT activity time

Table 10.4

PERT Activity Time Estimates and Computed Mean and Standard Deviations for Beta Distributions

Time Estimates				Beta Distribution Parameters	
Activity	a	m	b	Mean (t_e)	Standard Deviation (σ_e)
1-2	1	2	5	$1\frac{2}{3}$	2/3
1-3	2	4	5	$3\frac{5}{6}$	1/2
2-4	2	3	4	3	1/3
2-5	1	4	6	$3\frac{5}{6}$	5/6
3-5	3	5	9	$3\frac{2}{3}$	1
4-6	2	5	7	$4\frac{5}{6}$	5/6
5-6	3	4	5	4	1/3

It will be noted at this point that for purposes of analysis of PERT-CPM networks, the PERT mean time (t_e) is analogous to the CPM single-valued, expected time. For example, referring back to Table 10.2 (and Figure 10.3), in which activity time estimates were given, those values would be t_e values if it were a PERT network; thus, they would have been computed based on data similar to that given in Table 10.4. If it were a CPM network, the values attached to each activity would be simply the single-value time estimate obtained.

EVENT TIME COMPUTATIONS

The analysis of PERT-CPM networks includes determining several measures of performance: (1) earliest expected event time, (2) latest allowable event time, and (3) event slack.

Earliest Expected Event Time

The earliest expected event time is based on the activity time estimates provided directly in the case of CPM, or on the mean time (t_e) in the case of PERT. The earliest time an event in a network can be expected to "occur" is upon the *latest* completion of an activity terminating at that event. This is also known as the time of event "realization," and is denoted by T_E.

For example, in the PERT network of Figure 10.7, the event 4 (completion of the network) cannot occur until activities 2–4 and 3–4 are both completed. The basis for computation of the event realization time is the t_e values given on the network. It is apparent that activity 3–4 will be completed at time 7, whereas activity 2–4 will not be completed until time 12. Thus, the earliest expected realization time for event 4 is 12, or $T_E = 12$.

A second example of the earliest expected realization time for an event is given in Figure 10.8, for each event in the network. The first event (start of the project) is assigned a T_E value of zero. To get the T_E value for event 2, we add the activity time for activity 1–2 to T_E for event 1 (which is 0). Thus, we arrive at a T_E value of 3 for event 2. By a like manner, we obtain $T_E = 2$ for event 3.

Where more than one activity terminates at an event, the *latest*

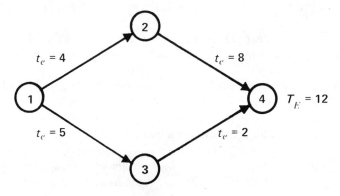

Figure 10.7
Earliest expected completion time

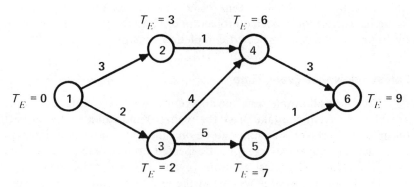

Figure 10.8
Network with T_E values

activity completion time determines the T_E value for that event (the time of realization of that event). Event 4 has activities 2–4 and 3–4 terminating at it. Therefore, the T_E value for event 4 is the time of latest completion of either activity 2–4 or activity 3–4. The activity 2–4 time (1) is added to the T_E value of 3 for event 2, yielding 4. The activity 3–4 time (4) is added to the T_E value of 2 for event 3, yielding 6. Thus, the T_E value for event 4 must be 6, the larger value. This analysis is summarized as follows:

Start Event			Activity	Sum of Activity Time and
Event No.	T_E	Activity	Time	Start Event T_E Value
2	3	2–4	1	4
3	2	3–4	4	6 (max)

It should become clear that event 4 is not realized until time 6, by simply summing the total activity times on each of the two activity paths leading up to event 4.

The T_E value for event 5 is simply the activity time for 3–5 added to the T_E value for event 3 ($5 + 2 = 7$). Since event 6 has two activities terminating at it, we must again determine which incoming activity is completed later. The analysis is summarized as follows:

Start Event			Activity	Sum of Activity Time and
Event No.	T_E	Activity	Time	Start Event T_E Value
4	6	4–6	3	9 (max)
5	7	5–6	1	8

Therefore, the T_E value for event 6 is 9. The T_E value for the last event in the network is the expected project time. Thus, the project represented by Figure 10.8 has an expected completion time of 9 days.

Latest Allowable Event Time

The latest allowable time for an event is the latest "calendar" time at which the event can take place (be realized) and still keep the project on time. The project is assumed to be on time if it can be completed no later than the previously computed expected project time (the terminal event T_E value). The latest allowable event time is denoted by T_L.

The procedure used is to start at the terminal event of the network and work backwards to the project start event. First, the terminal event T_L is set equal to its T_E value. The activity times for activities terminating at the last event are then subtracted from the last T_L value. Figure 10.9 illustrates a network for which the T_L values are shown for each event. The latest allowable time to start activity 4–6, and complete the project at time 9, is time 6 (9 – 3 = 6). The T_L for event 5 is determined by subtracting the activity 5–6 time from the T_L value of 9 for event 6 (9 – 1 = 8).

For the case in which two activities start from an event, a comparison must be made in the computation of the T_L value for that event. The T_L value will always be the *earlier* of the alternatives yielded. For example, the latest allowable time for event 3 to take place is at time 2, since a later time would throw the activity 3–4–6 sequence behind schedule. The determination is as follows for event 3: Subtract activity 3–5 time of 5 from event 5's T_L value of 8, yielding 3. Subtract activity 3–4 time of 4 from event 4's T_L of 6 yielding 2. Select the smaller value (earlier time) of 2 as T_L for event 3.

Event Slack

The slack at each event is computed as the difference between the earliest expected time and the latest allowable time. Slack is denoted as S for each event. Figure 10.10 shows the network of Figures 10.8 and 10.9 with the values of T_E, T_L, and S for each event shown.

DETERMINING THE CRITICAL PATH

The critical path of the network is the sequence of activities that constitutes the longest time path through the network, and thus

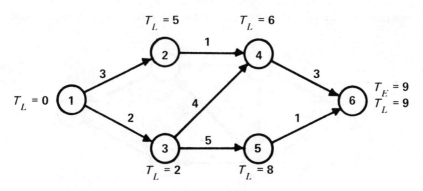

Figure 10.9
Network with T_L values

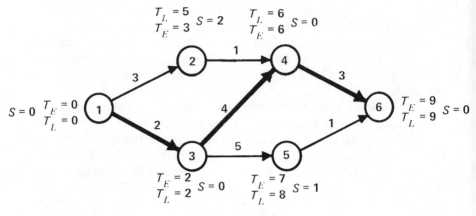

Figure 10.10
Network with T_E, T_L, and S values

determines the minimum time in which the project can be completed. The critical path can be traced through the zero slack events. For those cases in which zero slack exists, there is no difference between the earliest expected time and the latest allowable time. The events on the critical path will always have a slack of zero, since there is no time to spare on the critical path.

The critical path for the network of Figure 10.10, therefore, includes activities 1–3, 3–4, and 4–6 (or path 1–3–4–6). The events numbered 2 and 5 in the network are not on the critical path, and have slacks of 2 and 1, respectively. Although activity 1–2 is expected to be completed by time 3, it could be delayed by 2 days and still expect to complete the project on the scheduled time. Likewise, activity 3–5 could be delayed by one day and the project expected completion date would be unchanged.

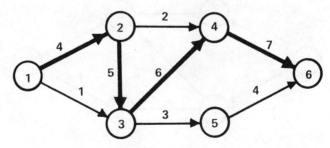

Figure 10.11
Network critical path

Occasionally small networks will yield ambiguous results when determining the critical path if care is not taken. For example, Figure 10.11 illustrates the case in which a slack of zero would be obtained for both events 2 and 4 (compute T_E, T_L, and S for each event). In this case, the critical path (darkened line) does not simply go from event 2 to event 4. This generally does not happen in large real-world networks; however, care must be taken to check that the critical path is correctly defined. The problem is easily resolved by keeping track of which activity causes a particular event to have a T_E value equal to its T_L value.

MANAGEMENT USES OF PERT-CPM NETWORKS

The primary reason for determining the T_E, T_L, and S values of the network events is to determine the critical path and the expected project time. Management will need to know which activities should be most closely managed to ensure on-time completion of the project.

Management may also want to consider shifting resources from noncritical activities to critical activities, if the resources are homogenous, such as some classes of nonskilled workers. Thus, it may be necessary to revise the original estimates for the project activities after resources are transferred, and recompute the T_E, T_L, and S values. A new critical path may even be obtained.

After arriving at the final network and critical path, the T_E values provide management with objective completion dates for various activities. The T_L and S values identify potential bottlenecks and sources of slack time.

MAKING PROBABILITY STATEMENTS ABOUT PROJECT COMPLETION TIME

It was previously shown that a standard deviation for each activity time could be calculated, for the PERT time estimate. The PERT technique further makes use of the central limit theorem of statistics to assume that the distribution of the overall project time will be normal. This is based upon the assumption that the summation of all expected activity times for activities on the critical path, yielding the overall expected project time, will be normally distributed.

Computation of Project Time Standard Deviation

The computation of the project time standard deviation is given as follows:

$$\sigma_{cp} = \sqrt{\Sigma \sigma_e^2}$$

where

    σ_{cp} = standard deviation for total expected project time (critical path)

    $\Sigma \sigma_e^2$ = sum of variances (standard deviations squared) for all activities on the critical path

For example, assume that the standard deviations for the critical-path activities of a network are 1, 3, 1, 2, and 1. The project time standard deviation would be determined as follows:

Critical Path Activities Only

σ_e Standard Deviation	σ_e^2 Variance
1	1
3	9
1	1
2	4
1	$\underline{1}$
	16

$$\sigma_{cp} = \sqrt{\Sigma \sigma_e^2} = \sqrt{16} = 4$$

Table 10.5 also illustrates the computation of the project standard deviation for an example network, with critical path 1–2–5–6. As an

Table 10.5
Computation of Project Standard Deviation

Activity	Mean (t_e)	Standard Deviation (σ_e)	σ_e^2
1-2*	18	4	16*
1-3	7	2	4
2-4	13	5	25
2-5*	25	3	9*
3-5	10	3	9
4-6	5	2	4
5-6*	9	3	9*
*critical		$\sigma_{cp} = \sqrt{16 + 9 + 9} = \sqrt{34} = 5.83$	

exercise, the reader should construct the network for the Table 10.5 project, and compute the T_E, T_L, and S values.

The assumption of normality and the computation of an overall standard deviation is not, as a matter of fact, limited to the overall project time. One may make the same assumption relative to the time for any event of the network; however, if the event is not on the critical path, some arbitrary decisions may be required as to which activity means and standard deviations to use.

Probability of Completing the Project On or Before a Specified Time

Since it has been assumed that the overall project time is approximated by a normal distribution, it is possible to make probability statements about completing the project on or before a specified time (or after a specified time). For example, assume that the expected project time (critical-path time) is 52 weeks, with a standard deviation of 5.83 weeks (computed as shown in Table 10.5). The probability of completing the project on or before 60 weeks would be determined as follows:

$$Z = \frac{60 - 52}{5.83} = \frac{8}{5.83} = 1.37 \text{ standard deviations}$$

By finding 1.37 standard deviations in the table of standard normal distribution values (Appendix XI), we see that $Z = 1.37$ corresponds to 0.91466. Thus, there is a 91.47 percent chance of completing the project on or before 60 weeks. Figure 10.12 illustrates the preceding analysis.

By the same approach, one could compute the probability of completing the project on or after a specified time. For example, what is the probability of completing the project on or after 54 weeks? The computation proceeds as follows:

$$Z = \frac{54 - 52}{5.83} = \frac{2}{5.83} = 0.34 \text{ standard deviations}$$

The corresponding area under the normal curve, to the right of the value 54, is $1.000 - 0.63307 = 0.3669$. Thus, the probability that the project will take 54 or more weeks is about 37 percent. Note that 0.63307 is the value found in the normal table for the area under the curve, to the *left* of the value 54. Since we desire the area under the curve to the right of 54, we calculate it as $1 - 0.63307$. This is allowable because the normal curve is perfectly symmetric.

Of course, no probability statements concerning project completion time can be made for CPM networks, since associated standard deviations for project activities are not available.

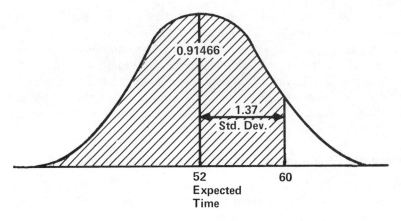

Figure 10.12
Normal distribution of expected project time

FORMULATION OF A PERT-CPM NETWORK AS A LINEAR PROGRAMMING MODEL

The PERT-CPM model can be formulated as a linear programming problem with relative ease. The benefit of such a formulation may be questionable from a practical point of view since computer programs for the specific purpose of PERT-CPM analysis have been developed. However, from a pedagogical point of view it is of considerable interest. Furthermore, an understanding of the linear programming formulation of the PERT-CPM model can provide the basis for a goal programming approach to analysis of such networks, in which other goals might be considered.

The PERT-CPM network can be formulated as a linear programming model as follows:

Minimize $Z = T_E(N)$
such that $\quad T_E(j) - T_E(i) \geq t_e(i,j)$, for all i and j
and $\quad\quad T_E(S) = 0$
where S = the source (project start) event number
$\quad\quad N$ = the sink (terminal) event number
$\quad\quad i$ = the start event number for each activity
$\quad\quad j$ = the end event number for each activity
$\quad (i, j)$ = the activity from event i to event j
$\quad t_e(i, j)$ = the expected time for activity (i, j)
$\quad T_E(S)$ = the T_E value for the source event (generally set to zero)

$T_E(N) =$ the T_E value for the sink event
$T_E(i) =$ the T_E value for the start event of activity (i, j)
$T_E(j) =$ the T_E value for the end event of activity (i, j)

The objective function of the preceding model specifies that the total expected project time is to be minimized. The second general constraint must be formulated for each activity in the network, and specifies that the earliest completion time at the end event of an activity, minus the earliest completion time at the start event of that same activity, must be at least equal to or greater than the expected time to complete the activity. The last constraint simply sets the T_E at the project start event to zero.

As an example, consider the PERT-CPM network shown in Figure 10–13. The linear programming formulation for the example network is:

$$\text{Min } Z = T_E(5)$$
$$\text{s.t. } T_E(2) - T_E(1) \geq t_e(1,2)$$
$$T_E(3) - T_E(1) \geq t_e(1,3)$$
$$T_E(4) - T_E(1) \geq t_e(1,4)$$
$$T_E(4) - T_E(2) \geq t_e(2,4)$$
$$T_E(4) - T_E(3) \geq t_e(3,4)$$
$$T_E(5) - T_E(3) \geq t_e(3,5)$$
$$T_E(5) - T_E(4) \geq t_e(4,5)$$

$$T_E(1) = 0$$

The above model can be further simplified by substituting the variable x for each of the T_E's, where the subscript for each x would be the value in the parenthesis (i.e., the event number). Performing this substitution of symbols, and substituting for each of the t_e's the associated activity times (shown on the network in Figure 10–13), we obtain the following:

$$\text{Min } Z = x_5$$
$$\text{s.t. } x_2 - x_1 \geq 2 \qquad (1)$$
$$x_3 - x_1 \geq 5 \qquad (2)$$
$$x_4 - x_1 \geq 6 \qquad (3)$$
$$x_4 - x_2 \geq 3 \qquad (4)$$
$$x_4 - x_3 \geq 4 \qquad (5)$$
$$x_5 - x_3 \geq 10 \qquad (6)$$
$$x_5 - x_4 \geq 7 \qquad (7)$$
$$x_1 = 0 \qquad (8)$$
$$\text{all } x_j \geq 0$$

The above linear programming model of the example PERT-CPM network can be solved by the usual procedure for any linear programming problem. The solution yielded would be as follows:

$x_1 = 0$ The T_E for event 1 is 0
$x_2 = 2$ The T_E for event 2 is 2
$x_3 = 5$ The T_E for event 3 is 5
$x_4 = 9$ The T_E for event 4 is 9
$x_5 = 16$ The T_E for event 5 is 16 (expected project time)
$Z = 16$ The minimum project time

The critical path could be identified by analysis of the dual solution to the above model. The dual solution variables would have values of one for the dual variables associated with the second, fifth, and seventh constraints. The second, fifth, and seventh constraints relate to the activities from events 1 to 3, 3 to 4, and 4 to 5, respectively. Thus, the critical path would be identified as 1–3–4–5.

COST NETWORKS AND PROJECT CRASHING

An extension of network time analysis is network cost analysis and project crashing. Although network cost analysis is typically associated with CPM (for historical development reasons), it can be applied to either PERT or CPM networks.

Cost Estimates

In network cost analysis, the costs associated with each activity are also estimated. Two types of cost are estimated: normal time cost, and crash cost. These costs are also associated with two time estimates for each activity: normal time, and crash time. In the case of CPM networks, this would require that a crash-time estimate be provided in addition to the normal expected time previously described. For PERT networks, the crash time estimate might be the most optimistic time estimate, a. The normal time estimate for PERT networks would be the t_e value.

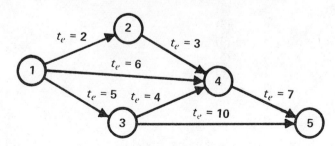

Figure 10.13
Example of PERT-CPM network for linear programming formulation

The relationship between normal time/cost and crash time/cost for an activity is generally assumed to be linear, for simplicity purposes. Such a relationship, for one activity, is illustrated in Figure 10.14. Thus, the crash cost per unit time can be estimated by computing the relative change in cost per unit change in time. For the example illustrated in Figure 10.14, the crash cost would be $100 per week, computed as follows:

$$\frac{\text{Crash cost} - \text{Normal cost}}{\text{Normal time} - \text{Crash time}} = \frac{400 - 100}{5 - 2} = \frac{300}{3} = \$100$$

The objective of crash-cost analysis is to reduce the total project completion time, while minimizing the cost of crashing. Special care is required during such analysis, however, since while crashing, the critical path may change, and an activity may be crashed without having an effect on the total project time.

Computation of Crash Cost

A simple example of the computation of crash costs will be illustrated, with the observation that such analysis can become quite complex very quickly. Thus, the use of computer programs is the only practical approach to crash-cost analysis for most real-world problems.

The example network is described in Table 10.6, with normal and

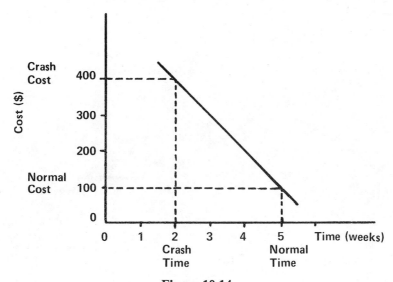

Figure 10.14
Activity time-cost relationship

crash times and costs listed for each activity. Also, the computed values of crash cost per week are given, computed as previously illustrated. Figure 10.15 illustrates the network graphically, with normal activity times, crash times (in parenthesis), and crash cost per week shown alongside each activity.

Step 1

The first step in the analysis is to compute the critical path through the network, for both normal and crash activity times. For our example, the critical path is found to be 1–2–5–6 in each case. Thus, normal and crash times are 44 weeks and 28 weeks, respectively. The project times and costs are summarized as follows:

	Critical Path	Time (weeks)	Cost
Normal times	1–2–5–6	44	$6400
Crash times	1–2–5–6	28	$9800

It is important to note that the crash-time critical path is not *necessarily* the same as the normal-time critical path. The crash-time critical path indicates the minimum possible project crash time, whereas the normal-time critical path is our point of departure for the crashing analysis.

The objective of crash-cost analysis is to determine the least cost required in order to complete the project in 28 weeks (crash time).

Step 2

First, we identify which activity on the critical path has the minimum crash cost (per week). In the example case, we are free to select from any one of the critical-path activities, since the crash cost per week

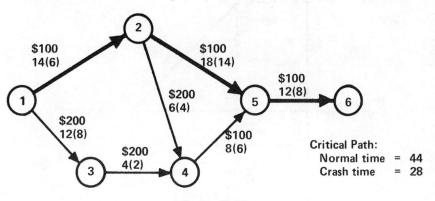

Figure 10.15
Cost network

Table 10.6
Crash Cost Network Description

	Time (weeks)			Cost (dollars)		
Activity	Normal	Crash		Normal	Crash	Crash Cost Per Week
1-2	14	6		1400	2200	100
1-3	12	8		1000	1800	200
2-5	18	14		1600	2000	100
2-4	6	4		800	1200	200
3-4	4	2		400	800	200
4-5	8	6		400	600	100
5-6	12	8		800	1200	100
				6400	9800	

is the same for each. Thus, we arbitrarily select activity 1–2 to crash. It is crashed by 8 weeks to its lower limit (6 weeks). The associated crashing cost is $800 ($100 × 8 weeks).

Step 3

We next revise the network, adjusting for the time and cost assigned to activity 1–2, as shown in Figure 10.16. The critical path(s) are redetermined, and found to consist of both paths 1–2–5–6 and 1–3–4–5–6. Note that activity times included in the computation are the times *not* in parenthesis. Activity 1–2 has been crashed to its limit of 6, while all other activities remain with normal times.

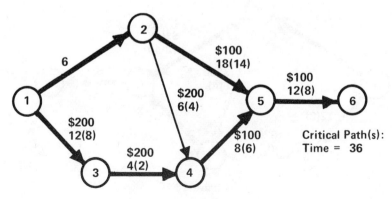

Figure 10.16
Cost network, with activity 1-2 crashed

Step 4

Again, we must identify which activity, on the critical path(s), has the minimum crashing cost (and will reduce total project time). Note that only by crashing activity 5–6 can we reduce total project time, without crashing more than one activity. Thus, we select activity 5–6 to crash. However, if we could reduce total project time at less cost by crashing two activities (one on each of the two critical paths), we would do so. In this case, it cannot be done at less cost. We crash activity 5–6 by 4 weeks, down to its 8-week limit, at a crashing cost of \$400.

Step 5

The network must now be again revised, taking into consideration the newly crashed activity. The revised network is illustrated in Figure 10.17. Although the critical-path (project) time has been reduced to 32 weeks, we still have the same two critical paths.

Step 6

We return to our attempt to select the activity(s) that can be crashed at minimum crashing cost (and reduce overall project time). It is important to note here that we *must* now crash not one, but two activities. This is because there is no longer one single activity through which both critical paths pass that has not been crashed. If only one activity were crashed, on one of the two critical paths, the other critical path would remain critical (unshortened) and thus the total project time would remain unchanged, but we would incur a crashing cost with no resulting benefit.

Thus, we must identify which two activities (one from each critical

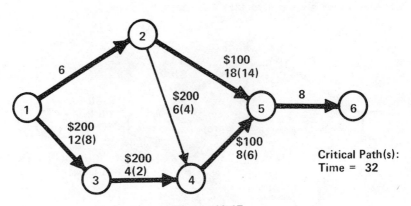

Figure 10.17
Cost network, with activities 1-2 and 5-6 crashed

path) can be crashed, at minimum crashing cost. In the example case, we have no choice on path 1–2–5–6 but to crash activity 2–5, since it is the only uncrashed activity on that path. However, if there were several uncrashed activities to select from on each critical path, we would select the two activities (one from each critical path) that involved the minimum aggregate weekly crashing cost.

We also will select activity 4–5 on path 1–3–4–5–6 to crash, since it has the minimum weekly crashing cost. However, we will crash each activity down only to the lower limit, established by one of them. In this case, since activity 4–5 can be crashed by only 2 weeks (down to a lower limit of 6 weeks), we also crash activity 2–5 by 2, down to a value of 16. The costs of crashing activities 2–5 and 4–5 are $200 each, yielding a total crashing cost of $400.

Step 7

We now revise the network, reflecting crashed activities, as illustrated in Figure 10.18. We observe that total project time has been reduced to 30 weeks, but we still have the same two critical paths.

Step 8

Since we still have crashing capability remaining in activity 2–5 (it was crashed from 18 to 16 weeks in step 6), we will now crash it, and one activity in path 1–3–4–5–6. Since both activities 1–3 and 3–4 have the same crashing cost, we will arbitrarily select activity 3–4 to crash.

Activities 2–5 and 3–4 are now crashed to each of their limits of 14

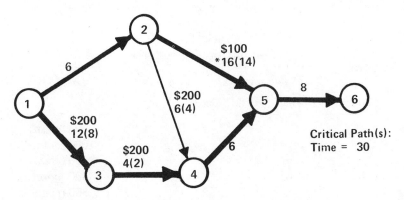

*Activity 2-5 partially crashed
by two time units

Figure 10.18
Cost network, with activities 1-2, 5-6, 4-5, and 2-5 crashed

and 2, respectively. The total cost of crashing is $200 for activity 2-5 and $400 for activity 3-4, yielding a crashing cost of $600.

Step 9

The network is again revised, yielding the diagram of Figure 10.19. Since one of the critical paths consists entirely of crashed activities, no further crashing can be performed.

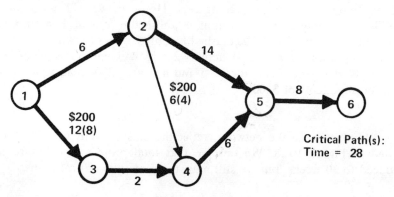

Figure 10.19
Cost network, with activities 1-2, 5-6, 4-5, 2-5, and 3-4 crashed

We have now achieved a minimum crash time for the network of 28 weeks, without crashing all network activities. Thus, the crash cost is less than the total crash cost for all activities of $9800, given previously in Table 10.6. It is, in fact, the minimum crash cost for the network.

Table 10.7
Cost of Crashing Network

Activity	Time (weeks) Normal	Time (weeks) Crash	Cost ($)
1-2		6	2200 (crash)
1-3	12		1000 (normal)
2-5		14	2000 (crash)
2-4	6		800 (normal)
3-4		2	800 (crash)
4-5		6	600 (crash)
5-6		8	1200 (crash)
		Total =	$8600

By returning to steps 2, 4, 6, and 8, we find that the incremental costs of crashing were: 800, 400, 400, and 600, yielding a total incremental crashing cost of $2200. The total cost of crashing the network is summarized in Table 10.7. The $8600 for crashing selected activities of the network as compared with $9800 for crashing all activities yields $1200 in savings. Note that the $8600 cost consists of the total normal cost of $6400 plus the incremental crashing cost of $2200.

SUMMARY

The basic modeling concepts of PERT-CPM networks have been presented, along with computational methods for analysis. Network cost and crashing analysis have also been described. Implicit in the PERT-CPM networks considered in this chapter has been the assumption that sufficient resources were available to carry out each of the activities, limited only by their precedence relationships. Another version of network analysis includes the case where scheduling of the activities is also dependent upon the availability of limited resources (such as manpower or equipment). Such networks are complex to analyze, and simulation is generally used.

Significant practical applications have been made of PERT-CPM type networks, and their value to management in planning, coordination, and control should not be underestimated. However, it must be added that substantial criticism has also been leveled at these tools of analysis. Certain questions have been raised concerning the correctness of some of the computational techniques employed. Also, the basic assumptions of PERT have been questioned. Finally, it has been pointed out that the model results are only as good as the time estimates provided. However, the convenient simplicity of the techniques in providing approximate solutions probably overshadows all but the last criticism. The last criticism is a problem common to all decision science models.

Finally, it is recommended that the reader avail himself of one of the multitude of computer programs available when employing PERT or CPM to large, complex real-world problems. For example, a FORTRAN program for PERT analysis is given on p. 375 of McMillan and Gonzalez (see References).

REFERENCES

Bedworth, D. D., *Industrial Systems: Planning, Analysis, Control*, Ronald Press, New York, 1973.

Evarts, H. F., *Introduction to PERT*, Allyn and Bacon, Boston, 1964.
Ford, L. R., Jr., and Fulkerson, D. R., *Flows in Networks*, Princeton Univ. Press, Princeton, N.J., 1962.
Levin, R., and Kirkpatrick, C. A., *Planning and Control with PERT/ CPM*, McGraw-Hill, New York, 1966.
McMillan, C., and Gonzalez, R. F., *Systems Analysis. A Computer Approach to Decision Models*. Richard D. Irwin, Homewood, Ill., 1973.
Moder, J. J., and Phillips, C. R., *Project Management with CPM and PERT*, Reinhold, New York, 1964.
Wiest, J. D., and Levy, L. K., *A Management Guide to PERT/CPM*, Prentice-Hall, Englewood Cliffs, N.J., 1969.

QUESTIONS

1. Would PERT-CPM models be described as planning and control models, or as optimization models?
2. Would PERT-CPM models be used for one-time projects or for repetitive projects?
3. Describe the major components of a PERT-CPM network model.
4. Describe what is meant by "critical path" in PERT-CPM networks.
5. Describe the meaning and purpose of the values T_E, T_L, and S in PERT-CPM network analysis.
6. Discuss the function served by an "event" in a PERT-CPM network.
7. What is the assumed distribution associated with an activity time in a PERT network? How are its parameters (mean and standard deviation) computed?
8. What is the assumed distribution of the overall project time in a PERT network? What is the basis for this assumption?
9. What are the estimates obtained for time and cost, for each activity, in a project crashing analysis? What is the assumption about the relationship between time and cost?
10. What is the objective of crash-cost analysis?

PROBLEMS

1. Construct (illustrate) a PERT-CPM network model for the project described by the following:

Activity	Start Event	End Event
1–2	1	2
2–3	2	3
2–4	2	4
3–5	3	5
4–5	4	5
4–6	4	6
5–7	5	7
6–7	6	7
5–8	5	8
7–8	7	8

2. In problem 1, assume that single estimates of expected time for each activity were obtained, as given in the following table. Determine the T_E, T_L, and S values for each event of the network, and identify the critical path.

Activity	Expected Time	Activity	Expected Time
1–2	6	4–6	1
2–3	4	5–7	3
2–4	5	6–7	4
3–5	2	5–8	9
4–5	4	7–8	7

3. Given the project network shown in the figure, with expected activity times (t_e) shown alongside each activity, determine:

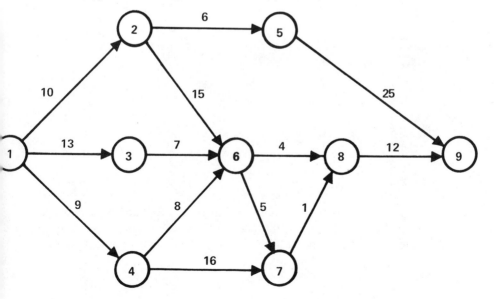

(a) Earliest expected event time for each event
(b) Latest allowable event time for each event
(c) Slack time for each event
(d) Network critical path
(e) Expected project time

4. Given the following (PERT) activity time estimates, determine the mean and standard deviation for each:

Activity	a	m	b
1–2	1	3	5
2–3	3	7	11
3–4	2	3	10
4–5	5	5	5
5–6	1	10	13
6–7	3	6	9

5. If the activities of problem 4 represent a project, what is the expected project time? What is the overall project time standard deviation?

6. Given the project described in the following table, which activities must be most closely controlled? Assume that resource requirements for completion of each activity are homogeneous; from which activities, and to which activities, should resources be transferred?

Activity	Most Optimistic Time	Most Likely Time	Most Pessimistic Time
1–2	4	6	8
1–3	1	2	3
2–4	1	1	1
2–5	1	3	5
3–5	2	3	10
4–6	3	4	5
5–6	2	4	12

7. In problem 3, assume that the variances (σ_e^2) for each activity are as given below. Determine the standard deviation for overall project time. Compute the probability the project will take 49 or less periods.

Activity	σ_e^2	Activity	σ_e^2
1–2	3	4–7	10
1–3	9	6–7	2
1–4	1	6–8	1
2–5	1	7–8	1
2–6	7	5–9	12
3–6	2	8–9	3
4–6	1		

8. Given a PERT network for which the expected project time has been determined to be 105 weeks, with project time standard deviation of 17 weeks, determine the probabilities of the following:

(a) The project time will be at most 88 weeks.
(b) The project time will be at least 54 weeks.
(c) The project time will be between 71 weeks and 139 weeks, inclusive.

9. Refer to the project network of problem 3. Assume that the activity 5–9 could not begin until all activities leading to event 6 had been completed.

(a) Redraw the project network of problem 3, including a dummy activity to reflect the above-stated requirement.
(b) Determine the critical path, expected project time, and slack at each event for the network.

10. Refer to the network in problem 6.

(a) Formulate the network as a linear programming problem.
(b) Formulate the initial simplex tableau for the linear programming problem, but do not solve.
(c) Refer the your solution to problem 6. What should you expect to get as the solution values for the real variables of your linear programming problem? What is the interpretation of these solution values?
(d) How would you identify the critical path of the network from your simplex solution?

11. The project network shown in the figure, with normal activity times, crash times (in parenthesis), and crash cost per time period all shown alongside each activity, is presented for analysis.

(a) Determine the critical path using normal activity times.
(b) Determine the critical path using activity crash times.

(c) Determine the minimum project time, crashing all activities.
(d) Which activity in the network should be crashed first? Why?
(e) Which activity in the network should be crashed second? Why?
(f) Given the answer to (c), what is the level to which activity 1–2 should be crashed? Answer the same for activity 3–4.
(g) Which is the last activity to be crashed, and to what level?
(h) What will be the incremental cost of crashing for each activity (to the extent crashed)? What will be the total incremental cost of crashing the project?
(i) Compare the answer of (h) to the total incremental cost of crashing all activities to the fullest extent possible. (For example, the cost of crashing activity 2–4 to the fullest extent possible would be: amount crashed, 4, times the cost per period of crashing, $8, which equals $32.)

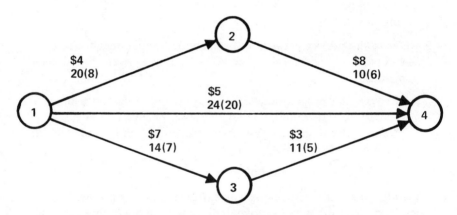

12. Given the project described in the following table, construct the associated network and determine the critical path using normal activity times. What is the expected project time using normal activity times? What is the critical path and expected project time if all activities are crashed? What is the minimum crash time for the project? Which activity in the network should be crashed first? Determine the minimum cost to crash the project. What is the cost savings, compared to crashing all project activities to the fullest extent?

Activity	Time		Cost	
	Normal	Crash	Normal	Crash
1–2	16	8	200	440
1–3	14	9	100	180
2–4	8	6	50	70
2–5	5	4	60	130
3–5	4	2	150	300
4–6	6	4	80	160
5–6	10	7	300	450
3–6	15	10	500	800

11 Game Theory

INTRODUCTION

Game theory is often considered as an extension, or subset, of decision theory, which was presented in Chapter 3. The word *game* is used to denote decisions under conditions of conflict or competition, and is not restricted to the theory of parlor games.

The conditions under which decisions must be made are often categorized as: (1) certainty, (2) risk, (3) uncertainty, or (4) conflict. The second and third categories of decision analysis were presented in Chapter 3, Decision Theory. The fourth category, decisions under conditions of conflict, is presented in this chapter, and is referred to as game theory.

The fundamental characteristic of game theory, which differentiates it from other topics of decision theory, is that in game theory it is assumed that the decision maker competes with other rational, intelligent, goal-seeking opponents. It will be recalled that the topic of decision theory included a passive opponent, i.e., the states of nature.

Game theory dates back to 1944 with the classic work of J. von Neumann and O. Morgenstern, *Theory of Games and Economic Behavior*. Although the book was hailed as a landmark in the history of decision theory, practical application of the theory to decisions involving conflict has been disappointing. It did, however, have a major impact on the development of linear programming and statistical decision theory.

Currently, the most important contribution of game theory is that the conceptual framework developed in game theory provides valuable insights for better understanding general decision problems. Thus, through a study of game theory, the decision maker may ultimately make more intelligent decisions. Game theory does not, however, generally provide a "technique" for problem solving, such as linear programming.

Game theory provides a framework for analyzing competitive situations, in which the competitors (or players) make use of logical thought processes and techniques of mathematics in order to determine an optimal strategy for "winning." Since many situations in business involve competition, game theory is of considerable theoretical interest.

TWO-PERSON ZERO-SUM GAMES

Game theory is generally divided according to the number of opponents (or players). The usual distinction is between two-person games, and games involving three or more persons. The theory of games of three or more persons (*n*-person games) is largely undeveloped, and it is precisely this limitation that has restricted the application of game theory from many real-world applications. However, much research has been done in game theory in recent years, and its theoretical potential remains sufficient to warrant a presentation of two-person games.

Game theory is further categorized according to the total payoff available to the players, with zero-sum or constant-sum games distinguished from nonzero or nonconstant-sum games. Again, the theory of nonzero-sum games remains relatively undeveloped. Therefore, the discussion of this chapter will be limited to the presentation and analysis of two-person zero-sum games.

Formulation of the Two-Person Zero-Sum Game

The two-person zero-sum game assumes that there are exactly two opponents. Each opponent or player must make his decision while considering the potential actions of his competitor. Let us identify the opponents as player A and player B.

Player A must select from among alternative strategies available to him, while considering the potential selection, by player B, from among strategies available to him. This is analogous to the situation facing the decision maker in decision theory, except that the states of nature faced by the decision theorist are now replaced by the various strategies available to the opponent of the game theorist.

Furthermore, it is assumed that the total combined payoff to both players is some constant sum. Putting it another way, the portion obtained by player A is lost to player B, who receives the remaining portion of the constant sum. For example, if two firms are competing for 100 percent of the market for a particular product, the portion obtained by firm A is exactly the portion lost by firm B. Since no more than 100 percent of the total market can be obtained by the two firms, the constant sum is 100 percent in this case. The term *zero sum* refers to the fact that the sum of A's positive payoff (gain) and B's negative payoff (loss) is zero.

The Payoff Matrix

It is also assumed that each player knows exactly the payoffs for every possible combination of strategies available to each player. Also, the payoffs are in a form that is transferable to either player with the same value to each; that is, the players' utilities regarding payoffs are the same.

Table 11.1 illustrates an example payoff matrix, showing the payoffs for player A resulting from all possible combinations of strategies for each player. It is important to note that only player A's gains are included in the payoff matrix. However, if the payoff matrix represents the percent market share obtained by player A, then player B in turn loses the market share that A gains, and the sum of the rewards is zero (zero sum).

For example, if player A selects strategy 1 and player B selects strategy *x*, then player A wins 80 percent while player B loses 80 percent, yielding a net sum of zero. Putting it in terms of a constant sum, if player A wins 80 percent of the market share, then player B receives the remaining 20 percent, yielding the constant sum of 100 percent. Either way of visualizing the problem is equivalent. It is common practice to represent the game payoffs by showing in the matrix the gains for the player on the side (which are thus losses for the player on the top);

Table 11.1
Payoffs for Player A

		Player B Strategies		
Strategies		*x*	*y*	*z*
Player A	1	80	40	75
	2	70	35	30

negative payoffs are losses for the player on the side (gains for the player on the top).

Analysis of the Game

Each player knows the strategies and payoffs available to himself and his competitor. Since the payoff matrix shows the gains for player A and the losses for player B, player A will attempt to maximize his gains while player B will attempt to minimize his losses.

Returning to the payoff matrix of Table 11.1, player A would evaluate his available strategies (1 and 2) by observing that if he selected strategy 1, player B could select strategy y, which would yield a payoff to A of 40 percent of the market. If player A selected strategy 2, player B could select strategy z, resulting in a payoff of 30 to A. Thus, player A, if he was a cautious individual, would select strategy 1, with a minimum possible payoff of 40, versus strategy 2, with a minimum possible payoff of 30.

Player B, in evaluating his alternative strategies, would observe that if he selected strategy x, player A could select strategy 1, yielding a loss of 80 for B. If B selected strategy y, player A could select strategy 1, yielding a loss of 40 for B. Finally, if B selected strategy z, player A could again select strategy 1, yielding a loss of 75 for B. Thus, player B would, if he was a cautious individual, select strategy y, where his maximum possible losses were minimized to 40 (versus maximum possible losses of 80 or 75 for strategies x or z, respectively).

The Value of the Game

The preceding example payoff matrix is again shown in Table 11.2, with players A and B's selection of strategies indicated. Also, the

Table 11.2
Payoff Matrix with Game Value

		Player B Strategies			
	Strategies	x	y	z	
Player A	1	80	(40)	75	← *Player A selection*
	2	70	35	30	
			Player B selection		

associated gain for player A and loss for player B is indicated by a circle around the value 40. The value of 40 is referred to as the *value of the game*.

Pure Strategies and Saddle Points

The preceding analysis of strategy selection by players A and B resulted in a solution at which each player would be satisfied to remain. In other words, if player A assumed that player B would attempt to minimize A's gains, and if player B assumed that player A would attempt to maximize B's losses, then each player would have no incentive to change his selection of strategy.

Since neither player would wish to risk changing his strategy from the single strategy selected, this type of result is referred to as a *pure strategy* (strategy 1 for player A, and strategy *y* for player B). If either player was motivated to select a different strategy, based on his observation of his opponent's strategy selection, then there would be no pure strategies.

Pure strategies will exist only when the solution has reached a point of equilibrium or steady state, referred to in game theory as a *saddle point*. The saddle point or equilibrium exists when neither player would change strategies, based on observation of his opponent's selection of a strategy. If player A knows that B has selected strategy *y*, his maximum gain is obtained by selecting strategy 1. Likewise, if player B knows that A has selected strategy 1, he will minimize losses by selecting strategy *y*. Thus, neither player has any incentive to move to a different strategy.

The term *saddle point* is used because a three-dimensional illustration of the gains for A and losses for B resembles a saddle. Figure 11.1 shows that when looking from north to south, the gains available to player A versus his strategies appears as an upward pointing ridge. On the other hand, when looking from east to west, the losses faced by player B versus his strategies appears as a downward pointing valley. The saddle point would occur simultaneously at the highest point of the valley faced by B and at the lowest point on the ridge available to A (i.e., the saddle point equals min-max losses and max-min gains).

The illustration of Figure 11.1 is slightly different from the previously discussed games in that the strategies available to each player are presented as a continuous range of values rather than as a number of discrete choices. This was done simply to facilitate the demonstration of the concept graphically.

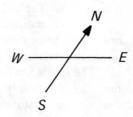

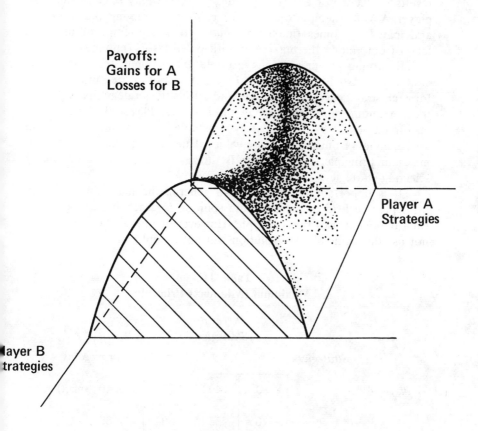

Figure 11.1
Three-dimensional view of player's payoffs versus strategies

The Maximin (Minimax) Principle

The principle employed for the analysis of the game originally presented in Table 11.1 is now given formally. It is the maximin (for gains) or the minimax (for losses) principle. This principle is the same as one of the principles (criterion) presented in the discussion of decisions under uncertainty in Chapter 3.

The fundamental assumption of the maximin (minimax) principle is that the decision maker is basically pessimistic about the decision environment (nature in the case of Chapter 3, and the competitor in the case of game theory). That is, the decision maker expects the worst results to occur, for any given strategy that he may select. Therefore, player A will attempt to maximize gains from among the minimum anticipated outcomes (maximin). Player B will attempt to minimize losses from among the maximum anticipated losses (minimax).

Returning to our previous example, the maximin (minimax) principle is illustrated in Table 11.3. Player A identifies the minimum gain for each strategy available to him, and selects the strategy that will yield the maximum gain from among those values. Player B identifies the maximum loss for each strategy available to him, and selects the minimum loss from among those values. Thus, player A makes use of the maximin principle, while player B utilizes the minimax principle, in selecting strategies.

It is important to note that, in general, the maximin (minimax) principle will lead to the optimum solution for each player as long as each opponent uses this principle. However, if one of the players does not use this principle, the solution will not be optimal.

Table 11.3
Maximum (Minimax) Principle

		Player B Strategies			Min of A's
Strategies		x	y	z	row gains
Player A	1	80	(40)	75	(40) (max)
	2	70	35	30	30
Max of B's col. losses:		80	(40) (min)	75	

A Further Example of the Maximin (Minimax) Principle

A second example will be given in which two firms (players) are competing for market share, but the range of alternatives for each opponent is greater. The payoff matrix for the example is given in Table 11.4.

The optimum solution is obtained by player A's selection of the maximin gain and player B's selection of the minimax loss. The solution again yields a saddle point, with the value of the game as 55. Player A selects the pure (single) strategy 2, while player B selects the pure strategy *y*.

The Rule of Dominance

Referring back to Tables 11.1 and 11.2, it is apparent that strategy 1 would result in the maximum gain for player A, regardless of which strategy player B selects. Thus, strategy 1 is said to *dominate* strategy 2. For cases in which a particular strategy is completely dominated by another strategy, the dominated strategy can be removed from the payoff matrix, since the player would never consider selecting it.

For player B in Tables 11.1 and 11.2, strategy *x* is dominated by strategy *y*, since the loss for strategy *x* is always greater than the loss for strategy *y*, regardless of which strategy A selects. (For that matter, strategy *x* is also dominated by strategy *z*.) Therefore, strategy *x* may be

Table 11.4
Payoff Matrix with Maximum (Minimax) Solution

	Strategies	w	x	y	z	Min of A's row gains
	1	40	80	35	60	35
	2	65	90	(55)	70	(55) (max)
Player A	3	55	40	45	75	40
	4	45	25	50	50	25
Max of B's col. losses:		65	90	(55) (min)	75	

Player B Strategies

removed from consideration. However, neither strategy y nor z is dominated by the other.

Table 11.5 illustrates the resulting payoff matrix, with dominated strategies crossed out. It is apparent that the resulting payoff matrix is trivial to evaluate. Player A can only select strategy 1 and player B will select strategy y in order to minimize losses to 40, rather than 75. However, we note that the resulting solution to the game is the same as was previously obtained.

The concept of dominance, illustrated for the preceding example, can be applied to any two-person zero-sum game, with any number of strategies for each player. For a payoff matrix of large size, the rule of dominance can be used to reduce the size of the payoff matrix considerably, prior to final analysis to determine the optimum strategy selection for each player.

The rule of dominance will also be applied to the second example, previously given in Table 11.4. First, rows 1 and 4 are dominated by row 2, therefore they can be crossed out or removed from the payoff matrix. The procedure is illustrated in Table 11.6.

By examining the remaining rows 2 and 3, we see that columns w and z are dominated by column y. Therefore, these columns are now crossed out (removed), as illustrated in Table 11.7.

Finally, by examining the remaining 2-by-2 payoff matrix, we see that row 2 dominates row 3. Thus, the final remaining payoff matrix consists of a single strategy for player A, with two strategies for player B, as given in Table 11.8. Since player B will select the minimum loss strategy, he will select strategy y. Thus, the saddle point solution again yields pure strategy 2 for player A and pure strategy y for player B, with the value of the game gain as 55.

Table 11.5
Payoff Matrix with Dominance

	Strategies	Player B Strategies		
		x	y	z
Player A	1	80	40	75
	2	~~70~~	~~35~~	~~30~~

Table 11.6
Payoff Matrix with Strategies 1 and 4 Dominated

	Strategies	w	x	y	z
			Player B Strategies		
Player A	1	~~40~~	~~80~~	~~35~~	~~60~~
	2	65	90	55	70
	3	55	40	45	75
	4	~~45~~	~~25~~	~~50~~	~~50~~

Table 11.7
Payoff Matrix with Strategies *w* and *z* Dominated

	Strategies	w	x	y	z
			Player B Strategies		
Player A	2	65	90	55	70
	3	55	40	45	75

Table 11.8
Final Payoff Matrix, with Dominated Strategies Removed

	Strategy	x	y
		Player B Strategies	
Player A	2	90	(55)

The rule of dominance is especially valuable for the evaluation of two-person zero-sum games where a saddle point (equilibrium) does not exist.

TWO-PERSON ZERO-SUM GAMES WITH MIXED STRATEGIES

It is entirely possible, even likely, that a two-person zero-sum game will not result in the selection of pure (single) strategies by the opponents. This is because no point of equilibrium can be reached, where pure strategies are selected. For this type of game situation, it is possible to obtain a steady-state solution by assuming that the players of the game will select mixed strategies.

A Non-Saddle-Point Solution

Consider, for example, the following situation in which a firm's management, and the union representing their employees, are in the process of a new contract negotiation. The hypothetical payoff matrix for the two groups (players) is given in Table 11.9.

We will assume that the payoffs are in cents per hour, and represent the overall value of the package of salary and fringe benefits increase per year for the upcoming contract period. The matrix payoffs, therefore, represent gains to the union (player A) and losses to management (player B). It is assumed that each group is completely aware of the payoffs that would result from the various possible combinations of strategies available to each player. Furthermore, they are in agreement concerning the valuation of the strategy combinations.

The union obviously wishes to maximize the gains for the employees they represent, while management wishes to minimize those gains (losses to the firm). If we presume that each of the union-management negotiators are prudent individuals (or groups), then we can employ the maximin (minimax) principle to analyze the game. The maximin (minimax) game results are illustrated in Table 11.10.

We discover, however, that there is not a common value for the game; that is, there is no saddle point. The union might select strategy 4 in order to maximize their minimum anticipated gains, and management might select strategy z in order to minimize their maximum anticipated losses. However, management would very quickly become dissatisfied with such a solution, since they could easily see that if the union selected strategy 4, management could reduce their losses to 50 by switching to

Table 11.9
Payoff Matrix for Union-Management Contract Negotiation

		Player B (Management) Strategies			
	Strategies	w	x	y	z
	1	75	105	65	45
	2	70	60	55	40
Player A (Union)	3	80	90	35	50
	4	95	100	50	55

Table 11.10
Non-Saddle Point Solution to Union-Management Game

		Player B (Management) Strategies				Min of row gains for A
	Strategies	w	x	y	z	
	1	75	105	65	45	45
	2	70	60	55	40	40
Player A (Union)	3	80	90	35	50	35
	4	95	100	50	55	50 (max)
Max of col. losses for B:		95	105	65	55 (min)	

strategy y. (Management would have initially avoided strategy y due to the possibility of the union selecting strategy 1, yielding a loss to management of 65 versus the maximum loss of 55 for strategy z.)

Let us assume that one player, in fact, makes the first move, which is then followed by the other, then back to the first player, and so on. This is analogous to one of the negotiators thinking out the potential strategy selection, prior to ever actually selecting a strategy. Assume that the union selects strategy 4. Management will immediately select strategy y, yielding a minimum loss to the firm of 50. The union will quickly respond by selecting strategy 1, resulting in a gain of 65 to the union employees. The union's move to select strategy 1 will be followed by management's moving to strategy z, reducing the union's gain to 45 (management's loss). The union will then, of course, move back to their initial selection of strategy 4. Thus, the game ends up in an infinite loop. The moves described are illustrated by the arrows in the payoff matrix of Table 11.10. The maximin (minimax) solution approach results in an indeterminate solution, as far as pure strategies are concerned. One of the players will always be dissatisfied.

Mixed Strategies

It is apparent from the cell values of the payoff matrix involved in the strategy-movement loop that the only relevant strategies to consider are strategies 1 and 4 for the union, and strategies y and z for management. This can be further verified by reducing the payoff matrix with the rule of dominance. Strategies 2 and 3 are dominated by strategies 1 and 4, respectively. Likewise, strategies w and x are both dominated by each of the strategies y and z. Thus, through the rule of

Table 11.11
Reduced Payoff Matrix of Union-Management Game

		Player B (Management) Strategies	
	Strategies	y	z
Player A (Union)	1	65	45
	4	50	55

dominance, the payoff matrix can be reduced to a 2-by-2 matrix, as given in Table 11.11.

The method of mixed strategies assumes that since neither player knows what strategy the other will select, each player will attempt to formulate a strategy which is indifferent to the other's strategy selection. This can be accomplished by randomly selecting between several strategies, according to a predefined plan. The random selection plan involves selecting each strategy a certain percent of the time, such that the player's *expected* gains (or losses) are equal, regardless of the opponent's selection of strategies. Selection of a strategy a given percent of the time is analogous to selection of a strategy with a given probability, on a one-time basis.

The technique for determining the percent (or probability) to be associated with a given strategy selection will be illustrated for the Table 11.11 game. Let us begin with player A (the union); he wishes to select strategy 1 or 4 according to probabilities such that his expected gains are the same regardless of player B's (management) selection of strategies y or z.

If player B selects strategy y, the possible payoffs to player A are 65 and 50. If player A selects strategy 1 with a probability of P (and therefore selects strategy 4 with a probability of $(1 - P)$, then his expected gains for this case are given by: $(P)(65) + (1 - P)(50)$. On the other hand, if player B selects strategy z, then player A's expected gains would be: $(P)(45) + (1 - P)(55)$. Now, in order for player A to be indifferent to which strategy player B selects, he wishes his expected gains to be equal for each of player B's possible moves. Thus, the two equations of expected value are set equal, and solved for P, as follows:

$$(P)(65) + (1 - P)(50) = (P)(45) + (1 - P)(55)$$
$$65P + 50 - 50P = 45P + 55 - 55P$$
$$25P = 5$$

$$P = \frac{5}{25} = \frac{1}{5} = 0.2$$

$$1 - P = 1 - 0.2 = 0.8$$

Therefore, player A would select strategy 1 with a probability of 0.2 and strategy 4 with a probability of 0.8, resulting in his expected gains being equal regardless of what player B decided to do.

Player B would likewise determine his appropriate probabilities for selecting strategies y and z, by equating his expected losses if A chooses 1 to the expected losses if A chooses 4, as follows:

$$(P)(65) + (1 - P)(45) = (P)(50) + (1 - P)(55)$$
$$25P = 10$$

$$P = \frac{10}{25} = \frac{2}{5} = 0.4$$

$$1 - P = 1 - 0.4 = 0.6$$

Therefore, player B would select strategy y with a probability of 0.4, and would select strategy z with a probability of 0.6.

We now find that we have a common value of the game (in terms of *expected* value), which is given as follows:

A's expected gains:

(1) if B selects y: $(0.2)(65) + (0.8)(50) = 53.0$
(2) if B selects z: $(0.2)(45) + (0.8)(55) = 53.0$

B's expected losses:

(1) if A selects 1: $(0.4)(65) + (0.6)(45) = 53.0$
(2) if A selects 4: $(0.4)(50) + (0.6)(55) = 53.0$

Thus, an equilibrium solution of sorts is reached, where each player mixes the selection of strategies according to prespecified probabilities of selection. The mixed-strategy solution yields an *expected* game value of 53.0. It should be pointed out that if the game were played many times according to the mixed-strategy plans, the resulting *average* value of the game would tend toward the expected value of 53.0. However, if the game was played only once, such as the union-management negotiation process, then, although the predecision expected value of the game was 53.0, the actual one-time result would be a single pure strategy for each player. Thus, either the union or management would be dissatisfied with the results. For example, when flipping a coin to determine who buys sodas, the *expected* result is that each player buys half the time. However, on a one-time basis, one player loses and the other wins.

Graphic Solution Method

A graphic solution to the mixed-strategy game can also be obtained when the number of strategies available to at least one of the players can be reduced through dominance to two alternatives. Since the previous example game was reduced to two alternative strategies for both players, it can be illustrated and solved graphically.

The example payoff matrix is again given in Table 11.12. The graphical approach consists of two graphs: (1) the payoffs (gains) available to player A versus his strategy options; and (2) the payoffs (losses) faced by player B versus his strategy options.

Table 11.12
2-by-2 Payoff Matrix

		Player B Strategies	
	Strategies	*y*	*z*
Player A	1	65	45
	4	50	55

The Graph for Player A

Figure 11.2 illustrates the graph of payoffs (gains) versus strategies for player A. The constraints are determined as follows. Player A determines the payoff for each alternative strategy available to him. If B selects strategy *y*, A will gain 65 by selecting strategy 1, and 50 by selecting strategy 4. Therefore, the value 65 is plotted along the vertical (payoff) axis under strategy 1, and the value 50 is plotted along the vertical axis under strategy 4. A straight line connecting the two points is then drawn. This line represents the maximum possible payoff to A, for all possible mixes of strategies 1 and 2, given that B selects strategy *y*.

If B selects strategy *z*, and A selects strategy 1, he then obtains a payoff of 45, whereas if A selects strategy 4, he receives a payoff of 55. The value 45 is plotted along the payoff axis under strategy 1, and the value 55 is plotted along the payoff axis under strategy 4. The straight line connecting the two points represents the maximum payoffs available to A for different mixes of strategies 1 and 4 if B selects strategy *z*.

Player A, being pessimistic in nature, will assume that player B will always select the alternative yielding the worst results for A. Thus, the payoffs (gains) available to A will be assumed to be represented by the lower of the two lines. Player A will then select a mix of strategies 1 and 4 such that he maximizes from among the minimum gains available to him. In this case, the optimum solution occurs at the intersection of the two payoff lines. At this point, the expected payoff to player A will be the same regardless of which strategy player B selects.

By looking at the probability values along the horizontal axis, we see that player A will select strategy 1 with a probability of 0.2, and strategy 4 with a probability of 0.8 (the sum of the two probabilities always, of course, being 1.0).

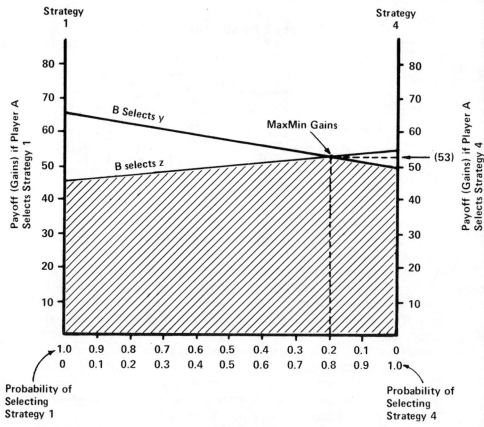

Figure 11.2
Payoff-versus-strategy graph for player A

The Graph for Player B

Figure 11.3 shows the graph of payoffs (losses) versus strategies for player B. Player B will incur a loss of 65 if he selects strategy y, and a loss of 45 if he selects strategy z, given that player A chooses strategy 1. Thus, the straight line connecting these two plotted values represents the minimum possible losses faced by player B if player A selects strategy 1.

If A chooses strategy 4, player B will incur a loss of 50 for strategy y, versus a loss of 55 for strategy z. The straight line connecting these two points represents the minimum losses faced by B if A selects strategy 4.

Player B will attempt to minimize from among the maximum losses, yielding the solution point at the intersection of the two payoff (loss) lines. Therefore, player B will select strategy y with a probability of 0.4, and strategy z with a probability of 0.6.

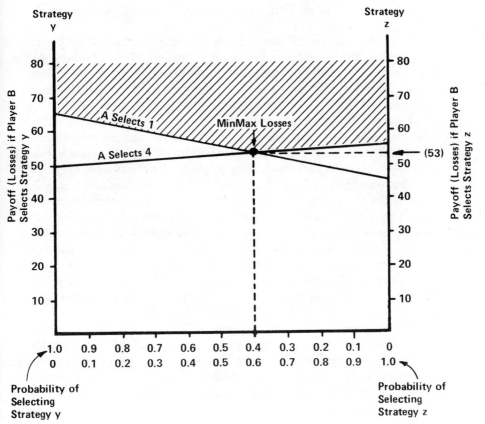

Figure 11.3
Payoff-versus-strategy graph for player B

Note that the expected value of the game for each of the two graphs is given by the location of the optimum point along the payoff axis, and it is 53 in each case. We have shown that the graphical approach yields the same results as were achieved previously by the mathematical approach.

A Further Graphic Example

It is also possible to solve a two-person zero-sum game graphically for one player, if the strategies available to that player have been reduced to two, even if the range of strategy alternatives for the opponent is three or more.

Consider the game given by the payoff matrix in Table 11.13. We see that by applying the maximin (minimax) principle, we are unable to obtain a saddle-point solution, and the matrix cannot be further reduced by the rule of dominance.

Since the game payoff matrix has not been reduced to a 2-by-2 size, it is not a simple matter to see how to go about determining mixed-strategy probabilities for player A (or for player B). However, for the player with just two alternative strategies, his mixed strategy probabilities can be easily determined by the graphic method.

Figure 11.4 illustrates the payoff-versus-strategy graph for player A. Note that there is a payoff line for each of the four strategies available to player B. These are developed by the previously discussed approach. For example, if player B chooses strategy w, player A obtains a payoff of 80 for selection of strategy 1, and a payoff of 20 for selection of strategy 2.

Each of the payoff lines can be thought of as a downward-pointing constraint. Thus, the cross-hatched region represents the area of feasible solution available to player A. Player A will attempt to maximize his payoffs (gains) subject to the given constraints. The point of optimum solution, therefore, occurs at the intersection of the two lines corresponding to "B selects y" and "B selects x." Player A will select strategy 1 with a probability of 0.6, and strategy 2 with a probability of 0.4, yielding an expected value for the game of 49.

Since the graph shows that only two of B's strategies are involved in the solution to A's mixed strategy probability determination, the reader can verify the graphic solution by solving for P and $(1 - P)$ by the previously shown mathematical method (i.e., equate A's expected payoffs for the case in which B selects strategy x to A's expected payoffs if B selects strategy y).

Table 11.13
2-by-4 Payoff Matrix

	Strategies	Player B Strategies w	x	y	z	Min of row payoffs for player A
Player A	1	80	(35)	55	50	(35) (max)
	2	20	70	40	60	20
Max of col. losses for player B		80	70	55 (min)	60	

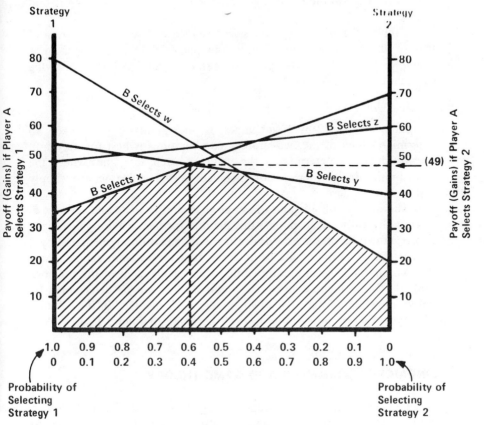

Figure 11.4
Payoff-versus-strategy graph for player A, while considering player B's four alternative strategies

The graphical method can be used to solve any 2-by-*n* game, for the player with the two strategy alternatives.

The Method of Subgames

The preceding discussion did not address itself to the mixed-strategy solution for player B, who faces four alternative strategies. One approach that may be used is to subdivide the game into several 2-by-2 subgames. For example, if the payoff matrix is 2-by-3 in size, it may be subdivided into three 2-by-2 subgames. The previous example, which involved a 2-by-4 payoff matrix, could be subdivided into six 2-by-2 subgames. In general, any 2-by-*n* game can be subdivided into a number of 2-by-2 subgames equal to the number of combinations of n things taken two at a time.

Each of the 2-by-2 subgames represents a different combination of two of the strategies available to the player with n strategies. For example, player B of the previous game would have the following combinations of two strategies:

(w, x), (w, y), (w, z), (x, y), (x, z), (y, z)

Each of the 2-by-2 subgames is then individually solved to determine which of the two-strategy combinations is best for player B. This is done by determining the value of each subgame, where the probabilities for strategies not included in the subgame are simply assumed to be zero.

The method of subgames is somewhat cumbersome and tedious to work with. Rather than pursue this method further, a more generalized approach will be presented, for dealing with games of larger than 2-by-2 size. It should be pointed out, however, that the two-strategy subgame that would yield the minimum game value for player B of the previous example would include strategies x and y. This can be determined by observing which of player B's two strategies are involved in the solution of player A's optimum solution. (See the graph of Figure 11.4.)

LINEAR PROGRAMMING AND GAME THEORY

The technique of linear programming, presented earlier in Chapters 4 and 5, may be applied to the two-person zero-sum game in order to solve for the probabilities associated with mixed strategies. The major advantage of using linear programming is that it can be applied to larger than 2-by-2 size games (i.e., 2-by-4, 3-by-3, etc.)

Let us return to the previous 2-by-4 game, given in Table 11.13 and illustrated for player A in Figure 11.4. We will now show how to formulate that game as a linear programming problem, in order to solve for each player's mixed strategies.

Linear Programming Formulation for Player A

We will first formulate the game for player A, since we know the solution from previous discussion. The reader can also get an intuitive feel for the linear programming approach by referring to the graph of Figure 11.4. We will represent the probabilities of selecting strategies 1 and 2 for player A as P_1 and P_2, respectively.

The payoff matrix is again given in Table 11.14. We know that if player B selects strategy w, then the expected mixed strategy payoff to player A is given by $80P_1 + 20P_2$.

Table 11.14
Payoff Matrix for the Linear Programming Example

		Player B Strategies			
Strategies		w	x	y	z
Player A	1	80	35	55	50
	2	20	70	40	60

Player A desires to select a mixed strategy, among strategies 1 and 2, such that the expected payoff to him is the same, regardless of B's action. In addition, player A's objective is to select his mixed strategy in such a way as to maximize his minimum expected payoffs.

The value of the game to A is determined by his strategy selection, regardless of whether his selection is optimal. Since A will attempt to maximize his expected payoffs, for the various strategies B might select, he will specify that his expected payoffs must be equal to or greater than the value of the game. (Then by maximizing the value of the game, A will maximize his expected payoffs.)

Let us denote the value of the game by the capital letter V. We can now write, in mathematical terms, the following expected payoffs to A for different strategies of B:

$$80P_1 + 20P_2 \geq V \qquad \text{Player B selects strategy } w$$
$$35P_1 + 70P_2 \geq V \qquad \text{Player B selects strategy } x$$
$$55P_1 + 40P_2 \geq V \qquad \text{Player B selects strategy } y$$
$$50P_1 + 60P_2 \geq V \qquad \text{Player B selects strategy } z$$

where

P_1 = probability that A will select strategy 1
P_2 = probability that A will select strategy 2

Since P_1 and P_2 are the probabilities with which A will make one move or the other, they must add up to one, or

$$P_1 + P_2 = 1.0$$

Player A's objective is to maximize his expected payoffs (gains), which he can achieve by maximizing the value of the game (V). Note that we have thus defined V as the criterion variable, and P_1 and P_2 as the decision variables.

Through a bit of algebraic manipulation, we can obtain the desired form for a linear programming solution. In order to remove the V's from the right-hand side of the constraints, we will divide all constraints and the last equation by V, yielding

$$\frac{80P_1}{V} + \frac{20P_2}{V} \geq 1$$

$$\frac{35P_1}{V} + \frac{70P_2}{V} \geq 1$$

$$\frac{55P_1}{V} + \frac{40P_2}{V} \geq 1$$

$$\frac{50P_1}{V} + \frac{60P_2}{V} \geq 1$$

$$\frac{P_1}{V} + \frac{P_2}{V} = \frac{1}{V}$$

We note that P_1 and P_2 are all divided by the value V. In order to simplify matters, we will denote P_1/V by p'_1, and P_2/V by p'_2. The objective of player A is to maximize the value of V, which we can also accomplish if we *minimize* the value of $1/V$ (as V becomes larger, the value of $1/V$ becomes smaller). We will now represent $1/V$ by v'.

The resulting linear programming problem can now be given as:

Minimize $v' = p'_1 + p'_2$
such that: $80p'_1 + 20p'_2 \geq 1$
              $35p'_1 + 70p'_2 \geq 1$
              $55p'_1 + 40p'_2 \geq 1$
              $50p'_1 + 60p'_2 \geq 1$

The simplex solution to the above linear programming problem yields the following optimal solution:

$$p'_1 = \frac{3}{245} \qquad p'_2 = \frac{2}{245} \quad \text{and} \quad v' = \frac{1}{49}$$

Since we earlier defined the relationships

$$p'_1 = \frac{P_1}{V} \qquad p'_2 = \frac{P_2}{V} \quad \text{and} \quad v' = \frac{1}{V}$$

we can now solve for P_1, P_2, and V, as follows.

$$V = \frac{1}{v'} \qquad P_1 = p'_1 V \quad \text{and} \quad P_2 = p'_2 V$$

which yields:

$$V = 49$$

$$P_1 = \left(\frac{3}{245}\right)(49) = \frac{3}{5} = 0.6$$

$$P_2 = \left(\frac{2}{245}\right)(49) = \frac{2}{5} = 0.4$$

Note that this is the same solution as we obtained earlier using the graphic method (see Figure 11.4).

Linear Programming Formulation for Player B

We will now demonstrate how player B could solve for his optimal mixed strategy, from among the four strategies available to him. Let us represent as the probabilities of selecting strategies w, x, y, or z the symbols P_w, P_x, P_y, and P_z.

Player B wishes to minimize his maximum expected losses, while facing the possibility that player A may select either of strategies 1 or 2. The expected losses to B, for each of player A's two alternatives are, $80P_w + 35P_x + 55P_y + 50P_z$, and $20P_w + 70P_x + 40P_y + 60P_z$. We will again denote the value of the game by V.

Player B's objective is to minimize the value of V such that

$$80P_w + 35P_x + 55P_y + 50P_z \leq V$$
$$20P_w + 70P_x + 55P_y + 60P_z \leq V$$

We also have

$$P_w + P_x + P_y + P_z = 1.0$$

We again divide each constraint through by V, yielding

$$\frac{80P_w}{V} + \frac{35P_x}{V} + \frac{55P_y}{V} + \frac{50P_z}{V} \leq 1.0$$

$$\frac{20P_w}{V} + \frac{70P_x}{V} + \frac{55P_y}{V} + \frac{60P_z}{V} \leq 1.0$$

$$\frac{P_w}{V} + \frac{P_x}{V} + \frac{P_y}{V} + \frac{P_z}{V} = \frac{1}{V}$$

The following new symbols are substituted for the above as:

$$p'_w = \frac{P_w}{V} \quad p'_x = \frac{P_x}{V} \quad p'_y = \frac{P_y}{V} \quad \text{and} \quad p'_z = \frac{P_z}{V}$$

Since player B wishes to minimize V, he also wishes to maximize $1/V$, which we will again denote by v'. Thus, we have the following linear programming problem:

Maximize $v' = p'_w + p'_x + p'_y + p'_z$

such that $80p'_w + 35p'_x + 55p'_y + 50p'_z \leq 1.0$

$\qquad\qquad 20p'_w + 70p'_x + 40p'_y + 60p'_z \leq 1.0$

The simplex solution to this problem is shown in Table 11.15. The solution mix is

$$p'_x = \frac{3}{490}$$

$$p'_y = \frac{1}{70}$$

and the solution value of the objective function variable (Z_j), which we have defined here to be v', is 1/49. These solution values are now converted back into the original variables:

$$V = \frac{1}{v'} \qquad P_x = p'_x V \quad \text{and} \quad P_y = p'_y V$$

yielding

$$V = 49$$

$$P_x = \left(\frac{3}{490}\right)(49) = \frac{3}{10} = 0.3$$

$$P_y = \left(\frac{1}{70}\right)(49) = \frac{7}{10} = 0.7$$

P_w and P_z will have solution values of zero; therefore, strategies w and z will not be employed by player B in his mixed-strategy solution. Recall that it was earlier stated that one could tell which strategies would be included in B's mixed-strategy solution from the graph of Figure 11.4.

One final note of interest, concerning the simplex solution procedure, relates to the dual solution of the linear programming problem. The dual solution values for the problem are located under the slack columns (S_1 and S_2), in the $C_j - Z_j$ row. S_1 is associated with constraint 1 (strategy 1 for player A) and S_2 is associated with constraint 2 (strategy 2 for player A). Note that the dual solution values (disregarding signs) are, in fact, the solution values for player A's mixed strategy; that is, the simplex solution to player A's linear programming formulation was:

$$p'_1 = \frac{3}{245},$$

$$p'_2 = \frac{2}{245},$$

which are the values found under S_1 and S_2, respectively, in the $C_j - Z_j$ row. Thus, it is only necessary to formulate the linear programming problem for one of the players, and both solutions can be read off the final simplex tableau.

Table 11.15
Simplex Solution for B's Strategy Mix

c_j			1	1	1	1	0	0
	Mix	Quantity	p'_w	p'_x	p'_y	p'_z	S_1	S_2
0	S_1	1	⑧⓪	35	55	50	1	0
0	S_2	1	20	70	40	60	0	1
	Z_j	0	0	0	0	0	0	0
	$C_j - Z_j$		1	1	1	1	0	0
1	p'_w	$\frac{1}{80}$	1	$\frac{7}{16}$	$\frac{11}{16}$	$\frac{5}{8}$	$\frac{1}{80}$	0
	S_2	$\frac{3}{4}$	0	$\frac{245}{4}$	$\frac{105}{4}$	$\frac{190}{4}$	$-\frac{1}{4}$	1
	Z_j	$\frac{1}{80}$	1	$\frac{7}{16}$	$\frac{11}{16}$	$\frac{5}{8}$	$\frac{1}{80}$	0
	$C_j - Z_j$		0	$\frac{9}{16}$	$\frac{5}{16}$	$\frac{3}{8}$	$-\frac{1}{80}$	0
1	p'_w	$\frac{1}{140}$	1	0	$\frac{1}{2}$	$\frac{2}{7}$	$\frac{1}{70}$	$-\frac{1}{140}$
1	p'_x	$\frac{3}{245}$	0	1	$\frac{3}{7}$	$\frac{38}{49}$	$-\frac{1}{245}$	$\frac{4}{245}$
	Z_j	$\frac{19}{980}$	1	1	$\frac{13}{14}$	$\frac{52}{49}$	$\frac{1}{98}$	$\frac{9}{980}$
	$C_j - Z_j$		0	0	$\frac{1}{14}$	$-\frac{3}{49}$	$-\frac{1}{98}$	$-\frac{9}{980}$
1	p'_y	$\frac{1}{70}$	2	0	1	$\frac{4}{7}$	$\frac{1}{35}$	$-\frac{1}{70}$
1	p'_x	$\frac{3}{490}$	$-\frac{6}{7}$	1	0	$\frac{26}{49}$	$-\frac{4}{245}$	$\frac{11}{490}$
	$Z_j(v')$	$\frac{1}{49}$	$\frac{8}{7}$	1	1	$\frac{54}{49}$	$\frac{3}{245}$	$\frac{2}{245}$
	$C_j - Z_j$		$-\frac{1}{7}$	0	0	$-\frac{5}{49}$	$-\frac{3}{245}$	$-\frac{2}{245}$
							p'_1	p'_2

REFERENCES

Baumol, W. J., *Economic Theory and Operations Analysis*, Prentice-Hall, Englewood Cliffs, N.J., 1961.

Dorfman, R., Samuelson, P. A., and Solow, R. M., *Linear Programming and Economic analysis*, McGraw-Hill, New York, 1958.

Kwak, N. K., *Mathematical Programming with Business Applications*, McGraw-Hill, New York, 1973.

Luce, R. D., and Raiffa, H., *Games and Decisions*, Wiley, New York, 1957.

Von Neumann, J., and Morgenstern, O., *Theory of Games and Economic Behavior*, Princeton Univ. Press, Princeton, N.J., 1944.

Williams, J. D., *The Compleat Strategyst*, rev. ed., McGraw-Hill, New York, 1966.

QUESTIONS

1. State the four major categories of conditions under which decisions are made. What are the distinguishing characteristics of each category of decision making?
2. Game theory is generally subdivided into two major categories according to the number of players. It is further divided into two categories according to payoffs. Describe each of the sets of categorizations for game theory. Which categories of game theory are well developed into a body of theory, and which are relatively undeveloped?
3. Discuss the rationale for studying game theory.
4. Discuss the meaning of "zero-sum" games.
5. Assume a game theory problem involving players A and B. What is the assumption about player A's knowledge concerning the alternatives and payoffs available to himself and to his opponent?
6. What is meant by the "value of the game" in game theory?
7. Discuss the meaning of "pure strategies" in game theory. What is a "saddle point"?
8. Describe the "maximin" (or "minimax") principle of game theory.
9. How does one strategy "dominate" another in game theory?
10. Describe "mixed strategies" and their use in game theory.

PROBLEMS

1. Given the following payoff matrix for a two-person zero-sum game, solve the game using the maximin (minimax) principle. Include in

your answer: (a) the strategy selection for each player; and (b) the value of the game to player A, and to player B. Can any strategies be eliminated by the rule of dominance? Does the game have a saddle point?

		Player B Strategies		
Strategies		X	Y	Z
Player A	1	− 500	− 100	700
	2	100	0	200
	3	500	− 200	− 700

2. Solve the following two-person zero-sum game using the maximin (minimax) principle. Determine the pure strategies for each player. What is the value of the game?

		Player B Strategies					
Strategies		U	V	W	X	Y	Z
	1	1	1	2	4	5	− 5
	2	3	− 3	4	3	2	4
Player A	3	6	2	3	5	7	5
	4	2	1	3	4	6	0

3. Show that by using the rule of dominance, the payoff matrix of problem 2 can be reduced to either a single row or a single column. Further show that the solution to the game, obtained from the reduced payoff matrix, is the same as was obtained in problem 2.

4. Determine algebraically the mixed strategies for each player, given the following payoff matrix. What is the expected gain for player A and the expected loss for player B?

		Player B Strategies	
Strategies		X	Y
Player A	1	60	50
	2	45	55

5. Consider the following two-person zero-sum game:

| | | Player B Strategies | | |
		X	Y	Z
	Strategies			
	1	500	600	300
Player A	2	100	325	250
	3	200	550	450

(a) Use the maximin (minimax) principle to determine if pure strategies exist.

(b) Identify the cycling path that will result (the movement from one payoff cell to another, as in Figure 11.10).

(c) Reduce the payoff matrix by the rule of dominance to a 2-by-2 matrix. Discuss the payoff cells remaining by referring to your answer to (b).

(d) Solve algebraically for the mixed-strategy probabilities for players A and B.

(e) Determine the expected gain for player A and the expected loss for player B. Discuss the meaning of this solution value.

6. Illustrate the graphical solution for the game given in problem 4, (a) for player A, and (b) for player B.

7. Illustrate a graphical solution for player B for the following game:

| | | Player B Strategies | |
		X	Y
	Strategies		
	1	85	15
	2	45	60
Player A	3	75	35
	4	20	70

8. Formulate the game given in problem 7 as a linear programming problem, and solve for the mixed-strategy probabilities for player B. Solve by the simplex method. Show that the mixed-strategy solution for player A is also given by the dual solution in the final simplex tableau.

9. Assume that two firms are competing for market share for a particular product. Each firm is considering what promotional strategy to employ for the coming period. Assume that the following

payoff matrix describes the increase in market share for firm A and the decrease in market share for firm B. Determine the optimal strategies for each firm.

		Firm B *Strategies*		
	Strategies	No promotion	Moderate promotion	Much promotion
	No promotion	5	0	– 10
Firm A	Moderate promotion	10	6	2
	Much promotion	20	15	10

(a) Which firm would be the winner, in terms of market share?
(b) Would the solution strategies necessarily maximize profits for either of the firms?
(c) What might the two firms do to maximize their joint profits?

10. Formulate the union-management game given as an example in the chapter (see Table 11.11) as a linear programming problem. Solve, using the simplex method, for management's mixed-strategy probabilities. Determine the union's mixed-strategy probabilities from the dual solution.

12 Simulation Analysis

INTRODUCTION

The subject matter of this chapter represents a major divergence from the previous chapters. In every case, previous chapters demonstrated an "analytic" solution, of some sort, to the model presented. For example, the break-even model was solved analytically by setting the linear profit equation equal to zero, and solving for the break-even quantity, Q_{BE}. The nonlinear profit model and the classic inventory (cost) models were solved analytically by the method of classical optimization. Linear programming, goal programming, and transportation problems were solved analytically by using algorithms (theoretically based step-by-step rules that obtain an optimal solution). The queueing equations were developed analytically, based upon probability theory.

The values of various alternatives, in decision theory and game theory, were computed analytically and evaluated according to various criteria, such as expected value, maximin, minimax, and so on. The critical path and expected project time for PERT-CPM networks were determined analytically.

The major emphasis of this book, therefore, has been on the formulation of the model, followed by an *analytic* solution to the model. In most cases, the analytic solution yielded an "optimum" solution to the decision variables. However, an analytic solution reflects the procedure by which the results are obtained, and does not necessarily imply "optimization" of the model. For example, the queueing equations yielded solutions in the form of "descriptors" of system performance. Of course, these model solutions were assumed to be input into a broader framework for the actual decision-making analysis.

Simulation provides an alternative to the analytic (or mathematical) solution procedure. The results, or output, of simulation, however, are always in the form of system "descriptors." The relationship of simulation to model construction and solution is illustrated in Figure 12.1. It should be added that although the simulation output is always in the form of descriptive results, it is most certainly possible to include, along with the simulator, a search rule to evaluate the simulation results and provide the optimum solution to the decision problem. This procedure is denoted in Figure 12.1 by the dotted line from the block containing descriptive results to the block containing optimization results.

SIMULATION DEFINED

The term *simulation* is used in this book to mean deriving measures of system performance by conducting sampling experiments on the model of the system. Presumably, the model of the system of interest includes the relevant components of the system, along with their relationships. The process of simulation involves "operating" (or running) the model to obtain operational information. Operating or running the model for some period is actually "sampling" from a model of the true system. The simulation process is achieved by generating inputs into the model, and measuring the performance variables of interest.

The simulation process, in general, is illustrated in Figure 12.2, and further shown in Figure 12.3 for a queueing analysis. Of course, the figures are oversimplified. For example, in Figure 12.3 we would also have to generate, as inputs, the service times, unless they were a known constant value.

Why Simulate?

It has often been said, "When all else fails, simulate." It is generally true that simulation should be used only if analytic solutions are not obtainable, or as a complement to analytic solutions. Since simulation of the model is closely akin to conducting sampling experiments on the real system, the results obtained are sample observations or sample statistics.

For example, if one were analyzing a single-channel, single-phase queueing system, the analytically derived queueing equation for mean number waiting would yield a value analogous to a population mean (μ),

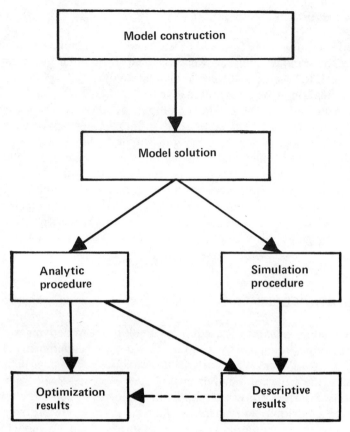

Figure 12.1
Relationship of simulation to model construction and solution

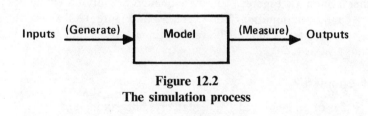

Figure 12.2
The simulation process

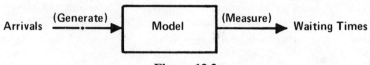

Figure 12.3
Simulation process, for queueing analysis

450

whereas simulation would yield a value analogous to a sample mean ($\bar{x}$). Whether or not the sample mean would approximate the steady-state mean of the queueing equation would depend upon the starting conditions of the simulation, and how long a period was simulated.

In any event, the simulation results do contain sampling variance (error), just as in the case of direct sampling from the population (or system). In cases where the sampling (simulation) is conducted over time, covariance is included in the results. Methods for dealing with such output are difficult at best.

On the other hand, models of systems are often too complex to solve analytically, and direct experimentation on the system is usually not practical. Thus, simulation provides a laboratory for experimentation and analysis of problems that often cannot be solved by other means.

Monte Carlo Simulation

A characteristic of systems, which often results in models which are too difficult to solve analytically, is that certain components must be represented as "random variables." These random variables are then represented in the model by probability distributions, and the model is referred to as a probabilistic or stochastic model. Almost all simulation studies involve the analysis of probabilistic models.

Monte Carlo is the technique of selecting values randomly from one or more probability distributions for use in a particular run of a simulation study. For example, in the case of the queueing simulation, the arrivals might be generated randomly according to the Poisson probability distribution. The random feature indicates that during any one time period, the number of arrivals could vary widely; however, over a large number of time periods, a frequency distribution of the number of arrivals would approximate a Poisson probability distribution.

Generally the origin of modern simulation methods, and the use of the Monte Carlo technique, are attributed to von Neumann, Ulam, and Fermi, who used the Monte Carlo simulation technique in conjunction with the development of the atomic bomb during World War II. It should be pointed out that simulation has also been used productively for the analysis of nonprobabilistic problems, such as evaluating multiple integrals and systems of differential equations. However, the discussion of this chapter will be limited to the use of simulation for analyzing probabilistic models.

Simulation has become an extremely important technique due to its relative flexibility in adapting to the complexities of real-world systems. However, a thorough treatment of the topic would constitute a book in itself, and only the fundamentals will be presented here.

SIMULATED SAMPLING

The fundamental basis of Monte Carlo simulation is the generation of the values of random variables that constitute an integral part of the model. Some examples of random variables, which are represented by probability distributions, are as follows:

Time between customer arrivals at a service location
Time between breakdowns of factory equipment
Service time, to serve customer or repair equipment
Time to complete an activity in a project
Demand per day for items in inventory
Lead time, in days, for an inventory order
Quantity of order size, when an order is received
Time to process an order after received
Sales of a particular item
Costs of a particular activity
Life of a particular asset

In fact, any variable of a model can be represented as a random variable, and assumed to follow some theoretical or empirical distribution.

A Simple Example

Let us assume that the probability distribution given in Table 12.1 represents the demand per day for a particular product. The objective of Monte Carlo simulation is to generate the quantity demanded on a particular day. This is achieved by "sampling" from the probability distribution.

The demand for a particular day could be randomly generated, according to the probability distribution given, by spinning a roulette

Table 12.1
Probability Distribution of Demand Per Day

D (Demand)	P(D)
14	0.2
15	0.4
16	0.2
17	0.1
18	0.1

wheel that was segmented as shown in Figure 12.4. We will assume that if the marker falls on a line, the value to the left of the line is taken. We will also assume that the person spinning the wheel cannot bias the results by starting at a certain place or spinning with a certain amount of force. Thus, the quantity demanded can be "randomly" generated, by a spin of the wheel. However, over a period of many days (many spins of the wheel), the relative frequency with which the values would be generated would approximate the probability distribution given in Table 12.1. The procedure illustrated is, in fact, the Monte Carlo method.

Computer-Generated Random Values

It is not generally practical to generate the values of the random variable by the preceding approach. Where it can be assumed that the random variable of interest follows some theoretical probability distribution (i.e., normal, Poisson, exponential, etc.), certain algorithms have been developed to generate the values of the random variable. These are

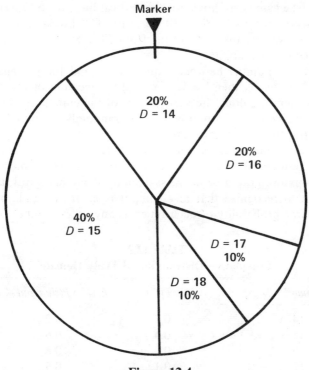

Figure 12.4
Simulated sampling

very convenient techniques for random value generation, and are well known. However, often the probability distribution may simply be based on historical data, and the resulting empirical distribution may not fit any known theoretical probability distribution.

We will now show how the values of a random variable following any empirical distribution can be generated. This discussion will also demonstrate the conceptual basis for random-value generation, in any Monte Carlo computer simulation.

First, let us return to the probability distribution of demand per day, given in Table 12.1, and now compute the *cumulative* probability distribution also. Table 12.2 gives the original probability distribution and the associated cumulative probabilities. The cumulative distribution, $P(\text{demand} \leq D)$, is also shown in Figure 12.5. Note that the length of the vertical lines, at each step, correspond exactly with the probability values for each demand quantity. For example, starting at the top, the vertical line directly above the value of 18 extends from 90 to 100 percent. This corresponds to the probability of 18 demanded (0.1, or 10 percent). The same case holds for the vertical line above 17, reflecting a probability of 0.1 ($90 - 80 = 10$ percent). The probability of 16 demanded is given by the vertical line from 60 to 80 percent, yielding 20 percent, or 0.2 probability.

Thus, if a number between 0 and 1 (or 0 and 100 percent) can be generated *randomly*, then by determining the location of the randomly generated number along the vertical axis of the cumulative probability distribution, we can obtain an associated randomly generated value for demand (on the horizontal axis).

There are numerous techniques available for randomly generating a number between 0 and 1. In fact, most computer centers have a random-number generator in the system, available upon call. It is quite important to recognize that any computer-generated random number has the same probability of occurrence as any other number between 0

Table 12.2
Cumulative Distribution of Daily Demand

Demand = D	P(D)	F(D) = P(demand ≤ D)
14	0.2	0.2
15	0.4	0.6
16	0.2	0.8
17	0.1	0.9
18	0.1	1.0

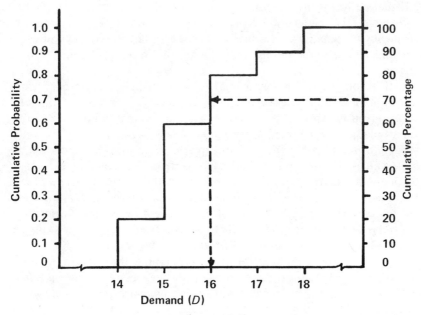

Figure 12.5
Cumulative distribution of daily demand

and 1. For example, if the random numbers were limited to the integers between 1 and 100, inclusive, then each value would have a probability of selection of 1/100. If the scale between 1 and 100 was subdivided into tenths, ranging from 0.1 to 100.0, then the probability of obtaining any one of the 1000 alternatives would be 1/1000. Most computer-generated random numbers are carried out to six or seven significant digits.

Figure 12.5 illustrates that if the value 0.700000 were randomly generated by the computer, we could then "transform" this random number into the associated demand quantity of 16, by making use of the cumulative distribution of demand. With a great many generations of random numbers between 0 and 1, we would obtain the value of 16 for demand 20 percent of the time (80 − 60).

Thus, it should become apparent that by using a computer random-number generator for generating numbers between 0 and 1 in conjunction with the cumulative distribution of a random variable, the values for any probability distribution can be randomly generated.

Figure 12.6 gives a flow diagram for the random generation of demand, according to the previously given cumulative probability distribution. A FORTRAN computer program is also given in Appendix

XII that performs the illustrated computations, for 1000 values of D. As an exercise, the reader should run the program, and develop the relative frequency of demand values printed out. The relative frequency of each demand level should closely approximate the initial probability distribution.

If a computer is not immediately available, the reader can "simulate" the experiment just given by reading down a column of random digits, given in Appendix XIII. By placing a decimal point prior to the values read, it can be seen that every value is between 0 and 1. Thus, the reading of a table of random digits replaces the computer generation of those values. As the random digits are read from the table, trace through the logic of Figure 12.6 and determine the value of demand associated with the random number. Remember that a probability distribution does not tell one what the exact value of demand will be; it simply indicates the relative frequency with which various demand values will be obtained over a large number of observations.

One final point should be made concerning the random-number generator. The values generated are actually between 0 and 1, *including* 0, but *excluding* 1. This point is not of serious concern, however, when values are generated to six or seven places accuracy. If the values were *truncated* at two or three places accuracy (analogous to reading only the first two or three columns of a seven digit column of numbers), it would, of course, become of concern. As an exercise, determine what values should be used in the decision blocks (diamonds) of Figure 12.6, if the random number (RN) were truncated to one place (one digit). Note that the values RN could take on would be 0 through 0.9, in increments of one tenth.

CONSTRUCTION OF THE SIMULATION MODEL

The essential, and probably most difficult, aspect of Monte Carlo simulation has been presented. Beyond the generation of the inputs (i.e., demand) to the model, it is simply a matter of developing the logical relationships for the model of the system. Most of the preceding chapters of the book have dealt with this topic to some extent.

However, since simulation models are "run" on computers, it is not necessary that the model be developed completely in the form of mathematical equations or inequalities. Rather, the model may consist of submodels or components, linked together by a *logical* relationship. The logical relationship is generally represented by the use of flowcharts or diagrams (such as Figure 12.6).

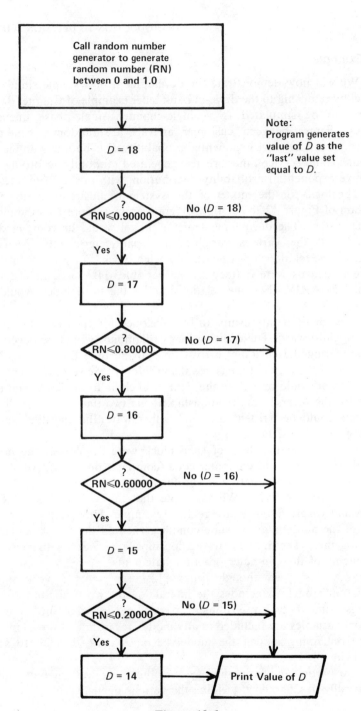

Figure 12.6
Flow diagram of random generation of demand

An Example

We will now demonstrate the development of a simple simulation model by returning to the drive-in bank teller example of Chapter 9. The system to be simulated is a single-channel, single-phase queueing process. Times between customer arrivals are randomly generated according to a negative exponential probability distribution, with mean 3 (minutes), and service times are also generated randomly according to a negative exponential probability distribution, with mean 2 (minutes).

The logic for the model of this system is illustrated in the flow diagram of Figure 12.7. The flow diagram, in fact, represents the model of the system. The development of the model would be completed by defining all the various variables and parameters, and specifying explicitly the relationships described in each block. For example, if time between arrivals were defined as the variable, TBA, and arrival time defined as ARIV, then the relationship for the third block would be $ARIV_n = TBA + ARIV_{n-1}$.

Most of the relationships to be developed for each diagram block are straightforward. The decision block (diamond) would be developed by comparing the customer arrival time to the time the server is first available. If the arrival time is less than (before) time server is available, the program would branch to the right. Branching to the left would take place for the reverse time relationship. If the two times were equal, the program could be written to branch either way (and the idle time or waiting time would be zero).

After the relationships of each block were developed, the model would be converted to computer code (computer program). An advantage of computer simulation is the facility to include decision blocks (e.g., "Is server busy?"). We also note that the relationships of each individual diagram block are relatively simple. However, the overall logic of the model may be quite complex when all the relationships are tied together. The individual relationships are tied together by the sequencing of the computer program statements.

Note that even though Figure 12.7 represents a very simple simulation model, it includes the interaction of two probability distributions (time between customer arrivals and service times). When random variables are included in any model, regardless of the simplicity of the remaining model, the model becomes quite difficult to solve analytically.

The particular waiting-line system illustrated was, in fact, solved analytically in Chapter 9, yielding the various queueing equations.

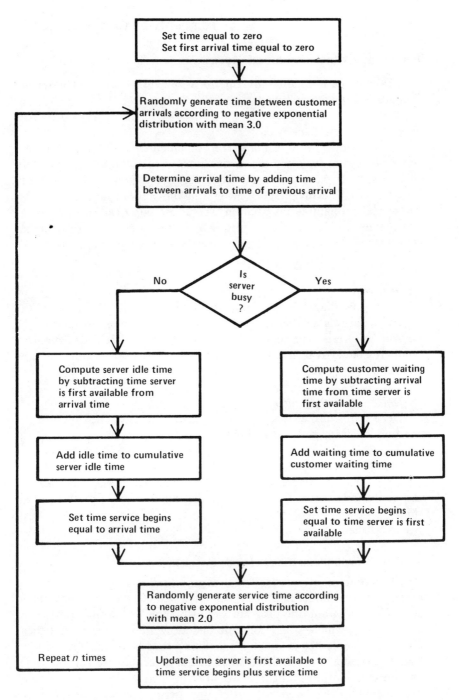

Figure 12.7
Flow diagram for simulation model of drive-in bank (single server)

Functions of the Simulation Model

The simulation model must perform several functions. The several functions are given as follows:

Random Variable Generation

The example given in Figure 12.7 included two blocks in which the times between arrivals and the service times were randomly generated. In this case, they were generated from negative exponential probability distributions. The advantage of generating the random variable from this theoretical probability distribution (versus an empirical distribution, as was previously illustrated in Figure 12.6) is demonstrated by the fact that only a single statement would be required in the program to perform this function.

Event Control

The flow diagram represents the flow of events. The logic of the program controls the sequence of events. Note that a key variable of the control feature is "the time the server is first available." The program compares the arrival time to this control variable to determine the flow of events.

System State Initialization

The status of the system must be defined initially. The first block of the flow diagram performed this function for our example.

System Performance Data Collection

Note that the diagram of Figure 12.7 included blocks that collected the cumulative server idle time and the cumulative customer waiting time. These are, of course, only two system descriptors that might have been collected.

Statistical Computations and Report Generation

This function was not shown in Figure 12.7; however, it would have come after the model had been simulated n times. After n runs of the simulation program, the program would branch to the final portion of the program, which would compute operating statistics and print them out. For example, the cumulative idle time would be divided by the total time the system was simulated to yield the percentage server idle time, and the cumulative waiting time would be divided by the total number of customers to yield the mean waiting time per customer. Other statistics relating to system performance could also be collected and printed out, such as the standard deviation, range, median, and a frequency distribution for the measured variable. A major advantage of simulation is its capability to collect and provide many different forms of statistical output.

Simulation Languages

It was stated that the construction of the simulation model, after construction of the system flow diagram and specification of model components, variables, parameters, and relationships, is generally followed by development of a computer program. However, the programming aspects of simulation can become quite complex.

Fortunately, generalized simulation languages have been developed to perform many of the previously discussed functions of a simulation study. In fact, some languages require no computer programming as such, at all.

The most generally known, and available, simulation languages are GASP, SIMSCRIPT, GPSS, and DYNAMO. These languages are designed to perform the common features of simulation. Such features include random-variable generation, event control, statistical computations, and report generation. Thus, with generalized simulation languages, the analyst orients himself to understanding and describing the system in a format that may make use of the selected simulation language.

Descriptions of the various simulation languages are given in simulation texts such as those listed in the references at the end of the chapter.

SYSTEM EXPERIMENTATION WITH SIMULATION

A generalized procedure for system experimentation with simulation is illustrated in Figure 12.8. After simulating the system n times, operating statistics are produced as program output. The operating statistics are generated for each of the performance characteristics of interest (i.e., mean number waiting, mean time waiting, percent server idle time, etc., in the case of a queueing system).

After simulating the system n times and obtaining output results, another case (experiment) may be considered. For example, in the simulation of an inventory system, one might be interested in the system performance for various combinations of r and Q (where r = reorder point and Q = quantity ordered). The inventory level at which a reorder

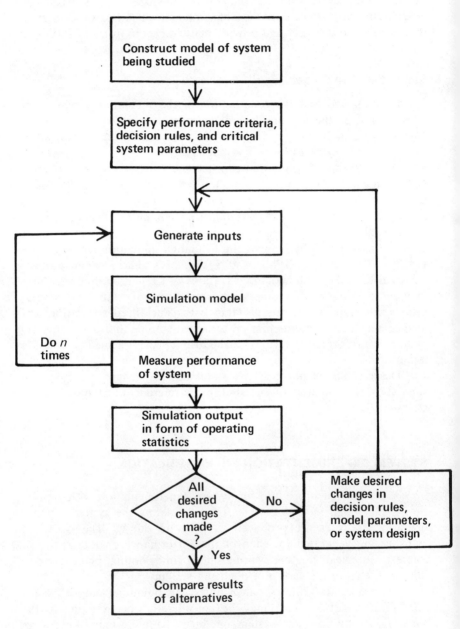

Figure 12.8
System experimentation with simulation

is made, r, and the order quantity, Q, are each "decision rules," to be evaluated. An example of a simulation experiment could be as follows:
Simulate the inventory system for the following cases:

Case	r	Q
1	50	400
2	55	400
3	60	400
4	65	400
5	50	500
6	55	500
7	60	500
8	65	500

The inventory system's performance would be evaluated for four different levels of r and two different levels of Q, yielding eight case combinations of r and Q (seven changes after the initial simulation with $r = 50$ and $Q = 400$).

The systems analyst might also be interested in the system performance when certain parameters are varied. This would be accomplished by changing parameter values, rather than decision rules, after each simulation. Changing parameter values provides the capability to conduct a "sensitivity analysis." For example, if demand for inventory was assumed to be normally distributed, with mean 20 and standard deviation 5, the analyst might wish to vary the mean value by plus and minus 10 percent, to see the effect on operating results. Such analysis might yield the conclusion that optimum decision rules are highly sensitive to certain system parameters.

Finally, simulation can be used to compare two or more entirely different system designs. For example, management might wish to know the expected results in a complete modernization of an existing system. If alternative designs were being considered, simulation could be used to provide estimates of system performance according to various operating characteristics. The existing system would probably be first simulated, to aid in validation of the model, followed by model changes to reflect the modernization alternatives.

APPLICATIONS OF SIMULATION

Simulation may be applied to any problem too difficult to model and solve by analytic means. Some eminent decision scientists have stated that any complex real-world problem should first be modeled and solved analytically, even if simplifying assumptions must be introduced, to gain an intuitive feel for the model components and system performance. This should then be followed up with a complete simulation model, including all the system complexities, to provide the final basis for decision making.

The technique of simulation has been applied to virtually every conceivable type of problem. Some examples are as follows:

Queueing Problems

A major area of application for simulation has been in the analysis of waiting-time problems. As Chapter 9 indicated, the assumptions required for analytic solution of queueing problems are quite restrictive. With few exceptions, simulation is the only available approach for considering such problems as multiple-phase queueing systems.

Inventory Problems

Chapter 8 introduced the case where the demand per day, during a constant lead time, was a random variable. However, if we consider the case where both demand per day and the lead time are random variables, the analysis becomes extremely difficult to handle by any means other than simulation. In addition, the inventory system might include the case where both the number of orders received per day and the size of the order are random variables. We would then have a joint probability distribution for demand during lead time, which was a function of three random variables, that could be analyzed only by simulation.

Network Problems

The PERT network included the case where the activity times were represented by the beta probability distribution. However, the analytical PERT solution does yield slightly biased results. This has been shown by simulating the network. Also the PERT approach is limited to the beta probability distribution. If it were shown from empirical data that the activity times followed some other distribution, the network could be analyzed with simulation.

A "canned" computer program has been developed, called GERTS, that will simulate networks that include not only probabilistic activity times, but also probabilistic branching—that is, the probability that an activity will be performed (occur) may be less than one. In PERT, all activities are assumed to occur with a probability of one. The GERTS simulator also allows other non-PERT features, such as looping of activities back to intermediate events, and multiple logic concerning event realization.

Production Problems

Various problems of production have been simulated, such as production scheduling, production sequencing, line balancing, plant layout, plant location analysis, and so on. It is surprising how often production problems resemble a queueing process of some sort. This is the reason for the popularity of illustrating simulation with a queueing example.

Repair and Replacement Problems

Since machine breakdowns or facility failures typically occur according to some probability distribution, such problems are most generally analyzed by simulation. Much analytical work, however, has also been done in this area. Simulation, in conjunction with analytical methods, provides a powerful means for studying such problems.

Finance Problems

Capital budgeting problems of finance include estimates of cash flows. These cash flows are composite results of many random variables. Simulation has been used to generate values of the various contributing factors to derive estimates of cash flows. A classic article by David B. Hertz in the January-February 1964 issue of *Harvard Business Review* illustrated the use of simulation for randomly generating the inputs into a rate of return calculation. The contributing inputs included such random variables as market size, selling price, growth rate, market share, and the like.

Marketing Problems

Marketing represents the ultimate in uncertainty. Simulation provides the opportunity for the marketing manager to experiment with alternative courses of action, when faced by a very large number of interacting random components, that vary widely. In addition, simulation may provide the marketer with insights into the operation of the market he faces. An example of a possible application for simulation, in the marketing environment, is where contract bidding is performed. The contractor can simulate the problem he faces and evaluate various alternative courses of action.

Public Service Operations

Recently such operations as police departments, fire departments, post offices, hospitals, court systems, airports, and other public systems have been analyzed by simulation. Typically, such operations are so complex that no other technique can be used to analyze the overall system.

The discussion of applications of simulation could go on and on. The fact is that simulation is a technique generally applicable to any complex system.

LIMITATIONS OF SIMULATION

Simulation does involve many difficult problems, some of which have not been resolved. For example, as was previously stated, simulation over time can yield statistical output containing covariance. The result is that simulation requires not only the ability to model and run the program, but also a considerable amount of statistical analysis expertise. Any large real-world simulation study should include a capable statistician on the staff, to assist in the analysis of output results. A technique known as spectral analysis has been found to be of considerable assistance in the analysis of output including covariance.

Another major problem of simulation involves validating the model. Actually there are two problems included. First, does the model correctly represent the true system of interest? Second, does the computer simulation program correctly simulate the model originally developed? Techniques and guidelines for validation have been developed, but this remains a serious problem in simulation. The old adage of "garbage-in, garbage-out" applies doubly to simulation analysis.

Some tactical problems continue to plague simulation analysts. One of these is starting conditions. Should we simulate the system by assuming the system is empty (analogous to opening up the store in the morning), or should we attempt to set up the simulation so that it will be as close to "normal operating conditions" as possible, at the start of a run? This may sound like a simple decision, but it is a serious problem for the actual construction of the simulation model.

Another tactical problem is, how do we know we have simulated the system long enough to reach steady state? Is there a steady state? Studies have shown that simulation takes a surprisingly long period of time to reach steady-state conditions. If we do not reach steady state, our output will be biased by the inclusion of "transient conditions."

The conclusion that must be reached regarding the discussed limitations of simulation is that although the novice can learn to simulate with little difficulty, simulation analysis of real-world problems should be performed by experts. This is, of course, true for any decision science technique, but it seems to be especially so for simulation.

REFERENCES

Greenberg, S., *GPSS Primer*, Wiley-Interscience, New York, 1972.

Meier, R. C., Newell, W. T., and Pazer, H. L., *Simulation in Business and Economics*, Prentice-Hall, Englewood Cliffs, N.J., 1969.

Mize, J., and Cox, G., *Essentials of Simulation*, Prentice-Hall, Englewood Cliffs, N.J., 1968.

Naylor, T. H., Balintfy, J. L., Burdick, D. S., and Chu, K., *Computer Simulation Techniques*, Wiley, New York, 1966.

Pritsker, A. A. B., *New GERT Concepts and a GERT Network Simulation Program*, Research Memorandum No. 71–8, Purdue University, Lafayette, Ind., 1971.

Pritsker, A. A. B., *The GASP IV Simulation Language*, Wiley, New York, 1974.

Wyman, F. P., *Simulation Modeling: A Guide to Using SIMSCRIPT*, Wiley, New York, 1970.

QUESTIONS

1. Define the term *simulation*, as it is used in this book.
2. Distinguish between analytic solution of a model and simulation of a model.
3. Discuss the type of results obtained from simulation of a model.
4. Would simulation normally be categorized as an optimization technique? Discuss your answer.
5. Under what circumstances would simulation most often be used? What single feature, or component, in a model is generally responsible for requiring simulation rather than analytic techniques of solution?
6. Define the Monte Carlo method. Give an illustration.
7. Discuss the concept of analyzing a simulation model by experimentation, as opposed to straightforward solution of a model for the optimum solution.
8. Discuss some simulation languages, and what features they provide.
9. Discuss some of the limitations of simulation.
10. Discuss some areas in which simulation has been applied.

PROBLEMS

1. Assume that the time between arrivals of oil tanker ships at an unloading dock is given by the following probability distribution.

Construct the cumulative probability distribution for this process, and illustrate graphically. Illustrate on the graph how the time between two ship arrivals can be obtained as a random value based on obtaining randomly a number between 0 and 1.

Time Between Ship Arrivals (in days)	Probability
1	0.05
2	0.10
3	0.20
4	0.30
5	0.20
6	0.10
7	0.05

2. Make use of the information in problem 1 and Appendix XIII (table of random numbers) to generate randomly the times between arrivals for the first 20 ships. In selecting random numbers from Appendix XIII, read sequentially down any column or across any row, two digits at a time. Complete a table of 20 observations, as follows:

Observation	Random Number	Time Between Arrivals
No ship—1st ship		
1st ship—2nd ship		
2nd ship—3rd ship		
.		
.		
.		
19th ship—20th ship		

3. Analyze the sampling results obtained in problem 2 by computing the frequency of various times between arrivals. Also, compute the relative frequency of times between arrivals (frequencies divided by 20). Compare your experimental results with the originally given probability distribution of problem 1. What statistical concept explains the difference between relative frequencies obtained and the originally specified probabilities?

4. Assume that the time required to unload, clean, and otherwise prepare a ship for departure is exactly 5 days. Using this information and the information given in problem 1, determine the values for the

following table of simulation results (let days start at day zero, so that the first ship arrives on day zero plus the first randomly generated time):

Ship Number	Arrival Day	Time to Arrival of Next Ship	Day Unloading Begins	Departure Day	Waiting Time	Number of Ships Waiting
1						
2						
3						
.						
.						
.						
20						

5. Compute the following summary statistics for the ship queueing simulation of problem 4:

   (a) Mean time between ship arrivals
   (b) Mean time ships wait for unloading
   (c) Mean number of ships waiting to unload
   (d) Mean time ships spend waiting and being unloaded
   (e) Mean number of ships waiting and being unloaded
   (f) Proportion of arrivals that enter an empty system
   (g) Frequency distribution of ship waiting times
   (h) Frequency distribution of number of ships waiting

6. Assume that the time required to unload, clean, and service ships is a random variable (rather than the constant 5 days assumed in problem 4), described by the probability distribution below. Complete the exercises prescribed in problems 1, 2, 3, 4, and 5 for the case assuming random unloading time. (Note that the simulation results will now include the joint interaction of two random variables, time between arrivals and unloading time, which would become much more difficult to solve by analytic means.)

Time to Unload, Clean, and Service a Ship (in days)	Probability
3	0.1
4	0.2
5	0.4
6	0.3

7. Assume that the inventory manager for a firm wishes to determine the expected (mean) demand for a particular good in stock during the reorder lead time (the time lapse from the stock reorder until the goods are received). This information is needed to determine how far in advance to reorder (the reorder point), before the stock level is reduced to zero. However, both the lead time, in days, and the demand per day for the good are random variables, described by the probability distributions below. Manually simulate the problem, using the table of random numbers (Appendix XIII) for 30 reorders, to estimate the demand during lead time. (Note: The number of days lead time for each reorder must first be randomly generated, followed by separate random generations of demand for *each* of the days of lead time.)

Lead Time	Probability	Demand Per Day	Probability
1	0.5	1	0.1
2	0.3	2	0.3
3	0.2	3	0.4
		4	0.2

8. Construct a frequency distribution of the demand during lead time, from the simulation results of problem 7. Also, construct a reverse cumulative frequency distribution of demand during lead time. (The *reverse* cumulative distribution is the number of times demand is *equal to or greater than* various demand levels. For example, the demand during lead time will be equal to or greater than 1 unit for all 30 of the reorders; however, it will be equal to or greater than 12 units demanded a very small number of times.)

9. Suppose the inventory manager of problem 7 wishes to set his reorder level so that the probability of a stock-out during lead time is no greater than 0.1 (the percentage of reorders for which shortages would be expected to occur is no more than 10 percent). This is referred to as a 90 percent service level—90 percent of the time, customers are served upon demand. At what level should the inventory manager set his reorder point? (Hint: Make use of the answer to problem 8.) At what point should the inventory manager reorder to maintain a service level of 80 percent? of 50 percent? of 20 percent? Note that by simply establishing a desired service level, the difficult question of stock-out cost is avoided by management, which may be necessary in some real-world applications.

10. Construct a flowchart model of some real-world system of interest, which could be used for constructing a simulation model. Make use of the concepts illustrated in Figures 12.7 and 12.8; however, do not simply duplicate the system of Figure 12.7. Be sure to identify the random variables that generate the inputs into the simulation, and the statistics to be gathered for measuring the system performance. Identify decision variables or rules, and model parameters that might be changed in an experimental analysis of the system.

13 Implementation of Decision Science

DEVELOPMENT OF DECISION SCIENCE

During the past 25 years, there has been significant progress in the field of decision science. Many new techniques have been developed through technical breakthroughs, new applications of existing techniques have been explored, and complex decision problems have been solved through the use of computers. The greatest advance in decision science, however, has occurred in the implementation of decision science for real-world decision problems. This progress indicates that decision science is entering the maturity stage of its development. The following sections discuss three broad phases in the development of decision science.

The Primitive Stage (Prior to the 1960s)

During this phase a handful of professionals began to apply quantitative tools to rather well-defined problems. The decision scientists were transferred from other disciplines, such as mathematics, statistics, natural sciences, and the like. They were primarily interested in learning and developing new techniques in order to find optimum solutions to clearly defined operational problems, that is, production scheduling, inventory problems, blending problems, and the like. During this phase, two well-known professional associations were organized: Operations Research Society of America (ORSA) and The Institute of Management Science (TIMS). Academic interest was very limited. In fact, there were only three universities with formal programs in decision science.

The Rapid Growth Stage (the 1960s)

This was the period during which a dramatic growth of decision science occurred in academic institutions. In the early 1960s, there were only six institutions that offered formal programs in decision science. Six years later, there were 37 institutions with formal degree programs in the decision science related fields. The profession has put its emphasis on the education of the future decision makers.

The rapid growth of decision science in academic institutions has brought some positive results in the field of management. First of all, it has provided a special impetus to utilize the enormous analytical power of computers. The computer technology allowed practical applications of many sophisticated decision science techniques to various operational and managerial problems. It was during this period when many computer manufacturers began to develop "canned" programs for easy applications of various techniques. Furthermore, many large organizations began to design the computer-based management information systems (MIS). The computer-based MIS required quantitative data inputs, systematic data analysis, and timely use of the data bank. Thus, decision science has become an important part of many organizations. Another important factor for the rapid growth of decision science was that college graduates with decision science education moved into various management positions. Consequently, management has become more understanding and appreciative of the potential contributions of decision science. This conducive environment has provided room for further growth of decision science. Perhaps the most important development during this phase was that for the first time a more realistic understanding of the role, value, and limitations of decision science began to emerge.

The enormous educational growth of decision science has also resulted in some negative aspects. Many decision scientists have put a great deal of energy into academic, theoretical, or pure research for the refinement of minute details of various techniques that had no or little relevance to real-world problems. Consequently, research was often conducted for the sake of research or publication. Many practitioners began to be disillusioned, partially due to their inability to comprehend the research work and partially because of the irrelevance of the study. Also, evidence of a tendency began to develop of emphasizing the techniques over the problems to be solved. In other words, some researchers tended to look for problems that could be simplified and solved by certain techniques. This "have-gun-will-travel" approach is indeed contradictory to the very purpose of decision science. There has been a lack of understanding of the decision environment, organizational values, conflicting nature of objectives, data requirements, time constraints, politics of the organization, and noneconomic ramifications of decision alternatives.

The Maturing Stage (the 1970s)

Although the maturing stage began earlier than 1970, it has become more evident during the years since then. The profession of decision science began a self-evaluation. The decision scientists started to ask the question, "Are we doing the job we are supposed to be doing?" Many leading decision scientists are not afraid to speak out about the failures of decision science as well as its successes. This phase can be characterized as follows:

1. A more pragmatic approach is being taken by both managers and decision scientists concerning the true value, role, and limitations of decision science.
2. A greater emphasis is being placed on the analysis of the decision environment and the nature of the problem, as compared to the previous emphasis on developing abstract models.
3. Decision scientists now recognize the importance of obtaining satisfactory solutions to certain problems rather than finding *the* optimum solution.
4. A greater effort is being placed on the better integration of environmental, behavioral, and quantitative analysis in problem solving. Managers and decision scientists are striving to gain a clearer understanding of the quantitative aspects of the problem and the impact of various model assumptions.
5. The computer technology is utilized more vigorously in pursuing heuristic solutions to ill-structured managerial problems. Decision scientists are attempting to develop processes for evolving successively better answers to the problem through the computer-based analysis.

The greater emphasis on the actual implementation of decision science indicates that the profession is moving in the right direction. During this period, a new professional organization has been formed among those who are more concerned about the actual implementation of decision science, American Institute for Decision Sciences (AIDS). The rapid growth of AIDS is another indication that decision scientists are determined to do their work through "tool-using rather than tool-tuning."

DECISION SCIENCE AND ENVIRONMENT

One of the primary incentives for man to pursue knowledge is the basic human and environmental problem of satisfying unlimited human desire with limited resources. This has always been the most troublesome human problem. Most human organizations, whether they are business enterprises, governmental agencies, or social institutions, have evolved in such a way as to narrow the gap between desires and resources.

There are two possible approaches that may be employed to solve this human problem. One is to increase available resources. For an individual, this approach may take the form of the Protestant work ethic, which calls for hard work to increase resources so that the individual can satisfy most of his desires. Or it may take a form of scientific endeavors that will enable him to utilize existing limited resources in a more efficient manner. Finally, it may mean a scientific breakthrough that creates new uses for relatively abundant resources, such as water, air, sunshine, and so on.

The second basic approach is for an individual to limit his desires so that the existing resources become sufficient to satisfy them. For example, one may choose to have a small cottage in the mountains and meditate ten hours, have only two meals, and work four hours per day. The two approaches we have cited are quite in contrast, but both have found wide practice in the history of human society.

The first approach is clearly a general philosophy of Western culture. One who accumulates wealth through hard work or innovative ideas becomes a successful person. The economic rewards of hard work also usually result in social and psychological rewards. In short, "money talks" for the fulfillment of human desires. It is quite common in this country to find a millionaire being respected even more highly than statesmen, artists, scholars, or religious leaders. Since we live in an environment of scarce resources (and they are becoming scarcer every day), it may be perfectly natural and appropriate for those who acquire greater control over resources to receive social respect.

The second approach has been a long-accepted practice, although it is gradually diminishing, in Eastern cultures. By exercising strong self-discipline, self-control, and sometimes even self-denial, one reduces his desires to the very minimal, let us say, to the subsistence level. This philosophy is broadly defined as asceticism. Ascetics usually introduce some philosophic or religious accent into their daily life in order to enrich their "inner" happiness. Physiologically, the practice of asceticism is far from a comfortable way of life. However, many have found the practice of asceticism a meaningful life style as they receive social respect for their philosophy, knowledge, and courage to endure physical hardships. If not completely ascetic, an austere way of life has long been advocated in many Asian countries as the gentlemanly life style. For example, even today, many Japanese millionaires spend their leisure by enjoying "small pleasures" at home, such as practicing calligraphy, playing "go" (complicated oriental chess-type game), composing poems, or watching the birds. It is interesting to note that traditionally the elite group in such societies comprised royalty, politicians, and scholars, all of whom were primarily engaged in the perpetuation of past norms and/or in literary or artistic endeavors. It now seems surprising upon reflection that the social elite group that advocated such a way of life not only controlled those who were directly involved in the actual production of goods and services but also received their respect.

The point of this discussion, aside from the pros and cons of Eastern and Western culture, is that in a society where limitation of human desires is a respected way of life, it is unlikely that decision science will find an important role to play. In other words, decision science becomes important in a cultural setting where the way of life is geared toward greater control over resources to fulfill desires. Therefore, decision science is not equally applicable to a given problem in different decision environments. Analysis of decision environment in terms of reality is an important prerequisite for an effective application of decision science.

The traditional economic theory postulates an "economic man," who is "economic" and also "rational." The economic man is an "optimizer" in the Western cultural sense. He is assumed to be one who allocates his resources in the most rational manner and has the knowledge of the relevant aspects of his environment. He is also assumed to possess a stable system of preferences and the skill to analyze the alternative courses of action in order to achieve his desires. In the classical economic theory, we often assume that the concept of economic man provides the basic foundation for the theory of the firm. In other words, we often think that the decision-making process of an organization is or should be like one employed by the economic man.

Recent developments in the theory of the firm have cast considerable doubt on whether the concept of economic man can be applied to the decision maker in today's complex organizations. According to broad empirical investigation, there is no evidence that any one individual is capable of performing a completely rational analysis for complex decision problems. Also, there is considerable doubt that the individual value system is exactly identical to that of the firm in determining what is best for the organization as a whole. Furthermore, the decision maker in reality is often quite incapable of identifying the optimum choice, either because of his lack of analytical ability or because of the complexity of the organizational environment.

The concept of economic man does not sufficiently provide either a descriptive or a normative model for the decision maker in an organization. Because of the organismic limitations of the decision maker, his decision making will at best be a crude approximation of global rationality. In this context, a management theorist has suggested that in today's complex organizational environment, the decision maker is not trying to optimize, instead he tries to satisfice.

There is an abundance of evidence that suggests that the practice of decision making is affected by the epistemological assumptions of the individual who makes the decision. Indeed, the practice of scientific methodology and rational choice is not always directly applicable to decision analysis. The decision maker is constantly concerned with his environment, and he always relates possible decision outcomes and their consequences to the environment with its unique conditions. Stated differently, the decision maker is extremely conscious of the implications of the decision to his surroundings rather than simply considering isolated economic payoffs. This concern with the environmental context of the decision prompts a variety of modifications that further removes him from the "rational" behavior.

The decision maker is then, in reality, one who attempts to employ an "approximate" rationality in order to maximize the attainment of organizational goals within the given set of constraints. He may fall far short of being a completely rational man, but his decision-making behavior may at least be "intentionally" rational. If we define decision science as a rational choice process within the context of the decision maker's environmental concern and his limited knowledge, ability, and information, the paradox between the economic man and decision maker in reality becomes increasingly vague. There still remains discrepancies between the theory of rationality and realities of human life. These discrepancies, however, may provide valuable information for the analysis of human behavior in the organizational environment. Nevertheless, it is outside the scope of this introductory text of decision science.

DECISION SCIENCE AND MANAGEMENT INFORMATION SYSTEMS

As we discussed in Chapter 1, the complexity of decision problems and the high cost associated with error in today's dynamic environment are forcing management to resort to more scientific approaches for decision analysis. For such a scientific decision analysis, the manager needs information that is timely, accurate, and pertinent for decision making. An effective management system is to provide such information

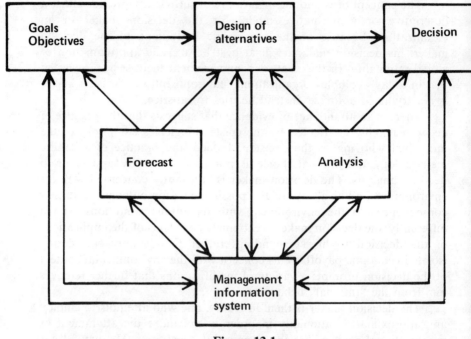

Figure 13.1
Management information system and decision analysis

to the decision maker. Figure 13.1 indicates the role of the information system in decision analysis.

Because advanced technology exists that can rapidly process quantitative information essential for managerial decisions, the role of decision science takes on a new significance. In essence, then, decision science provides much of the required information for decision analysis and such information is channeled through the management information system. Although they have different functions, both decision science and management information systems are integral factors for decision analysis. In fact, decision analysis, decision science, and management information systems are so closely interrelated that it is inconceivable to analyze one without the other two. The decision analysis is the primary function of the organization, the management information system makes that function possible, and decision science provides means to relate the two.

The process of a management information system is quite similar to that of decision science. In general, the process involves the following steps.

1. Identify the type of decisions that are being made in the organization. Analyze how these decisions are related to various organizational objectives.
2. Construct decision models by identifying decision variables, constraints or functional relationships among the variables, model parameters, and the objective function.
3. Identify data input requirements, data collection methods, and information-flow patterns.
4. Design a system of information feedback for control and updating of the decision models and the management information system.

In the above process, the second step is clearly the function of decision science. Therefore, without decision science it is impossible to design an effective management information system. It should be evident, then, that decision science is a crucial factor for the operation of any organization.

IMPLEMENTATION OF DECISION SCIENCE

In the early stages of decision science development, a practicing decision scientist had to be a super salesman as well as a competent professional. Indeed, decision science practitioners were lonely people; they were regarded by executives as "whiz kids" who talked only to each other and computers. As time has passed, however, the function of decision science has changed dramatically. Most executives and administrators now recognize its potential contributions. The "selling" of decision science, therefore, is not as hard a job as it would have been 20 years ago.

The most important phase of decision science application is the implementation of the model. Now that we have equipped ourselves with various techniques of decision science, it is appropriate to outline several phases we should follow in order to launch a successful application.

Management Participation

As described in Chapter 1, most decision science applications cut across the formal organization structure. Consequently, a successful application of decision science requires active participation on the part of top management. Sometimes top management provides verbal assurance of support to the decision analysis team but shies away from the project because they feel they are not competent enough to be directly involved. Such an attitude is deplorable and the decision science project may become a very expensive exercise.

Top management must take the initiative and responsibility to see that the right problems are analyzed and that appropriate procedures are followed to assure proper implementation. Because decision analysis is directly related to organizational objectives, active participation of top management is of paramount importance because they have better insight as to whether the project is being directed toward the overall organizational objectives rather than the interests of individual departments.

Sometimes, participation of top management is the only way to receive full cooperation from the operating manager, who is directly involved with the actual implementation of the model. Usually, the detailed information concerning variables, relationships, constraints, and work procedures that are important for the model formulation are obtained from the operating manager. Top management's participation and interest in the study determine the creditability of the model, as well as an objective analysis of the model results.

Analysis of Objectives, Goals, and Policies

Effective decision analysis obviously requires that organizational objectives should be analyzed as operational goals. It does not have any significant meaning if a firm simply presents such broad objectives as "customer satisfaction," "leadership in industry," "social responsibility," and so on. Based on a qualitative description of organizational objectives, operational goals must be established. Goals must be defined in such a way that they allow a means for quantitative self-evaluation. Moreover, relationships of the decision system under consideration must be quantitatively related to management goals.

Another important factor to be considered in the implementation of decision science is the analysis of organizational policies. It should be apparent that management goals cannot be completely specified until operating policies of the organization have been clearly determined. Indeed, management policies often are important model constraints. Hence, an incomplete analysis of operating policies often results in an unrealistic objective function and consequently misleading model outputs. Management policies not only encompass the operational aspects of the organization, but also reflect the philosophy of management concerning various exogenous and endogenous factors. For example, such considerations as social responsibilities, good citizenship, public image of the firm, stable employment level, and the like have become important policy matters in recent years. Organizations also have formal or informal policies concerning those who are directly affected by their operation—the owner, the employees, the customers, the dealers, the government, and its environmental conditions. Management policies impose restrictions not only on the determination of goals for a decision problem but also on the very nature of the decision to be made. Management policies must be clearly reflected in the model in order to derive a valid solution to the problem.

Formulating a Decision Science Model

After the decision problem is defined in terms of its goals, management policies concerning the problem, and the recognition of possible benefits of the analysis, the next step is to formulate the problem as a decision science model. Mathematical models are abstract symbolic representations of reality. It is out of place to emphasize all the benefits of mathematical models. But it must be pointed out that there are many pitfalls to be avoided in formulating the model. It should be remembered that a mathematical model is a simple representation of the problem. Therefore, the model should be a great deal simpler than reality; otherwise there would be no reason to construct the model in the first place. Decision science practitioners often take pride in formulating a model that is almost as complex and elaborate as the real-world problem. Once we heard a top executive of a firm announce at a professional meeting that the decision science group in his firm designed such a fantastic inventory model that there is only one computer in the world that has a large enough capacity to test the model. He also added that he could hardly wait to get a new computer to run the model. Now we wonder whether the executive and the decision science group are still working for the firm.

It should be clear that models must be simpler to understand and manipulate than reality. On the other hand, they should be capable of representing reality with an acceptable degree of accuracy and reliability. Fortunately, this is often possible because, although an analysis of a large number of components may be required to predict a phenomenon with perfect accuracy, a small number of components tend to account for most of the phenomenon. It is very important, therefore, to identify the right components and the correct interrelationships among them, as well as their relationships to the objective function.

Testing the Model and Solution

Decision science attempts to identify the "optimum" solution that allows the most effective achievement of organizational goals. The optimal solution is optimal only under the given model constraints and the objective function. As stated previously, since the model is only an abstract representation of the real problem, the model solution may not be the optimum for the real problem. However, as long as the model is carefully formulated to represent the problem, the solution would provide an effective guide to decision making. In order to determine the accuracy and reliability of the model the model and its solutions must be thoroughly tested. It is also important to test the model on a continuous time-interval basis so that significant changes in decision environment can be reflected in the model.

Final Implementation of the Solution

The final stage of decision science application is the actual implementation of the solution to the problem. This is, of course, the most critical phase, since this is where the benefits of the model are to be realized. In this stage, top management and operating managers play vital roles. Top management must approve the final solution after careful review, and operating managers take the responsibility of the model implementation. A continuous evaluation of the model to keep it current should also be the direct responsibility of the operating manager.

The primary function of decision scientists in this phase is to develop a general procedure to be followed in the model implementation. Also, they should assist operating personnel in an advisory capacity in analyzing the model results to see how they are related to the real operation of problems.

DECISION SCIENCE AND MANAGEMENT

The kind of picture we have drawn in this book may look rosy for decision science. In some organizations and for some decision scientists, the rosy picture may be justified. On the other hand, in some organizations things are not so rosy. In reality we often see that practicing managers and decision scientists operate as two separate groups, each with its own language, methods, and goals. Each has much to contribute to and learn from the other. C. P. Snow once observed that science and the humanities operate as two distinct cultures. This observation can be applied to the managers and decision scientists. Perhaps we need his advice; "What we need to do is humanize the scientist and simonize the humanist."

Reasons for Failure

There exists a definite gap between management practice and decision science. Clearly, decision science has contributed a great deal to the improvement of operational efficiency of many organizations. Many decision scientists, however, often tackle relatively unimportant problems with overwhelmingly sophisticated techniques, omit important decision variables in order to fit the problem to the technique, and design models that are comprehensible only to the theoreticians. In the process, decision scientists are losing their value to management. Managers, on the other hand, are not willing to base important decisions on the outcome of a process that they do not adequately understand. Furthermore, they are reluctant to learn some of the decision science techniques and change their usual way of decision making. There are many good reasons for the lack of true decision science applications in the real-world situations. C. Jackson Grayson, professor of decision science and the former chairman of the Price Commission in the federal government, lists the following reasons:

Shortage of Time

Most important decisions require immediate solution. There is not enough time to analyze the problem, collect the required data, design models, evaluate alternative courses of action, and analyze the impact of the decision. Decision scientists usually do not have the work experience to understand such time constraints. Consequently, time factors are usually left out as exogenous variables in the decision models. Managers prefer to use their own judgment rather than relying on such models.

Inaccessibility of Data

Often the required data for the decision model are inaccessible, nonexistent, or not in the form that are called for by the model. In order to develop a theoretically correct model, decision scientists insist on obtaining such data. Managers, in such instances, would simply skip the decision science study.

Resistance to Change

The typical manager does not have adequate knowledge to use decision science tools. On the other hand, he is very reluctant to change his old decision-making habits. It is not a surmountable task to educate and change the managers. Consequently, decision scientists must learn to operate within this decision environment.

Long Response Time

The decision scientists tend to approach a problem in a systematic manner, which requires considerable time. However, managers usually require a solution in a very short period of time. Consequently, managers would rather choose a "quick-and-dirty" solution rather than wait for a month to get a more rational solution. We have heard a story that a top manager was extremely unhappy with the marketing department because it took a month to compile the sales records for the preceding month. He instructed a decision scientist and a systems analyst to figure out a way to get the sales records within a day or two. Sure enough, they came up with a system and the sales records were on the manager's desk within two days. However, the computer output was so thick that it took the manager a month to read the report.

Simplifications and Assumptions

The decision science models require simplifications and assumptions. Often, models are based on such oversimplified assumptions that they no longer represent the real problem. For example, the time constraints, the data accessibility, personnel problems, bureaucratic power structures, political pressures, and the manager's priority structure for the objectives involved in the problem are often simplified out of the model altogether.

Then, what should be done to narrow the existing gap between management and decision science? C. Jackson Grayson recommends that decision scientists take an initiative in changing their work behavior. It is extremely difficult to change the work patterns of management. Furthermore, the endproduct is supposed to be management, not decision science. Decision scientists must learn to understand the real decision environment of management.

Once the president of a management-consulting firm told the following story to the audience in a professional meeting:

A recent Ph.D. in operations research was hired by a metropolitan city government. His job was to find a good location for a sewage disposal plant somewhere in one of the boroughs. A few weeks later he came to his supervisor. He had the model; he had spent an awful lot of money on computer time; and he announced "I've got the optimum location for it." When his supervisor heard "optimum" he started to duck, but thought he would listen to him anyway. Then the fellow showed how he came up with the location. Now, everybody who is high-up in any city administration (who has also got a little bit of brains and who has lasted more than six months) has an address book in his pocket, because it's great to know all the theories about public administration and city management, but before you do anything drastic, its nice to know who lives in the area that you are going to pick for the sewage disposal plant. And, by an odd coincidence, the optimum location picked was two blocks from the Chairman of the City Finance Committee's home. The supervisor suggested that that was not the "optimum" location, and this fellow got furious. He said, "I will tell you that this is the optimum location. Are you looking for a political solution or for a truthful solution?" The man who replaced the first fellow was put on that assignment and was told to find the best "workable" solution.

The above story tells us that decision scientists should know more than the analytical techniques to design the model. There have been several recent attempts to narrow the gap between management and decision science. First, there has been a rapid decentralization of decision science programs in industrial organizations. Instead of maintaining a decision science group, many firms have sprinkled decision scientists throughout the organization in situations where they can really help the organization. Many decision scientists are assigned to significant functional positions, or as aides to the top managers. They are given line responsibility for results. Another trend is the managers' demand for the decision model implementation by decision scientists. This approach would alleviate the problem of unworkable, theoretical model design on the part of decision scientists. A third trend has been a thorough on-the-job training of decision scientists about the functional, social, behavioral, and political aspects of the decision environment. It is the responsibility of management to expose decision scientists to the real-world decision environment.

In summary, nobody questions the potential contributions of decision science. The problem we face today in decision science is finding the best way to put decision science to work.

DECISION SCIENCE IN THE FUTURE

Decision science has advanced so dramatically during the past 25 years that it is at best speculation to discuss what decision science will be like in the future. But there have been several distinct movements that allow us to conjecture. These developments are in the areas of technical progress within the discipline itself, technological progress in other areas (such as computer science), and organizational impact of decision science. We shall discuss these trends in greater detail.

Technical Progress

In order to analyze the ever-increasing complexity of managerial problems, we need more sophisticated decision science techniques. Indeed, there have been several important advances made. First, several new techniques have been developed to solve complex decision problems. As we studied in Chapter 6, goal programming has been developed during the past five to ten years to solve managerial problems that involve multiple conflicting objectives. No doubt it is a significant new technique for decision science. A continuous development of new and better techniques is necessary to analyze many contemporary societal problems.

The second advance we have seen is in the expanded use of existing techniques. For example, there has been such an improvement in the efficiency of linear programming that it can be applied to a very large-scale problem involving tens of thousands of decision variables and several thousand constraints. We think a continuous refinement and expansion of existing techniques will take place in the future. This development will clearly lead to more extensive application of decision science techniques. Such development will no doubt increase the use of such tools as dynamic programming, nonlinear programming, integer programming, and various simulation methods.

A third area of advance in decision science is the development of more realistic descriptive models for managerial problems. Up until now, decision scientists have primarily engaged in the development of normative-type models. In other words, the model has been developed to get an answer that would tell the decision maker how the decision *ought to* be made. However, since the model has often been designed without the consideration of the decision maker's philosophy and other environmental aspects, the model result has found only occasional implementation. For example, suppose the decision maker has a very strong feeling toward the social responsibility of his organization. If the model yields a solution that calls for cutting off various community service activities of the organization, it will never be implemented. Many decision scientists are now attempting to design models that present satisficing results. In other words, the model incorporates most of the important environmental and philosophical aspects of the decision maker. Consequently, the model results would indicate the most satisfactory course of action within the frame of present decision process. Such a model will undoubtedly find greater acceptance as it considers the situation of how the decision *is* being made in the organization. The goal programming approach is based on this philosophy.

Technological Progress

The technical progress provides the necessary means to perform a systematic decision analysis. However, the actual applications of decision science to complex real-world problems require the use of electronic computers. The remarkable progress in computer technology, both in hardware and software areas, has allowed a greater sophistication of decision models. It is now possible to construct and solve very elaborate production, inventory, finance, scheduling, and marketing models that require a great memory capacity on the part of the computer. With the continuing inventions and innovations in computer science, the application of decision science is expected to become even a more important managerial function in the future.

Already, the time-sharing method has brought dramatic changes in decision analysis. With the convenience of a time-sharing facility, a continuous monitoring of the decision system is possible. For example, the production-inventory problem can be updated on a continuous basis without going through a periodic overhaul of the model. Also, such an access to time-sharing facility certainly provides strong incentives for the decision maker to utilize the modeling concept and decision science. With the progress we have seen in this area of computer technology, many repetitive-type operating problems may soon be analyzed by the computer. Another important advance in computer technology that has had a significant impact on the application of decision science is the standardization of various techniques in the form of "software packages." With further advances in this area, perhaps the application of the most widely used techniques may become routine.

Organizational Impact

At the beginning of the decision science application in various organizations, a decision scientist was an isolated person in the organization. He designed mathematical models whenever the need arose but remained isolated from the actual implementation and impact of the study. However, today, managerial personnel recognize the impact of decision science studies on the organization as well as on the work behavior of those directly affected by them. In large organizations, most top management personnel are involved either directly or indirectly with decision science projects. It has been the trend, therefore, that decision scientists report directly to top management. The decision science group (it may be called by various names in different organizations, such as operations research, management science, administrative analysis, managerial analysis, methods and analysis, corporate planning, and the like) has a continuous work load and inseparable work relations with various operational departments and service units (computer center, statistical records, etc.). Also, the recent trend of the decentralization of the decision science program may also result in a greater effectiveness of the decision science work.

Decision scientists are well-educated professionals with advanced degrees. They are usually specialists with narrow backgrounds. In order to play their roles effectively, they must learn the structure, functions, work methods, and behavioral aspects of the organization. Furthermore, they must be patient persuaders and advisers. In other words, the effective decision scientist must be a "specialist with a universal mind." Maybe we are asking for a superman. However, that is the type of person that is needed in today's complex decision environment.

REFERENCES

Astrom, V., "Culture, science and politics," in *The Making of Decisions: A Reader in Administrative Behavior*, W. J. Gore and J. W. Dyson (eds.), Free Press of Glencoe, London, 1964, pp. 85–92.

Boulding, K., "The specialist with a universal mind," *Management Science* **14**, No. 12 (1969), 647–653.

Churchman, C. W., Ackoff, R. L., and Arnoff, E. L., *Introduction to Operations Research*, Wiley, New York, 1958.

Grayson, C. J., Jr., "Management science and business practice," *Harvard Business Review*, (July-Aug. 1973), 41–48.

Halbrecht, H. Z., "If your students aren't marketable, what's your future?" *Decision Sciences* **4**, No. 3 (1973), xiii-xix.

Lee, S. M., *Goal Programming for Decision Analysis*, Auerbach, Philadelphia, 1972.

Magee, J. F., "Progress in the management sciences," *TIMS Interfaces* **3**, No. 2 (1973), 35–41.

McGuire, J. W., *Theories of Business Behavior*, Prentice-Hall, Englewood Cliffs, N.J., 1964.

Schubik, M., "Approaches to the study of decision-making relevant to the firm," in *The Making of Decisions: A Reader in Administrative Behavior*, W. J. Gore and J. W. Dyson (eds.), Free Press of Glencoe, London, 1964, pp. 31–50.

Simon, H. A., "A behavioral model of rational choice," *Quarterly Journal of Economics* **69**, No. 1 (1955), 99–118.

————, *Models of Man*, Wiley, New York, 1957.

————, *The New Science of Management Decision*, Harper, New York, 1960.

Wagner, H. M., *Principles of Management Science*, Prentice-Hall, Englewood Cliffs, N.J., 1970.

QUESTIONS

1. What are the three broad phases of decision science development?
2. What are some important characteristics of the maturing stage of decision science?
3. Contrast Western and Eastern ideologies concerning their respective economic approach to fulfill human desires. Are these ideologies changing? How and why?
4. Discuss the traditional concept of economic man in human organizations.
5. Is the decision maker in today's organizations basically the same as the economic man? Why or why not?
6. What is the relationship between decision science and management information systems?
7. What are some of the important factors for a successful implementation of decision science?
8. Is decision science always applicable to management problems? Why or why not?
9. Why is there a definite gap between management practice and decision science?
10. In your opinion, what should be done to narrow the gap between management practice and decision science?
11. What will be the most important technical progress of decision science you foresee in the future?
12. Do you think the electronic computer will play a greater role in decision science applications in the future? Why or why not?
13. What kind of organizational impact of decision science do you expect in the future? How should the organization resolve some of these problems?

APPENDIX I Classical Optimization

INTRODUCTION

The title of this Appendix implies that the subject matter is very old. This is, in fact, quite true. Calculus is the basic component to be presented and it dates back to Sir Isaac Newton (1642–1727) and Gottfried Leibniz (1646–1716), who are generally given credit for the invention of calculus. The concepts included here are, however, also the basis for many modern analytic solution techniques of business problems.

John von Neumann, one of the truly great scientists of the 20th century, has written*

"The calculus was the first achievement of modern mathematics, and it is difficult to overstate its importance. I think it defines more unequivocally than anything else the inception of modern mathematics ... ."

THE ESSENTIAL CONCEPT OF CLASSICAL OPTIMIZATION

The essential concept of classical optimization involves the *slope*, or rate of change, of a functional relationship. In our analysis of mathematical models of real-world systems we are most often interested in determining the optimum values of one or more *decision* variables. The

* Von Neumann, John, "The mathematician," in *The World of Mathematics*, Vol. 4, J. Newman (ed.), pp. 2053-2063.

mathematical model generally consists of decision variables and their functional relationship to some other dependent variable, such as total output, total profit, or total cost.

It is essential that we obtain a *general equation* of the *slope* of a mathematical function relating the dependent variable to the decision variables, if we are to determine the optimum solution. We can gain an intuitive understanding of this requirement by examining the following problem.

Let us assume that a production process involving one product and one resource input is to be analyzed. The objective is to maximize the dependent variable, output. The problem is to determine the optimum value of the decision variable, resource input, that will maximize output. The functional relationship of productive output to resource input is illustrated in Figure A.Ia.

We have the standard production function model of economic theory in which productive output increases as resource input increases up to a point, after which diminishing returns are experienced. Note that production output is maximized at the point where the curve (the functional relationship of output to input) stops rising and begins to fall. The *slope* of the curve at the point of maximum output is therefore *zero*. Thus, if we had a general equation of the slope, for all possible values of resource input, we could set the slope equation equal to zero and solve

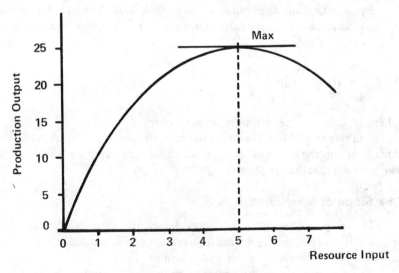

Figure A.Ia
Optimum input-output

for the input value that maximizes output. This is the essence of classical optimization.

For example, assume that the equation describing the relationship of output to input is

$$y = 10x - x^2$$

where y is output and x is input, and further assume that based on our knowledge of the above functional relationship we can determine, by some means not yet disclosed, a general equation for the slope of that functional relationship, for all possible values of x, given as follows:

$$y' = 10 - 2x$$

where y' is the slope, or rate of change in output. Now, if we set this equation for the slope equal to 0 and solve for x, we will determine the optimum value of input (x) that will maximize output (y), as follows:

$$
\begin{aligned}
10 - 2x &= 0 \\
2x &= 10 \\
x^* &= 5
\end{aligned}
$$

where x^* denotes the optimum level of input. The reader can verify that the solution technique does indeed maximize y by plotting the function $y = 10x - x^2$ for values of x ranging from 0 to 7 or 8. The high point of the curve will occur where x equals 5.

By substituting the value $x^* = 5$ back into the general model relating output to input, we can determine the optimum (maximum) level of output, as follows:

$$
\begin{aligned}
y &= 10x - x^2 \\
&= 10(5) - (5)^2 \\
y^* &= 25
\end{aligned}
$$

where y^* denotes the optimum level of output.

The purpose of this chapter is to illustrate how the general model (or equation) for the slope of a function can be determined and used in various optimization problems.

The Slope of a Function

The slope of a curve, or equivalently the rate of change of a mathematical function, is the central concept of differential calculus. Let us begin by discussing the slope of a straight line.

The slope of a straight line may be easily determined by selecting any two points along the x axis, say x_1 and x_2, and calculating the corresponding *change in y* (denoted by Δy) relative to the *change in x* (denoted by Δx). If we define the slope as b and further define y_1 and y_2 as the functional values corresponding to x_1 and x_2, respectively, then the slope is

$$b = \frac{\Delta y}{\Delta x} = \frac{y_2 - y_1}{x_2 - x_1}$$

as illustrated in Figure A.Ib.

Note that in the figure we have labeled the line $y = f(x)$, which is read "y equals a function of x," so that in Figure A.Ib, $y_1 = f(x_1)$ and $y_2 = f(x_2)$. Since $\Delta y = y_2 - y_1$, we have $\Delta y = f(x_2) - f(x_1)$. Also, since $\Delta x = x_2 - x_1$, then solving for x_2 we have $x_2 = x_1 + \Delta x$. Therefore, since $y_2 = f(x_2)$ it is also true that $y_2 = f(x_1 + \Delta x)$. Thus our formula for the slope may be written as

$$b = \frac{\Delta y}{\Delta x} = \frac{f(x_1 + \Delta x) - f(x_1)}{\Delta x}$$

The slope of the straight line, $y = f(x)$, is the same regardless of how small a change in x (Δx) we consider. The preceding equation is a general equation for the average rate of change in y relative to x. However, if we let Δx approach zero ($\Delta x \to 0$) but never quite equal zero, we obtain the *instantaneous* rate of change in y for a given value of x. This is written as

$$\underset{\Delta x \to 0}{limit} \frac{f(x_1 + \Delta x) - f(x_1)}{\Delta x} = \text{instantaneous rate of change in}$$
$$f(x) \text{ at } x = x_1$$

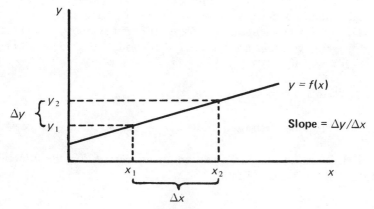

Figure A.Ib
Slope of a straight line

This is a very important point since, for a curved line, the average rate of change is not the same as the instantaneous rate of change, and it is the slope of a curve at a point that we are interested in for classical optimization. In order to determine the slope of a curve at a point, we must determine the slope of a straight line tangent to our curve at the point of interest. (A tangent is a straight line just touching the curve at one point in the portion of the curve being studied.)

By way of example, note in Figure A.Ic that as Δx becomes smaller and smaller ($\Delta x \to 0$), the straight line passing through point P pivots downward until it is tangent to the curve $f(x)$ at point P, corresponding to x_1. Therefore, the slope of our curved line at x_1 is given by the preceding slope equation for a straight line when Δx is infinitesimally small. It is, for all practical purposes, at the point $x = x_1$.

THE DERIVATIVE

The special kind of formula for slope given in the preceding section is called a *derivative*, and the process of calculating it is called differentiation. Thus, in general, the derivative of a function, $y = f(x)$, is given as

$$\lim_{\Delta x \to 0} \frac{f(x + \Delta x) - f(x)}{\Delta x} = \text{instantaneous rate of change in } f(x) \text{ for any } x$$

Again, this process obtains a *general* equation of the slope of a curve, for any point along the curve. The slope of $f(x)$ at a specific point on the curve is obtained by substituting into the slope equation the specific value of x corresponding to the point on the curve.

Derivatives are denoted by several different symbols. For example, the following symbols are all used to denote the derivatives of the function $y = f(x)$:

$$y', f'(x), f', \frac{dy}{dx}, \frac{d}{dx}f(x), D_x y, D_x f(x)$$

The symbols most often used in this text to denote the derivative will be y', $f'(x)$, and dy/dx.

Let us return to the equation given earlier for the functional relationship of output to input,

$$y = f(x) = 10x - x^2$$

The general model for the slope of this equation for any value of x is then given by determining the derivative of this function. We will first

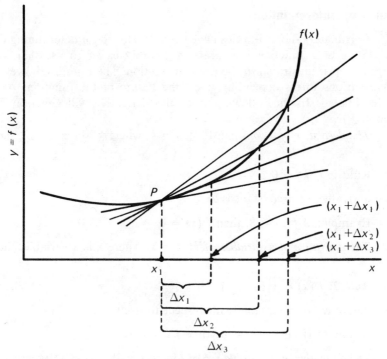

Figure A.Ic
Slope at a point on a curve

note that if $f(x) = 10x - x^2$, then $f(x + \Delta x) = 10(x + \Delta x) - (x + \Delta x)^2$. We simply substitute $(x + \Delta x)$ for x, in the equation. Therefore, we can write the derivative of our function as

$$\underset{\Delta x \to 0}{limit} \frac{f(x + \Delta x) - f(x)}{\Delta x} = \underset{\Delta x \to 0}{limit} \frac{[10(x + \Delta x) - (x + \Delta x)^2] - (10x - x^2)}{\Delta x}$$

$$= \underset{\Delta x \to 0}{limit} \frac{10\Delta x - 2x\,\Delta x - (\Delta x)^2}{\Delta x}$$

$$= \underset{\Delta x \to 0}{limit} \ 10 - 2x - \Delta x$$

and therefore as $\Delta x \to 0$, we obtain $f'(x) = 10 - 2x$.

We have obtained by differentiation the general model for the slope of the function $f(x) = 10x - x^2$, which is the same as was given without explanation in the initial optimization example. By substituting any value in for x, we obtain the slope of $f(x)$ at that point. For example, for $x = 5$, we obtain $10 - 2(5) = 0$, which, in the initial illustration, was shown graphically to be the case.

Rules of Differentiation

Fortunately short-cut rules have been developed for determining the derivative of a function that are considerably easier to use than the approach just illustrated in the previous section. The rules do, however, have various forms depending upon the nature of the function to be differentiated. In the following rules the derivative will generally be denoted by $f'(x)$.

The derivative of a constant. If $f(x) = k$, where k is a constant, then $f'(x) = 0$.

Rule 1: $f'(k) = 0$

The derivative of a constant is zero.

Example: If $f(x) = 8$, then $f'(x) = 0$.

The derivative of a variable. If $f(x) = x$, where x is a variable, then $f'(x) = 1$.

Rule 2: $f'(x) = 1$

The derivative of a variable with respect to itself is 1.

Example: If $f(x) = x = x^1$, then $f'(x) = 1$.

The derivative of a variable raised to a power. If $f(x) = x^n$, where x is a variable and n is a positive integer, then $f'(x) = nx^{n-1}$.

Rule 3: $f'(x^n) = nx^{n-1}$

The derivative of a variable raised to a positive integer power is the product of the original power times the variable raised to the original power minus one.

Example: If $f(x) = x^5$, then $f'(x) = 5x^4$.

The derivative of a constant times a function. If $f(x) = k \cdot g(x)$, where k is a constant, then $f'(x) = k \cdot g'(x)$.

Rule 4: $f'[k \cdot g(x)] = k \cdot g'(x)$

The derivative of a constant times a function is equal to the constant times the derivative of the function.

Example: If $f(x) = 7 \cdot g(x)$, then $f'(x) = 7 \cdot g'(x)$.
         If $g(x) = x^3$, then from rule 3, $g'(x) = 3x^2$,
         and therefore $f'(x) = 7(3x^2) = 21x^2$.

The derivative of the sum (or difference) of two functions. If $f(x) = g(x) + h(x)$, then $f'(x) = g'(x) + h'(x)$.

Rule 5: $f'[g(x) \pm h(x)] = g'(x) \pm h'(x)$

The derivative of the sum (or difference) of two functions is the sum (or difference) of the derivatives of the two functions.

Examples: If $f(x) = x^3 + x$, then $f'(x) = 3x^2 + 1$.
If $f(x) = x^5 - 3x^4$, then $f'(x) = 5x^4 - 12x^3$.

The derivative of the product of two functions. If $f(x) = g(x) \cdot h(x)$, then $f'(x) = g(x) \cdot h'(x) + h(x) \cdot g'(x)$.

Rule 6: $f'[g(x) \cdot h(x)] = g(x) \cdot h'(x) + h(x) \cdot g'(x)$

The derivative of the product of two functions is the product of the first function times the derivative of the second function, plus the second function times the derivative of the first function.

Example:* If $f(x) = (3x)(x^3)$, then $f'(x) = (3x)(3x^2) + (x^3)(3)$
$$= 9x^3 + 3x^3 = 12x^3$$

The derivative of the quotient of two functions. If $f(x) = g(x)/h(x)$, then $f'(x) = [h(x) \cdot g'(x) - g(x) \cdot h'(x)]/[h(x)]^2$

Rule 7: $f' \dfrac{g(x)}{h(x)} = \dfrac{h(x) \cdot g'(x) - g(x) \cdot h'(x)}{[h(x)]^2}$

The derivative of the quotient of two functions is the denominator times the derivative of the numerator minus the numerator times the derivative of the denominator all divided by the denominator squared.

Examples:* If $f(x) = \dfrac{x}{x}$, then $f'(x) = \dfrac{x \cdot 1 - x \cdot 1}{x^2} = \dfrac{x - x}{x^2} = \dfrac{0}{x^2} = 0$.

If $f(x) = \dfrac{x^4}{3x}$, then $f'(x) = \dfrac{(3x)(4x^3) - (x^4)(3)}{(3x)^2}$

$$= \dfrac{12x^4 - 3x^4}{9x^2} = \dfrac{9x^4}{9x^2} = x^2$$

If $f(x) = \dfrac{1}{x^3}$, then $f'(x) = \dfrac{x^3(0) - (1)(3x^2)}{(x^3)^2}$

$$= \dfrac{-3x^2}{x^6} = \dfrac{-3}{x^4}$$

Note that we could write $1/x^3$ as x^{-3} and use rule 3 to obtain the same answer: If $f(x) = x^{-3}$, then $f'(x) = -3x^{-4} = -3/x^4$.

* Of course the derivatives for the examples of rules 6 and 7 could have been easily determined by first computing the product (or quotient), and then differentiating the resulting function directly. However, for more complex functions, the formulas of rules 6 and 7 may be the only feasible approach.

The derivative of a function of a function (a composite function).

The chain rule: In order to demonstrate this method we will also use the notation for a derivative $f'(x) = dy/dx$, where $y = f(x)$. If $y = f(g(x))$, or $f(u)$, where $u = g(x)$, then $f'(g(x)) = f'(u) \cdot g'(x)$, more commonly given as:

Rule 8: $\dfrac{dy}{dx} = \dfrac{dy}{du} \cdot \dfrac{du}{dx}$

The derivative of the composite function $f(g(x))$ is given by setting $g(x) = u$ and differentiating $f(u)$ with respect to u, and multiplying the result by the derivative with respect to x of $g(x)$. In other words, we have

$$\frac{df(g(x))}{dx} = \frac{df(u)}{du} \cdot \frac{dg(x)}{dx}$$

Examples: If $f(g(x)) = (3x^2)^4$, then $f'(g(x)) = 4(3x^2)^3 \cdot (6x) = 648x^7$.
If $f(g(x)) = 2(3x - 5x^4)^3$, then $f'(g(x))$
$= 6(3x - 5x^4)^2 \cdot (3 - 20x^3)$.

The derivative of the exponential function. If $f(x) = e^x$, where e is the base of the natural logarithms, $2.71828 \ldots$, then $f'(x) = e^x$.

Rule 9: $f'(e^x) = e^x$

The derivative of e^x is itself. More generally, making use of rule 8, if $f(g(x)) = e^u$ where $u = g(x)$, then

$$f'(e^u) = e^u \cdot \frac{du}{dx} \quad \text{or} \quad f'(e^{g(x)}) = e^{g(x)} \cdot g'(x)$$

Examples: If $f(g(x)) = e^{5x}$, then $f'(g(x)) = e^{5x} \cdot 5 = 5e^{5x}$

If $f(g(x)) = e^{x^3}$, then $f'(g(x)) = e^{x^3} \cdot 3x^2 = 3x^2 e^{x^3}$

The derivative of the natural logarithm. If $f(x) = \ln x$, where $\ln = \log_e$, then $f'(x) = 1/x$.

Rule 10: $f'(\ln x) = \dfrac{1}{x}$

The derivative of the natural log of x is $1/x$. More generally, making use of rule 8, if $f(g(x)) = \ln u$, where $u = g(x)$, then

$$f'(\ln u) = \frac{1}{u} \cdot \frac{du}{dx} \quad \text{or} \quad f'(\ln g(x)) = \frac{1}{g(x)} \cdot g'(x)$$

Examples: If $f(g(x)) = \ln 5x$, then $f'(g(x)) = \dfrac{1}{5x} \cdot 5 = \dfrac{5}{5x} = \dfrac{1}{x}$.

If $f(g(x)) = \ln 3x^2$, then $f'(g(x)) = \dfrac{1}{3x^2} \cdot 6x = \dfrac{2}{x}$.

Higher-Order Derivatives

It has been shown that when we differentiate a function we obtain another function. It is reasonable, therefore, to assume that we could also differentiate the function that is the derivative of our initial function. For example, when we differentiate $f(x) = 10x - x^2$ we obtain $f'(x) = 10 - 2x$, which is the general model for the slope or rate of change of $f(x)$. If we differentiate $f'(x)$ we obtain $f''(x) = -2$, which is the rate of change in $f'(x)$. We can, in fact, carry the process of successive differentiation out as far as desired as long as there remains some function to differentiate. We denote first, second, third, and higher derivatives by $f'(x), f''(x), f'''(x)$, and so on, or by $f^{(iv)}(x), f^{(v)}(x)$, and so on.

By way of example, let us consider the "green monster" high-powered dragster. The vehicle contains enough fuel to operate 11 seconds and must travel 1/4 mile (1320 ft). Assume that its distance traveled, d ft, from the starting point after t seconds is given by the equation $d = t^3$. We can then determine the vehicle's speed (velocity) at any point in time after leaving the starting line by differentiating $d = t^3$ to obtain the general model for rate of change, which is $d' = 3t^2$. Likewise, the acceleration of the dragster at any point in time after starting is the second derivative of $d = t^3$, which is obtained by differentiating $d' = 3t^2$ to yield $d'' = 6t$.

The distance traveled, the instantaneous speed, and the acceleration after t seconds from the starting point are given in Table A.Ia.

Therefore, just as the vehicle passed the 1/4-mile point (very close to 11 seconds after starting) it would be traveling at a speed of about 361 ft/sec (or 246 miles/hr) and it would be accelerating at a rate of about 65.8 ft/sec (or 44.87 miles/hr).

We shall see in the following section that the second derivative is

Table A.Ia
Distance, Speed, and Acceleration

Seconds from Start	Distance Traveled (ft) $d = t^3$	Speed (ft/sec) $d' = 3t^2$	Acceleration (ft/sec^2) $d'' = 6t$
1	1	3	6
4	64	48	24
7	343	147	42
10	1000	300	60
10.97	1320	361	65.8
11	1331	363	66

also valuable for determining whether we have calculated a maximum or a minimum, when we set the slope equation equal to zero to solve for the optimum value of the decision variable. For more complex functions, higher than second derivatives may be used to determine whether a maximum or a minimum has been found.

MAXIMA AND MINIMA

We are now to the point in our discussion of calculus in which we can get back to some practical aspects. The objective of our using differential calculus is to determine maximum and minimum values of some function. Consider the function illustrated in Figure A.Id.

The figure illustrates a function of one variable, x. Also illustrated are several new terms. The *domain* is the range of values of x in which we are interested. The value of the function for the lower limit of the domain of x is given by A, whereas the value of the function for the upper limit of the domain of x is given by G. (Sometimes these are referred to as *endpoints*.) The domain limits (or endpoints) fall in a general category called *stationary* (or *critical*) points.

Some points other than endpoints are also stationary (critical) points. The requirement for a point (other than an endpoint) on $f(x)$ to be a stationary point is that the first derivative of the function is equal to zero at that point; that is, $f'(x) = 0$. All of the points B through F satisfy this condition. Two subsets of the stationary-point category are:

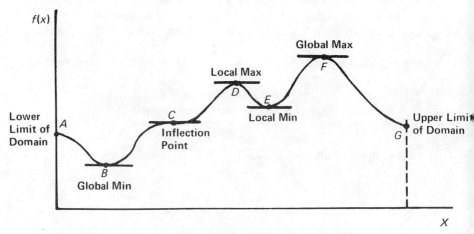

Figure A.Id
Maxima and minima

inflection points and *extreme points*. Extrema are further identified as either *local* or *global* extrema. In our analysis it is global extrema (or *absolute* extrema) that are of primary interest. Finally, an extreme point is either a *maximum* or a *minimum*.

In profit maximization we would generally attempt to determine the global "max," whereas in cost minimization the global "min" is of interest. It is important to point out that the global max or min of a function could be located at the lower or upper limits of the domain of the decision variable. In the illustration, however, this is not the case.

A *necessary condition* for identifying a stationary point, other than an endpoint, is to calculate the first derivative of the function, equate the first derivative to zero, and solve for the unknown (in this case x). As was previously pointed out, this is also a necessary condition for determining the extrema of a function; that is,

$$f'(x) = 0 \qquad \text{for } x = x^*$$

where x^* is defined as a value of x for which we have an extremum. Determining whether we have a relative max, a relative min, or a point of inflection requires further differentiation. Note that a *relative* max (min) simply indicates that it may be *either* a local or a global max (min).

A *sufficient condition* for x^* to be a relative *minimum* is

$$f''(x) > 0 \qquad \text{at } x = x^*$$

That is, the second derivation evaluated for the value x^* must be greater than zero. Likewise, a sufficient condition for x^* to be a relative *maximum* is

$$f''(x) < 0 \qquad \text{at } x = x^*$$

That is, the second derivative evaluated for the value x^* must be less than zero.

For the case in which the second derivative is equal to zero, that is, $f''(x) = 0$, it *generally* indicates a point of inflection. However, it may be necessary to examine higher derivatives. The general procedure for this case is as follows: Find the value of the lowest-order derivative that is *not* zero evaluated at x^*. If the *order* of the lowest-order nonzero derivative is even, the second-order derivative rules apply. If the order of the lowest-order nonzero derivative is odd, the critical point is an inflection point.

The preceding discussion is summarized in its simplest form in Figure A.Ie. Note that differentiation will *not* identify endpoints as extrema; only by comparison with other extrema can they be identified as local or global max (or min).

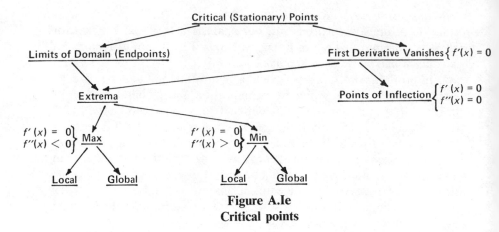

Figure A.Ie
Critical points

For a hypothetical function of the type illustrated in Figure A.If, with multiple critical points, it is necessary to compare the value of the function for the various extrema (including the limits of the domain) in order to determine the global (or absolute) max and min.

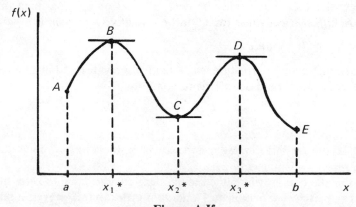

Figure A.If
Identification of extrema

In summary, let us say that we wish to determine the absolute (global) maximum and minimum for the function $y = f(x)$ in which the domain of x is given as: $a \leq x \leq b$.

I.   *Necessary Conditions*
      1. Calculate the equation for the first derivative [compute $f'(x)$].
      2. Set the first derivative equation equal to zero [set $f'(x) = 0$].
      3. Solve the equation of step 2 for x^* [solve $f'(x) = 0$].

II. *Sufficient Conditions*
1. Calculate the equation for the second derivative [compute $f''(x)$].
2. Determine the value of the second derivative for x^* [evaluate $f''(x^*)$].
3. If $f''(x^*)$ is negative, we have a relative maximum at x^*.
   If $f''(x^*)$ is positive, we have a relative minimum at x^*.
   If $f''(x^*)$ is equal to zero, we generally have a point of inflection.

III. *Determine Global Max and Min*
1. Substitute the value of x^* into the original equation [determine $f(x^*)$]; that is, solve for the value of y at $x = x^*$.
2. Substitute the value of a and b into the original equation [determine $f(a)$ and $f(b)$].
3. Compare all maxima to determine global max.
   Compare all minima to determine global min.

For the function illustrated in Figure A.If, we would obtain three values for x^* in step 3 of part I (for points B, C, and D on the function). There would then be two cases in which step 3 of part II would yield a negative value, and one case yielding a positive, since $f''(x_1^*) < 0$, $f''(x_3^*) < 0$, $f''(x_2^*) > 0$. Thus, we would have two relative maxima (points B and D) and one relative minimum (point C). Then, by substituting a, x_1^*, x_2^*, x_3^*, and b into $f(x)$ (to obtain the values for A, B, C, D, and E), we could determine the global max and min by inspection.

Some further discussion regarding the nature of functions often found in business problems is warranted at this point. It becomes much easier to deal with the problem of determining maximum or minimum values where the functions are either concave or convex. Both types of functions are illustrated in Figure A.Ig.

A function is said to be convex if a straight line connecting any two points on that function will fall entirely above the function (the dotted line in the figure). A function is said to be concave if a straight line connecting any two points on that function will fall entirely below the function.

If it is known that one has a convex function, the first derivative set equal to zero must yield at least a local minimum. The limit of the domain may still be the absolute min. Likewise, if it is known that one has a concave function, the first derivative set equal to zero must yield a local maximum.

For most cases in business analysis the function is assumed to be either concave or convex. Therefore, the most common problem in business will involve computing the first derivative, equating it to zero,

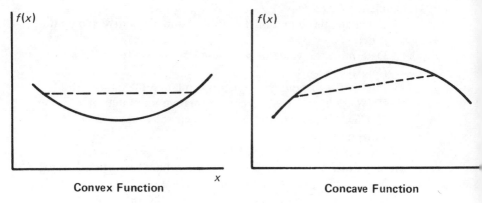

Figure A.Ig
Convex and concave functions

and solving for the extrema, and computing the second derivative and evaluating for the value of x^* to determine whether we have a max or a min. Although the optimum generally does not occur at a limit of the domain for unconstrained optimization problems, when we begin to analyze constrained optimization, the optimum is very likely to occur at the intersection of the objective function and a constraint, which is actually the redefined limit of the domain (endpoint) for our function being optimized.

Consider the following example of a problem in profit maximization. The profit model is

$$\Pi = f(TR,TC)$$
$$= TR - TC$$

where

Π = total profit
TR = total revenue
TC = total cost

Total revenue is assumed to be a function of price and quantity sold, as follows:

$$TR = f(P,Q)$$
$$= P{\cdot}Q$$

where P is price and Q is quantity sold. Total cost is assumed to be a function of fixed cost, variable cost, and quantity, as follows:

$$TC = f(FC,VC,Q)$$
$$= FC + VC{\cdot}Q$$

where

    FC = fixed cost
    VC = variable cost per unit
    Q = quantity sold

In addition, quantity sold is assumed to be a linear function of price (demand function), as follows:

$$Q = f(P)$$
$$= a - b \cdot P$$

where P is price and a and b are both positive parameters of the function (see graph). Figure A.Ih illustrates the assumed demand function. Thus we can substitute $a - b \cdot P$ back into the total revenue and total cost functions where Q appears, as follows:

$$TR = P \cdot Q$$
$$= P(a - b \cdot P)$$
$$= aP - b \cdot P^2$$
$$TC = FC + VC \cdot Q$$
$$= FC + VC(a - b \cdot P)$$
$$= FC + a \cdot VC - b \cdot P \cdot VC$$

Substituting back into our original profit equation, we have

$$\Pi = TR - TC$$
$$= (a \cdot P - b \cdot P^2) - (FC + a \cdot VC - b \cdot P \cdot VC)$$
$$= a \cdot P - b \cdot P^2 - FC - a \cdot VC + b \cdot P \cdot VC$$

Note that we now have the profit equation in terms of one decision

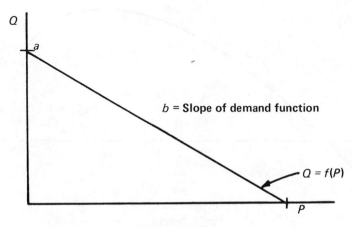

Figure A.Ih
Demand function

variable, price. This functional relationship is illustrated in Figure A.Ii.

We can now determine the optimum price to charge using our knowledge of calculus, as follows:

1 First derivative: $\dfrac{d\Pi}{dP} = a - 2b{\cdot}P + b{\cdot}VC$

2 Set equal to zero: $a - 2b{\cdot}P + b{\cdot}VC = 0$

3 Solve for P: $2b{\cdot}P = a + b{\cdot}VC$

$$P = \frac{a + b{\cdot}VC}{2b}$$

4 Second derivative: $\dfrac{d^2\Pi}{dP^2} = -2b$

5 Since $\dfrac{d^2\Pi}{dP^2} < 0$, we have a max.

Therefore, the optimum price to charge is $(a + b{\cdot}VC)/2b$ in order to maximize total profits (Π).

To take a specific example, let us assume the following:

Demand function: $Q = 10 - 2P$
Fixed Costs: $FC = \$1$
Variable Costs: $VC = \$3$ per unit

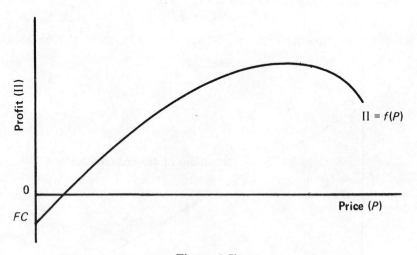

Figure A.Ii
Profit function

Thus, in our model we have

$$P = \frac{10 + 2(3)}{2(2)}$$

$$P^* = \$4.00$$

Note that we could have used the given values from the beginning, as follows:

$$\Pi = TR - TC$$
$$= P{\cdot}Q - FC - VC{\cdot}Q$$
$$= P(10 - 2P) - 1 - 3(10 - 2P)$$
$$= 10{\cdot}P - 2P^2 - 1 - 30 + 6P$$
$$= -2P^2 + 16P - 31$$

Differentiating and setting equal to zero, we have

$$\frac{d\Pi}{dP} = -4P + 16 = 0$$

or

$$P^* = 4$$

Note that fixed costs do not affect the answer. It is the *change* in profits relative to *change* in price that is important.

We can also determine the optimum value for quantity to be sold, and the maximum profit:

$$Q = 10 - 2P$$
$$= 10 - 2(4)$$
$$Q^{*,} = 2 \text{ units}$$
$$\Pi = P{\cdot}Q - FC - VC{\cdot}Q$$
$$= (4)(2) - 1 - (3)(2)$$
$$\Pi^* = \$1$$

The solution for profit might be in thousands or millions of dollars rather than simple units.

We have managed to convert the profit equation from a function of two variables into a function of one variable to determine the optimum solution. This, however, is not always possible. Advanced topics in optimization, such as partial differentiation, Lagrange multipliers, and nonlinear programming, are addressed to these problems. These topics are, however, beyond the desired scope of this text.

II Computer-Based
Solution of Linear Programming

SETTING UP THE LINEAR PROGRAM FOR THE COMPUTER

For illustrative purposes, let us consider the television manufacturing problem we discussed in Chapters 4 and 5:

$$\text{Maximize} \quad Z = \$100X_1 + \$80X_2$$
$$\text{subject to} \quad 2X_1 + 4X_2 \leq 80$$
$$3X_1 + X_2 \leq 60$$

The Objective Function

The program is designed to solve the minimization problem of linear programming. Therefore, if the problem is a maximization problem, it should be transformed to a minimization problem by multiplying the objective function by -1. The above problem is a maximization problem; thus, the objective function must be transformed to

$$\text{Minimize} \quad Z = -\$100X_1 - \$80X_2$$

Constraints

By following the usual simplex procedure, convert all constraints to equations by introducing slack variables and/or artificial variables. As was discussed in Chapter 5, the following procedure should be used:

1. Add a slack variable to a constraint containing "$\leq$."
2. Subtract a slack (surplus) variable and add an artificial variable to a constraint containing "$\geq$."

3. Add an artificial variable to a constraint containing "$=$."

In our example, the two constraints are both less-than-or-equal-to types. Therefore, they can be converted to equations as follows:

$$2X_1 + 4X_2 + X_3 = 80$$
$$3X_1 + X_2 + X_4 = 60$$

where X_3 is the slack variable for the first constraint and X_4 is the slack variable for the second constraint.

The New Objective Function

Now that we have introduced slack variables in the constraints, the objective function must include these slack variables. Thus, our objective function becomes:

$$\text{Minimize} \quad Z = -\$100X_1 - \$80X_2 + 0X_3 + 0X_4$$

Rearrangement of Constraints

We must rearrange the constraint equations in such a manner that the identity matrix (slack variables with $+1$ coefficients) comes first, followed by decision variables, and then surplus variables (slack variables with -1 coefficient). This rearrangement also applies to the objective function. Our example problem will have the following tableau:

C_j			0	0	-100	-80
	v	rhs	X_3	X_4	X_1	X_2
0	X_3	80	1	0	2	4
0	X_4	60	0	1	3	1

Treatment of Artificial Variables

If there are artificial variables in the problem, they should be assigned a very large positive value in the objective function. For example, if our problem has one more constraint, $X_1 + X_2 \geq 20$, it should be converted to

$$X_1 + X_2 - X_5 + X_6 = 20$$

where X_5 is a surplus variable and X_6 is an artificial variable. Thus, the objective function becomes

$$\text{Minimize} \quad Z = -\$100X_1 - 80X_2 + 0X_3 + 0X_4 + 0X_5 + 1000X_6$$

It is recommended that a physical rearrangement of constraints be made such that less-than-or-equal-to constraints come first, followed by greater-than-or-equal-to constraints, and finally exactly-equal-to constraints. For data input, constraints should be rearranged in such a manner that the identity matrix comes first (slack variables with $+1$ coefficients, then any artificial variables), followed by decision variables, then any surplus variables (slack variables with -1 coefficients). Also, the objective function should be arranged in the same column order. Suppose that our problem has the following model:

Minimize $Z = -\$100X_1 - \$80X_2 + \$0X_3 + \$0X_4 + \$0X_5 + 1000X_6$
subject to $2X_1 + 4X_2 + X_3 = 80$
$3X_1 + X_2 + X_4 = 60$
$X_1 + X_2 - X_5 + X_6 = 20$

Then, the rearranged format will be

C_j			0	0	1000	-100	-80	0
	v	rhs	X_3	X_4	X_6	X_1	X_2	X_5
0	X_3	80	1	0	0	2	4	0
0	X_4	60	0	1	0	3	1	0
1000	X_6	20	0	0	1	1	1	-1

PREPARING INPUT DATA CARDS

Title and Control Card

Columns	Description
1- 6	Alphanumeric problem label
11-13	Number of rows in initial solution (number of constraints)
14-16	Total number of variables in the problem (including all slack, decision, artificial, and surplus variables)
19	An integer (one) must appear here *at all times*
20-22	Number of decision variables
23-25	Problem type classification (minimization = -1, maximization = 1)
26-28	Sensitivity analysis (yes = 1, no = -1)
29-31	Number of $\leq$ type constraints

Example

We give here the set-up for our original example problem:

Maximize $\quad Z = \$100X_1 + \$80X_2 + \$0X_3 + \$0X_4$

subject to $\quad 2X_1 + 4X_2 + X_3 = 80$

$\qquad\qquad 3X_1 + X_2 + X_4 = 60$

Col.	6	13	16	19	22	25	28	31
EXAMPL	2	4	1	2	1	1	2	

Subscript Values of the Variables in the Initial Solution

List in row order the subscript values of the variables in the initial solution. A maximum of 26 values per card can be listed in integer fields of I3. Do not use columns 79 or 80.

Example

Col.	3	6
	3	4

The rhs Column

The right-hand-side (rhs) values of the constraints should be listed in floating-point fields of F11.3. A maximum of seven rhs values can be listed per card. Do not use columns 78, 79, or 80.

Example

Col.	11	22
	80.0	60.0

Contribution Coefficients

The contribution coefficients are the values assigned to the variables in the objective function. They should be listed in column order as determined in the revised function. A maximum of seven values can be listed in floating-point fields of F11.3. Do not use columns 78, 79, or 80.

Example

Col.	11	22	33	44
	0.0	0.0	−100.0	−80.0

Column Subscripts

Subscripts of the model variables should be listed in column order as determined in the revised constraint equations. A maximum of 26 values per card can be listed in integer fields of I3. Do not use columns 79 or 80.

Example

Col.	3	6	9	12
	3	4	1	2

Technological Coefficients

Technological coefficients of the problem are to be listed by row with a maximum of seven values per card in floating-point fields of F11.3, excluding columns 78, 79, or 80. Each new row must be punched on a new card.

Example

Col.	11	22	33	44
	1.0	0.0	2.0	4.0

	0.0	1.0	3.0	1.0

The number of input data cards will vary according to the nature of the given problem. However, by following the structure outlined here, the user can prepare acceptable data decks for any size problem. In addition, the user can process multiple data sets by stacking data sets behind each other. The problem will operate on each set until all the data have been exhausted.

The Final Card

The last card following the data decks must be a blank card.

ANALYSIS OF THE COMPUTER OUTPUT

The computer solution of linear programming (SIMPLP) provides the following output: the complete simplex solution on the iteration-by-iteration basis, the final solution listing, and sensitivity analysis.

The Simplex Solution

The computer program prints out the simplex solution through an iterative procedure. For our example, the simplex solution appears as follows:

ITERATION 0

C(I)	Basis	B(I)	C(J) = 0.000 X(3)	0.000 X(4)	−100.000 X(1)	−80.000 X(2)
0.00	X(3)	80.000	1.000	0.000	2.000	4.000
0.00	X(4)	60.000	0.000	1.000	3.000	1.000
	Z(J)	0.000	0.000	0.000	0.000	0.000
	Z(J) − C(J)		0.000	0.000	100.000	80.000

ITERATION 1

C(I)	Basis	B(I)	C(J) = 0.000 X(3)	0.000 X(4)	−100.000 X(1)	−80.000 X(2)
0.00	X(3)	40.00	1.000	−0.667	0.000	3.333
−100.00	X(1)	20.00	0.000	0.333	1.000	0.333
	Z(J)	−2000.00	0.000	−33.333	−100.000	−33.333
	Z(J) − C(J)		0.000	−33.333	0.000	46.667

ITERATION 2

C(I)	Basis	B(I)	C(J) 0.000 X(3)	0.000 X(4)	−100.000 X(1)	−80.000 X(2)
−80.00	X(2)	12.000	0.300	−0.200	0.000	1.000
−100.00	X(1)	16.000	−0.100	0.400	1.000	0.000
	Z(J)	−2560.000	−14.000	−24.000	−100.000	−80.000
	Z(J) − C(J)		−14.000	−24.000	0.000	0.000

OPTIMAL SOLUTION FOUND

Note: In this printout, "basis" is the same as v in the simplex tableau, B(I) is the same as rhs in the simplex tableau, and C(I) is the same as C_j in the simplex tableau.

The Final Solution

The final solution of the problem can be easily identified from the iteration 2 tableau. However, the computer program specifies the final solution as below:

```
***** FINAL SOLUTION *****
VARIABLE NO.                    VALUE
     X(2)                       12.000
     X(1)                       16.000
     Z =                        2560.000
```

The Sensitivity Analysis

The program performs the sensitivity analysis from the final simplex tableau. For our example, the following printout will result:

```
***** LP SENSITIVITY ANALYSIS *****
RIGHT-HAND-SIDE RANGING
```

CONSTRAINT NO.	LL	B(I)	UL
1	40.00	80.00	240.00
2	20.00	60.00	120.00

BASIS VARIABLE COEFFICIENT RANGING

VARIABLE NO.	LL	C(J)	UL
X(2)	33.33	80.00	200.00
X(1)	40.00	100.00	240.00

NON-BASIS VARIABLE COEFFICIENT RANGING

VARIABLE NO.	LL	C(J)	UL

Notes

1. The right-hand-side ranging is calculated from the final simplex tableau by the following procedure:

BASIS	*B(I)*	*X*(3)		
X(2)	12.000	0.300	12/ 0.3 = (40);	12/−0.3 = −40
X(1)	16.000	−0.100	16/−0.1 = −160 ;	16/ 0.1 =(160)

The smallest nonnegative value derived for the rhs/coefficient indicates the lower limit distance from the given rhs value (80 hours in assembly line 1). The smallest nonnegative value derived above is 40. Therefore, $80 - 40 = 40$ provides the lower limit of the range within which the solution mix (X_2 and X_1 in the solution basis) and the shadow price of \$14 for S_1 (X_3) do not change. The upper limit can be determined by finding the smallest nonnegative value when the rhs values are divided by the coefficients times (-1). This value is 160. Hence, $80 + 160 = 240$ provides the upper limit. The same procedure can be applied to the second assembly line (the X_4 column in the final simplex tableau).

2. The basis variable coefficient ranging is also calculated by a similar procedure. However, this procedure is based on the dual solution of the problem. From the final simplex tableau of the primal problem, we can evaluate the range in the following manner:

		Coefficient	
Column	$Z(J) - C(J)$	*in X(2) row*	
X(3)	-14	0.300	$-14/\ 0.3 = -46.67;$
X(4)	-24	-0.200	$-24/-0.2 = \boxed{120.00};$
			$-14/-0.3 = \boxed{46.67}$
			$-24/\ 0.2 = -120.00$

This time, the upper limit is found when the smallest nonnegative value is added to the original C_j (\$80 for X_2). Therefore, the upper limit will be $80 + 120 = 200$. The lower limit is found by dividing the $Z_j - C_j$ value by -1 times the coefficients and substracting the smallest nonnegative value from the C_j. Consequently, it is $80 - 46.67 = 33.33$. The solution mix would not change as long as the unit profit for X_2 is within this range. The same approach can be applied to C_j of X_1.

3. The nonbasis variable coefficient ranging can be performed in the same manner. In our problem, however, there are no nonbasis decision variables, since both decision variables are in the solution base.

```
      DIMENSION CNVP(10),CNVN(10),CJJP(10)                              LP=  10
      DIMENSION CI(10),NI(10),B(10),CJ(20),A(10,20),Z(20),ZC(20),NXJ(20) LP=  15
      DIMENSION NXI(20)                                                 LP=  20
      DIMENSION RHSP(10),RHSN(10),RHS(10)                               LP=  25
      DIMENSION BX(10),UL(10),SL(10)                                    LP=  30
      DIMENSION COFP(10),COFN(10),CUL(10),CLL(10),CJP(10)               LP=  35
      DIMENSION COFF(10)                                                LP=  40
    1 READ(5,61) PROB,PR,M,N,KODE,MN,PTYPE,NN,NS                        LP=  45
      IF(KODE)4,580,4                                                   LP=  50
    4 IF(MN)6,8,6                                                       LP=  55
    8 WRITE(6,10)                                                       LP=  60
   10 FORMAT('1','*** DATA ERROR ***')                                 LP=  65
      GO TO 580                                                        LP=  70
    6 READ(5,62)(NXI(I),I=1,M)                                          LP=  75
      READ(5,63)(B(I),I=1,M)                                            LP=  80
      READ(5,63)(CJ(J),J=1,N)                                           LP=  85
      READ(5,62)(NXJ(J),J=1,N)                                          LP=  90
      DO 5 I=1,M                                                        LP=  95
    5 BX(I)=B(I)                                                        LP= 100
      DO 7 I=1,M                                                        LP= 105
    7 READ(5,63)(A(I,J),J=1,N)                                          LP= 110
      DO 15 I=1,M                                                       LP= 115
      DO 15 J=1,N                                                       LP= 120
      IF (NXI(I)-NXJ(J)) 15,14,15                                       LP= 125
   14 CI(I)=CJ(J)                                                       LP= 130
   15 CONTINUE                                                          LP= 135
      ITER=0                                                            LP= 140
   21 DO 25 J=1,N                                                       LP= 145
      Z(J)=0.0                                                          LP= 150
      DO 24 I=1,M                                                       LP= 155
   24 Z(J)=Z(J)+CI(I)*A(I,J)                                            LP= 160
   25 ZC(J)=Z(J)-CJ(J)                                                  LP= 165
```

516

```
        OBJ=0.0
        DO 28 I=1,M
 28     OBJ=OBJ+CI(I)*B(I)
        WRITE(6,64)PROB,PR,ITER
        N1=1
        N2=10
 43     IF (N2-N) 45,45,44
 44     N2=N
 45     WRITE(6,65)(CJ(J),J=N1,N2)
        WRITE(6,66)(NXJ(J),J=N1,N2)
        WRITE(6,70)
        DO 48 I=1,M
 48     WRITE(6,67)CI(I),NXI(I),B(I),(A(I,J),J=N1,N2)
        WRITE(6,68)OBJ,(Z(J),J=N1,N2)
        WRITE(6,69)(ZC(J),J=N1,N2)
        IF(N2-N) 52,55,55
 52     N1=N1+10
        N2=N2+10
        GO TO 43
 55     CONTINUE
        ITER=ITER+1
        ZCM=ZC(1)
        JM=1
        DO 109 J=2,N
        IF (KODE) 106,105,106
105     IF (ZC(J)-ZCM) 107,109,109
106     IF (ZC(J)-ZCM) 109,109,107
107     ZCM=ZC(J)
        JM=J
109     CONTINUE
        IF (KODE) 122,121,122
121     IF (ZCM) 131,123,123
```

LP= 170
LP= 175
LP= 180
LP= 185
LP= 190
LP= 195
LP= 200
LP= 205
LP= 210
LP= 215
LP= 220
LP= 225
LP= 230
LP= 235
LP= 240
LP= 245
LP= 250
LP= 255
LP= 260
LP= 265
LP= 270
LP= 275
LP= 280
LP= 285
LP= 290
LP= 295
LP= 300
LP= 305
LP= 310
LP= 315
LP= 320
LP= 325

517

```
122     IF (ZCM) 123,123,131                                              LP=  330
123     MMN=M+MN; MO=M+1                                                  LP=  335
        IF(M.EQ.NS)GO TO 116                                              LP=  340
        DO 201 I=1,M                                                      LP=  345
        MXN=NS+1                                                          LP=  350
        DO 202 J=MXN,M                                                    LP=  355
        IF(NXI(I).EQ.NXJ(J)) GO TO 180                                    LP=  360
202     CONTINUE                                                          LP=  365
201     CONTINUE                                                          LP=  370
116     DO 194 K=MO,MMN                                                   LP=  375
        DO 192 I=1,M                                                      LP=  380
        IF(NXJ(K).EQ.NXI(I))GO TO 194                                     LP=  385
192     CONTINUE                                                          LP=  390
        IF(ZC(K).EQ.0.0)GO TO 196                                         LP=  395
194     CONTINUE                                                          LP=  400
        GO TO 124                                                         LP=  405
196     WRITE(6,197)                                                      LP=  410
197     FORMAT('-',5X,'ALTERNATE OPTIMAL SOLUTIONS EXIST')                LP=  415
124     WRITE(6,71)                                                       LP=  420
        DO 999 I=1,M                                                      LP=  425
        IF(B(I).NE.0.0) GO TO 999                                         LP=  430
        WRITE(6,998)                                                      LP=  435
998     FORMAT('+',28X,'--DEGENERATE SOLUTION')                          LP=  440
        GO TO 888                                                         LP=  445
999     CONTINUE                                                          LP=  450
888     IF(NN)204,126,204                                                 LP=  455
126     WRITE(6,127)                                                      LP=  460
127     FORMAT('-','*** DATA ERROR *** SENSITIVITY ANALYSIS (COL. 26-28,  LP=  465
       *DATA CARD #1)  CODE: -1=NO , 1=YES ')                            LP=  470
204     WRITE(6,73)                                                       LP=  475
73      FORMAT(1H1///)                                                    LP=  480
205     WRITE(6,206)                                                      LP=  485
```

```
206   FORMAT(' ',5X,'***** FINAL SOLUTION *****')                      LP=  490
      WRITE(6,207)                                                     LP=  495
207   FORMAT('-','   VARIABLE NO.',9X,'VALUE')                         LP=  500
      DO 210 I=1,M                                                     LP=  505
      WRITE(6,208)NXI(I),B(I)                                          LP=  510
208   FORMAT('0',2X,'X(',I2,')',11X,F10.3)                             LP=  515
210   CONTINUE                                                         LP=  520
      OBJP=ABS(OBJ)                                                    LP=  525
      WRITE(6,212)OBJP                                                 LP=  530
212   FORMAT(' ',5X,'Z =',10X,F10.3)                                   LP=  535
      IF(NN)128,128,280                                                LP=  540
128   GO TO 1                                                          LP=  545
180   WRITE(6,181)                                                     LP=  550
181   FORMAT('-',10X,'INFEASABLE SOLUTION')                            LP=  555
      WRITE(6,182)                                                     LP=  560
182   FORMAT('1')                                                      LP=  565
      GO TO 128                                                        LP=  570
131   XM=1.0E38                                                        LP=  575
      IM=0                                                             LP=  580
      DO 139 I=1,M                                                     LP=  585
      IF (A(I,JM)) 139,139,135                                         LP=  590
135   XX=B(I)/A(I,JM)                                                  LP=  595
      IF (XX-XM) 137,139,139                                           LP=  600
137   XM=XX                                                            LP=  605
      IM=I                                                             LP=  610
139   CONTINUE                                                         LP=  615
      IF (IM) 141,141,151                                              LP=  620
141   WRITE(6,72)                                                      LP=  625
      GO TO 1                                                          LP=  630
151   XX=A(IM,JM)                                                      LP=  635
      B(IM)=B(IM)/XX                                                   LP=  640
      DO 154 J=1,N                                                     LP=  645
```

519

```
154   A(IM,J)=A(IM,J)/XX                                                        LP= 650
      DO 161 I=1,M                                                              LP= 655
      IF (I-IM) 157,161,157                                                     LP= 660
157   XX=A(I,JM)                                                                LP= 665
      B(I)=B(I)-XX*B(IM)                                                        LP= 670
      DO 160 J=1,N                                                              LP= 675
160   A(I,J)=A(I,J)-XX*A(IM,J)                                                  LP= 680
161   CONTINUE                                                                  LP= 685
      CI(IM)=CJ(JM)                                                             LP= 690
      NXI(IM)=NXJ(JM)                                                           LP= 695
      GO TO 21                                                                  LP= 700
61    FORMAT(2A4,2X,7(I3))                                                      LP= 705
62    FORMAT(26I3,2X)                                                           LP= 710
63    FORMAT(7F11.3,3X)                                                         LP= 715
64    FORMAT(///' PROBLEM ',2A4,8X,'ITERATION',I3//)                           LP= 720
65    FORMAT(20X,'C(J)',1X,'=',1X,10F10.3 )                                     LP= 725
66    FORMAT('5X,'C(I)',2X,'BASIS',5X,'B(I)',3X,10(6H   X(I2,2H) )              LP= 730
57    FORMAT(1X,F8.2,1X,3H X(I2,1H), F10.3, 1X, 10F10.3)                        LP= 735
68    FORMAT(/11X,'Z(J)',1X,F10.3,1X,10F10.3)                                   LP= 740
69    FORMAT( 8X,'Z(J)-C(J)',10X,10F10.3 )                                      LP= 745
70    FORMAT(1H )                                                               LP= 750
71    FORMAT(///2X'OPTIMAL SOLUTION FOUND')                                     LP= 755
72    FORMAT(19H UNBOUNDED SOLUTION/19X,1H )                                    LP= 760
      *******RIGHT HAND SIDE RANGING                                           LP= 765
                                                                               LP= 770
      VARIABLE ID.                                                             LP= 775
      RHS(J) = INITIAL COMPUTED VALUE                                          LP= 780
      RHSP(J) = POSITIVE RHS(J) VALUES                                         LP= 785
      RHSN(J) = NEGATIVE RHS(J) VALUES                                         LP= 790
      RHSUP = SMALLEST POSITIVE VALUE SELECTED FROM RHSP(J),S                  LP= 795
      RHSLL = SMALLEST NEGATIVE VALUE SELECTED FROM RHSN(J),S                  LP= 800
      BX(J) = INITIAL TABLEAU RHS VALUES                                       LP= 805
```

520

```
C        UL(K) = COMPUTED UPPER LIMIT                                    LP= 810
C        SL(K) = COMPUTED LOWER LIMIT                                    LP= 815
C                                                                        LP= 820
280      WRITE(6,281)                                                    LP= 825
281      FORMAT('1',20X,'***** LP SENSITIVITY ANALYSIS *****')           LP= 830
         WRITE(6,291)                                                    LP= 835
291      FORMAT('-',12X,'RIGHT HAND SIDE RANGING')                       LP= 840
         WRITE(6,292)                                                    LP= 845
292      FORMAT('+',12X,'_____')            LP= 850
         WRITE(6,295)                                                    LP= 855
295      FORMAT('-','CONSTRAINT NO.',5X,'LL',8X,' B(I)',10X,'UL')        LP= 860
C                                                                        LP= 865
C        ASSIGN RHS + AND - VARIABLES LARGE NUMBERS                      LP= 870
C                                                                        LP= 875
285      DO 380 K=1,NS                                                   LP= 880
         DO 290 J=1,M                                                    LP= 885
         RHSP(J)=9999999;RHSN(J)=-9999999;RHS(J)=0.0                     LP= 890
290      CONTINUE                                                        LP= 895
C                                                                        LP= 900
C        ASSIGN INFINITE LARGE NUMBER IF A(I,J) = 0                      LP= 905
C                                                                        LP= 910
300      DO 330 J=1,M                                                    LP= 915
         IF(A(J,K)) 305,300,305                                         LP= 920
         RHS(J)=9999999;GO TO 320                                        LP= 925
C                                                                        LP= 930
C        ASSIGN INFINITE SMALL NUMBER IF B(J) = 0                        LP= 935
C                                                                        LP= 940
305      IF(B(J))315,310,315                                             LP= 945
310      IF(A(J,K).LT.0.0)RHS(J)=-.000001                               LP= 950
         IF(A(J,K).GT.0.0)RHS(J)=.000001                                LP= 955
         GO TO 320                                                       LP= 960
315      RHS(J)=B(J)/A(J,K)                                              LP= 965
```

```
320    RHS(J)=RHS(J)*(-1)                              LP=  970
C                                                      LP=  975
C      DETERMINE IF COMPUTED VALUES ARE + OR - VALUES  LP=  980
C                                                      LP=  985
       IF(RHS(J).GT.0.0)RHSP(J)=RHS(J)                 LP=  990
       IF(RHS(J).LT.0.0)RHSN(J)=RHS(J)                 LP=  995
330    CONTINUE                                        LP= 1000
C                                                      LP= 1005
C      SELECTION OF SMALLEST + AND - VALUES            LP= 1010
C                                                      LP= 1015
       J=1                                             LP= 1020
       RHSUP=RHSP(J);RHSLL=RHSN(J)                     LP= 1025
       DO 335 J=2,M                                    LP= 1030
       IF(RHSUP.EQ.0)RHSUP=RHSP(J)                     LP= 1035
       IF(RHSUP.GT.RHSP(J))RHSUP=RHSP(J)               LP= 1040
       IF(RHSLL.EQ.0)RHSLL=RHSN(J)                     LP= 1045
       IF(RHSLL.LT.RHSN(J))RHSLL=RHSN(J)               LP= 1050
335    CONTINUE                                        LP= 1055
C                                                      LP= 1060
C      DETERMINE IF INFINITE OR ZERO UL CHANGE FACTOR  LP= 1065
C                                                      LP= 1070
       IF(RHSUP.EQ.9999999)GO TO 340                   LP= 1075
       GO TO 345                                       LP= 1080
340    UL(K)=9999999;GO TO 350                         LP= 1085
345    IF(RHSUP.EQ.-000001)RHSUP=0.0                   LP= 1090
       UL(K)=BX(K)+RHSUP                               LP= 1095
350    IF(RHSLL.EQ.0.0) GO TO 355                      LP= 1100
       IF(RHSLL.EQ.-9999999) GO TO 355                 LP= 1105
       GO TO 360                                       LP= 1110
C                                                      LP= 1115
C      DETERMINE IF INFINITE OR ZERO LL CHANGE FACTOR  LP= 1120
C                                                      LP= 1125
```

```
355    SL(K)=-9999999;GO TO 370                                              LP= 1130
360    IF(RHSLL.EQ.-.000001)RHSLL=0.0                                        LP= 1135
365    SL(K)=BX(K)+RHSLL                                                     LP= 1140
370    WRITE(6,375)K,SL(K),BX(K),UL(K)                                       LP= 1145
375    FORMAT('0',4X,I2,1X,3(5X,F9.2))                                       LP= 1150
380    CONTINUE                                                              LP= 1155
C      ************BASIS VARIABLE COEFFICIENT RANGING                        LP= 1160
C                                                                            LP= 1165
C      VARIABLE ID                                                           LP= 1170
C      COFF(J) = INITIAL COMPUTED VALUES                                     LP= 1175
C      COFP(J) = POSITIVE VALUES OF COFF(J),S                                LP= 1180
C      COFN(J) = NEGATIVE VALUES OF COFF(J),S                                LP= 1185
C      COFUP = SMALLEST OF POSITIVE COFP(J),S                                LP= 1190
C      COFLL = SMALLEST OF NEGATIVE COFN(J),S                                LP= 1195
C      CUL(I) = COMPUTED UPPER LIMIT                                         LP= 1200
C      CLL(I) = COMPUTED LOWER LIMIT                                         LP= 1205
C                                                                            LP= 1210
387    IF(MN)387,387,390                                                     LP= 1215
       WRITE(6,388)                                                          LP= 1220
388    FORMAT('-',' *** DATA ERROR *** -- NO. OF REAL VARIABLES (COL. 20-    LP= 1225
      *22, DATA CARD #1)')                                                   LP= 1230
       GO TO 560                                                             LP= 1235
390    WRITE(6,391)                                                          LP= 1240
391    FORMAT('-',12X,'BASIS VARIABLE COEFFICIENT RANGING')                  LP= 1245
       WRITE(6,392)                                                          LP= 1250
392    FORMAT('+',12X,'_____')                                    LP= 1255
       WRITE(6,503)                                                          LP= 1260
C                                                                            LP= 1265
C      DETERMINE IF A BASIS VARIABLE                                         LP= 1270
C                                                                            LP= 1275
395    DO 480 I=1,M                                                          LP= 1280
       DO 400 K=MO,MMN                                                       LP= 1285
```

523

```
                                                                      LP= 1290
400   IF(NXI(I).EQ.NXJ(K))GO TO 405                                   LP= 1295
      CONTINUE                                                        LP= 1300
      GO TO 480                                                       LP= 1305
405   DO 401 J=1,N                                                    LP= 1310
      COFP(J)=9999999;COFN(J)=-9999999;COFF(J)=0.0                    LP= 1315
401   CONTINUE                                                        LP= 1320
C                                                                     LP= 1325
C     ASSIGN INFINITE LARGE NUMBER IF A(I,J) = 0                      LP= 1330
C                                                                     LP= 1335
      DO 430 J=1,N                                                    LP= 1340
      IF(A(I,J))415,410,415                                           LP= 1345
410   IF(ZC(J).GT.0)COFF(J)=9999999                                  LP= 1350
      IF(ZC(J).LT.0)COFF(J)=-9999999                                 LP= 1355
      GO TO 422                                                       LP= 1360
C                                                                     LP= 1365
C     ASSIGN INFINITE SMALL NUMBER IF Z(J)-C(J) = 0                   LP= 1370
C                                                                     LP= 1375
415   IF(ZC(J))421,420,421                                           LP= 1380
420   IF(A(I,J).GT.0)COFF(J)=.000001                                 LP= 1385
      IF(A(I,J).LT.0)COFF(J)=-.000001                                LP= 1390
      GO TO 422                                                       LP= 1395
421   COFF(J)=ZC(J)/A(I,J)                                           LP= 1400
422   COFF(J)=COFF(J)*(-1)                                           LP= 1405
      IF(NXI(I).EQ.NXJ(J))GO TO 430                                  LP= 1410
C                                                                     LP= 1415
C     DETERMINE IF + OR - COMPUTED VALUE                             LP= 1420
C                                                                     LP= 1425
      IF(COFF(J).GT.0)COFP(J)=COFF(J)                                LP= 1430
      IF(COFF(J).LT.0)COFN(J)=COFF(J)                                LP= 1435
430   CONTINUE                                                        LP= 1440
C                                                                     LP= 1445
C     SEARCH FOR SMALLEST + AND - VALUE COMPUTED
```

524

```
C         J=1
          COFUP=COFP(J);COFLL=COFN(J)                              LP= 1450
          DO 435 J=2,N                                             LP= 1455
          IF(COFUP.GT.COFP(J))COFUP=COFP(J)                        LP= 1460
          IF(COFLL.LT.COFN(J))COFLL=COFN(J)                        LP= 1465
  435     CONTINUE                                                 LP= 1470
C                                                                  LP= 1475
C         DETERMINE IF INFINITE OR ZERO UL CHANGE FACTOR           LP= 1480
C                                                                  LP= 1485
          IF(COFUP.EQ.9999999)GO TO 440                            LP= 1490
          GO TO 445                                                LP= 1495
  440     CUL(I)=9999999;GO TO 448                                 LP= 1500
          IF(COFUP.EQ..000001)COFUP=0.0                            LP= 1505
  445     CUL(I)=CJ(K)+COFUP                                       LP= 1510
C                                                                  LP= 1515
C         DETERMINE IF INFINITE OR ZERO LL CHANGE FACTOR           LP= 1520
C                                                                  LP= 1525
  448     IF(COFLL.EQ.-9999999)GO TO 450                           LP= 1530
          GO TO 455                                                LP= 1535
  450     CLL(I)=-9999999;GO TO 469                                LP= 1540
  455     IF(COFLL.EQ..000001)COFLL=0.0                            LP= 1545
  460     CLL(I)=CJ(K)+COFLL                                       LP= 1550
C                                                                  LP= 1555
C         REASSIGN + VALUE IF MAX TYPE PROBLEM                     LP= 1560
C                                                                  LP= 1565
  469     IF(PTYPE)470,555,462                                     LP= 1570
          CUL(I)=CUL(I)*(-1)                                       LP= 1575
          IF(CUL(I).LT.0.0)CUL(I)=0.0                              LP= 1580
          CLL(I)=CLL(I)*(-1)                                       LP= 1585
          CI(I)=CI(I)*(-1)                                         LP= 1590
  462     WRITE(6,475)NXI(I),CUL(I),CI(I),CLL(I)                   LP= 1595
                                                                   LP= 1600
                                                                   LP= 1605
```

525

```
      GO TO 480                                                          LP= 1610
 470  WRITE(6,475)NXI(I),CLL(I),CI(I),CUL(I)                             LP= 1615
 475  FORMAT('0',2X,'X(',I2,')',3(5X,F9.2))                             LP= 1620
 480  CONTINUE                                                           LP= 1625
C     ******** NON-BASIS COEFFICIENT RANGING                            LP= 1630
C                                                                        LP= 1635
C     VARIABLE ID                                                       LP= 1640
C        CNVP(K) = UPPER LIMIT                                          LP= 1645
C        CNVN(K) = LOWER LIMIT                                          LP= 1650
C        CJJP(K) = INITIAL COEFFICIENT VALUE                            LP= 1655
C                                                                        LP= 1660
      WRITE(6,501)                                                       LP= 1665
 501  FORMAT('-',12X,'NON-BASIS VARIABLE COEFFICIENT RANGING')          LP= 1670
      WRITE(6,502)                                                       LP= 1675
 502  FORMAT('+',12X,'_____')   LP= 1680
      WRITE(6,503)                                                       LP= 1685
 503  FORMAT('-','VARIABLE NO.',7X,'LL',8X,' C(J)',10X,'UL')            LP= 1690
C                                                                        LP= 1695
C     SEARCH FOR NON BASIS VARIABLE                                     LP= 1700
C                                                                        LP= 1705
      DO 550 K=MO,MMN                                                    LP= 1710
      DO 510 I=1,M                                                       LP= 1715
      IF(NXJ(K).EQ.NXI(I))GO TO 545                                     LP= 1720
 510  CONTINUE                                                           LP= 1725
      IF(PTYPE)520,555,515                                               LP= 1730
C                                                                        LP= 1735
C     MAX PROB -- DETERMINE UL CHANGE FACTOR                            LP= 1740
C                                                                        LP= 1745
 515  CNVP(K)=(CJ(K)+ZC(K))*(-1)                                        LP= 1750
      CNVN(K)=99999999                                                   LP= 1755
      CJ(K)=CJ(K)*(-1)                                                   LP= 1760
      GO TO 538                                                          LP= 1765
```

526

```
C
C      MIN PROB -- DETERMINE LL CHANGE FACTOR                          LP= 1770
C                                                                      LP= 1775
520    CNVP(K)=9999999                                                 LP= 1780
       CNVN(K)=CJ(K)+ZC(K)                                             LP= 1785
538    WRITE(6,475)NXJ(K),CNVN(K),CJ(K),CNVP(K)                        LP= 1790
545    IF(K.EQ.MMN)GO TO 560                                           LP= 1795
550    CONTINUE                                                        LP= 1800
555    WRITE(6,556)                                                    LP= 1805
556    FORMAT('-',' *** DATA ERROR *** -- UNDEFINED PROBLEM TYPE (COL. 22LP= 1810
      *-25, DATA CARD #1)  CODE: MIN=-1 ,  MAX=1')                     LP= 1815
560    WRITE(6,558)                                                    LP= 1820
558    FORMAT('1')                                                     LP= 1825
       GO TO 1                                                         LP= 1830
580    RETURN                                                          LP= 1835
       END                                                             LP= 1840
                                                                       LP= 1845
```

527

APPENDIX **III** Computer-Based Solution of Goal Programming

This appendix presents a computer-based solution procedure of goal programming. It presents a detailed description of a computer program of the simplex algorithm for goal programming. More specifically, it discusses the data input for the computer solution, the input process, the process for calculating the results, and finally the procedure for printout of the results. This computer program has been tested through many practical applications, and it has been proved efficient as long as the hardware has sufficient memory capacity for the problem.

SETTING UP THE GOAL PROGRAM FOR THE COMPUTER

For illustrative purposes, let us consider the textile-manufacturing problem discussed in Chapter 6:

$$\text{Minimize} \quad Z = P_1 d_1^- + P_2 d_4^+ + 5P_3 d_2^- + 3P_3 d_3^- + P_4 d_1^+$$
$$\text{subject to} \quad X_1 + X_2 + d_1^- - d_1^+ = 80$$
$$X_1 + d_2^- = 70$$
$$X_2 + d_3^- = 45$$
$$X_1 + X_2 + d_4^- - d_4^+ = 90$$

The computer program is designed in such a way that it will take care of the deviational and slack variables automatically. However, we have to specify the regular decision variables and their technological coefficients, the direction of constraints (equality or inequality), and the objective function. Thus, for the above problem, the information listed below is all that is required to formulate the problem.

```
Col. #   1    2
Row #   X₁   X₂  Sign   rhs
   1    1    1    B     80
   2    1         L     70
   3         1    L     45
   4    1    1    B     90
```

The symbols in the sign column will be explained below.

The computer solution setup of a goal programming requires five basic parts: (1) problem card, (2) the sign card, (3) the objective function, (4) the substitution rates, and (5) the right-hand side.

The Problem Card

The problem card is the first card and describes the parameters of the problem under consideration. The problem card setup is as follows:

Col. 1-4:   Punch PROB
Col. 5-7:   The number of rows
Col. 8-10:   The number of columns
Col. 11-13:   The number of priority factors

The rows, of course, refer to the number of constraints and goal equations. The columns refer to the number of real variables used in the problem (not including deviational and slack variables). The number of priority factors represents the number of actual priority levels only. Artificial priorities are automatically created by the program in order to create the first basis.

Example

The above illustrative problem is used to explain the problem card set-up. There are four rows, two real variables, and four priority factors in our problem:

```
Col. │ 1  2  3  4  5  6  7  8  9  10  11  12  13
     │ P  R  O  B  0  0  4  0  0   2   0   0   4
```

The Sign Card

The sign card describes the direction of constraints. There are four possibilities:

1. "E" for "exactly equal." No deviation in either direction is possible.

2. "G" for "greater than." This sign allows only the positive deviation from the right-hand side.
3. "L" for "less than." This sign allows only the negative deviation from the right-hand side.
4. "B" for "both directions are possible." This sign allows the minimization of either or both the negative and positive deviations from the goal or constraints.

One or both deviational variables of a constraint must appear in the objective function. If neither deviational variable appears in the objective function, it is possible that both deviational variables may end up in the basis and the constraint $d_i^- \cdot d_i^+ = 0$ will not be met. If both deviational variables appear in the objective function, they may be assigned different priority factors.

Example
For our problem, the sign card will be

Col.	1	2	3	4
	B	L	L	B

The Objective Function Cards

The objective function cards specify the priority factors, their locations, and the type of deviational variable (either positive or negative). The data cards for the objective function are prefaced by a name card with "OBJ" punched in the first three columns:

Col.	1	2	3	4	5
	O	B	J		

The data cards of the objective function define each element in the objective function in the following manner:

Col. 1-3:	Either the word "POS" for positive or "NEG" for negative should be punched. This specifies whether the positive or negative deviational variable is to be minimized at the stated priority level.
Col. 4-7:	Blank
Col. 8-9:	The row (ith) in which the deviational variable mentioned above appears.
Col. 10-12:	Blank

Col. 13-14: The priority level at which the deviational variable is to be minimized—the lower the subscript, the higher the priority.

Col. 15-25: The coefficient of the priority factor (differential weights). There must always be a value here. The program will not assume one. The decimal number should be punched, which enables one both to avoid having to right-justify the variable and to put in weights that are less than one.

Example

For our example, which had the objective function to minimize $Z = P_1 d_1^- + P_2 d_4^+ + 5P_3 d_2^- + 3P_3 d_3^- + P_4 d_1^+$, the objective function data cards will be as follows:

Col	Deviation	Row Deviation Appeared		Priority		Weights		
	1 2 3	8	9	13	14	20	21	22
	NEG	0	1	0	1	1	.	0
	POS	0	4	0	2	1	.	0
	NEG	0	2	0	3	5	.	0
	NEG	0	3	0	3	3	.	0
	POS	0	1	0	4	1	.	0

The Data Section Cards (Technological Coefficients)

The data section cards specify the technological coefficients of the decision variables. The data section cards must be prefaced by a card with the word "DATA" punched in the first four columns. This should be followed by cards with the following information:

Col. 1-7: Blank
Col. 8-9: The row (ith) in which the coefficient is located.
Col. 10-12: Blank
Col. 13-14: The column (jth) in which the coefficient is located.
Col. 15-25: The value of the coefficient to be placed in the above indexed location.

Example

For our example, the technological coefficients were as follows:

Col. #	1	2
Row #	X_1	X_2
1	1	1
2	1	
3		1
4	1	1

The above should be punched in the following manner:

	Matrix Row	Matrix Col.	Value in Indicated Position
Col.	8 9	17 18	20 21 22
	0 1	0 1	1 . 0
	0 1	0 2	1 . 0
	0 2	0 1	1 . 0
	0 3	0 2	1 . 0
	0 4	0 1	1 . 0
	0 4	0 1	1 . 0

The Right-Hand-Side Cards

The right-hand side is the last item to be read into the computer. The right-hand-side cards should be preceded by a card labeled "RIGHT" punched in the first four columns. The label card will be followed by the right-hand-side cards in the following mannner.

Col. 1-10:   Right-hand-side value for the first row
Col. 11-20:   Right-hand-side value for the second row
Col. 21-30:   Right-hand-side value for the third row

.   .

.   .

.   .

Col. 71-80:   Right-hand-side value for the eighth row

If there are more than eight rows, simply go to the next card.

Example

For our example, the right-hand-side card will be as follows:

Col.	10	20	30	40
	80.0	70.0	45.0	90.0

There is one more aspect of the computer solution that deserves our attention. If there exists goal decomposition, we may have two or more separate goals concerning a certain desired aspect of the decision problem. For example, in the textile manufacturing problem, we could reformulate the model as follows:

Minimize $Z = P_1 d_1^- + P_2 d_{11}^+ + 5P_3 d_2^- + 3P_3 d_3^- + P_4 d_1^+$

subject to $X_1 + X_2 + d_1^- - d_1^+ = 80$

$$X_1 + d_2^- = 70$$
$$X_2 + d_3^- = 45$$
$$d_{11}^- + d_1^+ - d_{11}^+ = 10$$

The fourth equation in the model represents a specified goal concerning the overtime operation of the manufacturing plant. Since this equation does not contain any decision variables, it is impossible to prepare data selection cards. In such a case, we can repeat the regular operation hour constraint and increase the rhs value by the allowed amount of overtime. Thus it becomes $X_1 + X_2 + d_4^- - d_4^+ = 90$.

This simple modification of the model enables one to set up the goal programming computer deck.

EXAMPLES OF COMPUTER DECK SETUP

The complete computer deck of goal programming should be arranged as explained above, in addition to necessary system cards specified by each computing facility. The order of cards for the computer deck setup can be simply demonstrated by Figure A.IIIa. The problem input deck represents the computer cards from PROB card to right-hand-side data card(s). The number of sign cards, objective data cards, data selection cards, and right-hand-side data cards vary according to the complexity and characteristics of the problem under analysis.

ANALYSIS OF THE COMPUTER OUTPUT

The computer solution of goal program provides the following output: complete printout of input data (the right-hand side, the substitution rates, and the objective function), the final simplex solution table (including $Z_j - C_j$ matrix and evaluation of objective function), slack analysis, variable analysis, and the analysis of the objective. In order to assist the potential user of this program, let us analyze each item of the output.

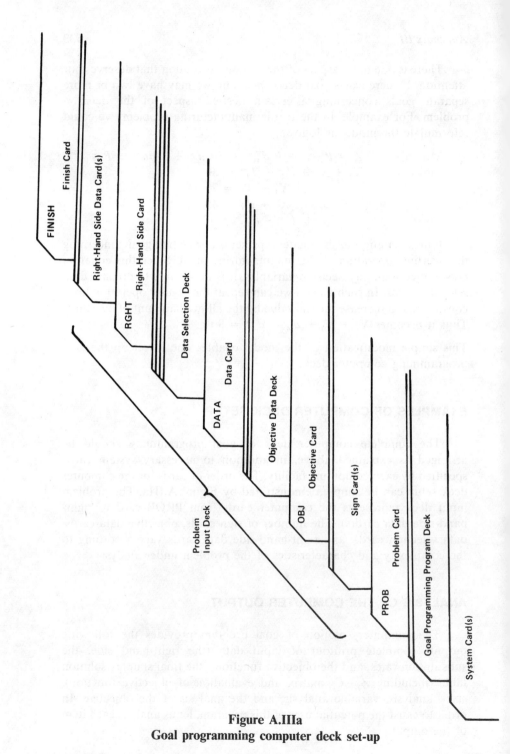

Figure A.IIIa
Goal programming computer deck set-up

Input Data

The computer prints out the complete input data so that the user of the program can easily recheck the data he has fed into the computer.

For our example, the computer printout of input data appears as follows:

THE RIGHT-HAND SIDE-INPUT   PAGE 01

1   80.00000
2   70.00000
3   45.0000
4   90.00000

THE SUBSTITUTION RATES-INPUT   PAGE 02

Row 1

| 1.000 | 0.0 | 0.0 | 0.0 | − 1.000 | 0.0 | 1.000 | 1.000 |

Row 2

| 0.0 | 1.000 | 0.0 | 0.0 | 0.0 | 0.0 | 1.000 | 0.0 |

Row 3

| 0.0 | 0.0 | 1.000 | 0.0 | 0.0 | 0.0 | 0.0 | 1.000 |

Row 4

| 0.0 | 0.0 | 0.0 | 1.000 | 0.0 | − 1.000 | 1.000 | 1.000 |

THE OBJECTIVE FUNCTION-INPUT   PAGE 03

PRIORITY 4

| 0.0 | 0.0 | 0.0 | 0.0 | 1.000 | 0.0 | 0.0 | 0.0 |

PRIORITY 3

| 0.0 | 5.000 | 3.000 | 0.0 | 0.0 | 0.0 | 0.0 | 0.0 |

PRIORITY 2

| 0.0 | 0.0 | 0.0 | 0.0 | 0.0 | 1.000 | 0.0 | 0.0 |

PRIORITY 1

| 1.000 | 0.0 | 0.0 | 0.0 | 0.0 | 0.0 | 0.0 | 0.0 |

SUMMARY OF INPUT INFORMATION   PAGE 04

NUMBER OF ROWS	4
NUMBER OF VARIABLES	8
NUMBER OF PRIORITIES	4
ADDED PRIORITES	0

Everything described above should be self-explanatory. It should be pointed out that in the substitution rates and the objective function matrices the first four columns represent negative deviation variables, followed by the two positive deviational variable columns and the two decision variables at the end.

The Final Simplex Solution

The computer program prints out the final simplex solution of the problem in the form of simplex matrix notation. This table is extremely useful for the user if he desires to perform postoptimal sensitivity analysis or parametric goal programming.

For our example, the final simplex solution printout appears as follows:

ITERATION 3   THE SIMPLEX SOLUTION   PAGE 05
THE RIGHT HAND SIDE

8	20.00000
7	70.00000
3	25.00000
5	10.00000

THE SUBSTITUTION RATES
ROW 1

0.0	-1.000	0.0	1.000	0.0	-1.000	0.0	1.000

ROW 2

0.0	1.000	0.0	0.0	0.0	0.0	1.000	0.0

ROW 3

0.0	1.000	1.000	-1.000	0.0	1.000	0.0	0.0

ROW 4

-1.000	0.0	0.0	1.000	1.000	-1.000	0.0	0.0

THE ZJ-CJ MATRIX
PRIORITY 4

-1.000	0.0	0.0	1.000	0.0	-1.000	0.0	0.0

PRIORITY 3

0.0	-2.000	0.0	-3.000	0.0	3.000	0.0	0.0

PRIORITY 2

0.0	0.0	0.0	0.0	0.0	-1.000	0.0	0.0

PRIORITY 1

-1.000	0.0	0.0	0.0	0.0	0.0	0.0	0.0

AN EVALUATION OF THE OBJECTIVE FUNCTION

4	10.00
3	75.00
2	0.0
1	0.0

The above printout can be interpreted this way:

The right-hand side. The numbers on the left-hand side are variable numbers for the basic variables (i.e., variable $8 = X_2$, variable $7 = X_1$, variable $3 = d_3^-$, and variable $5 = d_1^+$). The values on the right-hand side represent constants of the basic variables.

The substitution rates. The substitution rates matrix is again based on the column arrangement of d_i^-, d_i^+, X_j, in that order.

The ZJ-CJ matrix. This simplex criterion should be self-explanatory.

An evaluation of the objective function. This evaluation simply presents the Z_j values of goals. In other words, the values present the underattained portion of goals. It should be apparent in our example that the first two goals are completely attained, while the third and fourth goals are only partially attained.

The Slack Analysis

The slack analysis presents the values of the right-hand side and also values of the negative and positive variables for each equation. The slack analysis is an excellent vehicle to analyze the details of goal attainments when the problem is complex. Also, this analysis often proves to be very helpful in identifying errors when the model does not represent the exact decision environment.

For our example, the slack analysis appears as follows:

	SLACK ANALYSIS		PAGE 06
ROW	AVAILABLE	POS-SLK	NEG-SLK
1	80.00000	10.00000	0.0
2	70.0000	0.0	0.0
3	45.0000	0.0	25.00000
4	90.00000	0.0	0.0

Variable Analysis

The variable analysis presents the constants of only the basic decision variables. When the problem under consideration is a very complex one, the variable analysis is especially helpful because it presents only these constants, as compared to the final simplex solution table.

The variable analysis of our example appears as follows:

	VARIABLE ANALYSIS	PAGE 07
VARIABLE	AMOUNT	
2	20.00000	
1	70.00000	

It should be pointed out here that the variable numbers are rearranged. These numbers are variable numbers of the decision variables (i.e., X_j).

Analysis of the Objective

An analysis of the objective presents the Z_j value for the goals. These values represent the underattained portion of goals. If the model requires assignment of artificial priority to set up the initial table, the artificial priority will also be printed out.

For our example, the printout of the analysis of the objective appears as follows:

	ANALYSIS OF THE OBJECTIVE	PAGE 08
PRIORITY	UNDERACHIEVEMENT	
4	10.00000	
3	75.00000	
2	0.0	
1	0.0	

The following is the complete goal programming computer deck. This program is capable of solving problems for which the number of variables (including deviational variables) is less than or equal to 125. the number of rows is less than or equal to 60, and the number of priority levels is less than or equal to 10. If a problem is bigger than the above specified size, it can esaily be accommodated by expanding appropriate dimensions.

```
      DIMENSION RVLX(10,125)
      DIMENSION D(60,125)
      DIMENSION VALX(10,125)
      DIMENSION C(60,125)
      DIMENSION VALY(60,10)
      DIMENSION KEPT(60)
      DIMENSION RHS1(60)
      DIMENSION Y(60),IY(60)
      DIMENSION PRDT(60)
      DIMENSION AMT(60)
      DIMENSION ZVAL(10)
      DIMENSION DOD(60)
      DIMENSION DUD(125)
      DIMENSION X(125)
      GOAL PROGRAMMING
      CALL START(N,M,L,C,VALX,VALY,PRDT,RHS1,KPCK,KEPT,TEST)
      DO 21 J=1,M
   21 X(J)=J
      DO 20 I=1,N
   20 Y(I)=I
   15 FORMAT(I3,F12.2)
   12 FORMAT(10F12.3)
   13 FORMAT(8F9.0)
  213 FORMAT(F8.0,10X,F15.5)
  313 FORMAT(I3,10X,F20.5)
      DO 25 K=1,L
      DO 25 I=1,N
      VALY(I,K)=VALX(K,I)
   25 CONTINUE
      ITAB=0
C     BRING IN NEW VARIABLES
      ITER=0
```

```
C     CALCULATE NET CONTRIBUTION OF EACH VARIABLE (RVLX(K,J))
   31 L1=0
   32 K3=L-L1
   33 IF(K3-1) 800,40,40
   40 DO 60 K=1,K3
      DO 60 J=1,M
      SUMP=0.
      DO 50 I=1,N
      P=VALY(I,K)*C(I,J)
      SUMP=SUMP+P
   50 CONTINUE
      RVLX(K,J)=SUMP-VALX(K,J)
   60 CONTINUE
C     BRING IN X(K2)
      ZMAX=0.
      DO 90 J=1,M
      IF(K3-L) 92,70,70
   92 K4=K3+1
      DO 91 K=K4,L
      IF(RVLX(K,J)) 90,91,91
   91 CONTINUE
   70 IF(RVLX(K3,J)-ZMAX) 90,90,80
   80 ZMAX=RVLX(K3,J)
      K2=J
   90 CONTINUE
   95 IF(ZMAX) 790,790,100
C     WHICH VARIABLE IS REMOVED FROM THE BASIS
C     CALCULATE LIMITING AMT FOR EACH BASIS VARIABLE
  100 DO 150 I=1,N
      IF(PRDT(I)) 110,120,120
  110 WRITE(6,13) PRDT(I)
      GO TO 830
```

540

```
120 IF(C(I,K2)) 130,130,140
130 AMT(I)=-1.
    GO TO 150
140 AMT(I)=PRDT(I)/C(I,K2)
150 CONTINUE
C       SELECT SMALLEST POSITIVE LIMITING AMT
    I=1
160 IF(AMT(I)) 170,210,210
170 I=I+1
    IF(I-N) 160,160,180
180 WRITE(6,13) AMT(N)
    GO TO 830
210 ZMIN=AMT(I)
    K1=I
220 I=I+1
    IF(I-N) 230,230,300
230 IF(AMT(I)) 220,240,240
240 IF(ZMIN-AMT(I)) 220,220,210
C       REMOVE Y(K1)
300 Y(K1)=X(K2)
    DO 310 K=1,L
    VALY(K1,K)=VALX(K,K2)
310 CONTINUE
C       CALCULATE NEW RIGHT-HAND SIDES
    DO 400 I=1,N
    PRDT(I)=PRDT(I)-ZMIN*C(I,K2)
400 CONTINUE
    PRDT(K1)=ZMIN
C       CALCULATE NEW SUBSTITUTION RATES
    DO 500 J=1,M
    DO 500 I=1,N
    D(I,J)=C(I,J)-C(K1,J)* C(I,K2)/C(K1,K2)
```

```
  500 CONTINUE
      DO 510 J=1,M
      D(K1,J)=C(K1,J)/C(K1,K2)
  510 CONTINUE
      DO 520 J=1,M
      DO 520 I=1,N
      C(I,J)=D(I,J)
      IF(ABS(C(I,J)).LE.0.00001)C(I,J)=0.
  520 CONTINUE
      ITER=ITER+1
C     WRITE ALL TABLES OR JUST OPTIMAL TABLE
      IF(ITAB) 40,40,600
C     WRITE EACH TABLE
  600 WRITE(6,6001) ITER
 6001 FORMAT(1H1,10X,13HITERATIONS = ,I3,//)
      WRITE(6,5001)
      DO 610 I=1,N
      IY(I)=Y(I)
      WRITE(6,313) IY(I),IY(I),PRDT(I)
  610 CONTINUE
      WRITE(6,5002)
      DO 620 I=1,N
      WRITE(6,5006)I
      WRITE(6,12) (C(I,J),J=1,M)
  620 CONTINUE
      WRITE(6,5003)
 6813 DO 6814 K=1,L
      MM=L+1-K
      WRITE(6,5007) MM
      WRITE(6,12) (RVLX(K,J), J=1,M)
 6814 CONTINUE
      GO TO 40
```

542

```
C     MOVE TO NEXT LOWER PRIORITY LEVEL
790   LI=LI+1
      GO TO 32
C     WRITE FINAL RESULTS
800   WRITE(6,1015)
1015  FORMAT(1H1)
      WRITE(6,1014)ITER
1014  FORMAT(10X,'ITERATIONS............',I5)
      WRITE(6,5000)
5000  FORMAT(55X,'THE SIMPLEX SOLUTION',25X,'PAGE 05',//)
      WRITE(6,5001)
5001  FORMAT(//,' THE RIGHT HAND SIDE',//)
801   DO 810 I=1,N
      IY(I)=Y(I)
      WRITE(6,313) IY(I),PRDT(I)
810   CONTINUE
      WRITE(6,5002)
5002  FORMAT(//,' THE SUBSTITUTION RATES',//)
811   DO 812 I=1,N
      WRITE(6,5006)I
5006  FORMAT(1X,3HROW,I5)
      WRITE(6,12)(C(I,J),J=1,M)
812   CONTINUE
      WRITE(6,5003)
5003  FORMAT(//,' THE ZJ-CJ MATRIX',//)
813   DO 814 K=1,L
      MM=L+1-K
      WRITE(6,5007) MM
5007  FORMAT(1X,8HPRIORITY,I5)
      WRITE(6,12)(RVLX(K,J), J=1,M)
814   CONTINUE
C     EVALUATE OBJECTIVE FUNCTION
```

543

```
      DO 820 K=1,L
      ZVAL(K)=0.
      DO 820 I=1,N
      ZVAL(K)=ZVAL(K)+PRDT(I)*VALY(I,K)
  820 CONTINUE
      WRITE(6,5004)
 5004 FORMAT(' AN EVALUATION OF THE OBJECTIVE FUNCTION')
      DO 821 K=1,L
      KK=L-K
      IF(TEST.EQ.1.0)GO TO 89
      KK=KK+1
   89 WRITE(6,15) KK,ZVAL(K)
  821 CONTINUE
      CALL FINISH(RHS1,PRDT,VALY,L,KPCK,Y,N,KEPT,TEST)
  830 STOP
      END
      SUBROUTINE START(NROWS,NVAR,NPRT,C,VALX,VALY,RHS ,RHS1,KPCK,KEPT,T
     %EST)
C         THE START SUBROUTINE IS DESIGNED TO TAKE  INFORMATION IN A SPED-
C      IFIED FORMAT AND TRANSFORM IT INTO A SERIES OF USABLE MATRICIES.
C.........................................................................
      REAL NEG
      REAL L
      DIMENSION C(60,125),VALX(10,125)
      DIMENSION VALY(60,10)
      DIMENSION EQUALS(60),RVLX(10,125)
      DIMENSION RHS(60)
      DIMENSION KEPT(60)
      DIMENSION RHS1(60)
      NV=125
      NR=60
    1 FORMAT(A4,3I3)
```

544

```
      DATA POS,NEG/'POS ','NEG '/
      DATA DATA/'DATA'/
      DATA OBJ/'OBJ '/
      DATA PROB/'PROB'/
      DATA B /'B'/
      DATA E,G,L/'E','G','L'/
      DATA RGHT/'RGHT'/
      TEST=0.0
C
C.....................................................................
C
C     READ THE PROBLEM CARD  FOR THE NUMBER OF ROWS,VARIABLES, AND
C
C.....................................................................
C
   10 READ(5,1)ANAME,NROWS,NVAR,NPRT
      LISP=NPRT+1
      IF(NVAR.LE.0) GO TO 1020
      IF(NPRT.LE.0) GO TO 1020
      IF(NROWS.LE.0) GO TO 1020
      IF(ANAME.NE.PROB) GO TO 901
C
C.....................................................................
C
C     READ THE SIGN CARD.
C     IT WILL CONTAIN ONE OF THE FOLLOWING LETTERS FOR EACH ROW
C        FOR EQUALS                              E
C        FOR LESS THAN OR EQUAL TO               L
C        FOR GREATHER THAN OR EQUAL TO G
C        FOR BOTH DEVIATIONS                     B
C
C.....................................................................
C
      READ(5,11)(EQUALS(I),I=1,NROWS)
   11 FORMAT(80A1)
C
```

545

```
C       NART=0
C       COUNT THE NUMBER OF POSITIVE SLACK VARIABLES
C
        NFLDS=0
        DO 12 I=1,NROWS
        IF(EQUALS(I).EQ.B)NFLDS=NFLDS+1
   12   IF(EQUALS(I).EQ.G)NFLDS=NFLDS+1
C
C       TEST FOR SIZE
C
        NSIZE=NFLDS+NROWS+NVAR
        IF(NROWS.GT.NF) GO TO 911
        IF(NSIZE.GT.NV) GO TO 911
C
C
C       CLEAR ALL MATRICIES
C
        IF (NPRT.GT.NROWS) GO TO 1105
        NUM = NROWS
        GO TO 1106
 1105   NUM = NPRT
 1106   KDUD = NPRT + 1
        DO 16 J=1,NSIZE
        DO 16 I = 1, NUM
        KEPT(I)=0
        IF(I.GT.KDUD) GO TO 17
        K=I
        RVLX(K,J)=0.0
        VALX(K,J)=0.0
```

546

```
   17 IF(I.EQ.J) C(I,J)=1.0
      VALY(I,K)=0.0
      IF(I.NE.J) C(I,J)=0.0
   16 CONTINUE
      KPCK=0
      K=KDUD
C
C
C        ADJUST THE SLACK VARIABLES AND OBJECTIVE FUNCTION TO MEET THE
C        REQUIREMENTS OF THE SIGN
C
      DO 13 I=1,NROWS
      IF(EQUALS(I).EQ.E) GO TO 14
      IF(EQUALS(I).EQ.G) GO TO 15
      IF(EQUALS(I).EQ.L) GO TO 13
      IF(EQUALS(I).EQ.B)GO TO 18
      GO TO 910
   14 J=I
      VALX(K,J)=1.0
      NART=NART+1
      TEST=1.0
      GO TO 13
   15 KPCK=KPCK+1
      J=NROWS+KPCK
      C(I,J)=-1.0
      KEPT(I)=J
      J=I
      VALX(K,J)=1.
      NART=NART+1
      TEST=1.0
      GO TO 13
   18 KPCK=KPCK+1
```

547

```
      J=KPCK+NROWS
      C(I,J)=-1.0
      KEPT(I)=J
 13   CONTINUE
C
C
C     READ THE OBJECTIVE FUNCTION
C
 19   READ(5,21)ANAME
      I=0
      IF(ANAME.NE.OBJ) GO TO 920
      IF(ANAME.EQ.OBJ) GO TO 20
 20   READ(5,21)ANAME,I,M,TEMP
      IF(ANAME.EQ.DATA) GO TO 30
      IF(M.LE.0) GO TO 1022
      K=LISP-M
 21   FORMAT(A4,2I5,F16.0)
      IF(J.LE.0) GO TO 1022
      IF(K.GT.NPRT)  GO TO 1024
      IF(ANAME.EQ.NFG) GO TO 26
      IF(ANAME.EQ.POS) GO TO 25
      GO TO 27
 26   J=I
      VALX(K,J)=TEMP
      GO TO 20
 25   J=KEPT(I)
      IF (KEPT(I).EQ.0) GO TO 1026
      VALX(K,J)=TEMP
      GO TO 20
 27   IF(TEMP)926,20,926
C
C
```

548

```
C     READ THE DATA MATRIX IN
C.........................................
30    READ(5,21)ANAME,I,J,TEMP
      IF(ANAME.EQ.RGHT) GO TO 40
      IF(I.LE.0)  GO TO 1090
      IF(J.EQ.0) GO TO 1090
      J=KPCK+NROWS+J
      C(I,J)=TEMP
      GO TO 30
C
C
C     READ THE RIGHT HAND SIDE
C.........................................
40    READ(5,44)(RHS(I),I=1,NROWS)
44    FORMAT(8F10.0)
C
C
C     WRITE THE ABOVE RESULTS
C.........................................
5015  WRITE(6,5015)
      FORMAT(55X,'THE RIGHT HAND SIDE-INPUT',33X,'PAGE 01')
      DO 41 I=1,NROWS
      IF(RHS(I))941,42,43
42    RHS(I)=.00001
43    RHS1(I)=RHS(I)
      WRITE(6,1111)I,RHS(I)
1111  FORMAT(10X,I3,2X,F15.5 )
41    CONTINUE
      WRITE(6,620)
620   FORMAT(1H1)
      WRITE(6,5016)
5016  FORMAT(55X,'THE SUBSTITUTION RATES-INPUT',18X,'PAGE 02')
```

```
      DO 1112 I=1,NROWS
      WRITE(6,2519) I
 2519 FORMAT(1X,'ROW',I5)
 1112 WRITE(6,1113)(C(I,J),J=1,NSIZE)
 1113 FORMAT(10F12.3)
      WRITE(6,620)
      WRITE(6,5017)
 5017 FORMAT(55X,'THE OBJECTIVE FUNCTION-INPUT',19X,'PAGE 03')
      DO 1114 K=1,NPRT
      M=LISP-K
      WRITE(6,2150) M
 2150 FORMAT(' PRIORITY',I5)
 1114 WRITE(6,1113)(VALX(K,J),J=1,NSIZE)
      WRITE(6,620)
      WRITE(6,5018)
 5018 FORMAT(55X,'SUMMARY OF INPUT INFORMATION ',19X,'PAGE',' 04')
      NVAR=NSIZE
      WRITE(6,2017) NROWS,NVAR,NPRT,NAPT
 2017 FORMAT(10X,'NUMBER OF ROWS.......',I5,/,10X,'NUMBER OF VARIABLES
     *....' ,I5,/,10X,'NUMBER OF PRIORITIES...',I5,/,10X,'ADDED PRIOR
     2ITIES........',I5)
      IF(NART.GT.0)  NPRT=NPRT+1
      RETURN
  910 WRITE(6,914)
  914 FORMAT('PROGRAM CONTAINS AN ERROR EITHER IN THE NUMBER OF ROWS PUN
     1CHED OR IN THE SIGN CARD.THE VALUE IS SOMETHING OTHER THAN "E","G"
     2,OR"L"')
      GO TO 999
 1090 WRITE(6,1091)
 1091 FORMAT(' IMPROPER DATA COLUMN OR ROW DEFINITION')
      GO TO 999
  920 WRITE(6,921)
```

```
9210FORMAT(' AN OBJECTIVE CARD WITH THE VALUE',F16.3,'
     1IS FOUND BUT INSTRUCTIONS AS TO WHICH DEVIATION HAS BEEN NEGLECTED. I
     2EXAMINE YOUR DATA ')
      GO TO 999
1020 WRITE(6,1021)
1021 FORMAT(' NUMBER OF ROWS, VARIABLES, OR PRIORITIES CANNOT BE EQUA
     1L TO ZERO UNDER ANY CIRCUMSTANCES')
      GO TO 999
1022 WRITE(6,1023)
1023 FORMAT(' COLUMN VALUE OR PRIORITY VALUE IS EQUAL TO OR LESS THAN
     1ZERO
     1 ')
      GO TO 999
911 WRITE(6,912)
9120FORMAT(' THE NUMVER OF VARIABLES NEEDED TO COMPUTE THIS PROGRAM
     1IS TOO GREAT UNDER PRESENT DIMENSIONS. SEE YOUR PROGRAMMER FOR AL
     2TERING THIS RESTRICTION TO MEET YOUR NEEDS')
      GO TO 999
1026 WRITE(6,1027)
1027 FORMAT(' ATTEMPT IS MADE TO MINIMIZE NON EXISTANT POSITIVE DEVIA
     1TION')
      GO TO 999
1024 WRITE(6,1025)
1025 FORMAT(' OBJECTIVE FUNCTION PRIORITY EXCEEDS STATED NUMBER OF PRI
     1ORITIES')
      GO TO 999
901 WRITE(6,902)
902 FORMAT(' PROBLEM CAPD MISSING OR MISPUNCHED')
      GO TO 999
926 WRITE(6,927)
927 FORMAT(' A CARD IN THE OBJECTIVE SECTION DEFINED SOME VALUE FOR T
     1HE OBJECTIVE FUNCTION BUT FAILED TO DEFINE WHETHER THIS WAS TO AP
     2PLY TO THE POSITIVE OR NEGATIVE DEVIATION')
```

```
941 WRITE(6,942)
942 FORMAT(' NEGATIVE VALUES ARE NOT ALLOWED ON THE RIGHT HAND SIDE.
    1 CORRECT PROBLEM BY MULTIPLYING ENTIRE CONSTRAINT THROUGH BY MINU
    2S ONE.')
999 GO TO 999
    STOP
    END
    SUBROUTINE FINISH(RHS1,RHS,VALY,NPRT,KPCK,Y,NROWS,KEPT,TEST)
    REAL NEGSLK
    DIMENSION VALY(60,10)
    DIMENSION ZVAL(10)
    DIMENSION RHS(60)
    DIMENSION KEPT(60)
    DIMENSION Y(60),RHS1(60)
C   RHS1 IS THE RESERVED VECTOR OF RHS VALUES  FROM THE BEGINNING.
C   THE ENDING RHS VALUES ARE SUBTRACTED FROM THE BEGINNING ONES
C   AND THE RESULT IS PLACED INTO THE APPROPRIATE SLACK COLUMN.
C   THE REMAINDER OF THE VALUES  ARE PRINTED ON PAGE TWO OF THE RE-
C   SULTS.
C
C   SLACK ANALYSIS
C
    WRITE(6,21)
 21 FORMAT(1H1,120X,'PAGE   06'//,50X,'SLACK  ANALYSIS')
    1 FORMAT(////)
    WRITE(6,1)
    WRITE(6,8)
  8 FORMAT(10X,'ROW',6X,'AVAILABLE',12X,'POS-SLK',12X'NEG-SLK')
    WRITE(6,1)
    DO 19 I=1,NROWS
    NEGSLK=0.0
```

552

```
      POSSLK=0.0
      DO 11 J=1,NROWS
      M=Y(J)
      IF(I-M) 9,10,9
    9 IF(M-KEPT(I))    11,12,11
   11 CONTINUE
      GO TO 13
   10 NEGSLK=RHS(J)
      GO TO 13
   12 POSSLK=RHS(J)
   13 WRITE(6,14)I,RHS1(I),POSSLK,NEGSLK
   14 FORMAT(10X,I3,3F20.5)
   19 CONTINUE
   43 FORMAT(10X,I3,3X,F15.5)
C
C     VARIABLE AMOUNTS
C
      WRITE(6,44)
   44 FORMAT(1H1,120X,'PAGE 07'//,50X,'VARIABLE ANALYSIS')
      WRITE(6,45)
   45 FORMAT(////,7X,'VARIABLE          AMOUNT',//)
      DO 41 I=1,NROWS
      NCHCK=Y(I)-KPCK-NROWS
      IF(NCHCK)41,41,42
   42 WRITE(6,43)NCHCK,RHS(I)
   41 CONTINUE
      WRITE(6,72)
   72 FORMAT(1H1)
      WRITE(6,50)
   50 FORMAT(//,55X,'ANALYSIS OF THE OBJECTIVE',23X,'PAGE 8',////,50X,'P
     %RIORITY',10X,'UNDER-ACHIEVEMENT',/)
      DO 52 K=1,NPRT
```

553

```
      ZVAL(K)=0.0
      DO 51 I=1,NROWS
   51 ZVAL(K)=ZVAL(K) +VALY(I,K)*RHS(I)
      LISP=NPRT+1
      KK=LISP-K
      IF(TEST.EQ.0.0) GO TO 52
      KK=NPRT-K
      IF(KK.GT.0) GO TO 52
      KK=NPRT-K
      IF(KK.GT.0) GO TO 52
      WRITE(6,78) ZVAL(K)
   78 FORMAT(/,45X,'ARTIFICIAL',5X,F20.5)
      GO TO 77
   52 WRITE(6,53) KK,ZVAL(K)
   53 FORMAT(1H0,52X,I2,5X,F20.5)
   77 CONTINUE
      STOP
      END
```

APPENDIX IV Classical Optimization (Calculus) Approach to Solution of Classical Inventory Model

The general approach of classical optimization is to operate on the model function that is to be minimized (or maximized). In the case of the classic inventory model, it is C_t, the total inventory cost, that is to be minimized.

The method of classical optimization first observes that the lowest point on the C_t curve is at the point where that curve's slope is equal to zero. Thus, the objective is to determine a general statement (equation) of the slope of the C_t curve (equation). This is accomplished by calculus by simply taking the first derivative of the total cost function. Since it is the variable Q for which a solution value is desired, the slope function must be determined with respect to Q (which is the same manner in which the total function is specified). Thus, the first derivative of C_t is to be computed with respect to Q, as illustrated in the following. First, the decision variable is isolated at the end of each term of the C_t function, as follows:

$$C_t = C_1 \frac{D}{Q} + C_2 \frac{Q}{2}$$
$$= C_1 D Q^{-1} + \frac{1}{2} C_2 Q$$

Then the derivative of C_t with respect to Q, denoted by dC_t/dQ is as follows:

$$\frac{dC_t}{dQ} = -C_1 D Q^{-2} + \frac{1}{2} C_2$$

The simple formulas for differentiation are given in Appendix I on classical optimization.

The preceding equation is a general statement of the *slope* of C_t for various values of Q. Since the objective is to determine the value of Q that will achieve a minimun value of C_t, the general slope equation is simply set equal to zero, and solved in terms of Q, as follows:

$$- C_1 D Q^{-2} + \frac{1}{2} C_2 = 0$$

$$\frac{C_1 D}{Q^2} = \frac{C_2}{2}$$

$$\frac{Q^2}{C_1 D} = \frac{2}{C_2}$$

$$Q^2 = \frac{2 C_1 D}{C_2}$$

$$Q = \sqrt{\frac{2 C_1 D}{C_2}}$$

which is the same optimum solution obtained previously in the model discussion of the chapter.

APPENDIX V Classical Optimization Solution to Quantity Discount Inventory Model

We begin with the equation for the total inventory and goods cost and isolate the decision variable, Q:

$$C_t = C_1 \frac{D}{Q} + C_2 P \frac{Q}{2} + PD$$

$$= C_1 D Q^{-1} + \frac{1}{2} C_2 P Q + PD$$

Differentiating with respect to Q,

$$\frac{dC_t}{dQ} = -C_1 D Q^{-2} + \frac{1}{2} C_2 P$$

Setting this equal to zero and solving for the optimum value of Q,

$$\frac{-C_1 D}{Q^2} + \frac{C_2 P}{2} = 0$$

$$\frac{Q^2}{C_1 D} = \frac{2}{C_2 P}$$

$$Q^2 = \frac{2 C_1 D}{C_2 P}$$

$$Q_{opt} = \sqrt{\frac{2 C_1 D}{C_2 P}}$$

APPENDIX **VI** Derivation of Inventory Shortage Model

The inventory shortage model is derived by cost component in the following. First, the model variable definitions are as follows:

C_t = total annual inventory cost
C_o = total annual ordering cost
C_c = total annual carrying cost
C_s = total annual shortage cost
Q = quantity ordered, per order
B = quantity backordered (shortages), per order
S = maximum inventory level $(Q - B)$
D = annual demand
C_1 = ordering cost, per order
C_2 = carrying cost, per unit, per year
C_3 = shortage cost, per unit, per year
t_1 = time during which inventory is on hand
t_2 = time during which there is a shortage
t = time between receipt of orders
N = number of orders per year

The overall shortage model is

$$C_t = C_o + C_c + C_s$$

ORDERING COST

The ordering cost component of the model is unaffected by the allowance of shortages, and is respecified as follows:

558

$$C_o = C_1 \frac{D}{Q}$$

CARRYING COST

Since the maximum inventory level is given as S, which is equal to $Q - B$, the average inventory level during the period in which inventory is on hand (t_1) is $S/2$. Thus, the carrying cost during the period from receipt of one order to the next (t), is given as $C_2 t_1 S/2$. Note that t_1 is the time period for which there is inventory on hand.

The key to converting the preceding carrying-cost equation to an annual basis is to recognize that the geometrical relationship of t_1 to S is equal to the relationship of t to Q (i.e., similar triangles). Given that $t_1/S = t/Q$, we can then solve for t_1, yielding

$$t_1 = \frac{tS}{Q}$$

Then, by substituting this term into the previously described carrying-cost equation, $C_2 t_1 S/2$, we obtain,

$$\text{Carrying cost per order period} = C_2 \left(\frac{tS}{Q}\right) \frac{S}{2}$$

$$= \frac{C_2 t S^2}{2Q}$$

We next note that t is the time between order receipts, and there will be N orders per year. Thus, in order to convert the above to an annual basis we multiply t by N, that is, $tN = 1$ (year). Thus, the annual carrying cost equation becomes

$$C_c = \frac{C_2 S^2}{2Q}$$

SHORTAGE COST

Since B represents the maximum level of shortages, the average level of shortages during the period in which there is a shortage (t_2) will be $B/2$. Thus, the shortage cost during one order period (t), is given as $C_3 t_2 B/2$.

Again, the geometrical relationship of t_2 to B is equal to the relationship of t to Q. Thus, given that $t_2/B = t/Q$, we can solve for t_2, yielding

$$t_2 = \frac{tB}{Q}$$

Then, by substituting this term into the previously described shortage-cost equation, $C_3 t_2 B / 2$, we obtain

$$\text{Shortage cost per order period} = C_3\left(\frac{tB}{Q}\right)\frac{B}{2}$$

$$= \frac{C_3 t B^2}{2Q}$$

Again, since $tN = 1$ (year), we obtain the annual shortage cost as

$$C_s = \frac{C_3 B^2}{2Q}$$

Since $B = Q - S$, we can also state C_s as

$$C_s = \frac{C_3(Q - S)^2}{2Q}$$

Thus, the overall inventory model is

$$C_t = \frac{C_1 D}{Q} + \frac{C_2 S^2}{2Q} + \frac{C_3(Q - S)^2}{2Q}$$

APPENDIX **VII** Poisson Probability Values

r	0.10	0.20	0.30	0.40	λ 0.50	0.60	0.70	0.80	0.90	1.00
0	.9048	.8187	.7408	.6703	.6066	.5488	.4966	.4493	.4066	.3679
1	.0905	.1637	.2222	.2681	.3033	.3293	.3476	.3595	.3659	.3679
2	.0045	.0164	.0333	.0536	.0758	.0988	.1217	.1438	.1647	.1839
3	.0002	.0011	.0033	.0072	.0126	.0198	.0284	.0383	.0494	.0613
4	.0000	.0001	.0003	.0007	.0016	.0030	.0050	.0077	.0111	.0153
5	.0000	.0000	.0000	.0001	.0002	.0004	.0007	.0012	.0020	.0031
6	.0000	.0000	.0000	.0000	.0000	.0000	.0001	.0002	.0003	.0005
7	.0000	.0000	.0000	.0000	.0000	.0000	.0000	.0000	.0000	.0001

r	1.10	1.20	1.30	1.40	λ 1.50	1.60	1.70	1.80	1.90	2.00
0	.3329	.3012	.2725	.2466	.2231	.2019	.1827	.1653	.1496	.1353
1	.3662	.3614	.3543	.3452	.3347	.3230	.3106	.2975	.2842	.2707
2	.2014	.2169	.2303	.2417	.2510	.2584	.2640	.2678	.2700	.2707
3	.0738	.0867	.0998	.1128	.1255	.1378	.1496	.1607	.1710	.1804
4	.0203	.0260	.0324	.0395	.0471	.0551	.0636	.0723	.0812	.0902
5	.0045	.0062	.0084	.0111	.0141	.0176	.0216	.0260	.0309	.0361
6	.0008	.0012	.0018	.0026	.0035	.0047	.0061	.0078	.0098	.0120
7	.0001	.0002	.0003	.0005	.0008	.0011	.0015	.0020	.0027	.0034
8	.0000	.0000	.0001	.0001	.0001	.0002	.0003	.0005	.0006	.0009
9	.0000	.0000	.0000	.0000	.0000	.0000	.0001	.0001	.0001	.0002

r	2.10	2.20	2.30	2.40	λ 2.50	2.60	2.70	2.80	2.90	3.00
0	.1225	.1108	.1003	.0907	.0821	.0743	.0672	.0608	.0550	.0498
1	.2572	.2438	.2306	.2177	.2052	.1931	.1815	.1703	.1596	.1494
2	.2700	.2681	.2652	.2613	.2565	.2510	.2450	.2384	.2314	.2240
3	.1890	.1966	.2033	.2090	.2138	.2176	.2205	.2225	.2237	.2240
4	.0992	.1082	.1169	.1254	.1336	.1414	.1488	.1557	.1622	.1680
5	.0417	.0476	.0538	.0602	.0668	.0735	.0804	.0872	.0940	.1008
6	.0146	.0174	.0206	.0241	.0278	.0319	.0362	.0407	.0455	.0504
7	.0044	.0055	.0068	.0083	.0099	.0118	.0139	.0163	.0188	.0216
8	.0011	.0015	.0019	.0025	.0031	.0038	.0047	.0057	.0068	.0081
9	.0003	.0004	.0005	.0007	.0009	.0011	.0014	.0018	.0022	.0027
10	.0001	.0001	.0001	.0002	.0002	.0003	.0004	.0005	.0006	.0008
11	.0000	.0000	.0000	.0000	.0000	.0001	.0001	.0001	.0002	.0002
12	.0000	.0000	.0000	.0000	.0000	.0000	.0000	.0000	.0000	.0001

r	3.10	3.20	3.30	3.40	λ 3.50	3.60	3.70	3.80	3.90	4.00
0	.0450	.0408	.0369	.0334	.0302	.0273	.0247	.0224	.0202	.0183
1	.1397	.1304	.1217	.1135	.1057	.0984	.0915	.0850	.0789	.0733
2	.2165	.2087	.2008	.1929	.1850	.1771	.1692	.1615	.1539	.1465
3	.2237	.2226	.2209	.2186	.2158	.2125	.2087	.2046	.2001	.1954
4	.1733	.1781	.1823	.1858	.1888	.1912	.1931	.1944	.1951	.1954

r	3.10	3.20	3.30	3.40	λ 3.50	3.60	3.70	3.80	3.90	4.00
5	.1075	.1140	.1203	.1264	.1322	.1377	.1429	.1477	.1522	.1563
6	.0555	.0608	.0662	.0716	.0771	.0826	.0881	.0936	.0989	.1042
7	.0246	.0278	.0312	.0348	.0385	.0425	.0466	.0508	.0551	.0595
8	.0095	.0111	.0129	.0148	.0169	.0191	.0215	.0241	.0269	.0298
9	.0033	.0040	.0047	.0056	.0066	.0076	.0089	.0102	.0116	.0132
10	.0010	.0013	.0016	.0019	.0023	.0028	.0033	.0039	.0045	.0053
11	.0003	.0004	.0005	.0006	.0007	.0009	.0011	.0013	.0016	.0019
12	.0001	.0001	.0001	.0002	.0002	.0003	.0003	.0004	.0005	.0006
13	.0000	.0000	.0000	.0000	.0001	.0001	.0001	.0001	.0002	.0002
14	.0000	.0000	.0000	.0000	.0000	.0000	.0000	.0000	.0000	.0001

r	4.10	4.20	4.30	4.40	λ 4.50	4.60	4.70	4.80	4.90	5.00
0	.0166	.0150	.0136	.0123	.0111	.0101	.0091	.0082	.0074	.0067
1	.0679	.0630	.0583	.0540	.0500	.0462	.0427	.0395	.0365	.0337
2	.1393	.1323	.1254	.1188	.1125	.1063	.1005	.0948	.0894	.0842
3	.1904	.1852	.1798	.1743	.1687	.1631	.1574	.1517	.1460	.1404
4	.1951	.1944	.1933	.1917	.1898	.1875	.1849	.1820	.1789	.1755
5	.1600	.1633	.1662	.1687	.1708	.1725	.1738	.1747	.1753	.1755
6	.1093	.1143	.1191	.1237	.1281	.1323	.1362	.1398	.1432	.1462
7	.0640	.0686	.0732	.0778	.0824	.0869	.0914	.0959	.1002	.1044
8	.0328	.0360	.0393	.0428	.0463	.0500	.0537	.0575	.0614	.0653
9	.0150	.0168	.0188	.0209	.0232	.0255	.0281	.0307	.0334	.0363
10	.0061	.0071	.0081	.0092	.0104	.0118	.0132	.0147	.0164	.0181
11	.0023	.0027	.0032	.0037	.0043	.0049	.0056	.0064	.0073	.0082
12	.0008	.0009	.0011	.0013	.0016	.0019	.0022	.0026	.0030	.0034
13	.0002	.0003	.0004	.0005	.0006	.0007	.0008	.0009	.0011	.0013
14	.0001	.0001	.0001	.0001	.0002	.0002	.0003	.0003	.0004	.0005
15	.0000	.0000	.0000	.0000	.0001	.0001	.0001	.0001	.0001	.0002

r	5.10	5.20	5.30	5.40	λ 5.50	5.60	5.70	5.80	5.90	6.00
0	.0061	.0055	.0050	.0045	.0041	.0037	.0033	.0030	.0027	.0025
1	.0311	.0287	.0265	.0244	.0225	.0207	.0191	.0176	.0162	.0149
2	.0793	.0746	.0701	.0659	.0618	.0580	.0544	.0509	.0477	.0446
3	.1348	.1293	.1239	.1185	.1133	.1082	.1033	.0985	.0938	.0892
4	.1719	.1681	.1641	.1600	.1558	.1515	.1472	.1428	.1383	.1339
5	.1753	.1748	.1740	.1728	.1714	.1697	.1678	.1656	.1632	.1606
6	.1490	.1515	.1537	.1555	.1571	.1584	.1594	.1601	.1605	.1606
7	.1086	.1125	.1163	.1200	.1234	.1267	.1298	.1326	.1353	.1377
8	.0692	.0731	.0771	.0810	.0849	.0887	.0925	.0962	.0998	.1033
9	.0392	.0423	.0454	.0486	.0519	.0552	.0586	.0620	.0654	.0688
10	.0200	.0220	.0241	.0262	.0285	.0309	.0334	.0359	.0386	.0413
11	.0093	.0104	.0116	.0129	.0143	.0157	.0173	.0190	.0207	.0225
12	.0039	.0045	.0051	.0058	.0065	.0073	.0082	.0092	.0102	.0113
13	.0015	.0018	.0021	.0024	.0028	.0032	.0036	.0041	.0046	.0052
14	.0006	.0007	.0008	.0009	.0011	.0013	.0015	.0017	.0019	.0022
15	.0002	.0002	.0003	.0003	.0004	.0005	.0006	.0007	.0008	.0009
16	.0001	.0001	.0001	.0001	.0001	.0002	.0002	.0002	.0003	.0003
17	.0000	.0000	.0000	.0000	.0000	.0001	.0001	.0001	.0001	.0001

r	6.10	6.20	6.30	6.40	λ 6.50	6.60	6.70	6.80	6.90	7.00
0	.0022	.0020	.0018	.0017	.0015	.0014	.0012	.0011	.0010	.0009
1	.0137	.0126	.0116	.0106	.0098	.0090	.0082	.0076	.0070	.0064
2	.0417	.0390	.0364	.0340	.0318	.0296	.0276	.0258	.0240	.0223
3	.0848	.0806	.0765	.0726	.0688	.0652	.0617	.0584	.0552	.0521
4	.1294	.1249	.1205	.1161	.1118	.1076	.1034	.0992	.0952	.0912
5	.1579	.1549	.1519	.1487	.1454	.1420	.1385	.1349	.1314	.1277
6	.1605	.1601	.1595	.1586	.1575	.1562	.1546	.1529	.1511	.1490
7	.1399	.1418	.1435	.1450	.1462	.1472	.1480	.1486	.1489	.1490
8	.1066	.1099	.1130	.1160	.1188	.1215	.1240	.1263	.1284	.1304
9	.0723	.0757	.0791	.0825	.0858	.0891	.0923	.0954	.0985	.1014
10	.0441	.0469	.0498	.0528	.0558	.0588	.0618	.0649	.0679	.0710
11	.0244	.0265	.0285	.0307	.0330	.0353	.0377	.0401	.0426	.0452
12	.0124	.0137	.0150	.0164	.0179	.0194	.0210	.0227	.0245	.0263
13	.0058	.0065	.0073	.0081	.0089	.0099	.0108	.0119	.0130	.0142
14	.0025	.0029	.0033	.0037	.0041	.0046	.0052	.0058	.0064	.0071

r	6.10	6.20	6.30	6.40	λ 6.50	6.60	6.70	6.80	6.90	7.00
15	.0010	.0012	.0014	.0016	.0018	.0020	.0023	.0026	.0029	.0033
16	.0004	.0005	.0005	.0006	.0007	.0008	.0010	.0011	.0013	.0014
17	.0001	.0002	.0002	.0002	.0003	.0003	.0004	.0004	.0005	.0006
18	.0000	.0001	.0001	.0001	.0001	.0001	.0001	.0002	.0002	.0002
19	.0000	.0000	.0000	.0000	.0000	.0000	.0001	.0001	.0001	.0001

r	7.10	7.20	7.30	7.40	λ 7.50	7.60	7.70	7.80	7.90	8.00
0	.0008	.0007	.0007	.0006	.0006	.0005	.0005	.0004	.0004	.0003
1	.0059	.0054	.0049	.0045	.0041	.0038	.0035	.0032	.0029	.0027
2	.0208	.0194	.0180	.0167	.0156	.0145	.0134	.0125	.0116	.0107
3	.0492	.0464	.0438	.0413	.0389	.0366	.0345	.0324	.0305	.0286
4	.0874	.0836	.0799	.0764	.0729	.0696	.0663	.0632	.0602	.0573
5	.1241	.1204	.1167	.1130	.1094	.1057	.1021	.0986	.0951	.0916
6	.1468	.1445	.1420	.1394	.1367	.1339	.1311	.1282	.1252	.1221
7	.1489	.1486	.1481	.1474	.1465	.1454	.1442	.1428	.1413	.1396
8	.1321	.1337	.1351	.1363	.1373	.1381	.1388	.1392	.1395	.1396
9	.1042	.1070	.1096	.1121	.1144	.1167	.1187	.1207	.1224	.1241
10	.0740	.0770	.0800	.0829	.0858	.0887	.0914	.0941	.0967	.0993
11	.0478	.0504	.0531	.0558	.0585	.0613	.0640	.0667	.0695	.0722
12	.0283	.0303	.0323	.0344	.0366	.0388	.0411	.0434	.0457	.0481
13	.0154	.0168	.0181	.0196	.0211	.0227	.0243	.0260	.0278	.0296
14	.0078	.0086	.0095	.0104	.0113	.0123	.0134	.0145	.0157	.0169
15	.0037	.0041	.0046	.0051	.0057	.0062	.0069	.0075	.0083	.0090
16	.0016	.0019	.0021	.0024	.0026	.0030	.0033	.0037	.0041	.0045
17	.0007	.0008	.0009	.0010	.0012	.0013	.0015	.0017	.0019	.0021
18	.0003	.0003	.0004	.0004	.0005	.0006	.0006	.0007	.0008	.0009
19	.0001	.0001	.0001	.0002	.0002	.0002	.0003	.0003	.0003	.0004
20	.0000	.0000	.0000	.0001	.0001	.0001	.0001	.0001	.0001	.0002
21	.0000	.0000	.0000	.0000	.0000	.0000	.0000	.0000	.0001	.0001

r	8.10	8.20	8.30	8.40	λ 8.50	8.60	8.70	8.80	8.90	9.00
0	.0003	.0003	.0002	.0002	.0002	.0002	.0002	.0002	.0001	.0001
1	.0025	.0023	.0021	.0019	.0017	.0016	.0014	.0013	.0012	.0011
2	.0100	.0092	.0086	.0079	.0074	.0068	.0063	.0058	.0054	.0050
3	.0269	.0252	.0237	.0222	.0208	.0195	.0183	.0171	.0160	.0150
4	.0544	.0517	.0491	.0466	.0443	.0420	.0398	.0377	.0357	.0337
5	.0882	.0849	.0816	.0784	.0752	.0722	.0692	.0663	.0635	.0607
6	.1191	.1160	.1128	.1097	.1066	.1034	.1003	.0972	.0941	.0911
7	.1378	.1358	.1338	.1317	.1294	.1271	.1247	.1222	.1197	.1171
8	.1395	.1392	.1388	.1382	.1375	.1366	.1356	.1344	.1332	.1318
9	.1256	.1269	.1280	.1290	.1299	.1306	.1311	.1315	.1317	.1318
10	.1017	.1040	.1063	.1084	.1104	.1123	.1140	.1157	.1172	.1186
11	.0749	.0776	.0802	.0828	.0853	.0878	.0902	.0925	.0948	.0970
12	.0505	.0530	.0555	.0579	.0604	.0629	.0654	.0679	.0703	.0728
13	.0315	.0334	.0354	.0374	.0395	.0416	.0438	.0459	.0481	.0504
14	.0182	.0196	.0210	.0225	.0240	.0256	.0272	.0289	.0306	.0324
15	.0098	.0107	.0116	.0126	.0136	.0147	.0158	.0169	.0182	.0194
16	.0050	.0055	.0060	.0066	.0072	.0079	.0086	.0093	.0101	.0109
17	.0024	.0026	.0029	.0033	.0036	.0040	.0044	.0048	.0053	.0058
18	.0011	.0012	.0014	.0015	.0017	.0019	.0021	.0024	.0026	.0029
19	.0005	.0005	.0006	.0007	.0008	.0009	.0010	.0011	.0012	.0014
20	.0002	.0002	.0002	.0003	.0003	.0004	.0004	.0005	.0005	.0006
21	.0001	.0001	.0001	.0001	.0001	.0002	.0002	.0002	.0002	.0003
22	.0000	.0000	.0000	.0000	.0001	.0001	.0001	.0001	.0001	.0001

r	9.10	9.20	9.30	9.40	λ 9.50	9.60	9.70	9.80	9.90	10.00
0	.0001	.0001	.0001	.0001	.0001	.0001	.0001	.0001	.0001	.0000
1	.0010	.0009	.0009	.0008	.0007	.0007	.0006	.0005	.0005	.0005
2	.0046	.0043	.0040	.0037	.0034	.0031	.0029	.0027	.0025	.0023
3	.0140	.0131	.0123	.0115	.0107	.0100	.0093	.0087	.0081	.0076
4	.0319	.0302	.0285	.0269	.0254	.0240	.0226	.0213	.0201	.0189
5	.0581	.0555	.0530	.0506	.0483	.0460	.0439	.0418	.0398	.0378
6	.0881	.0851	.0822	.0793	.0764	.0736	.0709	.0682	.0656	.0631
7	.1145	.1118	.1091	.1064	.1037	.1010	.0982	.0955	.0928	.0901
8	.1302	.1286	.1269	.1251	.1232	.1212	.1191	.1170	.1148	.1126
9	.1317	.1315	.1311	.1306	.1300	.1293	.1284	.1274	.1263	.1251

r	9.10	9.20	9.30	9.40	λ 9.50	9.60	9.70	9.80	9.90	10.00
10	.1198	.1210	.1219	.1228	.1235	.1241	.1245	.1249	.1250	.1251
11	.0991	.1012	.1031	.1049	.1067	.1083	.1098	.1112	.1125	.1137
12	.0752	.0776	.0799	.0822	.0844	.0866	.0888	.0908	.0928	.0948
13	.0526	.0549	.0572	.0594	.0617	.0640	.0662	.0685	.0707	.0729
14	.0342	.0361	.0380	.0399	.0419	.0439	.0459	.0479	.0500	.0521
15	.0208	.0221	.0235	.0250	.0265	.0281	.0297	.0313	.0330	.0347
16	.0118	.0127	.0137	.0147	.0157	.0168	.0180	.0192	.0204	.0217
17	.0063	.0069	.0075	.0081	.0088	.0095	.0103	.0111	.0119	.0128
18	.0032	.0035	.0039	.0042	.0046	.0051	.0055	.0060	.0065	.0071
19	.0015	.0017	.0019	.0021	.0023	.0026	.0028	.0031	.0034	.0037
20	.0007	.0008	.0009	.0010	.0011	.0012	.0014	.0015	.0017	.0019
21	.0003	.0003	.0004	.0004	.0005	.0006	.0006	.0007	.0008	.0009
22	.0001	.0001	.0002	.0002	.0002	.0002	.0003	.0003	.0004	.0004
23	.0000	.0001	.0001	.0001	.0001	.0001	.0001	.0001	.0002	.0002
24	.0000	.0000	.0000	.0000	.0000	.0000	.0000	.0001	.0001	.0001

r	11.	12.	13.	14.	λ 15.	16.	17.	18.	19.	20.
0	.0000	.0000	.0000	.0000	.0000	.0000	.0000	.0000	.0000	.0000
1	.0002	.0001	.0000	.0000	.0000	.0000	.0000	.0000	.0000	.0000
2	.0010	.0004	.0002	.0001	.0000	.0000	.0000	.0000	.0000	.0000
3	.0037	.0018	.0008	.0004	.0002	.0001	.0000	.0000	.0000	.0000
4	.0102	.0053	.0027	.0013	.0006	.0003	.0001	.0001	.0000	.0000
5	.0224	.0127	.0070	.0037	.0019	.0010	.0005	.0002	.0001	.0001
6	.0411	.0255	.0152	.0087	.0048	.0026	.0014	.0007	.0004	.0002
7	.0646	.0437	.0281	.0174	.0104	.0060	.0034	.0019	.0010	.0005
8	.0888	.0655	.0457	.0304	.0194	.0120	.0072	.0042	.0024	.0013
9	.1085	.0874	.0661	.0473	.0324	.0213	.0135	.0083	.0050	.0029
10	.1194	.1048	.0859	.0663	.0486	.0341	.0230	.0150	.0095	.0058
11	.1194	.1144	.1015	.0844	.0663	.0496	.0355	.0245	.0164	.0106
12	.1094	.1144	.1099	.0984	.0829	.0661	.0504	.0368	.0259	.0176
13	.0926	.1056	.1099	.1060	.0956	.0814	.0658	.0509	.0378	.0271
14	.0728	.0905	.1021	.1060	.1024	.0930	.0800	.0655	.0514	.0387
15	.0534	.0724	.0885	.0989	.1024	.0992	.0906	.0786	.0650	.0516
16	.0367	.0543	.0719	.0866	.0960	.0992	.0963	.0884	.0772	.0646
17	.0237	.0383	.0550	.0713	.0847	.0934	.0963	.0936	.0863	.0760
18	.0145	.0256	.0397	.0554	.0706	.0830	.0909	.0936	.0911	.0844
19	.0084	.0161	.0272	.0409	.0557	.0699	.0814	.0887	.0911	.0888
20	.0046	.0097	.0177	.0286	.0418	.0559	.0692	.0798	.0866	.0888
21	.0024	.0055	.0109	.0191	.0299	.0426	.0560	.0684	.0783	.0846
22	.0012	.0030	.0065	.0121	.0204	.0310	.0433	.0560	.0676	.0769
23	.0006	.0016	.0037	.0074	.0133	.0216	.0320	.0438	.0559	.0669
24	.0003	.0008	.0020	.0043	.0083	.0144	.0226	.0329	.0442	.0557
25	.0001	.0004	.0010	.0024	.0050	.0092	.0154	.0237	.0336	.0446
26	.0000	.0002	.0005	.0013	.0029	.0057	.0101	.0164	.0246	.0343
27	.0000	.0001	.0002	.0007	.0016	.0034	.0063	.0109	.0173	.0254
28	.0000	.0000	.0001	.0003	.0009	.0019	.0038	.0070	.0117	.0181
29	.0000	.0000	.0001	.0002	.0004	.0011	.0023	.0044	.0077	.0125
30	.0000	.0000	.0000	.0001	.0002	.0006	.0013	.0026	.0049	.0083
31	.0000	.0000	.0000	.0000	.0001	.0003	.0007	.0015	.0030	.0054
32	.0000	.0000	.0000	.0000	.0001	.0001	.0004	.0009	.0018	.0034
33	.0000	.0000	.0000	.0000	.0000	.0001	.0002	.0005	.0010	.0020
34	.0000	.0000	.0000	.0000	.0000	.0000	.0001	.0002	.0006	.0012
35	.0000	.0000	.0000	.0000	.0000	.0000	.0000	.0001	.0003	.0007
36	.0000	.0000	.0000	.0000	.0000	.0000	.0000	.0001	.0002	.0004
37	.0000	.0000	.0000	.0000	.0000	.0000	.0000	.0000	.0001	.0002
38	.0000	.0000	.0000	.0000	.0000	.0000	.0000	.0000	.0000	.0001
39	.0000	.0000	.0000	.0000	.0000	.0000	.0000	.0000	.0000	.0001

r	25.0	30.0	40.0	50.0	λ 75.0	100.0
0	.0000	.0000	0	0	0	0
1	.0000	.0000	0	0	0	0
2	.0000	.0000	0	0	0	0
3	.0000	.0000	0	0	0	0
4	.0000	.0000	0	0	0	0
5	.0000	.0000	0	0	0	0
6	.0000	.0000	.0000	0	0	0
7	.0000	.0000	.0000	0	0	0
8	.0001	.0000	.0000	0	0	0
9	.0001	.0000	.0000	0	0	0
10	.0004	.0000	.0000	0	0	0
11	.0008	.0000	.0000	.0000	0	0
12	.0017	.0001	.0000	.0000	0	0
13	.0033	.0002	.0000	.0000	0	0
14	.0059	.0005	.0000	.0000	0	0
15	.0099	.0010	.0000	.0000	0	0
16	.0155	.0019	.0000	.0000	0	0
17	.0227	.0034	.0000	.0000	0	0
18	.0316	.0057	.0000	.0000	0	0
19	.0415	.0089	.0001	.0000	0	0
20	.0519	.0134	.0002	.0000	0	0
21	.0618	.0192	.0004	.0000	0	0
22	.0702	.0261	.0007	.0000	0	0
23	.0763	.0341	.0012	.0000	0	0
24	.0795	.0426	.0019	.0000	0	0
25	.0795	.0511	.0031	.0000	0	0
26	.0765	.0590	.0047	.0001	.0000	0
27	.0708	.0655	.0070	.0001	.0000	0
28	.0632	.0702	.0100	.0002	.0000	0
29	.0545	.0726	.0138	.0004	.0000	0
30	.0454	.0726	.0185	.0007	.0000	0
31	.0366	.0703	.0238	.0011	.0000	0
32	.0286	.0659	.0298	.0017	.0000	0
33	.0217	.0599	.0361	.0026	.0000	0
34	.0159	.0529	.0425	.0038	.0000	0
35	.0114	.0453	.0485	.0054	.0000	0
36	.0079	.0378	.0539	.0075	.0000	0
37	.0053	.0306	.0583	.0102	.0000	0
38	.0035	.0242	.0614	.0134	.0000	0
39	.0023	.0186	.0629	.0172	.0000	0
40	.0014	.0139	.0629	.0215	.0000	0
41	.0009	.0102	.0614	.0262	.0000	0
42	.0005	.0073	.0585	.0312	.0000	.0000
43	.0003	.0051	.0544	.0363	.0000	.0000
44	.0002	.0035	.0495	.0412	.0000	.0000
45	.0001	.0023	.0440	.0458	.0001	.0000
46	.0001	.0015	.0382	.0498	.0001	.0000
47	.0000	.0010	.0325	.0530	.0001	.0000
48	.0000	.0006	.0271	.0552	.0002	.0000
49	.0000	.0004	.0221	.0563	.0003	.0000
50	.0000	.0002	.0177	.0563	.0005	.0000
51	.0000	.0001	.0139	.0552	.0007	.0000
52	.0000	.0001	.0107	.0531	.0011	.0000
53	.0000	.0000	.0081	.0501	.0015	.0000
54	.0000	.0000	.0060	.0464	.0021	.0000
55	.0000	.0000	.0043	.0422	.0028	.0000
56	.0000	.0000	.0031	.0376	.0038	.0000
57	.0000	.0000	.0022	.0330	.0050	.0000
58	.0000	.0000	.0015	.0285	.0065	.0000
59	.0000	.0000	.0010	.0241	.0082	.0000
60	.0000	.0000	.0007	.0201	.0103	.0000
61	.0000	.0000	.0004	.0165	.0126	.0000
62	.0000	.0000	.0003	.0133	.0153	.0000
63	.0000	.0000	.0002	.0105	.0182	.0000
64	.0000	.0000	.0001	.0082	.0213	.0000
65	0	.0000	.0001	.0063	.0246	.0000
66	0	.0000	.0000	.0048	.0279	.0001
67	0	.0000	.0000	.0036	.0313	.0001
68	0	.0000	.0000	.0026	.0345	.0002
69	0	.0000	.0000	.0019	.0375	.0002

r	25.0	30.0	40.0	50.0	λ 75.0	100.0
70	.000	.0000	.0000	.0014	.0402	.0003
71	0	.0000	.0000	.0010	.0424	.0004
72	0	.0000	.0000	.0007	.0442	.0006
73	0	0	.0000	.0005	.0454	.0008
74	0	0	.0000	.0003	.0460	.0011
75	0	0	.0000	.0002	.0460	.0015
76	0	0	.0000	.0001	.0454	.0020
77	0	0	.0000	.0001	.0442	.0026
78	0	0	.0000	.0001	.0425	.0033
79	0	0	.0000	.0000	.0404	.0042
80	0	0	.0000	.0000	.0379	.0052
81	0	0	.0000	.0000	.0350	.0064
82	0	0	.0000	.0000	.0321	.0078
83	0	0	.0000	.0000	.0290	.0094
84	0	0	.0000	.0000	.0259	.0112
85	0	0	.0000	.0000	.0228	.0132
86	0	0	.0000	.0000	.0199	.0154
87	0	0	.0000	.0000	.0172	.0176
88	0	0	.0000	.0000	.0146	.0201
89	0	0	0	.0000	.0123	.0225
90	0	0	0	.0000	.0103	.0250
91	0	0	0	.0000	.0085	.0275
92	0	0	0	.0000	.0069	.0299
93	0	0	0	.0000	.0056	.0322
94	0	0	0	.0000	.0044	.0342
95	0	0	0	.0000	.0035	.0360
96	0	0	0	.0000	.0027	.0375
97	0	0	0	.0000	.0021	.0387
98	0	0	0	.0000	.0016	.0395
99	0	0	0	.0000	.0012	.0399
100	0	0	0	.0000	.0009	.0399
101	0	0	0	.0000	.0007	.0395
102	0	0	0	.0000	.0005	.0387
103	0	0	0	.0000	.0004	.0376
104	0	0	0	0	.0003	.0361
105	0	0	0	0	.0002	.0344
106	0	0	0	0	.0001	.0325
107	0	0	0	0	.0001	.0303
108	0	0	0	0	.0001	.0281
109	0	0	0	0	.0000	.0258
110	0	0	0	0	.0000	.0234
111	0	0	0	0	.0000	.0211
112	0	0	0	0	.0000	.0188
113	0	0	0	0	.0000	.0167
114	0	0	0	0	.0000	.0146
115	0	0	0	0	.0000	.0127
116	0	0	0	0	.0000	.0110
117	0	0	0	0	.0000	.0094
118	0	0	0	0	.0000	.0079
119	0	0	0	0	.0000	.0067
120	0	0	0	0	.0000	.0056
121	0	0	0	0	.0000	.0046
122	0	0	0	0	.0000	.0038
123	0	0	0	0	.0000	.0031
124	0	0	0	0	.0000	.0025
125	0	0	0	0	.0000	.0020
126	0	0	0	0	.0000	.0016
127	0	0	0	0	.0000	.0012
128	0	0	0	0	.0000	.0010
129	0	0	0	0	.0000	.0007
130	0	0	0	0	.0000	.0006
131	0	0	0	0	.0000	.0004
132	0	0	0	0	.0000	.0003
133	0	0	0	0	.0000	.0003
134	0	0	0	0	.0000	.0002
135	0	0	0	0	.0000	.0001
136	0	0	0	0	.0000	.0001
137	0	0	0	0	.0000	.0001
138	0	0	0	0	.0000	.0001

APPENDIX VIII Values of e^x and e^{-x}

x	e^x	e^{-x}	x	e^x	e^{-x}
0.00	1.000	1.000	3.00	20.086	0.050
0.10	1.105	0.905	3.10	22.198	0.045
0.20	1.221	0.819	3.20	24.533	0.041
0.30	1.350	0.741	3.30	27.113	0.037
0.40	1.492	0.670	3.40	29.964	0.033
0.50	1.649	0.607	3.50	33.115	0.030
0.60	1.822	0.549	3.60	36.598	0.027
0.70	2.014	0.497	3.70	40.447	0.025
0.80	2.226	0.449	3.80	44.701	0.022
0.90	2.460	0.407	3.90	49.402	0.020
1.00	2.718	0.368	4.00	54.598	0.018
1.10	3.004	0.333	4.10	60.340	0.017
1.20	3.320	0.301	4.20	66.686	0.015
1.30	3.669	0.273	4.30	73.700	0.014
1.40	4.055	0.247	4.40	81.451	0.012
1.50	4.482	0.223	4.50	90.017	0.011
1.60	4.953	0.202	4.60	99.484	0.010
1.70	5.474	0.183	4.70	109.95	0.009
1.80	6.050	0.165	4.80	121.51	0.008
1.90	6.686	0.150	4.90	134.29	0.007
2.00	7.389	0.135	5.00	148.41	0.007
2.10	8.166	0.122	5.10	164.02	0.006
2.20	9.025	0.111	5.20	181.27	0.006
2.30	9.974	0.100	5.30	200.34	0.005
2.40	11.023	0.091	5.40	221.41	0.005
2.50	12.182	0.082	5.50	244.69	0.004
2.60	13.464	0.074	5.60	270.43	0.004
2.70	14.880	0.067	5.70	298.87	0.003
2.80	16.445	0.061	5.80	330.30	0.003
2.90	18.174	0.055	5.90	365.04	0.003
3.00	20.086	0.050	6.00	403.43	0.002

APPENDIX IX Derivation of the Queueing Equations for the First Model

The first queueing model presented included the following assumptions: (1) Poisson arrivals and negative exponential service times, (2) infinite population and queue, (3) first-come, first-served queue discipline, (4) mean service rate (μ) is greater than mean arrival rate (λ), and (5) steady-state conditions.

The derivation of the queueing equations is an exercise in probability. Several approaches can be taken in showing this derivation. The approach taken here attempts to maximize the reader's intuitive understanding rather than performing elaborate mathematical computations. Although the intuitive approach is not as attractive from a theoretical point of view, it is hoped that an increase in understandability compensates for this lack of mathematical rigor. Only the student can answer this question.

As stated previously, it is assumed that we have steady-state conditions. Therefore, although many derivations of the queueing probabilities are initially developed as a function of time, and then later adjusted to reflect time independence, we shall simply begin our development of the equations with the assumption that the various probabilities considered are not dependent on how long the system has been operating.

The first point to be considered is the probability of an arrival or an end of service, during some increment of time. If the expected number of arrivals per hour (λ) is one, then what is the probability of an arrival during some very short increment of time? First we will assume that we divide the time period (one hour) into enough increments such that no more than one arrival could occur during any one time increment. If we divide the hour into minutes, then we have 60 time increments. If no more than one arrival could occur during any one of the 60 time increments, and we expect a total of one arrival during the hour, then the probability of one arrival during one time increment is 1/60. We get this by multiplying the expected number of arrivals in one hour by the time increment, 1/60 of an hour. If we expected 5 arrivals during an hour ($\lambda = 5$), then the probability of one arrival during one of the 60 increments would be $5 \times 1/60$ of an hour $= 5/60 = 1/12$. [If we draw one ball from an urn containing 60 balls, in which there are 5 red balls, then the probability of drawing a red ball is the number of red balls (5) times the probability of drawing any one of the 60 balls (1/60), yielding 5/60 or a probability of 1/12.] This is analogous to asking, what is the probability you will select the time increment containing the arrival (or arrivals).

Returning to our time increments, minutes are not actually very small time increments. Certainly more than one arrival may occur in one minute at many queueing systems. We, therefore, simply divide our time period into smaller time increments. Suppose we divide our hour into seconds, so that each time increment is 1/3600 of an hour. Therefore, if we expect one arrival in an hour, then the probability of an arrival during some time increment is $1 \times 1/3600 = 1/3600$. If we expected 5 arrivals in an hour, the probability of one arrival during one time increment is $5 \times 1/3600 = 5/3600 = 1/720$. We could next divide the hour into microseconds, and be reasonably sure that no more than one arrival will occur during one time increment.

If we assume that the fraction of an hour is represented by Δt, and that the mean (expected) arrival rate per hour is λ; then the probability of one arrival during Δt is equal to $\lambda(\Delta t)$. The exact same argument follows for the probability of one end of service during Δt, which is given by $\mu(\Delta t)$, where μ = mean (expected) service rate. Since we assume that no more than one arrival can occur during Δt, and no more than one end of service during Δt, we also assume that both an arrival and an end of service will not occur simultaneously during Δt. [Note that if $\lambda(\Delta t)$ is the probability of an arrival during Δt, and $\mu(\Delta t)$ is the probability of an end of service, then the joint probability of both occuring simultaneously is $\lambda(\Delta t)\mu(\Delta t) = \lambda\mu(\Delta t)^2$. If Δt is infinitesimally small, then $(\Delta t)^2$ will be virtually zero, and thus $\lambda(\Delta t)\mu(\Delta t) \cong 0$.]

Thus, there are three possible events during Δt, an addition of one unit in the system, a reduction of one unit in the system, or no change in the system (no arrival and no departure). If $\lambda(\Delta t)$ is the probability of an arrival during Δt, then $1 - \lambda(\Delta t)$ is the probability of no arrival. Likewise, $1 - \mu(\Delta t)$ is the probability of no departure from the system. The joint probability of no arrival and no departure is given by the product of the two events: $[1 - \lambda(\Delta t)][1 - \mu(\Delta t)] \quad =$

$1 - \lambda\Delta t - \mu\Delta t + \lambda\mu(\Delta t)^2$. The last term drops off for the same argument given previously $[(\Delta t)^2 \cong 0]$. Thus, we have as the probability of no change, $1 - (\lambda\Delta t + \mu\Delta t)$. The states of the system at time t and $t + \Delta t$, with the three possible events during Δt, are shown in Figure A.IXa (where k is the number of units in the system).

Of course, when there are zero units in the system ($k = 0$) at time t, then only two events can occur: Either there is no arrival, with probability $1 - \lambda\Delta t$, or there is an arrival, with probability $\lambda\Delta t$. When $k \geq 1$ at time t, all three events can occur, which is shown for the cases where $k = 1$, $k = 2$, and $k = n$, at time t. For example, for the general case where $k = n$ at time t, the probability of moving to $k = n-1$ at $t + \Delta t$ equals $\mu\Delta t$; the probability of moving to $k = n$ at $t + \Delta t$ equals $1 - (\lambda\Delta t + \mu\Delta t)$; and the probability of moving to $k = n + 1$ at $t + \Delta t$ equals $\lambda\Delta t$.

We will identify P as the probability of some number of units in the system (the state of the system), and denote by a subscript to P the number in the system. Thus, P_n is the probability of n units in the system. Referring to the figure, we see that there are two ways to have zero in the system at time $t + \Delta t$: When $k = 0$ at time t and no arrival occurs; and when $k = 1$ at time t and one departure occurs. The probability of zero in the system at time $t + \Delta t$ is then the probability of zero at time t times the probability of no arrival $[P_0(1 - \lambda\Delta t)]$, plus the probability of one at time t times the probability of one departure $[P_1(\mu\Delta t)]$, which yields

$$P_0 = P_0(1 - \lambda\Delta t) + P_1(\mu\Delta t) \qquad [1]$$

By referring again to the figure, we see that there are three ways to have one in the system at time $t + \Delta t$: When $k = 0$ at time t, and one arrival occurs during Δt; when $k = 1$ at time t, and no arrival or departure occurs; and when $k = 2$ at time t, and one departure occurs. Thus, the probability of one unit in the system is given by

$$P_1 = P_0(\lambda\Delta t) + P_1(1 - \lambda\Delta t - \mu\Delta t) + P_2(\mu\Delta t) \qquad [2]$$

For the general case, the probability of n units in the system at time $t + \Delta t$, is given by

$$P_n = P_{n-1}(\lambda\Delta t) + P_n(1 - \lambda\Delta t - \mu\Delta t) + P_{n+1}(\mu\Delta t) \qquad [3]$$

We next solve Eq. [1] for P_1 in terms of P_0, as follows:

$$P_0 = P_0(1 - \lambda\Delta t) + P_1(\mu\Delta t)$$
$$(\mu\Delta t)P_1 = P_0 - P_0(1 - \lambda\Delta t)$$
$$(\mu\Delta t)P_1 = P_0[1 - (1 - \lambda\Delta t)]$$
$$(\mu\Delta t)P_1 = P_0(\lambda\Delta t)$$

$$P_1 = P_0 \frac{\lambda\Delta t}{\mu\Delta t}$$

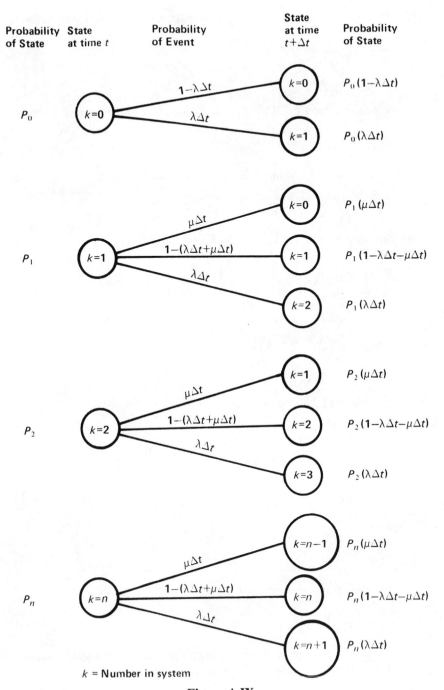

Probability of State	State at time t	Probability of Event	State at time $t+\Delta t$	Probability of State

P_0 $k=0$ $1-\lambda\Delta t$ $k=0$ $P_0(1-\lambda\Delta t)$

$\lambda\Delta t$ $k=1$ $P_0(\lambda\Delta t)$

P_1 $k=1$

$\mu\Delta t$ $k=0$ $P_1(\mu\Delta t)$

$1-(\lambda\Delta t+\mu\Delta t)$ $k=1$ $P_1(1-\lambda\Delta t-\mu\Delta t)$

$\lambda\Delta t$ $k=2$ $P_1(\lambda\Delta t)$

P_2 $k=2$

$\mu\Delta t$ $k=1$ $P_2(\mu\Delta t)$

$1-(\lambda\Delta t+\mu\Delta t)$ $k=2$ $P_2(1-\lambda\Delta t-\mu\Delta t)$

$\lambda\Delta t$ $k=3$ $P_2(\lambda\Delta t)$

P_n $k=n$

$\mu\Delta t$ $k=n-1$ $P_n(\mu\Delta t)$

$1-(\lambda\Delta t+\mu\Delta t)$ $k=n$ $P_n(1-\lambda\Delta t-\mu\Delta t)$

$\lambda\Delta t$ $k=n+1$ $P_n(\lambda\Delta t)$

k = Number in system

Figure A.IXa
Queueing system states

571

The Δt's cancel, and we get

$$P_1 = P_0\left(\frac{\lambda}{\mu}\right) \tag{4}$$

We next solve Eq. [3] for P_{n+1} in terms of P_n and P_{n-1}, which yields

$$P_{n+1} = P_n\left(\frac{\lambda + \mu}{\mu}\right) - P_{n-1}\left(\frac{\lambda}{\mu}\right)$$

and, substituting the value 1 for n, we get

$$P_2 = P_1\left(\frac{\lambda + \mu}{\mu}\right) - P_0\left(\frac{\lambda}{\mu}\right)$$

We can then substitute Eq. [4] for P_1, yielding

$$P_2 = P_0\left(\frac{\lambda}{\mu}\right)\left(\frac{\lambda + \mu}{\mu}\right) - P_0\left(\frac{\lambda}{\mu}\right)$$

$$= P_0\left[\left(\frac{\lambda}{\mu}\right)\left(\frac{\lambda + \mu}{\mu}\right) - \left(\frac{\lambda}{\mu}\right)\right] \tag{5}$$

$$= P_0\left[\frac{\lambda}{\mu}\left(\frac{\lambda + \mu}{\mu} - 1\right)\right]$$

$$= P_0\frac{\lambda^2 + \lambda\mu - \lambda\mu}{\mu^2}$$

$$P_2 = P_0\left(\frac{\lambda}{\mu}\right)^2$$

When we solve for P_3, we find that

$$P_3 = P_0\left(\frac{\lambda}{\mu}\right)^3 \tag{6}$$

Similarly,

$$P_4 = P_0\left(\frac{\lambda}{\mu}\right)^4 \tag{7}$$

and, by induction, we infer that

$$P_n = P_0\left(\frac{\lambda}{\mu}\right)^n \tag{8}$$

From our knowledge of probability theory, we know that the sum of the probabilities for all possible outcomes must sum to one. Thus we have

$$\sum_{n=0}^{\infty} P_n = 1.0 \tag{9}$$

Substituting Eq. [8] for P_n, we have

$$\sum_{n=0}^{\infty} P_0 \left(\frac{\lambda}{\mu}\right)^n = 1.0$$

or

$$P_0 = \frac{1}{\sum_{n=0}^{\infty} (\lambda/\mu)^n}$$

The denominator of the above expression is an infinite geometric series, which converges to

$$\sum_{n=0}^{\infty} \left(\frac{\lambda}{\mu}\right)^n = \frac{1}{1 - \lambda/\mu}$$

Thus, we have

$$P_0 = \left(\frac{1}{\dfrac{1}{1 - \lambda/\mu}}\right)$$

$$P_0 = 1 - \frac{\lambda}{\mu} \qquad\qquad [10]$$

Recalling from Eq. [8] that

$$P_n = P_0 \left(\frac{\lambda}{\mu}\right)^n$$

and substituting Eq. [10] for P_0 in this equation, we get

$$P_n = \left(1 - \frac{\lambda}{\mu}\right)\left(\frac{\lambda}{\mu}\right)^n \qquad\qquad [11]$$

Thus, for steady-state conditions, Eq. [10] yields the probability of no units in the system, and Eq. [11] yields the probability of n units in the system. Note that Eq. [11] reduces to Eq. [10] when $n = 0$.

The average of some variable X is, by definition, $\sum_{\text{all } X} X \cdot P_X$; therefore, the average number in the system (L) is given by

$$L = \sum_{n=0}^{\infty} n \cdot P_n$$

Thus, substituting Eq. [11] for P_n in the above expression, we get

$$L = \sum_{n=0}^{\infty} n \cdot \left(1 - \frac{\lambda}{\mu}\right)\left(\frac{\lambda}{\mu}\right)^n$$

$$= \left(1 - \frac{\lambda}{\mu}\right) \sum_{n=0}^{\infty} n \cdot \left(\frac{\lambda}{\mu}\right)^n$$

The term $\sum_{n=0}^{\infty} n(\lambda/\mu)^n$ is an infinite geometric series, which converges to

$$\sum_{n=0}^{\infty} n\left(\frac{\lambda}{\mu}\right)^n = \frac{\lambda/\mu}{(1 - \lambda/\mu)^2}$$

and therefore

$$L = \left(1 - \frac{\lambda}{\mu}\right)\left[\frac{\lambda/\mu}{(1 - \lambda/\mu)^2}\right]$$

which reduces to

$$L = \frac{\lambda}{\mu - \lambda} \qquad [12]$$

It is important to note that once any one of the values L, L_q, W, or W_q has been determined, the other three can be found directly.

If we expect λ arrivals per unit time, and if each of these arrivals spends an average time in the system of W, then the total time in the system for λ arrivals during that unit of time measure is λW. For example, if the average rate is two men per hour, and each arrival spends an average of three hours in the system then the total man-hours in the system during the hour of two arrivals is six. If the system is experiencing time in the system of six man-hours during each hour of operation, then this implies that there are six ($L = 6$) men in the system on the average. This gives us the relationship

$$L = \lambda W \qquad [13]$$

The same rationale can be given for the relationship of the number in the queue and the waiting time:

$$L_q = \lambda W_q \qquad [14]$$

The expected time (W) in the system must be equal to the expected time in the queue (W_q) plus the expected time in the service facility. We already know that the expected time in service is $1/\mu$. Therefore, we have

$$W = W_q + \frac{1}{\mu} \qquad\qquad\qquad [15]$$

Therefore, once we have solved for L by Eq. [12],

$$L = \frac{\lambda}{\mu - \lambda} \qquad \text{Mean number in the system}$$

We then get W from Eq. [13]:

$$W = \frac{L}{\lambda} \qquad \text{Mean time in the system}$$

and W_q is given by Eq. [15]:

$$W_q = W - \frac{1}{\mu} \qquad \text{Mean waiting time}$$

and finally L_q, from Eq. [14], is

$$L_q = \lambda W_q \qquad \text{Mean number in the queue}$$

The queueing equations for the other models presented in the chapter are in some cases developed by a similar process, and in other cases by a much more complex process. We will not extend the development beyond the elemental model.

APPENDIX X $P(0)$ for Multi-channel Poisson / Exponential Queueing Process: Probability of Zero in System

P(0) FOR MULTI-CHANNEL POISSON/EXPONENTIAL QUEUEING PROCESS: PROBABILITY OF ZERO IN SYSTEM

R=LAMDA/(S*MU)   NUMBER OF CHANNELS: S

R	2	3	4	5	6	7	8	9	10	15
0.02	0.96079	0.94177	0.92312	0.90484	0.88692	0.86936	0.85215	0.83527	0.81873	0.74082
0.04	0.92308	0.88692	0.85215	0.81873	0.78663	0.75578	0.72615	0.69768	0.67032	0.54881
0.06	0.88679	0.83526	0.78663	0.74082	0.69769	0.65705	0.61878	0.58275	0.54881	0.40657
0.08	0.85185	0.78659	0.72615	0.67032	0.61878	0.57121	0.52729	0.48675	0.44933	0.30119
0.10	0.81818	0.74074	0.67031	0.60653	0.54881	0.49659	0.44933	0.40657	0.36703	0.22313
0.12	0.78571	0.69753	0.61876	0.54881	0.48675	0.43171	0.38289	0.33960	0.30119	0.16530
0.14	0.75439	0.65679	0.57116	0.49657	0.43171	0.37531	0.32628	0.28365	0.24660	0.12246
0.16	0.72414	0.61838	0.52720	0.44931	0.38289	0.32628	0.27804	0.23693	0.20190	0.09072
0.18	0.69492	0.58214	0.48660	0.40653	0.33959	0.28365	0.23693	0.19790	0.16530	0.06721
0.20	0.66667	0.54795	0.44910	0.36782	0.30118	0.24659	0.20189	0.16530	0.13534	0.04979
0.22	0.63934	0.51567	0.41445	0.33277	0.26711	0.21437	0.17204	0.13807	0.11060	0.03688
0.24	0.61290	0.48519	0.38244	0.30105	0.23688	0.18636	0.14660	0.11532	0.09072	0.02732
0.26	0.58730	0.45640	0.35284	0.27233	0.21007	0.16200	0.12492	0.09632	0.07427	0.02024
0.28	0.56250	0.42918	0.32548	0.24633	0.18628	0.14082	0.10645	0.08045	0.06061	0.01500
0.30	0.53846	0.40346	0.30017	0.22277	0.16517	0.12241	0.09070	0.06720	0.04978	0.01111
0.32	0.51515	0.37913	0.27676	0.20144	0.14644	0.10639	0.07728	0.05612	0.04076	0.00823
0.34	0.49254	0.35610	0.25510	0.18211	0.12981	0.09247	0.06584	0.04687	0.03337	0.00610
0.36	0.47059	0.33431	0.23505	0.16460	0.11505	0.08035	0.05609	0.03915	0.02732	0.00452
0.38	0.44928	0.31367	0.21649	0.14872	0.10195	0.06981	0.04778	0.03269	0.02236	0.00335
0.40	0.42857	0.29412	0.19929	0.13433	0.09032	0.06065	0.04069	0.02729	0.01836	0.00248
0.42	0.40845	0.27559	0.18336	0.12128	0.07998	0.05267	0.03465	0.02279	0.01498	0.00184
0.44	0.38889	0.25802	0.16860	0.10944	0.07080	0.04573	0.02950	0.01902	0.01225	0.00136
0.46	0.36986	0.24135	0.15491	0.09870	0.06265	0.03968	0.02511	0.01587	0.01003	0.00101
0.48	0.35135	0.22554	0.14221	0.08895	0.05540	0.03442	0.02136	0.01324	0.00822	0.00075
0.50	0.33333	0.21053	0.13043	0.08010	0.04896	0.02984	0.01816	0.01104	0.00671	0.00055
0.52	0.31579	0.19627	0.11951	0.07207	0.04323	0.02586	0.01544	0.00920	0.00548	0.00041
0.54	0.29870	0.18273	0.10936	0.06477	0.03814	0.02239	0.01311	0.00767	0.00449	0.00030
0.56	0.28205	0.16986	0.09994	0.05814	0.03362	0.01936	0.01113	0.00638	0.00365	0.00022
0.58	0.26582	0.15762	0.09119	0.05212	0.02959	0.01673	0.00943	0.00531	0.00298	0.00017
0.60	0.25000	0.14599	0.08306	0.04665	0.02601	0.01443	0.00799	0.00441	0.00243	0.00012

0.62	0.23457	0.13491	0.07550	0.04167	0.02282	0.01243	0.00675	0.00366	0.00198	0.00009
0.64	0.21951	0.12438	0.06847	0.03715	0.01999	0.01069	0.00570	0.00303	0.00161	0.00007
0.66	0.20482	0.11435	0.06194	0.03304	0.01746	0.00918	0.00480	0.00251	0.00131	0.00005
0.68	0.19048	0.10479	0.05587	0.02930	0.01522	0.00786	0.00404	0.00207	0.00106	0.00004
0.70	0.17647	0.09569	0.05021	0.02590	0.01322	0.00670	0.00338	0.00170	0.00085	0.00003
0.72	0.16279	0.08702	0.04495	0.02280	0.01144	0.00570	0.00283	0.00140	0.00069	0.00002
0.74	0.14943	0.07875	0.04006	0.01999	0.00986	0.00483	0.00235	0.00114	0.00055	0.00001
0.76	0.13636	0.07087	0.03550	0.01743	0.00846	0.00407	0.00195	0.00093	0.00044	0.00001
0.78	0.12360	0.06335	0.03125	0.01510	0.00721	0.00341	0.00160	0.00075	0.00035	0.00001
0.80	0.11111	0.05618	0.02730	0.01299	0.00610	0.00284	0.00131	0.00060	0.00026	0.00001
0.82	0.09890	0.04933	0.02362	0.01106	0.00511	0.00234	0.00106	0.00048	0.00022	0.00000
0.84	0.08696	0.04280	0.02019	0.00931	0.00423	0.00190	0.00085	0.00038	0.00017	0.00000
0.86	0.07527	0.03656	0.01700	0.00772	0.00345	0.00153	0.00067	0.00029	0.00013	0.00000
0.88	0.06383	0.03060	0.01403	0.00627	0.00276	0.00120	0.00052	0.00022	0.00010	0.00000
0.90	0.05263	0.02491	0.01126	0.00496	0.00215	0.00092	0.00039	0.00017	0.00007	0.00000
0.92	0.04167	0.01947	0.00867	0.00377	0.00161	0.00068	0.00024	0.00012	0.00005	0.00000
0.94	0.03093	0.01427	0.00627	0.00268	0.00113	0.00047	0.00019	0.00008	0.00003	0.00000
0.96	0.02041	0.00930	0.00403	0.00170	0.00070	0.00029	0.00012	0.00005	0.00002	0.00000
0.98	0.01010	0.00454	0.00194	0.00081	0.00033	0.00013	0.00005	0.00002	0.00001	0.00000

APPENDIX **XI** Normal Probability Values

Z	.00	.01	.02	.03	.04	.05	.06	.07	.08	.09
0.0	.50000	.50399	.50798	.51197	.51595	.51994	.52392	.52790	.53188	.53586
0.1	.53983	.54380	.54776	.55172	.55567	.55962	.56356	.56749	.57142	.57535
0.2	.57926	.58317	.58706	.59095	.59483	.59871	.60257	.60642	.61026	.61409
0.3	.61791	.62172	.62552	.62930	.63307	.63683	.64058	.64431	.64803	.65173
0.4	.65542	.65910	.66276	.66640	.67003	.67364	.67724	.68082	.68439	.68793
0.5	.69146	.69497	.69847	.70194	.70540	.70884	.71226	.71566	.71904	.72240
0.6	.72575	.72907	.73237	.73536	.73891	.74215	.74537	.74857	.75175	.75490
0.7	.75804	.76115	.76424	.76730	.77035	.77337	.77637	.77935	.78230	.78524
0.8	.78814	.79103	.79389	.79673	.79955	.80234	.80511	.80785	.81057	.81327
0.9	.81594	.81859	.82121	.82381	.82639	.82894	.83147	.83398	.83646	.83891
1.0	.84134	.84375	.84614	.84849	.85083	.85314	.85543	.85769	.85993	.86214
1.1	.86433	.86650	.86864	.87076	.87286	.87493	.87698	.87900	.88100	.88298
1.2	.88493	.88686	.88877	.89065	.89251	.89435	.89617	.89796	.89973	.90147
1.3	.90320	.90490	.90658	.90824	.90988	.91149	.91309	.91466	.91621	.91774
1.4	.91924	.92073	.92220	.92364	.92507	.92647	.92785	.92922	.93056	.93189
1.5	.93319	.93448	.93574	.93699	.93822	.93943	.94062	.94179	.94295	.94408
1.6	.94520	.94630	.94738	.94845	.94950	.95053	.95154	.95254	.95352	.95449
1.7	.95543	.95637	.95728	.95818	.95907	.95994	.96080	.96164	.96246	.96327
1.8	.96407	.96485	.96562	.96638	.96712	.96784	.96856	.96926	.96995	.97062
1.9	.97128	.97193	.97257	.97320	.97381	.97441	.97500	.97558	.97615	.97670
2.0	.97725	.97784	.97831	.97882	.97932	.97982	.98030	.98077	.98124	.98169
2.1	.98214	.98257	.98300	.98341	.98382	.98422	.98461	.98500	.98537	.98574
2.2	.98610	.98645	.98679	.98713	.98745	.98778	.98809	.98840	.98870	.98899
2.3	.98928	.98956	.98983	.99010	.99036	.99061	.99086	.99111	.99134	.99158
2.4	.99180	.99202	.99224	.99245	.99266	.99286	.99305	.99324	.99343	.99361
2.5	.99379	.99396	.99413	.99430	.99446	.99461	.99477	.99492	.99506	.99520
2.6	.99534	.99547	.99560	.99573	.99585	.99598	.99609	.99621	.99632	.99643
2.7	.99653	.99664	.99674	.99683	.99693	.99702	.99711	.99720	.99728	.99736
2.8	.99744	.99752	.99760	.99767	.99774	.99781	.99788	.99795	.99801	.99807
2.9	.99813	.99819	.99825	.99831	.99836	.99841	.99846	.99851	.99856	.99861
3.0	.99865	.99869	.99874	.99878	.99882	.99886	.99899	.99893	.99896	.99900
3.1	.99903	.99906	.99910	.99913	.99916	.99918	.99921	.99924	.99926	.99929
3.2	.99931	.99934	.99936	.99938	.99940	.99942	.99944	.99946	.99948	.99950
3.3	.99952	.99953	.99955	.99957	.99958	.99960	.99961	.99962	.99964	.99965
3.4	.99966	.99968	.99969	.99970	.99971	.99972	.99973	.99974	.99975	.99976
3.5	.99977	.99978	.99978	.99979	.99980	.99981	.99981	.99982	.99983	.99983
3.6	.99984	.99985	.99985	.99986	.99986	.99987	.99987	.99988	.99988	.99989
3.7	.99989	.99990	.99990	.99990	.99991	.99991	.99992	.99992	.99992	.99992
3.8	.99993	.99993	.99993	.99994	.99994	.99994	.99994	.99995	.99995	.99995
3.9	.99995	.99995	.99996	.99996	.99996	.99996	.99996	.99996	.99997	.99997

APPENDIX **XII** Computer Program to Generate Value of Random Variable-Demand

```
C    PROGRAM TO RANDOMLY GENERATE
C    VALUES OF D (DEMAND) ACCORDING
C    TO PROBABILITY DISTRIBUTION
C    GIVEN IN TABLE 13-1
C
     N=1000
     ISEED=2671
     WRITE(6,10)
  10 FORMAT(///18X,'RN',10X,'D'//)
     DO 20 I=1,N
     RN=DRAND(ISEED)
     D=18.
     IF(RN.LE..9)D=17.
     IF(RN.LE..8)D=16.
     IF(RN.LE..6)D=15.
     IF(RN.LE..2)D=14.
  20 WRITE(6,30)I,RN,D
  30 FORMAT(6X,I5,3X,F10.8,F9.1)
     STOP
     END
     FUNCTION DRAND(ID)
C    SUBPROGRAM TO RANDOMLY
C    GENERATE RANDOM NUMBERS
C    (RN) BETWEEN 0 AND 1.0
C
     ID=ID*65539
     IF(ID)1,1,2
   1 ID=ID+2147483647+1
   2 DRAND=ID*.4656613E-9
     RETURN
     END
```

APPENDIX XIII Table of Random Numbers

```
39 65 76 45 45   19 90 69 64 61   20 26 36 31 62   58 24 97 14 97   95 06 70 99 00
73 71 23 70 90   65 97 60 12 11   31 56 34 19 19   47 83 75 51 33   30 62 38 20 46
72 20 47 33 84   51 67 47 97 19   98 40 07 17 66   23 05 09 51 80   59 78 11 52 49
75 17 25 69 17   17 95 21 78 58   24 33 45 77 48   69 81 84 09 29   93 22 70 45 80
37 48 79 88 74   63 52 06 34 30   01 31 60 10 27   35 07 79 71 53   28 99 52 01 41

02 89 08 16 94   85 53 83 29 95   56 27 09 24 43   21 78 55 09 82   72 61 88 73 61
87 18 15 70 07   37 79 49 12 38   48 13 93 55 96   41 92 45 71 51   09 18 25 58 94
98 83 71 70 15   89 09 39 59 24   00 06 41 41 20   14 36 59 25 47   54 45 17 24 89
10 08 58 07 04   76 62 16 48 68   58 76 17 14 86   59 53 11 52 21   66 04 18 72 87
47 90 56 37 31   71 82 13 50 41   27 55 10 24 92   28 04 67 53 44   95 23 00 84 47

93 05 31 03 07   34 18 04 52 35   74 13 39 35 22   68 95 23 92 35   36 63 70 35 33
21 89 11 47 99   11 20 99 45 18   76 51 94 84 86   13 79 93 37 55   98 16 04 41 67
95 18 94 06 97   27 37 83 28 71   79 57 95 13 91   09 61 87 25 21   56 20 11 32 44
97 08 31 55 73   10 65 81 92 59   77 31 61 95 46   20 44 90 32 64   26 99 76 75 63
69 26 88 86 13   59 71 74 17 32   48 38 75 93 29   73 37 32 04 05   60 82 29 20 25

41 47 10 25 03   87 63 93 95 17   81 83 83 04 49   77 45 85 50 51   79 88 01 97 30
91 94 14 63 62   08 61 74 51 69   92 79 43 89 79   29 18 94 51 23   14 85 11 47 23
80 06 54 18 47   08 52 85 08 40   48 40 35 94 22   72 65 71 08 86   50 03 42 99 36
67 72 77 63 99   89 85 84 46 06   64 71 06 21 66   89 37 20 70 01   61 65 70 22 12
59 40 24 13 75   42 29 72 23 19   06 94 76 10 08   81 30 15 39 14   81 83 17 16 33

63 62 06 34 41   79 53 36 02 95   94 61 09 43 62   20 21 14 68 86   84 95 48 46 45
78 47 23 53 90   79 93 96 38 63   34 85 52 05 09   85 43 01 72 73   14 93 87 81 40
87 68 62 15 43   97 48 72 66 48   53 16 71 13 81   59 97 50 99 52   24 62 20 42 31
47 60 92 10 77   26 97 05 73 51   88 46 38 03 58   72 68 49 29 31   75 70 16 08 24
56 88 87 59 41   06 87 37 78 48   65 88 69 58 39   88 02 84 27 83   85 81 56 39 38

22 17 68 65 84   87 02 22 57 51   68 69 80 95 44   11 29 01 95 80   49 34 35 86 47
19 36 27 59 46   39 77 32 77 09   79 57 92 36 59   89 74 39 82 15   08 58 94 34 74
16 77 23 02 77   28 06 24 25 93   22 45 44 84 11   87 80 61 65 31   09 71 91 74 25
78 43 76 71 61   97 67 63 99 61   80 45 67 93 82   59 73 19 85 23   53 33 65 97 21
03 28 28 26 08   69 30 16 09 05   53 58 47 70 93   66 56 45 65 79   45 56 20 19 47

04 31 17 21 56   33 73 99 19 87   26 72 39 27 67   53 77 57 68 93   60 61 97 22 61
61 06 98 03 91   87 14 77 43 96   43 00 65 98 50   45 60 33 01 07   98 99 46 50 47
23 68 35 26 00   99 53 93 61 28   52 70 05 48 34   56 65 05 61 86   90 92 10 70 80
15 39 25 70 99   93 86 52 77 65   15 33 59 05 28   22 87 26 07 47   86 96 98 29 06
58 71 96 30 24   18 46 23 34 27   85 13 99 24 44   49 18 09 79 49   74 16 32 23 02

93 22 53 64 39   07 10 63 76 35   87 03 04 79 88   08 13 13 85 51   55 34 57 72 69
78 76 58 54 74   92 38 70 96 92   52 06 79 79 45   82 63 18 27 44   69 66 92 19 09
61 81 31 96 82   00 57 25 60 59   46 72 60 18 77   55 66 12 62 11   08 99 55 64 57
42 88 07 10 05   24 98 65 63 21   47 21 61 88 32   27 80 30 21 60   10 92 35 36 12
77 94 30 05 39   28 10 99 00 27   12 73 73 99 12   49 99 57 94 82   96 88 57 17 91
```

Index